THE SOCIAL AND POLITICAL THOUGHT
OF LEON TROTSKY

THE SOCIAL AND POLITICAL THOUGHT OF LEON TROTSKY

BY

BARUCH KNEI-PAZ

The Hebrew University of Jerusalem

1978

CLARENDON PRESS · OXFORD

Oxford University Press, Walton Street, Oxford OX2 6DP

OXFORD   LONDON   GLASGOW   NEW YORK

TORONTO   MELBOURNE   WELLINGTON   CAPE TOWN

IBADAN   NAIROBI   DAR ES SALAAM   LUSAKA   ADDIS ABABA

KUALA LUMPUR   SINGAPORE   JAKARTA   HONG KONG   TOKYO

DELHI   BOMBAY   CALCUTTA   MADRAS   KARACHI

© *Oxford University Press 1978*

British Library Cataloguing in Publication Data
Knei-Paz, Baruch
   The social and political thought of Leon Trotsky.
   1. Communism
   I. Title
   335.43'3   HX312
   ISBN 0-19-827233-2

Printed in Great Britain by
Butler & Tanner Ltd.,
Frome and London

for
My Parents,
ZVI AND MIRIAM KNAPHEIS

PREFACE

THE SUBJECT of this book is, it would seem, sufficiently defined by its title; and the substantive issues which it proposes to deal with in the framework of a study of Leon Trotsky's social and political thought are set out in the introduction which follows this preface. Here I wish to describe the motives for undertaking such a study, the approach to the subject adopted, the problems encountered, and the manner of their resolution.

This study has had its origins in the present writer's interest in the relationship between ideas and historical events in general, and between Marxist ideas and the Russian Revolution of 1917 in particular. To speak of such a relationship is to speak not only of the correspondence between ideas and events; as often as not, it is to dwell on the divergence and conflict between the two and on the significance of this. Trotsky once wrote that the 'ideas and aims of those engaged in revolutionary struggle form a very important constituent element of a revolution'.[1] With this I fully agree. Although Marxism has traditionally frowned upon the notion that ideas shape history, the events of October 1917 and thereafter can hardly be comprehended outside the context of the impact of certain ideas—those of Marxism itself, or rather of a specifically conceived version of it—upon a small but quite extraordinary group of men and of their determination to implement, and if necessary impose, their intellectual convictions upon Russian society. But Trotsky went on to claim that 'never in all the past have the conceptions of a revolution in the minds of revolutionists approached so closely to the actual essence of the events as in 1917'.[2] This, in my view, is to presume more than the historical record can sustain. One of the underlying aims of the present study, there-fore, is to bring out not only the scope and impact of ideas but their limits as well: the extent, in other words, to which intellec-tual preconceptions 'in the minds of revolutionists' may be said

[1] Leon Trotsky, *The History of the Russian Revolution* (London, 1965), p. 1221. (Biblio-graphical details concerning this work are given in note 38 to chapter 2, below.)
[2] Loc. cit.

to have played a role in shaping history, and the extent to which such preconceptions were overpowered and made largely immaterial by the forces of reality.

No one who is even vaguely familiar with the biography of Trotsky will fail to see immediately the particular relevance of the uneasy relationship between ideas and events to Trotsky's own life and thought. Of all the 'makers' of October 1917, none, it seems, approached it with so complete a preconception of its character; none, moreover, was more totally committed to the socialist transformation of Russian society—and none was to emerge more bitterly disappointed and defeated by the eventual course of events. This historical image of Trotsky has become, admittedly, somewhat of a cliché by now. Nevertheless, it remains valid, though only if we add that Trotsky's 'ideas and aims' were 'betrayed' not so much by others—as he was prone to believe—as by the contradictions of his own intellectual preconceptions. In a sense, this study is an attempt to trace the origins and evolvement of such contradictions and, thereby, to throw some light as well on the immediate and subsequent character of the Russian Revolution. If excuse be needed, therefore, for the length and scope of this work, it is that I have also endeavoured—in the course of the examination of Trotsky's thought—to confront, and deal with, many of the issues, great and small, raised by that Revolution.

A great deal has been written about Trotsky's life and revolutionary career—both in and out of power—but relatively little about his social and political thought. This is perhaps only natural since his life contained many sensational moments and he is, even now, and perhaps not unjustly, considered to be the quintessential revolutionary in an age which has not lacked in revolutionary figures. Yet his achievements in the realm of theory and ideas is in many ways no less prodigious: he was among the first to analyse the emergence, in the twentieth century, of social change in backward societies, and among the first, as well, to attempt to explain the political consequences which would almost invariably grow out of such change. He wrote voluminously throughout his life, and the political thinker in him was no less an intrinsic part of his personality than the better-known man of action. It would be an exaggeration to say that his ideas have been neglected or that his writings are unknown; his name is, after all, automatically identified with the theory of the 'permanent revolution' and some of his works have always enjoyed a wide readership. But the theory of the 'permanent revolution', like other of his ideas, has had so many meanings attributed to it that it has lost meaning altogether and become more a label than a body of thought; and his works are read, it seems, more because they are now associated with a 'cult figure' than for any intrinsic value which they may have.[3]

Among the writings on Trotsky's thought, there are a few articles, or chapters in works devoted to wider subjects, which are useful as summaries of his views or of certain of his books.[4] But there is hardly a single work which has attempted to analyse his thought in any detail or to deal with it comprehensively. There exists, in fact, only one book, in Italian, which is entirely devoted to his ideas; it has many virtues but even it is based on limited sources and treats numerous aspects of Trotsky's thought in a cursory and very incomplete manner.[5] The late Isaac Deutscher's well-known three-volume biography has not a few pages and even chapters which discuss Trotsky's writings. But Deutscher's approach in this connection is not only largely uncritical; it is also lacking in any real analysis since it concentrates on merely summarizing, however colourfully, these writings. Moreover, Deutscher chooses to ignore many elements in Trotsky's thought, and others he fits into the preconceived notions of Soviet history and of Marxism, which characterize his biography as a whole.[6] For the rest, there exists

[3] The 'cult' element associated with Trotsky has given rise to a small industry of non-academic literature: a novel has been devoted to him (Bernard Wolfe, *The Great Prince Died*, London, 1959), a play (Peter Weiss, *Trotsky in Exile*, English translation London, 1971), and an illustrated biography (Francis Wyndham and David King, *Trotsky: A Documentary*, Harmondsworth and London, 1972). In addition, a film has been made about his assassination, with no less a 'screen star' than Richard Burton somewhat unconvincingly impersonating Trotsky.

[4] A list of the main writings on Trotsky's thought is provided in the bibliography at the end of this book.

[5] Guido Vestuti, *La Rivoluzione permanente: uno studio sulla politica di Trotsky* (Milan, 1960). A more recent work, Alain Brossat, *Aux Origines de la révolution permanente: la pensée politique du jeune Trotsky* (Paris, 1974) deals with the 1905 period mainly. See also Denise Avenas, *Économie et politique dans la pensée de Trotsky* (Paris, 1970).

[6] For an extreme, but not unfounded, critique of Deutscher's writings on Trotsky and in general, see Julius Jacobson, 'Isaac Deutscher: The Anatomy of an Apologist', in the book, edited by the same author, *Soviet Communism and the Socialist Vision* (New Brunswick, New Jersey, 1972), pp. 86–162. See also, in the same vein, Leopold Labedz,

a considerable literature which discusses Trotsky's ideas in the context of the Stalinist-Trotskyist controversy. The ideological confrontation between Stalin and Trotsky is, of course, a legitimate subject for research and debate—and it will be dealt with in the present study—but it has frequently been engulfed by purely polemical and partisan concerns.[7] It has also diverted attention from Trotsky's contribution to the field of social theory—a contribution which I hope will be made evident in this study—by unduly concentrating on ephemeral political issues of the past which are of little interest or importance today.

In view of the fact, therefore, that no treatment of Trotsky's thought exists which is at once comprehensive and free of partisanship of one kind or another, the intention of the present study is, firstly, to provide as complete an exposition of his thought and writings as is possible. This, however, may be little enough. It is also intended to discuss Trotsky's thought analytically and critically within the framework of a consistent interpretation of its significance, its virtues, and its flaws. Exposition and interpretation are clearly distinguished throughout, but I freely admit that certain themes or subjects have been more emphasized than others, that some works have been dealt with at length and others given short shrift, and that the whole has been put together in accordance with my own judgement of the relative importance and value of the various parts of Trotsky's literary output. Thus, for example, Trotsky's innumerable writings of the 1920s and 1930s on political events in Britain, France, Spain, etc., have been largely ignored since, in my view, they are either of little theoretical interest or whatever theoretical arguments they make are better gathered from other of his writings (as for instance, on the inter-war situation in

---

'Deutscher as Historian and Prophet', in *Survey* (Apr. 1962), pp. 120–44. A more moderate, but in its way no less damaging critique of Deutscher, is the review article by Alasdair MacIntyre, 'Trotsky in Exile', in *Encounter* (Dec. 1963), pp. 73–8. The present writer's differences with Deutscher will be evident from this study although, aside from a few comments in the footnotes, direct argument with him has been avoided.

[7] Works of this kind are legion and include, for example, some of Max Eastman's writings during the 1920s and thereafter. A more recent example, which involves also the Trotsky v. Lenin ideological controversy, is the volume edited by Nicolas Krassó, *Trotsky: The Great Debate Renewed* (St. Louis, 1972). See also Kostas Mavrakis, *Du Trotskysme* (Paris, 1973).

Germany).[8] Finally, it has been the intention, in the light of the interest declared at the outset of this preface, to grasp Trotsky's thought within the context of the specific theoretical problematics of the Russian Revolution, both before it transpired and after. This explains the arrangement of the study around the topic of the 'permanent revolution'—its theory, its practice, and its aftermath. But the wider implications of Trotsky's thought are also discussed, as are those of his ideas which dealt with other political or social questions, and such as concerned matters not strictly or mainly political in character.

The principal sources for this study are, of course, Trotsky's writings. The footnotes and the bibliography will give an idea of their scope. The writings span a period of forty years and if they were to be collected in one single edition they would easily fill, I venture to estimate, sixty to seventy thick volumes— without including the vast material contained in the Trotsky Archives at Harvard University. It has frequently been a source of amazement that Russian revolutionaries found the time and the energy to write so extensively; perhaps one should wonder that, having written so much, they found the time and the energy to make a revolution. At any rate, the very volume of Trotsky's own output and the range of its subject-matter presented the most obvious problem in the preparation of this study. It was resolved, one hopes, in the only way possible— as indicated above, through selection governed by the value of the material. The aim has been to be comprehensive, but not for the sake of sheer comprehensiveness.[9]

A somewhat more difficult 'methodological' problem, however, also arising from the extent of Trotsky's writings, concerned the question of whether to deal with his works in a chronological order or in accordance with specific subjects. The second of these alternatives was chosen, partly because a chronological approach would have involved a great deal of

---

[8] His views on Germany have been discussed as more or less representative of his views on Europe in general. By not discussing Britain specifically, it has been necessary to largely by-pass his well-known book, *Where is Britain Going?* which, however, is mainly a historical curiosity today.

[9] In view of the length of the book, this may sound like an ironical, if not tasteless, joke. But even after extensive selection, the range of the important material which had to be considered and incorporated remained enormous.

repetition, but mainly because the aim has been to concentrate on the over-all and completed character of his views and ideas, though always noting the actual course of their development. Since Trotsky returned to the same subjects at various times in his life, this approach has sometimes meant, especially in the first part of the study, traversing different historical periods; but the study as a whole has been set within a general chronological framework.

From the above it should be clear that while this book may be described as a work in the field of what is sometimes called the history of ideas, it is not in itself a work of history, much less a biographical study. Although ideas and their evolution have been related to events, the latter are dealt with in a cursory manner, partly for reasons of space, and partly because the events are by now so well known as to require no further elaboration, particularly in a work which is not devoted to the events themselves. Similarly, in the case of Trotsky's own life, biographical details are provided only where these are essential to the understanding of the origins of his ideas—as, for example, in the first chapter, which describes the earliest intellectual and environmental influences upon him. Thereafter, only the most important changes in his political and personal fortunes are referred to. There is, in any case, no lack of material on Trotsky's life and I have made no attempt to add to it. And since this is not a biography, neither have I attempted to evaluate, or pass judgement upon, Trotsky's political, as opposed to his intellectual, record—though it would be ridiculous to pretend that the two are entirely unrelated.

In the case of the ideas of others, with whom Trotsky often argued and clashed both before and after 1917, reasons of space were paramount in limiting the discussion of their points of view. Thus, for example, the thought of Lenin is often referred to, and sometimes compared with, that of Trotsky, but generally I have avoided detailed analysis of this kind. I have assumed that the reader is well enough acquainted with Lenin's writings and with those of other Russian revolutionaries and have referred to such writings only where they touched directly upon Trotsky's ideas. Sometimes this may leave the impression that Trotsky was the only one to propound certain views which were, in fact, common in Russian revolutionary circles; but my intention has been to give as complete a picture of Trotsky's thought as possible and not to carry out a comparative study. In the same way, although not a few of Trotsky's views about Russian history were derived from the work of others, I have not attempted to trace the intellectual or historical sources of all such views. Every thinker borrows from others and his thought will always be found to be eclectic to some extent; the emphasis, however, should be, I believe, on the particular synthesis he effects, which may then be taken to constitute the originality of his conception.

Finally, I wish to point out that this is not a work on 'Trotskyism' as a movement; I have eschewed entirely discussion of this subject, whether it involves its real or imaginary status during the 1920s or the more organized form it took in the 1930s and thereafter. Soviet diatribes, then and later, against 'Trotskyism' have been ignored altogether; and the writings of 'Trotskyists' have been considered only in so far as they concerned debates with Trotsky himself. To repeat, this is a study of Trotsky's own thought, not that of his opponents or followers, nor of the ideological and political movement which came to be identified with his name.[10]

I should like to express my gratitude to the following libraries in particular, and their librarians, for the use of their facilities and for the assistance which they so kindly provided me: the Bodleian Library at Oxford; the British Museum Reading Room (now the British Library); the Houghton Library at Harvard University; the New York Public Library; the Jewish National and University Library at the Hebrew University of Jerusalem; and St. Antony's College Library, Oxford.

I began this study while a doctoral student at St. Antony's College; and prepared it for publication when I returned to St. Antony's for a year as a Visiting Fellow. During both periods the College provided me with a home and an intellectual environment which I shall always recall with feelings of the deepest gratitude and nostalgia. I am greatly indebted to the

---

[10] There exists as yet no reliable history of the Trotskyist movement; but for a fully documented account of the early phase of Trotskyism's one conspicuous 'success story', see George Jan Lerski, *Origins of Trotskyism in Ceylon, 1935–1942* (Stanford, 1968). See also Robert J. Alexander, *Trotskyism in Latin America* (Stanford, 1973).

former Warden, Sir William Deakin, and to the present one, Raymond Carr, as well as to the former sub-Warden, Professor James Joll, for their many kindnesses. The Fellows of the College were invariably helpful and friendly, but I should like to mention in particular Dr. Richard Kindersley and Dr. Theodore Zeldin who offered advice and assistance on numerous occasions. My debt to Dr. Harold Shukman, also a Fellow of St. Antony's, is of a special kind since it is such as grows out of the closest of friendships and thus extends as well into areas which go far beyond the scope of this book.

Amongst many other debts accumulated at Oxford, that to the late Professor John Plamenatz will now for ever remain associated with the sadness incurred by his recent and untimely death; it has deprived me, as it has all his former students—not to mention others—of the further benefits of his unique critical perception and gentle, human concern. I am also much indebted to another friend and 'protector' at Oxford, the Warden of Rhodes House, Sir Edgar Williams, for his help and guidance in the course of many years. And to Peter Halban, Peter Janson-Smith and Peter Sutcliffe I am grateful for aid and advice at various stages of the publication process.

My other intellectual home, for some years now, has been the Hebrew University of Jerusalem, more specifically its Department of Political Science. My friends and colleagues there made every formal and informal effort to facilitate my work and to tolerate its sometimes eccentric pace and demands; I wish to thank the following especially: Professor Martin Seliger, Professor Shlomo Avineri, Dr. Emanuel Gutmann, and Dr. Zeev Sternhell. Professor J. L. Talmon, of the History Department, stimulated my thinking in the course of many conversations or subjects related to the concerns of this book. As for my students, from whom I am still learning, let it only be noted that in times of both war and peace they have managed to sustain an intellectual interest in the subject of this book—imposed upon them while still in the making—despite its apparent remoteness from the harsh realities of the Middle East. There are many others in Israel whom I should like to thank for this or that, but I will single out only three close friends, Dan Horowitz, Nissan Oren and Giora Teltsch, who have also been intellectual companions.

It remains to be said that, without contradicting all the above acknowledgements, my greatest personal as well as intellectual debt during the preparation of this work has been to Sir Isaiah Berlin, than whom there can have been no better teacher, supervisor and—I make so bold to say—friend. His patience, understanding and assistance, particularly during a very difficult period, were a constant source of encouragement and, indeed, were ultimately responsible for the completion of this work. His own writings have influenced me in numerous ways, some of which will surely be apparent in this study. I hope I have not disappointed all his efforts on my behalf.

The dedication of this book to my parents speaks, I think, for itself; and it would in any case be impossible to convey in words all that I owe them. No less difficult is the expression of gratitude to my wife Mira and, in a different sense, to my daughter Cigal: such things are sometimes best left unsaid, being so deeply felt.

Jerusalem   B.K.
Autumn 1975

CONTENTS

Part II: The Permanent Revolution: From Theory to Practice

EXPLANATORY NOTES

1. Throughout this study, the term 'Russian Revolution', when thus capitalized, designates specifically, and is used interchangeably with, the Bolshevik Revolution of October 1917 (or the October Revolution). The February Revolution is always identified as such, i.e. by its month. The fact that, according to the Western calendar, the February Revolution took place in March and the October Revolution in November, has thus been ignored from the point of view of the nomenclature here followed. In this connection it may be amusing to quote Trotsky himself on the problem of dates; noting that in his *History of the Russian Revolution* he 'felt obliged' to follow the old Russian calendar, he added in the preface to this work: 'The reader will be kind enough to remember that before overthrowing the Byzantine calendar, the revolution had to overthrow the institutions that clung to it.' However, in the few instances in the present book where specific dates are given, both the old Russian and its Western equivalent have been indicated.

2. Unless otherwise indicated, translations from Trotsky's works are my own. In a number of cases, however, I have consulted and exploited to the point of actual citation, existing translations, while nevertheless giving reference to the original Russian only, since modifications of the translations were generally necessary. The translation so used has been indicated as a rule at the first mention of the work concerned (but not thereafter), and in the section of the Bibliography listing Trotsky's writings.

3. In the transliteration of Russian names and titles of works, I have followed common usage for the former, and contrived the most approximate, but least cumbersome, phonetic rendition for the latter.

4. Unless otherwise indicated, all italics in quotations are from the original.

INTRODUCTION
(BY WAY OF A PROLOGUE)

Since the greatest enigma is the fact that a backward country was the *first* to place the proletariat in power, it behoves us to seek the solution of that enigma in the *peculiarities* of that backward country—that is, in its differences from other countries.[1]

No STUDENT of Marxism or of Russian history needs to be reminded that the spectacle of a revolution proclaiming itself to be socialist in character and goals, and triumphing in the Russia of 1917, raises the most fundamental problems of historical analysis and interpretation. In fact, more than half a century after the event, the Russian Revolution is still somewhat of an enigma, and certainly a source of unending debate, for the historian and for the student of political ideas alike. To grasp the dimensions of this enigma, one need only recall that at the beginning of 1917 the Tsar still ruled in the belief that he was divinely ordained to do so; that, at this same time, while the Russian intelligentsia lived with 'its head in the . . . twentieth century', its 'feet' were 'in the seventeenth',[2] mired in a primitive agricultural economy, in a vast peasant population culturally and socially impoverished; that the middle classes were economically and politically either insignificant or ineffective and that hardly a single 'bourgeois' institution had successfully penetrated the monolithic power of the autocracy and its hangers-on.

Why, the poet W. H. Auden once wondered, did 'old Russia suddenly mutate, into a proletarian state'?[3] Let us suspend judgement as to whether the result of the mutation was, in fact, a 'proletarian state' or merely a pretence to one; even if the

---

[1] All the epigraphs which appear at the heads of chapters are quotations from Trotsky's writings. In the above case the source is his *The History of the Russian Revolution*, pp. 19–20.

[2] Hugh Seton-Watson, *The Decline of Imperial Russia, 1855–1914* (New York, 1952), p. 24.

[3] Quoted in Lionel Kochan, *Russia in Revolution* (London, 1970), p. 11.

latter, Auden's question fairly summarizes the enigma and pithily contraposes its essential incongruities. Why was it, indeed, that a society so backward economically and politically, so much on the periphery of Europe and only vaguely and superficially—through military aspirations on the one hand and intellectual ones on the other—a part of it, so apparently immune to Western developments both in the realm of social change and institutional innovation—why was it that this society was the scene of the first 'proletarian' revolution, a revolution until then considered as compatible, if at all, only with the conditions prevailing in the advanced societies of the West?

To pose this question is, of course, to raise the standard historical 'problem' of the Russian Revolution and, thereby, what may by now be a somewhat commonplace issue, for it is a problem about which not a little has already been written and to which manifold answers have been suggested.[4] Yet it retains its power as a source of intellectual fascination; and, in any case, no one interested in the history of the Russian Marxist movement or in Russian Marxist thought, can avoid seeing it as emerging at every stage of his inquiries and constituting, in one way or another, their overriding theme. The problem, after all, was anticipated long before the Revolution, and it may be said to have been the source of almost every major theoretical and political controversy and rupture, of which there were not a few, in the Russian Social Democratic movement.

In particular, however, the problem of the relationship between backwardness and a socialist revolution occupied a central place in the thought of one Russian Marxist, who is the subject of the present study, and who, it will be argued, proposed the most original and, in some ways, the most convincing theoretical analysis, if not resolution, of its apparent contradictions. Leon Trotsky's analysis, moreover, had wider implications, for social theory in general and for the theory of revolution in particular. However, the untenable propositions and assumptions which it also contained threw much light, ironically, on the subsequent fate of the Russian Revolution. History,

---

[4] It would be hardly possible to list all the works, or even a selection of these, dealing with this subject; some of them, however, will be referred to in the course of this study. Arthur E. Adams (ed.), *The Russian Revolution and the Bolshevik Victory: Causes and Processes* (Lexington, Mass., 1972), contains a fairly representative sample of various views.

of course, is not merely a record of ideas or theories and an investigation of these certainly does not make other approaches to historical issues superfluous; in the present case, however, the playing out of ideas and theories reflects almost uncannily the course of reality itself, specifically both the logic and the incongruity of the actual meeting between a Marxist revolution and the 'Old Russia'.

Our subject, therefore, is a chapter, and a central one at that, both in the history of Marxist thought in general—considered as a product of Western social and intellectual developments—and in the history of Russian Marxism in particular—considered as belonging, in part at least, to a very different environment. From the final decade or so of the nineteenth century these histories overlapped in so far as the former was a model for the latter; but they also, and at an early stage, branched out in divergent directions, even while the model retained some of its influence. Thus the subject of our study must be examined in both historical contexts simultaneously, with a view to understanding the manner in which it remained within the tradition of Western Marxism and the point at which it contributed towards the creation of a considerably different tradition—though, in some ways which will become apparent in the course of the exposition, it may also be seen as unique in either context.[5]

To state all this is not to prejudge the issue of whether a connecting line may be drawn, and along what points, between the thought of Marx, and that of Trotsky or other Russian Marxists and, from there, to the character of the Russian Revolution itself; it is merely to stress the by now well-known fact that Marx's thought was open to, or at least not obviously incompatible with, being variously assimilated. To put the matter in a different but familiar way, the social and political thought of one Russian Marxist is here analysed, often explicitly but always tacitly, as an attempt to utilize, and thereby to develop in ways not always foreseen, a body of Western social thought and its political doctrine, for the understanding of the

[5] Western Marxism, of course, also contains a number of disparate traditions but, for our present purposes of distinguishing it from the Russian tradition—or rather from one main current of the latter—it may be considered as one whole, as having, that is, sufficiently common features marking it off from its Russian counterpart.

peculiar conditions and problems of Russian society at the outset of the twentieth century and during the subsequent four
decades. Today we have become accustomed to seeing Marxism as a doctrine with apparently greatest relevance and appeal
to non-Western or 'under-developed' societies. By looking at
the thought of Leon Trotsky we may be able to better comprehend why this should be so. In any case, the somewhat popular
view that Trotsky's thought was entirely within the European
Marxist tradition will be shown to be a misleading simplification; he, perhaps more than any other Marxist, was responsible
for transforming the geographical orientation of Marxist political theory in the twentieth century, though this has not been
generally recognized.

It may be objected that the adaptation of Marxism to Russian conditions was, in fact, a goal pursued by all Russian Marxists, from Plekhanov onwards, and by none more so than by
Lenin, and that, therefore, Trotsky was hardly unique in this
respect. However, it is the view of the present author that in
the case of Plekhanov, and of most other Russian Marxists as
well, no actual adaptation was carried out; their theory of a
Russian revolution consisted, on the whole, of a mere projection
of Marx's theory of Western historical development into
Russia's future. Whatever the merits of such an approach, it
cannot be said to have constituted a theoretical innovation;[6]
Marx's thought, in their hands, remained largely intact, or, to
use the standard term, it retained what was considered to be
its 'orthodox' character—and this in spite of the fact that Marx
himself, and Engels as well, had left the door open to the possibility that developments in Russia would follow a course very
different from that of Western history and might therefore issue
in a revolution equally different from any experienced in
Europe.[7] In the case of Lenin, the matter is admittedly somewhat more complicated and less obvious at first glance; but *his*
failure to adapt Marxist theory to Russia becomes just as

---

[6] This is not to say, of course, that Plekhanov or others did not contribute works of
merit and significance to Marxist theory in general. Trotsky himself always acknowledged Plekhanov's theoretical brilliance.

[7] The views of Marx and Engels on backwardness in general and on Russia in particular
are discussed in the Appendix which appears at the end of this study and which may
be read by way of background to the issues here alluded to and subsequently raised
throughout the study.

apparent when one recognizes that it was a Marxist *political movement* which Lenin in effect sought to accommodate to Russian conditions. Put another way, Lenin was not so much interested in the theoretical relevance of Marxism, nor in the theory, as such, of a socialist revolution, as in the manner in which a revolutionary movement (which happened to be governed by the Marxist ideology) should be organized in order that it might succeed in carrying out a revolution within the framework of the specific conditions prevailing in Russia.[8] It is almost impossible to overestimate the impact of what subsequently came to be known as Leninism (or Bolshevism) upon revolutionary movements and activities everywhere; but this has virtually nothing to do with the social theory itself of Marxism, to which Lenin added little and which he merely harnessed to his own theory of the revolutionary party.[9] The present study, therefore, takes as its point of departure the view that Trotsky's theory of a Russian revolution constituted the only sustained attempt to explain the manner in which both Marxism and a socialist revolution were immediately relevant to the Russia of the early twentieth century.

This theory was formulated largely before 1917, and following the events of that year Trotsky did not hesitate to claim that it had been confirmed by those events. Did it, does it, therefore, provide an unravelling to the enigma of the Russian Revolution, as Trotsky intended it to do? The analysis and critique of Trotsky's theory, from this point of view, make up the main body of this study and we shall not anticipate at this stage the ways in which, as has already been noted, the theory in fact did as much to unwittingly clarify the untenable elements in the juxtaposition of backwardness and socialist aspirations or possibilities, as to explain the tenable ones.

One aspect of this question, however, needs to be mentioned

[8] It seems legitimate to use the term 'Marxist ideology' in the context of Lenin's approach to Marxist theory; it was he, more than anyone else, who transformed the latter into an instrument for, primarily, political mobilization, whether of the masses or of the revolutionary élite. In this connection, see the study by Martin Seliger, *Ideology and Politics* (London, 1976).

[9] Once again, this is not to prejudge the connection between Marx's thought and the character of the Bolshevik Revolution or the operational, practical conclusions derived by Lenin. Nor is there any intention to imply that Lenin was not committed to Marxism or that, from a personal point of view, it did not form the foundation of his social and political beliefs.

here since it runs like a leitmotif through all that follows. As against Trotsky's approach to the interpretation of the Russian Revolution, there is a very different school of thought which, however, also believes that the Revolution presents no enigma: this is the school, occupying a prominent place in Western scholarship, which holds that the events of October 1917 and thereafter are simply and adequately explained by looking upon the Bolshevik seizure of power as merely a wild gamble that paid off. According to this view, political daring, determination and decisiveness, not to mention the pure chance of circumstances, were the factors which sealed the future of Russia and the triumph of the Marxist movement had therefore nothing to do with socialism or the logic of history or Marxism itself.[10] One need not accept the extreme formulation of this view—to the effect that all other factors were irrelevant—in order to agree that but for the person of Lenin, and the party, the methods and the mentality he almost single-handedly forged, we would not today be discussing the significance of a socialist revolution in Russia. As we shall see, Trotsky himself attributed to Lenin a crucial historical role, to the extent of admitting that without Lenin's leadership October 1917 would not have taken place. Yet the whole of his theory of a Russian revolution was founded on the proposition that history is *not* fortuitous or arbitrary. The relationship between chance and design, between individual choice or initiative and historical necessity, is a problem often encountered in Marxist theory. One of the aims of the present study, consequently, is to examine the persistent tension in the thought of Trotsky between the personal and the social, the subjective and the objective. We shall attempt to show why, after a long initial reluctance, he found it necessary in the end to see Russian Marxism as dependent on Bolshevism, and what the implications of this were for theory and practice alike. But this too was related to the problem of the backwardness of Russia; and it too may help to resolve the enigma of the Russian Revolution.

[10] For an extreme example of this school of thought, see Robert V. Daniels, *Red October* (New York, 1967). Daniels even argues that it was not so much Lenin's initiative or decisiveness which carried the day as his being *forced* to act, out of fear that if he did *not* gamble, then Kerensky's impending offensive against the Bolsheviks would effectively decimate the party.

Part I

THE THEORY OF THE PERMANENT REVOLUTION

CHAPTER ONE
MIND AND REALITY: IDEAS AND REVOLUTION

All through history, mind limps after reality.[1]

NOTHING IS more characteristic of the young Trotsky, as, indeed, of the familiar figure who was to emerge in later years, than his independence of mind and disdain for authority. By his own account, which is corroborated by all we know about him from other sources as well, he was by nature suspicious of all received opinion: in his autobiography he describes, not without a measure of self-delight, this ingrained scepticism, which often took the form of an almost exhibitionistic rebelliousness—against parents, teachers, schoolmates.[2] He had little patience with conventions, none at all with religious belief, and he was unable to comprehend how people could behave in ways contrary to the dictates of reason. He was also, however, even at an early age, somewhat flamboyant, attracted by and moved to side with, the colourful, the extravagant, even the ostentatious, in short, all that which could be proclaimed and done with flair and enthusiasm, of which qualities he had an abundance.

[1] Trotsky, *Literatura i Revolyutsiya* (Moscow, 1923), p. 15.
[2] *Moya Zhizn* (2 vols., Berlin, 1930). See I, pp. 17–126 for Trotsky's description of his childhood and early youth. The English translation of this autobiography was published in 1930 under the title *My Life* (reissued New York, 1960). The most complete biography of Trotsky is, of course, Isaac Deutscher's three-volume account, *The Prophet Armed, The Prophet Unarmed, The Prophet Outcast* (London, 1954, 1959, 1963). Max Eastman, *Leon Trotsky: The Portrait of a Youth* (New York, 1925) is a somewhat adulatory account of Trotsky's childhood and youth but has the advantage of being based on interviews with the subject. G. A. Ziv, *Trotsky: Kharakteristika po lichnym vospominaniam* (New York, 1921) consists of reminiscences by a friend from youth who, however, later became a political opponent. The sections devoted to Trotsky in Bertram D. Wolfe, *Three Who Made a Revolution* (Boston, 1955) are based almost entirely on Trotsky's autobiography and on Eastman and Ziv. There is also a somewhat forced psychoanalytical account: E. Victor Wolfenstein, *The Revolutionary Personality: Lenin, Trotsky, Gandhi* (Princeton, 1967). See also Edmund Wilson, *To the Finland Station* (London, 1960), pp. 406–31. A recent attempt at biography is Joel Carmichael, *Trotsky: An Appreciation of his Life* (London, 1975).

Together with this temperament there emerged, almost from the outset, a seemingly compulsive inclination towards the world of ideas, and of intellectual preoccupations in general, though there was not much in the immediate environment of his youth to encourage it. Born on 26 October 1879[3] in the remote village of Yanovka, in the Kherson province of the southern Ukraine—'a kingdom of wheat and sheep, living by laws all its own ... firmly guarded against the invasion of politics by its great open spaces and the absence of roads'[4]— Trotsky—or Lev Davidovich Bronstein as he was at birth and until 1902—was the son of a well-to-do and hard-working, but virtually illiterate, Jewish farm-owner who spoke an amalgam of Russian and Ukrainian, mostly the latter. The mother, in contrast, was literate, with some education, and of an urban background but, one has the impression from Trotsky's own description of her, a woman of limited depth. There could have been little in the home itself to satisfy Trotsky's native curiosity; each passing day, and life in general, was dominated by the 'rhythm of the toil on the farm' and 'nothing mattered except the price of grain on the world market'. Aside from a few months spent studying at a Jewish religious school in a nearby village, Trotsky hardly stepped outside Yanovka during the first nine years of his life.

In 1888, however, he was sent off to a *realschule* in Odessa, where he remained nearly seven years and where he was in-troduced to the opera, the theatre and, most of all, to books. For the latter he developed a boundless enthusiasm. His reading and his interests were at this time confined mainly to imagina-tive literature; he became fascinated with the world of letters and clearly yearned to enter it one day. Politics as such hardly impinged upon his consciousness at first. But, being sensitive and observant, he was growing more aware of the social charac-ter of his environment and developing a sense of its problems and iniquities. Moreover, at school, he often found himself in disciplinary difficulties as a result of his rebellious nature, his propensity for the dramatic confrontation over issues in dispute,

---

[3] About the coinciding, as it turned out, of this day and month with that of the Russian Revolution thirty-eight years later, Trotsky would only comment that 'mystics and Pythagoreans may draw from this whatever conclusions they like' (*Moya Zhizn*, I, p. 12).

[4] *Moya Zhizn*, I, p. 22.

and his aggressive, self-confident intellectual nonconformism.

All these characteristics, in fact, seemed to be at play in his initial, hostile encounter with Marxist ideas. When, at the age of sixteen or so, he began to take an interest in political questions, he was more easily drawn to Populism at first, not, it seems, out of any deep identification with its ideas, but, on the contrary, because it allowed him to give vent to his contumacy, and to his need for the demonstrative, without being constrained by any rigid doctrinal commitments. Marxism, on the other hand, whose general tenets he had vaguely become acquainted with, quite clearly repelled him at the outset. In his autobiography he tells why this was so. In 1896 he was completing his secondary education in Nikolayev, a provincial town near Odessa, and his thirst for knowledge was at its youthful height. He was reading voraciously, 'swallowing' books on philosophy, 'striving for a system'. But he resisted Marxism, 'partly because it seemed a completed system' and partly because it appeared to him 'narrow' and dry.[5] On joining a Populist circle, his attitude became, if anything, even more negative. In one of many similar outbursts of this time, he declared: 'A curse upon all Marxists, and upon those who want to bring dryness and hardness into all the relations of life.'[6] He was, for the time being, enticed by the grand ideal of Populism and repulsed and bored by what he then took to be the mechanical, economic laws of Marxism. But perhaps more than that, although searching for some ideal, he was unprepared to succumb to a 'completed system' which, he thought, would have left nothing to his own initiative and would have demanded of him discipline, loyalty and an end to personal freedom of belief and action.

Yet he was also eager to become involved in practical activity and in the 1890s Populism was already a spent force. In spite of himself, Marxism—in a still very undigested form—was taking a hold of him. Deciding with a friend to write a play in which a Marxist and a Populist would be protagonists, he found himself attributing 'courage and hope' to the former, 'feebleness' and 'failure' to the latter. Organizing a 'university' for

---

[5] Ibid., pp. 121–2.
[6] Eastman, op. cit., p. 67. The outburst was aimed at Alexandra Sokolovskaya, a Marxist within the Populist circle who later (1900) became Trotsky's first wife.

some twenty students, he took responsibility for the 'department of sociology'.[7] The year 1897 soon became a turning
point: he became convinced that revolutionary work must be
carried out amongst the workers, of whom there were about
ten thousand in Nikolayev, and, together with others, organized the South Russian Workers' Union for which he also
drafted a constitution 'along Social Democratic lines'. But in
January 1898 the organization was raided by the police and
Trotsky, together with some two hundred others, was arrested.

For two years he awaited trial, first in Nikolayev, then in
an Odessa prison. He used the time to become better versed
in Marxism; his knowledge of it was still rudimentary, based
more on hearsay than actual acquaintance with texts. He read
essays by the Italian Marxist Antonio Labriola and although
his 'ignorance' prevented him from understanding fully what
he read, after that, 'all the Russian proponents of the multiplicity of factors, Lavrov, Mikhailovsky, Kareyev and others,
seemed utterly ineffectual' to him.[8] He became interested in freemasonry and decided to write a treatise on it, using his newly
acquired and still elementary notion of 'historical materialism':

I made no new discoveries; all the methodological conclusions at
which I had arrived had been made long ago and were being applied
in practice. But I groped my way to them, and somewhat independently. I think this influenced the whole course of my subsequent intellectual development. In the writings of Marx, Engels, Plekhanov
and Mehring I later found confirmation for what in prison seemed
to me only a guess needing verification and theoretical justification.
I did not absorb historical materialism at once, dogmatically. The
dialectical method revealed itself to me for the first time not as abstract
definitions but as a living spring which I had found in the historical
process as I tried to understand it.[9]

By the end of 1899 the verdict against him was announced
and he was sentenced to four years of exile in Siberia. He was
first moved to a transfer prison in Moscow. There, for the first
time, he heard of Lenin and read, 'from cover to cover', the
latter's *The Development of Capitalism in Russia*, which had just

---

[7] *Moya Zhizn*, I, pp. 124 and 125.
[8] Ibid., p. 143.
[9] Ibid., p. 147. The work on freemasonry was later lost.

appeared.[10] In the autumn of 1900 he arrived in the east Siberian village of Ust-Kut, the place of his banishment. The harsh surroundings, however, did not detract him from pursuing his self-education. He continued his reading, studying Marx and others, and as he read, his conversion became complete: 'At the time of my exile, Marxism had definitely become the basis of my philosophy.'[11] However, 'now it was no longer a question of pure scientific study, but of the choice of a political path'.[12]

He also began writing, and publishing, mainly essays on literary and social subjects.[13] Analysing the works of Russian classic authors and of Ibsen, Nietzsche, Hauptmann and others, he dwelt on one principal theme: the relations between the individual and society.[14] 'I sat up night after night scratching up my manuscripts, as I tried to find the exact idea or the right word to express it. I was becoming a writer.'[15] Through these writings he was also becoming known to Social Democrats elsewhere.

His one purely political work during exile was an essay on party organization in which he argued for a centralized framework with a strong leadership.[16] This was widely circulated in mimeographed form and became the source of a lively controversy amongst the Social Democrats in Siberia. Two years later he would repudiate the apparent views this essay expressed, but meanwhile, shortly after he wrote it, he received a copy of Lenin's *What is to be Done?* which, of course, could only strengthen his convictions on this matter. He had as yet not recognized the full meaning of Lenin's ideas.

With the arrival of news and publications from abroad, and as his own intellectual development progressed, he became

[10] Ibid., p. 148.
[11] Ibid., p. 151.
[12] Ibid., p. 153.
[13] These early essays were first published in the Irkutsk newspaper *Vostochnoye Obozrenie* and later collected in volumes IV and XX of Trotsky's *Sochineniya*. (For a description of the *Sochineniya*, see the bibliography.)
[14] Trotsky's literary criticism during this and later periods will be discussed in chapter 11, below.
[15] *Moya Zhizn*, I, p. 151.
[16] Part of this unpublished essay was quoted by Trotsky in an appendix to his *Vtoroi Syezd RSDRP: Otchet Sibirskoi Delegatsii* (Geneva, 1903), pp. 31–2. This and his other writings on the subject of party organization are discussed in chapter 5, below.

more and more frustrated by his isolation from any kind of real activity. He yearned to break out of his provincial, barren milieu and plunge into the centre of revolutionary circles, whether in Russia or in Europe. Consequently, in the summer of 1902, he decided to escape his confinement.[17] This proved easier than he had expected; and he soon reached Samara where he established contact with the *Iskra* organization. Then, in the autumn, he decided to leave for abroad. After brief stop-overs in Vienna and Zurich, he arrived in October in London.[18]

There Lenin was waiting for him. Trotsky's published essays had earned him the reputation of a vivid, imaginative mind and Lenin was eager to meet this new convert to the revolutionary movement. He was not disappointed and the two immediately developed mutual respect for each other.[19] But the relationship between them, although generally a warm one, was mainly governed by intellectual and political interests. Trotsky developed closer friendships with some of the other members of the *Iskra* editorial board: Vera Zasulich and Paul Axelrod in particular. With Plekhanov, there was conflict from the outset, apparently growing out of the latter's disdain for the younger Trotsky's intellectual flourish and impudence. But Plekhanov also feared that Lenin courted Trotsky in order to build up a majority against him. When Lenin proposed that Trotsky be co-opted to the *Iskra* board, it was Plekhanov's opposition which prevented his election.[20] This did not stop Trotsky from pursuing active work: he lectured, travelled to meet Russian revolutionary émigrés in France, Switzerland, Belgium and Germany, and contributed regularly to the *Iskra* newspaper.

On political questions there seemed to be general agreement between Lenin and Trotsky. Thus when in 1903, at the famous Second Congress of the Russian Social Democrats, the two split irrevocably, it came as if without warning. But it was no less tempestuous for that. For reasons which will be discussed later in this study,[21] Trotsky now rejected all talk of a centralized

[17] It was at this time that he acquired the name Trotsky, 'borrowing' it from a gaoler he had come to know earlier while in prison in Odessa.
[18] See *Moya Zhizn*, I, chapter 10.
[19] See ibid., chapter 11, where Trotsky describes his first and subsequent meetings with Lenin in London.
[20] Ibid., pp. 180–1.
[21] See chapter 5, below.

party and it was he who now appeared as one of Lenin's main
opponents. At the Congress itself he lashed out at Lenin's 'dictatorial' views and later he did the same in a report on the proceedings which he composed in his official capacity as the dele-
gate of the Siberian Social Democratic Workers' Union.[22] A
year later he returned to the same subject in a long pamphlet:
this constituted an attack which was, if anything, even more
scathing, throwing doubt both on the motives of Lenin
personally and on the true meaning of the latter's declared
views.[23] It was the end of a brief partnership which would
not be renewed until the fateful days of some fourteen years
later.

For Trotsky the Congress also marked the beginning of his
isolation. He had opposed Lenin and the emerging Bolshevism
but he had not become a Menshevik.[24] Although in subsequent
years he would retain closer relations with the Menshevik faction than with the Bolshevik one, he felt at home in neither
camp. He was now without a 'roof', cut off by his own choice
from all organizational ties, a revolutionary without a revolutionary base. This was to be the source both of his intellectual
strength and his political weakness.

Trotsky's relatively brief but intensive 'Odyssey' from a provincial Populist circle to the centre of the Russian Social Democratic movement, from Nikolayev to Brussels and London, had
thus ended in frustration; in search of a base for political
activity, he reached it only to find himself rejecting it. Moreover, although he had in the course of that 'Odyssey' acquired
a 'system' of thought, he himself had only begun to contribute
to it. He had revealed a flourish for ideas and a powerful,
though sometimes overly florid, style for expressing them.[25]

[22] This report is the previously mentioned *Vtoroi Syezd RSDRP: Otchet Sibirskoi Delegatsii*.
[23] N. Trotsky, *Nashi Politicheskye Zadachi* (Geneva, 1904). This too is discussed in chapter
5, below. Trotsky used the initial N. for this and the previous work.
[24] However, he retained ties with individual Mensheviks and continued writing in Menshevik newspapers.
[25] The first to criticize his style as florid had been Plekhanov who used this as an argument against Trotsky's association with *Iskra*. Lenin, in a letter to Plekhanov, agreed
but believed Trotsky would 'outgrow' it. Trotsky himself was very sensitive to any
criticism of his style and accepted corrections sulkily. See *Moya Zhizn*, I, pp. 178 and
181.

There was passion and intelligence in what he wrote and a clear
conception of the issues involved. But his writings did not yet
fulfil his overall capacity for sustained theoretical reasoning.
And the political subjects with which he had dealt were chosen
more for their topicality than out of personal interest. He had
written about questions of party organization because these were
the issue of the day, not because he considered them generally
paramount. And although in so doing he had recognized their
importance and grasped the dangers involved in certain attitudes to them, the matter itself seemed to him, from the point
of view of his own intellectual evolution, peripheral. Broader
issues, involving the problem of the Marxist theory of revolution
and Russian social developments, were beginning to occupy his
attention. As was to occur throughout his life, political isolation
was an opportunity for thought and reflection, for 'systematic
work' in the realm of ideas.[26]

It was in this mood that in the spring of 1904, in Munich,
Trotsky met one Alexander Helphand, better known by his
pen-name Parvus. A Russian Jew who had left his native
country in 1887 and settled in Germany, Parvus was to have
one of the most chequered and mysterious careers in the annals
of Social Democracy.[27] But at this time he was considered one
of the most original thinkers in the movement, admired and
consulted by all, including Lenin. Although he had more or
less severed his ties with Russia and become involved primarily
in the German revolutionary movement, his home in Munich
was often frequented by Russian exiles. Here Trotsky, together
with his wife,[28] came to stay. The result was an 'intellectual
partnership'[29] out of which grew the initial sources of Trotsky's
theoretical conception of the Russian revolution. Later, in his
autobiography, Trotsky acknowledged this debt: 'He [Parvus],

[26] In this connection, see the remarks at the beginning of chapter 12, below.
[27] For a full account of his life, see the biography by Z. A. B. Zeman and W. B. Scharlau,
The Merchant of Revolution (London, 1965). See also Heinz Schurer, 'Alexander Helphand-Parvus: Russian Revolutionary and German Patriot', *The Russian Review* (Oct.
1959), pp. 313–31. On the influence of Parvus on Trotsky, see also W. B. Scharlau,
'Parvus und Trockij: 1904–1914. Ein Betrag zur Theorie der permanenten Revolution', in *Jahrbücher für Geschichte Osteuropas* (Oct. 1962), pp. 349–80.
[28] His second wife, Natalya Sedova; Trotsky's first wife, who had been banished with
him, remained behind when he escaped from Siberia.
[29] This is the title of the chapter Deutscher devotes to the Trotsky–Parvus relationship
(*The Prophet Armed*, p. 98).

possessed of wide vision, . . . brought me closer to the problems of the social revolution, and, for me, definitely transformed the conquest of power by the proletariat from an astronomical "final" goal to a practical task for our own day.'[30]

A bitter opponent of 'revisionism', Parvus in his pre-1904 writings had argued that the workers' movement must continuously agitate for revolution rather than wait for propitious conditions to develop of themselves. In his articles of the 1890s on Russia, he had clearly aligned himself on the side of those who held that Russian capitalism, however rudimentary, was now a permanent, irreversible phenomenon. Moreover, he had made a point of emphasizing the weakness of the Russian bourgeoisie and the consequent strategic importance of the working class.[31] Like others, Trotsky had read and been impressed both by the force of the arguments in these articles and the 'virile, muscular' style in which they had been presented.[32] But the real impact on Trotsky came from a series of articles, entitled 'War and Revolution', which Parvus published in *Iskra* during 1904.[33] They were occasioned by the outbreak of hostilities between Russia and Japan and opened with a sentence which immediately declared the ominous conclusion to which their arguments were devoted: 'The Russo-Japanese war is the blood-red dawn of coming great events.'[34]

Parvus's analysis in these articles centred on what he considered to be two new phenomena which now provided the key to further revolutionary developments: the phenomenon of war between capitalist nation-states and the phenomenon of Russia's direct involvement in world capitalist conflicts. Parvus was thus among the first to propose the 'imperialist war' thesis which was to become so popular in Marxist circles some ten years later. He argued that the world capitalist order, far from being a unified camp with one common interest, was in fact

[30] *Moya Zhizn*, I, p. 193. In 1940, in an appendix to his *Stalin* (New York, 1941), Trotsky wrote (pp. 429–30): 'There is no doubt that he [Parvus] exerted considerable influence on my personal development, especially with respect to the social-revolutionary understanding of our epoch.' See also his article 'Parvus', in *Nashe Slovo*, no. 15, 14 Feb. 1915.
[31] See Zeman and Scharlau, op. cit., pp. 24–5, 42–3.
[32] *Moya Zhizn*, I, p. 193.
[33] These were later reprinted in Parvus's book *Rossiya i revolyutsiya* (St. Petersburg, 1906), pp. 83ff. (The first article appeared in *Iskra*, no. 59, 10 Feb. 1904.)
[34] Parvus, op. cit., p. 83.

divided within itself and against itself through the growth of the nation-state. Once the basis of European stability, the nation-state was now a fetter upon further economic development. Competition for overseas markets, rival national economic interests, the insatiable need for continuous industrial expansion—all these were driving the European powers into what would eventually become a world-wide conflict.

As for Russia, her involvement in this lethal confrontation grew both out of her own capitalist ambitions and the particular instability of her social structure. On the one hand, she was obliged to fight over her interests abroad in order to remain an independent power; on the other, war was a way of diverting attention from domestic problems, of relieving or delaying pressure for internal social change. In fact, however, since Russia's external aspirations outran her internal capacities, the opposite would occur. War would upset the delicate internal balance, expose the obsolescence of the Tsarist autocracy and accelerate the process of social disintegration. Thus both international developments and her own precarious condition, obviously much more fragile than that of the European powers, would make her particularly vulnerable to a sudden upheaval. Moreover, once this upheaval came it would not be just a Russian affair; its repercussions would be world-wide:

The world process of capitalist development brings about a political upheaval in Russia. In turn, this will affect political development in all capitalist countries. The Russian revolution will shake the capitalist world. And the Russian proletariat will assume the role of the vanguard of the social revolution.[35]

This view of things later came to be known as the 'weakest link' thesis: the capitalist 'chain' breaking first at its most vulnerable point, namely, Russia. Parvus's prophetic conclusion, however, went far beyond anything anyone at the time was prepared to contemplate. Although the idea of Russia as the paradoxical spearhead of revolution had originally been suggested by Marx—though in a different context[36]—and, more recently, repeated by Karl Kautsky,[37] no one took it very

[35] Ibid., p. 133.
[36] See the Appendix at the end of this study.
[37] In an article, 'Slavyane i revolyutsiya', *Iskra*, no. 18, 10 Mar. 1902. See also Kautsky's later pamphlet, *Dvizhushchiya sily i perspektivy russkoi revolyutsii* (St. Petersburg, 1906).

seriously, certainly not the Russian Marxists themselves who, in accordance with their view of things, could not foresee anything more than a localized bourgeois revolution. The impact of the conclusion on Trotsky, however, was profound. The very sweep of the arguments, the imaginative leap over a conventional determinism, the intellectual courage of stating a paradox, all these found a response in Trotsky's own unorthodox nature. Above all, it appealed to his universal orientations: it offered the possibility of breaking out of a Russian self-centredness and relating, even linking, the Russian revolutionary movement to the whole gamut of world developments.

He himself was now engrossed in the writing of a brochure which would argue how hopeless was the prospect of a bourgeois-led revolution in Russia;[38] and as he completed it, events themselves seemed to be vindicating both his and Parvus's new-found insights. On 9/22 January 1905, workers in St. Petersburg, led by Father Gapon, marched in procession to the Tsar's Winter Palace; before the day was over, hundreds lay dead and wounded, victims of salvoes fired by the Tsar's troops, and Russia was on the brink of eruption. Trotsky, at the time in Geneva, decided to return to Russia immediately; on the way, he stopped in Munich to see Parvus and show him the manuscript of his brochure. In it Trotsky had written that the main revolutionary weapon in Russia would become the general strike of workers. Reading this, Parvus was impressed. 'The events', he told Trotsky, 'have fully confirmed this analysis.' And he added that now 'revolution in Russia may place a democratic workers' government in power'.[39] The two spent several days discussing both events and theory and Parvus agreed to write a preface to Trotsky's brochure. This preface, Trotsky was later to say, 'entered permanently into the history of the Russian Revolution'.[40]

In it[41] Parvus was primarily concerned to show how powerful

[38] *Do 9-go Yanvarya* (Geneva, 1905). Trotsky completed writing the brochure in December 1904 but when he submitted it for publication to the Mensheviks, it was at first turned down. It was finally published in the above edition in March 1905 with the presently to be discussed preface by Parvus. Later it was reprinted in Trotsky's *Sochineniya*, II, part 1, pp. 1–53. It is discussed in chapter 2, below.
[39] *Moya Zhizn*, I, pp. 192–3.
[40] *Stalin*, p. 430.
[41] Parvus, untitled 'Preface' (dated 18/31 Jan. 1905) to Trotsky's *Do 9-go Yanvarya* (Geneva, 1905), pp. iii–xiv. What follows is a summary of this preface.

a force the Russian proletariat had become and how all other opposition forces, including the peasants and the bourgeoisie, were dependent on it in any struggle with the autocracy. This, in his view, was due to the peculiar manner in which classes had developed in Russia. The bourgeoisie had not grown out of towns; instead a capitalist class was superimposed from above without the intermediate link of a radical middle class in the provinces. This was responsible for the subsequent weakness of the bourgeoisie, namely, its suspension from the air with no roots in the economic development of the country. One of the consequences of this was that the peasantry was unable to develop economically. In the absence both of a manufacturing industry and of bourgeois leadership, the peasants continued to pursue an undifferentiated agricultural economy or, at most, rudimentary production in arts and crafts. They remained an inchoate, disorganized mass ruled over by a bureaucracy resembling the Chinese model. Although restive and deprived, they of themselves could not spearhead a revolutionary drive. There thus remained only the proletariat which alone had had a social development of a revolutionary character. It too did not come into being via the economic evolution of the towns and the countryside—there had been none—but had been created by the industrial needs of the state. Thus, rapidly mobilized from amongst peasants seeking employment, and suddenly concentrated in large industrial centres, the workers filled a political vacuum, linking village with city, and constituting an intermediate element between the weak middle class and the powerful state. Their presence was now 'telescoping' events, since they were a directly involved party in the struggle of the bourgeoisie; unlike in the West, where this struggle was largely independent, in Russia it could succeed only by mobilizing the workers. In effect, however, this mobilization would not be the work of the bourgeoisie; the proletariat itself would plunge into the struggle of its own accord, dragging the bourgeoisie after it. The result would not be a simple restaging of the 'bourgeois revolution' but a phenomenon completely unique in history: a workers' government in a pre-democratic society.

Parvus believed that this would happen whatever the programme and position of the Social Democratic movement, for the whole basis of his argument was the spontaneous mass

nature of the development. The events of 1905 demonstrated
to him how far Russian Social Democracy was lagging after
events; it was the mass of workers themselves who were radical-
izing the revolution. Whatever the hesitations of its leadership,
the workers would stamp their own definitions on the revolutionary government: 'The Social Democracy will stand before
a dilemma: either to take responsibility for the actions of the
provisional government or to step aside from the working-class
movement. The workers will look to the provisional government as their own no matter what the Social Democracy does.'[42]

The manner in which the Marxist movement resolves this
dilemma will seal its fate:

The provisional revolutionary government will be a government of
the working-class democracy. If the Social Democracy stands at the
head of the revolutionary movement of the Russian proletariat, that
government will become a Social Democratic one. If not . . . the
Social Democracy will degenerate into an insignificant sect.[43]

In view of this, Parvus urged the movement to be in step
with the times, to throw overboard all its political caution and
theoretical doubts, to make itself the spokesman for the new
revolutionary fervour of the workers. With an eye on the 'revisionist' trend of Social Democracy in Germany, he proposed
clear tactical lines for radical action which would guard the
independence of the movement and prevent its appeasement
by temporary peasant and bourgeois allies. But his bold, far-
reaching conclusions stopped short of the most far-reaching
conclusion of all: he did not believe that the end of all this could
be a truly socialist revolution: 'A Social Democratic provisional
government will not be capable of accomplishing in Russia a
socialist revolution, but the mere fact of the liquidation of the
autocracy and of the establishment of a democratic republic
will create fertile ground for the political activity of Social
Democracy.'[44]

This somewhat left matters in the air. It implied that the
workers' government would be much confined in its scope; it
would be more radical, certainly, than a bourgeois regime but
also less radical than a socialist one. And what would be the
connection between democratic innovations and socialist ones

[42] Ibid., p. xi.   [43] Loc. cit.   [44] Loc. cit.

and how could one move from the one to the other? Parvus sensed the element of momentum and transition but did not work out its connecting links or the process as a whole, nor the actual relationship of all this to political developments elsewhere. Perhaps this was because, although he had provided the outlines of a social analysis of Russia's economic development, he had not explained the compatibility of her persistent backwardness with socialist institutions; the political strength, in other words, of the workers, due to Russia's peculiar social structure, did not in itself argue for the appropriateness of a workers' government, if this latter term was to be understood in its Marxist sense.

Even as it stood, however, Parvus's scenario was too much for his Russian colleagues. The Mensheviks' reaction to the idea of an immediate workers' government was predictable; but Lenin too was incredulous. It seemed to him an illusion, generated by imaginative impulse, rather than a realistic appreciation of the alignment of forces in Russia. 'This cannot be', he wrote, in the debate which ensued. 'This cannot be because only a revolutionary dictatorship supported by a colossal majority of the people can be at all lasting. . . . In trying to aim at an immediate socialist overturn, Social Democracy would only disgrace itself.'[45]

In fact, the only one who seems to have taken Parvus's preface to Trotsky's brochure seriously was Trotsky himself. In this brochure he too had concentrated on the unique features of what was taking place in Russian society. True, he had not been as bold as Parvus. Yet the impact of the latter's ideas on him was soon to be unmistakable; henceforth he would always see this as a turning-point in his intellectual development. It was the kind of imaginative prod which his mind needed to free itself from the worst confines of the 'completed system' of thought he had embraced only a few years before. In the said preface Parvus had written that 'events are revolutionizing the mind . . . revolution is driving political thought forward'.[46] Neither Parvus nor Trotsky had yet resolved the full implications of what still seemed to be only a bold hypothesis. But as

[45] Quoted in Solomon M. Schwarz, *The Russian Revolution of 1905* (Chicago and London, 1967), pp. 17 and 20.
[46] Parvus, 'Preface' to *Do 9-go Yanvarya*, p. iii.

Trotsky now hurried to be at the centre of those 'events' in Russia, his mind was working feverishly. Forced, in the summer of 1905, to go temporarily into hiding in Finland, after a brief stay in Russia and before returning again in October, he had a 'short interval of peace':

. . . I did intensive literary work and took short walks in the country. I read the papers with avidity, watched the parties take shape, clipped newspapers, and grouped and sifted facts. During that period, I finally formulated my conception of the inner forces of Russian society and of the prospects of the Russian revolution.[47]

A quarter of a century later, looking back upon the year 1905 and its impact on his life, Trotsky wrote in his autobiography: 'The revolution of 1905 made a break in the life of the country, in the life of the party and in my own life. The break was in the direction of greater maturity.'[48] This joining of the personal and the historical, of his own development with that of events, especially revolutionary ones, may already tell us something about Trotsky's unabashed sense of identification with the course of history, a subject we shall discuss later in this study.[49] But it also reveals the extent to which the events of 1905 aroused and provoked his intellectual capacities and shaped his subsequent political outlook. Thus in a remarkable passage, again in his autobiography, Trotsky observed:

No great work is possible without intuition—that is, without that subconscious sense which, although it may be developed and enriched by theoretical and practical work, must be ingrained in the very nature of the individual. Neither theoretical education nor practical routine can replace the political insight which enables one to apprehend a situation, weigh it as a whole, and foresee the future. This gift takes on decisive importance at a time of abrupt changes and breaks—the conditions of revolution. The events of 1905 revealed in me, I believe, this revolutionary intuition, and enabled me to rely on its assured support during my later life.[50]

Trotsky could hardly wait to give immediate expression in writing to the fruits of this 'intuition'. From the middle of October 1905, when he returned to Russia, until some six weeks

[47] *Moya Zhizn*, I, p. 197.   [48] Ibid., p. 210.
[49] See chapter 12, below.   [50] *Moya Zhizn*, I, pp. 212–13.

later, he would, as is well known, reach an early zenith in his revolutionary career as one of the outstanding leaders of the St. Petersburg Soviet. But the fifteen months between December 1905—when he would be arrested along with other members of the Soviet—and February 1907—when he would escape, again, from exile in Siberia—would be one of the most productive intellectual periods in his life. It was during this period of confinement that he wrote *Itogi i Perspektivy* (known in English as *Results and Prospects*), most of the essays in *Nasha Revolyutsiya* (Our Revolution), and the main parts of *1905*.[51] For all intents and purposes, the ideas he then developed represented an already completed, rather than tentative, theory of revolution, with which his name was henceforth to be linked, and in subsequent years he found it necessary only to refine this theory. The year 1905 was thus a landmark in his life, both as a revolutionary and as a thinker, for it was in the wake of the events of that year, and with the influence of Parvus still fresh, that he formulated, as he would write, 'the most finished statement in proof of the theory of permanent revolution'.[52]

What happened in 1905 to jar Trotsky's imagination and to set him on a course which he was to pursue throughout the rest of his life? In part, the general answer to this question is contained in a few lines from his dramatic speech to the Tsarist court trying him and his fellow members of the Soviet. The speech was delivered on 4/17 October 1906, and came in answer to the official charge that the accused had conspired to prepare an armed uprising against the state. In rejecting this charge, in the manner it was formulated, Trotsky sought to impart to the court a lesson in the workings of history:

The uprising of the masses, Messrs. Judges, is not something which is made, it occurs of its own accord. It is the result of social relations and not the product of a plan. It cannot be manufactured, it can only be foreseen. Through the operation of causes which depend as little on us as they do on the Imperial government, an open conflict had

---

[51] References to these works will be given in the following chapter. While in prison Trotsky also began writing a 'big work' on the theory of rent but he later lost the manuscript (see *Moya Zhizn*, I, p. 215).

[52] *Moya Zhizn*, I, p. 215.

become inescapable. Each day brought us closer and closer to it . . .
We, note well Messrs. Judges, never *prepared an uprising*, as the prosecu-
tor thinks and says, *we prepared for an uprising*.[53]

From this and other observations he was to make on what
happened in 1905, it is clear that the main impression of that
year on Trotsky was the sheer spontaneity of the events. He
was in particular impressed by the fact, as he took it to be, that
the revolutionary fervour of the masses, to which lip service had
been paid by Marxism so often in the past, was neither a myth
nor an illusion but a living reality. Similarly, he was now struck
by, on the one hand, the seeming inscrutability of history and,
on the other, the possibility of unravelling its logic. The determinist element in this he had of course inherited and assimilated
as every Marxist had done before him, but if in the past he
had understood it formally, he now believed himself to have
witnessed its reality. He had, in short, become fascinated by the
phenomenon, which to him at least now seemed beyond doubt,
that political developments *are* directly related to social and
economic substrata and that their nature is to be sought—and
'foreseen'—in social history. Finally, 1905 reaffirmed his view,
expressed so firmly against Lenin in 1903, that political leadership and organization were to be grasped as instrumental aids,
not as substitutes for, nor as the sources of, a mass movement.
    Curiously, however, the very same determinist element
which he now embraced, led him to think in what to others
at least seemed to be grossly non-determinist terms. The logic
which he claimed to perceive in history, at first intuitively, but
almost immediately afterwards through a long theoretical
analysis, was neither the universal logic attributed to Marx nor
the inexorable development of a Russian capitalism which his
co-Marxists were projecting into Russia's future. It was rather,
he believed, the logic of very peculiar conditions, making for
unique rather than universal circumstances, and subject to the
impact of a particular period in world history. The basic elements in Russia's impending future, as in that of all societies,
would be the same as in that European past which Marx had

[53] 'Moya rech pered sudom', in Trotsky, *1905* (4th Russian edition, Moscow, 1925),
p. 356. For bibliographical information concerning the book *1905*, see chapter 2, note
10. below.

described; but the pattern of their development in Russia would be different. If to foresee means not only to assimilate the ways of history but to transcend them as well, then mind, Trotsky seemed to believe, if it freed itself from the confines of functioning within the framework of hitherto experienced historical patterns alone, could also anticipate reality.

CHAPTER TWO

THE POLITICS OF BACKWARDNESS: THE REVOLUTION OF 1905

In Russian life, the Revolution of 1905 was the dress rehearsal for the Revolution of 1917.[1]

ON THE eve of what came to be known as the Revolution of 1905, Russia was a vast empire, part in Europe, part in Asia, with a population of nearly 150 million of whom some 80 per cent were peasants and the total composed of more than twenty nationalities;[2] with an economic system, part of which had been industrialized, the greater part of which, however, continued to be based on largely primitive agricultural production; a social structure and a cultural tradition remarkable for their combination of both backward and modern features; and the whole held together by a centralized, absolutist autocracy at the head of which stood a somewhat pathetic 'father figure' oblivious to the contradictions and ferment around him, waging war with Japan and everywhere pursuing 'big-power' pretensions.

In 1905 this enormous edifice was on the verge of collapse. Such a calamity had been long predicted by the numerous revolutionary and even non-revolutionary groups active in Russia. But as it unfolded during the months of 1905, it revealed features both unique and unforeseen.[3] Although the Revolution of 1905 was to enter history as a failed bourgeois revolution, its main impetus was not provided by the middle classes. Nor did the peasantry, an uncertain but potentially explosive force, stand at the centre of the widespread disturbances of that

---

[1] *Moya Zhizn*, I, p. 213.
[2] For a brief summary of demographic figures for Russia from 1897 to 1914, see J. N. Westwood, *Endurance and Endeavour: Russian History 1812–1971* (Oxford, 1973), pp. 171–4.
[3] For a general account of the Revolution, see Sidney Harcave, *The Russian Revolution of 1905* (London, 1970); for an account of Russian Social Democracy—especially the formation of its ideas—during the Revolution, see Schwarz, op. cit.

famous year. Instead, the most active, certainly the most precipitant social force, proved to be the still nascent working class.

It is true, of course, that during 1905 there were numerous peasant revolts and that the liberal bourgeoisie had clearly decided to lay claim to a substantial share of political power. Yet the latter, far from initiating the attack upon the autocracy, was simply swept into the general mood by events not of its own making. As for the peasantry, it rebelled in the only way it knew how: spontaneously, sporadically, without organization or leadership, and with only the vaguest notion of its goals. Neither of these social groups, whether independently or even together, posed an insurmountable threat to the autocracy. To an unprecedented extent, their effectiveness was dependent on that of a third group, the workers, who although on their own would have been similarly impotent, in conjunction with the others constituted the most decisive factor in undermining the regime's powers of resistance. It was the workers who had opened the whole drama with their St. Petersburg procession of 9/22 January; it was they who throughout the year threatened to paralyse the whole economy with general strikes in the major urban centres; and it was they who, as the events came to a head, issued the most radical demands. It was the workers also who, albeit briefly and to a limited extent, grasped at actual political power: in the middle of October they established the St. Petersburg Soviet of Workers' Deputies which, in that city, for a few weeks exercised independent authority.

The disproportionate importance of the Russian working class had been noticed by many prior to the events of 1905. But not even the most optimistic amongst them had quite foreseen the scope and intensity which characterized the workers' involvement in the Revolution. Lenin had indeed predicted that the proletariat would be the vanguard of a temporary alliance with the bourgeoisie and others too had spoken in not dissimilar terms.[4] Yet what happened in 1905 went beyond what even they had presumed for it raised for the first time, however tentatively, the possibility of a workers' seizure of power. This was surely incompatible with what the Russian Marxists had

[4] See Schwarz, op. cit., pp. 1–74, for a discussion of Menshevik and Bolshevik views before 1905.

in general anticipated, namely a 'bourgeois revolution' at best.[5]

But if, as everyone so matter-of-factly expected, the revolution in Russia was to usher in a period of 'bourgeois democracy', who and where were those social factors, more specifically that social class, which could translate this expectation into political reality? The weakness of the 'orthodox' Russian Marxist position was that it itself subscribed to a view of the Russian bourgeoisie which argued against the very prediction which it so confidently awaited to be fulfilled. For if the bourgeoisie, as all Marxists agreed, was weak, cowardly, dependent on the good graces of the state, and economically impotent, how could it be expected to stand at the head of a revolution? Surely such was not the condition of the European bourgeoisie on the eve of *its* political triumph? By the middle of 1905 the fundamental contradiction in the Marxist position was something which Lenin, for example, could no longer ignore. It was then, primarily in the work *Two Tactics of Social Democracy in the Democratic Revolution*,[6] that he finally despaired of bourgeois revolutionism and called for an alliance between workers and peasants against the state and against the bourgeoisie itself. But as the title of this work indicates, he continued to view the future within a traditional framework: the new alliance was a tactical alternative; as for the aim, a democratic, bourgeois republic, it remained unaffected. Moreover, if he had resolved one contradiction, he had introduced another, more serious one: how

[5] On the early history and ideas of the Russian Social Democratic movement, see also the following: Leopold Haimson, *The Russian Marxists and the Origins of Bolshevism* (Cambridge, Mass., 1955); J. L. H. Keep, *The Rise of Social Democracy in Russia* (Oxford, 1963); Richard Pipes, *Social Democracy and the St. Petersburg Labor Movement, 1885–1897* (Cambridge, Mass., 1963); Donald W. Treadgold, *Lenin and His Rivals: The Struggle for Russia's Future, 1898–1906* (New York, 1955); Allan K. Wildman, *The Making of a Workers' Revolution: Russian Social Democracy, 1891–1903* (Chicago and London, 1967). The most complete account of Lenin's ideas, before and after 1905, is Alfred G. Meyer, *Leninism* (New York, 1962). See also Adam B. Ulam, *The Bolsheviks* (New York, 1968). On Plekhanov, see Samuel H. Baron, *Plekhanov: The Father of Russian Marxism* (Stanford, 1963). For an account of Bolshevism by a former Menshevik leader, see Theodore Dan, *The Origins of Bolshevism* (London, 1964). On the ideas of the Legal Marxists, see Richard Kindersley, *The First Russian Revisionists* (Oxford, 1962). This list does not, of course, exhaust the literature on these subjects; other works will be referred to in the course of this study.
[6] The English version of this work is in Lenin, *Selected Works* (3 vols., Moscow, n.d. [1963]), I, pp. 485–597.

could two classes, the peasantry and the proletariat, make the revolution of a third, the bourgeoisie, particularly when the spearhead of this alliance, the workers, were said to be implacable enemies of the capitalist system? In due course, on the eve of his own triumph some twelve years later, Lenin would belatedly, and perhaps opportunistically, recognize and jettison this contradiction as well. But in the meantime not even he—much less the Mensheviks whose position at one point wavered but in the end altered not at all[7]—was prepared to repudiate what seemed the holiest of Marxist cows.

In a sense it may be said that such a repudiation was precisely what Trotsky in 1905 and thereafter resolved to make. As we have seen, the only Russian Social Democrat to draw more far-reaching conclusions, already at the outset of 1905, had been Parvus, and the first to become immediately a convert to these conclusions was his younger 'disciple', Trotsky. By the time he returned to Russia, in October of 1905, Trotsky was already convinced that he would be a witness to an event unlike anything imagined by his 'orthodox' colleagues. His actual experience of the Revolution of 1905[8] confirmed for him the hypotheses which he and Parvus had speculated upon during their discussions in Munich. The most daring of these hypotheses was that Russia was on the brink of a seizure of power by the workers, not the bourgeoisie; that, in fact, the latter was impossible in the context of Russian history and society; that, whether in 1905 or later, whenever it finally came, the upheaval in Russia would culminate with a workers' government in power. But while Parvus was the first to contemplate this prospect, it was Trotsky who was to give it the framework of a full theoretical construction.

To this end Trotsky attempted to do two main things: firstly, to describe and appraise the behaviour of social classes and their political movements as this emerged in 1905—the point of this would be to see in such behaviour a reflection in the mirror of Russian society; secondly, and consequently, to re-examine

---

[7] See Schwarz, op. cit., pp. 10–16 for the temporary influence on some Mensheviks of Parvus and Trotsky—through the newspaper *Nachalo* which the two were editing in 1905.
[8] For an account of Trotsky's role in 1905, see Deutscher, *The Prophet Armed*, chapter 5. Trotsky's own account is in *Moya Zhizn*, I, chapter 14.

Russia's social history with a view to arriving at a sociology of classes, of economics, and finally of revolutionary politics. Although obviously Trotsky did not sub-divide his writings in accordance with these two aims, but rather dealt with them jointly, in what follows we shall separate them in order the better to clarify the issues involved and the manner of Trotsky's argumentation.[9] The present chapter, therefore, will deal with Trotsky's analysis of the politics of 1905; the next chapter will consider his sociology of Russian society; and the chapter after that will discuss the culmination, so to speak, of Trotsky's investigations, namely, the theory of the permanent revolution.

1. Social Classes and Political Movements

(a) *The Bourgeoisie and Liberalism*

Trotsky's analysis of the Russian bourgeoisie and of Russian liberalism may be seen as an attempt to carry the generally accepted argument about the feebleness of the Russian middle classes to its logical conclusion. If the bourgeoisie was indeed so impotent a force, if it resembled its Western counterpart only in name, then it was incumbent, in his view, to draw practical, political conclusions which would take account of this anomaly. Not to do so meant to deny the relevance of social history to political events and this is precisely what he accused his Marxist colleagues of doing, that is, misunderstanding and ignoring the political reality which was taking shape around them, thereby also remaining fixed within theoretical preconceptions which did not conform to that reality.

In the next chapter we shall consider in detail Trotsky's contention that capitalism as such had not taken root in Russia, in spite of the changes of the two decades or so preceding 1905. As a point of departure for our present purposes we shall only note here that, in Trotsky's view, what passed for capitalism in Russia consisted of two artificial components: foreign capital and a handful of local entrepreneurs grown rich as a result of the industrial boom. But the former, he believed, was not only a non-indigenous factor, it was also, in the form of European

---

[9] The separation is thematic, not schematic, and thus in keeping with Trotsky's own conception of these subjects.

financiers, an ally of the autocracy; as for the latter, it was not only limited in numbers, it was also without indigenous social roots, and dependent on the state. Neither could possibly be interested in any radical transformation, much less the downfall, of the autocracy. Both were doing very well out of Tsarism. While the formal structure of capitalism may have been thus incorporated through the exigencies of financing industry, the 'infra-structure' was completely missing. For Trotsky grasped capitalism as a social and cultural system and not merely an economic arrangement. A big capitalist class, 'grafted onto' an economic policy, was not the equivalent of a bourgeois social class. The backbone of revolution is not the industrial baron, but the self-made middle classes who in the course of a long period succeed in penetrating the social organism and whose existence in fact transforms social life; not merely industrialization, but an urban life having certain identifiable cultural attributes, characterizes a bourgeois capitalist society. The absence of such components, a direct result of the peculiar development of Russia, was in Trotsky's view responsible for the weakness of the bourgeois liberal movement: it was without social foundations, itself an alien tissue 'grafted onto' a hostile body which could not but reject it.[10]

And, in fact, as one looks at the character of the Russian liberal movement as it began to take political shape at the outset of the twentieth century, it is this element of rootlessness which is most striking. Paul Milyukov, himself one of its leaders, defined Russian liberalism as 'not bourgeois but intellectual', and Max Weber once characterized it as 'the bearer of a political and socio-political idealism' which, however, was isolated

---

[10] Sources for Trotsky's views on Russian capitalism will be given in chapter 3, below, but for a succinct summary of his position see his book *1905* (4th Russian edition, Moscow, 1925), pp. 46–7. This is one of Trotsky's most important works and will be frequently referred to in the course of this study. It consists of essays and articles written during the period 1905–8 and first published in German under the title *Russland in der Revolution* (Dresden, 1910). The first Russian edition, containing some additions in the form of appendices, was published in Moscow in January 1922. The second and subsequent Russian editions are identical to the first except for one further appendix (pp. 294–309), based on articles written in 1922 (see chapter 3, note 48) and some minor additions to an article which previously appeared incomplete. All references are to the 4th Russian edition. (Most of the book may also be found in Trotsky's *Sochineniya*, II, part 2, pp. 3–205. For the English translation see Trotsky, *1905*, New York, 1972.)

from industrial and financial forces.[11] It consisted of two primary groupings: the gentry and the intelligentsia, the latter in
this connection meaning mainly members of the free professions. The gentry, as a part of the nobility, was, of course,
directly tied to the traditional social hierarchy; but, distinguished as it was from the older and original aristocracy by more
limited land holdings and more local administrative functions,
it soon developed a cohesion of its own.[12] The basis for the
cohesion became institutionalized from 1864 onward with the
establishment of the form of local self-government known as
the *zemstvo* or territorial assembly. Although delegates to these
assemblies could be elected from amongst non-noble land-
owners and even peasants, the gentry in fact always dominated
the institution. From this grew its struggle with the autocracy,
first for local autonomy and, later, for a share in the central
government as well. But the gentry, aside from the fact that
it for the most part leaned towards some kind of accommodation with the autocracy, and culturally remained rooted in the
land, did not succeed in transforming its liberal ideas into a
movement. There was a *zemstvo* movement, focused on rural
government reforms, but no liberal movement as such.

Only at the very beginning of the twentieth century did
organized liberalism come into being, and then it was no longer
the gentry that stood at its head but rather the intelligentsia
or professional middle class. The latter, at first in the employ
of the *zemstvos* as doctors, teachers, veterinarians, statisticians—
'the third element' as they came to be called—soon began to
exert political and ideological influence of their own and joined
hands with the upper intelligentsia—lawyers, academics, high
government officials—who were to be found outside the
zemstvos. Thus when in 1902 a liberal journal, *Osvobozhdenie*
(Liberation), began to appear, and a year later a liberal organization, *Soyuz osvobozhdeniya* (Union of Liberation), was established, it was not members of the gentry who were its main

[11] Quoted in Kochan, *Russia in Revolution*, p. 71. For a history of Russian liberalism,
see George Fischer, *Russian Liberalism: From Gentry to Intelligentsia* (Cambridge, Mass.,
1958) and Shmuel Galai, *The Liberation Movement in Russia, 1900–1905* (Cambridge,
1972).
[12] This distinction between 'gentry' and 'aristocracy' is the one made by Fischer, op.
cit., footnote pp. 5–6.

leaders, but men like Struve and Milyukov, representatives of
the intelligentsia. The effect of this, initially at least, was, on
the one hand, to push Russian liberalism leftward, into closer
ties with revolutionary groups and into more far-reaching
political demands. On the other hand, however, the shift from
gentry to intelligentsia accentuated the movement's social isolation. It now became the enclave of professional men with hardly
any influence on the court and without any place in the economic structure of the country, not even as representatives of
economic interests. This fact merely re-emphasized the difference between Russian liberalism and its Western counterpart: the latter was rooted in a *business* middle class, and became
the ideology of a completely transformed industrial, urban
society; the former, at first linked to a segment of the rural,
traditional milieu, remained suspended in the air, a refuge for
disenchanted members of the *professional* middle class, the
'bearers' of an 'idealism' far removed from the predominant
Russian reality.

It is this phenomenon of a movement, more specifically a
social class, in search of social roots, on the whole without success, and thus characterized by vacillation, uncertainty and
lack of confidence in the sphere of political action, which forms
the basis for Trotsky's critique of Russian liberalism, a critique
made first in the brochure *Do 9-go Yanvarya* (Until the 9th of
January), written at the end of 1904—and which had so
impressed Parvus—and followed by numerous other broadsides
both during and after the events of 1905.[13] These writings are
often polemical in nature, sometimes no more than scathing
diatribes against a political opponent, with few pretensions to
analytical detachment. But leaving aside the purely polemical
thrusts, they acutely expose what Trotsky saw as the liberals'
main weaknesses: their inability to stand at the head of a mass
movement, their fundamentally compromisory, even appeas-
ing attitude toward the monarchy, and their fear of unleashing
a revolutionary mood over which they would have no control

---

[13] Most of his important articles on Russian liberalism, as well as *Do 9-go Yanvarya*,
were collected by Trotsky in his *Nasha Revolyutsiya* (St. Petersburg, 1906), and subsequent references to them are as they appear in this edition. (These articles, together
with other writings on the same subject, may also be found in Trotsky's *Sochineniya*,
II, part 1.)

since, as they not incorrectly presumed, it would be directed as much against them as against the autocracy.

Until the 9th of January was occasioned by the heightened opposition campaign of the *zemstvos* which culminated in November 1904 with a convention and resolutions calling on the Tsar to revise the system of government and broaden the basis of popular representation. The first part of the brochure was devoted to showing how meek, in fact, and half-hearted, the demands of the liberal gentry were.[14] They were, in Trotsky's view, no so much demands as requests; instead of speaking in the clear language of ultimatums the *zemstvo* leaders were appealing to the good sense of the Tsar, pleading with him to 'join' them in bringing about reforms. The notion that the Tsar should be 'forced' to accede to changes had not crossed their minds. They could not imagine a social framework without the autocracy. This was not so much a consequence of the liberals' anti-revolutionism—though it was that as well—as of their fundamental desire for an accommodation with a slightly reformed *status quo*. Thus they shied away from explosive terms, refusing to 'call things by their right names, a constitution—a constitution, a republic—a republic, universal suffrage—universal suffrage':

The Russian liberals in general and *zemstvo* liberalism in particular have never attempted to break with the monarchy and are not attempting to do so now. On the contrary, they have been trying to convince the monarchy that the way to saving itself lies in the acceptance of the principles of liberalism.[15]

Hence their failure to repudiate the monarchical principle; hence their restrained tactics which revealed the 'whole soul of our privileged opposition':

Compromise instead of struggle. Rapprochement at all costs. Hence the drive to facilitate for absolutism the mental drama of such rapprochement. To organize itself not for the purpose of a struggle against the autocracy but for the purpose of making itself useful to it. Not to defeat the government but to lure it to its side, to be worthy of its gratitude and trust...[16]

---

[14] The support which the *zemstvos* had given to the war with Japan, Trotsky noted at the outset, exposed their inability to free themselves of a chauvinism which, in his view, was fundamentally no different from that of the most reactionary elements (*Do 9-go Yanvarya* in *Nasha Revolyutsiya*, pp. 19–21).

[15] Ibid., p. 28.   [16] Ibid., p. 22.

If anything, Trotsky's criticism of the liberal intelligentsia was even more scathing than his criticism of the gentry. For in the intelligentsia's vacillating attitude toward the idea of revolution he saw not only the betrayal of those very principles which it so passionately proclaimed but the final bankruptcy of Russian liberalism as a movement capable of transforming the political and social structure of Russia. What those liberals had failed to grasp, according to Trotsky, was that a bourgeois, democratic revolution was neither bourgeois, nor democratic, nor a revolution, unless the bourgeoisie itself acted in a revolutionary manner: 'Democracy, turning its back on revolution or nourishing illusions of a peaceful renovation of Russia, is undermining its own strength, its own future. Such a democracy is an inner contradiction. An anti-revolutionary democracy is no democracy at all.'[17]

Here, in Trotsky's view, was the fatal flaw in Russian liberalism. Lacking a mass movement, it was unable to gather enough momentum for a revolutionary assault on the autocracy. But anything short of a revolutionary assault could only end in the kind of compromise in which the monarchy would always have the upper hand. Thus the intelligentsia's demands for universal suffrage, for a constitution, for a national assembly, demands which, in Russia, were revolutionary in themselves, lacked the credibility which could only be generated by a movement with a mass base. This is why the autocracy could, formally, subscribe to certain liberal demands and, in practice, with impunity ignore them. The extent to which the intelligentsia recoiled from revolutionary change Trotsky perceived in its attitude toward the very masses who were now becoming active in politics. For these masses, peasants and workers, were not the masses of liberal reforms but of social changes which liberalism was not even prepared to contemplate. Thus while seeking some common front with peasants and workers, for lack of a mass-base of its own, liberalism simultaneously renounced a genuine alliance. More radical than the *zemstvo* gentry, the intelligentsia was yet less radical, in Trotsky's view, than the most conscious element of the masses, the workers. Thus it pleaded for deradicalization as the basis for a common front:

[17] Ibid., p. 39.

...shorn of its disguise, the liberals' demands [to the proletariat] amount to this: 'Remove yourselves—rid your revolutionary programme and your revolutionary tactics of all that which distinguishes you from us—abandon those demands which are not acceptable to the Moscow trader and the Tambov nobleman—in a word, betray those principles which you have proclaimed...'[18]

Trotsky completed the writing of *Until the 9th of January* in December 1904 but it was not published until the following March.[19] By then, of course, Russia was in the midst of an upheaval, with all segments of society participating in the assault on the autocracy. There is no question but that the liberals in the course of a few months had not only intensified but radicalized their demands. Trotsky acknowledged this openly. In his post-January 1905 articles he paid tribute to this move leftwards, somewhat revising his earlier analysis.[20] Moreover, he also acknowledged that the liberal intelligentsia had been strengthened by the entry of the capitalist bourgeoisie into the political arena and its identification with the liberal demands.[21] But all this, in his view, had not changed the essential alignment of political forces, for the shift leftwards had been universal and not limited to the liberals. In fact the liberals, both gentry and intelligentsia, as well as industrial interests, had upped their demands primarily as a result of the 'external pressure of revolutionary-democratic forces'.[22] They had, so to speak, been swept along on the wave of the mass ferment, becoming not so much intrinsically bolder as being compelled by events not of their own making to strike a pose more attuned to the mood of the country. In the case of 'commercial-industrial capital', an element of economic self-interest was at work—a constitutional state was certainly not incompatible with the development of an internal market—but here too, Trotsky believed, the primary motive was to keep as much in step with the times as possible.[23] By so doing, the liberal movement hoped both to stem, or at least appease, the masses, and somehow to remain at the

---

[18] Ibid., pp. 48–9.
[19] The delay in publication explains its title.
[20] See, for instance, the article 'Kapital v oppozitsii' in *Nasha Revolyutsiya*, pp. 74–94 and the pamphlet *Gospodin Petr Struve v politike* in ibid., pp. 177–223.
[21] See 'Kapital v oppozitsii', op cit.
[22] Ibid., p. 93.   [23] Ibid., p. 75.

head of the opposition to the government, thus preventing a flood which would sweep them aside:

> The liberals of the left wing will [at first] follow the people. They will soon attempt to take the people into their own hands. The people are a power. One must *master* them. But they are, too, a *revolutionary* power. One, therefore, must tame them. These are, evidently, the future tactics of the *Osvobozhdenie* group.[24]

But here again, Trotsky believed, the liberal flaw, its rootlessness and remoteness from the masses, was bound to reassert itself: at some point, the incompatibility of the mass social forces and the liberal goals would emerge, and the shift leftwards would become uneven with the liberals lagging behind, no longer able to swallow the implications of what was an essentially non-bourgeois movement. Thus the 'shift is not without limit'; for the liberal movement 'there does exist a certain limit which is basically determined by its class nature'.[25] Outflanked both ideologically and politically by a mass movement beyond its capacity to control, liberalism will find itself 'hopelessly dragging behind'.[26]

The intransigence of the autocracy may, in Trotsky's view, conceivably convince the intelligentsia, perhaps even other elements in the liberal movement, that the political structure could be changed only by revolution. However, on its own liberalism could not make this revolution; and with the masses it could not make *its* revolution. The upshot of this will be that, compelled to choose between the radicalism of the masses and some kind of peaceful, reformist accommodation with the autocracy, it will, even if unenthusiastically, submit to the second alternative. Thus it will be drawn back into the fold of its supposed adversary, contenting itself with the semblance of reform in the guise of fictional democratic institutions.[27]

---

[24] 'Posl Peterburgskikh sobitii' in *Nasha Revolyutsiya*, p. 66. See note 51, below, concerning this article.

[25] *Gospodin Petr Struve v politike*, in ibid., pp. 216–17.

[26] 'Posl Peterburgskikh sobitii', in ibid., p. 65. See also 'Otkritoe pismo professoru P. N. Milyukovu' in ibid., pp. 136–48 where Trotsky warned the liberals that they could not possibly keep pace with the masses nor confine them to their own constitutional limits.

[27] Trotsky made this 'prediction' in almost all of his writings composed during the events of 1905.

This prognosis of the future prospects and behaviour of liberalism was made by Trotsky already in the first months of 1905. Immediately following the events of that year, and indeed throughout the decade or so which separated it from the next Russian revolution, Trotsky, in drawing the 'lessons of the great year', saw this prognosis as having been confirmed. Thus on the twelfth anniversary of January 9th, looking back upon the behaviour of the liberals in 1905, he summarized it thus:

During the first period of the revolution, the activities of the proletariat were met with sympathy, even with support from liberal society. The Milyukovs hoped the proletariat would strike a blow at absolutism and make it more inclined to compromise with the bourgeoisie. Yet absolutism, for centuries the exclusive ruler of the people, was in no hurry to share its power with the liberal parties. In October 1905 the bourgeoisie learnt that it could not obtain power before the backbone of Tsarism was broken. This blessed goal could, apparently, be accomplished only by a victorious revolution. But the revolution put the working class in the foreground; it united it and solidified it not only in its struggle against Tsarism, but in its struggle against capital as well. The consequence was that each new revolutionary step of the proletariat—in October, November and December, the time of the Soviet—moved the liberals more and more in the direction of the monarchy. The hopes for revolutionary co-operation between the bourgeoisie and the proletariat turned out to be a forlorn Utopia.[28]

Similarly, in his very first stocktaking during 1906 and 1907, particularly in the book *1905*, he felt his analysis to have been confirmed.[29] He pointed out how qualified and tentative had been the support of industrial capitalism for the liberal movement. It was, it is true, attracted by the prospect of a 'strict and legal public order' which liberalism promised; but it needed 'even more a centralized government, that great giver of the good things of life'.[30] And when it perceived the actual

---

[28] 'Uroki velikogo goda', originally published in the New York Russian newspaper *Novyi Mir* 20 Jan. 1917 and republished in Trotsky, *Voina i Revolyutsiya* (2 vols., 2nd edition, Moscow–Petrograd, 1923–4), pp. 414–18. The quotation is here taken from the latter edition, II, p. 416.

[29] See especially *1905*, pp. 46–9 and 146–50. It should be stressed, however, that he did not ascribe the failure of the Revolution to the 'betrayal' of liberalism. Since, in his view, the events of 1905 did not depend on the liberals, the latter could be blamed only in part. More serious was the political unpreparedness of the workers. Trotsky's post-mortem is dealt with later in this chapter.

[30] *1905*, p. 47.

nature of mass agitation, particularly amongst its own workers, it quickly retreated to its protector the Tsar, thus leaving once again the intelligentsia suspended without any socio-economic backing. Not only heavy industry renegued; manufacturing interests also eventually closed rank with the authorities. Thus the Moscow textile industry, for instance, more independent of the state and interested in strengthening the purchasing power of consumers, at first joined vigorously the opposition and 'viewed the rising storm with undoubted benevolence':

But when the revolution revealed its social content and made the textile workers follow the course of the metal workers, the Moscow council returned all the more determinedly and 'ideologically' to the side of strong government. And counter-revolutionary capital, after joining counter-revolutionary landlordism, found its leader in the Moscow merchant Guchkov, the majority leader in the Third Duma.[31]

As for the liberal movement itself, all its contradictions and weaknesses were merely put under one roof when in 1905 the *zemstvo* constitutionalists and the Union of Liberation joined to form the Constitutional Democratic Party (Kadets):

The Kadet party was ... in its origin a union of the powerless *zemstvo* men with the generally weak intellectuals holding professional diplomas. The superficial character of *zemstvo* liberalism manifested itself clearly at the end of 1905, when the landlords, under the influence of agrarian disorders, quickly made their peace with the old order. And the liberal intelligentsia had to make a tearful departure from the manor house, where it had been—strictly speaking—only an adopted child, and look for recognition toward its historical family home, the city. But what company did it find there? A conservative big capital, a revolutionary proletariat, and an unbridgeable antagonism between them.[32]

It is this antagonism which, in Trotsky's view, was to spell the doom of liberalism in Russia and, with it, of the bourgeois revolution. No such antagonism existed in the West when there liberalism arose and triumphed, because in the West, at the time, no revolutionary proletariat existed. No liberal move-

---

[31] Loc. cit.   [32] Ibid., p. 49.

ment could cope with it, certainly not the Russian liberal movement:

And so a hopelessly belated, bourgeois intelligentsia, born to the sound of socialist curses, is suspended over the abyss of class contradictions, inured by the traditions of landlordism, and wrapped in professional prejudices, without initiative, without influence over the masses, and without faith in tomorrow.[33]

To Trotsky, the events of 1905 had made it clear that the liberal movement lacked the capacity to bring about a bourgeois revolution. The behaviour of other social forces, which in 1905 for the first time emerged as *political* forces, cast doubt, in his view, on the very idea of a bourgeois revolution in Russia.

(b) *The Peasantry and Agrarian Reform*

Until 1905, the peasants of Russia had been, for all intents and purposes, a dormant force. The subject more of romantic dreams than actual political activity, they had seen the hopes of 1861 frustrated by more than forty years of governmental intransigence toward their basic needs. But this had not resulted in any political activity on a mass scale nor made it much easier for those who championed their cause to organize their discontent into a genuine peasant movement. Even in 1905 no organization could claim to have captured their following, much less their unqualified and disciplined loyalty. But in 1905, for the first time, the peasants came to play a political role. Both in number and in scope their revolts against landlords and against agrarian policy in general increased. Still spontaneous rather than forethought, still uncoordinated rather than organized, these revolts were nevertheless an important part of the Revolution and a serious blow to the autocracy's confidence in its traditional social bulwark. During 1905, the Party of Socialist Revolutionaries (SRs), founded less than five years earlier as an amalgam of various former Populist groups, became a major force capitalizing on, though without really instigating, peasant revolts. An All-Russian Peasant Union, with organizations at local levels, was set up during the same year and for a while was effective in organizing peasant opposition. In 1905, therefore, it became clear that the peasants had

[33] Loc. cit.

finally emerged as a political force. Henceforth, it would be impossible to contemplate political action without taking the peasantry into account as a direct participant, certainly as an indispensable ally.[34]

But had their political baptism of 1905 led to the creation of an independent force, capable of swamping the rest of the revolutionary movement in accordance with the actual social distribution of the population? Had the power of the peasants become proportional to their numbers? And, moreover, were they a homogeneous body, with clearly defined goals and aspirations? What were, in fact, the social content and political implications of their revolts? Did their conception of the future—if such a conception could be said to exist at all—extend beyond the simple alleviation of general grievances and iniquities? Finally, how dependable would they be in the midst of the chaos of political warfare and how controllable by political leadership? In the wake of 1905, these questions became uppermost in the minds of revolutionary parties and leaders, not least within the Marxist movement itself.

Whatever his protestations in later years, there is little doubt that Trotsky's attitude toward the peasants in 1905, and subsequently, was fundamentally different from that of Lenin.[35] This does not mean that he underestimated the importance of the peasant question. On the contrary, the agrarian problem in general and the plight of the individual peasant in particular represented for him the single major crisis in Russian society, the most intractable of its dilemmas, the most malignant of its afflictions. It reflected as much the revolutionary potential of Russia as her backwardness. In fact, had the agrarian problem been on the way to resolution, the whole character of the Russian revolutionary movement would have been different. Nor did Trotsky doubt the revolutionary character of the 1905 peasant stirrings. He agreed that the land question could be

[34] On the history of the Russian peasantry and agrarian relations, see in particular Jerome Blum, *Lord and Peasant in Russia from the Ninth to the Nineteenth Century* (Princeton, 1961) and G. T. Robinson, *Rural Russia Under the Old Regime* (New York, 1932). On the peasant movement after 1905, see L. A. Owen, *The Russian Peasant Movement, 1906–1917* (London, 1937).

[35] Lenin's attitude toward the peasants is best seen in the previously mentioned *Two Tactics of Social Democracy in the Democratic Revolution*. Trotsky himself never wrote a work dealing specifically with the peasantry and his views on this subject are dispersed in various writings.

solved only by revolutionary means, and that the peasants would eventually solve it. He even praised the role of the Peasant Union in the events of 1905 as having been responsible for the general alarm which struck the government and nobility towards the end of that year.[36]

However, his view of the peasantry was always coloured by a fundamental pessimism both about its objective capacities everywhere and the actual manifestation of these in Russia. In *Results and Prospects*, surveying the general history of the peasantry's role in European politics, Trotsky wrote:

Shackled for centuries, poverty-ridden and furious, suffering at once all the elements of the old exploitation and the new, the peasantry at a certain moment constituted a vast reservoir of revolutionary strength; but, unorganized, scattered, isolated from the towns, the nerve centres of politics and culture, ignorant, limited in their horizons to the confines of their respective villages, indifferent to all that the town was thinking, the peasants could not play any role as a leading force.[37]

The epithets 'primitive', 'stupid', 'backward', appear frequently when Trotsky describes peasants. 'If it is true', he writes at one point in *1905*, 'that in general it is not political ideology which determines the development of the class struggle, it is three times more true with regard to peasants.'[38] He was always

---

[36] For Trotsky's account of the role of the peasants in 1905, see in particular *1905*, pp. 172–9.

[37] *Itogi i perspektivy* (in *Nasha Revolyutsiya*), p. 240. See also *1905*, p. 58. *Itogi i perspektivy* is, together with *1905*, the most important of Trotsky's early writings and the main source for his theory of the permanent revolution. It first appeared in 1906 in the above collection (pp. 224–86) and all subsequent references are to this edition. (For the English translation see *Results and Prospects*, in Leon Trotsky, *The Permanent Revolution and Results and Prospects*, London, 1962.)

[38] *1905*, p. 175. In the 1930s Trotsky made the following comment on the peasantry: 'Civilization has made the peasantry its pack animal. The bourgeoisie in the long run only changed the form of the pack. Barely tolerated on the threshold of the national life, the peasant stands essentially outside the threshold of science. The historian is ordinarily as little interested in him as the dramatic critic is in those grey figures who shift the scenery, carrying the heavens and earth on their backs, and scrub the dressing-rooms of the actors.' Trotsky, *The History of the Russian Revolution* (translated by Max Eastman, 3 vols. in single-volume edition, reissued London, 1965), p. 857. Eastman's translation is so meticulous (and was lauded by Trotsky himself: see his postscript at the end of the introduction to volumes 2 and 3, p. 514) that there seems to be no reason not to utilize it throughout. All subsequent references are to the London, 1965 edition. Citations, however, have been checked with the Russian original: *Istoriya Russkoi Revolyutsii* (2 vols., Berlin: vol. I, 1931; vol. II, parts 1 and 2, 1933).

repelled by the peasants' low level of culture, their moribund provincialism and their inability to give articulate expression to the cruel condition of their environment. It may be that he feared above all that should the numerical superiority of the peasants get a hold of the revolutionary movement, that movement would cut Russia off all that was progressive and enlightened in civilized life.[39]

Nevertheless, he did not really believe that the peasants, whatever their numbers, could come to dominate what he saw as the emerging pattern of mass opposition to the Tsarist regime. He did not see in them any capacity for political tenacity, so essential to political leadership. They were capable of spontaneous not organized rebellion, of impulsive actions, not carefully thought-out blows, of acts of desperation, not disciplined political gambits. The following passage from *1905* best sums up Trotsky's estimate of peasant revolutionism:

> The knot of Russian social and political barbarism is tied in the village; but this does not mean that the village has brought forth a class capable of cutting it. The peasantry, scattered among 500,000 settlements over the five million square versts of European Russia, has not acquired from its past any tradition of united struggle. Until the agrarian disorders of 1905–6, the task of the rebellious peasants was limited to expelling the landlords from their village, their *volost* or their *uyezd*. The landowning nobility could mobilize the centralized machinery of government against a peasant revolution. The peasantry could overcome it only by a simultaneous and resolute country-wide rising. But the living conditions of the peasants made them incapable of such a rising. A cretinous localism has been the historical curse of peasant risings, from which they can free themselves only in so far as they cease being purely peasant risings and merge with the revolutionary movements of new social classes.[40]

The peasants, therefore, were not, and could not be, an independent political, much less revolutionary, force. Historically, according to Trotsky, this had been true everywhere and Russia provided yet a further, and certainly more stark, confirmation of what European experience had already taught. The collapse of feudalism in Europe was first of all the work of the European

[39] Trotsky, however, could write with sensitivity about the hardships of the Russian peasant: see, for example, his *Sochineniya*, IV, pp. 17–42.
[40] *1905*, pp. 53–4.

bourgeoisie; its struggle against absolutism depended on the break-up of traditional land relations which were the basis of its adversary's social and political power. The peasant joined the struggle against the state only after the bourgeoisie had already undermined the stability of the countryside. In the process he became the ally of the bourgeoisie but always in the role of a junior partner, seldom aware of the larger implications of the transformation in which he had become involved. At no time was there any possibility of this alliance being turned upside down. In fact, the whole history of the growth of capitalism was the 'history of the subordination of the country to the town'.[41] The development of industry shifted power away from the countryside—where it had resided in the landed nobility—to the cities—where it came to reside in the hands of self-made capital. The latter then came to govern both economic production in agriculture and the new social relations—based on private property—which henceforth characterized the countryside. In this way the bourgeois aspirations of the peasant were fulfilled through the prerequisites of commerce and industrialism.[42] But on its own, the countryside could never have 'produced a class which could undertake the revolutionary task of abolishing feudalism'.[43] And if this was true in Europe, how much truer was it in Russia:

... we have enormous masses of rural revolutionaries. The peasants can constitute a prodigious force in the service of the revolution; but it would be unworthy ... to think that the party of the *muzhiks* is capable of taking the lead ... and of liberating, on its own initiative, the productive forces of the nation ... It is the town which possesses hegemony in modern society.[44]

If the development of Russia were analogous to that of Europe, the Russian bourgeoisie should now do for the Russian peasant what its counterpart did for the European peasant. But, in Trotsky's view, Russian development was not only not analogous but the Russian bourgeoisie was not even capable of struggling for its own interests and needs, much lesss those of another

[41] *Itogi i perspektivy*, p. 252.
[42] Trotsky attributed the failures of the revolutions of 1848 to the fact that the bourgeoisie at the time was unwilling to stand at the head of the peasant movements (see *1905*, pp. 54–5 and 57–8 and *Itogi i perspektivy*, pp. 239–40).
[43] *Itogi i perspektivy*, p. 253.   [44] *1905*, p. 251.

social class. 'Where', Trotsky asked, 'is that urban democracy which should drag after itself the whole nation?'[45] In fact, it was nowhere to be found. Imbedded in its landowning origins and influences, severed from the state-created, industrial élite, permeated by professional idealism, it was as far removed from national political leadership as the peasantry itself. Thus its attitude toward land reform, the pre-condition of the solution to the agrarian problem, was at best ambivalent, at times passive, at worst even one of opposition. It believed on the whole that the problem could be settled through legislative means, peacefully, gradually, without unduly and traumatically endangering the position of the landowning nobility. However, this nobility was not prepared to commit 'class suicide'; it would fight 'as ferociously as any ruling class engaged in a life-and-death struggle' to protect its 'soil'. 'The land question cannot be solved by a parliamentary agreement with the nobility, but only by the revolutionary pressure of the masses.'[46]

Yet the peasant masses themselves remained unreliable; torn between their new hunger for land and their age-old servility, they wavered between spontaneous rebellion and traditional obedience. The low level of ideological development prevented them deriving political conclusions from social conditions; they were at once the Tsar's most implacable enemies and his most loyal servants. Thus left to themselves, they would engage in contradictory and self-defeating activities:

The first wave of the Russian revolution [of 1905] was broken by the political stupidity of the peasant who first fought the landlord of his village to take over his land, and then put on the soldier's uniform and shot at workers. We may view the events of this revolution as a series of pitiless object lessons by which history knocks into the head of the peasant the awareness of the links which exist between his local need for land and the central problem of political power.[47]

The failures of the peasantry in 1905 were to be attributed to its social immaturity, cultural backwardness and political inexperience. The failure, however, did not represent the 'end of the road' for peasant revolutionism. On the contrary, 1905, according to Trotsky, marked the very beginning of peasant opposition, the continuation of which, though it might be

[45] Loc. cit.   [46] Ibid., p. 53.   [47] Ibid., p. 60.

delayed and diverted temporarily, would, in the long run, inevitably follow since agrarian reform would remain the central problem of Russian society. Such reform was fundamentally impossible without the transformation of the whole social and political structure of Russia. Sooner or later, the peasant would sense this to be so, would grasp instinctively that his own aspirations were dependent on this transformation. On his own, however, he could not undertake this task, because of his natural isolation from the centres of political and economic power and the narrowness of his vision. As always, therefore, he would need leadership; rejected by the bourgeoisie he would seek it elsewhere. He would find it when he perceived his own interests to have become bound up with the objectives of another social class. That movement would gain his loyalty which was most prepared to recognize the legitimacy of his claims as a precondition for its own:

In a revolution, the only party that can win the support of the peasantry is the party that leads the most revolutionary masses of the city, and that does not hesitate to assault feudal property because it is not afraid of the property-owning bourgeoisie. Only the Social Democracy is such a party today.[48]

(c) *The Proletariat and Social Democracy*

However unprecedented the spread of peasant rebellion in 1905, it could not have come as a complete surprise. After all, no one, whatever his political loyalties, could deny that the condition of the majority of peasants had, during the decades of industrialization, degenerated to the point of mass destitution. Moreover, it was widely recognized that the peasantry always represented a potential force which could, in one way or another, undermine the fragile base upon which the legitimacy of the Tsarist regime rested. Its numbers alone assured it of destructive power, if not of the power to provide an alternative regime of its own.

Certainly much more surprising must have been the emergence of the workers as a political force. Even more so than for the peasants, 1905 was for them the first real test of strength, a baptismal plunge into the chaos of Russian politics. Unlike

---

[48] Ibid., p. 55.

the peasants they were small in numbers; in relative terms an almost insignificant proportion of the population. Although highly concentrated, they were forbidden to form unions and thus lacked any organizational tradition. Ideologies and movements which appealed for their support were abundant, but their access to the workers was limited. Many workers remained tied to the village; all were probably uncertain of their social position *vis-à-vis* the countryside so that the conceptions of class solidarity and class consciousness must have been of the most rudimentary nature. Finally, their economic condition was not uniform; it depended on the industry in which they were employed or on the region in which they lived. Many were indeed destitute; but others were certainly better off than most peasants.

Yet there can be little doubt that during 1905 the same workers revealed a capacity for concerted action which went beyond anything that the peasants could muster. It is true, of course, that in the end they suffered defeat no less than others; but they proved more capable of translating economic power into political pressure than any other group. Trotsky was certainly right when he attributed this success to the fact that in Russia, as elsewhere, the creation of industry had the effect of introducing into society an element of economic vulnerability which was almost inconceivable within a purely agricultural economy.[49] An industrial economy, in contrast to the latter, was a *national* economy and when, as in Russia, the state itself was its begetter and overlord, the very existence of the state became dependent on the proper functioning of industry. It is in this sense that economics when industrialized are also politicized, and power becomes in great part subject to industrial effectiveness.

This general distinction between agricultural and industrial economies was the starting point for Trotsky's analysis of the political effectiveness of the proletariat. Of course, this was hardly an original idea; it was not even the exclusive insight of Marxism. Obviously, it is almost a banality that workers as a group constitute a unique source of political power as a result of their strategic economic functions. The point, however, is not the originality of the idea but the extent of its relevance

[49] See, for example, ibid., p. 239.

to Russia. No one had really assumed that the Russian proletariat had by 1905 acquired an economic position even analogous to its counterpart in the West. Nor had anyone really
assumed that it could acquire such a position without there first
being large-scale capitalist development which would see the
rise initially of the bourgeoisie and only thereafter of the working class. Finally, no one had assumed that the workers could
be a political force while their numbers were still so limited,
when, as Lenin argued in 1905, they still constituted a small
minority of the population. Trotsky's originality lay precisely
in the making of all these assumptions; together they would
form one of the basic foundations of his theory of a Russian
revolution.[50] But he also pointed to the very events of 1905 as
sufficient empirical proof for the special political strength and
maturity of the Russian workers.

Trotsky's account of the workers' participation in 1905
emphasized its many-faceted forms: the spontaneous mass
demonstration, the economic strike, the establishment of a rival
political authority. From the tragic procession of 9 January
to the collapse of the St. Petersburg Soviet on 3 December
the workers had travelled a long road which, however, had
ended in defeat. Nevertheless, in Trotsky's view, in the process
they had shed their 'political infancy', established their
superiority within the opposition camps and had made it clear
that without their leadership no revolution in Russia was now
conceivable.

The whole drama of 1905 had opened with a workers'
demonstration; but it had been spontaneous in nature, outside
the framework of party organizations and led by the improbable figure of Father Gapon, 'in perplexing manner placed by
history at the head of the working masses for several days'.[51]
Trotsky paid tribute to Gapon, whose memory, he said, 'will
always be dear to the revolutionary proletariat' for having
'opened the sluices of the revolutionary torrent'. Yet he could

[50] All the foregoing will be discussed in detail in chapters 3 and 4, below. Here only
Trotsky's evaluation of the political activities of the workers in 1905 is dealt with.
[51] 'Posl Peterburgskikh sobitii' in *Nasha Revolyutsiya*, p. 66. This article, written between
20 January and 2 February 1905 while Trotsky was in Geneva, was his first reaction
to the events of 9 January. It was composed as a separate piece but was later published
in the above collection as the concluding chapter to *Do 9-go Yanvarya*, pp. 63–73. (A
chapter in *1905*, pp. 74–82, is also devoted to 9 January.)

remain at the head of this torrent only briefly; having helped
to unleash it, he was himself overwhelmed by it, unprepared
for the actual forces it expressed. A second Gapon would 'now
look ridiculous' since the spontaneous upheaval would now
search for an organized framework, a plan of action, and a
clearly formulated revolutionary ideology.[52]

Whatever followed now, however, the spontaneity of the
opening act was unavoidable in its form; only in this way was
it possible to establish once and for all the revolutionary potential of the masses, 'no longer a theory, but a fact'. Scoffing at
the words of Struve, who only two days before the Petersburg
procession had written that 'there are no revolutionary people
in Russia as yet', Trotsky replied:

> The proletariat of Petersburg manifested ... political alertness and
> revolutionary energy ... the revolutionary proletariat of Petersburg
> is no romanticism, it is a living reality. So is the proletariat of other
> cities. An enormous wave is rolling over Russia. It has not yet quieted
> down. ... The proletariat has risen.[53]

For Trotsky, the events of January 1905 marked the beginning of a revolutionary uprising, but the spontaneity of the
masses, 'enough to *start* with', was 'not enough to *win*'.[54] Everything now depended on the extent to which an organized movement, representing the working masses, succeeded in mobilizing these masses through planned, unified action. There were
two dangers: the one, that the fervour of the masses would
outrun the preparedness of the movement; the other, that this
fervour would degenerate into local, uncoordinated and
scattered outbursts consuming 'precious revolutionary energy
with no results'. It was the task of the workers' movement,
therefore, to keep pace with the masses themselves and to provide them with that institutional framework which could turn
isolated, local risings into a 'national uprising':

> No local demonstration has a serious political significance any longer.
> After the Petersburg uprising, only an all-Russian uprising should
> take place ... Whatever spontaneous outbursts occur ... *they must
> be made use of to revolutionize and to solidify the masses, to popularize among
> them the idea of an all-Russian uprising* ...[55]

[52] Ibid., p. 72.   [53] Ibid., p. 66.
[54] Ibid., pp. 66–7.   [55] Ibid., p. 67.

This is the role which Trotsky now called upon the Social Democratic party to perform. It was the only party which could claim to be both revolutionary and integrally connected to the working masses; it was the only party which had both the necessary organizational facilities and a revolutionary theory, hence both political technique and slogans, 'political ideas'. The organization of a national uprising, which in Trotsky's view would determine the 'fate of the entire revolution', needed now to be the primary objective of the Social Democrats.[56]

In fact, of course, Trotsky, writing these lines at the beginning of 1905, had overestimated the capacity of the Social Democratic movement; it was as unprepared in 1905 to provide political leadership as were other movements. It too was overwhelmed by events, and overtaken by their sheer spontaneity. It was in any case split, with one faction, the Mensheviks, looking upon the events of 1905 as mainly a struggle of the bourgeoisie; and the second faction, the Bolsheviks, although in principle far more committed to direct action, almost completely left out of events and, in any case, also unprepared for the scope of the workers' agitation.[57] Trotsky was almost alone in his belief in a national uprising led by the workers.[58] Later he would attribute part of the failure of the workers in 1905 to this unpreparedness of the Social Democratic movement. The danger, of which Parvus had been the first to warn, that the workers would run ahead of the party, seemed to Trotsky to have materialized.

The autonomous development of political activity among the workers is one of the recurring, and central, themes in Trotsky's writings after 1905. In the unfolding of events he saw the workers as receiving and assimilating a political education. The spontaneous beginnings of January turned into the organized strikes of October and November. Here, Trotsky believed, were the real indications of how far the workers had grasped the source of their economic strength and how far they had learnt to translate it into political action. Already in 1904 Trotsky had predicted that the general strike would become the major

---

[56] Ibid., p. 72.
[57] See Schwarz, *The Russian Revolution of 1905, passim.*
[58] See again his speech to the Tsarist court, 'Moya rech pered sudom', in *1905*, pp. 346–60.

weapon in the hands of the workers.[59] He had then argued that spontaneous outbursts would be to no avail unless they were followed by united action which struck a blow at the economic underpinnings of the regime and which simultaneously attracted to its side the peasant population. He had made it clear that while the workers alone could immobilize the economy for a limited period, they could not hope to triumph in a decisive confrontation with the government without the support of the peasants.

What actually happened in October and November 1905 confirmed, in his view, both aspects of this forecast.[60] On the one hand, the strikes virtually brought Russia to a standstill; railways, factories, mines ground to a halt. As the strike-wave spread, the regime began to totter and, for the first time, to submit to its opponents' demands. On October 17/30, with the general strike showing no signs of abating, the Tsar took fright and issued a manifesto promising civil liberties, constitutional government and an extension of the franchise to those groups which had hitherto been completely excluded from voting rights. Although these promises fell short of a commitment to a Constituent Assembly, they represented a major concession on the part of the autocracy and a major victory for the workers. To Trotsky, the general strike proved once and for all the political superiority of town over countryside and proletariat over all other classes opposed to the regime:

The October strike was a demonstration of the hegemony of the proletariat in the bourgeois revolution and, at the same time, of the hegemony of the city over the countryside ... It is in vain that the reaction seeks to evaluate the proportional importance of the urban population and consoles itself by dreaming that Russia is still a nation of peasants. The political role of the modern city, like its economic role, cannot be measured by the simple numbers of its inhabitants. The retreat of the reaction before the strikes of the cities, in spite of the silence of the countryside, is the best proof that can be given of the dictatorship exercised by the city.[61]

In this sense Trotsky saw the strikes as a success, as having

[59] In an article written at the end of 1904, called 'Proletariat i revolyutsiya' and later published as part of *Do 9-go Yanvarya* in *Nasha Revolyutsiya*, pp. 54–63.
[60] Trotsky discussed the strikes of October and November in *1905*, pp. 83–97 and 153–60.   [61] *1905*, p. 96.

conclusively established the central role of the workers in Russian politics. But while these same workers were responsible for bringing matters to a head, their struggle simultaneously demonstrated that they too could not carry out an actual insurrection on their own. For they were dependent on the support of the peasants, and the peasants, donning their army uniforms, remained loyal to the government. Hence, at the crucial moment, the unarmed workers were barred by the bayonets of the peasants from turning the strike into an insurrection. Had they won over the peasants they would have won over the army and in that case the collapse of the regime would have been inevitable. In the event, however, the general strike, having exhausted its tasks without arms, had to withdraw when faced by arms.[62]

This was also to be the fate of the St. Petersburg Soviet. Like the demonstrations and the strikes, the Soviet was not the creation of the Social Democratic movement. It grew largely spontaneously, and without earlier preparation, from within various workers' groups, at first representatives of the printing shops, later of other trades as well, including the metal and textile industries. Eventually its membership exceeded 500 delegates. Neither the Bolsheviks, who had from the start given it a cool reception, nor the Mensheviks, who were far more enthusiastic and involved in it, controlled its affairs; together they had only six delegates in an Executive Committee of 31.[63] The Soviet was established in the middle of October and during the next six weeks it became a kind of focus for revolutionary activity, the body most responsible for directing and organizing the mass of workers. Its most dramatic figure throughout, even before its final days when he became its formal head, was Trotsky himself.[64]

If the general strikes had shown the scope of the workers' disruptive powers, the Soviet, according to Trotsky, demon-

---

[62] Ibid., pp. 99–100. Trotsky himself, as leader of the Soviet, had warned against a direct confrontation with the full force of the Tsar's army; and he had urged the cancellation of the strikes when they reached a point at which the danger of such a confrontation seemed imminent (see Deutscher, *The Prophet Armed*, pp. 134–5).

[63] Hugh Seton-Watson, *The Russian Empire, 1801–1917* (Oxford, 1967), p. 602.

[64] Trotsky's account of the Soviet is in *1905*, especially pp. 101–9, 200–11 and 225–45.

strated their capacity for innovating institutional alternatives.[65] Despite the lack of planning, the Soviet, Trotsky claimed, functioned efficiently and never strayed beyond the possibilities of its limits. But within these limits it exercised full authority without undermining its character as a representative organ. The Soviet, Trotsky wrote, was not established to create a workers' movement, much less an insurrection, but grew out of the movement itself, testifying to the fact that an organization is not necessary to initiate working-class activity but is essential only at a later stage to guide and co-ordinate such activity.[66] The Soviet was created because the workers needed an organization. This did not mean that the Soviet as such was to be subject to the moods and whims of the masses; on the contrary, its task, according to Trotsky, was to control the mass temperament, to lead the masses and, perhaps above all, to act as a check on their impulsiveness. Its very creation, Trotsky believed, bore witness to the advanced character of the workers' movement in Russia. Soviets sprung up elsewhere as well, in Moscow, Odessa and other cities; but the St. Petersburg Soviet was the 'model' for them all, the 'most important workers' organization which Russia has known to this day'.[67] The workers, by creating this organization, had shown that they were 'capable of creating authoritative power'.[68] But this power was unlike anything which had hitherto existed in Russia:

The Soviet is the first democratic power in modern Russian history. The Soviet is the organized power of the masses themselves over their component parts. It is a true, unadulterated democracy ... Through its members, through deputies elected by the working men, the Soviet

---

[65] *1905*, p. 227. This part of *1905* (pp. 225–45) was originally written, in a somewhat different form, as a chapter for the book *Istoriya soveta rabochikh deputatov St. Peterburga* (St. Petersburg, 1906) which Trotsky edited. It appears there under the title 'Sovet i revolyutsiya', pp. 9–21. Besides this and the introduction to the book, Trotsky contributed another chapter, 'Sovet i prokuratura', pp. 311–23, which was also included later in *1905*, pp. 331–45. The rest of the book, however, is by other participants in the Soviet.

[66] See, for example, Trotsky's comment in *Itogi i perspektivy*, pp. 242–3, where he attributed the creation of soviets in general to the 'masses themselves'. This theme runs throughout *1905*. Trotsky's view of the soviet as an instrument of revolution will be dealt with in chapter 5, below, in the context of his position on the issue of revolutionary organization and tactics.

[67] *1905*, p. 102. [68] Ibid., p. 227.

directs the social activities of the proletariat as a whole and of its various parts...[69]

It is clear, therefore, that for Trotsky the most important revelation of 1905, embodied in the St. Petersburg Soviet, was the extent to which Russian workers were capable of creating new and advanced institutions. The Soviet was not only unique by Russian standards; it was almost unique by Western standards too.[70] This did not contradict the social reality of Russia; rather, for Trotsky, it reflected the true distribution of economic and political powers in a society as topsy-turvy as Russia had become.

Nevertheless, in 1905, the Soviet, in spite of the wide support it had received from the workers, could not sustain itself, any more than the general strikes it directed could lead to a political collapse of the autocracy. At a certain stage, Trotsky believed, the task of the Soviet should have become the arming of the workers. But this it could not do so long as it had no access to the army through the peasants. And although it sought to give representation to peasant groups—the Socialist Revolutionaries were amongst its ranks—the peasant masses as a whole either remained indifferent or pursued their opposition independently. The results were that the Soviet could not risk unleashing the full force of the workers' opposition, that it spent much of its time walking the thin line between opposition based on various forms of demonstrations and revolutionary offensive, and that in the end it surrendered rather than face a violent confrontation with the stronger forces ranged against it:

All the oppressed, all the unfortunate, all honest elements of the city, all those who were striving towards a better life, were instinctively or consciously on the side of the Soviet ... The Soviet was actually or potentially a representative of an overwhelming majority of the population. Its enemies in the capital would not have been dangerous had they not been protected by absolutism, which based its powers on the most backward elements of an army recruited from peasants.

---

[69] Ibid., pp. 227–8.
[70] The precedent for it in the West was, according to Trotsky, the Paris Commune; see the preface Trotsky wrote in December 1905, under the title 'Cherez tritsat pyat let, 1871–1906' to a Russian edition of Marx's *The Paris Commune*, published as Karl Marx, *Parizhskaya kommuna* (St. Petersburg, 1906).

The weakness of the Soviet was not its own weakness; it was the weakness of a purely urban revolution.[71]

And what, in view of all this, were the conclusions to be drawn about the Social Democratic party? At the beginning of 1905 Trotsky had urged the party to stand at the head of the workers, to become their spokesman and organizational arm, even to act as co-ordinator of a national uprising. But with the birth of the Soviet, he became convinced that these tasks were beyond the capacity of the party and more naturally belonged to the Soviet. In fact, the very creation of the Soviet signified to Trotsky that the party had failed to fill the organizational vacuum. It was split both institutionally and ideologically; it was neither structured nor organized in a way which could accommodate the emerging pattern of the workers' direct involvement in politics.[72] From the very outset Trotsky argued that the Soviet should be as representative a body as possible, a united front of all workers of whatever political affiliation, unencumbered by factional squabbles. Only in this way could it hope both to gain wide support and to exploit to the full the strength of numbers. The emergence of the Soviet as the fulcrum of the workers' activities demonstrated to Trotsky the fundamental differences of organization and tasks between this new phenomenon and the party. In a passage in *1905*, remarkable for its anti-party sentiments, he summarized these differences:

The Social Democratic party, which within its clandestine confines narrowly united several hundred and, through the circulation of ideas, several thousand, workers in Petersburg, was in a position to give the masses slogans which would clarify their natural experience in the flashing light of political thought; but this party was not capable of uniting through a living bond, in a single *organization*, the thousands and thousands of men of whom the mass is composed: in effect, it always carried out its essential work in secret laboratories, in the dens of conspiracy which the masses ignored ... The difficulties, on the one hand, which existed between the two equally strong factions of Social Democracy and their struggle, on the other, with the Socialist Revolutionaries, made absolutely indispensable the creation of an *impartial* organization. To have the authority of the masses on the very

---

[71] *1905*, p. 229.   [72] Ibid., pp. 236–8.

morrow of its formation, it had to be instituted on the basis of a very wide representation.[73]

Elsewhere in *1905* he added:

... the Soviet was in reality the embryo of a revolutionary government ... Prior to the Soviet there had been many revolutionary organizations among the industrial workers, mostly Social Democratic ones. But these were organizations *within* the proletariat; their immediate aim was to struggle for influence over the masses. The Soviet became immediately the organization *of* the proletariat; its aim was to struggle for revolutionary power.[74]

We shall, in a later chapter, return in greater detail to Trotsky's views on party organization at this and other times.[75] In the meantime, however, we may conclude that in the light of his experience of 1905, Trotsky had become convinced that the Social Democratic party, whether for reasons of its specific problems in 1905 or its intrinsic structure, could not command the political or organizational loyalty of the working-class population. In effect, he claimed, it was being outstripped by events; the workers themselves had proved more militant than the party had apparently expected, while its structure remained geared more to pre-revolutionary agitation than to revolutionary leadership. Henceforth, not the party, but those organizations created by the workers themselves in the very midst of revolutionary activity, would control the fate of the revolution itself. Once again this was for Trotsky a reflection of the unique and peculiar features he perceived in the development of Russian politics and society.

2. The Emerging Pattern of Russian Politics

A quarter of a century after 1905 Trotsky would summarize the results of that year in the pithy sentence: 'Although with a few broken ribs, Tsarism came out of the experience of 1905 alive and strong enough.'[76] This had become obvious to him already by the end of 1905, for he did not take seriously the promises made by the government in the October manifesto

[73] Ibid., p. 102.   [74] Ibid., p. 226.
[75] See chapter 5, below, where Trotsky's views on the Soviet are also discussed again.
[76] *History of the Russian Revolution*, I, p. 34.

and did not, in any case, attribute much importance to the scope of the concessions.[77] If, therefore, at the outset of 1905 he had been not unoptimistic about the prospects of revolution, and in the course of the year had even been carried away by the sight of the escalating mass disturbances, at the close of it and immediately thereafter—contemplating that 'experience' within the walls of the prison where he now sat—he could not but conclude that the Revolution was hardly a revolution at all and that it had, at any rate, ended in failure. This was true not only in the obvious sense that power had not been wrested away from the autocracy; not only in the sense that Russia's political structure remained fundamentally intact; but in the sense also that the revolutionary forces themselves had emerged routed and in disarray. The extent of defeat in this latter sense, if not immediately obvious, became evident in the light of the exhaustion and over-all decline of political activity, among workers and peasants alike, during subsequent years.

For Trotsky, the reasons for the failure of 1905 had little to do with the so-called cowardice or impotence of the liberals, except that this explained the impossibility of a bourgeois revolution. But the revolution was for him only ostensibly a liberal-bourgeois affair; fundamentally it had a mass character. The weakness, therefore, of the liberal movement was in this sense irrelevant; the more relevant problem was why the Revolution of 1905, *as a revolution of workers and peasants*, had collapsed. There were, in Trotsky's view, two main reasons, closely related: on the one hand, the continued political subservience of the peasant to the regime, which took the form of loyalty in the army;[78] on the other, the inability of the workers to force an alliance with the peasant masses, so that the city remained isolated from the countryside. In the one case, the peasants, though now in opposition when outside the army, in the end remained the autocracy's main bulwark; in the other, the workers, though now turning the city into the centre of political activity, were yet unable to impose its emerging hegemony over the whole country. The one case showed, according to Trotsky, that the peasants had still not grasped the relation-

---

[77] For Trotsky's evaluation of the October manifesto, see *1905*, pp. 114–18. 'Everything has been given', he wrote (p. 118), 'and nothing has been given.'

[78] The problem of winning over the army was discussed by Trotsky in *1905*, pp. 238ff.

ship between opposition and political power, between demands for social reform and the need to seize the reins of government; thus rebellion did not flow over into revolution. The second case was a reflection of the fact that while the workers could act in a revolutionary manner, did think in terms of power, they did not understand the importance of creating a wider social movement which would encompass all the masses. The upshot was the absence of a united front, with city and country-side acting largely independently of each other, and the consequent diffusion and dissipation of the potential power of the masses. Thus 1905 ended as it had begun: widespread opposition, involving all sectors of Russian society, but no *national* uprising.[79]

Yet the failures of the Revolution, according to Trotsky, had to be seen within the context and the possibilities of 1905; they reflected temporary weaknesses, not constants which would remain forever barriers to effective action. In fact, Trotsky believed, the Revolution revealed how far the political character of the masses was changing, with the obvious implications of this for the future which, in his view, could consequently only be a source of confidence to a Social Democrat. Aside from the fact that no society could undergo an upheaval of such proportions as 1905 without it leaving a permanent impression on its collective consciousness—and that this in itself was therefore a factor which would play a role in the future—the Revolution, in Trotsky's view, had made concrete the hitherto imperceptible emergence onto the Russian political scene of new realities. The myth of the peasants as an eternally docile, apolitical force, had been laid to rest for ever. Whatever their shortcomings, confusions, and immaturity in 1905, they had proved not only their fundamental dissatisfaction with things as they were, but also their preparedness to give expression to their grievances; henceforth, they could no longer be ruled out as a force to be reckoned with. However, the most significant development, for the long run, was the role and involvement of the workers. With unprecedented rapidity, with little or no previous experience of political activity of a non-clandestine nature, they had assumed in the course of 1905 the most radical and the most determined

[79] This is the central theme of Trotsky's 'summary' of the 1905 events; see *1905*, pp. 225–45.

posture. They had not only stolen the thunder of the liberals, they had in fact emerged as *the* revolutionary force in Russia. The liberals had shown themselves to be both non-revolutionary and irrelevant. The peasants, it is true, would be, like the workers, indispensable to any future assault on the autocracy, but, unlike the workers, they would always lack the initiative and the capacity for either political or ideological leadership. A revolution in Russia would thus depend on workers and peasants alike but it was the former who would constitute its moving and shaping force. 'Neither the peasantry, nor the middle class, nor the intelligentsia', Trotsky had declared in March 1905, 'can play an independent revolutionary role in any way equivalent to that of the proletariat.'[80] Nothing that happened in the course of the year changed his mind on this point and he would continuously repeat it in subsequent years.

We shall not pause at this stage to criticize Trotsky's conclusions, for the issues involved here—the actual strength of Russian workers, the viability of a workers' government in Russian conditions, the significance of the Soviet, the role of the peasants and the supposed subservient function of party organization—are best considered in the light of his whole theory of the Russian revolution to which subsequent chapters of this study are devoted and where the criticisms are raised. At this point in our exposition, in order to understand the sources of that theory, let us only summarize the main thesis which Trotsky attempted to draw from the events of 1905. This was that the Revolution signified the emergence of a new pattern of politics in Russia—and one, moreover, which had no precedent in the European past. Its most prominent feature was the direct confrontation, in a pre-bourgeois society, between workers and government, between an industrial, labour class and a traditional aristocracy, between socialist ideas and those of absolutism—and this at a time when the workers were a minority and the peasants still the overwhelming majority of the population. What else was this pattern of politics, Trotsky concluded, with all its apparent contradictions and possibilities, except the pattern characteristic of a backward society, or rather of a society backward in a peculiar manner?

[80] In the article 'Politicheskie pisma', *Iskra*, no. 93, 17 Mar. 1905.

If politics, as Trotsky believed, were the visible expression or protuberance—Marx's 'superstructure'—of social change and development, then the emerging pattern of Russian politics had to be grasped as a reflection of the hidden underside of Russian backwardness. To expose the latter, and thereby also the full implications—the contradictions and possibilities—of the pattern itself, it was necessary, Trotsky believed, to probe into social history.

CHAPTER THREE

THE SOCIOLOGY OF BACKWARDNESS: COMBINED DEVELOPMENT

The most primitive beginnings and the latest European endings.[1]

DID ANYONE, beyond a Tolstoy, still believe at the outset of the twentieth century that Russia, unlike the West, should or could strive to create some pastoral idyll, based on her peasants and on simple but fundamental values, thus avoiding what Marx once called the 'fatal vicissitudes', the 'pitiless laws' and the 'deleterious influences'[2] of the modern capitalist world? By then, if not before, the old Populist dream of a Russian socialism growing out of indigenous rural institutions—the *obshchina* or village commune in particular—had been largely exploded by the seemingly inexorable developments of the last decades of the nineteenth century—and even Tolstoy was now regarded as somewhat of an eccentric, albeit a respected and powerful one. At the time of the Revolution of 1905 Russia was not yet—not even nearly—an industrial, much less a capitalist, nation, but evolution in this direction seemed irreversible.[3]

The problem of the gap, or at any rate the difference, between Russia and the West did not, of course, arise originally at this time. It is a theme running through Russian history from at least the reign of Peter the Great, and in the nineteenth century it may be said to have pervaded in an obsessive manner the whole of the country's cultural and intellectual life—its literature, its social thought, its educational system, its 'high

---

[1] Trotsky, *1905*, p. 304.

[2] Marx used these epithets when discussing the issue whether Russia could avoid capitalism; see the Appendix, below.

[3] On the Marxist–Populist argument concerning the nature of Russia's future, see A. P. Mendel, *Dilemmas of Progress in Tsarist Russia: Legal Marxism and Legal Populism* (Cambridge, Mass., 1961). On the ideas of the various leading Populists, see Franco Venturi, *Roots of Revolution* (London, 1960), and the introduction to this work by Isaiah Berlin.

society'—though reactions to the West as a model to be imitated could be as passionately negative as positive. Whatever the reaction, however, comparison became unavoidable. And, in fact, the more Russia came to resemble the West, the more her backwardness seemed to protrude. If this is a paradox it is one arising from the very concept of backwardness—as it took root in Russia and as it will concern us in what follows.[4]

Backwardness is a term signifying a certain relation; there are obviously no absolute criteria according to which a society may be described as backward and only comparison—in terms of some preconceived normative scale—makes it so. The standard of comparison may be arbitrary and it is certainly always historically conditioned. Yet such comparison is commonplace and, in so far as it relates to certain general features of societies, hardly in dispute: thus an agricultural society, to take an obvious example, is said to be backward, an industrial one advanced; authority based on religious precepts is characteristic of backwardness, that based on secular, positive laws, of modernity; and so on.[5] Some societies, in this sense, are of course less or more backward than others but beyond the question of extent there is another sense in which not all societies are backward in the same way. Such societies as have been designated 'primitive' by anthropologists, or others which Marx called 'Asiatic', are certainly backward according to the accepted Western norms—which are, in fact, the norms of comparison. But in their case, backwardness is a designation

---

[4] 'Backwardness' (as well as the adjective 'backward') and 'underdevelopment' (as well as 'underdeveloped') are terms frequently used interchangeably in the modern literature on this subject. In what follows, although no essential distinction is intended and the two sets of terms may generally be taken to correspond, 'backwardness' and 'backward' have been used throughout, and this for three reasons: firstly, they are the terms Trotsky used himself (*otstalost* and *otstalyi* in Russian); secondly, 'underdevelopment' and 'underdeveloped' appear to be terms which were applied to particular regions of the world in the context of post-World War II history; and, thirdly, the words 'underdevelopment' and 'underdeveloped' do not seem to convey the clear social and historical demarcation of uniqueness which is an integral part of Trotsky's conception of backwardness. The latter term, it is true, is sometimes taken to be offensive; but obviously no moral judgement whatever is intended and it is used throughout as a neutral, descriptive term.

[5] It should be stressed again that these are descriptive definitions, though the notion that one form of society is more 'progressive' or in any sense 'better' than another—a notion which, as will be seen, is inherent in Trotsky's comparison of Russian with Western societies—is, of course, a normative one.

imposed from outside and unrecognized, or rather meaningless, from the point of view of the societies themselves, and this for the very reason that Western norms have either not penetrated them or have not been assimilated or adopted, even by their intellectual, political, or other élites.[6] It is otherwise with a second category of societies where backwardness is internally recognized or felt, for, if in the case of 'primitive' or 'Asiatic' societies, change, development—what is commonly called 'progress'—are largely unknown features, and backwardness does not constitute a problem, in the case of the latter such features are as if a product of their consciousness of being backward and, for them, backwardness itself becomes a social and political problem.

Such a distinction is crucial, for Russia at the beginning of the twentieth century and before obviously belonged to the second category. And it is this phenomenon of backwardness which concerned Trotsky. He was interested not in backward ('primitive') societies where stability, continuity, harmony even, were seemingly eternal features, but rather in a backward society where the very opposite was the case. He was preoccupied, we may say, with the problem of change, and with backwardness as a source of change and, ultimately, of revolutionary change. The point of departure for him was, therefore, the series of questions: Under what conditions does backwardness become a social and political problem? Under what conditions does it generate conflict? Under what conditions may it be seen as the motive force of revolution? And what kind of revolution? At the back of all this stood the paradox we referred to earlier, of Russia's backwardness seemingly becoming the more conspicuous, and the more unbearable, the more she became like the West.

1. Social and Economic Development of Russia: The Impact of the West[7]

Results and Prospects, written and first published in 1906, was Trotsky's first major work devoted to social theory and was to

---

[6] For a discussion of the theoretical literature on 'primitive' or 'traditional' societies, see Georges Balandier, *Political Anthropology* (Harmondsworth, 1972).

[7] As was explained in the preface, this study of Trotsky's thought, though set within a general chronological framework, is arranged according to subject matter. Consequently, in this and the following chapter in particular, the exposition and analysis

remain, together with parts of *1905*, his fullest account of the sociology of Russian historical development.[8] Its first chapter begins with the following paragraph:

If we compare social development in Russia with social development in European countries—taking the latter as one from the point of view of that which their history has in common and which distinguishes it from the history of Russia—then we can say that the main characteristic of Russian social development emerges to be its comparative primitiveness and slowness.[9]

Twenty-five years later, opening his monumental *History of the Russian Revolution*, Trotsky would write: 'The fundamental and most stable feature of Russian history is the slow tempo of her development, with the economic backwardness, primitiveness of social forms and low level of culture resulting from it.'[10]

Backwardness or primitiveness, this obvious but striking feature of Russian development, was at the root of the whole of Trotsky's analysis of Russian society. Yet the important element for Trotsky in this backwardness was that it was never really total. In fact, Russian social development never 'remained isolated and under the influence of inner tendencies only'; on the contrary, 'Russian social life, built up on a certain internal economic foundation, has all the time been under the influence, even under the pressure, of its external social-historical milieu'.[11] This then was the *sui generis* element which, on the one hand, distinguished Russia from Asiatic societies and, on the other, made comparison with the West relevant.

of Trotsky's views of Russian society and his theory of revolution are based on his writings both during the period following 1905 and in later years as well, including the 1920s and 1930s. This seems legitimate for a number of reasons: firstly, the subject is theoretical and not strictly dependent on this or that particular event; secondly, Trotsky's conception of the Russian revolution was based on conclusions reached from an analysis of Russian history and society before 1905; thirdly, Trotsky's later writings are consistent with his earlier ones, being based on the same theoretical assumptions. The later writings are a refinement of the earlier ones and do not constitute a separate body of work: there is no 'younger Trotsky' as against an 'older one'. The present approach allows us, therefore, to see Trotsky's thought in its wholeness. (See also chapter 4, note 13, below.)

[8] References to *Itogi i perspektivy* are, as previously, to the edition appearing in the collection *Nasha Revolyutsiya* (St. Petersburg, 1906), pp. 224–86.

[9] *Itogi i perspektivy*, p. 224.

[10] *History of the Russian Revolution*, I, p. 25. Trotsky, of course, was not using here the term 'primitiveness' in its anthropological sense but as a synonym for backwardness.

[11] *Itogi i perspektivy*, p. 225.

The 'external social-historical milieu' of which Trotsky spoke was not that of the East; had it been only that it would not have differed in its essentials from the kind of external contacts which characterized the relations of a China or an India with their neighbours. In the case of Russia, geography had 'blessed' her with borders in Europe; and geography, according to Trotsky, determined her destiny no less, perhaps more, than that of other countries. Thus not the Tatars, in his view, were the real danger or the main influence; with them she could stand on a par even given the primitiveness of her economic foundations. The primary hazard was from the West, from Lithuania, Poland, Sweden, from societies whose economic organizations were on a higher level than that of Russia. To such societies Russia might have easily succumbed had she not chosen to fight them off by adopting their own methods. In fact, of course, she did not really choose, she was forced to do so, by the very exigencies of self-preservation. Consequently, it was these societies and not the Tatars who 'compelled Old Russia to introduce firearms and create standing regiments ... who later on forced her to form knightly cavalry and infantry forces':[12]

> The East gave Russia the Tatar yoke, which entered as an important element into the structure of the Russian state. The West was a still more threatening foe—but at the same time a teacher. Russia was unable to settle in the forms of the East because she was continually having to adapt herself to military and economic pressure from the West.[13]

Confronted by the Western threat, Russia thus developed a military technology. This initial influence was not directly economic but it had economic implications and, eventually, consequences. To prepare her own army for a clash with stronger neighbours she had to modernize her military might; the Russian state was thus impelled to create 'an industry, a technique, to engage in her services military specialists ... to establish naval schools, factories, [and so on]'.[14] Henceforth she was irre-

[12] Ibid., p. 226.
[13] *History of the Russian Revolution*, I, p. 26.
[14] *1905*, p. 18. (References to this work are, as previously, to the 4th Russian edition, Moscow, 1925.)

versibly set on a course not only different but unique since it would involve the maintenance of contradictory economic foundations.

Trotsky traced how during an extended period almost the whole of Russia's internal resources were devoted to military and defence needs. Most of the state budget was earmarked for the upkeep of troops: in the second half of the eighteenth century as much as 70 per cent, in the first half of the nineteenth never less than 50 per cent.[15] The only possible source for such funds was the peasantry which, as a result, bore the brunt of the financial pressures. The peasants were subjected to arbitrary taxation rates, always excessive and always beyond their means. The consequence was a disruption of peasant life and economy:

The state pounced upon the 'essential product' of the peasant, deprived him of his livelihood, caused him to flee from the land upon which he had not even had time to settle—and thus hampered the growth of the population and the development of the productive forces . . . Inasmuch as it took away an important part of the essential product it destroyed even those primitive production bases upon which it depended.[16]

Simultaneously, however, the state was undermining the possessing classes on whom too it had to depend to a disproportionate extent. Determined to increase the size of its coffers, the state controlled and regimented the nobility, and in this way succeeded in swallowing up a large part of the 'surplus product'. This naturally retarded the development of this sector of society as well, which was either 'bureaucratized'—recruited into administrative service—or, in any case, already stagnated by the system of serfdom which discouraged the growth of an independent non-agricultural based class. The Emancipation of 1861 came, from the point of view of the nobility, too late; by then its strength and resources had been sapped. As for the peasants, Trotsky believed that the Emancipation simply unharnessed them that they might be the more easily recruited into the armed forces and the more efficiently taxed through the com-

[15] Ibid., p. 19.
[16] *Itogi i perspektivy*, p. 226; see also *1905*, p. 20.

munes—without, however, opening up for them any realistically new prospects.[17]

Thus the effects of external exigencies, initially at least, were harmful economically; but socially certain 'progressive' changes were instituted, not because the state was interested in social reforms but because they were necessitated by external needs; in all likelihood they would not have been carried out had it been simply a matter of internal pressures. The Emancipation itself was an example of this, even if it did not have immediate social consequences. Another was the already noted need to introduce at least a minimally advanced economic infra-structure for military production, one which would be initially burdensome from the point of view of the economy as a whole, but which would eventually serve as the basis for further social development. Still another was the evolution of a contradictory policy toward the possessing classes: on the one hand, as Trotsky had argued, the state, by economically undermining the 'estates',[18] was preventing their growth and social differentiation; but, on the other hand, the 'state needed a hierarchical organization of estates'[19] in order to survive, since its military goals could not be realized without a *functional* differentiation of its élites. Thus it had to have and create entrepreneurs as well as army officers, merchants as well as bureaucrats. This had the effect of introducing the kind of distinctions which had also characterized the early development of Western society and which, there, eventually led to a confrontation between state interests and those of the estates, culminating in the triumph of the latter.

In Russia, however, the differentiation between estates subsequently culminated in another way. This was again initially due to the fact that the estates had never been allowed to become independent economically. And since differentiation was a function of state military and foreign interests, it

---

[17] *1905*, p. 19; *Itogi i perspektivy*, p. 226. Trotsky argued that the decision to emancipate the peasants was governed by industrial needs, that is, by the need to create a free labour force.

[18] By 'estate' Trotsky meant a social group which had certain rights and obligations formally defined by law and recognized as such by the state; an 'estate' was not equivalent to the Marxist notion of 'class' though it was that 'pre-capitalist' social grouping from which a class might later develop.

[19] *Itogi i perspektivy*, p. 226.

remained under the aegis of the autocracy itself. This is not to say that the estates had themselves been created by the state. Trotsky rejected as an exaggeration the view, which he attributed to Milyukov,[20] that 'while in the West the estates created the state, in Russia state power created the estates':

Estates cannot be created by state action, by law. Before one or another social group can take shape as a privileged estate with the help of state power, it must have developed economically with all its social advantages. Estates cannot be manufactured according to a previously established scale of ranks or according to the code of the Légion d'Honneur. State power can but assist, with all its resources, the elementary economic process which brings forward higher economic formations.[21]

So the basis for economic differentiation had already come into being in Russia. Nevertheless, it was rudimentary and stultified; and because of the particular power of the Russian state, a power growing directly out of the military edifice it had created for the defence of the nation, the estates could never align themselves *vis-à-vis* the state from an independent position. Thus the state did with them as it more or less wished: '... while undermining the economic foundations of [the estates'] development, it simultaneously strove to force the development of these foundations by government measures, and—like any other state—strove to turn this development of estates to its own advantage.'[22]

The result was that a real struggle between state and estates could never materialize; the balance of powers was too one-sided, the Tsar's 'freedom of movement incomparably greater than that of the king in European monarchies'.[23] The estates developed, but as an appendage to the state, functioning at its 'discretion' and in its service, lacking autonomous power or even status, leading an almost parasitical existence. In this way, the phenomenon known as Russian despotism became possible: a huge, centralized and bureaucratic autocracy, unmediated by any social grouping, between it and the masses no social,

---

[20] See P. Milyukov, *Ocherki po istorii russkoi kultury* (St. Petersburg, 1896). Trotsky, however, drew freely on Milyukov's work.

[21] *Itogi i perspektivy*, p. 227. Trotsky's difference with Milyukov derived, of course, from the Marxist view that economics precedes social formations. See also *1905*, p. 21.

[22] *Itogi i perspektivy*, p. 226.   [23] *1905*, p. 21.

economic or political bridge. Tsarism became an 'intermediate
form, standing between European absolutism and Asian
despotism, and perhaps approaching, if anything, the latter'.[24]
Yet Trotsky stressed that this very fact, this impurity or uniqueness of form, both political and economic, was a direct, even
if protracted, result of the impact of the West upon Russia;
moreover, its significance was that *it* is what limited Russian
backwardness, or rather reduced the extent of her backwardness, and made later 'advanced' development possible. Simultaneously, however, it made internal instability and, eventually, conflict inevitable.

To show this, Trotsky now traced the further development
of the Russian economy. However much the state squeezed
internal resources, it remained short of the necessary means for
pursuing its military goals. There was, in any case, a limit to
what the Russian economy could provide: it was, after all, still
based on 'primitive economic foundations' and it was not growing from within because the state had largely prevented this
from becoming possible. But the more it stood in the way of
natural economic growth, the more the state found itself
endangered by the lack of it; military confrontation with the
West could not succeed, in the end, without further economic
emulation of the West. To resist the latter or compete with it,
it had to copy its methods again:

Thus the Russian state, erected on the basis of Russian economic conditions, was being pushed forward by the friendly, and even more
by the hostile, pressure of the neighbouring state organizations, which
had grown up on a higher economic basis. From a certain moment—
especially from the end of the seventeenth century—the state strove
with all its power to accelerate the country's natural economic development. New branches of handicraft, machinery, factories, big industry, capital, were, so to say, artificially grafted onto the natural
economic stem. Capitalism seemed to be an offspring of the state.[25]

The word 'artificially' must be here stressed as representing
the key to Trotsky's conception of Russian history during the
eighteenth and nineteenth centuries.[26] What developed during

[24] Loc. cit.   [25] *Itogi i perspektivy*, p. 228.
[26] 'From this standpoint', Trotsky added (ibid., p. 228), 'it could be said that all Russian
science is the artificial product of government effort, an artificial grafting on the natural
stem of national ignorance.' And in a footnote he claimed that the school system was
also 'artificial', governed by state needs.

this modern period was 'artificial' because, firstly, it was not initiated or even demanded by internal needs or classes and thus not dictated by any response to internal social or economic interests; and, secondly, because it was not motivated by a desire to develop industrial forces but 'by purely fiscal and in part military-technical considerations'.[27] Does this mean that in Trotsky's view the development of capitalist foundations, which now proceeded apace, was not inevitable in Russia? It was not inevitable if one sees Russia as a free agent, or a separate, independent entity outside the European framework. In that case, there were not sufficient internal reasons or social groups for instigating industrial growth. But, in fact, it *was* inevitable because the whole point about Russia's history is that she was not a free agent, not an isolated Eastern or Asiatic society, but subject to the continuous pressures of the West. Thus from the point of view of her internal social structure, new economic forms were bound to appear artificial and not organic; from the point of view of her external needs, they were both unavoidable and rational.

But by the time this came to be, the 'internalization' of external needs had itself affected the social structure. The differentiation of estates, of which Trotsky had spoken earlier, though it had not gone deep, had yet created the inevitable structural changes. These same estates could not independently initiate economic activity, but they were so placed now that should the initiative come from above they would respond positively to it. Thus the state did not build in a vacuum. The formal prerequisite—economic and functional differentiation—was already there; with it a dormant, latent but unequivocal trend had been created. The state now gave it the push it needed. This did not make new economic forms any less artificial—considering the general level and extent of economic and social development—but neither were they completely without foundations.[28]

They could not, however, be introduced through internal resources alone since these resources were insufficient to provide the kind of financial effort which was needed to establish industry. Having no independent economic base, deprived of its 'surplus product' by the state, the propertied classes had no

---

[27] Ibid., p. 229.   [28] Loc. cit.

capital of their own. And without capital the state could not
'graft on' capitalism. So it did the only thing possible: it turned
to the European bourgeoisie. Thus began the era of the direct
intervention of European business interests in the internal
economy of Russia. Henceforth the state was to be in pawn to
the 'European Stock Exchange', a prisoner of huge and exorbi-
tant loans. On the one hand, these loans were essential to the
modernization of the Russian economy; on the other, since
their repayment could be effected only through higher taxation, they would lead to the further impoverishment of the
general population and, simultaneously, would prevent the
accumulation of internal wealth.[29] Thus, from the outset, while
a modern economy was being created it was already undermined, a house built on sand.

In the meantime, however, the state could live under the
illusion of unchallenged strength. The huge army which it built
up, larger than anything which even France knew before or
after 1789, assured the Tsar of 'internal domination'.[30] And,
of course, it allowed him not only to ensure the defence of his
frontiers, but to dabble in European matters: Alexander I in
1815, Nicholas I in 1848, and so forth. The semblance of power
was sufficient to divert each Tsar from the internal contradictions of what had been created. Russia was indeed an autocracy, institutionally resembling some Asiatic despotism; but
the assimilation of 'European technique and capital armed
[her] with all the resources which are the attribute of great
Western powers'.[31] And this, naturally, only whetted her appe-
tite; in the course of the latter part of the nineteenth century
she plunged ahead, confronting the world like an 'invincible
power'.[32]

2. The Impact of Industrialization

(a) *Innovation and Backwardness*

In the last two decades or so of the nineteenth century, in a
programme of industrialization unprecedented for its speed and
scope, Russia may be said to have entered—however in-
completely and however guardedly—the modern industrial age.

---

[29] Ibid., p. 230; *1905*, pp. 19–20.   [30] *Itogi i perspektivy*, pp. 229–30.
[31] *1905*, p. 21.   [32] *Itogi i perspektivy*, p. 230.

By Western standards, of course, her progress still did not amount to very much; even at the end of this period, all the determination, effort and financial acumen of a Witte notwithstanding, Russia was far from taking her place amongst the handful of European nations which could then be described as either industrial or advanced. And the over-all character of the country was not appreciably transformed. But the pace and extent of her industrial growth, in relation to her own immediate past, was truly astonishing.[33]

The Russian state did not embark on its policy of industrial expansion as a response to inner pressures and interests; as Trotsky had tried to show, and as was discussed in the previous section, these were prevented from emerging by the state's domination of its privileged classes and of economic development as a whole. The policy of industrialization was rather governed—as other economic innovations had been in the past—by *external* pressures and fears—by the fear, above all, as Witte had often expressed it, that otherwise Russia would become a virtual colony of European powers.[34] Industrialization, therefore, was to be imposed from above, by whatever means necessary, and upon a largely agricultural society presumably ill-prepared for it. However, the surprising thing, according to Trotsky, is how far this 'artificial' approach, this 'grafting on' of industry, succeeded. Russia's 'industrial revolution' in fact revealed, in Trotsky's view, the great extent of the capacities of a backward society to absorb innovations—and thereby exposed, again, a seeming paradox: backwardness was no barrier to the rapid assimilation of, and adaptation to, the most modern techniques of economic production. On the contrary, not only was a backward society capable of quickly adopting new economic forms, it also had the capacity for perfecting them, in a way which even advanced economies had not succeeded in doing.

In the second of the essays comprising the book *1905*, Trotsky

---

[33] Seton-Watson, *The Russian Empire, 1801–1917*, chapter 14, summarizes the most important facts and figures on Russia's industrialization during this period. On the motives and problems of industrialization, see T. H. Von Laue, *Sergei Witte and the Industrialization of Russia* (New York and London, 1963). On Russia's economic development in general during the nineteenth century, see Alexander Gerschenkron, *Economic Backwardness in Historical Perspective* (Cambridge, Mass., 1966).

[34] See Von Laue, op. cit., especially chapter 1.

presented figures which in his view attested to this phenomenon. So long as the state's commitment to industrialization
was either half-hearted or partial, the process was slow and
almost insignificant; but once the commitment became final
and determined, industry literally sprang up from the ground.
Thus, for example, it was during the last decade of the nineteenth century that 40 per cent of all enterprises first appeared.
Similarly with production: in 1767 Russia produced 10 million
poods of pig-iron; a hundred years later, in 1866, she had
reached only 19 million poods.[35] But by 1896 she was producing
98 million poods and, in 1904, 180 million.[36] Trotsky cited
similar figures for petroleum production.

   But even more significant than the scope of growth was, in
Trotsky's view, the manner in which industry had become
organized and eventually structured. Since industrialization
was to be rapid, it could not grow out of already existing enterprises. There was, as a result, no gradual development, no
normal extension of existing facilities, no organic growth. Instead, new industries were simply created. One consequence
of this, which would later have an impact on Russia's class
structure, was that the small manufacturer, the artisan, the
middle producer, was either ignored or wiped out, since he was
unable to keep pace with technical change and the financial
exigencies of accelerated development. Thus a disproportionate
part of industrial production became concentrated in large industries, set up and financed by the state, unrelated organically
to the rest of the Russian economy. It is these industries which
gave Russia her industrial character; the small and middle
sized industries, so important in the development of the West,
never played a central role in Russia.[37] Trotsky provided the
following figures to show how extensive this phenomenon was:
at the turn of the century, nearly 43 per cent of all industrial
workers were employed in 453 enterprises of 1,000 workers or
more each; the rest were dispersed amongst nearly 34,000
enterprises employing less than 1,000 workers each. Similarly,
nearly one-half of all enterprises realized profits amounting to
less than 10 per cent of total commercial and industrial profits;
while less than 2 per cent of the enterprises accounted for 45

[35] The Russian pood is equivalent to 16·3 kilograms.
[36] *1905*, p. 30.   [37] Ibid., pp. 30–1.

per cent of all profits.[38] Comparing industrial concentration to
that of Germany and Belgium, Trotsky tried to show again how
seemingly paradoxical Russian development was. In Germany,
in 1895, only 296 enterprises employed 1,000 or more workers
each, accounting for ten per cent of all workers. According to
the corresponding figures for Russia in 1902, there were 302
enterprises employing 1,000 or more workers each and accounting for nearly 40 per cent of total workers. In the case of
Belgium, also in 1895, 184 enterprises employed 500 or more
workers each, amounting to 28 per cent of all workers; in
Russia, in 1902 again, enterprises employing 500 or more
workers each numbered 726 and represented nearly 54 per cent
of all workers.[39]

Trotsky's statistics, although obviously selective, are generally borne out by other sources.[40] There is room in them for
greater refinement of detail; but there can be no argument
about the over-all correctness of the phenomenon they portrayed, namely, of a backward society assimilating in an extremely short span of time the most advanced forms of industrial
production, of which the outstanding was the large factory or
enterprise built on the principle of the high concentration of
workers. Moreover, as Trotsky pointed out elsewhere,[41] this was
accompanied by the introduction of the latest machinery and
production methods, by the use of finance capital, by high
exploitation of natural resources, by a policy of protective
tariffs, by the extensive development of railways and communications and by the creation of large urban centres—in short,

[38] Ibid., pp. 31–2.
[39] Ibid., pp. 32–3. The table which Trotsky gave on page 33 includes far more details
than can be here summarized. In *The History of the Russian Revolution*, I, pp. 31–2, Trotsky
made the following comparison with the United States: 'Small enterprises, involving
less than 100 workers, employed in the United States, in 1914, 35 per cent of the total
of industrial workers, but in Russia only 17·8 per cent. The two countries had an
approximately indentical relative quantity of enterprises involving 100 to 1,000
workers. But the giant enterprises, above 1,000 workers each, employed in the United
States 17·8 per cent of the workers and in Russia 41·4 per cent! For the most important
industrial districts the latter percentage is still higher; for the Petrograd district 44·4
per cent, for the Moscow district even 57·3 per cent.'
[40] See, for example, M. I. Tugan-Baranovsky, *Russkaya fabrika v proshlom i nastoyashchem*
(3rd edition, Moscow, 1934, first published in 1900); see also, Seton-Watson, *The Decline of Imperial Russia, 1855–1914*, chapter 4 and the same author's *The Russian Empire,
1801–1917*, chapter 14.
[41] *1905*, pp. 26–9; *Itogi i perspektivy*, pp. 230ff.; *History of the Russian Revolution*, I, chapter
1, *passim*.

by all those features which were both the pre-conditions and the permanent characteristics of an industrial economy.

Trotsky's emphasis on the advanced nature of the development of Russian industry was not intended to conceal either the limits of this development or the very different, and still dominant, features of Russian society; he did not mean it to be an argument, so common and prevalent at the time amongst Russian Marxists, which would show that Russia was becoming a capitalist country like any other and that it was now only a matter of time before this process was culminated. On the contrary, the emphasis on industrial capacities was placed by Trotsky in the context of the more general reality, and was meant in fact as an argument against seeing Russia in either white or black terms, as either capitalist or 'feudal', or becoming the one and ceasing to be the other. For the whole point of emphasis was that while the state, on the one hand, was prepared to introduce modern industry, and on a scale necessary for its purposes, on the other, it was determined not to allow parallel changes in society and politics. The state believed, in other words, that it could industrialize without disturbing either existing social relations or its traditional political authority and institutions. Hence it by-passed or largely ignored Russia's existing economic foundations (though this was also governed by considerations of speed, since to have built on these foundations would have meant delaying the pace of industrialization); hence industry was 'grafted on', in the tradition of Russia's other periodic bursts of modernization, or adaptation to the outside world, a tradition going back to Peter the Great and even beyond. The consequence was, not unlike analogous adaptations in the past, that an industrial sector was created without really affecting, much less transforming, the traditional economy of the country: the two were simply made to co-exist side by side. And the state thus continued to rest on the traditional pillars of its power and legitimacy: the peasantry and the landowning nobility. This, according to Trotsky, accounted for the stark contradictions of Russian society in the wake of industrialization. In a vivid passage in *1905* he described the phenomenon thus:

In Europe 5·4 million square kilometres, in Asia 17·5 million, and a population of 150 million. In this enormous area, all epochs of human development: from the primitive savagery of the northern forests, where men eat raw fish and worship trees, to the most modern social relations of the capitalist city ... The most concentrated industry in Europe, based on the most backward agriculture in Europe. The most colossal governmental apparatus in the world, exploiting all the achievements of technical progress—to arrest the historical progress of its own country.[42]

Such contradictions in Russia's social and economic reality made it impossible to classify the country under standard 'either-or' categories. Russia's industrial progress, Trotsky wrote in later years, was difficult to reconcile with a conventional, 'banal' notion of backwardness. 'However', he added, 'it does not disprove ... backwardness, but dialectically completes it.'[43] By this he meant that the concept of backwardness had to be grasped in terms of the very contradictions and incongruities which were to be found in the reality of which it was an abstraction.

Had the state therefore succeeded in isolating the economic—that is, industry—from the social and political, and from the old economic foundations? Had it managed to create an industrial island thereby satisfying its external needs and ambitions without disturbing the greater empire over which it presided? True, the co-existence of the primitive and the modern suggested that the gamble had indeed come off, and may even be perpetuated indefinitely. But this, in Trotsky's view, was to take the situation as it was and project it into the future, without taking account of its internal mechanisms. Precisely because Russian backwardness did not conform to static categories, precisely because it was dynamic, the notion that it could persist in its initial form was questionable in the first place. Contradictions being incompatible they cannot be expected to be sustained for ever. The contradiction between the modernity of industry and the primitiveness of agriculture was obvious; but industry itself was creating new contradictions of its own so that other elements were penetrating the Russian social structure. The whole was in fact assuming a different character, though one peculiar, again, to the specifically Russian path of historical development. The underside of Russian

[42] *1905*, p. 44.
[43] *History of the Russian Revolution*, I, p. 32.

society, during the period roughly corresponding to that of industrialization, was, Trotsky would now argue, changing
beyond recognition.

(b) *The Russian Town*

Before industrialization, Trotsky noted, Russian towns had no
economic function.[44] They were 'administrative, military, tax-
collecting centres'; their inhabitants, who were 'employed in
one form of state service or another, lived at the expense of the
exchequer'.[45] The population for the most part consisted of
officials, some merchants, and peasants 'seeking refuge within
city walls'.[46] The towns were thus not centres of production,
not even economic units. On the contrary, the 'Russian towns,
like the towns under the Asiatic despotisms . . . played only the
role of *consumers*'.[47] And this was in complete contrast with the
growth of towns and cities in the West:

The guild craft was the basis of the [European] medieval city culture,
which radiated also into the village. Medieval science, scholasticism,
religious reformation, grew out of the craft–guild soil . . . The craft–
guild culture of the West formed itself on a relatively high level of
economic development when all the fundamental processes of the
manufacturing industries had been distinguished from agriculture,
had been converted into independent crafts, had created their own
organizations, their own focuses—the cities—and at first a limited . . .
but nevertheless stable, market. At the basis of the medieval European
city therefore lay a comparatively high differentiation of industry, giving rise to regular interrelations between the city centre and its agricultural periphery.[48]

None of this had happened in Russia. Instead here manufacturing industry and the crafts remained in the country,
attached to agriculture:

Our economic backwardness . . . found its expression in the fact that
craft, not yet separated from agriculture, preserved the form of home

[44] Trotsky's analysis of the growth of Russian towns owed much to the ideas of Parvus
(see chapter 1, pp. 19–20, above) but both in fact drew on the work of Milyukov.
[45] *Itogi i perspektivy*, p. 232.   [46] *1905*, p. 46.
[47] *Itogi i perspektivy*, p. 232.
[48] Appendix I to vol. I of *The History of the Russian Revolution*, pp. 474 and 475. This
appendix consists of excerpts from two articles written for *Pravda*, 1 and 2 July 1922
and later published as an appendix to the second and subsequent editions of *1905* (4th
edition, pp. 294–309). (See chapter 2, note 10.)

industry. Here we were nearer to India than to Europe, just as our medieval cities were nearer to the Asiatic than the European type ... Our Reformation remained at the stage of the peasant sect, because it found no leadership from the cities. Primitiveness and backwardness here cry to the heavens ...[49]

When Europe industrialized, it did so on the foundations of the cities which had been created: from their midst came the skills, the organizational techniques, the entrepreneurial acumen, the divisions of labour which were later incorporated into modern industry. The switch from an agricultural to an industrial economy, having been mediated through the cities, was smooth, gradual, natural. A solid non-agricultural, independent economic basis had been forged; when industrialization came it did not need to depend on agriculture. Moreover, Trotsky believed, in the West the emergence of new classes in itself attested to the smoothness of the change-over. The growth of independent town manufacturing concerns and industries created an independent class, the bourgeoisie, strong enough to tear itself away from agriculture, eventually powerful enough and broad enough to confront the absolutist state.

When Russia industrialized, however, it did so without independent towns. Instead, industrialization itself created urban, economic centres—another example of the peculiarities of backward development. Thus just as an enormous industrial structure was created where almost none had existed before, so an enormous urban population came into being virtually overnight. Trotsky noted that in 1724, that is, at the end of the reign of Peter I, the town population numbered 328,000, or 3 per cent of the total inhabitants of the country. In 1796 it had reached 1,300,000 or about 4 per cent of the total; in 1812 it stood at 1,653,000 or 4·4 per cent, and in 1851 at 3,482,000 or 7·8 per cent. This relatively slow pace of growth was then followed by a spectacular leap: according to the census of 1897 the population of the towns was now 16,289,000,

[49] Ibid., pp. 474, 475. See also p. 29 of *The History of the Russian Revolution*, where Trotsky wrote: 'The insignificance of the Russian cities, which more than anything else promoted the development of an Asiatic state, also made impossible a Reformation—that is, a replacement of the feudal-bureaucratic orthodoxy by some sort of modernized kind of Christianity adapted to the demands of a bourgeois society. The struggle against the state church did not go farther than the creation of peasant sects, the faction of the Old Believers being the most powerful among them.'

although this still accounted for only about 13 per cent of the total population.[50] Trotsky cited other statistics to show the suddenness of urban growth. Between 1885 and 1897 the increase in the urban population was equivalent to 33·8 per cent, or more than twice the increase in the population of Russia as a whole (15·25 per cent), and nearly three times the increase in the rural population (12·7 per cent). Some individual cities had even more rapid increases. Thus Moscow, for instance, during the period of the 35 years before 1905 grew from 604,000 to 1,359,000, i.e. by 123 per cent.[51]

The importance of these changes, however, was not reflected in numbers alone. The very nature of the town or city had been transformed. The modern Russian town had become a commercial and industrial centre. And the social and economic character of its inhabitants had changed accordingly.[52]

(c) *The Industrial Bourgeoisie*

Two prerequisites, according to Trotsky, are necessary for the growth and development of a bourgeoisie: firstly, that a part of the nobility (or gentry) break away from the traditional, individual land economy and turn to commercial interests, initially agricultural, eventually manufacturing and industrial; and, secondly, that that portion of the peasantry engaged in arts and crafts become attached to the towns, gradually independent of agriculture, eventually the nucleus of that which is properly called the pre-industrial, urban bourgeoisie.[53] In the case of Russia, Trotsky wrote, both these prerequisites remained unfulfilled: the nobility, for the most part, remained tied to the land since, among other things, it was prevented by the state from striking out on its own; the land remained for it its social and economic basis, the state its protector. Even after 1905, when it became politically active, it was primarily to defend its land interests, at a time when the state, under pressure from other sectors, seemed on the verge of abandoning

---

[50] *Itogi i perspektivy*, pp. 231–2. Trotsky acknowledged that these figures were taken from Milyukov. He repeated them in his *1905*, p. 45.

[51] *Itogi i perspektivy*, p. 232; *1905*, p. 45.

[52] For further details of Trotsky's view of Russian urban development, see *Itogi i perspektivy*, chapters 2 and 3, *passim*; *1905*, pp. 46ff.; *History of the Russian Revolution* I, chapter 1, *passim* and Appendix I, *passim*.

[53] See, for example, *Itogi i petspektivy*, p. 233.

its protector role.[54] As for the artisans, who, according to the 1897 census, numbered four million, they remained tied to the village and the countryside, and eventually were engulfed, and thus nullified as an independent force, by the sudden coming of large industry which 'proletarianized' them; they 'had no time to develop'.[55] So a Russian bourgeoisie had no roots from which to grow; and the liberal, democratic ideas which later appeared amongst a segment of the intelligentsia were to be plagued by this fact for ever—as Trotsky argued in another context.[56] Whatever bourgeoisie there was at the end of the nineteenth century consisted for the most part of members of the professions, bureaucrats and only a small class of merchants, with the whole lacking any 'bourgeois ethos' or class solidarity.[57]

If, however, a pre-industrial urban bourgeoisie, which Trotsky considered so essential to the subsequent growth of an independent bourgeoisie, had never come into being, a post-industrial business or 'capitalist class' did suddenly spring up. This, for Trotsky, was another example of the 'uneven', seemingly illogical development of social phenomena in Russia. Of these business men, although most were also merchants of one kind or another, some were also big entrepreneurs, real capitalists, created by the state to run the huge industries, making large profits and undoubtedly enjoying a certain degree of influence in court circles. To Trotsky, the existence of such capitalists showed that just as in industrial production Russia had skipped over various stages to reach the most advanced methods, so in a parallel and related way, in fact in a way growing directly out of this 'short-cut', she had skipped over various social stages to create the most advanced capitalist class. But just as in the

---

[54] *1905*, pp. 51–2.　　　　[55] *1905*, p. 46; *Itogi i perspektivy*, p. 233.
[56] See chapter 2, pp. 31n., above.
[57] According to the 1897 census, to which Trotsky often referred, 'merchants' numbered 281,179. Approximately 220,000 persons (just over 500,000 with dependants) were listed as belonging to the professions of whom over 166,000 were teachers, some 21,000 occupied in the arts and literary professions, another 21,000 in the medical professions, 4,000 engineers and technologists, and nearly 9,000 barristers and attorneys. Persons employed in the central government numbered nearly 100,000 (about 270,000 with dependants) and in local government, i.e. *zemstvo* employees, some 105,000 (300,000 with dependants). The categories were not always clearly defined and there was probably some overlapping, but the figures provide an approximately accurate picture. See Seton-Watson, *The Russian Empire, 1801–1917*, pp. 535–6.

economy there was no mediation between the lower, agricultural foundations and the higher, industrial ones, so in the social
structure there was no mediation between, on the one hand,
the lower classes and, on the other, the upper classes engaged
in industrial production. And for this very reason the capitalist
class was itself fundamentally weak for it lacked a wider social
basis on which it could rely in a confrontation with the state.[58]
Moreover, it lacked the tradition of fighting for its interests:
'Big capital obtained its economic rule without a struggle.'[59]
It had been directly created at the beckoning of the state, not
in opposition to it, or out of a natural evolution of internal economic forces. And it had for the same reason no cause to confront the state; its profits were, after all, substantial, its alliance
with the state amply rewarding. Finally, whatever the size of
the profits, and however generous the favours of the state, the
source of it all was foreign capital. Without the latter, the whole
industrial edifice would collapse. So the capitalists, no less than
the state, were dependent on foreign capital and this flowed
through the state, so they were first of all dependent upon it.
And as for the European bourgeoisie, the purveyor of the capital, it was hardly interested in the collapse of the Russian autocracy:

> The aristocracy of the stock exchange, which dominates European
> countries and which, without making any special effort, turned the
> Tsarist government into its vassal, did not want to join the bourgeois
> opposition in Russia . . .[60]

> The European stock exchange was even directly interested in the
> maintenance of absolutism, for no other government could guarantee
> such usurious interest.[61]

Thus Russia's backwardness, according to Trotsky, was also
incongruous when viewed in the context of the development
of her bourgeoisie. Here too there was the same 'uneven', assymetrical development which characterized the rest of Russian
society: there were 'big capitalists' but hardly any bourgeoisie
in the wide social sense, industrial economic interests but no

---

[58] *Itogi i perspektivy*, pp. 233–6; *1905*, pp. 46–7.
[59] *1905*, p. 46.   [60] Ibid., pp. 46–7.
[61] *Itogi i perspektivy*, p. 235. See also Appendix I, *History of the Russian Revolution*, 1, pp.
475–7.

bourgeois class interests or solidarity, upper middle-class luxury but no middle-class ethos or culture. Consequently, between the top and bottom of Russian society, as between the top and bottom of the economy, there was still a vacuum:

The social character of the Russian bourgeoisie and its political physiognomy were determined by the condition of origin and the structure of Russian industry. The extreme concentration of this industry alone meant that between the capitalist leaders and the popular masses there was no hierarchy of transitional layers ...[62]

Between the masses and the autocracy there stood a capitalist bourgeoisie, very small in numbers, isolated from the 'people', half-foreign, without historical traditions and inspired only by the greed for gain.[63]

(d) *The New Proletariat*

The whole of Trotsky's survey of Russian society in the wake of industrialization was meant to lead up to and culminate with the proletariat, which Trotsky saw as the most conspicuous and the most significant example of the dynamics of Russian backwardness.

Trotsky stressed the fact that the Russian proletariat was created in a matter of decades only.[64] In the West this class had emerged more or less gradually and, in any case, following the development of a working town population. In Russia, together with industrialization, the workers were formed suddenly, and before 'producing' towns had come into existence, before such towns could provide a nascent working-class reservoir for new industry. In fact, the growth of towns was parallel to that of the workers, for it was in effect the creation of new workers which created cities. A working-class population came into being before a bourgeoisie, and the towns and cities became centres largely of the former and not the latter.[65]

If the circumstances of the birth of the Russian proletariat were thus unique, so was the source from which it was mobilized. In the West, the workers also came initially from peasant backgrounds but via a protracted and transforming detour; they

---

[62] *History of the Russian Revolution*, I, p. 32. [63] *Itogi i perspektivy*, p. 236.
[64] See, for example, *1905*, pp. 50–1.
[65] But, as Trotsky noted in *1905*, p. 45, many industrial enterprises and thus workers were located outside towns.

became first agricultural labourers, later wage-earners in the craft industry attached to towns, only afterwards employees of large industrial factories. In Russia, there was hardly an intermediary process; here, according to Trotsky, the workers 'were thrown into the factory cauldron snatched directly from the plough'.[66] There being an insufficient labour force in the towns, industry reached into the vast agricultural reservoir, where destitution made wage-labour attractive to the peasant:

... the reservoir from which the Russian working class formed itself was not the craft-guild, but agriculture, not the city but the country. Moreover, in Russia the proletariat did not arise gradually through the ages, carrying with itself the burden of the past as in England, but in leaps involving sharp changes of environment, ties, relations, and a sharp break with the past.[67]

For many the 'break with the past' was only partial: they took work in the towns but continued to live in the village. Thus they commuted between an industrial milieu and the old rural one. For this very reason such workers were more conscious of the contrasts between the past and the present, between an old and traditional way of life and a new, urban one. The lack of a transitional period, of an opportunity for psychological adjustment to new patterns of existence, was emotionally unsettling, but, simultaneously, made the Russian worker more sharply aware of his social roots:

The Russian proletariat was forever repeating the short history of its origin. While in the metal industry ... a layer of hereditary proletarians was crystallized out, having made a complete break with the country, in the Urals the prevailing type was half-proletarian, half-peasant. A yearly inflow of fresh labour forces from the country in all the industrial districts kept renewing the bonds of the proletariat with its fundamental social reservoir.[68]

How large was the proletariat? Basing himself on the statistics of the 1897 census, Trotsky gave the total figure of 9,372,000 which, together with dependants, he claimed to account for 27·6 per cent of the entire population.[69] But this

---

[66] Appendix I, *History of the Russian Revolution*, I, p. 476.
[67] *History of the Russian Revolution*, I, p. 33.   [68] Loc. cit.
[69] *1905*, p. 50 (the figure appearing there is actually 9,272,000 but this is an obvious printing error since the total adds up to 9,372,000).

was an obvious exaggeration; the total figure included some six million not involved in industry at all, but employed in agriculture, in fishing, in hunting, or as artisans, servants and house-porters. Trotsky's criterion seems to have been wage-labour but this surely included many, like the above categories, who could be considered working class only in the loosest meaning of the term. A more reasonable approximate total figure is 3,000,000, which was the estimate of M. I. Tugan-Baranovsky, who had made a special study of the question.[70] And this figure in fact approximates to the total, about 3·3 million, which Trotsky listed, in accordance with the census, as employed in mining and manufacturing industries, in transport, in construction, and in commercial enterprises.[71] Moreover, it was this category which Trotsky himself considered as being the most relevant, the most socially and politically aware. The lower figure was, of course, small in relation to the rest of the population but Trotsky emphasized its *absolute* significance: '... to judge the actual and potential importance of the ... proletariat by its relative numbers would be to fall into the gross error of failing to perceive the social relations behind the bare figures.'[72]

Thus, firstly, he stressed that the figure of some three million (or about ten million with dependants) was large in absolute terms, that is, it constituted a population having an independent force of numbers; it was not some tiny marginal group. Secondly, it was fairly homogeneous, subject to more or less similar economic conditions, and sharing a common environment. Thirdly, it was highly concentrated, either in places of work or by regions; it was not so dispersed as the peasantry, whose large numbers lost much of their significance as a result. The proletariat formed 'the core of the population of every city of any economic or political importance'.[73] Finally, it was strategically located economically; the most important forms of economic production were dependent upon it in Russia, as in

[70] In his *Russkaya fabrika v proshlom i nastoyashchem*, pp. 265 and 289–90.
[71] *1905*, p. 50. [72] Loc. cit.
[73] Loc. cit. According to the 1897 census, the population of towns included 13,386,392 persons who came under the category of *meshchane*. This category consisted of small shop-keepers, white-collar employees, artisans, and urban workers. It may be assumed that far the greatest proportion belonged to the last classification, i.e. workers and their dependants. See Seton-Watson, *The Russian Empire, 1801–1917*, p. 535.

the West, as were the railroads without which the whole industrial framework could not function.[74] The combination of
numbers, high concentration, homogeneity of environment,
proximity to more advanced forms of life, had, in Trotsky's
view, turned the workers into an independent class, having its
own cultural characteristics. Notwithstanding its still existing
ties with the countryside, it was, he believed, a new force within
the Russian social structure.

Trotsky emphasized again and again the fact that the Russian proletariat was created before a Russian bourgeoisie; that,
moreover, it came into existence and became a social class
before the fundamentally agricultural economy of Russia was
transformed into an industrial, much less capitalist, one; that,
finally, its economic importance was far greater than that of
the older, more established social classes. All these factors for
him constituted additional elements in the peculiarity of Russian development in general, Russian backwardness in particular. This was best brought out, in his view, by the fact that in
Western Europe, at the time of its 'bourgeois revolutions', no
working class 'in the modern sense' had existed, while in Russia,
a nation without a bourgeoisie, much less a bourgois revolution,
a substantial modern proletariat was already an obvious social
factor.[75] If, therefore, one returned to that vacuum which
Trotsky claimed had been created in Russian society by the
absence of an independent middle class, one would find,
according to him, that this vacuum between the state and the
masses was now being filled in a unique way, by a new social
force, and with political implications far beyond itself. These
implications would constitute the basis for Trotsky's reformulation of the Marxist theory of revolution and of much else
besides.

3. Backwardness and 'Combined Development'

(a) *The Unique and the Universal*

If one compares the writings of Trotsky, on whatever subject,
with those of many other Russian Marxists, and not least Lenin,
one is immediately struck by one obvious difference of
approach: while they continuously quote Marx, either in sup-

---

[74] *1905*, p. 50.   [75] *History of the Russian Revolution*, I, pp. 33–4.

port of general propositions or even as an authority for their claims concerning the specific case of Russia, Trotsky almost never does so. One will find in his work few examples of the 'Marx said so' kind of argument which so often, in others, appears as a substitute for actual analysis. Trotsky generally avoided resorting to the authority of texts because he grasped Marxism as a tool, not as a 'completed system'. Thus already in *Results and Prospects* he felt compelled to declare, in the context of a rejoinder to those who would 'convert a historically-relative comment by Marx into a supra-historical axiom', that 'Marxism is above all a method of analysis—not analysis of texts, but analysis of social relations'.[76]

It would be a gross exaggeration to say that he considered Marxism an open system, subject to continuous change and redefinition. To the end of his life he remained committed to its fundamental propositions; and, in fact, at the end of his life he became involved in a largely insipid debate during which he defended some of Marxism's least inspiring orthodoxies.[77] But he was also always opposed to the view that Marx had solved all theoretical problems or that the task of a Marxist was simply to apply mechanically what he had read in the pages of Marx. Moreover, in his analysis of Russian society, he was only too conscious of the fact that Marx had only barely touched upon the general problem of backwardness and had largely ignored the peculiar dynamics of development in a backward society. He was, of course, aware of Marx's writings on 'Asiatic' societies, of Marx's conception of capitalism as a universalizing force in the world and of Marx's analysis of German backwardness. In fact, one may see Trotsky's theses on backwardness as, in a sense, an extension of some of Marx's ideas. Nevertheless, Trotsky was also aware that these theses went far beyond what Marx had written and that the political conclusions he was to draw from them certainly went far beyond what Marxists at the time were prepared to accept.

Trotsky did not consider his social and political analysis of Russia as in any way contradicting Marx; rather, in his view, it contributed to a better understanding of the unique conditions which made themselves felt within the context of universal history. It was important, he believed, to clarify and emphasize

[76] *Itogi i perspektivy*, p. 246.   [77] See chapter 11, pp. 485ff., below.

the former in order to grasp the character of the latter. This is the procedure he followed in his analysis of Russian backwardness and its implications. History was indeed becoming more universal but through different processes:

Pedants... believe that the history of one capitalist nation must repeat itself in the history of any other capitalist nation, with larger or smaller divergences. What these pedants fail to see is that the world is now undergoing a unified process of capitalist development which absorbs all the countries it meets on its way and creates in them a social amalgam combining the local and general conditions of capitalism. The actual nature of this amalgam cannot be determined by mouthing historical clichés, but only by applying a materialistic analysis.[78]

Trotsky claimed that those 'mouthing clichés' were as often Marxists themselves as westernizing liberals who welcomed capitalism for reasons of their own. He attributed this to the original Marxist controversy with the Populists who had argued for a non-capitalist future for Russia; in this controversy, perhaps initially for tactical reasons, the Marxists went to the other extreme: 'In its struggle with Populism, Russian Marxism, demonstrating the identity of the laws of development for all countries, not infrequently fell into a dogmatic mechanization revealing a tendency to pour out the baby with the bathwater.'[79]

What was needed, therefore, was not party polemics but independent analysis, not simply a tactical political stance but a recognition of the complexities of historical development and of the uniqueness of its various examples:

Where lies the essence of [the backwardness of Russia]? In that the indubitable and irrefutable belatedness of Russia's development under influence and pressure of the higher culture from the West, results not in a simple repetition of the West European historical process, but in the creation of profound *peculiarities* demanding independent study ... Not to see [the] immense peculiarity of our historical development means not to see our whole history.[80]

The whole of Trotsky's analysis of Russian history and social development had been based on making conspicuous their

[78] *1905*, pp. 55–6.
[79] Appendix I, *History of the Russian Revolution*, I, p. 471.
[80] Ibid., pp. 472, 474.

unique, peculiar features. Drawing together the threads of his investigation, Trotsky attempted to formulate a general, theoretical proposition governing the phenomenon of backwardness.

(b) *'The Law of Combined Development'*

The laws of history have nothing in common with a pedantic schematism. Unevenness, the most general law of the historic process, reveals itself most sharply and complexly in the destiny of the backward countries. Under the whip of external necessity, their backward culture is compelled to make leaps. From the universal law of unevenness thus derives another law which, for the lack of a better name, we may call the law of *combined development*—by which we mean a drawing together of the different stages of the journey, a combining of separate steps, an amalgam of archaic with more contemporary forms. Without this law, to be taken of course in its whole material content, it is impossible to understand the history of Russia, and indeed of any country of the second, third or tenth cultural class.[81]

Let us ignore Trotsky's use in this passage, as elsewhere, of the term 'law': it need not be taken literally and Trotsky's purpose will be served even if it is seen as designating only a general proposition or observation about historical development.[82] On this basis, Trotsky's meaning here and in other writings on this subject may be summarized as follows.[83] In so far as the pattern

---

[81] *History of the Russian Revolution*, I, pp. 27–8. Trotsky coined the term 'the law of combined development' only in this and subsequent works, that is, only in the 1930s. The term itself does not appear in his earlier writings. Nevertheless, the concept and idea of 'combined development' is quite clearly present already in 1905–6; only the actual name for it is missing (thus, see for instance, *Itogi i perspektivy*, p. 235 and chapter 3, pp. 236–44, *passim*, as well as *1905*, pp. 56–7). Consequently, the later use of the term does not represent a new concept but simply the naming of an old one.

[82] For a critique of the Marxist concept of historical 'laws' and for the distinction between a 'law' and a 'trend', see Karl Popper, *The Poverty of Historicism* (London, 1960), especially Part IV.

[83] Trotsky discussed the concept of 'combined development' in the following works in particular: *History of the Russian Revolution*, I, pp. 26–8; 30–2; 33–4; 35; 66; 72 and Appendix I, pp. 471–7, *passim*; Appendix II to vol. III of the above, especially pp. 1219–20; 'Chto takoe oktyabrskaya revolyutsiya?', Trotsky Archives, T3470, translated into English as *In Defence of October* (Colombo, 1962)—this is a speech Trotsky delivered in Copenhagen in November 1932; 'Predislovie', Archives, T4262, (this is the preface Trotsky wrote in 1938 to the book by H. Isaacs, *The Tragedy of the Chinese Revolution*, London, 1938, where it appears on pp. xi–xxv); 'Tri kontseptsii russkoi revolyutsii', Archives, T4684 (this appears as an appendix to his *Stalin*, pp. 422–34). (For a description of the Trotsky Archives, see the Bibliography.)

of internal historical development of each country, and in particular backward ones, is concerned, there is no universal history. Societies develop in accordance with their own social, economic, cultural and other origins and characteristics. There is no reason to believe that all, sooner or later, evolve in the same direction on their own. This much may be obvious; what is less obvious, or so Trotsky believes, since his Marxist colleagues do not accept it, is that even at that point at which universal history—or rather European history, more specifically capitalism—does impinge on the particular, thereby guaranteeing that all countries will be drawn into the same future, the subsequent development or path towards this future in the countries affected does not take a form common to European history. Though Trotsky does not say so, this may be taken as a negation of Marx's famous remark that capitalism 'creates a world after its own image'.[84] If this is true it is true for Trotsky only in the sense that the impact of capitalism compels all countries to break out of their egocentricity, to live, as well, outside their own particular history. But it does not lead to a reproduction of capitalism. The introduction of new, advanced forms of life, particularly economic, instead of provoking development in accordance with certain preconceived stages— characteristic of some European countries within the context of *their* history—creates an 'amalgam' which is unique, and which represents the peculiar juxtaposition of backward forms with the new ones, and therefore precludes a simple reproduction of the European past.

For the point of this juxtaposition is that the new forms bear no relation to the old, much less do they evolve from them. On the contrary, the new forms are at first simply *appended* to the backward society. And this accounts for 'combined development' in the sense of the adoption, at virtually one stroke, of the latest forms.[85] At the point of adoption, therefore, society

---

[84] The remark occurs in the *Communist Manifesto*: see Karl Marx and Frederick Engels, *Selected Works* (2 vols., Moscow, 1955), I, p. 38.

[85] It may be relevant to note in this context Trotsky's view of the human capacity for adaptability: 'Living beings, including man of course, go through similar stages of development in accordance with their ages. In a normal five-year-old child, we find a certain correspondence between the weight, size and the internal organs. But it is quite otherwise with human consciousness. In contrast with anatomy and physiology, psychology, both individual and collective, is distinguished by exceptional capacity of ab-

may be said to change not from within but from without, not by evolving but by 'grafting on', appending, new ways of life. If this is the case then the notion that each society must experience the same processes in order to arrive at the same result is based on a misunderstanding because, in effect, there are no processes or stages as yet but only a leap. In appending new forms, the backward society takes not their beginnings, nor the stages of their evolution, but the finished product itself. In fact it goes even further; it copies not the product as it exists in its countries of origin but its 'ideal type', and it is able to do so for the very reason that it is in a position to append instead of going through the process of development. This explains why the new forms, in a backward society, appear more perfected than in an advanced society where they are approximations only to the 'ideal' for having been arrived at piecemeal and within the framework of historical possibilities. Put another way, this means that a backward society can 'exploit' or take advantage of the history of the advanced; it need not repeat the mistakes, the tribulations of trial and error, which are the lot of those who are first in history and, for being first, do not know exactly where they are headed nor how to get there. The backward society need not grope in the dark; it enjoys the fruit of others' labour. Taking the finished product, it perfects it; and by perfecting it, it may also outstrip its predecessors, a paradox not unknown in history:

Although compelled to follow after the advanced countries, a backward country does not take things in the same order. The privilege of historic backwardness—and such a privilege exists—permits, or rather compels, the adoption of whatever is ready in advance of any specified date, skipping a whole series of intermediate stages. Savages throw away their bows and arrows for rifles all at once, without travelling the road which lay between those two weapons in the past. The European colonists in America did not begin history all over again from the beginning. The fact that Germany and the United States

---

sorption, flexibility and elasticity; therein consists the aristocratic advantage of man over his nearest zoological relatives, the apes. The absorptive and flexible psyche confers on the so-called social "organisms", as distinguished from the real, that is biological organisms, an exceptional variability of internal structure as a necessary condition for historical progress.' From 'Chto takoe oktyabrskaya revolyutsiya?', Archives, T3470 (the 1932 Copenhagen speech).

have now economically outstripped England was made possible by
the very backwardness of their capitalist development.[86]

Of course, all this does not mean that every backward society
will automatically exploit the advantages afforded by history.
Emulation of Europe or the adoption of new economic forms
is itself a function of the impact of Europe, which in the particular case of Russia took the form of a threat to her survival as
an independent country. Elsewhere, in countries which had
already lost their independence—Europe's colonies—the impact may be no less traumatic, and may be expected to lead
eventually to no less a determination to emulate in order to
acquire independence.[87] In each case the 'amalgam' will be different, depending on the local 'ingredients', but the phenomenon of 'combined development' will always emerge.

But since this phenomenon is the very opposite of internal
evolution, old forms will persist, or will be made to persist, at
the outset. The example of Russia showed this clearly and,
Trotsky believed, in three different, though not unrelated,
spheres. Firstly, there had been 'combined development' in the
intellectual and cultural sphere. The Russian intelligentsia was
a product of the emulation of the West, an élite schooled in
Western patterns of thought and culture, 'skipping' over its own
traditions, for the most part completely at home in the prevailing European atmosphere. However, this occurred while the
underlying 'backward' culture of Russia remained undis-
turbed, completely untouched by this élite. Thus, incidentally,
the problem of the 'two cultures', or of a 'vertical culture', and
the sense of alienation of the one from the other, the severance
of élite from masses.[88] Secondly, 'combined development' had
emerged 'most forcibly' in the economic sphere. Adopting
Western methods of production, Russian industry became in
some ways more modern than the modern. It absorbed the most
advanced techniques and machinery, it built some of the most

---

[86] *History of the Russian Revolution*, I, pp. 26–7. On Trotsky's view that being first in
industrialization, as in the case of England, may prove to be a disadvantage in the
long run, see his *Kuda idet Angliya?* (Moscow–Leningrad, 1925), especially pp. 46–7
(English translation, *Where is Britain Going?*, London, 1926).

[87] See, in general, his work *Problems of the Chinese Revolution* (London, 1969, first
published in English 1932).

[88] See the Appendix to *Stalin*, p. 422.

concentrated large industries, it achieved in only a short period an 'extraordinary' rate of growth. Here too there was a 'skipping' over epochs, rather than a repetition of the long, drawnout process which had characterized the development of industry in the West.[89] And here too, the fundamental economic character of the country as a whole remained largely unaffected; the peasant, agriculture, primitive methods of working the land, together with rural poverty and destitution—all these combined to dominate the general economic picture. Finally, there had been 'combined development' in the social sphere; rapid urbanization and the emergence of a proletariat *before* a bourgeoisie, while, concurrently, the old nobility retained its social position and the old political structure, the autocracy, retained its power. Again, this was an example of 'archaic' forms co-existing with 'contemporary' ones.[90]

Yet such co-existence is, and must be, only temporary; it characterizes the initial period during which 'combined development' is taking place. The irony of 'combined development', of the advantages of backwardness, is that it also accelerates the forces of social disintegration. The juxtaposition of the old and the new becomes ultimately unbearable, for two reasons: firstly, because the old is now clearly seen to be inferior; secondly, because the new, though not having evolved from society, now affects it by introducing into it its own consequences. In the case of the first reason, the pressure for doing away with the old must increase amongst those who are still subject to it; rationally this should evoke a welcome response amongst those who first introduced the new, since the remnants of backwardness prevent the full exploitation of a country's potential—but, as in the case of Russia, this would also mean undermining their own position. However, it is the second reason, the 'by-products' unleashed by the new, primarily economic forms, which is finally responsible for the disintegration of the society. Economics has its own momentum; new methods demand new social arrangements so that new segments of society are created and others are uprooted. Some are catapulted to the very forefront of the new economic methods, others are undermined by them, still others experience a radical change in expectations though without any real possibility of

[89] *History of the Russian Revolution*, I, p. 31.   [90] Ibid., p. 27.

their fulfilment. 'Combined development' now issues in a vicious circle: the more pronounced it is, the more contradictions it creates and the more it makes necessary their resolution. Politics and society lag behind economics but the latter is continually undermining the old character of the former. Sooner or later the vicious circle will be broken; the contradictions will become intolerable, the antagonisms aggravated, the incompatibilities unresolvable within the existing framework. Economics will unhinge the delicate social balance and this will make the political structure vulnerable. Backwardness, once the characteristic of a stagnant but relatively stable society, will have become the source of instability, change and, finally, revolution. In fact, the peculiar nature and dynamics of this kind of backwardness, will have 'made revolution inevitable'.[91] And this too, according to Trotsky, will take the form of a new, combined 'amalgam'.[92]

Trotsky's Theory of Backwardness: An Overview and Evaluation

Trotsky's analysis of Russian society was meant to be linked directly—and was so linked in his writings—to a theory of the Russian revolution, specifically to what came to be known as 'the theory of the permanent revolution'. The present study, in the following chapter, will attempt to show how, according to Trotsky, the one arises out of the other. But his theory or conception of backwardness may also be judged on its own grounds—irrespective of the political or revolutionary theory derived from it—as a sociological generalization.

Before evaluating Trotsky's theory of backwardness, however, it may be useful to draw together its various elements, as these emerged in the exposition, and summarize its main points of analysis and its conclusions. What follows is presented in a manner more systematic than it appears in Trotsky's writings

[91] *Itogi i perspecktivy*, p. 231.
[92] In a work first published in 1915, Thorstein Veblen spoke of the 'merits of borrowing' and of the 'penalty of taking the lead' in explaining the relative industrial advance of Germany *vis-à-vis* England. Veblen's thesis is clearly affiliated to Trotsky's idea of 'combined development', especially to the notion of the advantages of backwardness; see Thorstein Veblen, *Imperial Germany and the Industrial Revolution* (London, 1939), especially pp. 19ff. and 88ff.

but scrupulously attempts not to overstep the bounds of his meaning:

1. Backwardness is a condition (and a term) which characterizes or describes two essentially different types of societies. The one is a static, even stagnant, society whose internal mode of production and social structure remain what they have fundamentally always been and are incapable of generating change from within. This, roughly speaking, is the type of society called by Marx Oriental or whose 'mode of production' he defined as Asiatic. The second type is a society which originally may have been of the first type but which in the course of time, and for various historical reasons, has been subjected to the impact of other societies, defined as 'advanced' or Western. In this case, change becomes a fundamental characteristic of backwardness and the interrelationship between this backward society and the advanced ones becomes crucial to an understanding of developments in the former particularly. Russia, for example, belongs to this second category of backwardness and it is this category which is the subject of sociological and revolutionary as opposed to anthropological analysis.

2. The impact of an advanced society on a backward one may be said to be traumatic: ultimately, it forces the backward society to adopt new forms of economic production, it undermines the traditional social hierarchy, it infects and transforms the existing élites, it introduces new patterns of thought and, throughout, it creates comparative norms. To a large extent all this is true even if the impact is the result of a 'colonial-imperialist' relationship. But the effect is far more extreme and more rapid where the impact precedes the colonial period (as in the case of Russia), and where the backward society has remained fundamentally independent. In that case, the very exigencies of the struggle for retaining independence lead to a more extensive adoption of new methods of economic and social organization and thus to a more widespread disintegration of the traditional methods and forms of life. The process whereby this occurs may now be traced.

3. The confrontation between the backward and the advanced

initially leads the former to seek to adopt, in part at least, those aspects of the latter which are the source of its strength, since only in this way can the latter be withstood, i.e. on its own grounds. This involves primarily the copying of methods of economic production but such copying cannot be effected without simultaneously copying, or unleashing, those social relations which these methods demand. This presents a dilemma to the political authority—the state—of the backward society: how to change methods of production without overly disturbing traditional social relations. The state meets the dilemma by pursuing the former while attempting to take greater control of the latter, through bureaucratic interference, complete domination of the economy and especially capital formation, prevention of the growth of independent economic powers and, finally, force and oppression. In fact, however, new social relations can never be completely suppressed or even controlled, and they develop in spite of the state's efforts.

4. In copying an advanced society, the backward society is working according to a ready-made model. This may suggest that it necessarily must reproduce both the paths followed by the advanced society in reaching that model as well as the actual model itself. In fact, of course, the advantage of a 'late-comer' is that, with hindsight and through the experience of the 'pioneer', it can move directly towards the end-product, skipping various stages, avoiding the *process* of development, imposing upon itself the result of it only. But this not only shortens the time-span; it introduces in fact a *different* process and leads in the end to the creation of a different model, which subsumes that of the advanced society and goes beyond it. This is so because of the previously mentioned disruption of old social relations, the innovative nature of the new ones and the peculiar intermixing of the whole.

5. The skipping of developmental stages creates curious results, for by leaping over forms of production the backward society is also by-passing social forms. Those social groupings which would have come into being had there been no skipping over stages, i.e. had there been an adoption of earlier forms of production, do *not* come into being. On the other hand, such social

groupings as constitute the pre-conditions of the latest model *do* crystallize. Simultaneously, the main elements of the traditional society remain: the old political authority, because of the power it has accumulated and its control over the economy; and the old agricultural sector because its break-up need be only partial and limited in order to make the new sector viable for immediate purposes. Thus, as in the case of Russia, the overall curious result is: political absolutism, aristocratic privileges and a large agricultural population, together with advanced industry, urbanization, a working class, but—no middle class.

6. This situation is characteristic of the unique process through which the backward society has travelled, namely, 'uneven and combined development'. The situation may be broken down into the following attributes:

(a) Backwardness, far from being total, is only partial, and in some ways the backward society is as advanced as any other.

(b) Conversely, sectors of the society have not changed at all, ostensibly at least, so that the over-all impact is that of lopsidedness, uneven distribution of new forms of production, the polarization of society into various groups not directly or logically related to one another.

(c) The juxtaposition of very old and very new creates stark anomalies and a general non-rationalized economic and social structure, i.e. one that is in many ways counter-productive or self-defeating.

(d) The co-existence within one social framework of two fundamentally different and contradictory 'models' of society arouses comparison, awareness of alternatives and, eventually, a *consciousness* of backwardness, i.e. a consciousness of the fact that the society is, in comparison with others, in some important senses defective.

(e) New methods of production create new goals and aspirations which are at variance with previous ones but since the former have not been wholly adopted and the latter not wholly abandoned there is both confusion over goals and a clash between them.

(f) The contradictions inherent in uneven, non-uniform development, the growth of a consciousness of backwardness and of alternatives, the conflict over goals, all these create disharmony, instability, and a political situation which is potentially explosive.

7. The sociological and historical analysis of backwardness stops where political analysis begins: the former analysis has shown that backwardness of the type described above is a source of change resulting in serious social problems. The political analysis which will follow will show that these problems can be resolved only by revolution, and that this revolution will have a peculiar character arising directly from the peculiar character of this backwardness. The 'revolution of backwardness' thus forms a separate, though related, subject.

Alexander Gerschenkron, the historian of Russian economic development, has written:

A good deal of our thinking about industrialization of backward countries is dominated—consciously or unconsciously—by the grand Marxian generalization according to which it is the history of advanced or established industrial countries which traces out the road of development for the more backward countries ... There is little doubt that in some broad sense this generalization has validity ... But one should beware of accepting such a generalization too whole-heartedly. For the half-truth that it contains is likely to conceal the existence of the other half—that is to say, in several very important respects the development of a backward country may, by the very virtue of its backwardness, tend to differ fundamentally from that of an advanced country.[93]

[93] Gerschenkron, op. cit., pp. 6–7. The following is a very selected list of works on backwardness or underdevelopment which deal directly with the kinds of issues raised by Trotsky's writings on this subject (though hardly any seem to be aware of Trotsky's contribution to this field): Wilard A. Beling and George O. Totten (eds.), *Developing Nations: Quest for a Model* (New York, 1970), particularly the contributions by Reinhard Bendix, 'What is Modernization?' and Alberto Guerreiro-Ramos, 'Modernization: Towards a Possibility Model'; Otto Feinstein (ed.), *Two Worlds of Change: Readings in Economic Development* (New York, 1964), particularly the contributions by Simon Kuznets, 'Underdeveloped Countries and the Pre-Industrial Phase in the Advanced Countries', and Paul A. Baran, 'On the Political Economy of Backwardness'; Bert F. Hoselitz (ed.), *The Progress of Underdeveloped Areas* (Chicago, 1952); Harvey Leibenstein, *Economic Backwardness and Economic Growth* (New York and London, 1957); W. W. Rostow, *The Stages of Economic Growth* (2nd edition, Cambridge, 1971). For the historical background to economic developments in the twentieth century, see Karl Polanyi, *The Great Transformation* (Boston, 1957). Two examples of works written from a Marxist point of view are Paul A. Baran, *The Political Economy of Growth* (2nd edition, New

This passage, though it was not intended as such, may be taken as a fair summation of Trotsky's views. Of course, Trotsky believed his conception of backwardness and change to be consistent with Marx. And, in so far as it concentrated on the initial issue of the impact of the West, through capitalism, upon Russia, on the impingement, that is, of 'universal' history upon particular history, it was consistent with Marx's ideas. But in a more fundamental way, it should now be clear, it diverged from Marx, and certainly from Marx as he was understood by his Russian followers. For the conclusions Trotsky reached were, firstly, that a backward society such as Russia need not and, in fact, could not, develop that social structure and way of life which characterized the West, namely, capitalism; and, secondly, that the implication of this was not that Russia would avoid capitalism by withdrawing to some indigenous social form but that she would by-pass capitalism. At some point in the 1870s and the beginning of the 1880s this possibility had crossed Marx's mind. But Marx remained sceptical and, in effect, did not really adopt this view and certainly not in the context which Trotsky later raised; it was basically at odds with Marx's European-centred perspective.[94] Russian Marxists, in any case, may be said to have interpreted Marx as rejecting the notion of Russia's avoiding capitalism, and to have agreed with this rejection. That they considered the notion un-Marxist, if not anti-Marxist, was in no small measure responsible for their refusal, at least until 1917 when some changed their minds, to accept Trotsky's analysis.[95]

Yet there is an important sense in which they were right and Trotsky wrong. The conception of backwardness as Trotsky presented it was founded on the premiss that 'history does not repeat itself',[96] that historical analogies though useful are

---

York and London, 1962), and David Horowitz, *Imperialism and Revolution* (Harmondsworth, 1971). The latter work adopts many of Trotsky's views. For a concise summary of Russia's unique features of development, see Boris Brutzkus, 'The Historical Peculiarities of the Social and Economic Development of Russia', in Reinhard Bendix and S. M. Lipset (eds.), *Class, Status and Power* (Chicago, 1953), pp. 121–35.

[94] See the Appendix, below.

[95] Lenin's views of Russian capitalism were first defined in his *The Development of Capitalism in Russia*, published originally in 1899, which clearly saw capitalism in Russia to be inevitable.

[96] *Itogi i perspektivy*, p. 236.

limited, that the past of one part of the world transforms the future of another, that, consequently, the task of social analysis was to clarify the unique, albeit in relation to universal factors. As such, his conception constituted the only original effort to break out of the bounds of historically preconceived notions and to account for the refusal of the present to comply with these notions. More than others, Trotsky thus strove to use Marxism as a 'tool' not a conclusion. For this reason, he was less vulnerable to the charge of a mechanical historicism than others. But the analysis of the unique case which he studied, Russia, hinged on a correct reading of the actual *scope* of the changes to which the country had been subjected. Everything depended on how far Russia had in fact subsumed or assimilated the past and present of Western Europe, how far therefore she could put herself beyond that past and present. Trotsky did not stress changes at the expense of persisting elements; both the new and the old constituted an integral part of his view of Russia in particular, and of backwardness in general. But throughout his writings on this subject there runs an ambiguity over the nature of the changes themselves.

This ambiguity arose out of a failure to distinguish sufficiently between two related but far from interchangeable concepts: industrialization and modernization.[97] Although he was clearly aware of the distinction, he often ignored it, with the result that at certain crucial points his analysis of backwardness verged on questionable assumptions. Without exhausting the possibilities of exact definition, the general properties distinguishing these two concepts may be described as follows:[98]

Industrialization is that process whereby facilities for the production of industrial goods are created and both concentration and dependence on the latter are replacing concentration and

[97] As technical terms, industrialization and modernization, and particularly the latter, are of course a product of modern social science. Although Trotsky speaks of 'modernizing', the term modernization itself does not as such appear in his writings. But the concept is clearly implied throughout, and he is fully aware of its meaning.

[98] These descriptions are *historical*, not 'eternal', i.e. their content may change in the future, but this is the meaning they have had in the past and present. Moreover, the actual properties may vary greatly in number and extent from country to country; they should be taken as in a sense more ideal than real. The literature on modernization is vast but two summary accounts may be mentioned: C. E. Black, *The Dynamics of Modernization: A Study in Comparative History* (New York, 1967); S. N. Eisenstadt, *Modernization: Protest and Change* (Englewood Cliffs, N.J., 1966).

dependence on the production of agricultural goods. The process involves the following elements: (a) the exploitation of natural resources and the development of transport facilities; (b) the acquisition of scientific knowledge and technical skills; (c) the concentration of labour, i.e. of a labour force, in central urban areas around places of work; (d) production for collective, as opposed to personal, consumption, i.e. not specifically for the individual's needs but for the needs of society as a whole.

Modernization is that process whereby the following elements or changes are introduced into the over-all social and economic structure: (a) industrial production; (b) a state administration or bureaucracy to deal with national economic planning and to provide services (as opposed to one concerned only, or primarily, with purely political and military affairs); (c) investment in science and technology; (d) universal school education, institutions of higher learning, and encouragement of the growth of the latter and access to them; (e) a technological communications network capable of reaching rapidly most, if not the whole of, the population; (f) the formulation of national goals, widely enough accepted so that members of the society will be attracted towards them; (g) capacities for the mobilization of human and natural resources in accordance with these goals; (h) national, as opposed to only, or primarily, local or regional cultural forms and orientations; (i) some form of egalitarian ideology, at least in the sense of political equality;[99] (j) social and economic mobility, i.e. possibilities of change and improvement; (k) political institutions based on some form of representation.[100]

Looked at in this way, it is clear that although modernization involves industrialization it is far from exhausted by it. To put it another way, the process of industrialization may take place, may even be in large part completed, without leading to modernization, though it may force the partial adoption of some other aspects of the latter. Far more than change in economic production is necessary to bring about modernization.

---

[99] The extent of this can vary greatly, from formal legal equality to the actual pursuit of economic equality. But even 'lip service' to some concept of equality, e.g. 'men are born inherently equal', in so far as it constitutes at least a formal aspect of national ideology, may be sufficient.

[100] This too may vary greatly and does not imply actual democratic institutions but rather some democratic ideology, e.g. popular sovereignty.

And unless one adopts a strictly deterministic, Marxist viewpoint, there is no reason why a change in economic production should call into being all the essential properties of modernization.

Perhaps it was the Marxist framework of his thought which caused Trotsky to confuse unquestionable signs of industrialization with the sufficient conditions of modernization. Whatever the case, he sometimes wrote as if the two were identical, or nearly enough so. In fact, however, using such distinctions as outlined above, he should have drawn a more refined contrast between Russia and Western Europe, or between a backward society such as Russia and advanced societies such as England and France. In accordance with these distinctions, Russia was a society undergoing the process of industrialization—though even this was only partly true—but hardly at all the process of modernization. It is undeniable that in some ways she had been modernized: there was a state administration concerned with economic planning; there were institutions of higher learning and an intellectual élite; there was some conception, though not on a mass level, of certain national goals; and there were perhaps some signs of the other aspects of the process of modernization. But, on the whole, not only were these elements limited but others were almost completely absent: no universal education, no real national culture stronger than the roots of regionalism or of the nationalities, no wide-spread egalitarian ideology, no representative institutions, and so on. It is not even clear to what extent she could be defined as an industrialized society: as Trotsky himself recognized, industrialization was only partial and uneven, and dependence on agricultural production for the servicing of loans in effect increased instead of lessening. Moreover, it is not even possible to say that there was a clear trend towards modernization, although a move in this direction may be said to have occurred later, in the years prior to 1917. For the great mass of the people, in any case, those changes which had taken place, did not mean involvement in a new, modern world. Although since Peter the Great Russia had periodically revamped herself in response to outside pressures, the changes were either too limited, or merely superficial, or affecting only small segments of the society. Usually they were followed by periods of reaction and where they were aimed at the masses, as in Emancipation, they proved to be half-hearted and unfulfilled. In fact Russia may be taken to be a classic example, as Trotsky himself recognized, of a society in which economic and administrative change is pursued largely without reference to social and political institutions, in which society and politics lag behind economics.[101] Hence, on the one hand, industrialization, partial at least; hence, on the other, no modernization.

What made modernization possible, and eventually a culminated process, in parts of Western Europe? This is the kind of historical question which Marx may have asked himself and, in fact, his search for an answer to it may be seen as the pervading theme of his work. This theme is relevant here because it concerned the very issue over which Trotsky's view of backward development diverged from Marx's view of development in general. If Trotsky sometimes confused industrialization with modernization, Marx, in his turn, often identified the two with *capitalism*. Sometimes in his work capitalism appears as the result of these processes, sometimes as their precipitant, or necessary and sufficient condition, but always inevitably linked. Yet it is clear that although historically, for certain countries, this may have been true, there is in fact no necessary relationship between the processes and capitalism. It is perfectly conceivable for a society to become industrialized and modernized without beginning or ending with capitalism (though Marx, of course, did not see it as the ultimate end). If in Marx's time there were no examples to sustain this, developments since his time—ironically, in those very countries in particular where Marxism became the official ideology—have at least partly confirmed it.[102] Yet Marx's observations, pertaining as they did to a certain point in history, were legitimate, though their projection upon the future may have been much less so. From his historical perspective, he could hardly do otherwise than to link capitalism with industrial society, and with progress and advancement

---

[101] This phenomenon has been repeated in contemporary backward or underdeveloped societies though in a different sense: not the unwillingness but the inability of the central political authority, the state, to transform its social milieu, i.e. traditional society, in accordance with its economic and political ambitions.

[102] This is, of course, precisely what Trotsky sought to predict, i.e. that a modern society could be created without going through the capitalist stage of development.

in general. But that he linked it necessarily and inevitably arose not from his account of history but his interpretation of it, that is, from that fundamental thesis which saw historical change as the function of a class society. Dividing society into classes, he attributed to them roles, each being in turn the 'bearer' of some form of economic organization or system. Thus for him classes were logically linked to certain social processes; thus he could not conceive of a separation of economic forms from certain changes, of classes from these economic forms and hence changes, of capitalism from advanced society. Thus the importance of the bourgeoisie and, later, the proletariat. This was, of course, the very kernel of Marx's thought, what made him into a social theorist and not a chronicler of history, and what eventually also turned Marx into Marxism. But it was this also which made it impossible for him to conceive of modern society without the capitalist phase. And his interpretation of a particular period in Western history was certainly turned into a 'supra-historical axiom'.

The originality of Trotsky lay in the fact that he was able to break out of Marx's historical framework as well as out of Marx's European self-centredness. Trotsky had, of course, the advantage of belonging to a different, and later, historical epoch. But this was the very reason why he refused, even if not in a fully declared way, to remain locked within Marx's suppositions; that is, he took the time element to be crucial, and history as continuously transforming the possibilities of the future. Thus he abandoned fundamentally the link between modern society and capitalism and he saw the former as attainable without the latter. This is why also, he, more than other Russian Marxists, was able to make not only a distinction between industrial society and capitalism, but to question the very possibility of the latter, in a sense beyond the merely industrial features, actually developing in Russia. In fact, he claimed, capitalism as such did not and could not come into being, and only a non-capitalist, partially industrialized society had been created.

The crucial distinction, however, was still between an industrial and a modern society and how one could progress from the one to the other. The advantage of Marx's analysis was that it provided the propelling force, the agent of change, namely, a class, the bourgeoisie; the weakness of Trotsky's analysis was that it was forced to blur the distinction between the one and the other since it could not account for the transition. The importance of this distinction now becomes clear: to bring about the process of modernization, an agent of change, a social or political force, is required. In the West, for its own historical reasons, this agent was a bourgeoisie which saw in modernization—economic, social and political—the predicate for the fulfilment of its position and aspirations in society. Thus modernization was, in the West, a function of deeply rooted social interests. This did not mean, as Marx may have thought, that everywhere else this scenario would have to be repeated, that elsewhere too only the bourgeoisie could and would play this role of agent of social change. In a backward society, in the twentieth century, the absence of a bourgeoisie obviously precluded the re-enactment of Western history. But it did not preclude another social force from assuming a similar role. The most obvious alternative was the existing political authority itself, namely, the state, backed by its own administrative élite. Yet in Russia this alternative did not materialize; as Trotsky had argued, the state either could not or would not undertake the role. On the contrary, the Russian state stopped always short of going beyond industrialization. This was because its interests were economic-military not economic-social, as Trotsky stressed. The consequence was, to repeat, industrialization without modernization.

But if there had been no modernization, how much had really changed in Russia? In effect, very little, only segments of the formal economic framework. And if this was so, then Trotsky's concept of 'combined development', although in itself a brilliant heuristic generalization, must be seen to assume a quite different dimension. It correctly identified the dynamics of economic change. But it was an exaggeration as far as social and political change was concerned. Thus, in so far as it claimed to link industrial with other changes, it was largely a misrepresentation of reality. Again, it has to be emphasized that Trotsky was aware of the limits of its applicability: he returned persistently to the manifold ways in which Russia lagged behind modern or advanced societies, he stressed again and again the restricted nature of over-all social change in Russia. But, equally, it is clear why at a certain point he had to leave the distinction between industrialization and modernization blurred and ambiguous. For his purposes, modernization was essential, since without it he could not claim that the actual character of Russian society, particularly the character of its social classes, had undergone radical change. He had to assume, in particular, that the Russian workers had become a *social*, not merely wage-earning, class in the full Marxist sense, analogous to its counterpart in Western Europe; he had to assume that a new social and political culture, having a mass basis, had come into being. Modernization, as he recognized, was in fact a pre-condition for the kind of new advanced society which he was to envisage for Russia. If the modernizing process was not a fact, what chance was there for this new society? In this sense, the pessimism or cautious reservations of the more orthodox Russian Marxists—who, however, did not provide any real, immediate theoretical alternative—was better grounded in Russian reality than the optimism of Trotsky. The ambiguity subsumed under this optimism was in fact to occupy, and plague, his thought in these and later years. In the next chapter we shall see how the limits of 'combined development' were even more conspicuous within the context of Trotsky's theory of revolution. And in subsequent chapters we shall see the practical dilemmas as well, of which such limits were the roots.

Nevertheless, he was right in one respect. The continued tension between new economic institutions and old social and political ones, the disharmony between economics on the one hand and society and politics on the other, could not persist. Industrialization need not lead to modernization but in that case it itself could not be completed. In so far as the Russian state was determined to build an industrial edifice it was itself becoming committed to some form of modernization, as well as creating demands for it. It is possible, therefore, that at some point the state, however reluctantly, but in accordance with its own military-economic needs, would assume the role of an agent of social change. And the attempts at reform, particularly in agriculture, during the decade or so which followed 1905, seemed to confirm this at least partly. If so, the possibility of gradual, even peaceful change did not appear to be ruled out. Trotsky, however, was convinced that this possibility did not in fact exist. To initiate the kind of changes which were required, the autocracy would in effect have to decree itself out of existence. Was this a reasonable prospect? Trotsky believed that it obviously was not. He was therefore convinced that these changes would be brought about by different forces, that the collapse, consequently, of the old regime and the old society had become imminent, that, to repeat, the 'entire preceding social development [had] made revolution inevitable'.[103]

[103] *Itogi i perspektivy*, p. 231.

CHAPTER FOUR

THE REVOLUTION OF BACKWARDNESS: THE PERMANENT REVOLUTION

> History does not repeat itself. However much one may compare the Russian revolution with the Great French Revolution, the former can never be transformed into a repetition of the latter. The nineteenth century has not passed in vain.[1]

TROTSKY'S THEORY of the 'permanent revolution' was first formulated during the period immediately following upon 1905.[2] From the outset, and throughout the decade or so thereafter, it stood in direct opposition to the whole theoretical atmosphere prevalent in the Russian Social Democratic movement. Nearly a quarter of a century after he originally broached the theory, Trotsky recalled what it was that he had then attempted to do:

Vulgar 'Marxism' has worked out a pattern of historical development according to which every bourgeois society sooner or later secures a democratic regime, after which the proletariat, under conditions of democracy is gradually organized and educated for socialism . . . Both [reformists and formal revolutionists] considered democracy and socialism, for all peoples and countries, as two states in the development of society which are not only entirely distinct but also separated by great distances of time from each other. This view was predominant also among those Russian Marxists who, in the period of 1905, belonged to the left wing of the Second International. Plekhanov, the brilliant progenitor of Russian Marxism, considered the idea of the dictatorship of the proletariat a delusion in contemporary Russia. The same standpoint was defended not only by the Mensheviks but also by the overwhelming majority of the leading Bolsheviks . . . The

---

[1] Trotsky, *Itogi i perspektivy*, p. 236.
[2] The origin of the phrase 'permanent revolution' and its adoption by Trotsky are discussed later in this chapter, pp. 152ff., below.

theory of the permanent revolution, which originated in 1905, declared war upon these ideas and moods.[3]

Although a revolutionary theory has obvious implications for revolutionary tactics, Trotsky did not propose his new ideas as a tactical manœuvre. He believed that they grew directly out of the specific conditions of Russia, that they were governed by historical necessity, not by a voluntaristic opportunism.[4] His argument with both the Mensheviks and the Bolsheviks was therefore over the essential, substantive issues involved in transplanting Marxism to Russian soil. In fact, as we shall see, he became so convinced of the correctness of his analysis and thus of the inevitability of his prophecies that he eventually underestimated the role which organizational tactics would play in their fulfilment. He was to grasp the curious relation between his theory and *praxis* much later; in the meantime, in 1905–6, he believed that he already saw the inevitable shape of things to come in Russia. And it was different from anything which the West had experienced; it was therefore essential, in his view, to free oneself of preconceived categories, derived from Western history, and accept the possibility of unprecedented patterns of revolution. Thus he wrote, in 1906:

The Marxists [in Russia] are now confronted by a task of quite another kind: to discover the 'possibilities' of the developing revolution by means of an analysis of its internal mechanism. It would be a stupid error simply to identify our revolution with the events of 1789–93 or of 1848. Historical analogies . . . cannot take the place of social analysis. The Russian revolution has a quite peculiar character, which emerges as the result of our entire social and historical development and which, in its turn, opens before us quite new historical prospects.[5]

---

[3] Introduction to the first Russian edition of *Permanentnaya Revolyutsiya* (Berlin, 1930), pp. 14–15. Similar statements by Trotsky may be found elsewhere as well; see, for instance, 'Tri kontseptsii russkoi revolyutsii', Archives, T4684 (English version in *Stalin*, pp. 422–34) and the preface to the 1919 Russian reissue of *Itogi i perspektivy* (Moscow, 1919), pp. 3–9. However, in these same writings Trotsky also tried to minimize the over-all gap between himself and Lenin, in order to refute Stalin's charges at the time that his (Trotsky's) views were always anti-Leninist and that he was consistently an opponent of Bolshevism.

[4] See, for example, the preface to *Nasha Revolyutsiya*, p. xvii, where he said of his theory: 'It is not an idea we raise as a premise to our tactics. [It] is a conclusion derived from the interrelationships of the revolution. We would be despicable subjectivists if our tactics were nothing more than a practical application of this abstract idea.'

[5] *Itogi i perspektivy*, p. 224.

1. 1789–1848–1905

The recognition of unique features had been the basis of Trotsky's analysis of Russia's social and historical development; the problem of revolution, he believed, had to be approached with the same preparedness to recognize the fact that history had not exhausted the variety of revolutionary possibilities. Historical comparisons were as important for the differences they yielded as the apparent universal factors they pointed to in a general way. In the third chapter of his *Results and Prospects*, entitled '1789–1848–1905', Trotsky briefly surveyed past revolutions in an attempt to show how unique each was, and how useless it was, therefore, to substitute 'historical analogies' for 'social analysis'.

The French Revolution of 1789 was, in Trotsky's view, an example *par excellence* of a national revolution. Though it was a revolution led by a particular class, the bourgeoisie, that class spoke in the name of the nation as a whole. It rallied behind itself peasants as well as workers, it proclaimed universal ideas, it took upon itself 'the task of leadership in the struggle for a new order, not only against the outworn institutions of France but also against the reactionary forces of Europe as a whole'.[6] Thus the revolution against absolutism was a *national* revolution, made possible by the correspondence between the bourgeoisie's 'consciousness' and that of society, arising from a general consensus among classes about the kind of social and political framework which France should adopt.[7]

In 1848, however, when the revolutionary scene shifted to Germany and Austria, no one class was capable of playing a national role. The bourgeoisie, according to Trotsky, was too weak to tear itself away from landed interests, while the peasants, 'scattered, isolated . . . stupid, limited in their horizons to the confines of their respective villages, could not have

---

[6] Ibid., p. 237. No attempt is here made to comment upon the degree of correctness of Trotsky's interpretation of the revolutions of 1789 and 1848.

[7] Ibid., p. 239. In *The History of the Russian Revolution*, III, pp. 857–8, Trotsky indirectly admitted that his earlier views (he had repeated them in *1905* as well, see p. 57), particularly with regard to the relationship in 1789–93 between the bourgeoisie and the peasantry, had been misconceived: he now attributed to the Parisian *sans-culottes* the main role of liberating the French peasants.

any significance as a leading force'.[8] Finally, the proletariat, a new force, was yet too small and inexperienced, too immature to step into the revolutionary vacuum created by the withdrawal of the bourgeoisie. Thus while in 1848 the existing regimes no longer had the capacity to rule, they were still able to save themselves since there was no one to take their place. The general impotence of the various social classes only reflected the absence of consensus amongst them about the future of German and Austrian society, and their inability, therefore, to unite in a common front.

Nevertheless, beginning with 1848, it became clear that sooner or later a new social force would assume the revolutionary role reserved in the past for the bourgeoisie. The proletariat had proved too weak in 1848 not because it was a spent force but, on the contrary, because it was one which was just in the process of consolidating itself. However, though it was now inheriting the revolutionary role left vacant by the bourgeoisie, it could not perform it in a manner analogous to that of the bourgeoisie. Henceforth, as Marx and Lassalle had perceived immediately, a national revolution would no longer be possible:

. . . already in the middle of the nineteenth century the problem of political emancipation could not be solved by the unanimous and concerted tactics of the pressure of the whole nation. Only the independent tactics of the proletariat, gathering strength from its class position, and only from its class position, could have secured victory for the revolution.[9]

The fact that Germany raised the original historical paradox of a working class becoming a political, even revolutionary, force *before* the bourgeoisie had carried out its own revolution, was of course not lost on Trotsky.[10] In an embryonic way, Trotsky believed, this was the first example of the unprecedented possibilities inherent in a backward nation, such as Germany was at the time in comparison with England or France. In fact, it was this backwardness which explained why the revolution in Germany took on an extreme class character: for backwardness signified social disharmony between major social

---

[8] *Itogi i perspektivy*, p. 240.　　　[9] Ibid., p. 242.

[10] Nor, of course, on Marx; see this chapter, pp. 156ff., below.

groups, the persistence of anomalies in the midst of partial change. France, in 1789–93, effected a political revolution as the culmination of a social revolution which had already transformed the country. Germany, in 1848, had undergone only a partial social revolution, as a result of which she remained suspended between two worlds, and nothing illustrated this so much as the inability of the bourgeoisie to commit itself wholeheartedly to the new world. The proletariat, a product of the latter, thus began to emerge as the force which would make a political revolution in order to complete the social one, and it would have to do so as much against the bourgeois powers still tied to the past as against the feudal powers still entrenched in it. On the one hand, this would lead to class polarization, the sharpening of class divisions and antagonism, the juxtaposition of contradictory class interests and aims. On the other hand, the proletariat's programme, although ostensibly at variance with what the rest of society was prepared to accept, would in fact represent what the nation as a whole *needed* in order to overcome its backwardness, in order to bring its social revolution to completion. Thus the 'execution of those tasks which the nation as a whole is unable to carry out' fell to the lot of the proletariat.[11]

If all this was true of Germany in 1848, it was even truer, according to Trotsky, of Russia in 1905. Once again the 'classic' precedent of 1789 was hardly relevant; once again the difference lay in the fact that Russia was a backward society, undergoing change but incapable of completing a social revolution; once again there was the phenomenon of a revolutionary working class ranged against a society over which the bourgeoisie did not rule. The pattern of class formation and development was thus in Russia, as in Germany, different from what Marx had perceived it to be in England and France. In Russia, however, the situation was even more extreme than it had been in Germany, for here the bourgeoisie was almost non-existent while the working class was qualitatively more developed, the

---

[11] *Itogi i perspektivy*, p. 237. There is in this view of the specifically *class* struggle in the name of *universal* goals, an allusion to Marx's notion of the proletariat as a universal class, a notion which first appears in Marx's early writings (see Karl Marx, *Early Writings*, translated and edited by T. B. Bottomore, London, 1963, especially pp. 58–9). In Marx as well, of course, it is linked to the general question of modernization which Trotsky here hinted at and which will be raised again later in this chapter.

product of the most advanced forms of twentieth-century industry and urbanization. The strength of the proletariat was therefore multiplied, and the prospects of a political revolution, as a pre-condition of total social change, at the head of which would stand the workers, had become immediate. A national revolution, however, was even more impossible than in Germany a half century earlier. But the class revolution, in the name of 'the nation as a whole', which had failed in 1848, was no longer remote in 1905. It was necessary, therefore, to get away from the precedent of 1789 and adopt a new perspective upon 1905 and beyond.

The twentieth century, Trotsky consequently believed, stood on the threshold of a new kind of revolution, what we may call, following his meaning, the *revolution of backwardness*[12]—though its ultimate success would depend on developments in advanced countries as well. The theory of the permanent revolution, with which the name of Trotsky became linked from 1905–6 onwards, was therefore an attempt to explain a peculiarly twentieth-century phenomenon.

2. The New Model and the Old[13]

The administrative, military and financial power of absolutism, thanks to which it could exist in spite of social development, not only

---

[12] The term 'revolution of backwardness' does not appear as such in Trotsky's writings but it may be taken to identify the meaning of his whole theory of the Russian revolution.
[13] In the presentation and analysis which follow of Trotsky's theory of the permanent revolution, the main sources used are Trotsky's writings during the 1905–8 period. It would not be difficult to base oneself on these sources alone since all the essentials of the theory were formulated during this period. Nevertheless, Trotsky returned to the subject in the 1920s and 1930s in a fairly extensive way. What he then wrote neither altered nor added anything essential to the original formulation of the theory. Nevertheless, Trotsky was then able to make certain refinements and to go into greater detail about the actual 'mechanism', as he called it, of the permanent revolution. In order to present the theory as a whole, and in the most coherent way, it therefore seemed sensible to ignore the difference in period between his various writings on the permanent revolution and to deal with them as one in theoretical terms. Naturally, the later writings also refer to specific political questions of the post-1917 period. But wherever this is so, it has been excluded from the present purely theoretical discussion, thus avoiding historical confusion, and relegated to the next chapter where questions of the concrete application of the theory are discussed. Of the earlier works, *Itogi i perspektivy* is the main source for the theory of the permanent revolution. Of the later works, the most important is *Permanentnaya Revolyutsiya*. But various other writings are also referred to and details of these will be found in the text and notes which follow. (See also chapter 3, note 7, above.)

did not exclude the possibility of revolution . . . but, on the contrary, made revolution the only way out; furthermore, this revolution was guaranteed in advance an all the more radical character in proportion as the great might of absolutism dug an abyss between itself and the nation.[14]

Having thus argued that revolution in Russia had become inevitable, Trotsky now sought to construct the kind of revolutionary 'scenario' which would reflect the peculiarities of Russia's social development and project the necessary political confrontations arising from it. In so doing, he was, of course, working within a Marxist framework; that is, the scenario would have to incorporate the basic ingredients of the Marxist view of revolution—class struggle, the distribution of economic power, the objective conditions arising from particular productive functions, the strategic importance of a specific social environment, and so on. But this general framework, which Trotsky accepted as the universally valid 'method' of Marxist social analysis, did not determine the actual content which it encompassed. In his view a method of social investigation could not provide in advance all the possible particular political forms which social relations may give rise to; nor did it obligate whoever adopted the method to either postulate in advance, or arrive at, an inevitable internal structure for this framework. Quoting some sentences from Karl Kautsky in which the latter attacked those who used the materialist conception of history 'not as *method of investigation* but merely as a ready-made *stereotype*', Trotsky noted: 'We particularly recommend these lines to our Russian Marxists, who replace independent analysis of social relations by deductions from texts, selected to serve every occasion in life.'[15] The 'stereotyped' form of thinking arose, in Trotsky's view, from a confusion of method with its results in a particular case; more specifically, from a confusion of Marx's method of social analysis with Marx's conclusions about the particular example of Western capitalism. It was this confusion which had led to the assumption that Western capitalism was both a prototype for all societies and the sole pre-condition for the socialist revolution. In fact, however, for Trotsky the original Marxist model was valid only in a specific historical and social context; a different context required a different model.[16]

The theory of the permanent revolution derived from the construction of just such a different model. It may be best visualized at first by presenting it in diagrammatic form in juxtaposition with the generally accepted classical Marxist model (though it must be stressed that the diagrams as such do not appear in Trotsky's writings and are merely a short-hand way of translating and illustrating his distinction between the two models):

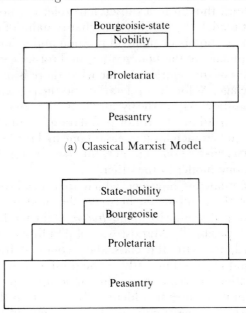

(a) Classical Marxist Model

(b) Trotsky's Model

These diagrams do not pretend to be complete or exact replicas, but necessarily crude abstractions. Reality is too diverse to be conveniently fitted into straight lines and rectangles; and these diagrams should be seen as an aid to explication, not a substitute for it. The explication itself will follow. Moreover, in both diagrams, the drawn sizes of the 'rectangles' should not be taken to represent the actual size or distribution of the different class-populations; they are only a rough approximation. Nor is there necessarily any relationship in size as *between* the models. Similarly, the diagrams ignore the sub-divisions which can be made within a particular class, e.g., petty-bourgeoisie as opposed to capitalist bourgeoisie, industrial as opposed to agricultural proletariat, subdivisions which do not affect the general, over-all picture which Trotsky's new model seeks to convey.

---

[16] It can hardly be said that Trotsky's argument convincingly resolves the whole problem of methodology and content in Marxism. The argument is certainly an oversim-

This somewhat schematic and obviously oversimplified presentation of the two models has nevertheless the advantage of making clearer both the differences and similarities between them. The differences are as follows: whereas in the Marxist model it is the bourgeoisie which stands at the top of the 'pyramid' by virtue of owning or controlling the means of production and exercising domination over political institutions, in Trotsky's model this position is reserved for the autocracy and, to some extent, though in a subservient role, the nobility. In the Marxist model, the nobility (or what remains of it) has no independent economic or political position and is, so to speak, under the tutelage of the bourgeoisie; in Trotsky's model it is the condition of the bourgeoisie, or what there is of it, which is one of tutelage. As for the proletariat and the peasantry, their respective positions within the pyramids are the same, but there are obvious variations in size of population: a much smaller proletarian and a much larger peasant one in Trotsky's model; and, of course, *vis-à-vis* one another, the size relationship is different from one model to the other.

It is the similarities, however, which are crucial to grasping the value of the comparison between the models. There is, firstly, the over-all similarity in the *structure* of the models, which represents a specifically Marxist way of dividing society, that is, in accordance with the class and economic framework. Secondly, and most importantly, is the similarity of the proletariat's position in relation to the uppermost part of the structures: in both cases it is identically placed, in the formal sense at least. The positioning is also the same, of course, in the case of the peasantry but less significant, since in both models there is as if no direct formal contact between it and the 'ruling' elements.

What phenomena can be noted in these comparisons in accordance with Trotsky's social and political analysis of Russia?

---

plification, though he is not concerned in this particular context with arguing the case of Marxism as an objective science—which is, of course, at the root of the problem. The short answer to the distinction he makes is that Marxist methodology *does* influence and even prejudge both content and results. But this is a wider issue than the one Trotsky is dealing with here: he may be said to be merely pleading for greater sophistication in distinguishing historical developments. See also the sub-section 'The Unique and the Universal' in chapter 3, above, and the conclusions to the same chapter.

There is first of all the phenomenon of a proletariat which is *not* the product of capitalist development but of the process of industrialization as such. Moreover, this process does not bring into being bourgeois-capitalism but rather a form of *state capitalism*. Although Trotsky does not actually use this term—he would discuss it years later in a different though not unrelated context[17]—it is clearly what he has in mind. Not capitalism in the socio-cultural Marxist sense, involving a middle-class, private ownership of means of production, private capital, bourgeois morality and ideological forms, and so on, has been created in Russia, but industrial production and entrepreneurship under the tutelage of the state.

However, as far as the proletariat is concerned, this difference is, in Trotsky's view, purely academic. The workers' economic position, their mode and conditions of labour, their immediate environment, namely, the factory and the city, are identical in both kinds of 'capitalism' since the constant framework is industry. Identical also are the principles of wage-labour and the grossly uneven distribution of property. Since the nature and place of their economic occupation and the influence of their socio-cultural surroundings are the same, their ideological and political inclinations should also be of the same kind. What does differ from one form of capitalism to another is not the nature of the 'adversary'—in both cases it is the same fundamental system of economic arrangement—but his actual identity. Whereas in the Marxist model the proletariat stands in opposition to the bourgeoisie, in Trotsky's model it is turned against the autocracy and against the latter's 'appendage', or instrument, the state, and only incidentally against the bourgeoisie in so far as this latter clings to its protector. It is in this sense, therefore, that Trotsky believes that in so far as a revolutionary situation and a revolutionary force exist in Russia they correspond to their counterparts in the advanced Western societies. In both cases, the revolution is of the workers against their 'employers' and, as Trotsky will argue, in the name of socialism.

But Trotsky's model, as here presented, does not *of itself* define or describe—neither, for that matter, does Marx's—either a revolutionary situation or the revolutionary potential

[17] See chapter 10, below, where Trotsky's critique of Stalinism is discussed.

of the social forces it encompasses, much less the logic of a specifically *socialist* revolution; it does no more than illustrate the
main class divisions which exist and the positions of the classes
in relation to one another. The revolutionary issues need to be
argued by reference to factors that cannot be portrayed in a
formal model, by reference, namely, to the social dynamics of
the society itself. The answer to the first issue—in what sense
is the Russian situation a revolutionary one—may be said to
have been inherent in Trotsky's sociological analysis of Russia's
backwardness; it centres on the fundamental disharmonies of
Russian society or, to put it in the usual Marxist terminology,
on the discrepancy, which Trotsky claims to have now arisen,
between the means of production (industrial or becoming so),
and the relations of production (still adapted to a semi-feudal
environment).[18] But a revolutionary situation need not actually
lead to revolution; whether it does or not will depend on two
general and related factors: the capacity of the existing rulers
to adapt themselves or respond to social and political demands,
or, conversely, the capacity of the ruled to act in a revolutionary
way, that is, to grasp power. The first of these factors Trotsky
had discounted in its entirety; he does not believe that the autocracy can adapt itself or respond adequately, since adequately
here means in effect self-dismemberment or self-liquidation,
and no ruling élite can be expected to commit suicide of its own
volition. There therefore remains the question of the revolutionary capacity or potential of the ruled: are they in a position
to overthrow the autocracy and establish a new government
and, eventually, a new society? If so, what kind of government
must this be and what kind of society will it aim at? These questions remain unanswered and to deal with them properly it is
necessary to turn from the schematic presentation to a detailed
explication of Trotsky's model of the revolution of backwardness, to the theory itself of the permanent revolution.

3. The Proletariat and Revolution

In a backward society, torn between the contradictions of past
and present, a revolution which is national in scope is imposs-

[18] This follows, of course, Marx's well-known definition of the conditions of revolution
in his 'Preface to *A Contribution to the Critique of Political Economy*' (in Marx–Engels,
Selected Works, I, pp. 361–5).

ible; the main classes, separated by the social cleavages of back-wardness, cannot unite behind an agreed revolutionary pro-gramme. The revolution, Trotsky believed, will therefore triumph as a class revolution or it will not triumph at all.[19] In that case, however, the class standing at the head of the revolu-tion must be powerful enough to withstand not only the regime it seeks to overthrow but the social forces which cling to it and which will rally to its defence. Was the proletariat in Russia sufficiently significant to confront the rest of society? Here Trotsky raised again[20] the question of the weight of numbers: did its minority status contradict the proletariat's potential as a revolutionary force? Must this potential come to fruitation only when the proletariat in Russia reached the proportions of its counterpart in the advanced countries of the West, that is only when Russia herself had been turned, presumably, into a fully modern, industrial nation? In replying to these ques-tions, Trotsky again pointed to the peculiar features of the Rus-sian condition when compared either with the past or present of the West.

Mere numbers, he argued, were misleading; statistics said nothing about the nature of the categories which they formally defined, percentages and proportions did not exhaust the possi-bilities of relations. The importance of the proletariat was only partly a function of numbers; it was, rather, more a function of its social character. This character was in turn the product of the industrial and geographical milieu in which the worker found himself and of the economic position he occupied. In Russia, since industry was erected not from its foundations but from its highest forms, the worker was immediately thrown into the most technologically advanced environment. This hap-pened while the rest of the population remained at its previously low level. Thus in relation to that population, the worker's im-portance rose out of proportion to his numbers. Similarly, the worker found himself in the modern city, whose industrial and commercial character bore no resemblance to the larger countryside but whose resultant strategic importance could not

[19] Trotsky agreed with Plekhanov's well-known statement that the victory of the Rus-sian proletariat was possible only as a revolutionary victory—or not at all (see his 1907 speech to the Fifth London Congress of the RSDRP, in *1905*, p. 252).
[20] See chapter 3, pp. 84–6, above.

be measured by its relative numbers only. The Russian worker's environment, therefore, coincided with the most advanced features of Russian society; in so far as it was these features which must eventually predominate, their force expressed the force of the worker:

> ...it is clear that the importance of a proletariat—given identical numbers—increases in proportion to the amount of productive forces which it sets in motion. That is to say, a worker in a large factory is, all other things being equal, of greater social magnitude than a handicraft worker, and an urban worker of greater magnitude than a country worker. In other words, the political role of the proletariat is the more important in proportion as large-scale production dominates small production, industry dominates agriculture and the town dominates the country. If we take the history of Germany or of England in the period when the proletariat of these countries formed the same proportion of the nation as the proletariat now forms in Russia, we shall see that they not only did not play, but by their objective importance could not play, such a role as the Russian proletariat plays today.[21]

It followed, therefore, according to Trotsky, that 'the attempt to define in advance what proportion of the whole population must be proletarian at the moment of the conquest of political power is a fruitless task'.[22] But even more significant, in his view, was the strategic location of the workers *vis-à-vis*

---

[21] *Itogi i perspektivy*, p. 269. In *The History of the Russian Revolution*, 1, pp. 33–4, Trotsky wrote: 'England achieved her Puritan revolution when her whole population was not more than $5\frac{1}{2}$ millions, of whom half a million were to be found in London. France, in the epoch of her revolution, had in Paris only half a million out of a population of 25 million. Russia at the beginning of the twentieth century had a population of about 150 million of whom more than 3 million were in Petrograd and Moscow. Behind these comparative figures lurk enormous social differences. Not only England of the seventeenth century, but also France of the eighteenth, had no proletariat in the modern sense. In Russia, however, the working class in all branches of labour, both city and village, numbered in 1905 no less than 10 million, which with their families amounts to more than 25 million—that is to say, more than the whole population of France in the epoch of the great revolution. Advancing from the sturdy artisans and independent peasants of the army of Cromwell—thorugh the *sans-culottes* of Paris—to the industrial proletarians of St. Petersburg, the revolution had deeply changed its social mechanism, its methods, and therewith its aims.' (The figure of 10 million which Trotsky gives as the number of Russian workers in 1905 is, of course, misleading since it includes many categories which hardly fit the description 'proletarian'. The actual figure is probably closer to 3 million—though this does not necessarily affect Trotsky's argument. See chapter 3, p. 85, above.)

[22] *Itogi i perspektivy*, p. 270.

the economic structure: their potential, which they had confirmed in 1905, to paralyze industry, and their potential equally—also at least partially confirmed—to dominate urban centres. But beyond these elements there was a further factor, which Trotsky viewed as a kind of advantage arising from backwardness. This was the non-capitalist nature of Russian industry which far from arguing for the weakness of the Russian proletariat in fact was the real source of its revolutionary potential. To show why this was so, Trotsky compared the development of Russian industry with that of the West. The experience in the latter showed, in his view, that where industry had been built through capitalism, there the bourgeoisie had been able to attain power which was out of all proportion to *its* numerical inferiority, since the capitalist framework had given it the means by which to dominate the whole structure of society, to impose upon it a way of life which extended beyond the purely economic. Assimilated into this capitalist socio-cultural framework, the proletariat in the West, for the time being at least, had not been able to exploit its superior numbers in accordance with objective proportions. In Russia, however, a different picture had emerged. Here, the advance of industry, without the capitalist framework, left the methods of production exposed; industry was like the skeleton of a building, so much the easier to raze. Thus in relation to the bourgeoisie the workers were obviously more powerful; but the point was that they were more powerful in relation to the whole industrial edifice, for the state, though it nourished industry and lived off capitalism, had not, and could not, itself introduce those socio-cultural elements of capitalism which in the West created political power. In effect, its political power—which was primarily based on a large army—did not embody that economic power which should have been derived from industry. Instead, it was the proletariat which, in a sense by default, inherited this economic power. Industry without capitalism, in short, meant not only a working class without a bourgeoisie, but a working class with the capacity to rule over industry.[23] Trotsky did not conclude, of course, that this comparison implied that the Western proletariat was doomed to be for ever ruled by its capitalist employers. On the contrary, in the long run the proletariat

[23] See especially sections 4 and 7 of *Itogi i perspektivy*, and *1905*, pp. 25–60, *passim*.

there was more powerful and would assert itself in accordance with its objective strength in proportion as the capitalist system itself, for economic reasons, degenerated. In the short run, however, it was in a country such as Russia that the workers could make themselves felt more forcefully:

> There is no doubt that the numbers, the concentration, the culture and the political importance of the industrial proletariat depend on the extent to which capitalist industry is developed. But this dependence is not direct. Between the productive forces of a country and the political strength of its classes there cut across at any given moment various social and political factors of a national and international character and these displace and even sometimes completely alter the political expression of economic relations. In spite of the fact that the productive forces of the United States are ten times as great as those of Russia, nevertheless the political role of the Russian proletariat, its influence on the politics of its own country and the possibility of its influencing the politics of the world in the near future, are incomparably greater than in the case of the proletariat of the United States.[24]

Trotsky therefore concluded, in a sentence to which he would later point as embodying his major prophecy of 1906, that: 'In an economically backward country the proletariat can come to power sooner than in a capitalist, advanced country.'[25]

4. The Proletariat and 'Socialist Consciousness'

Assuming for the moment that Trotsky's evaluation of the relative strength of the Russian working class was correct, there still remains the question to what extent this class may be said to have attained a 'socialist consciousness'. This question has nothing necessarily to do with the earlier issue, namely the *revolutionary* consciousness of the workers, since their revolutionism may take merely the form of some spontaneous opposition to social and economic conditions without any specific conception of alternative ones except in the vague, general sense. Were the workers oriented towards socialism? It must be admitted that Trotsky nowhere answered this question satisfactorily, though he dealt with it at some length. The importance of a

---

[24] *Itogi i perspektivy*, pp. 246–7. Trotsky went on to cite an approximately similar comparison of the United States and Russia made by Karl Kautsky.
[25] Ibid., p. 245.

positive reply could hardly be exaggerated; it was in effect one of the preconditions for the validity of the theory of the permanent revolution. Since throughout the formulation of this theory in 1906 Trotsky discounted, or rather relegated to a subsidiary position, the role of party organization and party leadership, the more or less independent socialist orientation of the working masses became a crucial factor in assuming the specifically socialist content of their revolution. Nevertheless, the positive reply which he gave, as he had to, in effect begged the question.

In the seventh chapter of *Results and Prospects*, Trotsky rejected the view that a socialist consciousness was a function of a high stage of capitalist development. Were this to be so, he argued, then it would logically follow that one needed merely to wait until capitalist society had made itself so technologically efficient as to transform all production into a 'single automatic mechanism, belonging to a single syndicate and requiring as living labour only a single trained orangoutang',[26] whereupon society would presumably peacefully become socialist, without revolution, without a dictatorship of the proletariat, since everyone would have been conditioned into a socialist consciousness by the existence of, in effect, already socialized production and consumption. The absurdity of this, Trotsky wrote, was like the logical absurdity which would arise if one were to take the Marxist notion of the proletarianization of the masses under capitalism and turn it into a programme, that is, work towards the goal (in effect wait for its fulfilment) of everyone becoming a worker, joining a trade union or political organization, becoming 'united by a spirit of solidarity and singleness of aim', whereupon, once again, 'socialism could be realized peaceably by a unanimous, conscious "civil act" at some time in the twenty-first or twenty-second century'.[27]

But this automatic abolition of capitalism was, of course, impossible because the so-called 'prerequisites' of socialism—the concentration of production, the development of technique, the growth of consciousness among the masses—although they develop simultaneously, also 'retard and *limit* each other' creating disharmony, or the lack of parallel uniformity: 'Each of these processes [i.e. prerequisites] at a higher level demands a certain

[26] Ibid., p. 261. [27] Ibid., p. 264.

development of another process at a lower level. But the complete development of each of them is incompatible with the complete development of the others.'[28]

The schematic, mechanistic logic, applied to the development of capitalism, ended in absurdities because it concentrated only on quantitative changes, forgetting that at a certain point there occurred a qualitative leap which transformed hitherto evolutionary change into a situation which could be changed only by revolution:

. . . those processes which are historically prior conditions for socialism . . . having reached a certain stage which is determined by numerous circumstances—a stage, however, which is a long way away from the mathematical limit of these processes—undergo a qualitative change and, in their complex combination, bring about what we understand by the name of revolution.[29]

Trotsky's general argument may be said to have been quite impeccable as far as it went; but it did not yet answer the specific question whether a 'qualitative change' in consciousness had in fact taken place among Russian workers. Here he fluctuated between the view that this was, in fact, the case and a considerably different view, according to which the workers' gravitation towards socialism appeared as an instinctive, spontaneous phenomenon. On the one hand, Trotsky claimed that the very existence of large-scale enterprises, as the natural milieu of the worker, implanted the notion of socialized production. The more technologically advanced industry became and the more conscious the worker became of the possibilities of producing efficiently for society as a whole, the more the worker saw that this was in fact not being done, and could not be done, because the advantages of technological progress were nullified by the system of private ownership. The worker came to recognize that poverty was a function not of scarcity as such but of the manner in which production was planned and its goods distributed. In this sense, socialist consciousness was a consequence not of a population which was predominantly proletarian but of a proletariat, numerically small though it may have been, which was exposed to advanced forms of production.[30]

On the other hand, Trotsky admitted that the system of capi-

[28] Ibid., p. 263.   [29] Ibid., p. 264.   [30] Ibid., pp. 264–7.

talist production, even in its peculiar and retarded Russian form, engendered egoism, economic opportunism and narrow-mindedness among workers as well, not just employers. 'The individual struggle for existence, the ever-widening abyss of poverty, the differentiation in the ranks of the workers themselves, the pressure of the ignorant masses from below' prevented the 'splendid shoots of idealism, comradely solidarity and self-sacrifice' from becoming fully developed.[31] This undoubtedly undermined the worker's collective consciousness, and his rational grasp of the implications and consequences of the economic system by which he was employed. Still, it could not, in Trotsky's view, destroy that inner impulse which told the worker that the solution to his problems was bound up with the collapse of that system:

... despite his remaining philistinely egoistic, and without his exceeding in 'human' worth the average representative of the bourgeois classes, the average worker knows from experience that his *most basic requirements and natural desires can be satisfied only on the ruins of the capitalist system.*[32]

Trotsky spoke of three factors as constituting the 'prerequisites of socialism'. The first he called the 'productive-technical' prerequisite, namely, the condition prevailing when 'the development of productive forces has reached the stage at which large enterprises are more productive than small ones'.[33] The second was the 'social-economic' prerequisite, the existence of a social force, the proletariat, which by virtue of its economic role was potentially the most powerful of classes and was objectively interested in socialism.[34] The final prerequisite was political-revolutionary, the 'dictatorship of the proletariat' which made possible the actual transition to socialism.[35] Trotsky saw the first two prerequisites as being satisfied more or less automatically by the very creation of the modern industrial framework. It was the last, however, which was a direct result of socialist consciousness. For a 'dictatorship of the proletariat' to become possible, it was essential that the proletariat 'should be *conscious* of its objective interests; it is necessary that it should understand that there is no way out for it except through socialism'. This meant that the conquest of power was the 'conscious

[31] Ibid., p. 273. [32] Loc. cit. [33] Ibid., p. 265.
[34] Ibid., p. 267. [35] Ibid., p. 271.

action of a revolutionary class'.[36] How far did such consciousness exist among Russian workers? In effect Trotsky conceded
that it was far from being fully developed, that the proletariat
was not composed entirely of 'conscious socialists'. But he
rejected the view that an 'overwhelming majority' of the
workers needed to be 'conscious socialists'; it was sufficient that
there be a conscious nucleus, a 'revolutionary army' acting as
the spearhead for the rest of the workers who would join this
army once 'open battle' was declared.[37] Trotsky claimed that
the absence of a proletariat entirely composed of 'conscious
socialists' was a condition characteristic not only of Russia but
also of capitalist societies. Actually, he believed, it could not be
otherwise, for the very existence of capitalism infected and distorted the consciousness of the masses. A full 'moral regeneration', which was the aim of socialism, was impossible within
the confines of a non-socialist society; those who preached that
human nature must be transformed before socialism can be
embarked upon, would 'put off socialism for several centuries'.[38] Socialist man was a product of socialism itself; the pre-
socialist society could only create men who 'strove towards
socialism':

If socialism aimed at creating a new human nature within the limits
of the old society it would be nothing more than a new edition of
the moralistic utopias. Socialism does not aim at creating a socialist
psychology as a prerequisite to socialism but at creating socialist conditions as a prerequisite to socialist psychology.[39]

It is clear that here, in Trotsky's discussion of the proletariat
and socialist consciousness, the most conspicuous elements of
'voluntarism' are revealed. He made more concessions to 'élitism' as well here than anywhere else in his early writings. His
position was, of course, far removed from that of Lenin for he
did not have an organizational élite in mind, but it was equally
remote from that of Menshevism.[40] And, although he acknowledged the limits of the workers' socialist consciousness, he made

[36] Ibid., p. 272.
[37] Ibid., pp. 264 and 272. It should be emphasized that when Trotsky spoke of this
nucleus or 'revolutionary army' he did *not* mean a party of professional revolutionaries
but workers themselves, albeit the 'cream', so to speak, of the proletariat.
[38] Ibid., p. 272.   [39] Ibid., p. 273.
[40] See his strictures against Blanquism, ibid., p. 272.

less of this than he perhaps should have. Many years later, after 1917, he would, in contrast, continually stress the limits. All the 'minuses' of the proletariat, he would then write, their 'illiteracy, backwardness, the absence [among them] of organizational habits, of system in labour, of cultural and technical education . . . we are feeling at every step'.[41] This would mean that the Russian workers' past had badly prepared them for socialism; and that the absence among them of a 'socialist consciousness' would complicate and transmute the tasks of the post-revolutionary regime.

5. The Proletariat and the Peasantry: A National Uprising

Not for a moment did Trotsky imagine that the Russian workers could by themselves overthrow the autocracy, much less conquer power in isolation from all other classes. In spite of the class nature which he attributed to the revolution, the initial conquest of power was a political question which did depend on numbers and on the actual alignment of numerical forces. The attitude of the peasantry was therefore crucial. This did not mean, conversely, that the overwhelming peasant majority could make a revolution on its own: we have seen why Trotsky discounted completely the prospect of a specifically peasant revolution.[42] It did mean, however, that a revolution of the workers was impossible without the initial support of the peasants. But the alliance which he therefore postulated as a pre-condition of success did not as a result mean that a *national* revolution was in the offing after all, and not only because the bourgeoisie would be excluded. The particular conditions of Russia made it essential, in his view, to distinguish between two concepts, which in the context of the theory of the permanent

[41] Appendix I, *History of the Russian Revolution*, I, p. 476.
[42] See chapter 2, pp. 41–7, above. In *The History of the Russian Revolution*, I, pp. 29–30, Trotsky wrote: 'Fifteen years before the great French Revolution there developed in Russia a movement of the Cossacks, peasants and worker-serfs of the Urals, known as the Pugatchev Rebellion. What was lacking to this menacing popular uprising in order to covert it into a revolution? A Third Estate. Without the industrial democracy of the cities a peasant war could not develop into a revolution, just as the peasant sects could not rise to the height of a Reformation. The result of the Pugatchev Rebellion was just the opposite—a strengthening of bureaucratic absolutism as the guardian of the interests of the nobility, a guardian which had again justified itself in the hours of danger.'

revolution appeared as chronologically separate: on the one hand, a *national uprising*, on the other, the *class revolution* as such. The one pertained to the period of the actual overthrow of the autocracy and the establishment of a new regime, the other to the actual transformation of Russian society. The one was, in the literal sense, a political revolution, the other a social revolution. Naturally, in practice, this distinction could not be strictly maintained; the dividing line between political and social was in many ways blurred, and was as much a short-hand way of conceptualizing the revolution as a description of its actual progress. Nevertheless, it helped to explain the peculiar over-all process which the revolution would undergo. Thus in his writings during 1905 itself Trotsky had spoken of a 'national uprising' as the first stage of the revolution;[43] and in *Results and Prospects* he wrote that the 'proletariat can achieve power by relying upon a national upsurge and national enthusiasm'. And he continued: 'The proletariat will enter the government as the revolutionary representative of the nation, as the recognized national leader in the struggle against absolutism and feudal barbarism.'[44]

The necessity of the alliance between workers and peasants arose out of the potential strength of the peasantry, its wrecking power, when in opposition to the revolution. Therefore it had to be won over; but this meant that it should remain not merely neutral but that it should actually participate on the side of the workers—for in this way alone could the autocracy be disarmed and the uprising in turn armed. In other words, winning over the peasantry meant in effect winning over the army. But it was clear that the alliance was merely strategic; it was an alliance arising out of the existence of a common enemy, not a common vision of the future, out of an agreement over what was to be done away with not what was to take its place. The national uprising was thus the *political form* which the revolution initially took. This at first camouflaged but did not subsume the *social content* which the revolution bore and which was its driving force. However, the longer the new revolutionary regime, made possible by the alliance, maintained itself, the more, Trotsky believed, would the social content transform the political form—and not vice versa—the more, in other

[43] See chapter 2, pp. 50–1, above.   [44] *Itogi i perspektivy*, p. 254.

words, would the alliance be torn asunder. It was at this point, therefore, that the actual mechanism of the permanent revolution emerged.

6. The Permanent Revolution: Stages, Process, Momentum

Let us now reconstruct Trotsky's actual scenario of the permanent revolution. Bringing together, firstly, the various threads from which it is suspended, the scenario may be said to unfold against the following background: The particular correlation of forces in Russia at the beginning of the twentieth century had driven the proletariat to the forefront of the opposition to the autocracy. In one sense, this was as logical as the revolutionary role of workers in advanced Western societies, since in Russia too the workers were the product of an industrial and economic system made to function at their expense, and the fact that this system in Russia had different origins did not affect this reality. However, the persistence, concurrently, in Russia of a primitive economy and social system involved the existence of another class, the peasantry, whose problems could be solved only by revolutionary means, and made it impossible for the proletariat to pursue the solution to *its* problems in isolation from that class. The resultant alliance, growing out of mutual dependence, was tactical but not arbitrary; it was dictated, in effect predetermined, by the peculiarities of the socio-historical context. This did not mean that the alliance could be effectively concluded at any given moment; various subjective factors might delay and undermine it, as had been the case in 1905. But in the long run—the clearer it became to both partners that neither could do without the other—it had to materialize. The initial task of such an alliance would be the overthrow of the existing political authority. But this was little enough; once in power it would immediately confront social issues, the resolution of which would demand of the new regime that it define its social character and philosophy. Thus, the future of an originally political alliance would be determined by the social policies which it would become necessary to pursue. And these, in turn, would determine the future of the revolution itself.

This was the immediate social and political background. The

scenario which Trotsky now unfolded may be said to consist
of three acts, each flowing into another.[45] The first 'act' may
be entitled the 'emancipation of the peasant'. It would open
with a new regime in power, its social composition heterogeneous but its leading element clearly apparent. Although it
'can and should' include representatives of the peasantry, the
urban petty-bourgeoisie, the intellectuals, it is the representatives of the proletariat 'who will form within it a solid
majority'.[46] It cannot be otherwise, according to Trotsky: the
bourgeois element, or rather a small minority thereof, will have
joined the revolution only after the fact, having played almost
no role in it, and bringing with it neither economic nor social
power; the peasants, without whom the revolution would indeed have been impossible, would nevertheless be subservient
in view of the concentration of organizational power in the cities
and not the countryside, a fact which in turn reflected the domination of town over country and industry over agriculture. The
new government would thus be a coalition of diverse oppo-
sitional forces, but it is the proletariat whose participation
would be 'dominating and leading':

One may, of course, describe such a government as the dictatorship
of the proletariat and peasantry, a dictatorship of the proletariat, peasantry and intelligentsia, or even a coalition government of the working class and the petty-bourgeoisie; but the question nevertheless
remains: who is to wield the hegemony in the government itself, and
through it in the country?

From what we have said . . . it will be clear how we regard the
idea of a 'proletarian and peasant dictatorship'. It is not really a matter of whether we regard it as admissible in principle, whether 'we
do or do not desire' such a form of political co-operation. We simply
think that it is unrealisable—at least in a direct, immediate sense.
Indeed, such a coalition presupposes either that one of the existing
bourgeois parties commands influence over the peasantry or that the
peasantry will have created a powerful independent party of its own;
but we have attempted to show that neither the one nor the other
is possible.[47]

[45] It should be stressed, however, that the end of each 'act' in reality is less fixed than
it would be were the 'scenario' to be presented in 'theatrical' form: the metaphor should
not be equated with the actual drama.

[46] *Itogi i perspektivy*, p. 250.

[47] Ibid., pp. 250 and 253. Although Trotsky did not mention Lenin it is obviously to
him that these words were addressed in the first instance.

Nevertheless, the dominance of the proletarian over the peasant and bourgeois representatives would not reflect, at this stage, the order of social priorities which the new government would set itself and pursue. On the contrary, although its initial steps would be as essential to it as to its collaborators, they would put into effect policies whose aim was to serve and satisfy the interests primarily of the non-proletarian elements, peasant as well as bourgeois. Here Trotsky had in mind not only those first measures whose objectives were, as he put it, 'cleansing the Augean stables of the old regime and driving out its inmates' which would 'meet with the active support of the whole nation'.[48] Beyond this elementary task, the government, at the instigation of the proletariat, would seek to institute democratic rights and to alleviate, as far as was feasible immediately, the predicament of the peasants:

The dominance of the proletariat will mean not only democratic equality, free self-government, the transference of the whole burden of taxation to the rich classes, the dissolution of the standing army in the armed people and the abolition of compulsory church imposts, but also recognition of all revolutionary changes—expropriations— in land relationships carried out by the peasants. The proletariat will make these changes the starting-point for further state measures in agriculture.[49]

Thus the spontaneous 'grabbing' of land by peasants in the wake of the revolutionary fervour would receive the official sanction of the new government and would presumably be even encouraged by it. Its immediate social effect would be the expropriation of the landed nobility, the 'abolition of feudalism'. It was in this sense, Trotsky declared emphatically, that '*the proletariat in power will stand before the peasants as the class which has emancipated it*':[50]

Under such conditions the Russian peasantry in the first and most difficult period of the revolution will be interested in the maintenance of a proletarian regime ('workers' democracy'), at all events not less than was the French peasantry in the maintenance of the military regime of Napoleon Bonaparte, which guaranteed to the new property-owners, by the force of its bayonets, the inviolability of its holdings. And this means that the representative body of the nation,

---

[48] Ibid., p. 254.   [49] Ibid., pp. 251–2.   [50] Ibid., p. 251.

convened under the leadership of the proletariat, which has secured the support of the peasantry, will be nothing else than a democratic dress for the rule of the proletariat.[51]

But if this agrarian policy was the 'starting-point', what 'further state measures' could the government take? Here, following Trotsky, we arrive at a crucial point, the stage at which the first 'act' fades into the second, almost imperceptibly at first, but ever more sharply, without, in a sense, the actors themselves being aware of the change of scenery. It is here, in effect, that Trotsky claimed to identify the first emergence within the revolution of its 'permanent' character; for while the movement was from one stage to another, the stages became apparent only as the peripheries of a process and the whole was driven forward by the internal momentum of the revolutionary mechanism. The 'separateness' of the stages was a schematic abstraction, to be made, perhaps, when the history of the revolution came to be recorded; the revolution itself, the living reality of it, was an uninterrupted process, a spectrum whose colours shaded off into one another progressively.

If the first act was sudden, immediate and short-lived, the second was one of transition. It slid into view as a result, initially, of the agricultural question and came into full focus at the moment that the government, almost concurrently, turned to industrial issues. The expropriation of privately-owned estates does not itself solve the agrarian problem; for a part of the peasantry at least it may even aggravate it since the effective result of unplanned, spontaneous and therefore arbitrary distribution of land would be to favour some peasants at the expense of others. To break up large estates and parcel them out to small producers would be no solution since it would perpetuate primitive and inefficient methods of agricultural production. Furthermore, the immediate nationalization and 'equalization of the use of land' would be not only economically wasteful and even ruinous but politically suicidal: it would arouse the immediate opposition of the mass of the peasantry for whom emancipation meant *private* land not state or public holdings; it would mean alienating the peasantry even before the regime had had time to establish itself.[52] Trotsky would

[51] Ibid., p. 252.   [52] Ibid., pp. 257–8 and 275–7.

clearly prefer to avoid or delay an extremist policy one way or another; far more desirable was a piecemeal, pragmatic approach which would avoid precipitating a clash of interests within the government, the effect of which would only lead to a weakening of the proletariat's support in the countryside.

Yet the relationship with the peasantry even under conditions of general appeasement would remain problematical. On the one hand there would be the tension growing out of the general social incompatibility between the two classes; on the other, appeasement could not go so far as to permit the formation of a set pattern of agricultural relations and production which were in opposition to the long-term interests of the workers:

Though the absence of accumulated bourgeois-individualistic traditions and anti-proletarian prejudices among the peasantry and intellectuals will assist the proletariat to come into power, it is necessary, on the other hand, to bear in mind that this absence of prejudices is due not to political consciousness but to political barbarism, social formlessness, primitiveness and lack of character.[53]

This bitter reality was not a reliable basis for the stable sharing of power; and it would assert itself the moment that the proletariat attempted to carry out its minimal obligations towards that part of the peasantry with which its ties were closest, the agricultural proletariat:

The abolition of feudalism will meet with support from the entire peasantry, as the burden-bearing estate. A progressive income-tax will also be supported by the great majority of the peasantry. But any legislation carried through for the purpose of protecting the agricultural proletariat will not only not receive the active sympathy of the majority, but will even meet with the active opposition of a minority of the peasantry.[54]

Yet such legislation could not be avoided by the workers. Moreover, it was the best possible condition under which to prepare for the confrontation with the peasantry. It would not arouse the great mass of peasants, as other extreme measures might, and it would both split the peasantry and turn parts of it against the countryside as allies of the workers. The inevitable clash thus did not erupt suddenly and immediately, but

[53] Ibid., pp. 254–5.   [54] Ibid., p. 255.

gradually, and followed a tactical path aimed both at minimum resistance and the accumulation of support:

> The proletariat will find itself compelled to carry the class struggle
> into the villages and in this manner destroy that community of interest
> which is undoubtedly to be found among all peasants, although within
> comparatively narrow limits. From the very first moment after its tak-
> ing power, the proletariat will have to find support in the antagonism
> between the village poor and the village rich, between the agricultural
> proletariat and the agricultural bourgeoisie.[55]

Though for politically tactical reasons the conflict with the
peasantry should be confined to these limits for as long as possible and not aggravated by an immediate extremist solution
of the agrarian question, the further degeneration of relations
between workers and peasants was inevitable, Trotsky believed.
The fault lay not so much in post-revolutionary phenomena
as in the forced nature of the original alliance. Since it was
created for the purposes of the uprising itself, its possibilities
would be exhausted with the overthrow of the autocracy and
the introduction of basic democratic forms. Beyond these immediate objectives there was not, and could not be, agreement.
Thus the clash which would now come would be only a reflection of the original and fundamental lack of consent on social
issues. The parting of the ways would mark the disintegration
of the national coalition and the coming to the fore of purely
class interests:

> Every passing day will deepen the policy of the proletariat in power
> and more and more define its *class character*. Side by side with that,
> the revolutionary ties between the proletariat and the nation will be
> broken, the class disintegration of the peasantry will assume political
> form, and the antagonism between the component sections will grow
> in proportion as the policy of the workers' government defines itself,
> ceasing to be a general-democratic and becoming a class policy.[56]

The severity of this process was not confined to problems of
agriculture, however; it might begin there but in the meantime
it would have extended to problems of industry, that is, to those
problems which directly affected the interests of the workers
themselves. Here too, the most moderate reforms, the most elementary fulfilment of workers' demands, would lead to a

[55] Loc. cit.   [56] Ibid., p. 254.

sharpening of the class struggle, at first on a different front, and to the eventual isolation of the proletariat from the nation. The reaction of the 'capitalists' to such basic demands for reform would be out of all proportion to the substance and scope of these demands. Trotsky gave two examples of this: the demand for an eight-hour day and the demand for an alleviation of the problem of unemployment. In themselves, he noted, these were not radical demands; in fact, in the case of the eight-hour day, it 'by no means contradicted capitalist relations'.[57] But the introduction of this reform in the immediate wake of a revolution within which the proletariat occupied the dominant position, would arouse suspicion and would be interpreted as a direct challenge to property interests. It would be seen as only the first of a long line of demands, the ultimate aim of which was to undermine private property, and which had therefore to be resisted at the very outset. So the eight-hour day itself would lead to panic-riddled counter-measures, to 'organized and determined resistance' by owners of industrial concerns, which would take the form of lock-outs or the closing down of factories.

Hundreds of thousands of workers would find themselves thrown onto the streets. What should the government do? . . . Under the political domination of the proletariat [in contrast to one dominated by the bourgeoisie], the introduction of an eight-hour day should lead to altogether different consequences. For a government that wants to rely upon the proletariat, and not on capital, as liberalism does . . . there would be only one way out: expropriation of the closed factories and the organization of production in them on a socialized basis.[58]

A similar course of events would follow, in Trotsky's view, in the case of the attempt at dealing with the problem of unemployment. The attempt itself could not be avoided since the workers' representatives could hardly reject their constituents' demands in this sphere by replying with 'arguments about the bourgeois character of the revolution'.[59] Suppose then that the government committed itself to maintaining the unemployed, in whatever form: this would be a threat to the existence of a 'reserve army of labour' upon which industrial owners relied; it would constitute a 'shift' in economic power to the benefit

---

[57] Ibid., p. 256.   [58] Ibid., pp. 256–7.   [59] Ibid., p. 257.

of the workers; and it would be completely unacceptable to the industrialists:

> There is nothing left for the capitalists to do then but to resort to the lock-out, that is, to close the factories. It is quite clear that the employers can stand the closing down of production much longer than the workers and therefore there is only one reply that a workers' government can give to a general lock-out: the expropriation of the factories and the introduction in at least the largest of them of state or communal production.[60]

Thus the proletariat does not *begin* with radical measures; but it is forced into them, driven not so much by its own will as the momentum of the revolutionary process, unfolding in concrete, day-to-day questions. Somewhere during this process the dividing line between the first and the second 'act' is traversed until the revolution becomes quite clearly identifiable as completely different in character from what it had been at its outset. Minimal demands become converted into maximal ones, elementary claims are transformed by a process of radicalization. This prompted Trotsky to note how absurd was the notion that a workers' government, even during its first days in power, could make a distinction between its 'minimum and maximum' programmes, between its short-term aims and its long-term ones. The two were inextricably mingled from the outset, by the very fact that the workers would be in actual power, and not simply a pressure group standing outside government. It is not the 'original intention' of the proletariat's representatives but their role in the government—not as 'powerless hostages' but as the 'leading force'—which would destroy the borderline between minimum and maximum programmes, both 'in principle and in immediate practice'.[61] In effect, Trotsky suggested, the actual scope of the workers' programme could not be predicted in advance since it was a function of the revolutionary process itself, of the possibilities it might open up, and not of a carefully worked-out plan.

This did not mean, however, that the process or transition from the first to the second stage or act could itself be aborted; this much, he believed, was guaranteed by the existence of a workers' government. This, after all, was the unique feature

---

[60] Loc. cit.   [61] Ibid., pp. 256, 258, 275.

of a revolution in Russia, namely, that it would immediately catapult the proletariat into the dominant position of actual rule. The fact that this would happen in a country which had not had a bourgeois revolution or government, did not mean that therefore a different class would carry out a bourgeois revolution. The 'substitution' of one class by another was not merely a technical detail, a change in instruments; it was a change in the whole character of the revolution, in its entire social content. Thus the idea that in Russia the only detour from past revolutionary models would be that the proletariat would make the bourgeois revolution and thereby rest content, was an idea divorced from the logic of social conditions and class behaviour. 'A proletarian government under no circumstances can confine itself' to a bourgeois revolution:

To imagine that it is the business of Social Democrats to enter a provisional government and lead it during the period of revolutionary-democratic reforms, fighting for them to have a most radical character, and relying for this purpose upon the organized proletariat—and then, after the democratic programme has been carried out, to leave the edifice they have constructed so as to make way for the bourgeois parties and themselves go into opposition, thus opening up a period of parliamentary politics, is to imagine the thing in a way that would compromise the very idea of a workers' government. This is not because it is inadmissable 'in principle'—putting the question in this abstract form is devoid of meaning—but because it is absolutely unreal, it is utopianism of the worst sort—a sort of revolutionary-philistine utopianism.[62]

The fact is, Trotsky argued, that a revolution led by the proletariat could not be defined as a bourgeois revolution, though amongst its initial aims were certain bourgeois institutional forms. Such forms, however, were themselves transitory and could exist only so long as they provided a basis for further development. They were never entirely completed, for before that could happen social policies were instituted by the workers' government which made different institutional forms necessary. In this way the revolution passed from the tasks arising out of the country's backwardness—its failure in the past to make bourgeois-democratic changes—to tasks arising out of its advanced structures—its success in adopting a modern

[62] Ibid., pp. 255–6.

industry. Since it was the workers, the product of the latter, who stood at the head of the revolution, it was the modern tasks which eventually had to become paramount. Thus, in effect, a bourgeois revolution in the twentieth century was impossible; in the 'given world-historical conditions ... the revolution at the beginning of the twentieth century . . . discovers before it the prospect . . . of breaking through the barriers . . . of the bourgeois revolution'.[63] The idea that Trotsky was therefore proposing was the 'idea of *uninterrupted revolution* ... an idea that connects the liquidation of absolutism and feudalism with a socialist revolution'.[64]

However, he warned, it would be no less utopian to believe that the transition to this stage of the revolution guaranteed the actual triumph of socialism. The socialist transformation itself still lay in a relatively distant future and was far from being a certainty. The most that could be said for this stage was that it would have irreversibly broken with its bourgeois beginnings and begun to lay the foundations of a socialized society. It would have placed '*collectivism on the order of the day*'[65] as its distinguishing feature, not as a completed task but as a policy to be pursued. It would have begun instituting the principle of collectivism in industry and in agriculture but in a limited manner and only in the most receptive sectors of the economy. It would be greatly constrained by the strength of the opposition it would encounter and by the objective technical difficulties of organizing production in a country such as Russia. The opposition would come both from the 'capitalists' and the peasants. The former, however, could be relatively easily dealt with; it was the latter who would have the potential power of breaking the back of the workers, of arresting the further extension of socialist policies. The more class oriented, that is collectivist, the policies of the workers became, the more adamant would be the opposition of the peasantry until, finally, it would turn 'its hostile face towards the proletariat':

[63] Ibid., p. 249.
[64] Ibid., pp. 258 and 259. This is the only place in *Itogi i perspektivy* where the phrase 'uninterrupted revolution' (*niepreryvnaya revolyutsiya*) actually appears. The phrase '*permanentnaya revolyutsiya*' does not appear at all but in later years Trotsky accepted this latter as the identifying name for his theory of the Russian revolution (see this chapter, pp. 152ff., below).
[65] Ibid., p. 258.

The primitiveness and petty-bourgeois character of the peasantry, its limited rural outlook, its isolation from world-political ties and allegiances, will create terrible difficulties for the consolidation of the revolutionary policy of the proletariat in power . . . The more definite and determined the policy of the proletariat in power becomes, the narrower and more shaky does the ground beneath its feet become. All this is extremely probable and even inevitable.[66]

The resulting political problems of 'continuing' the revolution single-handed would, however, be further aggravated by social and economic difficulties. And nothing would be more difficult than the actual organization of 'social production'. The fundamental poverty of the country, the lack of experience in planning and self-management, the problems of coordinating agricultural and industrial production, the shortage of technique and know-how, all these would undermine the new government's capacity to go beyond the most elementary stages of collectivism. A 'number of oases' would be created but, on the whole, nothing which even approached a socialist society:

It would be absurd to suppose that it is only necessary for the proletariat to take power and then by passing a few decrees to substitute socialism for capitalism. An economic system is not the product of the actions of the government ... [and] a government of the proletariat is not a government that can perform miracles.[67]

In effect, therefore, the second stage or 'act' of the revolution would have here exhausted itself. Though its bourgeois beginnings would have been transcended, though the groundwork for socialist policies would have been prepared, the further development of the revolution through internal forces would have become impossible. This was the point at which the full indigenous potential of the Russian proletariat, in fact of Russian society, would have reached its limits. It would now, moreover, be threatened by virtual collapse, having aroused the opposition of the peasant masses. Politically, therefore, it would stand isolated, vulnerable, in danger of being liquidated by a counter-revolution. If the workers had come to power because of the particular advantages offered by Russia's backwardness, it was

[66] Ibid., p. 255.
[67] Ibid., p. 274. (Trotsky was here quoting from an article he had written in November 1905 for the newspaper *Nachalo*. It may be found also in *Nasha Revolyutsiya*, pp. 168–73.)

the disadvantages of that backwardness which would now make their position unmaintainable. Their prospects of sustaining themselves and their policies would no longer be dependent on them but on developments which were for the most part beyond their control. Everything, in fact, would now depend not on what happened inside Russia but outside. The permanent revolution, begun within national boundaries, had now to spill over onto the international arena.

7. The World Revolution

If, in the first place, Trotsky had made the workers' seizure of power dependent on peasant support, in the last resort their retention of power and the future of socialism in Russia were to be dependent on the support of the European proletariat. Trotsky's analysis of Russian society had stressed, as we have seen, the advantages of backwardness; but it could not, and was not meant to, deny the ultimate reality of backwardness itself. He did not believe that socialism could be realized in any one country alone; how much more so was this the case in a country such as Russia? Thus in the penultimate chapter of *Results and Prospects* he felt compelled to declare this in emphatic terms: '*Without the direct state support of the European proletariat the working class of Russia cannot remain in power and convert its temporary dominance into a lasting socialist dictatorship.*'[68] And in the last paragraph of the book he repeated this warning:

Left to its own resources the working class of Russia will inevitably be crushed by the counter-revolution the moment the peasantry turns its back on it. It will have no alternative but to link the fate of its political rule, and, hence, the fate of the whole Russian revolution, with the fate of the socialist revolution in Europe.[69]

In between these two passages he tried to show that the prospects of such a revolution in Europe, the prospects in effect of a *world* socialist revolution, were fully within the bounds of any realistic appraisal of the situation in Europe.

What did he expect to happen? In the first place he assumed, quite reasonably, that a workers' government in Russia would arouse more than a passing curiosity in Europe. It would, in

[68] Ibid., p. 278.   [69] Ibid., pp. 285–6.

fact, be seen as a direct threat to European stability, not only because it would bring to an end Europe's financial stake in Russia but because it would also break the hitherto unchallenged universal power of European capitalism. A direct European reaction was therefore extremely probable and this, in his view, was a further reason why the workers in Russia, already besieged by the peasantry, could not hope to complete their revolution without the help of the European proletariat. But in that case, whether in fact they 'carry the revolution onto European soil' by their 'own initiative' is irrelevant; they will be '*compelled* to do so by the forces of the European, feudal-bourgeois reaction'.[70] They will be compelled, in other words, to begin exporting their revolution, to become involved in the internal politics of other countries, to support the struggle of workers' movements elsewhere. Not loyalty to a world socialist ideal will motivate them, but their own interests, their own desire for survival. This in itself, however, did not guarantee success; the workers' government in Russia could assist the European revolutionary movement, it could not create it. The extent of its success would, of course, depend on two factors beyond its direct control: the resilience of the European bourgeoisie, and the actual power of the European proletariat.

As for the first, Trotsky believed that it was already on the brink of exhaustion. This was so, in his view, not only for the well-known reasons of fundamental economic instability, aggravated by a cruel competition for world markets, but the inability of the bourgeoisie to camouflage its interests, as it had done in the past, under supposedly national aspirations and unity. Having placed 'huge masses of men under arms', the bourgeois governments could not throw them into war without facing the prospect of rebellion. A national war, that modern means for detracting from, and even averting, internal disintegration, had become impossible everywhere:

In the old capitalist countries there are no 'national' demands, i.e. demands of bourgeois society as a whole, of which the ruling bourgeoisie could claim to be the champion. The governments of Britain, France, Germany and Austria are unable to conduct national wars. The vital interests of the masses, the interests of the oppressed nationalities, or the barbarous internal politics of a neighbouring

[70] Ibid., p. 280.

country, are not able to drive a single bourgeois government into a war which could have a liberating and therefore a national character. On the other hand, the interests of capitalist grabbing, which so often induce now one and now another government to clank its spurs and rattle its sabre in the face of the world, cannot arouse any response among the masses. For that reason the bourgeoisie either cannot or will not proclaim or conduct any national wars.[71]

Should, however, war become unavoidable in Europe it will 'inevitably [lead to] a European revolution'. No one realized this better than the European bourgeoisie itself which now lived in 'fear of the revolt of the proletariat'.[72] And this fact, according to Trotsky, testified to the strength of the proletariat in the 'old capitalist countries':

. . . even without the outside pressure of events such as war or bankruptcy, revolution may arise in the near future in one of the European countries as a consequence of the extreme sharpening of the class struggle. We will not attempt to build assumptions now as to which of the European countries will be the first to take the path of revolution; of one thing there is no doubt, and that is that the class contradictions in all European countries during recent times have reached a high level of intensivity.[73]

Trotsky admitted, however, that objective revolutionary conditions in Europe had been inadequately exploited by the various Social Democratic movements. In Germany, in particular, the success of the Social Democratic party had been its undoing: having built a mass movement it had become more infatuated with the movement as an end in itself than with the ends for which it had been created. It had become conservative and inert. This was so much so that Social Democracy itself had emerged as an obstacle to revolution, preferring the gains of the moment to the risks of an open struggle for power.[74] This was partly why, in Trotsky's view, the long-expected revolution in Germany had failed to materialize, why the centre of working-class radicalism had shifted away from Europe and to the

[71] Ibid., p. 282. To anyone reading this after 1914, Trotsky's prognosis must have appeared bitterly laughable. But Trotsky's reaction to World War I would be that the mutual slaughter resulting, in effect, in defeat for all, only vindicated the bankruptcy of 'national' wars. However this would not, of course, explain the behaviour of European Social Democracy or of the European working class. For more on this, see chapter 8, below.

[72] Ibid., p. 283.   [73] Ibid., p. 284.   [74] Ibid., p. 285.

less organized but more active movements in the East. But Trotsky believed that a workers' revolution in Russia would have the effect of jolting the Western parties into action. In the case of Germany, it would make itself felt in two ways: firstly, by sparking off rebellion in German (and Austrian) held parts of Poland; secondly, by providing the encouragement of a successful precedent. In the first eventuality, the attempt of the German and Austrian governments to put down the Polish rebellion would have to be met by the direct intervention of the Russian revolutionary government, as an 'act of self-defence'. The hazards of war for Russia, however, would be offset by the sure prospect that in such a conflict she would gain the support of the German and Austrian proletariat, thus instigating civil war in those two countries. Trotsky confidently predicted that 'a war between feudal-bourgeois Germany and revolutionary Russia would lead inevitably to a proletarian revolution in Germany'.[75] This would happen against the background of the Russian precedent whose impact on the 'consciousness and temper' of the European working class would be such as to create the 'necessary prerequisites for revolution':

The tremendous influence of the Russian revolution indicates that it will destroy party routine and conservatism and place the question of an open trial of strength between the proletariat and capitalist reaction on the order of the day. . . . The revolution in the East will infect the Western proletariat with a revolutionary idealism and provoke a desire to speak to its enemies 'in Russian'.[76]

That Trotsky found it necessary to make so much—too much, as we know—out of the prospects of a 'world revolution' cannot be attributed simply to his intrinsic 'internationalism'. To look at the matter in terms of his character alone is to obscure the very particular source of his theoretical and practical concern. His emphasis on a general European conflagration grew not so much out of a European outlook as out of the specific problems of revolution in Russia. Trotsky's contemporaries also tied the fate of the Russian revolution to that of Europe but they assumed that Europe was still the revolutionary centre of the world. Trotsky, in contrast, claimed that the centre had in fact shifted eastwards. He was, following Parvus, the first to

---

[75] Ibid., pp. 280–1.   [76] Ibid., p. 285.

predict that a workers' government would come to power in Russia before it did so anywhere in Europe. The theory of the permanent revolution represented an attempt to explain the logic and mechanics of this phenomenon. But the problem of maintaining a *socialist* government in Russia could not be resolved without reference to Europe. Backwardness carried a high price—dependence, in the end, on others. Thus, in Trotsky's view, the age-old relationship of Russia to the West was to be resurrected in the twentieth century, though with a new twist. Thus the necessity, for Russia, of a world revolution was, in a sense, a legacy of Russia's past. For this reason the world revolution was an inseparable part of the permanent revolution, its third and final 'act', or the ultimate link, as Trotsky saw it, between backwardness and the modern world.

8. The Theory of the Permanent Revolution Restated

The foregoing exposition of the theory of the permanent revolution was based entirely on Trotsky's writings in the period immediately following 1905, particularly on *Results and Prospects.* Since our approach in this study is not strictly chronological but based on the logic of the subject matter, we may turn to one of Trotsky's much later works by way of concluding the present discussion.

In 1928, Karl Radek, until that year one of Trotsky's most loyal supporters within the Soviet Communist party, wrote an article attacking the theory of the permanent revolution.[77] By that time, Trotsky's political career was at its end; he had been banished to Alma-Ata in Central Asia, his name had been discredited, his views and deeds widely denounced. Attacks on the theory of the permanent revolution were now nothing new: they had begun in 1924 and were the ideological basis for the

---

[77] A manuscript copy of this article is in the Trotsky Archives: Karl Radek, 'Razvitie i znachenie lozunga proletarskoi diktatury'. At the time he wrote this article, Radek was in exile in Siberia as a consequence of his membership in the Joint Opposition and his support of Trotsky against Stalin's policy of 'socialism in one country'. The article was apparently an attempt to regain the good graces of Stalin; later, in 1929, he renounced Trotsky completely and declared his acceptance of Stalin's policies. He was rehabilitated and became a leading propagandist for 'socialism in one country'. In 1936, however, he was arrested, tried and, apparently in 1939, executed. See Warren Lerner, *Karl Radek: The Last Internationalist* (Stanford, 1970), chapter 8. Chapter 7 of the same book deals with the relations between Trotsky and Radek.

gradual exclusion of Trotsky from all political functions.[78] Thus Radek's article merely repeated already well-known accusations of doctrinal heresy. But the fact that it was written by one who in the past had been such an ardent supporter of the theory must have particularly stung Trotsky. In the event, he composed during 1928 an extended reply to Radek which became a book under the title *Permanentnaya Revolyutsiya* (The Permanent Revolution).[79] The book is primarily a polemic against Radek and, of course, Stalin; it is also marred by Trotsky's exaggerated efforts to show how close he and Lenin had always been theoretically.[80] But underneath the polemics there is a restatement, by way of defence, of the theory of the permanent revolution, which aims at clarifying and refining the views first expressed following 1905. For this reason, and despite the fact that the book adds nothing essentially new to those views, it is worth summarizing briefly.[81]

The Permanent Revolution concentrates on three main issues: the role of the peasantry in a workers' revolution, the bourgeois features of the revolution and its transition to a socialist or collectivist phase, and the importance of the world revolution. The first issue is the most extensively discussed since the main charge against Trotsky had been that he had not only underestimated but ignored the peasants, that his rejection of Lenin's formula—'the dictatorship of the proletariat and peasantry'—constituted a gross error which alone discredited the theory of the permanent revolution. Trotsky now admitted the rejection but not the error, and claimed, although in an intentionally restrained, even oblique manner, to have been right against

[78] Trotsky's controversy with Stalin over the question of 'socialism in one country' is discussed in chapter 9, below.
[79] All references are to the first Russian edition published in Berlin in 1930. (For the English translation see Trotsky, *The Permanent Revolution* and *Results and Prospects*, London, 1962.)
[80] Quoting Lenin had by then become standard practice; and the legitimacy of one's views depended on such quotations. In spite of himself—and his many apologies in the book—Trotsky, for obvious political reasons, adopted this practice. The result is that he minimizes the differences between himself and Lenin, calling them 'tactical' when in fact they were quite substantial.
[81] In what follows, all those portions of the book which relate to the post-1917 period have been excluded and relegated to later chapters where questions of the concrete application of the theory are discussed. Here purely theoretical issues only are raised.

Lenin.[82] Far from ignoring the peasants, Trotsky argued, he had based his whole theory precisely on the fact that their position had become so intolerable as to make them a revolutionary force, a force, moreover, without which a Russian revolution would have been inconceivable. The agrarian problem had become the most severe of Russia's dilemmas and it could no longer be solved except through an agrarian revolution. But an agrarian revolution was not necessarily a peasant revolution, though it was, of course, impossible without the participation of the peasants. The question which had to be asked in 1905 was whether the peasants themselves were capable of solving their problems, of acting, that is, as an independent political force. And about this there were not two points of view; Bolsheviks as well as Mensheviks agreed that this was out of the question, that without the leadership of either the bourgeoisie or the proletariat, the peasants could not carry out a revolution. The Mensheviks, of course, believed that the bourgeoisie would ultimately make their own revolution, thereby settling the agrarian problem as well. But if the impossibility of a bourgeois revolution was not clear to them, as it should have been, in 1905, it certainly became incontrovertible in the course of time. The issue was therefore the relationship between the peasantry and the proletariat. Neither could act without the other, so much was obvious. But did their necessary alliance imply an equal distribution of power and, therefore, of roles? Over this differences of opinion arose. Lenin, correctly perceiving that their joint revolution would be initially an agrarian revolution, assumed as a result that it would take the form of a dictatorship of both classes. As a formal, 'algebraic' proposition this was unexceptionable. But it did not resolve the question of how the fundamental social incompatibility between workers and peasants could be reconciled.[83]

The truth of the matter, Trotsky observed, was that no such reconciliation was possible and the alliance had to be seen as

[82] For obvious tactical reasons, he avoided throughout the book any outright criticism of Lenin. Thus he spoke of the need to see Lenin's views on the issue of the peasants as continuously 'developing', as raising tentative possibilities rather than final conclusions, as being rooted in a specific historical context, and so on—whereas, in fact, Lenin's mind was far more made up than this would imply. See *Permanentnaya Revolyutsiya*, chapter 3, *passim*.
[83] Ibid., pp. 9 and 165.

a purely temporary political stratagem. To attribute to it more permanent features would mean undermining the goals which were a part of the workers' programme; it would mean arresting the revolution at its agrarian stage. This was so because while the workers could identify with peasant aspirations, the peasants could not identify with those of the workers; a reconciliation between them therefore implied numerous concessions on the part of the workers and none on the part of the peasants. In that case, however, the proposed dictatorship was in effect of the peasants alone and the whole revolution stood in danger of collapsing for there was no guarantee that the peasants could in fact act in this independent capacity. On the contrary, they could act as a revolutionary force only by attaching themselves to, and being dragged along by, another class which, though weaker numerically, was stronger in terms of its political organization and social consciousness. The role of the peasants, therefore, had to be grasped not in its formal sense—it did not matter what one *called* the revolutionary dictatorship—but in concrete political terms—the actual distribution of power in a revolutionary regime. The only realistic conclusion was that the dictatorship must be of the proletariat alone:

Not for nothing did the radical thinkers occasionally refer to the peasant as the Sphinx of Russian history. The question of the nature of the revolutionary dictatorship . . . is inseparably bound up with the question of the possibility of a revolutionary peasant party hostile to the liberal bourgeoisie and independent of the proletariat. The decisive meaning of the latter question is not hard to grasp. Were the peasantry capable of creating their own independent party in the epoch of the democratic revolution, then the democratic dictatorship could be realized in its truest and most direct sense, and the question of the participation of the proletarian minority in the revolutionary government would have an important, it is true, but subordinate significance. The case is entirely otherwise if we proceed from the fact that the peasantry, because of its intermediate position and the heterogeneity of its social composition, can have neither an independent policy nor an independent party, but is compelled, in the revolutionary epoch, to choose between the policy of the bourgeoisie and the policy of the proletariat. Only this evaluation of the political nature of the peasantry opens up the prospect of the dictatorship of the proletariat growing directly out of the democratic revolution. In this, naturally, there lies no 'denial', 'ignoring' or 'underestimation' of the peasantry. Without the decisive significance of the agrarian question for the life of the whole of society and without the great depth and gigantic sweep of the peasant revolution there could not even be any talk of the proletarian dictatorship in Russia. But the fact that the *agrarian* revolution created the conditions for the dictatorship of the *proletariat* grew out of the inability of the peasantry to solve its own historical problem with its own forces and under its own leadership.[84]

The second issue with which Trotsky dealt in *The Permanent Revolution* was that of the transition from purely bourgeois objectives to socialist ones. The opponents of the theory of the permanent revolution had accused Trotsky of political adventurism'; he had assumed, they claimed, that whole historical stages can be 'skipped' or 'leapt over', that a backward autocratic society could be immediately transformed into a socialist one. To these charges Trotsky now answered that they were partly a deliberate misrepresentation of his theory and partly a misunderstanding of it. The misrepresentation was contained in the charge that he chose to neglect the necessarily bourgeois stage which must precede a socialist revolution. But this was like the charge that he had ignored the peasants, Trotsky observed. In fact he had never denied that amongst the tasks of the revolution would be some purely bourgeois-democratic ones; after all, this is what the agrarian revolution was all about, and this is what was to be initially involved in the overthrow of the autocracy. To this extent he had always agreed with Lenin, that in the absence of an independent bourgeoisie it was incumbent upon the proletariat to carry out bourgeois reforms. But to designate, consequently, the revolution as bourgeois in character was to speak of its short-term objectives not its ultimate prospects. 'I never denied', Trotsky wrote, 'the *bourgeois* character of the revolution in the sense of its immediate historical tasks, but only in the sense of its driving forces and its perspectives.'[85] A revolution, in other words, had to be defined by its *telos*, its ultimate end, not its intermediate stages. But having a *telos* it was also an 'organic' whole; and thus the attempt to

---

[84] Ibid., pp. 71–2. Trotsky dealt with the peasant issue in a somewhat rambling and disjointed fashion, but the most important passages appear on pages 8–10, 47, 70–84, 104–6 and 112–18.

[85] Ibid., p. 56.

distinguish between stages as clearly separate and unrelated was 'vulgar Marxism'. Social relations develop and evolve, stages grow one into another, and revolution is an on-going process not a clearly demarcated time-table. The failure to grasp this dynamic character of social life, particularly in a time of revolution, was the source of the misunderstanding of the concept of a *permanent* revolution. It led to a 'metaphysical posing of the question concerning the "bourgeois" or the "socialist" character of the revolution'[86] which could only end in a schematic, unrealistic view of history. As against this, to grasp the revolution as a process was to grasp the full extent of its possibilities, to see beyond the present and into the future. The *telos* of a process was not exhausted by its beginnings but it could be perceived through them. The peculiar beginnings of the Russian revolution must therefore determine its ultimate character; the 'immediate tasks' of those beginnings were bourgeois, but the instrument for implementing the tasks contained the seed of their ultimate evolution:

. . . the dictatorship of the proletariat does not come *after* the completion of the democratic revolution . . . No, the dictatorship of the proletariat appeared probable and even inevitable on the basis of the bourgeois revolution precisely because there was no other power and no other way to solve the tasks of the agrarian revolution. But exactly this opens up the prospect of a democratic revolution growing over into the socialist revolution.[87]

Trotsky emphasized that a revolution was just this process of 'growing over',[88] not a skipping over stages. The notion that socialism could be suddenly and immediately made to flower in the soil of feudal autocracy was, he agreed, indeed absurd. But it was not a notion, he said, which emerged in the theory of the permanent revolution. On the contrary, that theory excluded it entirely; it saw the revolution as the means through which society only accelerated or completed the processes of change which were already inherent in it. It was precisely because these processes could not culminate within the old framework that revolution became necessary. The result was not some artificial tampering with history but its natural

---

[86] Ibid., p. 116.   [87] Ibid., pp. 58–9.
[88] The Russian word he used was *pererostanie*.

evolution: 'In Russia ... history combined the main content of the bourgeois revolution with the first stage of the proletarian revolution—did not mix them up but combined them organically.'[89]

There was no 'leaping' over stages here, no miraculous transformations; there was only the possibility of 'telescoping' the stages into 'embryonic forms',[90] of shortening the time period of historical changes which would otherwise be the work of centuries. That such an accelerated pace was possible in Russia was to be directly explained by Russian backwardness. Because the tasks of the past—the agrarian revolution—were not carried out in the past by those who should have done so, namely, the bourgeoisie, they must now be carried out by others, namely, the proletariat. Had there been an agrarian revolution, the Russian proletariat, because of Russia's backwardness, would have been the last in Europe to come to power. As it was, backwardness both prevented an agrarian revolution and propelled the Russian proletariat into power ahead of European workers. Thus the tasks of the past were combined with those of the present and thus arose the possibility of shortening the gap between them.[91]

But this, again, was not an abstract 'leap'[92] into the future. It was 'no isolated leap of the proletariat'; rather it was the 'reconstruction of the whole nation under the leadership of the proletariat'.[93] The combining of stages made possible a short-cut into the modern world; the delays and omissions of the past were made up for by the possibilities of the present. In a word, this was how a backward country caught up with history. 'That is how', Trotsky wrote, 'from 1905 onwards, I conceived and interpreted the prospect of the permanent revolution.'[94] It was the continuous, unbroken evolution of tasks which gave the revolution its 'uninterrupted' character.[95] Rather than stopping at any particular stage, the revolution 'grew over' into more advanced phases; the complete 'reconstruction of the

---

[89] Ibid., p. 123.   [90] Ibid., p. 124.
[91] Ibid., pp. 58–9, 113, 116, 125.   [92] In Russian, *skachek*.
[93] Ibid., p. 64.   [94] Loc. cit.
[95] Throughout the book Trotsky used the term 'uninterrupted' as interchangeable or synonymous with 'permanent'; sometimes he wrote 'permanent' and, in brackets, added 'uninterrupted'—see, for instance, ibid., p. 58.

nation', its modernization, was the work of one revolutionary process, telescoped into one historical epoch.

However, the actual completion of this task depended also on a more or less simultaneous revolution in Europe. This raised the third and, in a sense, the most important issue which Trotsky had to confront at the time of writing *The Permanent Revolution*. He was as convinced, twelve years after October 1917, as he had been some twelve years before, that a workers' revolution confined to the frontiers of Russia stood in danger of collapsing. A backward country may have the first workers' revolution but it could not arrive at *socialism* before the advanced countries or outside the context of world history. He listed this as one of the 'basic postulates' of the theory of the permanent revolution:[96]

Backward countries may, under certain conditions, arrive at the dictatorship of the proletariat sooner than advanced countries, but they will arrive later than the latter at socialism. . . . In a country where the proletariat has power in its hands as the result of the democratic revolution, the subsequent fate of the dictatorship and socialism depends in the last analysis not only and not so much upon the national productive forces as upon the development of the international socialist revolution.[97]

Similarly, in the introduction to the book he stated that whenever the question, 'Do you really believe that Russia is ripe for the socialist revolution?', was asked of him, he 'always answered': 'No, I do not. But world economy as a whole, and European economy in the first place, is fully ripe for the socialist revolution. Whether the dictatorship of the proletariat in Russia leads to socialism or not, and at what tempo and through what stages, will depend upon the fate of European and world capitalism.'[98]

By 1929, Trotsky's optimism about a European revolution had become naturally more guarded but far from exhausted.[99] In any case, he could see no other way of saving Russia for

---

[96] At the end of *Permanentnaya Revolyutsiya*, pp. 164–70, Trotsky appended a list of fourteen 'basic postulates' which, he said, constituted the 'principal conclusions' of the theory of the permanent revolution.

[97] Ibid., p. 168.　　　　　[98] Ibid., p. 11.

[99] His views on revolutionary prospects in Europe are discussed in chapters 8 and 9, below.

socialism. He believed that Russia on her own had by then more or less exhausted all her internal possibilities. The dictatorship of the proletariat, he thought, had been turned into fact; the foundations for collectivism had been prepared; but further development in this latter direction was no longer feasible. Not only was socialist policy becoming sterile as a result of the limitations imposed upon it by national boundaries; there was the further danger that the economic scarcities of the country would undermine even the rudiments of 'national reconstruction'. It was at this point, therefore, that the primitive foundations of the old society might re-assert themselves; backwardness, the source of revolutionary change, might become a fetter upon change itself. A proletarian regime would be hard-pressed to remain in one place, much less advance.[100] Under such conditions socialism was out of the question; and the future of the socialist revolution was thus more than ever bound up with world history:

The completion of the socialist revolution within national limits is unthinkable. . . . The socialist revolution begins on the national arena, it unfolds on the international arena, and is completed on the world arena. Thus, the socialist revolution becomes a permanent revolution in a newer and broader sense of the word; it attains completion only in the final victory of the new society on our entire planet.[101]

The Permanent Revolution: Scope and Limits

The words 'permanent revolution' do not appear in *Results and Prospects*; there, as we have seen, Trotsky referred to his conception of the Russian revolution as that of an 'uninterrupted revolution' (*niepreryvnaya revolyutsiya*). 'Permanent revolution' (*permanentnaya revolyutsiya*) came to be generally used in later years to identify Trotsky's ideas but it is fairly certain that it was not he himself who first coined this 'title'. Although he referred to it in an article of 1908,[102] it would seem that by then

---

[100] See Trotsky's introduction, written in March 1930, to the German edition of *Permanentnaya Revolyutsiya* and published in Russian as 'Dve kontsentsii', in *Byulleten Oppozitsii* (June–July 1930), pp. 30–6.
[101] *Permanentnaya Revolyutsiya*, p. 167.
[102] The article was first published in the Polish journal *Przedgląd Social-Demokratyczny* (July 1908), pp. 405–18, under the title 'W czym sie róznimy' (Over what do we

this is how his theory of the revolution was already dubbed by others.[103] Nevertheless, he did not, in this article, object to the title—though he objected to the 'vulgarization' of the idea by its opponents[104]—and, in subsequent years, he was to use it regularly himself without ever raising the question of its appropriateness. In the 1919 preface to the Russian re-issue of *Results and Prospects* he presented the contents of the book as an analysis of the 'viewpoint of the permanent revolution' which, he said, he had 'maintained in the course of fifteen years';[105] and in the 1922 preface to the first Russian edition of *1905*—the book, we may recall, originally appeared in German, in 1910—although he said of 'permanent revolution' that it was a somewhat 'sententious expression', he readily accepted and used the appellation.[106] Thereafter, of course, he always referred to it as 'my theory of the permanent revolution', though using the title interchangeably with the phrase 'uninterrupted revolution', as in the book *The Permanent Revolution* which we have discussed above.[107]

Whoever first coined the term 'permanent revolution', however, and whatever Trotsky's acceptance of it, there is no doubt that it was an unfortunate choice—and not only because it is obviously non-Russian in origin. We have used it throughout this study because that is how the theory it designates came to be known and that is how, after all, Trotsky himself agreed to call it. But it *is* somewhat sententious or bombastic, and it is even misleading. It has sometimes been taken to mean the idea of an unending, eternally ongoing transformation in the lives of men, a kind of 'permanent' state of deliberate change

---

differ?). The Russian version is in Trotsky's *1905*, pp. 270–86. See especially pp. 272–3: this appears to be the first time that Trotsky used the words 'the permanent revolution'. (In the first Russian edition of *1905*, the article appears in an incomplete form, with some passages—included in all subsequent editions—missing.)

[103] According to Trotsky (in the above article) the Menshevik Martynov thus referred to the theory.

[104] See *1905*, p. 272 where he stated that he never claimed, as had been attributed to him, that Russia could leap straight into socialism.

[105] *Itogi i perspektivy: dvizhushchie sily revolyutsii* (Moscow, 1919), p. 5.

[106] The preface appears also in the 4th Russian edition of *1905*, where the words cited are on page 4.

[107] He persisted in using this 'title' even though by then the words 'permanent revolution' had acquired an anti-Leninist label in the Soviet Union.

of one's environment, and perhaps even revolt against it.[108] Neither this, nor some metaphysical senses which have been attributed to it, has anything to do with Trotsky's meaning— as he would say in later years, the idea of 'permanent revolt seems to me simply nonsense'.[109] The theory he promulgated pertained to the specific historical context of a country such as Russia was at the beginning of the twentieth century, and was intended to explain the specific possibility of combining a bourgeois with a proletarian revolution. But 'permanent' hardly describes this process since it is not an unending one and there is nothing eternal about it. Indeed, 'uninterrupted', that is, moving without break or pause from one historical conjunction—the bourgeois—to another—the socialist—was the best choice of term. 'Continuous', or even 'expanding', would also have been more appropriate than 'permanent' for continuity of stages and expansion of revolutionary tasks were ideas at the very core of the theory.

But we shall not quibble over semantics; obviously what is important is to grasp the content of the theory: the name by which it goes need not detract us from the substance of that content. And in view of the fact that the theory has become famous by that name it would be hopeless probably, and perhaps pedantic, to rename it at so late a date.

There is, however, another reason for retaining the name as it came to be known, and that is that the phrase 'permanent revolution' (with a slight variation) is to be found in none other than Karl Marx himself. Although the idea of a continuous revolution seems to have originated in French socialist circles during the second quarter of the nineteenth century[110] and the

---

[108] Similarities between it and revolutionary ideas attributed to Mao Tse-tung have also been noted: see Stuart R. Schram, *The Political Thought of Mao Tse-tung* (Harmondsworth, 1969), pp. 98–101. See also Lee Chen-Chung, 'Trotsky's Theory of the "Permanent Revolution" and Mao Tse-tung's Theory of the "Continuous Revolution"', *Issues and Studies* (Apr. 1972), pp. 29–39. Trotsky, however, is considered a heretic no less in China than in the Soviet Union.

[109] 'Dva pisma v redaktsiyu *New York Times*', in *Byulleten Oppozitsii* (Jan. 1940), p. 13. Nor does Trotsky's use of the term bear any relation to its meaning in Sigmund Neumann's *Permanent Revolution: Totalitarianism in the Age of International Civil War* (2nd edition, New York, 1965), *passim*, or in Bertrand de Jouvenel's *Power: The Natural History of its Growth* (London, 1948), pp. 136ff.

[110] See J. L. Talmon, *Political Messianism: The Romantic Phase* (London, 1960). See also Schwarz, *The Russian Revolution of 1905*, p. 246.

words 'la révolution en permanence' even appear in Proudhon,[111] the meaning which is closest to that of Trotsky's intention is clearly evident only in some of Marx's writings. To see the affinity, therefore, as well as the differences, and thereby the place of Trotsky's theory within the Marxist canon and tradition, it seems worthwhile to look briefly at Marx's use of the phrase and the idea.

It occurs twice in the well-known 1850 *Address of the Central Committee to the Communist League*.[112] Discussing the objectives towards which the League should strive, Marx declared:

While the democratic petty bourgeois wish to bring the revolution to a conclusion as quickly as possible ... it is our interest and our task to make the *revolution permanent*, until all more or less possessing classes have been forced out of their position of dominance, until the proletariat has conquered state power, and the association of proletarians, not only in one country, but in all the dominant countries of the world, has advanced so far that competition among the proletarians of these countries has ceased and that at least the decisive productive forces are concentrated in the hands of the proletarians.[113]

And in the concluding passage of the *Address*, Marx stated:

[The German workers] themselves must do the utmost for their final victory by clarifying their minds as to what their class interests are,

[111] P.-J. Proudhon, *Idées révolutionnaires* (Paris, 1849), p. 255. Proudhon and other French socialists had in mind the idea of a continuous revolution transforming the lives of men and finally culminating in a socialist society. This, of course, has little to do with Trotsky's notion of the permanent revolution as a revolution characteristic of a backward society.
[112] Marx-Engels, *Selected Works*, I, pp. 106–17 (the *Address* was drawn up by Marx together with Engels). Marx first used the term 'permanent revolution' in 1843 (see his 'On the Jewish Question', in Bottomore, ed., Karl Marx, *Early Writings*, p. 16) and again in 1844, in the joint work with Engels, *The Holy Family* (Moscow, 1956, p. 166), where he wrote that Napoleon had 'substituted permanent war for permanent revolution'. But Marx's meaning in both instances seems to have been more figurative than literal. However, in another 1843 article, without using the term itself, Marx already hinted at the idea he would express in 1850; speaking of the political backwardness of Germany, he noted that 'the struggle against the political present of the Germans is a struggle against the past of the modern nations ... In politics, the Germans have *thought* what other nations have *done*'. ('Contribution to the Critique of Hegel's Philosophy of Right: Introduction', in Bottomore, ed., op. cit., pp. 47, 51.) The glaring gap between German reality and that of the advanced nations, Marx argued, made Germany more vulnerable to a radical revolution. (Since, however, Marx's early writings remained unknown until the 1920s, they have no relevance in the present context of the development of the idea of the permanent revolution.)
[113] Marx-Engels, *Selected Works*, I, p. 110 (italics added).

by taking up their position as an independent party as soon as possible and by not allowing themselves to be seduced for a single moment by the hypocritical phrases of the democratic petty bourgeois into refraining from the independent organization of the party of the proletariat. Their battle cry must be: The Revolution in Permanence.[114]

In the same year, that is 1850, Marx wrote and published the long, and also well-known, article, *The Class Struggles in France, 1848–1850*.[115] Here too the idea of a 'permanent revolution' is mentioned directly. It comes in the context of a definition of what Marx called 'revolutionary socialism' in France:

> . . . the *proletariat* rallies more and more round *revolutionary socialism*, round *communism*, for which the bourgeoisie has itself invented the name of *Blanqui*. This socialism is the *declaration of the permanence of the revolution*; [it is] the *class dictatorship* of the proletariat as the necessary transit point to the *abolition of class distinctions generally*, to the abolition of all the social relations of production on which they rest, to the abolition of all the social relations that correspond to these relations of production, to the revolutionizing of all the ideas that result from these social relations.[116]

This is the last time that Marx referred to the subject of 'permanent revolution' directly, though his 1882 preface to the Russian edition of the *Communist Manifesto* may be seen as implying the idea anew, in a different context.[117] On the basis of these three references alone it is difficult to gather the precise meaning which Marx attached to 'permanent revolution', but the general conception becomes clear when analysed in the particular context of the period 1848–50.

The notion of the proletariat as a 'universal class' which would liberate not only itself but the whole of society is to be found in the earliest of Marx's writings.[118] That the notion should have arisen in the context, in fact, of the German situation of the time was not fortuitous. Already in the early 1840s

---

[114] Ibid., p. 117.

[115] Ibid., pp. 139–242.

[116] Ibid., pp. 222–3. This passage is immediately followed by the sentence: 'The scope of this exposition does not permit of developing the subject further.'

[117] See the Appendix, below.

[118] See in particular the previously mentioned 'Contribution to the Critique of Hegel's Philosophy of Right: Introduction' (in Bottomore, ed., op. cit. pp. 43–59) at the end of which Marx speaks of the complete 'emancipation' of Germany as possible only through the proletariat.

Marx was preoccupied by the fact not only of Germany's retarded social and political development in comparison with England or France but also of the apparent inability of the German bourgeoisie to rise to a dominating position in German society even at so late a date. He stressed, however, that a proletariat had begun to constitute itself as a significant political force in Germany *before* a bourgeois revolution. Thus the idea that Germany's political development might follow a path different from that of England and France had already impressed itself upon him in the early 1840s and grew for him out of the very backwardness which he perceived in Germany. He thus contemplated the prospect of a truly radical revolution in German society because of this, hitherto unique, historical juxtaposition of bourgeoisie and proletariat.[119] In 1848, in the *Communist Manifesto*, at a time when the prospects of a bourgeois revolution in Germany looked propitious, he nevertheless stressed again the importance of the proletariat:

The Communists turn their attention chiefly to Germany, because that country is on the eve of a bourgeois revolution that is bound to be carried out under more advanced conditions of European civilization, and with a much more developed proletariat, than that of England in the seventeenth, and of France in the eighteenth century, and because the bourgeois revolution in Germany will be but the prelude to an immediately-following proletarian revolution.[120]

This passage is significant in a number of respects. Firstly, it shows explicitly Marx's grasp of the fact that a belated bourgeois revolution in Germany, carried out when some other countries of Europe were at a more advanced stage, must be different in character from previous bourgeois revolutions. On the basis of this passage alone it is clear that Marx's view of the possibilities of social development was not uniform or mechanistic. Secondly, the expectation that a proletarian revolution would follow 'immediately' suggests that Marx contemplated a kind of momentum within the revolution which would carry it beyond its initial, ostensible goals. The affinity of this, as of the previous point, to Trotsky's later theory of the

---

[119] It is thus interesting that Marx's view of the proletariat as a revolutionary class was first formed in the context of a 'backward' Germany and only later in the context of the 'advanced' nations.

[120] Marx–Engels, *Selected Works*, I, p. 65.

permanent revolution in Russia is obvious enough so as to require no comment. Thirdly, however, it is also clear that Marx still envisaged the bourgeois and proletarian revolutions as separate, even if now directly interrelated, stages. Whatever the time gap between these revolutions, Marx saw them as distinct events.

By 1850, however, the prospects of a bourgeois revolution in Germany had subsided and Marx's optimism of 1848 was replaced by obvious disappointment, and despair with the emerging reality. As has often been noted, for a short period during that year Marx appears to have adopted an almost 'Blanquist' attitude toward revolution.[121] The *Address* and the *Class Struggles*, in any case, clearly indicate that his position had become very radical and very impatient indeed. Was the consequent stratagem of the 'revolution in permanence' tantamount to the idea which arose for Trotsky more than a half century later in Russia? There are a number of reasons for thinking that it was not, in fact, an exact precedent. In the first place, although the passages from the *Address* and the *Class Struggles* which have been quoted suggest that Marx, at least momentarily, envisaged a more direct revolutionary role for the proletariat, both in Germany and in France, they also show that only in the case of France did he anticipate a workers' government, a 'class dictatorship'. But since France was a post-bourgeois, advanced nation, such an expectation is not at variance with Marx's standard 'time-table' for the socialist revolution; in the context of France, therefore, the use of the term 'permanence of the revolution' may be taken to be simply a declaration to go unrelentingly beyond the half-measures of non-communist socialist movements and pursue immediately, full revolutionary socialist goals. In the case of Germany, the question of an immediate workers' government does not arise at all; on the contrary, the passage from the *Address* where Marx declared that it is 'our task to make revolution permanent' is followed almost immediately by the sentence: 'That, during the further development of the revolution, the petty-bourgeois

---

[121] For different interpretations of Marx's attitude during the 1848–50 period, see Shlomo Avineri, *The Social and Political Thought of Karl Marx* (Cambridge, 1968), chapters 7 and 8, and George Lichtheim, *Marxism: An Historical and Critical Study* (2nd edition, London, 1964), chapters 3 and 6.

democracy will for a moment obtain predominating influence in Germany is not open to doubt.'[122] And in what follows it is clear that Marx was using the expression 'a moment' in a figurative sense.[123] In fact, the penultimate paragraph of the *Address* is cautious and subordinates developments in Germany to those in France:

If the German workers are not able to attain power and achieve their own class interests without completely going through a lengthy revolutionary development, they at least know for a certainty this time that the first act of this approaching revolutionary drama will coincide with the direct victory of their own class in France and will be very much accelerated by it.[124]

Thus 'revolution in permanence' in Germany meant to Marx at most the organization and arming of the workers as an independent political movement which will prepare itself for the period immediately following the bourgeois revolution. It meant that the workers, after such a revolution, would at once proceed with their own revolutionary campaign. Basically, therefore, the *Address* of 1850 was a reformulation of the passage on Germany in the *Communist Manifesto* of 1848.

Although this excursion into the texts of Marx shows, therefore, that the 'permanent revolution' did not mean to him what it later meant to Trotsky, it also serves to emphasize one important common feature, namely, the relationship which both saw between backwardness and revolution. As has been noted, Marx already in his earliest writings drew a connection between belated development and radical politics. During the 1848–50 period he translated this into actual political terms, foreseeing the prospect of accelerated revolutionary development in Germany. Thereafter, while less confident about the future of revolution in 'backward' Germany,[125] he became fascinated by the prospects of revolution in the 'backward' East, including

[122] Marx–Engels, *Selected Works*, I, p. 110.
[123] Ibid., pp. 111–16, which show that Marx foresaw a prolonged period of struggle against a bourgeois regime.
[124] Ibid., p. 116. For Trotsky's own—brief, polemical and tendentious—discussion of Marx's 1850 position, see *Permanentnaya Revolyutsiya*, pp. 132–4.
[125] Following 1850 Marx consistently opposed every 'Blanquist' revolutionary policy in Germany and elsewhere. See Avineri, op. cit., pp. 197–201.

Russia. Nevertheless, he never worked out the full connection between backwardness and revolutionary socialism. But it remains a fact that the context within which Trotsky later formulated the theory of the permanent revolution was one which had already concentrated the mind of Marx. The importance of this affinity is not, of course, that Trotsky's ideas are somehow 'legitimized' by Marx; this is irrelevant, even if it were true, and, in fact, it is not true as far as the content of these ideas is actually concerned. The importance lies, rather, in the historical issue of the relationship between Marxism and backward societies in the twentieth century. The by now commonplace paradox of Marxist movements coming to power in such societies may be partially explained by an element which Marx already noticed and was only able to hint at but which Trotsky eventually transformed into the very *revolutionary* core of Marxism.

It is interesting to note that while for Marx the spectacle of revolution in the East was problematic, that while he remained uneasy about the shift in revolutionary activity away from Europe which was to some extent already becoming evident in his own time, Trotsky in 1905–6 saw in this the most logical of developments. In part this is to be explained by Trotsky's adherence to the notion, which had by then become prevalent, that all nations were now engulfed within the expanding, capitalist orbit. According to this view, the weakest link in the chain, as Parvus had argued in 1904, would be the first to crack. But this thesis did not explain why Marxism or Social Democracy should inherit the subsequent allegiance of significant social forces in a backward country. Thus although Trotsky accepted the view that the world had become one large 'capitalist camp', this was more responsible for his subsequent linkage of the Russian revolution to events in the West, than for his initial prognosis that a workers' revolution was most likely to occur first in a backward society. As we have seen, Trotsky envisaged not only a workers' revolution, not only a workers' government, but a government which would almost immediately drive towards socialist or collectivist reforms. This went beyond even what Parvus had anticipated, and Trotsky was right when he wrote in *The Permanent Revolution* that, although Parvus's views 'bordered closely on mine', they were not 'identical' and 'actually differed' from them.[126] It is worth quoting the full distinction which Trotsky then made between his and Parvus's views in order to grasp the radical manner in which Trotsky, alone amongst all Russian Marxists, proposed to connect backwardness directly with a Marxist revolution:

Parvus was not of the opinion that a workers' government in Russia could move in the direction of the socialist revolution, that is, that in the process of fulfilling the democratic tasks it could grow over into the socialist dictatorship. . . . Parvus confined the tasks of the workers' government to the *democratic* tasks. . . . What Parvus had in mind even at that time was the establishment of a workers' regime after the 'Australian' model . . . that is . . . a regime in which the workers' party does indeed govern but does not rule, and carries out its reformist demands only as a supplement to the programme of the bourgeoisie.[127]

That Trotsky, who always acknowledged his intellectual indebtedness to Parvus,[128] nevertheless emphasized their differences was not due to some academic concern for historical precision. The distinction between his and Parvus's conceptions of the workers' government was crucial; the point was that, in Trotsky's view, a workers' government could *not* confine itself to 'democratic tasks', or 'reformist demands', and this for two reasons: firstly, because the opposition it would encounter, by virtue of being a *workers'* government, could be confronted and overcome only by a greater control and transformation of society, and this could be achieved only through the introduction of state and collectivist measures; secondly, because the most pressing social and economic problems of Russia could not be solved through purely democratic reforms. Trotsky's

---

[126] *Permanentnaya Revolyutsiya*, pp. 64–5. During 1905, in the German Social-Democratic journal *Die Neue Zeit*, articles appeared by Rosa Luxemburg, Karl Kautsky and Franz Mehring which spoke of a 'permanent revolution' in Russia; all, however, had in mind the bringing of the *democratic* revolution to completion, i.e. not stopping at half-way compromises with the autocracy. None imagined an immediate socialist revolution.
[127] Ibid., p. 65. It should be added, however, that although this is not an incorrect representation of Parvus's views, Parvus also expected the transition to socialism to become more likely *because* 'democratic tasks' were to be carried out by a workers' government.
[128] Trotsky's tributes to Parvus were noted in chapter 1, pp. 16–17 and 19, and in note 30 of the same chapter.

theory of the permanent revolution, by basing itself on the peculiar nature of Russia's backwardness, sought to explain the logic of these reasons within their actual geographical and historical context. Here, in fact, was the link which Trotsky claimed to perceive between the old world and the new, between backwardness and socialism. It is important, therefore, to examine the significance which Trotsky attached to these particular reasons.

The matter is best dealt with by raising again the main conclusion Trotsky had reached when asking himself, in the course of his survey of Russian society, what it is that had made revolution in Russia inevitable. The short answer he had given may be paraphrased as follows: a regime which itself had set in motion economic and demographic changes, was unprepared to countenance the necessary social and political changes which must follow. Determined to modernize a part of Russia's productive capacities, it yet shied away from any real modernization which went beyond the purely technical industrial sphere, or that part of it in which it was interested. But the middle course it chose was the worst from every point of view: on the one hand, such changes as were introduced were sufficient to undermine, though not transform, the traditional character of Russia and thus create new social forces, new needs and new aspirations; on the other, they were insufficient to ensure the successful pursuit of the regime's own declared foreign-military goals. The result was that internally it could not cope with increased demands for further change (thus the revolution of 1905 and, later, 1917), and externally it could not cope with the threat from its enemies or fulfil its foreign policy ambitions (thus the debacle of the war with Japan and, later, of the First World War). Although the external threat could be rolled back only through a response to the internal demands, that is, only through a more complete transformation of Russian society, such a transformation, as the regime rightly recognized, would ultimately end in the virtual liquidation of the regime itself. In short, therefore, the existing socio-political structure was incapable of modernizing Russia; in fact, it had become a fetter upon further development.

The concept of modernization—understood as change in accordance with Western and socialist standards or norms—which appears in various unmistakable guises in Trotsky's writings, may be said to emerge as the corollary of his concept of backwardness. Is this not what the theory of the permanent revolution was all about in fact? In the light of the concept of modernization, the full significance of what Trotsky took to be the transition to socialism can be seen to unfold. To return to his fundamental reasons for the inevitability of this transition: the first was that a workers' government would be driven into collectivist measures by its opponents; the second that such measures were in any case necessary to deal with economic problems. What Trotsky perceived in 1905, and what he later claimed to see, in even more extreme form, in 1917, was the problem of the lack of consensus and uniformity which characterizes societies, particularly backward societies, which are in a period of change, disruption and uprooting. The kind of national consensus which he attributed to the revolutionary forces in France in 1789, where, he believed, it was not so much the social structure, as political institutions which had to be overthrown, was, in his view, impossible in the Russia of 1905 or thereafter. Hence, a national uprising but no national revolution; hence, agreement as to what had to be destroyed but no agreement as to what should take its place; hence, a general commitment to change, but no commitment to all that a plunge into the modern world implied. At a certain stage of the upheaval, tradition-bound forces—the nobility, the bourgeoisie, above all the peasantry—would rebel against the revolution itself. State or collectivist measures would have to be implemented, because to stop short of these would be to stop short of actual modernization; it would be, at best, to limit modernization to minimal agrarian reforms, at worst to return to the *status quo ante*. Without consensus, without agreement about the future, a dictatorship—of the workers, the only force prepared and capable of carrying out modernization—becomes essential and inevitable. The complete transformation of a changed but still backward society becomes the prerogative of a new state power. Thus, Trotsky believed, collectivist measures, supported by state power, would be a substitute for national consensus, would provide the far-reaching control and domination necessary to pull Russia out of her past.[129]

[129] The implications of this, which were to become only too clear after 1917, are discussed in Part II of this study.

Besides, there was, in his view, no other way of dealing with even the most fundamental economic problems. Here too Trotsky may be seen to have been stipulating a condition arising from his conception of what modernization in a backward society involved. Put succinctly, Trotsky recognized that the problems of agriculture had become inseparable from those of industry, and vice versa; the solution to the one dictated the solution to the other. A simple distribution of land was inconceivable: were it to go uncontrolled, not only would chaos in agriculture ensue, but industry would remain dependent on the uncertainties of the countryside. The development of industry had to be accompanied both by control over agriculture and a diminution of the agricultural sector. Moreover, since, in Trotsky's view, the solution to industrial problems lay in socialization and planning, the agricultural sector would have to be brought into the same collectivist orbit, sooner or later. Thus the solution of the agrarian problem, carried out in the twentieth century, that is, in the presence of industry, assumes a completely different character from its solution elsewhere, in a pre-industrial era. Thus a long-delayed peasant uprising, led not by the bourgeoisie as in the past, but by the proletariat, cannot conclude with a seventeenth or eighteenth-century settlement of the land problem. And the historical juxtaposition of an agricultural and an industrial revolt leads to a specifically twentieth-century revolution. In the passage which follows, Trotsky, writing after 1917, isolated this phenomenon as the key to what eventually occurred in Russia:

The law of combined development of backward countries—in the sense of a peculiar mixture of backward elements with the most modern factors—here rises before us in its most finished form, and offers a key to the fundamental riddle of the Russian revolution. If the agrarian problem, as a heritage from the barbarism of the old Russian history, had been solved by the bourgeoisie, if it could have been solved by them, the Russian proletariat could not possibly have come to power in 1917. In order to realize the Soviet state, there was required a drawing together and mutual penetration of two factors belonging to completely different historic species: a peasant war—that is, a movement characteristic of the dawn of bourgeois development—and a proletarian insurrection, the movement signalling its decline. That is the essence of 1917.[130]

[130] *History of the Russian Revolution,* I, p. 72. See also 'Dve kontsentsii' (*Byulleten Oppozitsii,* June–July 1930), p. 32.

And, we may add, the 'essence' of Trotsky's theory of the permanent revolution is that, taking the combined nature of backward development as its point of departure, it sought to explain the mechanism—both historical and political—which governed the coincidence of two revolutions in time. Perhaps, after all, Trotsky should have named it from the outset the theory of the 'combined revolution.'

Marx believed that capitalism was a 'universalizing' force, bringing all those whom it touched within its orbit, creating, as he said, 'a world after its own image'. There was a great deal of truth in this, of course, in the sense that no country subject to the impact of Europe could long remain shut off within its own past. The irony was, however, that it was not so much capitalism as such, as its negation, the idea of socialism, and in particular the Marxist idea of socialism when translated into a political movement, which was to bring not a few backward countries, and first of all Russia, within the orbit of 'universal history', or rather within the orbit of modern modes of economic production and social organization. In the event, of course—and as we have seen Trotsky argue—the ultimate impact of capitalism was *not* to create 'a world after its own image'.

Could a world, in those backward countries, come into being, however, after the image of *socialism*? The view that the Russian Revolution was what is sometimes called the 'revolution of modernization' has by now a long tradition in Western scholarship.[131] We have tried to show that it was already inherent in, in fact the core of, Trotsky's theory of the Russian revolution, before that event actually materialized, and that it derived from elements present, though not fully worked out, in Marx's thought itself. Still, Marx was not so much concerned with modernization, which he considered the product largely of

---

[131] See, for example, the following works: John H. Kautsky, *Political Change in Underdeveloped Countries* (New York, 1962) and the same author's *Communism and the Politics of Development* (New York, 1968); Barrington Moore, Jr., *Soviet Politics—The Dilemma of Power: The Role of Ideas in Social Change* (New York, 1965) and the same author's *Social Origins of Dictatorship and Democracy* (Harmondsworth, 1969), especially chapter 9; Adam B. Ulam, *The Unfinished Revolution* (New York, 1960); T. H. Von Laue, *Why Lenin? Why Stalin?* (Philadelphia and New York, 1964).

capitalism, as with the social and moral framework within which modernization had now to be accommodated, namely, the presumably classless and free society of socialism. Having modernized its methods of social production and having thereby made possible the solution to all economic problems, society, Marx believed, could now 'modernize', that is, transform accordingly, its social, human relations. It is for this reason that Marx was sceptical about the prospects of socialism in backward countries—material change, modernization of the means and capacities for production, was both a practical precondition of socialism and an 'ideational' one since the need for, and the consciousness of, socialism arose only in the wake of the possibilities and alternatives created by material change itself.[132]

Trotsky's theory of the permanent revolution was not only a theory of how material change—modernization in this sense—could be brought about in a backward country. On the contrary, it argued that the modernization of material conditions should and could proceed hand in hand with their accommodation within the socialist framework of which Marx had spoken; that, in other words, a 'socialist psychology', as he called it, and by which he meant, of course, a socialist consciousness, should and could arise before or, at best, concurrently with, the creation of both the material pre-conditions of socialism and the actual conditions themselves of socialism. Thus the notion of modernization in Trotsky's thought was that of modernization in accordance with both the material and moral precepts of socialism. To return to the question we posed above: Trotsky *did* believe that a backward country could be remoulded in the image of socialism.

The problem is, of course, that this belief grew as much out of wishful thinking and questionable assumptions as out of a persuasive theoretical analysis of all the difficulties inherent in the above conception of modernization, in the transformation,

---

[132] Marx did not, of course, write a work specifically devoted to modernization; but all his social and economic writings may be seen to be concerned with this subject in one way or another; see in particular Karl Marx, *Pre-Capitalist Economic Formations* (E. J. Hobsbawm, ed., London, 1964) and *Marx's Grundrisse* (David McLellan, ed., London, 1971). On the theme of modernization in Marx's thought, see Robert C. Tucker, *The Marxian Revolutionary Idea* (London, 1970).

that is, of Russia into a socialist society. It is true that Trotsky could always fall back on the crucial condition he had stipulated—the European revolution—and, in fact, in later years he would repeat again and again that he had always made socialism in Russia dependent on socialism in Europe.[133] But the idea that revolution in Russia would spark off a general conflagration in Europe which, in turn, would presumably rescue Russian socialism, was itself a not insubstantial bit of wishful thinking. In the first place, it was based on the assumption, albeit one shared by Marxists in general, that revolutionary socialism was still a force in Europe, as relevant to advanced societies as Trotsky now claimed it to be to backward ones, that Europe could no more solve its problems without revolution than Russia could hers. In the second place, it did not have much to do with the question of the possibility of socialism in Russia. Let us, for the sake of argument, grant Trotsky the benefit of the doubt: the view, in any case, that European capitalism in the years prior to World War I was disintegrating, the view, later, that the War was the final drama of this disintegration, may have proved to be misguided and illusory but it was not preposterous at the time. Suppose then that the collapse of capitalism would have even seen the emergence of workers' governments in Europe—would this have made the transition to socialism in Russia that much more certain? No doubt the 'direct state support of the European proletariat' (to repeat Trotsky's words in *Results and Prospects*) would have made life much less complicated for a Russian 'workers' government'; but this is still to beg the question of whether Russia was 'ripe' for socialism, of whether socialism could be made to grow on primarily backward foundations. A socialist Europe could certainly assist Russia materially; it is, however, too much to believe that it could make up for the country's social and cultural limitations.[134]

In point of fact, the theory of the permanent revolution, though it made socialism in Russia *ultimately* dependent on Europe, was first of all based on certain overly optimistic

---

[133] See chapters 8 and 9, below.

[134] The persistent problems confronting underdeveloped countries today, no matter what the extent of the material aid they receive, show that backwardness cannot be overcome by material means alone, or even primarily.

assumptions about the internal, independent capacities of Russian society. We have argued in the previous chapter that Trotsky, in spite of his awareness of the over-all poverty—in all its senses—of Russian society, nevertheless exaggerated the extent of the socio-cultural changes which had taken place in it by the beginning of the twentieth century. He could hardly do otherwise and sound convincing, for not to assume such changes was to project socialism into a virtual vacuum—and, after all, the whole point of the theory of the permanent revolution, as of the notion of 'combined development', was that a basis for socialism had already been created.

On the other hand, not even Trotsky could argue—since this *was* preposterous—that this basis was such as emerges with the evolution of society towards socialism—a basis Marx had assumed to arise in the 'womb' of capitalist society as it 'transcended' itself. Here it is not difficult to see the kind of position to which Trotsky's theory actually committed him, though without his realizing it. What, after all, is the purpose, the function, of revolution in the Marxist view of things? Let us leave aside the question, which cannot be dealt with here, and which has been much debated in the literature on Marxism, of what Marx's own over-all position on the issue of revolutionary activism was (we have merely touched upon it in the context of some of his 1848–50 writings).[135] But in accordance with the general historical theories of Marxism it can be argued that political revolution is legitimate only when it emerges as the last act, so to speak, of a *social revolution*. The latter is the kind of broad transformation through which a society passes over an 'epoch' and as a result largely of internal economic forces outside its control and consciousness. It is once this social revolution has more or less culminated that the question of political revolution arises: it becomes necessary when, despite such changes, old and now inadequate political and other institutions continue, for one reason or another, to persist or maintain themselves, and are a 'fetter' upon further development. The role of political revolution, in that case, is to force politics and the remnants of the past to conform to the new character of society. This way of looking at the Marxist theory of revolution may be too sche-

---

[135] For the view that Marx was very cautious about propounding revolutionary action, see Avineri, op. cit., especially pp. 146ff. and 215–20.

matic and an oversimplification, and it is certainly at variance with Marxism's own historical role, but it is not incompatible with its historical thesis about politics lagging behind economics and social reality in general.[136]

Now it is obviously true that by the beginning of the twentieth century Russian political and other institutions were no longer adequate, and were incompatible with the changes which had taken place in Russian society. A case for political revolution can, accordingly, be not unreasonably made out even on non-Marxist grounds. But the nature of the institutional changes required depended, of course, on the nature of the economic and social changes which had emerged. Thus it was common to speak of the need for 'democratic' institutions as being the most logical at that point in Russia's development. It is true, of course, and it is the most persuasive, the most cogently argued element in Trotsky's thought, that such a purely formalist approach neglected the fact that Russian development did not conform to the pre-conditions which would make democratic institutions viable. Conversely, however, to argue that a socialist government, socialist institutions, were on the order of the day was to argue that a *political* revolution had to precede the social one, that institutions had to be created which not only did not have roots in social life but took precedence over it. Trotsky had in fact committed himself to the view that socialism was to be imposed from above, that state institutions would carry out that revolution which society itself was either incapable of, or unprepared to give birth to, that, in a word, revolution would make society conform to politics and to political ideology—a curious and far-reaching reversal of the Marxist view of historical change.

We know that this is precisely what was eventually to happen, that the Soviet government was to pursue—at first hesitantly but at last unrelentingly—a policy of the wilful transformation of society from above. No one, however, perhaps not even Lenin, who is commonly identified with this approach to

[136] In his famous summary of his views of history, 'Preface to *A Contribution to the Critique of Political Economy*' (in Marx–Engels, *Selected Works*, I, pp. 361–5), Marx spoke of the 'epoch of social revolution' and nowhere mentioned the question of a political revolution. However, see the critical analysis of this 'Preface'—which exposes the vagueness of its concepts—in John Plamenatz, *German Marxism and Russian Communism* (London, 1954), chapter 2.

politics, which Stalin later perfected, was more responsible for
providing it with its initial, theoretical justification than
Trotsky. It is not surprising, therefore, that following 1905
Trotsky was looked upon as somewhat of a reckless adventurist,
a revolutionist *par excellence*. Even Lenin thought him too
extreme, though Lenin may have been worried as much by the
practical possibilities of Trotsky's ideas as their ideological pedigree.[137] As for Trotsky, he was of course not unaware of the
revolutionary activism to which he alone for a long time was
committed. There is an interesting and revealing passage in an
article of 1908 where Trotsky summarizes the differences
between the Menshevik and Bolshevik factions and, implicitly,
between them and himself:

Whereas the Mensheviks, proceeding from the abstract notion that
'our revolution is a bourgeois revolution', arrive at the idea that the
proletariat must adapt all its tactics to the behaviour of the liberal
bourgeoisie in order to ensure the transfer of state power to that bourgeoisie, the Bolsheviks proceed from an equally abstract notion—
'democratic dictatorship, not socialist dictatorship'—and arrive at
the idea of a proletariat in possession of state power imposing a bourgeois-democratic limitation upon itself. It is true that the difference
between them in this matter is very considerable: while the anti-revolutionary aspects of Menshevism have already become fully apparent,
those of Bolshevism are likely to become a serious threat in the event
of victory ... both Mensheviks and Bolsheviks become scared of the
consequences of the class struggle and hope to limit it by their metaphysical constructs.[138]

[137] As has been often noted, in September 1905 Lenin momentarily entertained the
possibility that Russia might have her democratic and socialist revolutions simultaneously and even propounded that this be the goal of the Social Democrats. Thus he
wrote: 'From the democratic revolution we shall begin immediately and within the
extent of our strength—the strength of the conscious and organized proletariat—to
go on to the socialist revolution. We stand for uninterrupted revolution. We shall not
stop halfway.' (Lenin, *Sochineniya*, 4th edition, IX, p. 213.) But this seems to have been
an impulsive reaction to the events of 1905, for almost immediately thereafter Lenin
returned to the orthodox view that Russia must first go through a bourgeois revolution
before there could be talk of a socialist one—a view he would uphold until 1917. In
Permanentnaya Revolyutsiya (pp. 39–40), Trotsky claimed that Lenin never read his *Itogi
i perspektivy* or other writings on the theory of the permanent revolution; by this Trotsky
wanted to show that Lenin was both unacquainted with the theory and never actually
rejected it. In fact, of course, Lenin's whole position was at odds with that of Trotsky
and the latter's attempt in *Permanentnaya Revolyutsiya* to blur the differences between
them is hardly to the credit of his historical or intellectual integrity.
[138] *1905*, p. 285. This is the article referred to in note 102, above. The passage quoted
is quite prescient if we recall the vacillations of the Bolsheviks before Lenin's arrival

It remains true, however, that Trotsky never saw the implications of his revolutionary theory in the manner in which they have been here interpreted, and the extreme materialization of which he would in later years devote himself to denouncing. It remains true also that, despite what has been here said, there is a fundamental difference in character and mentality between Trotsky and Lenin, not to mention Stalin. Why is it that Trotsky appears to us to have been more genuinely attached to the ideals of socialism than either of these men, or rather to that conception of a modern Russia which took due account of both material and moral conditions? The answer to this, as to the question why Trotsky did not see the implications of his ideas, is that these ideas were not formulated as an exercise in ideological justification but out of a conviction that they scrupulously reflected Russian reality. Thus Trotsky did genuinely believe that that reality was ready to absorb socialist ideas and a 'workers' government'. Thus he genuinely believed, above all, in the vitality of the Russian proletariat. Earlier in this study we noted his reaction to the workers' participation in the Revolution of 1905 and the impact of this upon him.[139] In fact, the whole of his exaggerated view of the extent to which Russia had been transformed by industrialization may be attributed to his conviction—which must now appear either perverse or simply naïve—that the Russian proletariat was an independent, vital revolutionary force, both in the sense of its economic-based political strength, as well as that of its consciousness, idealism, and devotion to socialist goals.[140]

in Petrograd in April 1917. In 1922, when including the article in *1905*, Trotsky added the footnote (at the bottom of the same page): 'This threat [i.e. that Bolshevism will prove to be 'scared'], as we know, never materialized because, under the leadership of comrade Lenin, the Bolsheviks (though not without an internal struggle) revamped their policy on this fundamental question in the spring of 1917, that is, before the seizure of power.' See also a letter he wrote in 1921 where, while reaffirming the correctness of his theory of the permanent revolution and declaring that in his differences with the Bolsheviks he had '[not been] wrong on everything', he admitted that he had drawn 'incorrect' conclusions about the revolutionary potential of the Bolshevik faction (*The Trotsky Papers, 1917–1922*, The Hague, II, 1971, pp. 642–5).
[139] See chapter 1, pp. 23ff., above.
[140] Another Marxist who believed in workers' consciousness and participation, and upon whom the events of 1905 in Russia also had a profound impact, was Rosa Luxemburg (see her 1906 pamphlet *The Mass Strike: The Political Party and the Trade Unions*, English version reissued New York, 1971). In his autobiography (*Moya Zhizn*, I, pp.

This also explains his attitude, from the time of the fateful Second Congress of Russian Social Democrats in 1903, and until 1917, to the question of revolutionary organization and of the relationship in general between masses and party. If what he believed about Russian workers was true, then the theory of the permanent revolution had no need to take undue account of the organizational instrument which would set the mechanism of the revolution in motion—the workers themselves, Trotsky thought, were the instrument, the agent and the vehicle, of social change. Thus the issue we have discussed above, of a political revolution imposed from above, did not arise for him, for the revolution would be of the workers themselves. And, indeed, this accounts for his bitter and unequivocal opposition to Lenin until 1917, an opposition which grew precisely out of the fact that Trotsky considered, not incorrectly, Lenin's conception of the party to represent an attempt to impose the revolution from above.

It was Lenin, of course, who was to take the first step towards a possible reconciliation with Trotsky. Though Lenin's famous 'April Theses' of 1917 were obviously not governed by this consideration, they enabled Trotsky to think that on the question

---

232–3) Trotsky claimed that Rosa Luxemburg in 1907 (at the Fifth Congress of the RSDRP in London, which she attended) agreed with his theory of the permanent revolution; Deutscher (in *The Prophet Armed*, p. 178) repeats this claim as fact without providing any further evidence for it. There are, of course, many affinities between Trotsky and Rosa Luxemburg but no basis, in fact, to show that the latter was a proponent of permanent revolution. Her above-mentioned pamphlet reveals an awareness of the peculiar rapidity of developments in Russia but there is no suggestion in it that Russia is ripe for a socialist revolution. Nor does her 1905 *Neue Zeit* article ('Nach dem ersten Akt', *Die Neue Zeit*, 4 Feb. 1905, pp. 610–14), in which she speaks of maintaining the Russian revolution 'in permanence', reveal any adoption of Trotsky's standpoint. As was pointed out earlier (see note 126, above) she urged only that the democratic (i.e. bourgeois) revolution be perpetuated until all its demands had been met and the autocracy brought down. Rosa Luxemburg's biographer also finds no basis for Trotsky's (or Deutscher's) claim: see J. P. Nettl, *Rosa Luxemburg* (2 vols., London, 1966), I, p. 339, and II, p. 504. Only after 1917 could she, like Lenin (see next note), be said to have approached a position similar to Trotsky's: see her pamphlet *The Russian Revolution* (written in 1918) which, however, is also a far-reaching critique of Bolshevik policies. In later years Trotsky embraced Rosa Luxemburg as a 'spiritual light' unto the Fourth International: see his 'Rosa Luxemburg i Chetvertyi Internatsional', Archives, T3677. See also his article 'Ruki proch ot Rozy Luxemburg!', in *Byulleten Oppozitsii* (July 1932), pp. 11–16. For an earlier tribute to her, see the speech he delivered in the Petrograd Soviet in January 1919, following her and Karl Liebknecht's murder: 'Mucheniki Tretego Internatsionala: Karl Liebknecht i Rosa Luxemburg', in Trotsky's *Sochineniya*, VIII, pp. 82–94.

of the permanent revolution the two were now of one mind.[141] Yet nothing so bears witness to Trotsky's overestimation of the workers and of mass consciousness—and, perhaps, to his own eventual though unstated recognition of this fact—as the actual motive for his reconciliation with Lenin and with Bolshevism. In the midst of 1917 it must have become obvious to him that the mechanism of the permanent revolution could *not* be set in motion without a revolutionary organization. In the theory of that revolution, the party proved to be the missing link, or—

[141] The second of Lenin's 'Theses' declared: 'It is a specific feature of the present situation in Russia that it represents a *transition* from the first stage of the revolution—which, owing to the insufficient class-consciousness and organization of the proletariat, placed power in the hands of the bourgeoisie—to its *second* stage, which must place power in the hands of the proletariat and the poorest sections of the peasants.' (Lenin, *Selected Works*, II, p. 46.) For an assessment of Lenin's volte-face of April 1917, see Jonathan Frankel, 'Lenin's Doctrinal Revolution of April 1917', *Journal of Contemporary History* (Apr. 1969), pp. 117–42. Although in 1915 Lenin had spoken of the 'growing over' (*pererastanie*) of the bourgeois into the socialist revolution (see Meyer, *Leninism*, p. 143 and Trotsky, *Permanentnaya Revolyutsiya*, p. 21), his 'April Theses' represent a sudden and complete change of view, i.e. an abandonment of the traditional 'different and separate stages' theory. While it is true that Lenin never identified himself directly with Trotsky's theory of the permanent revolution, in effect his 'Theses' were tantamount to an acceptance of the theory. In *Moya Zhizn*, II, p. 281, Trotsky writes that A. A. Joffe had once told him about a conversation he (Joffe) had had with Lenin in 1919 on the subject of the permanent revolution and, according to Joffe, Lenin had said: 'Yes, Trotsky proved to be right.' In ibid., p. 284, Trotsky quotes from the letter Joffe wrote him before committing suicide in November 1927: '. . . with my own ears I heard Lenin admit that even in 1905, you, and not he, were right.' (The full text of Joffe's letter is reproduced in Trotsky, *The Real Situation in Russia*, New York, 1928, pp. 325–32.) See also Trotsky's reference to the conversation between Joffe and Lenin in *Permanentnaya Revolyutsiya*, footnote pp. 40–1. There can be no doubt that Lenin's 'conversion' in 1917 was a typical example of his theoretical flexibility or, to put it another way, of his capacity and readiness to abandon old doctrines for new ones more suited to the needs of the moment, in this case the need for a theoretical justification for the seizure of power. If Lenin's approach to theory in 1917 was opportunistic, this cannot be said of Trotsky who, after all, had propounded the permanent revolution theory since 1905 (although an element of opportunism was certainly present in *his* conversion to Bolshevism). In general it may be said that the approach of the two men to theory and doctrine was fundamentally different, that of Lenin being consistently instrumental. This also explains the fact that whatever Lenin's identification with Trotsky's theory, in later years he would be less reliant than Trotsky on a European revolution and more prepared to pursue internal policies irrespective of external developments. In the 1920s and 1930s Trotsky would argue that Stalinism was a deviation from Leninism; as we shall see, there would be much exaggeration in this argument (see especially chapter 10, pp. 428ff., below). Thus Trotsky was probably right to claim that Lenin had embraced the theory of the permanent revolution; but he attributed too much importance to this, assuming that Lenin had thereby committed himself to all that he, Trotsky, saw as flowing from this theory. After 1917 he never quite grasped Lenin's political mentality and acumen.

since Trotsky had considered it superfluous—the rejected link. If, therefore, in 1917, Lenin tacitly at least accepted Trotsky's theory of the Russian revolution, the problem of the missing link explains why, in the same year, the theory could not be put into practice without Lenin and the Bolsheviks.[142] But the extent to which the recognition, and the acceptance, of *this* fact by Trotsky involved a radical transformation in his thought in general, and in his attitude to party organization in particular, will become even more apparent in a full consideration of his earlier views on the role and importance of the revolutionary party.

[142] Trotsky, of course, took October 1917 to be a vindication of his theory. Of his numerous claims to this effect, see for example *Permanentnaya Revolyutsiya*, p. 118, where he declared: 'The *fundamental* train of thought which I developed twenty-three years ago in *Results and Prospects*, I consider confirmed by events as completely correct.'

CHAPTER FIVE

THE SUBSTITUTE LINK:
THE REVOLUTIONARY PARTY

[Throughout our history] the intelligentsia has substituted itself for political parties, classes and the people as a whole ... [its] role as ideological standard-bearer has been bound up with the country's political life not through the class which it wished to serve but only through the 'idea' of that class. Thus it was with the first circles of the Marxist intelligentsia.[1]

TROTSKY'S THEORY of the permanent revolution was not incompatible with—in fact, as has been suggested and will be further argued, it was ultimately dependent upon—the Bolshevik conception of the revolutionary party; but nothing that he wrote until 1917 on party or organizational issues could possibly be reconciled with that conception. In his opposition to Lenin, Trotsky took a position as extreme and as unrelentingly aggressive as any of Lenin's Menshevik critics. This was already so before 1905; and in the wake of 1905 his views, though they could hardly become more extreme, were reinforced by a sense of vindication. In the decade or so which followed, Trotsky, it is true, was to make numerous efforts to unite anew the Social Democratic movement—but on such a wide basis as would have effectively forced Lenin to abandon 'Bolshevism'. Thus, when in 1917 Trotsky joined the Bolsheviks, this was not the consequence of any evolution in his party views: the change of mind was sudden, abrupt and total. This transformation can certainly be explained; and it may even be seen—though with some hindsight—as having been predictable, in view of the militant, radical position to which his theory of the Russian revolution had committed him.

Whatever the case, however, Trotsky's views on party questions, being so disparate, cannot be defined in terms of one

[1] Trotsky, 'Ob intelligentsii', in *Literatura i Revolyutsiya* (Moscow, 1923), pp. 262 and 269.

single conception; and they must, therefore, be considered within the context of different historical periods: before 1905, when he first defined his position; 1905 and after, when he redefined it in the light of the Revolution of that year; and from 1917 onwards when he abandoned it and took up the opposite Bolshevik position. The distinction between the first two periods does not involve a break; there is in fact a continuity between them. But as on so many other issues, so on party questions, 1905 seemed to Trotsky to provide a practical lesson. As for the period beginning after February 1917, it may serve us—in view of all that his new views involved—as a transition point to the actual practice, as opposed to theory, of the Russian Revolution.

1. Before 1905

The question of party organization and activity constitutes the main subject of Trotsky's earliest political writings.[2] In fact, almost his first work of a purely political nature is an essay which deals with this very question. It was composed in 1901, during Trotsky's first exile in Siberia, and copies of it were circulated amongst Social Democrats in the Siberian colonies. It was never published, however, and only a brief extract from it, which Trotsky later included in another work, survives. This other work is the published version of a report Trotsky wrote in 1903, immediately following the Second Congress of the Social Democratic party, on behalf of the Siberian delegation, and which appeared under the title *Vtoroi Syezd RSDRP (Otchet Sibirskoi Delegatsii)* (The Second Congress of the RSDRP: Report of the Siberian Delegation).[3] A year later, in August 1904, there appeared his first extensive work, *Nashi Politicheskye*

---

[2] As opposed to writings on literary or cultural subjects. Of his other political writings before 1902, the previously mentioned work on freemasonry was lost while in manuscript (see chapter 1, p. 12, above). He also co-authored, in 1900, a pamphlet on the Nikolayev labour movement which was published in Y. M. Steklov and L. Trotsky, *Iz rabochego dvizheniya v Odesse i Nikolaeve* (Geneva, 1900).

[3] Geneva, 1903; hereafter referred to in the notes as *Vtoroi Syezd*. (The extract from the 1901 essay is on p. 32.) This published version of the report, Trotsky wrote in the preface (p. 4), differed only slightly from the original version and only the afterword (pp. 32–6), containing in part the above extract, was added for publication. The Siberian delegation consisted of Trotsky and one other representative, V. Mandelberg.

Zadachi (Our Political Tasks).[4] This was a pamphlet of more than a hundred pages, devoted entirely to the organizational and political issues which had split the party in 1903 and constituting perhaps the most vitriolic, though not unreasoned, attack then or ever against Lenin and the Bolshevik position. Together, these two works, closely related in time, content and views, provide a complete statement of Trotsky's thought during the period before 1905 on questions of party organization in particular, and on the role of the revolutionary party in general.

(a) *Centralism*

In his autobiography Trotsky noted that the '1901 essay'[5] dealt with the question of 'the necessity for creating a centralized party' and that 'it was discussed with avidity' among the Siberian revolutionaries.[6] Indeed, the impression it seems to have made was that Trotsky was a proponent of such a 'necessity', for in his 1903 *Report* he attempted to explain, albeit indirectly, why at the Congress he had sided against Lenin, in spite of the views which he had expressed in the essay. Moreover, in a long footnote to the *Report* he added, apologetically, that at the time of writing the essay he was 'completely cut off from practical and literary work' amongst Russian Social Democrats and it was therefore composed 'under the influence of scrappy information'.[7] He admitted that at the time 'some comrades did find ... the essay to be "Populist" in character (in view of its "non-democratic" tendencies)'.[8] However, in quoting the essay he in fact contraposed it to the Bolshevik views; to his mind there was no contradiction between it and opposition to such views. The '1901 essay' had indeed argued for 'centralism', he wrote, but a centralism entirely different from that which Lenin had introduced at the Congress.[9] The

---

[4] Geneva, 1904. The sub-title of this work is 'Takticheskie i organizatsionniye voprosy'. As in the previous work, Trotsky here used the initial N., instead of L. Both works were published under the imprint of the party press. As far as is known to the present writer, no English translations of these works have ever appeared.

[5] Since Trotsky did not say what the original title of the essay was, it will be referred to in this form.

[6] *Moya Zhizn*, I, p. 157.   [7] *Vtoroi Syezd*, p. 31.   [8] Ibid., p. 32.

[9] In the same footnote he added ironically that those who then accused him of 'non-democratic tendencies' have in the meantime 'gone so far on the road of centralism that the author of the "Report" now appears to them infected with "anti-centralist" prejudices. So rapidly does our fatherland move on the road of progress.' Loc. cit.

problem to which he had in 1901 given his attention was how
to manage a movement which because of its size and dispersal
over a large territory had become seemingly unmanageable.
In the essay he had defined the problem as follows: 'We seem
to have found ourselves ... in the situation of those inexperienced magicians who by means of trite devices have called to
life a tremendous force and when it had to be mastered,
appeared to be bankrupt.'[10]

Trotsky added that in the essay he had declared there to be
'only one way out: an all-party organization with a Central
Committee at the top'.[11] He then quoted directly three paragraphs from the essay, the first of which reads as follows:

In the case that any one of the local organizations refuses to recognize
the authority of the Central Committee, the latter will have the power
and the right not to recognize this organization. It will cut off that
organization from the whole revolutionary world, severing all relations with it; it will stop the flow to it of literature and other facilities,
will dispatch into the field its own detachment and, supplying the
latter with all necessary means, will declare it to be the local committee.[12]

This was as extreme a position as it would have been possible
to take on the role and authority of the Central Committee and,
in the light of this passage, it is no wonder that Trotsky's essay
was interpreted by some to embody 'non-democratic tendencies'. But the other two paragraphs which Trotsky quoted
serve at least to tone down this position, if not to nullify it:

But such a 'heroic' measure might have only exceptional application.
As a general rule, the application of material repression would appear
absurd: it would mean that the Central Committee was swimming
against the all-party current—a hopeless dream.

If the Central Committee were to possess organizational tact and
an understanding of the tasks of the movement, conflicts between it
and the local committees would become impossible since, given a
normal development of matters, the orders of the Central Committee

[10] This sentence, given as a direct quotation from the essay, appears also in the footnote,
ibid. pp. 31–2.
[11] This, again, is in the footnote (p. 32) but as a paraphrase and not a direct quotation
from the essay.
[12] Ibid., p. 32. This and the following quotations, which together constitute the whole
of the extract from the essay, were given by Trotsky in the body of the text.

would constitute merely the formulation of all-party interests ...
Keeping vigilant watch that the local committees stay in step with
the party, the Central Committee would, however, refrain from an
interference in the internal life of the local organizations.[13]

Since the original '1901 essay' has not survived in its entirety
there is no way of knowing which part of the extract—the first
paragraph or the last two—reflects the intention and general
tone of its source. It may be that, having changed his mind
in 1903, Trotsky was then concerned to give prominence to
the qualifications of his '1901 essay'. Whatever the case, the
tempering of a strong Central Committee by a vital, broadly
based rank-and-file movement *does* reflect Trotsky's views two
and three years later. Both in the *Report* and in *Our Political
Tasks* he clearly emerged as a supporter of centralism, but a
centralism governed by scrupulous democratic arrangements;
he argued for the importance of organization to the revolutionary movement, but as the servant of that movement and
not its master; he admitted the need for direction and leadership but as means towards the creation of a genuine working-
class movement, not as a self-perpetuating hierarchy outside
its control and severed from it.

The Second Congress of the party had brought to an end
Trotsky's brief collaboration with Lenin and the *Report* shows
how profoundly he had been repelled by Lenin's wrecking tactics. A sort of shock of recognition runs through its pages; it
reveals an angry disillusionment with the Social Democratic
movement in general and its Leninist wing in particular.
Trotsky's reaction is almost like that of an idealistic but naïve
neophyte who, seeing his idols for the first time at close range,
suddenly realizes how distorted by distance had been his view
of reality. He had come to the Congress believing that there
the achievements of the various local organizations would be
expressed by a 'collectively worked-out programme'; instead,
everything already accomplished had been 'erased' by the factionalism and personal strife among delegates. As a result,

[13] Loc. cit. Trotsky put the last paragraph in italics. Deutscher, in *The Prophet Armed*,
p. 45, quotes only the first paragraph and does not mention at all the rest of the extract;
he is thus able to conclude that originally, i.e. in 1901, Trotsky 'expounded broadly
a view of the organization and the discipline of the party identical with that which
was later to become the hall-mark of Bolshevism'. The next two paragraphs, however,
show this to be too unequivocal a conclusion.

rather than 'building', the Congress had 'destroyed'.[14] He had also believed that a Congress was not convened in order to 'create' a movement but to 'register' its progress and take note of its internal developments, thereby arriving at an over-all consensus, not divided, 'particularistic' loyalties: 'A party is not an arithmetical sum of local committees. A party is an integral organism. Thus the Congress is capable of "creating" a party only in so far as a party has already been created by the prolonged organizational work of technical and ideological consolidation.'[15]

Instead, however, first the particularism of the 'Bund', then the obduracy of the 'hard *Iskra* men' had split the party into warring factions thus raising doubt whether there was 'justification in calling ourselves a Social Democratic party'.[16] The Congress had in fact become a 'destructive force' and Lenin in particular, 'with the talent and energy characteristic of him, assumed the role of the party's disorganizer'.[17] To attribute the whole of the blame for what had happened at the Congress to Lenin would be to 'simplify' the issue; particularism and intransigence had revealed themselves to be widespread traits. But it was Lenin, in Trotsky's view, who more than anyone else represented this tendency and it was he who was most responsible for the failure to achieve unity.

Unity, in fact, appears to have been almost an end in itself for Trotsky, and at the Second Congress he was already playing the role of the 'conciliator', a role he would also take upon himself throughout the years following 1903. But the pursuit of unity did not lead him into embracing a mid-way or compromise position between the factions. On the contrary, on all the major issues he took a definite, independent stand and his opposition to Lenin was motivated not only by the latter's disruptive influence but by the very content of the proposals and ideas which Lenin introduced. No one, not even among those who would become the leading figures of Menshevism, was more adamantly opposed to the organizational principles of Lenin than Trotsky. Thus while in the *Report* he denounced firstly the element of factionalism as such, it is Lenin's view of centralism which was the main object of his attack.

[14] *Vtoroi Syezd*, pp. 7 and 8.   [15] Ibid., p. 6.
[16] Ibid., p. 7.   [17] Ibid., p. 11.

It is unnecessary here to go into the detailed criticism which Trotsky gave of the various administrative arrangements proposed by Lenin; the argument as to the composition of the various party organs—the *Iskra* board, the Central Committee, the Council—and their interrelationship was highly technical and not particularly interesting, though, of course, it was over such ostensibly 'technical' issues that the party had split.[18] What is important is Trotsky's general principles as to party organization and his fundamental grounds for opposing the kind of centralism advocated by Lenin. As to the first, it is abundantly clear where Trotsky's sympathies lay; he was above all a supporter of Social Democracy as a broad, mass movement. Nothing was more repugnant to him than what he called the 'abstract' centralism of Lenin, 'devoid of revolutionary content', representing an autonomous institutional structure whose relationship to the movement as a whole was 'purely formal'.[19] Lenin, in Trotsky's view, was obsessed by the need for 'control' over the party's membership and this inevitably led him into a position which precluded both the spontaneous growth of the movement and the development of local organizations closely attached to their grassroots origins. Were it not for the stultifying effect it would have on the movement, Lenin's formalism could be discounted as an 'innocent office man's dream';[20] and, in fact, formal and abstract though it was, and therefore unrealizable in reality, its impact would be to undermine the party as the representative of Social Democracy. It could not stem the growth of political and revolutionary consciousness among the workers but its consequence would be to sever the party from just this growth. While an organizationally impeccable structure was built up, its relevance to the workers' movement would be purely legalistic. Rather than submitting to the demands of the party, the workers' local organizations and committees would ignore it. Denunciations by the party would have no effect; if the party was out of touch with the rank-and-file, the latter would go its own way. The end result would be

---

[18] For the official transcript of the proceedings at the Second Congress, see *Vtoroi Syezd RSDRP: Protokoly* (Moscow, 1932), which should not, of course, be confused with Trotsky's report. A brief account of the proceedings is in Leonard Schapiro, *The Communist Party of the Soviet Union* (London, 1963), chapter 2. Most of the works cited in note 5, chapter 2, above, also discuss various aspects of the Congress.

[19] *Vtoroi Syezd*, pp. 12 and 13.   [20] Ibid., p. 14.

an organization without a movement or at least an organization overtaken by its movement. Conversely, there would emerge a movement without an organization, or at least a movement lacking a real central organization, a movement whose dispersed nature would remain a problem. The answer to this problem for Trotsky lay therefore not in 'purely formal', legalistic arrangements, but in an organization which allowed local branches the maximum freedom of action compatible with unity; and unity was to be interpreted not as a straitjacket but as an organic framework, not as an arbitrarily determined set of criteria but as the shape which a movement assumes through its own internal growth. The task of the party organization was to coordinate activities and policies, not prescribe the legal aegis under which they were to be carried out. The more sensitive the party organs, and particularly the Central Committee, to local organizations, the more would the latter turn to it for guidance and, therefore, the more effective would the principle of centralism—a centralism freely accepted, not imposed—become.[21]

As against this view of centralism, there was, Trotsky continued, the formula proposed by Lenin. Beneath the seemingly innocuous differences in the party statutes drafted by Lenin and Martov to define party members—the one spoke of 'personal participation', the other of 'personal co-operation'—there were hidden, according to Trotsky, fundamentally different attitudes towards the character of the party.[22] The one would limit its scope, the other extend it as far as possible. That he, Trotsky, was at one with Martov on this question was a direct consequence of this different attitude. And, in fact, over this issue the Martov version received the support of the majority. However, the subsequent split, which resulted in a triumph for Lenin—and hence the right to the 'Bolshevik' label—and

[21] Ibid., pp. 14–15. Trotsky's warning about the lack of preparedness of the Social Democratic party anticipated that of Parvus a year later: see chapter 1, pp. 20–1, above.

[22] According to Lenin's draft, a party member was one 'who accepts the party's programme, and supports the party both materially and by personal participation in one of the party organizations'. Martov's draft also stipulated the acceptance of the programme and material support but instead of 'personal participation' it sought to include anyone 'who gives the party his regular personal co-operation, under the direction of one of the party organizations'. Ibid., p. 14 and Schapiro, op. cit., p. 49.

which ostensibly concerned only the composition of the various party organs—the *Iskra* board, the Central Committee, the Party Council—revealed, in Trotsky's view, the further ulterior motives of Lenin.[23] These were nothing less than to make a mockery of internal democracy. The Leninist concept of centralism, as this split showed, was directed at elevating not a principle of organization but one of 'hegemony'. What in fact emerged, according to Trotsky, was not so much a struggle for principles as a 'struggle for power'.[24] Lenin's real concern was to gain control over the whole party apparatus, to introduce the kind of organizational uniformity which would make the independence of the various organs a fiction, and subject the whole to his own personal domination. To achieve this goal he pursued a policy based on mistrust and conflict among the party leadership. He declared a 'state of siege' against his opponents' views. He was determined to bring about a direct confrontation. All this he achieved, and in so doing succeeded in aggrandizing his own position. But he was driven to this not only by his own personal ambitions but by the whole 'system' of thought to which he subscribed and which he personified. Thus the clue to Lenin's concept of centralism was to be sought not only in the man but in the concept itself:

We are talking about a 'struggle for power' but we do not give these words a personal content. The personal struggle seemed to demonstrate a principle of a, so to speak, non-personal character. It was the conclusion of a system. The 'state of siege' on which Comrade Lenin so energetically insisted, demands 'firmness of power'. The practice of organized mistrust demands an iron fist. A system of terror is crowned by the emergence of a Robespierre. Comrade Lenin made a mental roll-call of the party personnel and arrived at the conclusion that he himself was to be the iron fist—and he alone. And he was right. The hegemony of Social Democracy in the struggle for liberation has led, in accordance with the logic of the state of siege, to the hegemony of Lenin over Social Democracy. In this context, the 'struggle for power' has lost its personal character—it has emerged as the last link of a system. Its success has been the success of the system. The more ruinous, therefore, might it be for the party.[25]

[23] For Trotsky's dissection of Lenin's tactics and proposed manipulation of the various party organs, see *Vtoroi Syezd*, pp. 15–20 and 21–6.
[24] Ibid., p. 20. [25] Ibid., pp. 20–1.

This theme of the direct 'link' which existed between a man's ideas and his subsequent rise to a position of personal power was stressed by Trotsky in the final pages of the *Report*. The phenomenon of Lenin's struggle for personal domination was not accidental, he believed, not to be attributed simply to the character of this particular man. It was, in Trotsky's view, the logical consequence of a centralism which emphasized 'control' at the expense of natural growth and development. The confrontation at the Congress, which took the form of elections to the Central Committee and to the *Iskra* editorial board, was thus a confrontation not only between different personalities but between the 'tactics of a normal constitutional structure and the tactics of a state of siege, strengthened by dictatorship'.[26] Not centralism had triumphed in the end but 'egocentrism', not the 'collective principle' but 'narrow practicism'.[27] The Central Committee in its Leninist guise could be expected to exhibit neither 'independent will nor independent thinking'; since 'free initiative', so essential to 'creative work', sometimes led to 'disobedience', creative work too could be expected to disappear. Instead the party would have a Central Committee whose task it would be to act as a 'watchtower' over centralism, 'dissolve opposition' and 'slam shut the doors of the party'. The 'fist' had become the symbol of the party, the 'crowning' act of Lenin's creation.[28] Once again Trotsky returned to the Robespierre analogy, this time with vivid detail:

... the process of self-devourment has begun ... Comrade Lenin has transformed the modest [party] Council into an all-mighty Committee of Public Safety so that he may play the role of an 'incorrupt' Robespierre. All that has stood in the way has had to be swept away so that Comrade Lenin ... could become, through the medium of the Council, the man who unhampered plants a 'republic of virtue and terror'. Robespierre's dictatorship through the Committee of Public Safety was able to keep itself alive, firstly, only by a fixed selection of 'reliable' persons from the Committee itself and, secondly, by replacing the holders of all distinguished state posts with the protégés of the 'Incorruptible'. Otherwise, the omnipotent dictator would have hung in the air. In our caricature Robespierrade, the first condition was attained through the dismissal of the old [*Iskra*] editorial board;

[26] Ibid., p. 21.   [27] Ibid., p. 27.   [28] Ibid., p. 28.

the second was secured immediately through the fixed selection of persons to the first triumvirate of the Central Committee and, afterwards, by passing all the candidates through the filter of 'unanimity' and 'mutual co-operation'. Appointments to all other official posts will depend on the discretion of the Central Committee whose own work is under the vigilant control of the Council. Such, comrades, is the administrative apparatus which must rule over the republic of orthodox 'virtue' and centralist 'terror'.[29]

Trotsky did not believe that Lenin's 'regime' could last for long; like that of the original Robespierre, it too had to collapse because of 'too little bread and too many executions'.[30] The danger, however, was that in the process of falling it would pull down with itself the whole of the party—as Robespierre had pulled down the whole of democracy:

We stand at present before the real danger that the inevitable and approaching downfall of Lenin's 'centralism' will compromise in the eyes of many Russian comrades the idea of centralism in general ... The disappointment which [the regime] will inevitably cause may turn out to be fatal not only for the Robespierres ... of centralism, but also for the idea of a united fighting party organization. Then the masters of the situation will be the 'Thermidorians' of socialist opportunism and the doors of the party will be really wide-open.[31]

Although Trotsky's *Report* was couched in the most strident language and its opposition to Lenin was as uncompromising as could be, even it appeared almost moderate when compared to both the language and content of *Our Political Tasks*. During the one-year interval separating the writing of these pamphlets, Trotsky's wrath did not subside; on the contrary, the 1904 piece shows how inured he had become in his antagonism toward 'Leninism'. While *Our Political Tasks* is full of insights and

---

[29] Ibid., p. 29. In his postscript to *Vtoroi Syezd*, Trotsky replied mockingly to Lenin's complaint at being compared to Robespierre: 'It is a pity he [Lenin] has taken the Robespierre [comparison] in earnest; [our] report . . . spoke only of a caricature Robespierre. The latter differs from its great historical model approximately as a vulgar farce differs from a historic tragedy.' Ibid., p. 33.

[30] Ibid., p. 29.

[31] Ibid., pp. 29–30. In the postscript to the *Report* Trotsky described Lenin's view of the party as constituting a 'trend' within Russian Social Democracy toward 'bureaucratic centralism' (ibid., p. 34). He did not, however, elaborate on the meaning of this term, which would become so relevant many years later (see chapter 10, below). The postscript adds little to the *Report* itself and is couched in purely polemical language.

an uncanny sense of the portents of the 'organizational issue', it is also perhaps the most violent of Trotsky's works. Derogatory epithets abound in it; Lenin, for instance, is described as 'demagogical', 'malicious', 'repulsive'. The whole is unabashedly polemical. Moreover, the work is dedicated to 'my dear teacher Paul Borisovitch Axelrod' and is clearly in part a defence of Menshevism against Bolshevism, though it is the attack on the latter which takes precedence. Once again, therefore, on the issues of party structure and the role of the party, Trotsky found himself identifying with the Mensheviks and this in spite of the fact that, for other reasons, he was at this time in the process of breaking all formal ties with them. Nevertheless, characteristically, his main concern remained that the factional hatchets be buried and that unity be re-established.

In spite of the polemical nature of the work and its vituperative language, it does not lack for a reasoned analysis of the issues involved. In fact, it may be said to begin where the *Report* left off and to develop, as the earlier pamphlet did not, a full theoretical critique of the Leninist conception of the party. Thus where the *Report* only hinted at certain of the theoretical implications of 'Leninism', *Our Political Tasks* declared and argued these openly. The chief of these was that 'Leninism' led directly to conspiracy. Trotsky believed that there now existed a clear danger that Russian Social Democracy would be transformed from a—potentially—mass movement into a clique of conspirators; that, moreover, this clique, without any justification and in a purely arbitrary manner, would declare itself to represent the working class; and that, finally, to the extent that it succeeded in giving the impression that this was what it represented, it would be in a position to 'substitute' itself for that class, thereby bringing about a catastrophe for both Social Democracy and the workers.

Before proceeding, however, to Trotsky's detailed critique of Lenin and Bolshevism it is best to give a brief summary of his own views of party organization and tasks as they emerge in the work. Trotsky's central proposition was the one he had briefly touched upon in the *Report*, namely, that a party organizational structure must be adapted to the movement and not vice versa, and that this structure must be so built as to make possible the widest participation of workers—otherwise the structure would become either redundant or destructive. Trotsky remained, as he continuously repeated, a staunch advocate of centralism but he interpreted centralism to be a system of organizational 'co-ordination' (*soglasovanie*) not a system of organizational rule. He took the main problem of Russian Social Democracy to be, once again, the isolation and dispersal of its branches or local committees. Moreover, he recognized that a Social Democratic movement as such did not yet exist—between the intellectual leadership and the working class there had been only the most rudimentary of contact, much less union. The tasks of organization were therefore twofold: firstly, to create the kind of central coordination which would overcome the limitations of purely local activities; secondly, to create the kind of organization which was best equipped both to reach the workers and bring them to identify themselves with the party. As we shall presently see, his opposition to Lenin grew out of the conviction that the latter's principles of party organization would not only not serve these objectives but would undermine them. He was, in short, a proponent of a mass movement because only such a movement seemed to him to be politically realistic while all other substitutes were either doomed to fail or, at best, could only succeed as non-Marxist, non-working-class movements.

Trotsky did not exclude the possibility that the workers' movement for social and economic change might develop outside the confines of the Social Democratic party. In fact, the fear that this is precisely what might happen pervades *Our Political Tasks*. Partly, the danger of this arose, in his view, from the overly cautious and restrained trends within Social Democracy. While this would be one of the main themes of his later works, it was already broached here.[32] This was the basis for Trotsky's criticism of 'Economism', as it had been, of course, for Lenin as well.[33] At the same time, he saw the danger of alienating the workers as attributable also to purely organi-

---

[32] It should be remembered that at the time he wrote *Nashi Politicheskye Zadachi* the idea of the permanent revolution had not yet occurred to him. Only towards the very end of 1904 and the beginning of 1905 did he begin to formulate this idea and only then did he begin to denounce systematically the 'minimalist' tendencies of Social Democracy.

[33] For his rejection of 'Economism', see in particular pp. 6–14 and 27–39 of *Nashi Politicheskye Zadachi*.

zational mistakes. The problem could be stated as one of mobilization: how to organize direct support amongst a population which was ripe for political activity but lacked political experience? That such ripeness was not of itself a sufficient guarantee for success could be seen, according to Trotsky, in the well-intentioned but wrong-headed approach of the 'Economists'. Eschewing direct political organization for piecemeal economic reforms through existing institutions, they were beginning to lag behind the political consciousness of the workers themselves. Unlike Lenin, Trotsky was prepared to admit that 'Economism' had initially a useful role to play: at a time when the workers had no conception whatever of the possibilities of organizing and campaigning for reform, those of the 'Economists' who went amongst them had succeeded in spreading the elementary ideas of organization.[34] This served at least to awaken the workers from their apathy. But once awakened their pace of development was so rapid as to outstrip the 'Economist' idea of trade-unionism. Moreover, their importance as a social force had grown so greatly that it was precisely political activity which was now paramount. 'Economism' was as a consequence becoming irrelevant. The real danger, however, was that Social Democracy as a whole would be left behind because it could not keep pace with the spontaneous growth of a radical, revolutionary consciousness among the masses. Under such circumstances, the revolution might catch Social Democracy 'unawares ... unprepared ... in a political sleep which could turn into political death'.[35]

The alternative to 'Economism', however, was not the other extreme, an organization so politicized as to exclude all but the most professional of revolutionaries. The Leninist approach was self-defeating: preparing themselves for revolution, the Bolsheviks would have no one to fight it with once it came. The very opposite of this approach was now required: not the exclusion of the mass of workers but their inclusion, not a stringent organizational framework but one loose enough to embrace all those who were its potential allies. If the party closed its doors to the workers, the latter would only 'turn their backs on us'. This 'tragic prospect' could be avoided only by 'consolidating our political, moral and organizational ties with the con-

[34] Ibid., pp. 6–14.   [35] Ibid., p. 85.

scious elements of the working class'.[36] The principal task of the party, therefore, was nothing less than the creation, within its own walls, of a mass movement.

The methods which Trotsky proposed to achieve this objective suggest how sympathetic he in fact was to the spirit, if not the letter, of 'Economism'. He would have no truck, of course, with their 'economic' outlook nor with what he took to be their political naïveté, their gradualism, their cautiousness, their fundamentally non-revolutionary character. But he placed the same stress on direct contact with, and work amongst the proletariat, on the priorities which must be assigned to propaganda and education, and on the need for involving the workers in the day-to-day work of the party. In fact, he was so extremely devoted to, and optimistic about, these methods as to appear himself to be somewhat innocent-minded. Perhaps the exaggerated emphasis which he gave to these tactics should be attributed to the context within which it was presented: he was arguing with Lenin and Lenin seemed to him to have abandoned completely the workers themselves. In this sense, Trotsky's exhortations were intended to remind the party what Marxist socialism was all about. Thus it was both in the hope of revolutionary success and 'in the name of Marxism' that he admonished the party to keep clearly in mind that the fundamental basis of its movement was the proletariat. The assimilation of Marxism amongst the intelligentsia was only a beginning, a pre-condition for the further development of a Marxist movement. The only sufficient condition for its growth, and one that could not be replaced by organizational manipulation, was a 'politically developed proletariat'.[37] To this end the tasks of education were central and their potential benefits two-fold: in the course of actively aiding the workers to develop their awareness both of themselves and of the world around them, the party would gather direct support amongst them. The process of education would naturally result in a broad mobilization. Unfortunately this was the very task which the party was either forgetting or relegating to the sphere of lip-service:

I remember the times [when] the propagandist set himself the goal of making clear to the worker ... his [the worker's] place in the

[36] Ibid., p. 67.   [37] Ibid., p. 23.

universe. The propagandist began with cosmology. Then he separated, happily, man from ape. Proceeding through the history of culture he reached (with difficulty) capitalism, then socialism. The basic idea of all this was to turn the simple proletarian into a Social Democrat imbued with a complete materialistic world outlook. Today, this re-spectable doctrinairism is already out of fashion, and much for-gotten—re-emerging, as it would appear, only in its most miserable caricatured form.[38]

Many of the pages of *Our Political Tasks* were therefore devoted to the need for educating the masses.[39] Throughout, this exhortation was accompanied by a recognition that work amongst the proletariat must have as its purpose not only peda-gogic results but political ones as well.[40] The education of workers was, for Trotsky, a commitment to involving them directly in the activities and decisions of the party. The similari-ties which have often been drawn between Trotsky and Rosa Luxemburg are, in the light at least of the 1904 pamphlet, well-founded. Here too a boundless, almost naïve, romantic optim-ism characterized Trotsky's views on worker participation, so much so, in fact, that one may be permitted to wonder whether he was not exaggerating intentionally in order to offset Lenin's opposite extremism. Whatever the case, there can be no doubt about Trotsky's fundamental orientation. He was completely committed to the idea of mass participation, both as a Marxist and as a revolutionary, and he saw in it the only sure road to success. 'The *self-activity* (*samodiatelnost*) of the proletariat', he wrote at one point, 'has become a living slogan and, let us hope, that in the future it will be rejuvenating.'[41] Elsewhere, he went so far as to predicate the legitimacy of party decisions on rank-and-file consent: 'It is essential that each of our principal de-cisions be their [the workers'] decision.'[42] 'Active participation of all' (*aktivnoe uchastie vsiekh*) was a phrase he stressed fre-quently[43] and the 'collective struggle of the proletariat'[44] was

[38] Ibid., p. 84. In the paragraph which follows he added: 'The great but doctrinaire task of explaining to the worker his place in the divine macrocosm has been transformed into the succinct bureaucratic idea: explaining to the member of the organization his place in the Leninist microcosm.'

[39] See in particular ibid., pp. 42–6.

[40] See in particular the section on pp. 46–50 which is entitled 'From Pedagogy to Tactics'.

[41] Ibid., p. 47.   [42] Ibid., p. 67.

[43] See, for instance, ibid., pp. 81 and 82.   [44] Ibid., p. 74.

a slogan he meant to be taken literally. He was aware of the need for discipline and did not question the crucial nature of its importance but he rejected a mechanical form of discipline which turned the individual into a robot and which sought to incorporate the kind of obedience characteristic of the capitalist factory production system or of the 'barracks regime': 'The task of Social Democracy should be to set the proletariat against a system of discipline which replaces the working of human thought by the rhythm of physical movements.'[45] It is no exaggeration, therefore, to attribute to Trotsky a position which was in all fundamentals compatible with a democratic view of party organization; and he himself stressed throughout, that that which was essential above all to the further development of the Social Democratic movement was the democratization of party life.[46]

He did not see, however, any contradiction between this objective and the organization of the party on the principles of centralism. Again, he took centralism to be an instrumental arrangement, a 'technical' method of organizing party work so as to get around the special difficulties of constructing a political movement in a country such as Russia. 'The task of the present decisive moment', he wrote, 'consists in this: to gather together all organized elements now in existence, uniting them for the purpose of systematic and centralized, not scattered and dispersed work.'[47] At present, according to Trotsky, Russian Social Democracy was not so much a party as a loose association of local organizations and committees. Though ostensibly all these marched under the same banner and subscribed to the principles of unity, in fact most of the time the one did not know what the other was doing. The situation was aggravated by the necessarily clandestine nature of their activities. Action on a national scope was thus limited, and the movement was weakened not so much by ideological as by geographical division. But this was precisely the kind of problem which could be rectified by organizational means. Centralism was, therefore, a way, firstly, for creating a national headquarters; secondly, for erecting the kind of administrative

[45] Loc. cit.
[46] See in particular the sub-section on pp. 64–9, entitled 'Democratism'.
[47] Ibid., pp. 85–6.

mechanism which, through its permanent contact with all organizations, could quickly and efficiently coordinate among them. Finally, its task was to concern itself with over-all planning and supervision and to provide leadership from the centre.[48]

But all this was to be subject to the principle that local organizations retained as far as possible an independent status. The task of the central organization was to bring about unity but not through compulsion and regimentation. It was as much incumbent upon the party's national institutions to adapt themselves to the local ones as it was for the latter to aspire to work within the context of the over-all movement. Nor was it in the interest of the party Central Committee to take over the function of the local committees; on the contrary, the retention of initiative as well as primary authority by local committees were points which Trotsky stressed in particular. He believed that the vitality of the movement could be assured only if it flowed from below upwards, from those who were in closest and most frequent contact with the wide membership of the party. To impose authority from above was to make sterile the whole organism and to sever it from the realities of its environment. Finally, the aim of centralism was not to create authority and power but to erect an institutional framework which would make possible 'collective-coordinated' action and methods of struggle. Centralism as such could provide only the technical aids for the realization of this aim; its ultimate attainment 'lay along the road of struggle, errors, education—not in the "factory school" but in the school of political life . . .'.[49] 'Active participation' was therefore a fundamental and indispensable feature of this centralism. 'Of course', Trotsky added, 'I am talking about a "European" centralism and not about an autocratic "Asiatic" centralism. The latter does not *presuppose* but rather *excludes* such participation.'[50]

(b) 'Substitutionism'

Although in *Our Political Tasks* Trotsky was concerned with formulating a position of his own on party organizational issues,

---

[48] Trotsky's views on centralism are scattered throughout the pamphlet; but see in particular the section 'Organizational Problems', pp. 57–90.
[49] Ibid., p. 74.   [50] Ibid., p. 81.

it was his criticism and refutation of 'Leninism' which occupied a central place in the pamphlet. The whole work was in fact an argument with Lenin—sometimes crude, often extreme and always passionate. But beneath the polemics, beneath the almost violent language and the personal denigration of Lenin, there lay a critique which even today, and perhaps especially today when the subsequent evolution of Bolshevism is a matter of common historical knowledge, constitutes the most cogent analysis—dissection would perhaps be a more appropriate word—of the Bolshevik phenomenon. In 1904, when Bolshevism still appeared to be not so much an independent force as the heresy of a single man, it was possible to react to Trotsky's pamphlet as if it were just another diatribe, just another addition to the Menshevik arsenal. And, of course, such diatribes were not lacking; Trotsky's was among the first but it was one of many and the others also pointed to the anti-democratic, the élitist, the conspiratorial elements or tendencies in Bolshevism. Today, however, although *Our Political Tasks* remains one of Trotsky's most neglected works—it has, for instance, never been translated into English, not even by Trotsky's contemporary followers (perhaps *because* of its anti-Leninism)—its partisan features are less important than the insight it provides into the nature of what is in many ways a specifically twentieth-century phenomenon—the revolutionary political party in the age of democratic universal ideologies. Far from lacking an understanding of organizational questions, of the relationship between party and power—a charge often made against him[51]—Trotsky here revealed an acute grasp of the power which such a party may accumulate, and of the manner in which it may degenerate precisely because it presumed to speak in the name of a democratic, mass ideology. His critique of Bolshevism raised the specific issue of organizational techniques as well as the wider issues of the autonomy of political action and the role of intellectuals in politics.

The issue between Menshevism and Bolshevism, according to Trotsky, came down to this: who will constitute the core of the Social Democratic movement, the workers themselves or

[51] For a particularly crude example of this kind of criticism of Trotsky, which is often accompanied by an *ex post facto* justification of Leninism, see Nicolas Krassó, 'Trotsky's Marxism', *New Left Review*, no. 44, 1967, pp. 64–86.

the party leadership? The issue was ostensibly one of organizational tactics but in fact, he believed, it involved the character of the whole movement. It was not just a matter of which approach offered the best prospect of success—though this was certainly a major consideration—but whether the choice of one approach over another would not lead to a transformation of revolutionary goals. Trotsky thought that it must do so, that here the means used must affect the ends.[52] The object of the Social Democratic movement was not revolution as such but a socialist revolution. The essence of Marxism was that the character of a revolution was governed by the social character of those who were its makers. A socialist revolution was the work of the proletariat; it was its 'objective conditions', its consciousness, its vision of the future, which determined the content of socialism. Moreover, a socialist revolution presupposed a commitment to the principles of a real, not fictional, democracy: equality, freedom of choice, self-determination and liberation from the hierarchical power structures which have characterized societies heretofore. These elements of the future socialist society had to be already embodied within the organization of the movement which aspired to that society. An organization which failed to incorporate these ideals into its structure, was an organization whose ideals were at odds with socialism. An organization which adopted the principles of hierarchy and division of labour, while paying merely lip service to socialist principles, would perpetuate them also in the event that it succeeded. The end result, according to Trotsky, would be that not a socialist revolution, but one only purporting to be socialist, would emerge.

These views were at the basis of Trotsky's attack on the methods of organization advocated by Lenin. According to Trotsky, what was at stake in the controversy with Lenin was not so much the system of organization but the working class itself. To adopt the tactics proposed by Bolshevism was, in effect, to subscribe to the view that the workers were no more than a hindrance to revolution, and in general an irrelevancy. What Lenin was demanding was nothing less than their neutralization so that the party, or rather its select leadership, could pursue the business of revolution without interference from sup-

[52] *Nashi Politicheskye Zadachi*, p. 67.

posedly unreliable and inexperienced elements. The workers to Lenin were an unpredictable, uncontrollable mass; their ideological and political consciousness was limited, their capacity for organized activity was sporadic and their understanding of the realities of political struggle was governed by narrow class interests. Thus the basis of the Marxist movement, the class upon which Marx had placed the hopes of the future, now emerged as an undifferentiated mass which, were it to take an active part in the revolutionary struggle, would only complicate matters for those who were involved in revolution in a full-time capacity. It was the latter, the professionals, the experts, the trained revolutionaries who, for Lenin, constituted the agents of revolution. Thus if Lenin were to have his way, the workers would be replaced by a band of professional revolutionaries, dedicated, disciplined, obedient and above all, subject to no control. The organization of the party would become autonomous, almost sovereign, a power unto itself; the function of the proletariat would be to remain passive except when called upon by the organization to demonstrate its support and solidarity. In effect, therefore, what Lenin was advocating was to 'substitute' the working class by a narrow political instrument which would take it upon itself to speak in the name of Marxism and in the name of the workers themselves. This system of organization Trotsky called 'substitutionism' (*zamestitelstvo*). It stood in direct opposition to the system of organization traditionally identified with Marxism and now represented in Russia by Menshevism:

The difference between these systems ... is decisive in defining the character of our party's work. In one case, we have a system of *thinking for* the proletariat, of the political *substitution* of the proletariat; in the other, a system of *educating* politically the proletariat, *mobilizing* it, so that it may exercise effective pressure on the will of all groups and parties. These two systems produce political results which are, objectively, totally different.[53]

Under the pretence of guarding the 'orthodox purity' of the movement, the system of 'substitutionism' would have the effect, according to Trotsky, of 'undermining the very foundations'

[53] Ibid., p. 50. This paragraph begins a sub-section titled: 'Away with political substitutionism!'

of the movement.[54] Lacking all confidence in the ability of the workers to become a conscious social force, it appropriated their tasks, sacrificed in advance the objectives of co-operation between party and masses, and then presumed to speak in the name of 'our proletariat'.[55] This in itself was bad enough, but what was even worse was the fact that thereby the whole purpose of a party was made redundant: 'substitutionism' assumed that 'objective interests' functioned in a mechanical way, that once called upon to give their support the workers would automatically fall into line and that there was thus no need to prepare them for the decisive moment. In fact, 'objective interests' were only a beginning; they had to be translated into operational terms:

> Marxism teaches that the interests of the proletariat are determined by the objective conditions of its existence. These interests are so powerful and ineluctable that they ultimately compel the proletariat to make them traverse its field of conscience, that is, to turn the realization of their *objective* interests into a *subjective* interest. Between these two factors—the objective fact of the proletariat's class interest and its·subjective conscience—lies the road of the blows and setbacks of life, of errors and disappointments, of fluctuations and defeats. The tactical wisdom of the tasks of the proletarian party is situated entirely between these two factors and consists in shortening and making easier the road which lies between them.[56]

The method of 'substitutionism' was thus a 'simplification' of revolutionary tactics. But that it should have emerged in the Russian Social Democratic movement was not accidental but rather a reflection of the special difficulties of that movement. The greater the distance between objective and subjective interests, that is, the 'weaker the political culture of the proletariat', the greater the temptation to seek a simpler, shorter route to power.[57] Although it was the antithesis of 'Economism', 'substitutionism' shared with the latter a similar despair about the Russian working class:[58] both assumed that Russian workers were incapable of political action, were limited by their primitive beginnings, and governed by purely immediate needs. 'Economism' as a result had sought to concentrate on

---

[54] Ibid., p. 67.   [55] Ibid., p. 51.
[56] Ibid., p. 52.   [57] Ibid., p. 53.
[58] Trotsky's comparison of 'Economism' with 'substitutionism' is on pp. 53–4.

exclusively 'subjective interests', unmediated by the ultimate 'objective' condition of the workers; thus its approach had been non-political, consisting merely of the piecemeal alleviation of immediate deprivations. Bolshevik 'substitutionism', on the other hand, had simply taken for granted the universal 'objective' interests of workers but without pursuing its corollary, the translation of such interests into a conscious, subjective aspiration. It therefore 'substituted' itself for the workers: the required unity of 'objective' and 'subjective' being, in its view, impossible on the mass level, it was nevertheless sufficiently fulfilled if it existed among a select leadership. Thus, in the Bolshevik case, instead of 'economists' there were 'politicists' who took it upon themselves to act in the name of the masses. Nevertheless, in spite of the entirely different conclusions each had arrived at in the sphere of tactics, both represented a symptom of pessimism and despair about the workers, both 'recoiled before the "distance" which separates objective interests from subjective ones'.[59] In the end, according to Trotsky, both abandoned the whole problem of tactics: the one by choosing to avoid politics, the other by choosing to restrict politics to professionals. Both manifested a 'sort of *passivity* in the face of the colossal tactical difficulties'[60] which confronted the Social Democratic movement. Finally, the 'political self-denial of the "Economists", like the "political substitutionism" of their antipodes, were nothing else than the attempt of a young Social Democratic party "to play tricks" with history': 'If the "Economists" have sought to flee from the enormity of their tasks by assigning themselves the humble role of marching *at the tail of history*, the "politicists" have resolved the problem by striving to transform history *into their own tail*.'[61]

The method of 'substitutionism' was, in other words, an attempt to find a short-cut to success. Instead of undertaking the difficult but necessary task of surmounting the 'distance' between objective class interests and their conscious, subjective assimilation, the 'substitutionists' wanted to circumvent it entirely. In Trotsky's view, however, the short-cut was an illusion; the fact that the Russian proletariat was less developed than its Western counterparts, meant only that the educational and organizational tasks of the Russian party were that much more

[59] Ibid., p. 54.   [60] Ibid., p. 53.   [61] Ibid., p. 54.

essential.[62] To succumb to the temptation of 'thinking for' the
workers was to become reconciled to a narrow, sectarian movement, lacking a fundamental mass basis. It is clear that Trotsky
not only believed that the 'substitutionist' approach was bound
to lead to failure but that it was an evil in itself. It gave the
party a conspiratorial image, it undermined its social mission
of educating the workers, it cut off its social roots, it created
the false impression that politics constituted an independent,
autonomous area of activity, unrelated to what was happening
in society itself. The way of 'conspiracy', Trotsky declared, was
not the way of a movement which sought the self-realization
of a social class rather than the satisfaction of the political ambitions of certain individuals with particularist interests.[63] If
Social Democracy was to succeed it had to succeed as a mass
movement; if it pursued the way of 'substitutionism' it would
either fail or it would succeed as a party which had jettisoned
Social Democracy.[64] If it abandoned the workers it would have
separated '*revolutionary* activity from *socialist* activity'.[65]

As for inner-party democracy itself, it would be, in Trotsky's
view, the first victim of 'substitutionism'. The notions of discipline and division of work propagated by Lenin constituted an
extension of these methods of organization as they existed in
bourgeois society.[66] The same hierarchical, non-democratic,
power-oriented system of organization which was endemic to
class society pervaded the Bolshevik conception of centralism.
As in the former, so in the latter, the division of labour based
on expertise and professionalism perpetuated the alienation
of work from its social context. In place of social education
it encouraged merely technical education. Party members
became functionaries and the organization as a whole was
transformed into a 'bureaucratic' structure.[67] The question of

[62] Less than a year later, as we have seen, Trotsky would argue that the special conditions prevailing in Russia had in fact made the Russian workers more revolutionary,
more 'conscious' than those in the West. See chapter 4, pp. 118ff., above.
[63] Ibid., p. 58.
[64] See pp. 58–9 where Trotsky implies that Lenin's tactics have begun to resemble those
of the Socialist-Revolutionaries.
[65] Ibid., p. 64.
[66] See the sub-section on pp. 59–64 for Trotsky's identification of Lenin's division of
labour with that prevailing in capitalist society.
[67] See ibid., p. 84 where Trotsky hints at the same notion of 'bureaucratic centralism'
which he had first suggested in *Vtoroi Syezd* (see note 31, above).

external tactics was here directly related to internal organization; Lenin's centralism, having first excluded the possibility
of building a mass party, would instead make possible only a
self-enclosed, self-perpetuating organizational clique seeking to
dominate and manipulate the movement as a whole. It would
become a system for instituting the principle of authority. And
its consequence would be authoritarianism; having once
embraced the idea of 'substitutionism', Lenin would not stop
until he had made it pervasive. It was in this context that one
of Trotsky's most famous observations appeared:

In inner-party politics, these methods [of Lenin] lead, as we shall yet
see, to this: the party organization substitutes itself for the party, the
Central Committee substitutes itself for the organization and, finally,
a 'dictator' substitutes himself for the Central Committee.[68]

(c) *Jacobinism*

The final chapter of *Our Political Tasks* is entitled 'Jacobinism
and Social Democracy' and it constitutes the most far-reaching
projection of the implications of Leninism. The idea that Lenin
was emerging as a Russian Robespierre had already struck
Trotsky, as we have seen, when he wrote his *Report* of 1903.
But there he had used it primarily as an analogy, by way of
illustrating a point; here he analysed the full meaning of Jacobinism as a political and social phenomenon re-appearing in
the context of Russian Social Democracy. His target was the
notion that there was some common ground between Jacobinism and Social Democracy, a notion expressed in Lenin's
famous statement that 'a revolutionary Social Democrat is a
Jacobin who is indissolubly bound to the organization of the
proletariat and aware of its class interests'.[69] In this single sentence Lenin had summarized his characteristic approach to the
relationship between social doctrine and revolutionary practice: the former defined the goals of the latter but not its
methods. Practice grew not so much out of doctrine as out of
the realities of politics. That a socialist revolutionary could
adopt the methods of a bourgeois revolutionary was due to the
fact that there were certain universal constants in the making

---

[68] Ibid., p. 54.
[69] Trotsky opens the final chapter, p. 90, by citing this statement by Lenin.

of revolutions; the social content of revolutions may change but their methods remained essentially the same.

Yet this was precisely the notion which Trotsky rejected and was determined to refute. Doctrine (or ideology) and practice—organization, tactics, and so on—were not only related, in his view, but mutually dependent; a Social Democrat could no more be a Jacobin than a French Jacobin could have been—or a Russian 'Jacobin' could be today—a Social Democrat. The two exclude and contradict each other; the practice of the one grows as much out of proletarian socialism as that of the other grows out of bourgeois capitalism. Thus, Trotsky declared, a 'Jacobin-Social-Democrat' was an impossible hybrid; inevitably he would be more Jacobin than Social Democrat. A choice had to be made: either 'Jacobin *or* Social Democrat', a choice between 'two worlds, two doctrines, two tactics, two mentalities, separated by an abyss'.[70]

The final chapter was therefore devoted to an analysis of the distinguishing features of Jacobinism and Social Democracy. Trotsky took these titles to represent social and historical categories, not politically autonomous universals. They had their roots both in the possibilities and limitations created by a particular historical context. They were as distant from one another as the realities of the twentieth century were distant from the realities of the eighteenth:

Jacobinism is not a supra-social 'revolutionary' category but a historical product. Jacobinism is the highest moment reached by the tension of revolutionary energy during the epoch of the self-emancipation of bourgeois society. It is the maximum radicalism which could be produced by bourgeois society—not by the development of its internal contradictions but by the suppression and stifling of these: in theory, by appealing to the rights of the abstract man and the abstract citizen, in practice, with the help of the guillotine.[71]

The Jacobins, Trotsky continued, had been Utopians and idealists. They wanted to establish an egalitarian republic on the foundations of private property, and a republic of reason and virtue within the framework of class exploitation. And when the contradictions inherent in these juxtapositions became overwhelming, they activated the guillotine. For them

[70] *Nashi Politicheskye Zadachi*, p. 93 and repeated on p. 95.
[71] Ibid., p. 91.

the principles of universal morality had the force of an absolute 'Idea', an absolute 'Truth'. And they believed that 'no heta- comb could be spared in building a pedestal for this "Truth"'. Their 'absolute belief in a metaphysical idea' was accompanied by an 'absolute disbelief in living people'. The inevitable result of this was suspicion towards the outside world and degenera- tion within their own ranks. Lacking all understanding of the mechanism of social processes, they could not see that the social forces which had been liberated by revolution could be sup- pressed not by the guillotine but only if history were to come to an end. But far from ending, history continued to play out its drama in accordance with the clash of contradictions newly released by the events which began in 1789.[72]

'How different', Trotsky exclaimed, 'from this historical fate [of Jacobinism] is the fate of Social Democracy, the party of such optimistic perspectives.'[73] The future of this party rested not on idealism, much less on Utopianism, not on some meta- physical truth, but on the very realities of social developments. It drew its support not from an abstract idea but a concrete, living class. It sought not to suppress or even close its eyes to social contradictions, but to allow them to work themselves out fully. Here lay the distinction between the fictional consent of bourgeois society and the real struggle for liberation which was at the core of revolutionary socialism. The Jacobin suspected social antagonism; the Social Democrats accepted it as the in- evitable feature of the pre-socialist society. That which finally had led to the decay of Jacobinism—the inescapable reality of conflict—was the source of the strength and confidence of Social Democracy.[74] The diametrically opposed differences between the two were expressed both in thought and in practice:

They [the Jacobins] were Utopians; we aspire to express objective tendencies. They were idealists from foot to head; we are materialists from head to foot. They were rationalists, we are dialecticians. They believed in the saving force of a supra-class truth before which all should kneel. We believe only in the class force of the revolutionary proletariat. . . . Their method was to guillotine the slightest deviations, ours is to overcome differences ideologically and politically. They cut off heads, we enlighten them with class consciousness.[75]

[72] Ibid., p. 92.
[74] Ibid., p. 93.
[73] Loc. cit.
[75] Ibid., pp. 93–4.

Trotsky's contrasts, it is obvious, resembled more that between two 'ideal types' than actual realities. Certainly, in spite of Trotsky's protestations of realism, his comparison contained an idealization of Social Democracy. But whatever its exaggerations, it made clear, at least, what Trotsky's own view of good and evil was. His denunciation of political 'decapitation', as he called it, and by which he meant not only physical terror but the methods of expulsion and purge as well, was uncompromising. The way to real unity, for him, was through the free clash of ideas, not the beheading or excommunication of opponents. The latter methods he considered not only repugnant, but folly: 'Hydra's heads', he remarked, 'sprout continually anew and such as contain the ideas of virtue and truth, as defined by the executioners, become rarer and rarer.'[76]

Yet this digression into historical comparison served only as an introduction to Trotsky's main purpose in the final chapter of *Our Political Tasks*. This purpose was to show that far from being a historical curiosity, Jacobinism was a phenomenon which as a *political*, if not social, force could be resurrected. Though having nothing to do with Social Democracy, it appeared as a threatening tendency in all revolutionary movements. This is the most interesting aspect of what Trotsky had to say here; for although he was much too sanguine about the ultimate defeat of this tendency, he grasped fully its endemic character. Despite all the superior qualities which he attributed to Social Democracy, it too was susceptible to Jacobinism. What followed, therefore, was the most extreme condemnation of the 'new Jacobins' and the 'new Robespierre': the Bolsheviks and Lenin.

The characteristics of Jacobinism which Trotsky assigned to Lenin and the Bolsheviks all bore, he said, the stamp of the original: suspiciousness, doctrinairism, intolerance, the thirst for power, the propensity to use the hammer where a gavel would do and, finally, the overwhelming ambition to retain absolute control over purity of thought and unity of action. But French Jacobinism, Trotsky remarked, at least had the fascination which derives from originality. The new Jacobinism, being a re-enactment of the old, struck him as a caricature, a parody of an already witnessed drama. And this in spite, perhaps even

[76] Ibid., p. 94.

because, of its different, Russian setting. Indeed, everything about Bolshevism and Lenin seemed inflated and exaggerated to Trotsky. Robespierre's aphorism—'I know only two parties, the good and the bad citizens'—was, according to Trotsky, 'engraved on the heart of Maximilian Lenin ... in a crude form'.[77] Speaking of Lenin's distrust of those around him, Trotsky wrote: 'This malicious and morally repulsive suspiciousness of Lenin [is] a flat caricature of the tragic intolerance of Jacobinism.'[78]

But it is not Trotsky's personal aesthetic sensitivities, of course, which need concern us here. What is far more important is the political danger which he saw inherent in Bolshevism. He believed that unless the methods of Lenin and his followers were denounced and rejected, in fact exorcised, by the party, it would live under the threat of 'complete decay—political, moral and theoretical'.[79] He did not believe that Bolshevism could triumph as a true representative of the working class but he did not underestimate its capacity for destroying Social Democracy as the movement of the workers. It was precisely because Lenin had wedded Jacobinism to Social Democracy that, in Trotsky's view, the latter stood in danger of degenerating. For him it was a marriage of two incompatibles: the theory and methods of bourgeois radicalism gone wild, with the theory and methods of socialist radicalism imbedded in democratic principles. The whole point about Social Democracy was that its approach to organization and tactics, as well as its confidence in its ultimate success, were based on the fundamental axiom that a workers' movement was the product of education, struggle, development, the free and open competition of ideas. Instead Bolshevism appeared as the offshoot of the manipulative, élitist mind. Seeing enemies everywhere, almost paranoiac in its attitude toward dissension, it sought to liquidate all differences of opinion—not through the natural process of coexistence and conciliation but through 'decapitation'. Lenin thought that there was only one truth and he was its guardian; and if only everyone were to see this, how much simpler everything would be.[80] This utter self-conviction, this complete belief in one's self-righteousness to the exclusion of the legitimacy of

[77] Ibid., p. 96.
[79] Loc. cit.
[78] Ibid., p. 98.
[80] Ibid., pp. 96 and 97.

all other viewpoints, was to Trotsky the pretext upon which a new wave of terror would be launched. What was at stake here was not only the rightness or wrongness of Lenin's own views—this was an issue unto itself and Trotsky had already expressed his opinion on Bolshevik centralism and 'substitution-ism'—but the very principles which were to govern the internal political life of the party. More specifically, the issue was whether the party of Social Democracy could tolerate within its midst a 'regime of terror' headed by a 'dictator'.[81] If it could, if it would, then it had to realize that the end would be not only a dictatorship over the party but a 'dictatorship over the proletariat'.[82] Citing the programmes of Lenin's followers in the Urals, Trotsky argued that Marx's concept of the dictatorship *of* the proletariat was now being interpreted as a dictatorship *over* the proletariat.[83] And this was not 'simply a local Ural absurdity... a curiosity';[84] it confirmed the worst prediction made about Bolshevism before the appearance of the Ural example and it was a 'symptom' of the serious danger threatening the party as a whole:

... the dictatorship over the proletariat [means] not the self-activity of the working class which has taken into its hands the destinies of society, but a 'powerful, commanding organization', ruling over the proletariat and, through it, over society, thus securing presumably the transition to socialism.[85]

The prophetic element in this, as in so much of the pamphlet, is too obvious to need commenting upon. Similarly uncanny was Trotsky's perception that the 'substitution of the dictator-ship of the proletariat' went hand in hand with the 'logic of Blanquism';[86] and this tendency towards the 'conspiratorial seizure of power' Trotsky also attributed to the 'political back-wardness' of Russia which made its revolutionaries 'more susceptible to Jacobinism than to reformism'.[87] This was the corollary of his earlier observation that the distance between the proletariat's 'objective interests' and its 'subjective, con-

---

[81] Ibid., p. 97.

[82] 'Dictatorship over the proletariat' is the title of the second and last sub-section, pp. 101–7, of the final chapter. Trotsky would use this same phrase many years later in the context of Stalinism (see chapter 10, below).

[83] Ibid., pp. 101–2.   [84] Ibid., p. 106.   [85] Ibid., p. 102.

[86] Loc. cit.   [87] Ibid., p. 104.

scious' ones was so wide in Russia as to cause despair amongst Social Democrats. This was, he hinted, the source of the Jacobin, as well as the Blanquist, danger. In these last pages of *Our Political Tasks*, Trotsky also hinted at a phenomenon which would become central to his later views of the problems of party organization and leadership: this was the phenomenon of the particular attraction which Jacobin and Blanquist conspiracy and opportunism had for the Russian intelligentsia, and the latter's 'impatience' with the longer, tiring process of educating and preparing the working class for revolution.[88]

Dedication to the latter process remained his own 'credo'. He repeated again that there was no short-cut to the success of Marxist socialism except through the conscious self-mobilization of large numbers of workers for the revolutionary struggle. And the pre-condition for this was, as he emphasized again in a final plea for tolerance and diversity, a movement which was open to a wide spectrum of ideas, however at odds they might be one with another, and which welcomed 'competition ... between different trends within socialism'.[89]

As to the ultimate fate of the relationship between the Social Democratic party and the working class, Trotsky was confident that the latter would not allow itself to be manipulated: '*A proletariat capable of dictatorship over society will not tolerate a dictatorship over itself.*'[90] He believed that the party, temporarily diverted from its proper course by the machinations of Lenin, would eventually return to its true tasks, would re-adjust itself by forging close and inextricable bonds with the workers. It therefore emerges that his warnings about the hazards of Bolshevism were not, in fact, prophecies which he himself thought would be fulfilled. At the very least, he could not imagine the triumph of Bolshevism as a socialist, Marxist movement; why this could not be he had amply shown in his analysis of the fundamental incompatibility between Social Democracy and Jacobinism. What he had not shown, however, was why, as he further believed, Bolshevism as such was bound to collapse. Some thirteen years later he himself would stand, together with Lenin, at the head of a triumphant Bolshevism. Yet *Our Political Tasks*

[88] Ibid., pp. 104 and 106. Trotsky's attitude toward intellectuals in revolutionary politics is discussed later in this chapter.
[89] Ibid., p. 105.   [90] Loc. cit. (italics added).

ends with the prediction that the Bolsheviks, the purveyors of
the 'organizational fetish', will inevitably disintegrate.[91] This
conclusion is very much at odds with the rest of the pamphlet.
Imbued with a historical optimism which would mislead him
in the future as well, Trotsky had in the end forsaken that more
realistic intuition which was also a quality of his mind and
which had otherwise characterized and informed his polemic
of 1904.

2. 1905 and After

Our Political Tasks opened with a preface which Trotsky wrote
towards the end of August 1904, immediately prior to the publication of the pamphlet and some months after the text itself
had apparently been completed. By then Lenin's ascendancy
in the party had been considerably halted; his faction had
suffered reverses and it seemed that the danger of Bolshevism
had been rolled back. Trotsky's preface made note of this fact
and celebrated what its author hoped would be the end of internecine warfare. He now called for consolidation and systematic
work; but far from gloating over the apparent recovery of Menshevism he argued that it should liquidate itself as a faction.
The schisms of the past should be buried for ever and one united
Social Democratic party resurrected, not identified with any
one narrow trend but representing the over-all outlook of Social
Democracy.[92]

The 'conciliator' in Trotsky was thus immediately at work.[93]
But the split in the party was more embedded than he imagined
and, as the coming years were to show, all his efforts would
come to naught. In the meantime, however, events outside the
party were beginning to transform the political environment
in which it existed. Within a matter of months, it seemed to
Trotsky, the dream of a radical working class was on its way
to becoming a reality. What was both puzzling and encouraging was that in so far as such a reality was taking shape, it was
doing so independently of the party. Trotsky's assumption had
been—and it was an assumption shared by all Social Demo-

---

[91] Ibid., p. 107.   [92] Ibid., pp. viii–ix.
[93] Trotsky's 'conciliationism' came to the fore particularly after 1907; see below, pp.
213–14.

crats—that the radicalization of the workers would be a slow and drawn-out process. And he took it for granted that the party would play a central role in this process. Now it appeared clear to him that it was neither dependent on the party nor was it the goal of an unspecified future. As we have seen, this new reality immediately took his mind away from party matters; for the first time he turned to a systematic analysis of Russian society, an analysis which ended with the theory of the permanent revolution. This, for him, constituted the unlocking of the puzzle and a justification for the encouragement he felt. He now had to admit, in contrast to what he still thought at the time of writing *Our Political Tasks*, that the objective conditions of the Russian working class were such as to make the prospects of revolution more, rather than less, realistic than those of the European revolution. In the course of his analysis of Russian conditions, he began to perceive also that the main problem of the Social Democratic movement would be not to pull the workers behind it but to keep pace with them. This possibility, however, had already struck him in *Our Political Tasks* when he visualized a situation in which the workers, alienated by the party's inner squabblings and controversies, would 'turn their backs' on it and go their own way. In 1905 it became clear that if the workers had not specifically rejected the party, they had at least unequivocally chosen to act outside its confines. The workers' movement was largely spontaneous indeed and as the year 1905 unfolded the Social Democratic party seemed to be virtually an irrelevancy. Trotsky himself had by now severed most of his formal ties with the Mensheviks so that he himself was already an independent figure. His own subsequent experience, his newly arrived at conception of the Russian revolution, and the instability of the Social Democratic party combined to reinforce his pre-1905 view that the Bolshevik approach to party organization was totally mistaken.

(a) *The Party and the Soviets*

We have already dwelt on the extent to which the events of 1905 impressed upon Trotsky the view that the future of the workers' movement, including ultimately the socialist revolution, lay in mass action.[94] If before 1905 such a view was still

[94] See chapter 1, pp. 23ff., above.

in the realm of theoretical argument, after 1905 it appeared to Trotsky to have been empirically vindicated. If anything, therefore, his attitude became even more extreme. On the one hand, he now urged the complete reconstruction of the party in accordance with the new reality of a proletariat which had proved its capacity for both radical and mass participation in politics.[95] 'The gates of the party', he wrote, 'must be flung wide open, without fear of the proletarian elemental force.'[96] On the other hand, he became convinced that not even a reconstructed mass party could exhaust, or even provide the framework for, the organizational possibilities which now presented themselves. The experience of 1905, the experience of revolution, taught, he believed, that organizational instruments arise and are created in the very midst of revolution. One such instrument was the Soviet; it had been born in the heat of battle and it, more than any other institution, had come to express the will of the workers.

Trotsky's attitude toward the Soviet has been indicated in a previous chapter[97] and we return to it briefly here only to emphasize its effect on his view of the role of the Social Democratic party. The most interesting of his writings in this connection are the sections, previously referred to, in his book *1905*, 'summing up' the lessons of that year.[98] They show the extent to which he was prepared to forsake the concept of party and of organizational loyalty for the sake of mass effectiveness.

At the beginning of 1905 Trotsky, as we have seen, had urged the Social Democratic party to stand at the head of the workers and lead them. But the dangers he had warned of in 1903 and 1904, that internal splits and insufficient contact with the masses would isolate the party, had, in his view, unfortunately materialized in 1905. The party was no longer suited to act as the vehicle for revolutionary leadership.

What was needed now was an organization that could command the loyalty of the masses at a time when the latter were less interested in organizational and ideological niceties and more in effective action and solidarity. Thus, Trotsky wrote,

[95] See, for instance, his article 'Nuzhno stroit partiyu', first published in *Nachalo*, no. 12, 27 Nov. 1905 and reprinted by Trotsky in his *Nasha Revolyutsiya*, pp. 173–6.
[96] 'Nuzhno stroit partiyu', p. 175.
[97] See chapter 2, pp. 53–7, above.
[98] *1905*, pp. 101–9 and 225–45.

the 'creation of an *impartial* [non-party] organization' was rendered 'absolutely indispensable': 'To have the authority of the masses on the very morrow of its formation, it had to be instituted on the basis of a very wide representation.'[99] Such an organization was the Soviet. In 'summing up' the essential nature of this institution, Trotsky wrote:

The Soviet organized the working masses, directed the political strikes and demonstrations, armed the workers, and protected the population against pogroms. Similar tasks were carried out by other revolutionary organizations before the Soviet came into being, concurrently with it, and after it. But this did not give them the influence which the Soviet enjoyed. The secret of this influence lay in the fact that the Soviet grew organically out of the proletariat, in the course of the latter's direct struggle for power as determined by actual events. If the workers themselves, on the one hand, and the reactionary press, on the other, gave the Soviet the name of 'workers' government', this reflected the fact that the Soviet was in reality the embryo of a revolutionary government. The Soviet represented power in so far as power was assured by the revolutionary strength of the working class districts; it struggled directly for power in so far as power still remained in the hands of the military police monarchy.[100]

The Soviet, in his view, had therefore become the workers' most natural organization. Did this mean that the Soviet had replaced the Social Democratic party as the organ of the working class in time of revolution? In purely organizational terms, this was precisely what Trotsky now believed. The exigencies of revolution, the need for as wide a revolutionary front as possible, ruled out the narrow, clandestine basis of the party. But it did not rule out the influence of the party as the source of the Soviet's—and the revolution's—ideology. If the Soviet was not the monopoly of Social Democracy, it was nevertheless governed by the ideas of *social democracy*, that is, the ideas of proletarian socialism. And in so far as the party remained loyal to its ideological roots, it retained the capacity for influencing and even ultimately guiding the work of the Soviet. In a sense, though not in a formal one, this is what happened, according to Trotsky:

The party, from the outset, retained the possibility of exploiting the immense advantages deriving from its Marxist training; because it

[99] *1905*, p. 102.   [100] Ibid., pp. 225–6.

was capable of clearly orienting its political thinking in the vast
'chaos', it was able, almost without effort, to transform the Soviet—
which formally was a non-party organization—into the organizational instrument of its own influence.[101]

One can therefore summarize Trotsky's views on the
workers-party-Soviet relationship as follows: in *preparing for*
revolution, it is the party which strives to educate and influence
the workers; in *carrying out* a revolution, it is the workers themselves who create the most appropriate organization, the
Soviet: at such a time, it is the masses who 'sweep the party
forward', a phenomenon which 'will occur in every revolution,
however powerful its organization'.[102] Concurrently, however,
the party assumes the role of the source of theoretical and ideological inspiration, influence and guidance. Put another way,
the party is the organization of the workers during the *pre-revolutionary* period; it ceases to be such an organization during the
revolutionary period and becomes an appendage to the workers—
and to the Soviet—themselves.[103]

This view of the party as providing a general programme
of social action while the masses themselves constitute the executive arm, verges, of course, on the politically naïve. But it
indicates again how convinced Trotsky had become of the
reality and viability of mass action.[104] In the years after 1905,
he held this view not out of idealistic or romantic considerations, but because he in fact believed that this approach to the
workers' movement offered the best prospects of success. He
believed, in other words, that only a genuinely mass movement
could bring about a socialist revolution. Simultaneously, this
position was bound up with the wider revolutionary conception—the theory of the permanent revolution—which he
had formulated in the wake of 1905. That conception had been

[101] Ibid., p. 226.   [102] Ibid., p. 237.

[103] A similar argument was developed by Trotsky in his *V zashchitu partii* (St. Petersburg,
1907), pp. 75–121. This book is a collection of various articles and letters written during
1906.

[104] In 'Posl Peterburgskikh sobitii' (*Nasha Revolyutsiya*, pp. 63–4)—this article was his
first reaction to the events of January 1905—Trotsky declared: 'How invincibly elo-
quent are facts! How utterly powerless are words! The masses have made themselves
heard! . . . The revolutionary masses are no more a theory, they are a fact.' A similar
excitement at the prospect of mass revolutionary action overtook him even before
January 1905; see the article, written in December 1904, 'Proletariat i revolyutsiya',
in ibid., pp. 54–63.

much influenced by the mass phenomena which Trotsky was a witness to in 1905; and one of its basic assumptions was that the Russian proletariat would act as a mass social and political force. As we have seen from his 1903 and subsequent writings, he was not blind to the danger that a political party could assume a politically autonomous role; but he refused to believe that it could thereby control and dominate the workers. Rather he believed that the reverse would happen.

The years which followed 1905 were a period largely devoid of revolutionary activity, for Trotsky as for the Russian revolutionary movement in general. Although for Russia this was to be a period of far-reaching reforms—in local self-government, in education, and, above all, in agrarian policy—to Russian revolutionaries it signified the 'years of reaction'.[105] The government's virtual '*coup d'état*' of June 1907 and subsequent renegation on its political concessions of 1905 put an end even to formal parliamentary agitation. The revolutionary wave of 1905 not only subsided, it seemed to have exhausted itself. Amongst the intelligentsia the earlier infatuation with politics was replaced by a withdrawal into less immediate and less concrete concerns. The former 'legal Marxists', later members of the Union of Liberation, among them Struve and Berdyaev, turned against revolution and to religion. In literary and artistic circles, although this was to be a great period of innovation, there was a similar tendency towards concern for more ethereal matters, as represented by the growth of such literary schools as Symbolism. Moreover, in the wake of Stolypin's plans for the regeneration of Russia, national sentiments reasserted themselves. On the whole, there was at best a wait-and-see attitude, at worst a general resignation to the autocracy and a greater concern for personal security rather than the health of society as a whole.

As for the Social Democratic movement itself, it was in

---

[105] For a succinct account of the reforms of these years, see Harold Shukman, *Lenin and the Russian Revolution* (New York, 1968), chapter 6. For a brief assessment of Stolypin's reforms and economic changes after 1907, see Alexander Gerschenkron, 'Patterns of Economic Development', in C. E. Black (ed.), *The Transformation of Russian Society* (Cambridge, Mass., 1960), pp. 52–61. See also Harry T. Willetts, 'The Agrarian Problem', in George Katkov *et al.* (eds.), *Russia Enters the Twentieth Century, 1894–1917* (London, 1971), pp. 111–37.

shambles. The party had held its Fourth Congress in April 1906 and ostensibly some formal unity had been restored. But the Bolshevik faction continued to retain a separate organization and in the years that followed became more and more estranged from the rest of the party. Arguments over underground as against parliamentary activity, over 'liquidationism'—Lenin's name for what he took to be a movement to destroy the party apparatus—as well as over the old issue of a revolutionary élite as against a mass movement, became even more intense and made reconciliation impossible. At any rate, Lenin himself was obviously not interested in unity, at least not on any terms but his own, and by 1912 he resolved to turn his faction into an independent party, though claiming for it the 'RSDRP' label. As against this, later in the same year, various, largely Menshevik, elements formed yet another grouping known as the 'August Bloc' which was, however, no more than a loose meeting of minds. The Bolsheviks, ostensibly more consolidated, were in fact plagued by internal splits and scandals. In 1908 a form of philosophical revolutionism, more metaphysical than political, formulated by Bogdanov, had threatened to distract the Bolsheviks from their traditional down-to-earth attitudes and Lenin had had to fight it off with a major polemic.[106] In later years, the Bolsheviks went through a version of their own 'Azeff affair' with the discovery in 1913 that their Duma leader, Roman Malinovsky, was a police agent. No faction, therefore, was in a healthy state and in spite of the numerous attempts at 'conciliation' and rebuilding this was the period during which the Russian Social Democratic movement reached its lowest depths. Membership figures dropped drastically, repression by the authorities became more efficient, and much of the leadership was forced to go into exile. In part, the troubles of the movement derived from its endemic factionalism and discord; but the underlying cause of its eclipse was the general decline of interest in political, and certainly revolutionary, activities.[107]

The disarray in the movement naturally frustrated the effectiveness of its leading figures. Like everyone else, but perhaps more so, Trotsky was to suffer the effects of this general chaos

---

[106] This was his well-known *Materialism and Empirio-Criticism*, published in 1909.
[107] A full account of the problems of the Social Democrats during the post-1905 period is given in Schapiro, op. cit., chapters 4–7. See also Shukman, op. cit., chapter 7.

The Revolutionary Party

213

within the revolutionary ranks. In 1905 he had reached the pinnacle of revolutionary activity. The year which followed was spent in prison but it was a year of intensive thinking and writing during which he formulated the ideas that would become permanently associated with his name. But now, as his biographer has written, only the 'doldrums'[108] awaited him. He had broken with both the main wings of the party already before 1905 and had made his name independently, without their assistance. In the years which were now to follow he was to remain irreconcilably at odds with these wings. He had neither faction nor following, and his own self-willed, contumacious nature, his inability to submit to party discipline, made reconciliation impossible. Moreover, in the wake of the defeat and the reversals which the revolution was to suffer, and the seeming quietism which overtook Russian society, his bold, radical ideas, his vision of a national uprising leading to a workers' government, appeared to be completely out of touch with reality. Hardly anyone was to take the theory of the permanent revolution seriously; for years the general attitude toward it would be that it was a brilliant but eccentric product of a mind endowed with too much imagination.[109]

The pitiful condition of the Social Democratic movement was apparent to Trotsky immediately. He had returned to St. Petersburg in March 1907, after an adventurous escape from exile in Siberia,[110] and from there, via Finland, he made his way to London, where he attended the Fifth Congress of the party. The Congress, which met in April–May 1907, was ostensibly that of a united party. In the course of its deliberations, however, it became clear how divided in fact its members were. No one could as yet guess that this would be the last Congress of the party in the form in which it had existed since its first one in 1898,[111] but the depth of the split between Mensheviks

[108] This is the title Deutscher gives to the chapter of his biography of Trotsky dealing with the years 1907–14 (*The Prophet Armed*, p. 175).
[109] See, for example, the criticisms of Trotsky in F. A. Cherevanin, *Proletariat v revolyutsii* (Moscow, 1907).
[110] Trotsky's own colourful account of his journey into exile and his escape from it is in *1905*, pp. 361–422. It was also published in a separate edition under the title *Tuda i Obratno* (Petrograd, 1919). The account is an excellent example of Trotsky's powers of description, even when, as in this case, he was not writing about politics.
[111] The next Congress, the Sixth, was not to convene until ten years later (26 July–3 Aug. 1917) when it would be that of the Bolsheviks exclusively. In between there

and Bolsheviks was evident to all. The main issue, as always, was the fundamental character of the movement and, as always, the factions could not agree. While the Mensheviks emphasized the need for building up a mass following, Lenin stuck to his conception of a clandestine organization. Trotsky stood outside the factions and equally castigated both. Although his main address at the Congress was directed primarily against the Mensheviks, he was no less critical of Lenin's views.[112] He was typically at odds with everyone and, no less typically, made this clearly known to all. Nevertheless, he was eager to bring about a reconciliation between the factions since he believed that the strength and effectiveness of the party could only be assured through actual unity.

This was in fact the policy which he was to propagate throughout the subsequent years. Although he remained more closely associated with the Mensheviks, and used their newspapers to denounce Lenin's factionalism, he became the chief 'conciliator', striving always to salvage a basis for unity. But no such basis existed and all his attempts, such as the 'August Bloc' of 1912 of which he was the main initiator, only seemed to exacerbate the inured antagonism between the main protagonists. Worst of all, seeking a synthesis of the best of two worlds, he aroused and earned the antipathy of both. Sometimes alternatively, sometimes simultaneously, he appeared as the enemy of each and this deepened his isolation, paralyzed his effectiveness, and frustrated his ambitions. Then, as before and as would happen again, albeit under different circumstances, he revealed an incapacity to make his way in the twisting corridors of party politics, and, above all, an incapacity to emerge as a leader during mundane times. The result was that from 1907 to 1914, living in Vienna and occupying himself mainly with journalistic work, he failed completely to exert influence one way or another.[113]

<hr>

would be a number of Conferences of the party, at the Sixth of which, in January 1912, the split would become final.

[112] The speech appears as an appendix in *1905*, pp. 249–56 and will be referred to later in this chapter.

[113] From October 1908 and until 1912 he edited the Viennese *Pravda*; although he did not turn it into the organ of the Mensheviks, but used it instead for preaching party unity, the contributors to the paper were Mensheviks. In April 1912 the Bolsheviks began to publish a paper with the same name, thus ending the career of the

(b) *The Party and Intellectuals*

But if, therefore, these were for Trotsky years of political stultification, from an intellectual and cultural point of view this was to be a period for him of new influences and great personal development. He had first come to Europe in 1902 but his sojourn then had been relatively brief and, at the time, events in Russia were developing so dramatically that it was hardly possible for him to immerse himself in the European milieu. Now, during his second 'exile', there was to be not only more time, but also less to take his mind off the European world: although Trotsky considered the fact of political quiet in Russia to be the proverbial calm before the storm, there was not much that a Russian revolutionary could do in the meantime. Besides, unlike some Russian revolutionary émigrés, and particularly Lenin, who seem to have been largely impervious to a change in environment and did not, in any case, allow it to divert them from their total immersion in Russian affairs, Trotsky was by nature open and receptive to new influences, and his range of interests, as we shall see later in this study, was always variegated. It did not take him very long to become, not only accustomed to the very different social and cultural milieu of Europe, but to feel himself completely at home in it.[114] He easily broke out of the closed and narrow circle of Russian émigrés. He read European literature, visited the famous art galleries, perfected his knowledge of languages, especially German, and, concurrently, plunged into the affairs of European Social Democracy. Although temperamentally and politically he was often at odds with the leading European socialists of the time—the Adlers, Hilferding, Kautsky—he nevertheless struck up close friendships with them.[115] He frequented literary gatherings and

---

Viennese *Pravda* and initiating that of its famous successor. Later Trotsky contributed to other newspapers, among them *Luch* and *Kievskaya Mysl*, on political as well as cultural and literary subjects. His articles in these newspapers were reprinted in volumes IV, VI, VIII, and IX of his *Sochineniya*.

[114] His own description of this period and milieu is in *Moya Zhizn*, I, pp. 231 ff.

[115] His sketches of these and other European personalities were later published together in a collection *Godi velikogo pereloma: Lyudi staroi i novoi epokh* (Moscow, 1919) and in his *Sochineniya*, VIII. Here, as well as in his autobiography (I, pp. 236–48), he emphasized that the friendships were more intellectual than political: he saw the European socialists as fundamentally non-revolutionary.

political meetings, partook of the local custom of long conversations in cafés and wrote copiously about cultural matters.[116] Although these years were spent mostly in Vienna, he made numerous trips to other European centres—Paris, London, Munich—as well as to the European 'periphery', the Balkans.[117]

One of the results of this involvement in European cultural circles was that Trotsky developed a curious ambivalence towards the intellectual community and intellectuals in general. On the one hand, he was full of admiration, even awe, for the artistic, literary and cognitive products of this community, and he himself sought to absorb its highest attainments; in fact, he was so overwhelmed by European standards and achievements that he developed almost an inferiority complex about most things Russian—though, it should be added, he was not so humble as to think *himself* inferior. Together with this deference to European culture, however, there went a certain disdain for the European intelligentsia, its way of life, its somewhat easygoing and scholastic manner, its fundamental acceptance, as he saw it, of bourgeois institutions and, above all, its reluctance, or at least hesitation, to act in a forcefully political manner. Trotsky, the man of letters, was naturally drawn to the intellectual circles; but the revolutionary in him was repelled, and perturbed, even alarmed, by what he considered to be their tempering influence on political struggle. This ambivalence had a direct impact on his attitude towards intellectuals in politics, particularly in revolutionary politics; he became sceptical about the value of the intelligentsia's support for Social Democracy in general, and Russian Social Democracy in particular. In the latter case, he came to believe that the very inferiority which he attributed to the Russian intelligentsia made its involvement in the party organization and in the movement especially ominous. And all this had a direct relevance, of course, to the issue of the character and composition of the Social Democratic organization.

---

[116] His writings on literary and cultural matters, which originally appeared mainly in the journal *Kievskaya Mysl*, were later collected in *Literatura i Revolyutsiya*, (Moscow, 1923), pp. 193–392 and in his *Sochineniya*, XX, pp. 267–497.
[117] For his dispatches from the Balkans, as the correspondent of *Kievskaya Mysl*, see his *Sochineniya*, VI and IX.

In this connection, two of his articles from this period are particularly striking: the one, 'The Intelligentsia and Socialism', written in 1910, deals with the general subject of its title;[118] the other, 'Concerning the Intelligentsia', written in 1912, analyses the specific case of Russian intellectuals and Russian socialism.[119]

The central thesis of the first article is that the intelligentsia was far less independent of its immediate social and political environment than it itself liked to think. It was, Trotsky argued, a social, rather than a moral, category, like every other occupational grouping. The European intelligentsia in particular, though it had reached the heights of theoretical and critical thinking, had widened its ties with the established order rather than severing them. The special status which it enjoyed, the relative comforts it received, it owed to the benefaction of a bourgeois society wealthy enough to dispense such luxuries. An unequivocal commitment to socialism would involve a readiness to sacrifice such advantages, a readiness to accept the kind of equal, non-privileged conditions and treatment to which others were subject. It was not surprising, therefore, Trotsky continued, that the vast majority of the intelligentsia—by which he meant intellectuals, writers and artists, and the professionally educated—had so far failed to join the socialist movement. The opportunities which modern bourgeois society offered the educated were far more enticing than the ideals of socialism. In fact, the 'more definitely socialism has revealed its content, the more easy it has made it for each and all to understand its mission in history, the more decidedly have the intelligentsia recoiled from it'.[120]

As for those intellectuals[121] who had joined the socialist camp,

---

[118] 'Intelligentsiya i sotsializm', in *Literatura i Revolyutsiya*, pp. 344–57. All references are to this edition. This article originally appeared in 1910 in the St. Petersburg journal *Sovremenny Mir* and was written as a review of Max Adler's pamphlet, published in the same year in Vienna, *Der Sozialismus und die Intellektuellen*. (The article may also be found in Trotsky's *Sochineniya*, XX, pp. 452–65.)

[119] 'Ob intelligentsii', in *Literatura i Revolyutsiya*, pp. 255–69. (This was originally published in *Kievskaya Mysl*, 4, 12 Mar. 1912 and is also included in Trotsky's *Sochineniya*, XX, pp. 327–42.)

[120] 'Intelligentsiya i sotsializm', p. 348.

[121] Trotsky did not distinguish between 'intellectuals' and the concept of the 'intelligentsia' and treated the two interchangeably even though he sometimes spoke of those involved in purely cognitive pursuits—thinkers—and sometimes of those involved in

even they continued to hold on to the prejudices which came
from favoured status. It was significant, Trotsky claimed, that
the first great influx of intellectuals into the socialist movement
had taken place at the very beginning of its history, when it
was without a mass following. Then the intellectual's individualistic psychology could find an outlet in the scope which
the movement provided for theoretical argument and purely
ideological pursuits. As the movement grew—the more in fact
it succeeded in drawing into its ranks the mass of workers—
the more difficult it became for the intellectual to retain his
prominence. The simultaneous shift from theoretical to practical work, the concrete application of the principles of collectivism, had similarly limited the prospects for individual activity
and contributions. Discipline, self-restraint, organizational co-
ordination, had tempered the intellectual's enthusiasm and
frustrated his personal ambitions:

A worker comes to socialism as part of a whole, along with his class
... The intellectual, however, comes to socialism by severing his class
umbilical cord, as an individual, as a personality, and inevitably seeks
to exert influence as an individual. But just here he comes up against
obstacles—and as time passes the greater do these obstacles become.
At the beginning of the Social Democratic movement, every intellectual who joined, even if not above the average, won for himself a place
in the working-class movement. Today every newcomer finds, in the
Western European countries, the colossal structure of working-class
democracy already in existence ... The organizational apparatus of
Social Democracy stands between the intelligentsia and socialism like
a watershed ...[122]

The growth of the socialist movement, in Trotsky's view,
tended therefore to 'alienate' the intelligentsia. One of the
results of this, if it did not lead to the outright abandonment
of the movement, was the development amongst the socialist
intelligentsia of an idealistic strain, which was accompanied
either by a passivity towards revolutionary action in general,
or else by pathetic individual acts of rebellion. In the one case,
it was the older 'ideologues' who became merely onlookers;

---

the professions—lawyers, doctors, etc. This lack of differentiation is a fault, of course,
since his criticism as to the dependence of the intelligentsia on bourgeois society is not
uniformly valid.

[122] Ibid., pp. 349–50.

in the other, it was the young, particularly the students, who exhibited anarchic, though impassioned, tendencies.[123]

If in this 1910 article Trotsky did not mention a further possible consequence of the intellectual's alienation from a mass movement, namely, the emergence of a domineering vanguardism, this was perhaps because the very mass nature of European Social Democracy seemed to him to preclude such a possibility. But this was the very consequence which he emphasized in his essay of two years later when writing on the subject of the Russian intelligentsia. 'Concerning the Intelligentsia' is perhaps one of the most unflattering protrayals ever drawn of the character of Russian culture and its begetters. Although Trotsky was fully aware and admiring of the great achievements of ninetenth-century Russian literature and arts, the poverty which he claimed permeated Russian social thought symptomised for him the fundamental malaise of Russian culture. Comparing Russian social thought with that of Western Europe, he found the former to be primitive, imitative and stylized, sometimes petrified in an imaginary past—as, for example, Populism—and sometimes given to romantic and utopian flights of fancy into the future—as, for example, the anarchism of a Bakunin or a Tolstoy.

In the context of the present chapter, however, it is not so much Trotsky's description of the poverty of Russian social thought, as the peculiar character he attributed to the Russian intelligentsia, that is relevant. He began the essay by asking why it was that the Russian intelligentsia was so obsessed with itself, and so convinced of its superiority, so concerned with its historical mission. How was it, he wondered, that a book such as Ivanov-Razumnik's *History of Russian Social Thought* could be written, in which the whole of Russian history was identified with the intelligentsia? Whence the 'self-styled Messianism' of the intelligentsia, its belief that it will 'save the entire world

[123] See ibid., pp. 352–5, for Trotsky's analysis of the psychology of student revolutionism. Trotsky noted the schizophrenic character of the student condition—rebellion against an older generation, and at the same time acceptance of the social and cultural benefits which that generation made possible. He pointed also to the fundamental romanticism of student politics, its Quixotic qualities, its instability, its fluctuations, its readiness to join any cause—whatever its ideological content—which promised an outlet for militantism. All this, he said, was 'characteristic not of a class or of an idea but of an age-group'. The whole analysis reads as if it were a reaction to the student politics of the 1960s.

from the coming kingdom of the boors'? The answer, he
believed, lay in the 'fatal curse of Russian history': in the
'submissiveness' of the peasant masses and in their 'backwardness, poverty and cultural pauperism'.[124] The traditional
docility of the masses, their indifference, apathy and complacency in the face of the worst miseries and injustices, isolated
the intelligentsia's own tradition of protest and opposition. And
the Western roots of the Russian intelligentsia's culture opened
a chasm between it and the masses which was more pronounced, more abysmal, more abnormal than anywhere in
the West. In its own country the Russian intelligentsia found
itself rootless, alienated, suspended above a hostile and un-
comprehending environment. And as a result it had sought
refuge in itself. Rejected, and at the same time repelled by, the
masses, despairing of the abyss separating it and the people,
it withdrew into its own shell and there wove for itself an ethereal realm of ideas. Thus the impractical, idealistic nature of
its thought, removed from all social reality. Borrowing social
ideas from Western sources and unable to plant them in Russian
soil, it turned them into metaphysical abstracts: the concept
of freedom, in the West rooted in definite social, political, historical conditions, became for the Russian intelligentsia an
absolute, an ideal form empty of all meaning, pursued as an
aspiration of the soul and not as a concrete political objective:

> In Europe, with its cultural order and defined intellectual capital . . .
> you will not find absolute freedom . . . the activities of European politi-
> cal parties and their leaders are determined by the nature of the objec-
> tive situation. It is hardly the same with us, where the intelligentsia
> is not bound by anything . . . 'They', in Europe, are bound by plans,
> conventions, textbooks, programmatic definitions of class interests,
> while I am absolutely free amidst my social steppes . . . The absolutely
> free Russian *intelligent* . . . learns from Europe, taking its latest
> ideas and words, and then rebels against their stipulated, limited,
> 'Western' meaning. He assimilates them to his absolute 'freedom';
> in other words, he empties them of meaning . . . This 'freedom' hangs
> like a curse over the whole history of the Russian intelligentsia.[125]

And how, in spite of its estrangement from social reality, had
the intelligentsia managed to survive? Firstly, by means of 'ter-

---

[124] 'Ob intelligentsii', in *Literatura i Revolyutsiya*, p. 257.
[125] Ibid., pp. 263–4.

rible moral exertions, concentrated asceticism ... fanaticism in the world of ideas, relentless self-limitation, an opinionated and suspicious attitude, and unflagging surveillance of one's own purity'.[126] And, secondly, by making its conscience that of Russia, its history that of the country as a whole. Thus its self-centredness, its vanity, its obsession with itself; the 'fatal discrepancy between ideology and practical, living social reality' had been transformed by the intelligentsia into a 'justification of its unabashed haughtiness'.[127] Thus also its sense of moral superiority, its love-hate relationship with the masses, its assumption of a special role and position in society, of a self-imposed mission, and its presumption to represent the true soul and destiny of Russia:

'Look', they [the intelligentsia] say, 'at the kind of people we are: special, chosen, anti-philistine, seeking the City of the Future. If we are to speak frankly and tell the whole truth, we must admit that the Russian people are savages; they don't wash their hands and don't rinse their water-buckets. The intelligentsia, however, has suffered crucifixion for the people's welfare. It has taken all the anguish of the truth upon itself. For a century and a half it has never hesitated to offer its very life for the passion that consumes it.'[128]

Having once convinced itself—by way of compensation for its fundamental social estrangement—of its calling, its 'chosen' status, nothing in the realm of reality could divert the intelligentsia from its self-defined purpose, neither the complacency nor even the opposition of the very masses it claimed to serve. If the Russian people were submissive to the established order, then the intelligentsia would pursue its—and *their* supposed—goals without them, and with ever greater zeal. And so it had done, according to Trotsky, but at the price of complete and hopeless political isolation, and insignificant, at best imaginary, results. In the end, the intelligentsia's 'delusions of grandeur' and its continued failures to arouse the masses led to the emergence of the specifically Russian phenomenon of 'substitution-ism'. Presuming to represent the people, it soon identified itself

---

[126] Ibid., p. 267. Nevertheless, Trotsky added, being so severed from any concrete commitment, the intelligentsia could permit itself frequent changes of ideological loyalties: 'It is ... well known that when it comes to the consistency of the intelligentsia's faith, its refusal to swallow gnats hardly prevents it from gulping down two-humped camels.'
[127] Ibid., p. 262.   [128] Loc. cit.

with them: 'It has lived through entire cultural epochs—for
the sake of the people. It has selected the roads of development—again for the people.'[129] At first this phenomenon took
the form of 'substitution' for a class, as in the case of the
Decembrists:

> Count Rastopchin once made the ironic comment about the
> Decembrist uprising of 1825 that in France the 'rabble' brought about
> a revolution to make itself equal with the aristocracy whereas our
> aristocrats made a revolution in the interest of the 'rabble' ... The
> Decembrists acted out a part that the Russian intelligentsia has re-
> enacted more than once. The Decembrists acted in a 'substitutive'
> fashion for the interests of a class that had not yet emerged in Russia.
> They 'substituted' themselves for bourgeois liberalism.[130]

Subsequently, this acting by proxy, in the name of a social
class, was extended to cover the masses in general, and the
phenomenon turned out to be characteristic of all Russian revolutionary movements, Populism as well as Marxism:

> The substitution of non-existent or feebly developed classes, a function
> masking the social weakness of the intelligentsia, has now become an
> ideological necessity for it and almost a political profession. At first
> the aristocratic intelligentsia substituted itself for the 'rabble'; then
> the Populist-commoner substituted himself for the peasantry; finally,
> the Marxist-*intelligent* substituted himself for the proletariat.[131]

There is in all this the unmistakable ring, of course, of the
Trotsky of 1904, of *Our Political Tasks*. Then too he had found
it necessary to stress the 'substitutionist' tendencies in Russian
Marxism, particularly as these were expressed through Lenin
and the Bolsheviks. In 1912, although he did not mention Lenin
and the Bolsheviks—there were instead allusions to the former
'legal Marxists' Berdyaev and Struve—he saw the problem of
the Marxist leadership—the social composition and character
of its members—in the wider context of Russian social history.
Thus the source of the élitist, vanguard tendencies was not only
the Social Democratic revolutionary movement itself, nor just
organizational arrangements—issues he had raised in 1904—
but the whole tradition of Russian social movements. In this

---

[129] Loc. cit. For 'substitutionism' Trotsky used the same Russian word (*zamestitelstvo*)
as in *Nashi Politicheskye Zadachi*.
[130] Ibid., p. 268.   [131] Loc. cit.

way Trotsky linked the 'first Marxist circles' to Russia's revolutionary past, in particular to Populism, the Populism, of course, of clandestine, conspiratorial, and élitist traditions. And, beyond this, he showed that such traditions, which were for him the concrete, political expression of social estrangement, were themselves directly linked to the specific conditions of Russian society: its general backwardness, the low cultural level of its masses, and its social formlessness, that is, the absence in it, until very late, of structured, vital classes. This last was for Trotsky the crux of the matter; in Europe, with its highly developed class structure in general, and its highly organized, because large and mature, proletariat, no one could presume to substitute himself for the masses. On the contrary, the danger there was that Social Democracy would be too cautious, too tied down by its mass organizational base, too pedantic in its insistence on mass democracy and consent, and thus, ultimately, too conservative.[132] In Russia, on the other hand, social backwardness, the weakness of the class structure, had encouraged isolated individuals to take it upon themselves to represent not so much a class as the 'idea' of it.

Finally, in 'Concerning the Intelligentsia', Trotsky, by linking the issue of 'substitutionism' to the psychology of the intelligentsia, revealed to what extent he had become suspicious of 'intellectuals' in politics, and how far removed on this point, as on so many others, he was from Lenin. This suspiciousness extended not only to the Russian intelligentsia; as we have seen, in his earlier, 1910 essay, he was no less sceptical about the European intelligentsia, though for other reasons as well. In both cases, however, he distrusted the individual motives and ambitions of the intellectuals, especially of those who were unprepared to come to terms with what he believed to be the inherently mass character of the revolutionary movement. As always, therefore, Trotsky remained a champion of the masses, and of the mass party and movement. And, again as always, he was confident that it was just such a movement which was

---

[132] In *Moya Zhizn*, I, pp. 233–4, Trotsky noted that in 1908 he 'wrote a book on German Social Democracy for a Bolshevik printing house in St. Petersburg. There, for the second time—the first was in 1905—I set forth the idea that the gigantic machine of German Social Democracy might, at a critical moment for the bourgeois society, prove to be the mainstay of the conservative order'. Unfortunately, it has proved impossible to locate a copy of this book; nor is it to be found in Trotsky's *Sochineniya*.

asserting itself in Russia, turning the 'substitutionism' of the intelligentsia into a historical curiosity. 'Concerning the Intelligentsia', for the most part an essay in despondency over Russia's past, concluded nevertheless with a typical optimistic flourish:

> During the years 1905–6 large social entities appeared on the historical scene: classes with their own interests and their own demands. At one stroke Russian events leaped into world history, arousing a powerful response in Europe and in Asia. Political ideas ceased to be ethereal spirits wafted down from some ideological heaven; the epoch of the intelligentsia's substitutionism came to an end, historically exhausting itself . . .
>
> It is nonsense to think that after a great effort history must turn back on itself . . . The Karatayev-like quality,[133] the ahistorical character of our masses, has disappeared forever. There can be no returning to it. And together with this we are through for good with the apostolate of the intelligentsia . . .
>
> History does not repeat itself. However great the intelligentsia's past significance may have been, henceforth its role can be only auxiliary and subordinate. Heroic substitutionism is passing away with its epoch into eternity.[134]

Having so acutely portrayed the social roots of 'substitutionism', Trotsky in the end seemed to covert it into a mere historical episode. Even assuming that 1905 was a watershed in Russian history, did it necessarily follow that, 'at one stroke', all that made for 'substitutionism' in Russian society and culture had been wiped out? Had everything in fact changed so suddenly and drastically? At the very least, a degree of cautious scepticism should have informed Trotsky's attitude toward 1905 and after. Instead, as his final riposte, he chose—here as elsewhere, on this issue as on so many others—to make what was merely a declaration of faith. In the light of his own analysis of the persistent conditions in Russia's history making for 'substitutionism', this declaration was a gross *non sequitur*. Once again, therefore, his abiding optimism, his faith in the historical process, betrayed Trotsky's better judgement. He refused to believe in the tenacity of old cultural patterns and he was determined to believe in the power of the new.

[133] Trotsky's reference is to the character Platon Karatayev, in Tolstoy's *War and Peace*, who symbolized the peasant's characteristics of submissiveness and obedience.
[134] 'Ob intelligentsii', p. 269. The final words of the article are: 'The future [will be] wiser and stronger than the past.'

Conclusion: 1917 and After

To the very eve of 1917 Trotsky remained an anti-Bolshevik. He continued to believe that the fate of the Russian revolution would be determined by the impact of social forces, of which the direct intervention of the great mass of the Russian proletariat would be the final expression. He refuted the view that revolutions are 'made', that they are the product of a party organization, that they depend on a party's 'slogans' and 'tactics'.[135] It was important, in his view, to build the right organization and to choose the right tactics in order to ensure that the party did not fall out of touch with its constituents and was not left behind when the revolution came. But the *coming* of the revolution did not depend on the party; it would come with or without the party and it would be carried to its conclusion by the workers themselves.

All this, of course, put him in direct opposition to the kind of approach associated with Lenin and the Bolsheviks. Yet the moment the revolutionary crisis of 1917 unfolded, Trotsky completely changed his political loyalties. In a matter of months, from being one of the most extreme critics of Bolshevism he turned into a firm supporter, a full-fledged member, and the leader of its October insurrection.[136] In one stroke, the bitter controversies of fourteen years were buried; he abandoned his

---

[135] See, for instance, his article 'Borba za vlast', originally published in *Nashe Slovo*, 17 Oct. 1915, and included as an appendix in *1905*, where he wrote: 'Of course, parties are not classes. Between the position of a party and the interests of the social stratum on which it rests, there may be a lack of correspondence and this may later be converted into a profound contradiction. The behaviour of a party may change under the influence of the mood of the popular masses. This is indisputable. But, in that case, it is all the more essential for us, in our calculations, to stop relying on less stable and less trustworthy elements, such as party slogans and party tactics, and concentrate on more enduring historical factors: the social structure of the nation, the correlation of class forces, the tendencies of development.' *1905*, pp. 288–9.

[136] At the time of the February Revolution, Trotsky was in New York. He succeeded in getting to Russia by the middle of May, after spending most of April in an internment camp in Nova Scotia. At the outset, he functioned as a member of the *Mezhrayonka*, the Inter-Borough Organization, a Petrograd association of non-Bolsheviks and non-Mensheviks opposed to the Provisional Government. He met Lenin shortly after his arrival and at first turned down Lenin's offer to join the Bolsheviks, though he already admitted that there was no longer any political distance between them. He became formally a member of the Bolshevik party in September. See *Moya Zhizn*, II, pp. 5–41.

role of 'conciliator', denounced the Mensheviks, and became as if a long-standing ally of Lenin.[137]

How can this sudden and drastic volte-face be explained? There is, of course, the simple explanation which, for being simple is not therefore necessarily wrong, namely, that Trotsky was thirsting for power and chose to join Lenin because the latter seemed the only one to share the same ambition. Whether one accepts this thesis or not—and this is not the place to analyse it—one still needs to provide a further dimension to Trotsky's conversion: how could he reconcile himself, from the theoretical point of view, to 'Leninism'? That Lenin after April 1917 appeared to have accepted implicitly Trotsky's theory of the permanent revolution explains why *Lenin* could welcome Trotsky; since, however, Lenin did not thereby abandon his party views, it does not explain why Trotsky could now accept Lenin, why Trotsky, that is, could now ignore the party issues over which their differences were, if anything, even more acrimonious than over the separate, though related, question of the 'permanent revolution'.

If one looks at Trotsky's own attempts in later years to explain his rapprochement with Lenin, what stands out is in fact his general avoidance of any real discussion of the whole 'affair'. Of course, he could hardly avoid referring to it entirely if only because, after Lenin's death, the fact of his anti-Bolshevik past was to be continually raised against him. But almost all his references to the reconciliation—as, indeed, almost everything he would write about Lenin—are marred by an otherwise uncharacteristic element of hero worship; one can only guess how much of this was genuine and how much necessitated by the subsequent elevation of the dead Lenin and his views to a position of sacrosanct authority.[138] Whatever the case, it forced Trotsky into a perfunctory dismissal of the issues involved; so much so, in fact, that one sometimes gets the impression that his pre-1917 differences with Lenin were not so much

---

[137] The Bolsheviks, of course, were themselves at odds with Lenin at the outset and Trotsky sided with Lenin against the more moderate elements in the party.

[138] The general impression, however, is that it was genuine. Lenin seems to have been the only man to whom Trotsky was prepared to defer and he himself certainly contributed no small amount, whatever his motivation, to the growth of the Lenin personality cult. See chapter 12, below, where his relationship to, and writings on, Lenin are discussed.

fundamental as involving merely a question of emphasis. What he wrote in his autobiography, for instance, is typical of this 'playing down' of the nature of the original controversy:

Revolutionary centralism is a harsh, imperative and exacting principle. It often takes the form of absolute ruthlessness in its relation to individual members, to whole groups of former associates ... It is only the most impassioned, revolutionary striving for a definite end—a striving that is utterly free from anything base or personal—that can justify such a personal ruthlessness ... There is no doubt that at that time [i.e. 1903] I did not fully realize what an intense and imperious centralism the revolutionary party would need to lead millions of people in a war against the old order ... I still could not see Lenin's centralism as the logical conclusion of a clear revolutionary concept.[139]

In all this there is not even a hint of the real nature of Trotsky's pre-1917 opposition to Lenin's centralism; on the basis of what he here said one could hardly guess that the issues Trotsky had once raised were those of inner-party democracy, of mass participation, of the free development of ideas and trends, and that he had denounced Lenin's centralism precisely because its ruthlessness led, in his view, to 'substitutionism', to Jacobinism, to a dictatorship over the proletariat. In all of his post-1917 works there is only one direct reference to his anti-Bolshevik writings of 1903 and 1904. It occurs in his last major work, the biography of Stalin, but even here he simply dismissed *Our Political Tasks* as containing 'not a little that is immature and erroneous in my criticism of Lenin'.[140] Neither here, nor anywhere else, did he actually discuss his 'errors'; everywhere he deemed it sufficient either to cite the superior political foresights of Lenin, or to relegate the whole matter to a merely organizational or tactical realm which, at the time, he had presumably failed to grasp.[141]

[139] *Moya Zhizn*, I, pp. 187–8. See also the unpublished defence of his past, which he composed at the end of 1924, in the Trotsky Archives, T2969.

[140] *Stalin*, p. 62. He added, however, that the 1904 pamphlet also contained 'pages which present a fairly accurate characterization of the cast of thought of the "committeemen" of those days'. Yet Lenin is entirely absolved of this 'cast of thought' and it is Stalin who is its embodiment. Earlier, however (ibid., p. 58) he allowed himself a word of criticism against Lenin's *What is to be Done?*, claiming that Lenin also recognized some of its 'erroneousness'.

[141] It has to be said that besides the gap which it leaves in the development of his thought, this evasion of the real issues involved shows how far political exigencies had, in this connection at least, undermined his intellectual integrity.

We cannot hope, therefore, to extract from Trotsky's own words a convincing theoretical explanation of his conversion to Bolshevism. Yet, unwittingly, he himself provided at least a clue to the kind of explanation which it is possible to infer. An example of this is the manner in which he accounted for his 'conciliationist' position prior to 1917. 'My conciliationism', he wrote in one place, 'flowed from a sort of social-revolutionary *fatalism*. I believed that the logic of the class struggle would compel both factions [i.e. the Mensheviks and the Bolsheviks] to pursue the same revolutionary line.'[142] And, elsewhere, he elaborated on this:

> The policy of conciliation thrived on the hope that the course of events itself would prompt the necessary tactic. But that *fatalistic optimism* meant in practice not only repudiation of factional struggle but the very idea of a party, because, if 'the course of events' is capable of directly dictating to the masses the correct policy, what is the use of any special unification of the proletarian vanguard, the working out of a programme, the choice of leaders, the training in a spirit of discipline?[143]

At the very least this constituted, albeit without any further development of the necessary conclusion, an admission that Trotsky had underestimated the role in revolution of purely political devices. In effect, it was a recognition of the indispensability of the revolutionary élite—the 'vanguard', the 'leaders', the 'very idea of a party'. The crucial terms in the above two quotations are 'fatalism' and 'fatalistic optimism'. They signify not only that Trotsky had eventually perceived the flaws in his thought growing out of an optimistic evaluation of the working class, but that he now grasped the relationship between society and politics in a manner which was largely absent from his writings before 1917. Then he had linked social development and political action in a deterministic way: the one would naturally follow from the other, as if in a directly causal relationship; given certain socio-economic processes, the masses would behave in a predictable, necessary way. This, Trotsky now admitted, was 'fatalistic optimism' and it therefore excluded, what eventually could *not* be excluded, the revolutionary vanguard. *Why*, however, did the masses not behave in a manner

[142] *Permanentnaya Revolyutsiya*, p. 48 (italics added).
[143] *Stalin*, p. 112 (italics added).

which should have been predictable on the basis of a social theory such as Marxism, thus necessitating both the mediation and the direct intervention of the political vanguard, the political party? Once again, though this time perhaps less unwittingly, Trotsky himself provided the outlines of a possible explanation. In his biography of Stalin, he posed the question whether 'Stalinism was already rooted in Bolshevik centralism' and he answered it as follows:

Upon analysis this inference crumbles to dust, disclosing an astounding paucity of historical content. Of course, there are dangers of one kind or another in the very process of stringently picking and choosing persons of advanced views and welding them into a tightly centralized organization. But the roots of such dangers will never be found in the so-called 'principle' of centralism; rather they should be sought in the lack of homogeneity and the backwardness of the toilers—that is, in the general social conditions which make imperative that very centripetal leadership of the class by its vanguard. The key to the dynamic problem of leadership of the class is in the actual interrelationships between the political machine and its party, between the vanguard and its class, between centralism and democracy. These interrelationships cannot, of their nature, be established *a priori* and remain immutable. They are dependent on concrete historical conditions; their mobile balance is regulated by the vital struggle of tendencies, which, as represented by their extreme wings, oscillate between the despotism of the political machine and the impotence of phrasemongering.[144]

The first thing to be noted about this passage is its raising of the point Trotsky had argued before 1917, namely, the relationship between the dangers of vanguardism and the backwardness of the social environment. Indeed, as we shall see, this would be at the root of his later analysis of Stalinism.[145] But in view of this, it may be noted how unconvincing was Trotsky's attempt to separate such dangers from the 'principle' of centralism; for if the dangers of vanguardism were a function of backwardness, so, for that matter, must be the necessity for centralism itself. But whatever the case, centralism of a *particular* kind, Bolshevik centralism, arose as a direct necessity of *particular*

---

[144] Ibid., pp. 61–2. This paragraph immediately precedes Trotsky's above-mentioned reference to his *Nashi Politicheskye Zadachi*.
[145] See chapter 10, below.

social conditions. Put concretely, this meant that the conditions of Russia, if they were to issue in a 'workers' government', made necessary a *Bolshevik* party organization. And this is precisely what Trotsky had come to accept in 1917. He had in effect become reconciled to the impossibility of carrying out the socialist revolution in Russia without Bolshevism.

One final example will serve to complete this picture of Trotsky's position after 1917 on the relationship between objective and subjective or voluntaristic factors. It pertains to his and Lenin's special roles in the triumph of the October Revolution. Speculating on 'what might have been' in 1917, Trotsky wrote, in 1935:

> Had I not been present in 1917 in Petersburg the October Revolution would still have taken place—*on the condition that Lenin was present and in command.* If neither Lenin nor I had been present in Petersburg, there would have been no October Revolution: the leadership of the Bolshevik party would have prevented it from occurring—of this I have not the slightest doubt! If Lenin had not been in Petersburg, I doubt whether I could have managed to conquer the resistance of the Bolshevik leaders.[146]

This surely represents Trotsky's ultimate concession to the element of the instrumental in the success of revolution. The view that one or two men could determine the fate of a revolution was a view which he could not possibly have contemplated before 1917 and which he had in fact rejected *in toto.* Here, however, the 'vanguard' was reduced to its absolute extreme: not even the party, but one individual, Lenin (or, *perhaps,* Trotsky himself) became the effective and indispensable instrument of revolution. Trotsky did not mean by this, of course, anything so absurd as that Lenin *alone* was indispensable: without a situation of chaos, such as reigned in Russia in the months prior to October, and without rebellious masses, all revolutionary leaders were impotent. Lenin was a necessary, though not sufficient, 'condition'. The masses too were necessary; but neither did they constitute a sufficient 'condition'. In this precisely, however, lay Trotsky's change of mind—for prior to 1917 the

---

[146] Trotsky, *Diary in Exile, 1935,* translated by Elena Zarudnaya (London, 1959), pp. 53–4. Trotsky's views on the individual and history, including the example of Lenin, are discussed in chapter 12, below.

revolutionary masses alone were for him a *sufficient* condition for the triumph of the Russian revolution.[147]

We may therefore summarize the matter in the following way. In spite of the 'fatalistic optimism' which, by his own admission, characterized Trotsky's thinking, his own theory of the permanent revolution committed him to the most radical position on the question of a workers' revolution. Returning to Russia after February, he was convinced that all he had written and predicted over more than a decade was now unfolding in reality. But he must have become equally aware that left to their own initiative the masses might compromise with less than now seemed, to him, attainable. Russia was in revolt, but chaos, uncertainty, the absence of a clear political orientation, were factors more in evidence than unity of thought and action. What was needed now was a strong guiding hand, an organization of determined leaders, capable of taking control, and unafraid of power. And although the Bolsheviks too were vacillating at first, they were, in principle, and as was to emerge, the most prepared for these tasks.

If this was the political basis for Trotsky's joining hands with Bolshevism, there was in perspective a wider dimension to the new alliance. Here it is necessary to recall a theme touched upon in previous chapters.[148] Trotsky's theory of the permanent revolution was indeed the most far-reaching of the revolutionary programmes within Russian Social Democracy. But as an *operational* programme it was fundamentally defective. It put, as we have seen, too much faith in the political and social

---

[147] In 1932 Trotsky listed the following 'necessary historical prerequisites' for the events of 1917: '1. The rotting away of the old ruling classes—the nobility, the monarchy, the bureaucracy; 2. The political weakness of the bourgeoisie, which had no roots in the masses of the people; 3. The revolutionary character of the agrarian question; 4. The revolutionary character of the problem of the oppressed nationalities; 5. The significant social burdens weighing on the proletariat; 6. The Revolution of 1905 [which] was the great school, or in Lenin's phrase, "the dress rehearsal" of the Revolution of 1917 ... 7. The imperialist war [which] sharpened all the contradictions, tore the backward masses out of their immobility and thus prepared for the grandiose scale of the catastrophe. But all these conditions, which were fully sufficient for the *outbreak of the revolution* (i.e. of October), were insufficient to assure the *victory of the proletariat* in the revolution. For this victory one more condition was necessary: the Bolshevik party.' ('Chto takoe Oktyabrskaya revolyutsiya?', Archives, T3470—this is the 1932 Copenhagen speech.)

[148] See chapter 3, pp. 98ff. and chapter 4, pp. 165ff., above.

maturity of the Russian working class. It overestimated the workers' capacity for spontaneous self-organization as well as their commitment to the goals of socialism. It left too much to the so-called 'inexorable forces' of history, and it assumed a pace of social development amongst the proletariat which was at variance with reality—and this latter in spite of Trotsky's constant recognition of the pervasiveness of Russian backwardness. Yet this backwardness was more profound than even Trotsky had imagined. Russia had changed, but without undergoing that *social* revolution which a Marxist theory of revolution postulated as the pre-condition of the *political* socialist revolution. The proletariat in Russia was not yet that agent of social change which the European bourgeoisie, according to Marxism, had been in its own time. The masses were indeed eager for change but they could not be said to have any defined conception of its nature and content. Thus some other agent of change was needed if the revolution was to follow a path which Trotsky had laid down for it. In his theory of the permanent revolution the operational link between society and politics was missing. In the end, therefore, he was forced to come to terms with a substitute link, that very phenomenon which he had first denounced in 1903 as a perverted form of revolutionary organization, and the roots of which he later saw in the social and cultural backwardnews of Russia. Then he had dismissed its prospects of success; now he both revised his evaluation of its prospects and himself joined hands with it. He believed now that between the theory of the permanent revolution and that of the vanguard party there was no basic incompatibility. Thus, as he wrote in his autobiography, like the time in 1902, when as a young and still unknown revolutionary escaping Siberian exile and seeking a revolutionary base he had come knocking at Lenin's door in London, so now again he 'came to Lenin':

As I look back now on the past, I am not sorry. I came to Lenin for the second time later than many others, but I came in my own way, after I had gone through and had weighed the experience of the revolution, the counter-revolution and the Imperialist war. I came, as a result, more surely and seriously than those 'disciples' who, during the master's life, repeated his words and gestures . . . but, after his death, proved to be nothing but helpless epigones and unconscious tools in the hands of hostile forces.[149]

Subsequently in this study we shall return to the issues which have been here discussed, for, in one form or another, they would continuously re-assert themselves in the context of the attempt to 'build socialism' in Russia. Henceforth, indeed, Trotsky would be a faithful 'disciple' of Bolshevism; but more agonizingly than some other 'disciples', faithful in their own way, he would spend the rest of his life, in thought and in practice, grappling with his, and Russia's, contradictions of 1917.

[149] *Moya Zhizn*, I, p. 190.

Part II

THE PERMANENT REVOLUTION: FROM THEORY TO PRACTICE

CHAPTER SIX

THE POLITICAL REVOLUTION

> The road to socialism lies through a period of the highest
> possible intensification of the principle of the state . . . Just
> as a lamp, before going out shoots up in a brilliant flame,
> so the state, before disappearing, assumes the form of the
> dictatorship of the proletariat, that is, the most ruthless
> form of the state, which embraces the life of the citizens
> authoritatively in every direction.[1]

THE MEN who seized and consolidated power in Russia during and after October 1917 were committed to a society the likes of which the world had not yet seen. Whatever our verdict on the nature of the seizure itself of power and on the manner in which the latter came to be wielded, there can be no doubt about the renovating intentions of the new Soviet regime. Russian society was to be transformed, one way or another, and not in order to resemble some existing social model, but rather one which so far had taken shape only in the imagination of men. However incongruous the leap from Russian backwardness to modern socialism, this was precisely the goal which the Soviet regime proclaimed it would pursue.

Yet the incongruity of it all was overwhelming. Hardly any of the pre-conditions which socialist thinkers of most persuasions, and not least Marx, postulated as essential for the transition to socialism were to be found in the Russia of 1917. Russia was an impoverished and not an affluent society, her economy was primarily agricultural and not industrial, the most numerous class, by far, was the peasantry and not the proletariat, her political experience encompassed almost nothing of elections, representative government, civil rights, or free organization and, finally, though the list could be extended, she was culturally backward, a nation the majority of whose population was illiterate, and with her fair share of what Marx once called 'the idiocy of village life'. Suspended above this reality, a

[1] Trotsky, *Terrorizm i Kommunizm* (*Sochineniya*, XII, p. 161).

government declaring itself to be motivated by Marxist ideas and intent on introducing socialism, was indeed a spectacle at which it was permissible to stare in awe and disbelief, and with not a little scepticism.

In Part I of the present study, an analysis was made of how one of the men at the head of this new government sought to explain, before the event itself, the historical logic of this incongruity. Trotsky's theory of the permanent revolution, which we have defined as the revolution of backwardness, was dedicated to the proposition that such a state of affairs, far from constituting one of those jokes which history plays upon the reason of man, was perfectly compatible with those laws of society which Marxism had claimed to discover. Whatever the actual validity of Trotsky's theory, he could indeed at least claim to be the most vindicated of men in so far as the initial stage of his prognosis was concerned. Or so it appeared. In fact, the very seizure of power took a form which he had not originally contemplated. And, in any case, the seeming incongruity between backwardness and socialism had yet to be resolved in practice.

In this, Part II of our study, we shall examine the manner in which, during the years following 1917, Trotsky proposed to carry the 'permanent revolution' to its conclusion, that is, to create those conditions which would, presumably, make socialism a reality. This will not take us into a consideration of his own activities or political record during this period—a subject outside the confines of this study—but of the ideas and arguments he raised and the policies he sought to disseminate. There is, of course, an overlapping between the subject of his deeds and that of his ideas—and, certainly, not seldom a contradiction between the two—but it should be possible to concentrate on the latter as forming a field of inquiry unto itself. To put the matter more simply, in what follows we shall be concerned not with what he did but with what he thought should be done.[2] Accordingly, the present chapter will discuss Trotsky's views on those aspects of a socialist revolution which pertain to the seizure and consolidation of power; the next chapter will deal with his ideas on issues of social and economic

[2] No attempt is therefore made to assess Trotsky's political record while in power, a subject outside the scope of this study.

change; and the chapter after that with the relationship, as Trotsky saw it, between the Russian Revolution and the 'world revolution'.

1. Insurrection and the Making of Revolution

At the close of the last chapter we discussed in a general way the reasons for Trotsky's reconciliation in 1917 with Lenin and the Bolshevik party. To appreciate his subsequent views on the kind of political institutions and policies required of a socialist government to consolidate its power, it is necessary to look first at the manner in which he interpreted the period from February to October, and the circumstances of the actual Bolshevik seizure of power—a subject which constitutes an aspect of the 'party question' but which also throws light on Trotsky's general conception of revolution and political power.

Throughout the period 1907–17 Trotsky, of course, never for a moment doubted that sooner or later 1905 would be repeated in Russia—and that the next time round it would end differently. The 'years of reaction' were for him simply a sort of lull in the fighting; ultimately political disturbances and general unrest must break out again.[3] The outbreak of war convinced him that this would be the event which would finally consolidate the forces of opposition, unleash all the pent-up radicalism of the masses, and strike the death blow at Tsarism.[4] Thus when the news of the first disturbances of January and February reached him—at the time he was in New York—he immediately drew the parallel with 1905. 'The streets of Petrograd', he began an article, 'again speak the language of 1905.'[5] After tracing briefly the resurgence of the masses over the intervening years, he concluded: '. . . we are witnessing the beginning of the second Russian Revolution.'[6] A few days later he learned that the Tsar had abdicated and that the liberals had

[3] For his views of the 1907–17 period, see, in particular, his articles in *Pravda* (Viennese), especially those collected in his *Sochineniya*, IV, pp. 245–310.
[4] His main work on the World War is *Voina i Internatsional* included in the collection *Voina i Revolyutsiya*, (2 vols., 2nd edition, Moscow–Petrograd, 1923), I, pp. 75–154. The work will be referred to, in another context, in chapter 8, below.
[5] 'U poroga revolyutsii', in *Sochineniya*, III, part 1, p. 3. (Originally published in *Novyi Mir*, no. 934, 13 Mar. 1917.)
[6] Ibid., p. 5.

taken over the reins of government. Without the slightest hesitation he declared that they could not possibly hold on and that
what had happened was only the beginning:

Should the Russian revolution stop today as the representatives of
liberalism advocate, tomorrow the reaction of the Tsar, the nobility
and the bureaucracy would gather power and drive Milyukov and
Guchkov from their insecure ministerial trenches, as did the Prussian
reaction years ago with the representatives of Prussian liberalism. But
the Russian revolution will not stop. The time will come and the
revolution will make a clean sweep of the bourgeois liberals blocking
its way, as it is now making a clean sweep of the Tsarist reaction.[7]

In the following days Trotsky wrote further newspaper
articles analysing what he called 'the internal forces of the
revolution', by which he meant the ways in which the development of events was being driven of itself. The 'scenario' of the
permanent revolution, which he had drawn up more than a
decade ago, was clearly in his mind. What he expected to
happen now was that, firstly, a rival workers' institution, the
Soviet, would be resurrected to function independently, and
in opposition to the Provisional Government, preparing itself
for an eventual seizure of all government power.[8] Secondly, he
expected the problem of a conclusion to the war to dominate
events; the Provisional Government, dependent, in his view,
on winning the favours of the 'bourgeois' allies, would not dare
to sign an independent peace with Germany; but the Russian
workers would not agree to continuing the 'imperialist' war;
and their opposition to it, together with the inability of the
liberals to pursue the war successfully, would accelerate the process leading to a workers' government. And such a government,
Trotsky believed, 'will be a mortal blow to the Hohenzollerns
because it will give a powerful stimulus to the revolutionary
movement of the German proletariat and of the working
masses of all other countries'.[9] This was, of course, the prognosis
Trotsky had originally marked out in his theory of the perma-

[7] 'Dva litsa: vnutrennie sily russkoi revolyutsii', in *Sochineniya*, III, part 1, p. 11. (Originally published in *Novyi Mir*, no. 938, 17 Mar. 1917.)
[8] 'Narastayushchii konflikt', in *Sochineniya*, III, part 1, pp. 11–13. (Originally in *Novyi
Mir*, no. 940, 19 Mar. 1917.)
[9] 'Voina ili mir?', in *Sochineniya*, III, part 1, p. 16. (Originally in *Novyi Mir*, no. 941,
20 Mar. 1917.)

nent revolution: the coming to power of a workers' government first in Russia and, from thence, the spread of the revolution until it engulfed the whole of Europe and beyond. Observing, from afar, the first developments in Russia, Trotsky believed that his theory was now indeed being played out in practice.

But by the time, in May, of his return to Russia, the first act of this drama—the coming to power of a workers' government—was still far from being a foregone conclusion. On his arrival, Trotsky immediately made his way to the Petrograd Soviet and there he declared in a speech which had wide impact:

What do we recommend? I think that the next step should be the handing over of all power to the Soviet of Workers' and Soldiers' Deputies. Only with authority concentrated in one hand can Russia be saved. Long live the Russian revolution as the prologue to the world revolution.[10]

In keeping, perhaps, with the atmosphere of the place at which he spoke, this was more rhetorical flourish than anything else. In fact, he was already beginning to draw close to Lenin and to the idea of an insurrectionary *coup*. Together with Lenin he quickly abandoned the slogan 'All Power to the Soviets' once it became clear that the latter were prepared to co-operate with the government.[11] Immediately following the 'July Days' he declared his solidarity with the Bolsheviks in an open letter to the Provisional Government: 'The fact that I am . . . not a member of the Bolshevik party is not due to political differences but to certain circumstances in our party history which have now lost all significance.'[12] More and more he came to see the need for 'vanguard' action. Thus in a pamphlet written in August and early September he defined the tasks of the party as follows:

It is impossible for us to predict all the twists and turns of the path of history. As a political party, we cannot be held responsible for the

[10] 'Rech na zasedanii Petrogradskogo Soveta', in *Sochineniya*, III, part 1, p. 46. The speech was delivered on 5/18 May 1917 (the day after Trotsky's arrival in Russia) and was originally published in *Izvestiya*, no. 60, 7 May 1917.
[11] See, for example, his article 'Dvoebezvlastie', in *Sochineniya*, III, part 1, pp. 61–9. This article originally appeared in the first issue, dated 2/15 June 1917, of the newspaper *Vpered* which Trotsky himself founded and which was to be the organ of the Inter-Borough Organization (the *Mezhrayonka*). Only sixteen issues of the paper appeared before the organization merged with the Bolsheviks.
[12] 'Pismo vremennomu pravitelstvu', in *Sochineniya*, III, part 1, p. 166. The letter, dated 10/23 July 1917, was originally published in *Novaya Zhizn*, no. 73, 13/26 July 1917.

course of history. But we are all more responsible to our class; to render it capable of carrying out its mission in all the deviations of the historical journey—that is our fundamental political duty ... It is now incumbent on our party, on its energy, its solicitude, its insistence, to draw all inexorable conclusions from the present situation, and, at the head of the disinherited and exhausted masses, to wage a determined battle for their revolutionary dictatorship.[13]

He was thus prepared now to ignore every trend or grouping which was opposed to, or even merely reluctant to, seize power in the name of the working class. He did not, of course, abandon the idea of the Soviet as representing the organized interests of the workers: this was, after all, the body upon which he had placed all his revolutionary hopes both in 1905 and thereafter. But this did not prevent him from circumventing and ignoring the views of the Petrograd Soviet when its Executive Committee emerged as 'compromisers', co-operating with the Provisional Government. How could he justify his new position that only the party knew best and was the only truly representative organ of the workers—for this was in effect what he was now arguing—in spite of the fact that the Bolsheviks were everywhere a minority? Years later, in his *History of the Russian Revolution*, he provided a rationalization, a typically brilliant one, but a rationalization nevertheless, for the insurrection by a minority which he was then already contemplating.[14] Analysing what he called the 'phenomenon of dual power' (*dvoevlastie*) which had arisen following February, he perceived in it a typical Russian twist. The normal character of this phenomenon he described as follows:

The historic preparation of a revolution brings about, in the pre-revolutionary period, a situation in which the class which is called to realize the new social system, although not yet master of the country, has actually concentrated in its hands a significant share of the state power, while the official apparatus of the government is still in the hands of the old lords. That is the initial dual power in every revolution.[15]

The 'Russian twist', however, was the chronic 'anomaly' of the Russian bourgeoisie, an 'old, historically belated . . . worn

[13] 'Chto zhe dalshe?', in *Sochineniya*, III, part 1, p. 242. The pamphlet was originally serialized during August and September in the Bolshevik paper *Proletarii*.
[14] *The History of the Russian Revolution*, I, chapter II, pp. 223–32.
[15] Ibid., p. 224.

out' class: 'If on coming to power it encounters an antagonist already sufficiently mature and reaching out its hand toward the helm of state, then instead of one unstable, two-power equilibrium, the political revolution produces another, still less stable.'[16] This interpretation was in keeping with Trotsky's view that the Russian revolution could not be bourgeois in nature. Yet he went on to admit that the instability of dual power might also swing in favour of the bourgeoisie; thus there was a real possibility that it would come to 'dominate the old state apparatus' and the Soviets would be unable to 'form the foundation of a new state':

The Mensheviks and the Socialist Revolutionaries were steering toward the first solution, the Bolsheviks toward the second. The oppressed classes, who, as Marat observed, did not possess in the past the knowledge, or skill, or leadership to carry through what they had begun, were armed in the Russian revolution of the twentieth century with all three. The Bolsheviks were victorious.[17]

Thus Trotsky made the victory of the Bolshevik party a direct function of the Russian proletariat. The determinism of this was, of course, far from being obvious and was certainly unproven. And he himself, a paragraph later, vacillated again toward the instrumental view: 'The relation of class forces is not a mathematical quantity permitting *a priori* computations. When the old regime is thrown out of equilibrium, a new correlation of forces can be established only as the result of a trial by battle. That is revolution.'[18]

In fact what Trotsky had in mind was the necessary prelude to revolution: insurrection, that actual seizure of power by force which would in its wake make possible the carrying out of a political revolution. Trotsky was to be the leader of the insurrection, the October 1917 which has entered history, and he has left us one of the best theoretical analyses by a participant of its nature. This is the chapter in *The History of the Russian Revolution* entitled 'The Art of Insurrection'.[19] If it fails in the end to convince, it is because Trotsky himself, struggling with the eternal issue of the pre-determined as against the self-willed,

[16] Loc. cit.   [17] Ibid., pp. 230–1.   [18] Ibid., p. 231.
[19] Ibid., III, pp. 1017–47. Most of this chapter is a theoretical analysis of the insurrection; thereafter in the *History* Trotsky reverted to the account of the actual events of October. (His *Uroki Oktyabrya*, Berlin, 1925, was mainly a polemical treatment of 1917.)

emerges now on the one side, now on the other. The argument he conducted in this chapter was as if between the theory of the permanent revolution and the theory of Bolshevism; but a synthesis of the two eluded him.

Was the insurrection a conspiracy? In Trotsky's view it both was and wasn't. An insurrection could never be entirely spontaneous, for if it were it would be merely chaotic, lacking direction and, at best, would culminate in a situation of anarchy, with the government overthrown but no one to replace it. Thus an 'element of conspiracy almost always enters to some degree into any insurrection':[20]

Just as a blacksmith cannot seize the red hot iron in his naked hand, so the proletariat cannot directly seize the power; it has to have an organization accommodated to this task. The co-ordination of the mass insurrection with the conspiracy, the subordination of the conspiracy to the insurrection, the organization of the insurrection through the conspiracy, constitutes that complex and responsible department of revolutionary politics which Marx and Engels called the 'art of insurrection'. It presupposes a correct general leadership of the masses, a flexible orientation in changing conditions, a thought-out plan of attack, cautiousness in technical preparation, and a daring blow.[21]

This is not to say, Trotsky continued, that a conspiracy could take the place of insurrection the way Blanqui imagined. Power cannot be seized in a vacuum, without regard for the prevailing social and political conditions. Nevertheless, Blanqui had been right in the sense that given all the right conditions, even then the successful seizure of power depended on the organizational instruments at one's disposal. The proletariat needed more than a spontaneous insurrection: 'It needs a suitable organization, it needs a plan; it needs a conspiracy.'[22] This the party provides, though it does so by utilizing other organizations, either soviets or such workers' bodies as are 'more or less equivalent to soviets':

When headed by a revolutionary party the soviet consciously and in good reason strives towards a conquest of power. Accommodating itself to changes in the political situation and the mood of the masses, it prepares the military bases of the insurrection, unites the shock

[20] Ibid., pp. 1017–18.   [21] Ibid., p. 1019.   [22] Ibid., p. 1020.

troops upon a single scheme of action, works out a plan for the offensive and for the final assault. And this means bringing organized conspiracy into mass insurrection.[23]

This joining of organized conspiracy to spontaneous insurrection assures that insurrection will be, 'like war, a continuation of politics with other instruments'.[24] However, the spontaneity of the insurrection is itself left in doubt since in analysing the 'art of insurrection' Trotsky attached particular importance to the choosing of the right moment for it; and this element of timing is provided by the party and its leadership. The latter do not wait for the masses to rise, nor do they necessarily follow the masses;[25] rather it is they who choose the most propitious moment.[26] Granted that the masses cannot be aroused unless they are already in a condition of potential ourburst, still the insurrection, it appears from Trotsky's account, is as much a matter of organization as of spontaneity. Much of Trotsky's analysis of it, in fact, was given over to the *technique* of organizing, planning and staging it. Throughout he assumed that the support of the masses for the party—intent in this way to seize power—was intrinsic. Thus the organized element emerged as an expression of the popular will. This was not, for Trotsky, a matter of pure democratic arithmetic; one did not hold a referendum on whether the majority were in favour of seizing power and by whom. Rather it was a matter of sensing the mood of the people and properly estimating the 'correlation of forces'; such forces were not merely numerical, though numbers were obviously important, but strategic. Quoting Lenin approvingly, Trotsky claimed that it was the large city centres which were crucial, which decided the fate of the insurrection, even if rural support was not immediately forthcoming: 'It was in this dynamic sense that Lenin spoke of the majority of the people, and that was the sole real meaning of the concept of majority.'[27] From this it was but one step for Trotsky to the ultimate Leninist revolutionary premise:

The proletariat can become imbued with the confidence necessary for a governmental overthrow only if a clear prospect opens before

[23] Ibid., p. 1021.   [24] Ibid., p. 1023.
[25] Trotsky attributed the fiasco of the 'July Days' to the inability of the party to contain a spontaneous, if misguided, mass initiative; see ibid., II, pp. 544–95.
[26] Ibid., III, p. 1022.   [27] Ibid., pp. 1028–9.

it, only if it has had an opportunity to test out in action a correlation of forces which is changing to its advantage, only if it feels above it a far-sighted, firm and confident leadership. This brings us to the last premiss—by no means the last in importance—of the conquest of power: the revolutionary party as a tightly welded and tempered vanguard of the class.[28]

And a few pages later Trotsky laid down the ultimate claim to legitimacy:

The Bolsheviks took the people as preceding history had created them, and as they were called to achieve the revolution. The Bolsheviks saw it as their mission to stand at the head of that people. Those against the insurrection were 'everybody'—except the Bolsheviks. *But the Bolsheviks were the people.*[29]

Is this not the same identification of élite with masses which, in his 1912 essay on the Russian intelligentsia, Trotsky had ascribed to the pretensions of that intelligentsia? Of course, Trotsky believed that the success of the Bolshevik insurrection was the initial vindication of his theory of the Russian revolution, of his views concerning socialism and backwardness, of his fundamental premise that in Russia the bourgeois stage of the revolution would be short-lived and would quickly pass over to the collectivist stage. Thus he claimed to see a kind of 'dialectical synthesis' between his theory and the Bolshevik practice; and this is perhaps best expressed in the following metaphor which he employed: 'Without a guiding organization the energy of the masses would dissipate like steam not enclosed in a piston-box. But nevertheless what moves things is not the piston or the box, but the steam.'[30] How could he know, however, that the 'piston-box' and the 'steam' were in this case parts of the same machine? He assumed it, of course, on the basis of his theoretical preconceptions, for the empirical evidence for it was at best dubious. And in assuming it, he—and the Bolsheviks—determined the character of the political revolution proper which could now be launched.

---

[28] Ibid., p. 1024.
[29] Ibid., p. 1029 (italics added). This aspect of Trotsky's post-1917 view of the relationship between party and masses is neglected in the otherwise cogent account of Trotsky's attitudes toward mass action by Norman Geras, 'Political Participation in the Revolutionary Thought of Leon Trotsky', in Geraint Parry (ed.), *Participation in Politics* (Manchester, 1972), pp. 151–68.
[30] Ibid., I, p. 19.

2. Terrrorism and the Dictatorship of the Proletariat

In the summer of 1918 Karl Kautsky published a pamphlet under the title *The Dictatorship of the Proletariat*.[31] In it he argued that the Soviet dictatorship was not that of a class but of a party, that power had come to be wielded by a handful of men and that in the end this would undermine, perhaps make impossible, the goals of socialism.[32] This evoked an immediate reply from Lenin, the famous *The Proletarian Revolution and the Renegade Kautsky*.[33] In 1919 Kautsky returned to the attack in no less stringent terms with his *Terrorism and Communism*.[34] This time it was Trotsky who replied. In 1920, while engulfed in the conduct of the Civil War, he found time to compose a major work, bearing the same title as that of the Kautsky book.[35]

Although at the turn of the century Kautsky had entertained the possibility that Russia may be among the first to achieve a radical government,[36] in his work of 1919 he argued that the attempt to effect a socialist transformation of the country was premature. In his view socialism could not be realized anywhere except on a democratic basis; and where the majority of the population rejected socialism there was no alternative but to postpone its implementation until that level of political and cultural development had been reached which would create a socialist majority. The Bolsheviks in Russia, faced with a hostile population, had decided, according to Kautsky, to ignore all opposition and to impose socialism from above. The

[31] English translation by H. J. Stenning, London 1919, reprinted Ann Arbor, 1964.
[32] Rosa Luxemburg, though highly critical of Kautsky's position, also denounced the Soviet government for turning the dictatorship of the proletariat into a dictatorship of the party. See her *The Russian Revolution* (Ann Arbor, 1961). This work was written in 1918 but not published until 1922.
[33] First published in 1918.
[34] English translation by W. H. Kerridge, London, 1920. First German edition, *Terrorismus und Kommunismus* (Berlin, 1919).
[35] *Terrorizm i Kommunizm* (Petrograd, 1920). The work was republished in Trotsky's *Sochineniya*, XII, pp. 9–180. All subsequent references are to this latter edition. The first English translation appeared under the title *The Defence of Terrorism* (London, 1921). The first American edition bore the title *Dictatorship v. Democracy* (New York, 1922). A more recent English edition, with the original title, *Terrorism and Communism*, was issued at Ann Arbor, 1961. The final section of this work (*Sochineniya*, pp. 108–77) deals with questions of economics and labour and will be referred to in the next chapter.
[36] See his article referred to in chapter 1, note 37, above.

consequence has been the worst of political excesses—the dictatorship of a minority, bureaucratization, force and terror. A backward, unprepared Russia was being forced to leap all at once into the socialist millennium. But in fact, in Kautsky's view, dictatorship would lead not to socialism but to a new form of barbarism.

In considering Trotsky's reply we may profitably pass over that part of it which was an attack on what he saw as Kautsky's devotion to the 'fiction' of 'bourgeois democracy'; Trotsky here added nothing new to the well-known Marxist critique of democratic or parliamentary institutions.[37] The unique aspect of Trotsky's book and that which, not unjustly, has been responsible for its notoriety, lies in its views on the use of force, compulsion and terror. He went far beyond the position merely that in time of revolution and civil war such methods were unavoidable. Trotsky's attitude was far more positive; he made a virtue of necessity and argued for the use of these methods as measures necessary not only for the protection of the Soviet regime but for the advance of socialism. Thus he declared at the outset: 'Who aims at the end cannot reject the means.'[38] And it is clear from the rest of the book that he saw no contradiction between the means used and the goal aimed at.

Trotsky's defence of the use of terrorism by the Soviet government was therefore based on an extreme form of utilitarianism. The 'sacredness of human life' was not rejected in principle; but it was not for Trotsky a value so absolute as to overshadow all other values. Just as there may be justifiable grounds for killing in war or as a means of self-defence, so the taking of human life was not only a necessary evil but an expedient act in time of revolution. 'If human life in general is sacred and inviolable, we must deny ourselves, not only the use of terror, not only war, but also revolution itself.'[39] However, those who now most vociferously denounced the use of terror by the revolutionary regime, were the very persons who, according to Trotsky, in the past had themselves used terror, intimidation and repression to protect their own interests. The principle of the 'sacredness of human life' was not one which they had themselves adhered to or intended adhering to and it was a principle

[37] See, especially, pp. 34–44 of *Terrorizm i Kommunizm* (*Sochineniya*, XII).
[38] Ibid., p. 25.   [39] Ibid., p. 63.

which could become truly inviolable only in the context of a
new social system to which the revolution itself was devoted.
'To make the individual sacred we must destroy the social order
which crucifies him. And this problem can only be solved by
blood and iron.'[40]

What, however, made one terror (the Red) better than
another (the White)? Trotsky quite clearly identified the
superiority of one terror over another with the superiority of
the cause in the name of which it was used. And, in the case
of the Russian Revolution, the struggle was between progress
and reaction, the new order against the old, the forces of light
against the forces of darkness. What justified the Red Terror
was the nature of the goal it was used to advance, the goal of
socialism in general, the classless society in particular. The
terror of those who opposed the revolution was aimed at con-
serving a social regime serving the interests of the few; that of
the revolution itself sought a social regime serving the interests
of all.[41] For this reason also, the latter was more effective than
the former: 'Terror is helpless . . . if it is employed by reaction
against a historically rising class. But terror can be very efficient
against a reactionary class which does not want to leave the
scene of activity.'[42] 'But where', Trotsky asked, 'is [the] guarantee . . . that it is in fact [the Bolshevik] party which expresses the
interests of historical development?' And he replied: 'We have
suppressed the Mensheviks and the S.R.'s—and they have disappeared. This criterion is sufficient for us.'[43] So Trotsky saw
history marching on the side of the righteous and victory
became a criterion for the justness of the cause. It followed,
therefore, that 'the man who recognizes the revolutionary historic importance of the very fact of the existence of the Soviet
system must also sanction the Red Terror'.[44] And as to the
'degree' of terror employed, it was not a question of 'principle'
but of 'expediency'.[45]

It would be superfluous to remark that this way of justifying
the use of violence and compulsion is reminiscent not only of
Rousseau's famous adage about 'forcing men to be free' but
also of the legitimacy attributed to the worst excesses of certain

[40] Ibid., p. 64.
[41] Ibid., p. 60; also p. 163.
[42] Ibid., p. 59.
[43] Ibid., p. 106.
[44] Ibid., p. 65.
[45] Ibid., p. 59.

twentieth-century regimes, amongst them the Soviet one which would one day turn its terror on Trotsky himself.[46] But even more glib was the manner in which Trotsky sanctioned the terror by attributing it directly to the will of a class. He took it for granted that the working class itself was exercising control and direction of the use of terror. There is not the slightest suggestion throughout the book that it was the Bolshevik party, much less a handful of men, which decided how and against whom terror was to be activated. And this is, of course, because Trotsky identified the party directly with the proletariat. Thus it was the working class itself which had 'recourse to severe measures of state terror', which would 'suppress . . . all attempts to tear power out of its hands',[47] and so on.

Trotsky's arguments in defence of terrorism were also characteristic of his defence of the Soviet dictatorship, the 'dictatorship of the proletariat'. The possibility of sustaining a revolutionary regime through formal democracy was dismissed out of hand by Trotsky. The concept of the parliamentary majority was a 'fetishism';[48] it was a form of rule typical of bourgeois society in which, in any case, not the majority ruled, except as a fiction, but the vested economic interests. The dictatorship of the proletariat, conversely, was that form of government which assured true representation of the majority, which made possible the organization of state power against the still unrelenting forces of reaction and which enabled the working class to lay the foundations for the eventual transformation of society:

It is clear that if our problem is the abolition of private property in the means of production, the only road to its solution lies through the concentration of state power in its entirety in the hands of the proletariat and the setting up of the transitional period of an exceptional regime—a regime in which the ruling class is guided, not by general principles calculated for a prolonged period but by considerations of revolutionary policy.[49]

---

[46] In later years, however, Trotsky would distinguish between this terror and that of Stalin (see chapter 10, below).

[47] Ibid., pp. 58 and 59.

[48] Ibid., p. 24. Trotsky justified the dissolution of the Constituent Assembly on the grounds that it would have been either a hindrance to revolutionary policy or superfluous (ibid., pp. 44–9).

[49] Ibid., p. 23.

Political force, in the form of this dictatorship of the proletariat, was an essential and unavoidable feature of revolutionary transition. The social basis of society could not be changed by parliamentary legislation, even if it were to receive the backing of the majority, since bourgeois interests would themselves resort to extra-parliamentary means to subvert the effects of such legislation. Compromise on issues affecting the fundamental fabric of society was impossible; on such issues, 'only force can be the deciding factor'.[50] Thus the dictatorship of the proletariat was the framework of revolution itself, the form of government which, facilitating a monopoly of power, created the political conditions for effecting social change. And though this dictatorship had as its ultimate purpose the abolition of state power, it was itself the most extreme form of such power, being decreed by the exigencies of revolutionary struggle.[51]

Trotsky applied the means-end principle to the dictatorship of the proletariat in the same way he had done in the case of terrorism. 'The man who repudiates the dictatorship of the proletariat', he declared, 'repudiates the socialist revolution and digs the grave of socialism.'[52] However, as in the case of terrorism, so here, the question arose as to what was the actual role of the proletariat. In what sense was the dictatorship that *of* the proletariat, in what sense was it *in the name of* the proletariat? It was precisely this question which Kautsky had stressed in his attack on the Soviet dictatorship. Trotsky replied as follows:

We have more than once been accused of having substituted for the dictatorship of the Soviets the dictatorship of our party. Yet it can be said with complete justice that the dictatorship of the Soviets became possible only by means of the dictatorship of the party. It is thanks to the clarity of its theoretical vision and its strong revolutionary organization that the party has afforded to the Soviets the possibility of becoming transformed from shapeless parliaments of labour into the apparatus of the supremacy of labour. In this 'substitution' of the power of the party for the power of the working class there is nothing accidental, and in reality there is no substitution at all. The Communists express the fundamental interests of the working class. It is quite natural that, in the period in which history brings

[50] Loc. cit.   [51] Ibid., p. 161.   [52] Ibid., p. 26.

up those interests, in all their magnitude, on the order of the day, the Communists have become the recognized representatives of the working class as a whole.[53]

It was only natural, therefore, that while the Soviets were the 'organs of power', 'general control' was concentrated in the hands of the party; it was the party which had the 'final word in all fundamental questions' and its Central Committee the ultimate powers of decision: 'This affords extreme economy of time and energy and in the most difficult and complicated circumstances gives a guarantee for the necessary unity of action.'[54] So much had Trotsky become enamoured of the party, in fact, that he now considered the 'progress of the socialist revolution in every [other] country' as 'depending' on the creation of 'just as authoritative a Communist party' as in Soviet Russia.[55] The future of socialism, in short, had become directly linked with the undisputed authority of the political vanguard.[56]

---

[53] Ibid., p. 106.   [54] Ibid., p. 104.   [55] Loc. cit.

[56] Two chapters of *Terrorizm i Kommunizm* (pp. 69–89 and 90–5) are devoted by Trotsky to an analysis of the Paris Commune of 1871. Kautsky had given over a large part of his *Terrorism and Communism* to a discussion of the Commune with a view to showing how the latter differed from the Soviet dictatorship of the proletariat. In Kautsky's view, the Commune had shown a respect both for human life and the principles of democracy, a respect totally absent in the Soviet case. In replying to this denigrating comparison, Trotsky argued that, in the first place, the Commune was 'the living negation of formal democracy . . . [it was] the dictatorship of working class Paris over the peasant country' (p. 83); and, in the second place, to the extent that it placed humanitarian considerations above long-term political ones it merely hastened its own demise and its final disaster. In fact, the differences between the Commune and the Soviet regime, according to Trotsky, grew partly out of the lessons which the latter has learned from the Commune's failure: the need for a central organization, discipline, strong leadership, ruthlessness towards enemies, and absolute control of the organs of government and force. Trotsky concluded this analysis by interpreting Marx to have taken a similar view of the defects of the Commune. In brief, those very elements which Kautsky had deemed praiseworthy in the Commune, were, in Trotsky's view, the source of its weakness. For other of Trotsky's writings on the Commune, see the following: 'Cherez tritsat pyat let, 1871–1906', written in late 1905 as a preface to Karl Marx, *Parizhskaya Kommuna* (St. Petersburg, 1906); (this preface, parts of which were later incorporated by Trotsky in his *Itogi i perspektivy*, deals primarily with the post-1905 situation in Russia, and only secondarily with the Commune); 'Pod znamenem Kommuny', in *Novyi Mir*, No. 938, 17 Mar. 1917 (reprinted in *Voina i Revolyutsiya*, II, pp. 412–14); 'Les Leçons de la Commune', written in February 1921 as a preface to C. Talès, *La Commune de 1871* (Paris, 1924). In all these writings, the Commune is described as the original example of the dictatorship of the proletariat. For Trotsky's pre-1917 writings on terrorism, see his *Sochineniya*, IV, pp. 338–69 where he denounces individual terrorism.

3. Civil War and the Red Army

Trotsky wrote voluminously about the creation of the Red Army and the conduct of the Civil War, tasks for which he himself was responsible.[57] It would be impossible to do justice to these writings in a study of this nature and the most that can be attempted is a summary of the more theoretical aspects of his military views as they bear upon questions here discussed, and as they relate to social and political questions in general.[58]

The most frequently cited of authorities in Trotsky's writings on war is Clausewitz; and this is not surprising since Clausewitz's famous principle that war is a continuation of politics by other means is precisely the principle which governed Trotsky's approach to the Civil War.[59] He saw the War as an integral part of the revolution, as the ultimate extension of the class struggle, and as the most direct of initial instruments for consolidating political gains. He did not exclude the possibility that in certain countries, under particular circumstances, civil war would not follow a revolutionary insurrection; in such countries social change might have proceeded so far that by the time of revolution the power of the old classes would have been eroded entirely. Historically, nevertheless, whether in England or in France, civil war and revolution were directly bound up, in Trotsky's view, and the former represented the direct, violent

[57] For his own account and evaluation of his role in the Civil War, see *Moya Zhizn*, II, pp. 140–95. The following are the main collections of his writings on military affairs in general, and the Red Army and the Civil War in particular: *Kak vooruzhalas revolyutsiya* (3 vols. in 5 parts, Moscow, 1923–5); *Sochineniya*, XVII, part 1, pp. 225–389 and part 2, pp. 3–514; *The Trotsky Papers, 1917–1922*, vol. I: 1917–19, vol. II: 1920–2, edited and annotated by Jan M. Meijer (The Hague, 1964 and 1971). The last collection consists of 796 documents (in the original Russian with a facing English translation) acquired from Trotsky in 1936 by the International Institute of Social History at Amsterdam. Copies of these documents are also available in the Trotsky Archives at Harvard. The documents comprise mainly brief dispatches from and to Trotsky at the front. They are essential to the historian of the Civil War but have almost no bearing on the subject of the present study.

[58] In this connection, see Deutscher, *The Prophet Armed*, pp. 477–85. Deutscher, basing himself on Karl Radek (presumably the latter's *Portrety i pamflety*, Moscow, 1927) claims that the main influence on Trotsky's military thinking was Jaures's *L'Armée nouvelle* (Paris, 1911).

[59] For an example of Trotsky's complete identification with Clausewitz's axiom, see his article 'Novaya kniga F. Engelsa', in *Pravda*, no. 71, 28 Mar. 1924. This article was written as a review of Engels' *Notes on the War, 1870–71*, published in Vienna in 1923.

confrontation between the old and the new forces. So it was in Russia; the Civil War was a particular form of politics, practiced during a stage when non-violent forms for resolving the class struggle were no longer effective. In pursuing the Civil War, the Russian proletariat, together with the peasants, was simply continuing its political struggle against Tsarism and bourgeois liberalism.[60]

In organizing the Red Army, Trotsky envisaged the eventual creation of a new kind of fighting force, a people's army. Thus he accepted in principle Jaurès's idea of people's militias as opposed to a professional standing army; in practice, however, he strove to create a very different kind of military force. He believed that a democratic people's army was a goal for the future; he did not think that it could be established so long as the remnants of the old social system were not completely eradicated, and certainly not during a time of civil war when the immediate objective of rapid victory left neither time nor resources for a fundamental social reorganization of the fighting forces. Above all, however, he thought the militia system could come into being only when the social and economic system had already been modernized, when mass education, high cultural standards, and a collective consciousness had been achieved. The general backwardness of Russia, the low cultural level of the peasants who fought in the Red Army, the lack of technical skills and facilities—all these meant that the idea of a people's army was premature. In any case, a fully democratized army was, like the fully democratized society, a function of the triumph of socialism and the withering away of the state.[61]

In the meantime, therefore, Trotsky argued for the creation of an army on principles not fundamentally different from those characterizing all armies. Thus the Red Army was to be primarily a standing army based on orthodox rules of hierarchy

[60] See in particular 'Voprosy grazhdanskoi voiny', in Trotsky's *Sochineniya*, XII, pp. 379–402. This is a speech delivered by Trotsky before the Military Science Society on 29 July 1924.

[61] For Trotsky's views on the limitations which backwardness imposed on army organization, see 'Novaya kniga F. Engelsa', op. cit. At the 8th Party Congress in March 1919 Trotsky submitted his 'Theses' on the creation of the Red Army in which he accepted in principle the militia idea but urged its postponement until proper social conditions had been created; see 'Nasha politika v dele sozdaniya armii', in *Kak vooruzhalas revolyutsiya*, I, pp. 186–95 (also in *Sochineniya*, XVII, part 1, pp. 377–89).

and command. Specialists and experts would be recruited and encouraged as would officers of the Tsarist regime who agreed to fight now in the ranks of the revolution. The elective principle, whereby commanders were chosen by their men, was to be rejected entirely in favour of the orthodox system of appointments by superiors. Discipline was to be inculcated according to well-established military practice.[62] In fact, all of Trotsky's efforts were concentrated on creating a highly centralized, modern army based on proven methods of organization and command, and eschewing tendencies towards partisan detachments or guerilla warfare. Although, simultaneously, Trotsky established the political commissar system in the army, his approach to military organization was fundamentally traditional and conservative.[63]

This is not to say that he denied the existence of non-military differences between the Red Army and other armies of the past and present. On the contrary, the social structure which he claimed was emerging and would eventually dominate the army, as well as the nature of the goals to which it was devoted, transformed it, in his view, from the very beginning into a unique military body. Despite the traditional principles of military organization, made necessary by the realities of Russia's internal and external conditions, the spirit of the army, Trotsky believed, was unlike that of other fighting forces. This was so because, above all, an alliance, based on collectivist concerns and the recognition of a common enemy, was being forged between workers and peasants in the army. Ties between troops and officers, although governed by military rules, were nevertheless more intimate because of the sense of common purpose and the vision of an egalitarian society. Officers themselves were more and more being recruited from among peasants and workers, thus breaking down traditional class barriers to

[62] This approach was laid down by Trotsky immediately after his appointment as Commissar of War; see his address of 28 Mar. 1918 to the Moscow City Conference of the Russian Communist Party, published as 'Trud, distsiplina, poryadok spasut sotsialistichesku sovetskuyu respubliku', in *Sochineniya*, XVII, part 1, pp. 155–72 (also in *Kak vooruzhalas revolyutsiya*, I, pp. 31–45).

[63] For his definition of the division of functions between commanding officer and commissar—the one responsible for military operations, the other for morale and loyalty—see his speech of 7 June 1918 to the First All-Russian Congress of Military Commissars, published as 'Organizatsiya Krasnoi Armii', in *Kak vooruzhalas revolyutsiya*, I, pp. 127–31 (also in *Sochineniya*, XVII, part 1, pp. 264–9).

mobility. The Red Army, as the army fighting for the secure-
ment of the basis from which the future socialist society would
be constructed, was inculcating its men with ideals, with a spirit
of co-operation, with a readiness for self-sacrifice. The Red
Army was indeed a *class* army, Trotsky declared, as was inevitable during a period of Civil War when military confrontation
itself was the result of irreconcilable social class divisions. But
its victory, in so far as it promoted the eventual abolition of
all class divisions, would be a national victory, that is, of the
people themselves and not of certain narrow interests.[64]

These views of the uniqueness of the Red Army did not, however, lead Trotsky into confusing political ideology with the
principles of military practice. On the contrary, he became the
most adamant opponent of the tendency amongst some officers
to seek out a specifically Marxist military strategy. Just as later
he would oppose the concept of a 'proletarian culture', so now
he denounced the concept of a proletarian military strategy.[65]
In fact, he went so far as to argue that Marxism, like any other
theory of society, was not only unhelpful in clarifying purely
military problems but irrelevant in this context.[66] The view he
took was that military doctrine, and war in general, was an
art and not a science, and as such depended not so much on
theoretical precepts as on the skills learned from experience and
on knowledge of an empirical nature:

There is not and there never has been a military 'science'. There does
exist a whole number of sciences upon which military affairs rest . . .

[64] These somewhat rhetorical views run through many of Trotsky's pronouncements
on the Red Army; for particular examples see the speech, delivered on 24 Sept. 1919,
and published as 'Ne sdadimsya, vyderzhim, pobedim!', in *Sochineniya*, XVII, part
2, pp. 219–24 and the article of August 1919, 'Programma militsii i ee akademicheskii
kritik', in *Kak vooruzhalas revolyutsiya*, II, part 1, pp. 115–21. Trotsky at this time was
beginning to urge experimentation with the militia system, though within the framework of the highly centralized Red Army.
[65] On his views concerning 'proletarian culture', see the following chapter.
[66] Trotsky's major writings dealing with these questions, on which the summary which
follows is based, are: 'Vstupitelnoe i zaklyuchitelnoe slovo na diskusii o voennoi doktrine', in *Kak vooruzhalas revolyutsiya*, III, part 2, pp. 201–9 (originally two speeches
delivered on 1 Nov. 1921 to the Scientific Military Society); 'Voennaya doktrina ili
mnimo-voennoe doktrinstvo', in ibid., pp. 210–40 (written in Nov.–Dec. 1921); 'Doklad
i zaklyuchitelnoe slovo', in ibid., pp. 242–70 (a report delivered to a conference of
Military Delegates at the 11th Party Congress on 1 Apr. 1922); 'Voennoe znanie i
marksizm', in ibid., pp. 271–89 (speech of 8 May 1922 to the Scientific Military
Society).

from geography to psychology . . . but war itself is not a science—
it is a practical art, a skill . . . War cannot be turned into a science
because of its very nature, no more than it is possible to turn architecture, commerce or a veterinary's occupation into a science. What
is commonly called the theory of war or military science represents
not a totality of scientific laws explaining objective events but an
aggregate of practical usages, methods of adaptation and proficiencies
corresponding to a specific task: the task of crushing the enemy.[67]

This being so there could be no one unified, all-embracing
military doctrine prescribing strategy for all events. Strategy
was always suited to particular conditions—of equipment,
numbers, geography, nature of the enemy and so on—and had
therefore to be continuously adapted as these changed. Flexibility and an empirically open approach needed to be the
guidelines in formulating strategy. Trotsky lashed out at those
who would decree some single strategic axiom—either 'always
attack' or 'always plan so as to assure manœuvrability' or some
other such general precept; in certain conditions defence was
more important than offence, and entrenchment more than
movement.[68] To create the pretence of a unified military doctrine was to be 'lured into a mystical or metaphysical trap';[69]
and to assume that commitment to Marxism was commitment
to some one military strategy was to confuse social theory with
the practice of an instrumental skill:

Just how is it possible to construct the usage of a military trade or
art by means of a Marxist method? This is the same thing as trying
to construct a theory of architecture or a text book on veterinary medicine with the aid of the Marxist method . . .[70]

To play chess 'according to Marx' is altogether impossible, just as
it is impossible to wage war 'according to Marx'.[71]

If there could not be an original 'Marxist' military doctrine,
the Red Army, like all armies, should feel free to borrow and
learn from all sources experienced in the art of war, and it must

---

[67] 'Doklad i zaklyuchitelnoe slovo', p. 244.
[68] Ibid., pp. 243 and 249–52; also 'Vstupitelnoe i zaklyuchitelnoe slovo na diskusii o
voennoi doktrine', pp. 205–7 and 'Voennaya doktrina ili mnimo-voennoe doktrinstvo',
pp. 222ff.
[69] 'Vstupitelnoe i zaklyuchitelnoe slovo . . .', p. 201.
[70] 'Doklad i zaklyuchitelnoe slovo', p. 244.
[71] 'Voennoe znanie i marksizm', p. 277.

jettison, as well, the notion that a specifically 'national' doctrine could be developed. The latter was merely a pretext for becoming imbedded in traditional ways of waging war without examining their efficacy. Trotsky's approach was, therefore, to create an atmosphere of openness to new ideas and a preparedness to experiment.[72] Above all, he warned against the concept of a 'proletarian' military strategy. The organization and social structure of the socialist army should not be confounded with its technique; the former defined its unique political characteristics, the latter was the result of purely military considerations. There was no more a proletarian strategy of war than there was a bourgeois one; under a socialist as under a capitalist government there was only the art itself of military strategy.[73]

In his speeches and writings on military affairs Trotsky always stressed the serious nature of the problems created for the Red Army by the economic and technical backwardness and the cultural poverty of Russian society. Yet the Red Army was not the only Soviet institution whose possibilities were narrowed by the limits of Russia's internal capacities. The character which the new political structure itself assumed in the initial years reflected the reality of these limits. Though Trotsky did not, and perhaps could not, say so, the 'dictatorship of the proletariat', in the actual form it took, and not the form it was ideologically presumed to have, was as much a product of Russia's backwardness as of Marxist notions about such a regime characterizing the 'transition to socialism'. If the Red Army could not be transformed into a people's army, this was, as Trotsky admitted, because democratization required both social cohesion and a high level of social development. But the absence of these was surely a general problem of Russian society and would have its impact on other institutions—and aspirations—as well.

A case, of course, could be made out—and this Trotsky tried to do in his *Terrorism and Communism*—that the extreme nature of the 'dictatorship of the proletariat' was governed by the ex-

---

[72] 'Vstupitelnoe i zaklyuchitelnoe slovo . . .', pp. 207–8 and 'Voennaya doktrina ili mnimo-voennoe doktrinstvo', pp. 215–18.
[73] 'Voennaya doktrina ili mnimo-voennoe doktrinstvo', pp. 213–15 and 'Doklad i zaklyuchitelnoe slovo', pp. 268–9.

igencies of the Civil War. Had not Marx himself spoken of such a dictatorship even in countries much more advanced than Russia? And, indeed, Marx had assumed that the dictatorship was necessary because no deposed class would surrender without a fight.[74] But had he also assumed that it would be necessary in order to create the new socialist society? There can be, of course, different views about this, and it is impossible to determine with any certainty what Marx thought would be the exact point at which the 'dictatorship of the proletariat' would become superfluous and the state 'wither away'. But this much is certain, that Marx, on the basis of his own social theories, could not expect such a dictatorship to arise where the conditions for socialism, and the need for it, had not already evolved of themselves. Given such conditions and given the support of the workers for socialism, the problem of democracy would presumably fall into place, would be resolved in the natural course of developments. One may question the validity of this as well, but the least that could be said for it was that it was not arbitrarily derived but based on a certain logic, even if the fundamental axioms of that logic were themselves a matter for debate.

The point about the 'dictatorship of the proletariat' in the new Soviet republic was that, being based on a quite different logic, not only could it not begin to disappear the moment it had secured the victory of the revolution, or of the class it claimed to represent, but it would have to increase its domination over society. The political revolution was but a preliminary; to transform society it would be necessary, sooner or later, that the dictatorship become, if anything, more omnipotent. Given the poverty of the foundations upon which the dictatorship stood, the social revolution, if it was to take place at all, would have to be imposed from above. Was Trotsky prepared for this? As we shall now see, in the economic, though not the socio-cultural realm, he was both prepared and determined that it should happen. One may doubt, however, whether at the time he recognized the full implications of this.

[74] For Marx's view of the 'dictatorship of the proletariat', see in particular the *Communist Manifesto* and *The Class Struggles in France*. Lenin's conception of it is in his *State and Revolution*.

CHAPTER SEVEN

THE SOCIAL REVOLUTION

> Once having taken power, it is impossible to accept one
> set of consequences at will and refuse to accept others . . .
> And, once having taken over production, the proletariat
> is obliged, under the pressure of iron necessity, to learn
> by its own experience a most difficult art—that of organiz-
> ing a socialist economy. Having mounted the saddle, the
> rider is obliged to guide the horse—on peril of breaking
> his neck.[1]

IN RETROSPECT, it is clear that Russia in 1917, and in the
years thereafter, was the first 'under-developed country'—if
this term is understood to signify not only a backward society
but one determined, in so far at least as its government is concerned, to overcome its backwardness. By now the analogy
between Russia and subsequent 'under-developed countries' is,
of course, a truism and we shall not belabour it. It may be noted,
however, that the situation confronting the Soviet government
in 1917 and later may serve as a model of the dilemmas which
were to arise, albeit with obvious local variations, elsewhere;
and though the intended manner of the eventual resolution of
these dilemmas—wilfully, rapidly, totally, and in accordance
with those standards of a modern society which were and are
associated with the West—may or may not serve as a model
for others, it had implications beyond itself, both as regards the
methods to be used, and the goals to be sought, or options available.

The main obstacles to change in Russia were, of course, the
primitiveness of economic production and the paucity of
material resources—not potential, for Russia was not naturally
poor, but actual. The lack of internal capital, of machinery,
of basic commodities, and the limited trade possibilities resulting from the fact that agriculture was the only source of
exports—all these, not to mention other factors, combined to

---

[1] Trotsky, *Terrorizm i Kommunizm* (*Sochineniya*, XII, pp. 99–100).

create the need for contradictory economic policies which, sooner or later, would issue in a well-known vicious circle: on the one hand, to raise capital and sustain the economy, agriculture had to be encouraged; on the other hand, to transform the economy, agriculture had to be undermined, or exploited, for the sake of industry.

Beyond this, however, there lay obstacles to change which were of a different kind and ultimately of a more complicated nature. Even if one assumes that in principle a way can be found out of purely economic problems, their practical resolution is obviously dependent on the degree of social and cultural change, on the nature of the human resources available at any one time. In 1917, and for many years to come, Russia was characterized by all those features now commonly associated with 'under-development': inured traditional ways and norms of life; a largely uneducated population; the absence of initiative and ambition or, as it has sometimes been called, the spirit and the ethic of modern economic life; and, perhaps above all, the lack of a vital, homogeneous social class capable of spearheading change. Russia, of course, was always far more Westernized than most, if not all, 'under-developed countries'. Everything is relative; but there is a point at which differences in degree do not affect similarities in kind.

How were these problems to be overcome? In examining Trotsky's ideas in this connection, it is important to note at the outset that just as in 1917 he had become reconciled to the fact that the revolutionary party would have to act as the political substitute for the workers, so in subsequent years he would resign himself to the fact that the party (or government) must continue substituting itself in the economic and social revolution as well. The idea, in other words, that the workers could fill the social void created by the absence of a middle class was seen, even by him, to be a fiction. However, it is also important to point out that although at one level he was to address himself to problems of economic reconstruction or modernization as such, his animating motivation remained to bring about change in accordance with *socialist* principles. For the truth of this we need not rely upon his rhetoric alone; we may look—as we shall do now—at the different ways in which he approached economic problems as against social and cultural ones, ways which show that he clearly distinguished between change as such, and socialist change; and we may look as well—as we shall do in the next chapter—at the importance he simultaneously attached to a world revolution and the consequent limits he attributed to the possibilities of socialism in Russia alone.

1. Economic Reconstruction

The economic history of the early years[2] of Soviet Russia is conveniently divided into two periods: that of War Communism, from the middle of 1918 to the middle of 1921, and that of the New Economic Policy (NEP), from the middle of 1921 to approximately 1926.[3] Because of the very different character of these two periods—and of the problems raised by them—our discussion of Trotsky's economic views will proceed in accordance with this division.

(a) *The Period of War Communism*

Whether War Communism was introduced as a result chiefly of practical considerations—the extremely difficult conditions created by the Civil War—or whether it was motivated primarily by the ideological preconceptions of the Soviet regime, is a question over which there is some disagreement among historians of the Soviet economy.[4] Probably both factors played their role; but what is certain is that if conditions did dictate the adoption of War Communism, the regime had no difficulty in justifying it ideologically. For the policies pursued and defined under this rubric involved the most intensive socialization by the state. Almost all industry was nationalized, private

---

[2] This chapter deals with the period extending roughly from 1918 to 1927, that is, to the virtual end of the New Economic Policy and to the effective exclusion of Trotsky from all power.

[3] Officially, NEP was not abandoned until some years later (on its tenth anniversary in 1931 it was still claimed to be in effect); in fact, however, the turn against the conception of NEP, and policies aimed at reducing the growth of the private sector, began in 1926. For accounts of the first decade of the Soviet economy, see in particular the following: E. H. Carr's *History of Soviet Russia*, especially *The Bolshevik Revolution, 1917–1923*, II (Harmondsworth, 1966), *The Interregnum, 1923–1924* (Harmondsworth, 1969), and *Socialism in One Country, 1924–1926*, I (Harmondsworth, 1970); Maurice Dobb, *Soviet Economic Development Since 1917* (6th edition, London, 1966); Alec Nove, *An Economic History of the U.S.S.R.* (Harmondsworth, 1969).

[4] See Nove, op. cit., pp. 78–82 and Dobb, op. cit., pp. 122–4.

trade was banned, agricultural surpluses were requisitioned and peasants prevented from freely marketing their products, money exchange was partially eliminated, and workers and trade unions virtually militarized. All this in the end led to near disaster, to an almost complete economic collapse,[5] but at the height of War Communism there were not a few Bolsheviks who believed that it would lead rapidly to the creation of an economic foundation for socialism.

The whole of Trotsky's position on War Communism indicates that he was among the most conspicuous of these optimistic Bolsheviks.[6] Whatever may have motivated others in supporting War Communism, it is abundantly clear that Trotsky himself saw it as first and foremost an instrument for the rapid socialization of Russia, and only secondarily as a stop-gap policy for dealing with the particular problems created by Civil War. We may take as a central text an expanded version of a report which Trotsky delivered to the Third All-Russian Congress of Trade Unions in January 1920, supplementing it with references to other of his speeches and articles, in order to see how enthusiastic Trotsky was about the measures adopted during War Communism and how convinced that only such measures could succeed in transforming Russian society in preparation for socialism.[7]

Preoccupied with the Civil War, Trotsky had turned his mind to economic matters only towards the end of 1919. From the very outset his views inclined towards extremist solutions. In the middle of December 1919 he submitted to the party's Central Committee a set of proposals for dealing with the economic situation of which the most daring was the militarization

---

[5] This is not to imply that War Communism alone was responsible for the chaos which reigned in the Russian economy by 1921. Obviously, the economy was in ruins as a result of the Civil War itself. But it is clear that the policies of War Communism, far from alleviating the situation, exacerbated it.

[6] The main source for Trotsky's economic views during the period of War Communism is volume XV of his *Sochineniya*, which is entirely devoted to economic subjects.

[7] The original report bears the long title 'O mobilizatsii industrialnogo proletariata, trudovoi povinnosti, militarizatsii khozyaistva i primenenii voinskich chastei dlya khozyaistvennykh nuzhd'. It was first published in *Pravda*, no. 14, 22 Jan. 1920 (and republished in its original form in *Sochineniya*, XV, pp. 107–14). However, Trotsky later expanded the contents of the report with extracts from other reports and included the whole as chapter 8 of his *Terrorizm i Kommunizm* (in *Sochineniya*, XII, pp. 127–67). All subsequent references are to this expanded version.

of labour.[8] Here for the first time he suggested that the Red Army be used to direct demobilized soldiers, by compulsion if necessary, towards essential jobs in the economy.[9] In spite of the immediate controversy which this proposal aroused, Trotsky not only clung to the idea but initiated a campaign to have it accepted. Towards the middle of January 1920 he appeared before trade union leaders and argued that the economic situation was so critical that the most drastic of solutions, the complete militarization of labour, even if it involved the most extreme use of force and compulsion, was absolutely essential.[10] Although Lenin supported Trotsky's proposal, it continued to be widely opposed.

But it is only in the report to the Congress of Trade Unions later in January—more exactly in the expanded version of that report which he published in 1920 as part of his *Terrorism and Communism*—that he made clear the broader reasons for the labour militarization proposal. Although he was convinced that it was also vital for dealing with the immediate problems of the economy, his real concern was with establishing the social foundations of the future, the groundwork for the collectivist society. Thus the report began with a definition of the importance which Trotsky attached to the form of the organization of labour: 'The organization of labour is in its essence the organization of the new society; every historical form of society is in its foundation a form of labour organization.'[11] And he continued with a general statement about the nature of labour and the place of discipline:

As a general rule, man strives to avoid labour. Love of work is not at all an inborn characteristic: it is created by economic pressure and

[8] 'Perekhod ko vseobshchei trudovoi povinnosti v svazi s militsionnoi sistemoi', in *Sochineniya*, XV, pp. 10–14 (originally in *Pravda*, no. 283, 17 Dec. 1919).
[9] However, the need for imposing discipline and control over labour was first emphasized by Trotsky as early as March 1918; see his 'Trud, distsiplina, poryadok' in *Sochineniya*, XVII, part 1, pp. 155–72.
[10] 'Khozyaistvennoe polozhenie respubliki i osnovnye zadachi vosstanovleniya promyshlennosti', in *Sochineniya*, XV, pp. 27–52. Trotsky's view, from 1920 onwards, that trade unions should be merely an appendage of the state is well-known, as is Lenin's difference over this issue with Trotsky: see Carr, *The Bolshevik Revolution*, II, pp. 200–29. The anti-trade union bias remained deeply ingrained in Trotsky; see, for example, his extreme strictures in later years against syndicalism, collected in the pamphlet *Leon Trotsky on the Trade Unions* (New York, 1969).
[11] *Terrorizm i Kommunizm* (*Sochineniya*, XII), p. 127.

social education. One may even say that man is a fairly lazy animal. It is on this characteristic, in reality, that all human progress is, to a large extent, founded; for if man did not strive to spend his energy economically, if he did not seek to acquire the maximum quantity of products in return for the minimum quantity of energy, there would have been no technical development or social culture. From this it appears, therefore, that human laziness is a progressive force . . . We must not, however, draw the conclusion from this that the party and the trade unions must encourage this characteristic as if it were a moral duty. No, no! We have enough of it as it is. The problem confronting social organization is, in fact, to set 'laziness' within a definite framework, to discipline it, and to pull mankind together with the aid of methods and measures invented by mankind itself.[12]

But this is only by way of a preliminary justification for the imposition of discipline upon labour; for Trotsky was concerned not merely with education and propaganda towards regular habits of work, but *compelling* and *coercing* workers to function and produce in a manner determined by their political leadership. In fact, though he paid lip service to the need for persuasion, for pointing out to workers the importance of discipline and of the fulfilment of production goals, he did not really believe that such an approach would have any appreciable effect. He argued instead that the best form of education was in fact compulsion; the worker would learn to work if he was forced to do so. But how was compulsion to be justified? In the same way, Trotsky believed, that the 'dictatorship of the proletariat' and civil war were justified: in order to protect a workers' government, a dictatorship was essential; in order to save the Soviet Republic, a ruthless war was necessary. The battle on the military front having been won, the main threat to Soviet Russia was now an economic collapse. All means necessary for preventing this collapse, for preserving the revolution, were justified; and the militarization of labour was the *sine qua non* of survival.[13] The problem of the restoration of the economy was the problem of labour power, its mobilization and proper distribution. Were it possible to acquire labour freely or to depend on more than just a minimal spirit of voluntarism, the Soviet government would do so. Since it was not possible to do so, compulsion and coercion were justified. So the population

[12] Ibid., p. 128.   [13] Ibid., p. 135.

had to be seen as a single 'reservoir' of labour power from which the government could extract as it deemed necessary.[14]

Beyond this immediate justification for the recourse to compulsion, however, there lay the larger question of the 'road to socialism'. Not only was compulsory and militarized labour essential to restore the economy, it was a necessary aspect of the transition to socialism. It is this claim which was the most interesting element in Trotsky's views, and which immediately raised anew the issue of socialism and backwardness. Thus he affirmed: 'It is beyond question that to step from bourgeois anarchy to socialist economy without a revolutionary dictatorship, and without compulsory forms of economic organization, is impossible.'[15] And he added:

We [are for] regulated labour on the basis of an economic plan, obligatory for the whole people and consequently compulsory for each worker in the country. Without this we cannot even dream of a transition to socialism. The element of material, physical compulsion may be greater or less; that depends on many conditions—on the degree of wealth or poverty of the country, on the heritage of the past, on the general level of culture, on the condition of transport, on the administrative apparatus, etc., etc. But obligation and, consequently, compulsion, are essential conditions for overcoming bourgeois anarchy, securing socialization of the means of production and labour, and reconstructing economic life on the basis of a single plan.[16]

The compulsory militarization of labour was thus for Trotsky the 'inevitable method' of labour organization 'during the period of transition from capitalism to socialism'.[17] Why was it essential and inevitable? In fact, precisely because the transition was not so much from capitalism as from a semblance of it. The very fact of the backwardness of Russian capitalism meant that Russian society lacked the habits of labour and social production:

Russian capitalism, as a consequence of its lateness, its lack of independence, and its resulting parasitic features, has had much less time than European capitalism to technically educate the labouring masses, to train and discipline them for production. The problem is now in its entirety imposed upon the industrial organizations of the proletariat.[18]

[14] Ibid., pp. 129–30. [15] Ibid., p. 133. [16] Ibid., p. 134.
[17] Ibid., p. 137. [18] Ibid., p. 142.

Thus in a backward country such as Russia, the by-passing of the full capitalist stage of development meant that it became the task of the workers' government, 'under the leadership of its vanguard', to educate the working class.[19] But since this could not be done by market mechanisms as in bourgeois society, compulsion became unavoidable and, in fact, desirable. Bourgeois methods—scarcity, unemployment, surplus labour, and the consequent necessity of the worker to accept capitalist conditions in order to subsist—were in any case themselves forms of coercion, though paraded under the fiction of free labour. The difference between this coercion and that of the workers' state was that the latter openly advocated it and admitted to it, making no pretence at concealing coercion since it was 'in the interests of the workers themselves'.[20] 'Repression for the attainment of economic ends', Trotsky wrote, 'is a necessary weapon of the socialist dictatorship.'[21] The task of the Soviet government was to create those qualities of work and production which Russian history failed to create: the spirit of competition, of personal initiative, of self-discipline, of pride in work done, together with a consciousness of the idea of social, collective production, co-operation, solidarity and mutual responsibility.[22]

There was yet a further justification, in Trotsky's view, for the use of coercion in the name of socialism and this was that socialism would in the long-run shorten the period of hardship which separated the backward society from its modern future; imposing burdens at the outset, it would lighten the future in a way which would have been impossible had the society been transformed in accordance with the capitalist method:

If Russian capitalism developed not from stage to stage, but leaping over a series of stages, and instituted American factories in the midst of primitive steppes, the more is such a forced march possible for a socialist economy. After we have conquered our terrible misery, have accumulated small supplies of raw material and food, and have improved our transport, we shall be able to leap over a whole series of intermediate stages, benefiting by the fact that we are not bound by the claims of private property and that therefore we are able to

[19] Ibid., p. 140.   [20] Loc. cit.
[21] Ibid., p. 143.   [22] Ibid., pp. 143 and 157–8.

subordinate all undertakings and all the elements of economic life to a single state plan.[23]

This reads almost like the view, which years later was to become widely entertained in many under-developed countries, that socialism, especially its Russian Marxist variety, was the quickest road to modernization. And this is undoubtedly what Trotsky himself believed both before 1917, when he claimed to disentangle theoretically the way out of Russia's social impasse and economic backwardness, and now, in 1920, as he formulated concrete proposals for economic reconstruction. The point in what Trotsky was saying, however, seems to be not that the socialist road was quicker for being only socialist, but that it was quicker for being also compulsory; and, indeed, who could deny that coercion brought more rapid results than the attempts to persuade and the freedom to abstain, than a system which relied on attaining actual consensus on policies? Whatever his own criticism of coercion less than a decade later, it is clear that this was precisely the manner in which Trotsky grasped the advantages of coercion during these early years of the Soviet regime. Without regimentation imposed from above, the road to modern society would be long and uncertain; and without a modern society, Russia could not become socialist. In any case, what would be the point, Trotsky wondered, of seeking consensus and social responsibility in a country so politically inexperienced and so socially divided as Russia was?[24]

But was not the very idea of compulsion anathema to the socialist mind? On the contrary: in Trotsky's view it was intrinsically a part of the way to socialism in a backward society, though not of socialism itself. The period of transition was in fact a period entirely characterized by the use of unpalatable but necessary and desirable methods. Thus Trotsky could write: 'The very principle of compulsory labour service is for the Communist quite unquestionable. "He who works not, neither shall he eat." And as all must eat, all are obliged to work.'[25] And so the 'element of state compulsion not only does

---

[23] Ibid., p. 153.
[24] This theme runs through the whole of the report, but see especially pp. 158ff.
[25] Ibid., p. 129.

not disappear from the historical arena, but on the contrary will still play, for a considerable period, an extremely prominent part'.[26]

Yet there was a difference, in Trotsky's view, between this compulsion and that practised by non-socialist regimes. Morally, not to mention socially, it was superior and justified because it was 'applied by a workers' and peasants' government in the name of the interests of the labouring masses'.[27] The difference, therefore, between Soviet and other compulsion, Trotsky declared, was 'defined by a fundamental test: who is in power?'.[28]

(b) *The Period of the New Economic Policy*

Whatever the motivations—pragmatic or ideological—for the introduction of War Communism in 1918, there can be no doubt as to the reasons which led to the turn-about of 1921 and which culminated in NEP. Although later some of those— particularly Bukharin—who defended NEP appeared to do so out of personal ideological inclinations, the immediate reasons for the change in policy were purely practical.[29] The Soviet economy in 1921 was simply collapsing; chaos reigned in production and distribution, and large-scale famine led to untold deaths. In part this was certainly due to the objective factor of the Civil War; but the policies of War Communism not only could not cope with the situation, they were in fact preventing recovery. Moreover, the situation was beginning to have political repercussions—peasant riots, strikes by workers, and the traumatic mutiny of sailors at Kronstadt. By the time of this last event, in February–March 1921, Lenin and others had

[26] Ibid., p. 128.
[27] Ibid., p. 163.
[28] Loc. cit. For almost all of Trotsky's writings on the organization, mobilization, and militarization of labour, see *Sochineniya*, XV, pp. 3–206 and 251–342. It would have been merely tedious to give an account of these writings, and superfluous, since they add only dry economic details to the central ideas expressed in the report which has formed the basis of this section.
[29] For a brief account of Bukharin's political and economic views, see Sidney Heitman, 'Between Lenin and Stalin: Nikolai Bukharin', in Leopold Labedz (ed.), *Revisionism* (London, 1962), pp. 77–90. An excellent biography of Bukharin is now available; see Stephen F. Cohen, *Bukharin and the Bolshevik Revolution: A Political Biography 1888–1938* (London, 1974). Unfortunately, the biography reached this author too late to be referred to in the present study.

become convinced that a completely new approach, in effect a major retreat, was essential to save the revolution and, of course, the government. The result was NEP, an economic policy which re-introduced private enterprise, particularly private agriculture, but private manufacturing as well, and though leaving the 'commanding heights' of the economy— banking, foreign trade and large-scale industry—in the hands of the state, marked a significant shift away from the ideological goals of Bolshevism.[30]

Lenin did not succeed in introducing NEP without opposition and while most of the party eventually fell into line, by the time of his death in January 1924 a great debate over the future of the Soviet economy, and thus that of NEP, was unfolding.[31] In this debate, Trotsky was to become involved in a characteristically exuberant and direct manner; and it was he who became the political and ideological leader of that grouping which came to be identified as the Left, and which urged not only the rejection of NEP but a return to the direct path to socialism.[32]

He did not, it is true, voice objections when NEP was first debated and introduced, and seemed to simply go along with the general consensus in the party.[33] But from the outset he was

[30] Full accounts of NEP are given in the works, previously cited, by Carr, Dobb and Nove (see note 3, above).

[31] The most complete account of this debate is Alexander Erlich, *The Soviet Industrialization Debate, 1924–1928* (Cambridge, Mass., 1960). See also M. Lewin, *Russian Peasants and Soviet Power* (London, 1968), chapter 6 for the views of the main protagonists (Bukharin, Preobrazhensky, Trotsky, and Stalin).

[32] In what follows, as in the previous section of this chapter, no attempt is made to evaluate Trotsky's economic opinions from a purely, or even primarily, *economic* point of view. Within the context of this study, what is of interest is the political (or ideological) aspect of his economic views, and the light it throws on his general social and political ideas.

[33] Ironically, Trotsky was amongst the first to raise a proposal, as early as February 1920, for a change of course which would involve, partially at least, an abandonment of War Communism. The proposal sticks out from the rest of his economic statements and writings, for both before and almost immediately afterward he held and propagated views of a completely different nature. On this one occasion, addressing the Central Committee of the party, he suddenly proposed that the extreme restrictions placed on the peasantry be removed. (See 'Osnovnye voprosy prodovolstvennoi i zemelnoi politiki', *Sochineniya*, XVII, part 2, pp. 543–4.) He urged that the requisitioning of agricultural products be terminated, that the peasant be allowed to sell freely and make a profit, that industrial products be more widely used as a form of payment. He expressed the view that the existing restrictions were discouraging the peasant from cultivating his land beyond his own family needs, thus preventing much-needed surplus

critical of its effects on what he considered the essential methods to be followed by a socialist-oriented economy; and he refused to accept a uniform or extreme application of NEP. Thus in a memorandum of August 1921 to the Central Committee he urged the retention of central, all-encompassing planning, in spite of its being in contradiction with the conception of NEP, and demanded the establishment of a 'central economic authority'.[34] Thereafter, as before, he was the leading proponent of comprehensive planning and of Gosplan (the State Economic Planning Commission).[35] And in the course of time he became more and more convinced that while NEP had succeeded in revitalizing agriculture—this was, after all, its main intention—it was unable to confront, much less solve, the fundamental problems of the Russian economy, particularly the problem of industrialization. From the end of 1922 onwards, therefore, he began to expound a position which would become one side of the forthcoming 'great debate' on the future of the Soviet economy.

In a speech in October 1922 Trotsky first raised the idea which would be identified with this position, the idea, that is, of 'primitive socialist accumulation'.[36] The gist of the speech

---

production. And he concluded that the present policy was not only lowering agricultural production but also 'bringing about the automization of the industrial proletariat and threatens to disorganize completely the economic life of the country' (ibid., p. 544). Did he really have in mind a retreat from War Communism and the adoption of a programme not unlike that which later came to be identified with NEP? Or was this, as his biographer has suggested, an impulsive, emotional reaction to the economic havoc of which he had suddenly become aware? (See Deutscher, *The Prophet Armed*, p. 496.) Whatever the case, the proposal was turned down by the Central Committee and Trotsky never raised it again, returning instead to his earlier and much more characteristic views. In his autobiography, recalling his 1920 proposal, Trotsky stated that he had then concluded that 'War Communism must be abandoned' and that 'to revive our economic life the element of personal interest must be introduced at all costs' (*Moya Zhizn*, II, p. 198). But this was clearly an attempt to minimize, *ex post facto*, his later opposition to NEP (and thus his differences with Lenin) and cannot be taken as sufficient evidence for a real change of mind; and, in any case, it does not explain the fact that he dropped the whole idea immediately, never to return to it again.

[34] Memorandum to Central Committee on planning, 7 Aug. 1921, Archives, T774.
[35] For his views on planning, see *Sochineniya*, XV, pp. 207–48.
[36] The speech was delivered to the fifth Komsomol Congress on 11 Oct. 1922 and is in *Sochineniya*, XXI, pp. 294–317. The term 'primitive socialist accumulation' was apparently first coined by Vladimir Smirnov who at the time worked as an economist for Gosplan. It was, of course, used by way of analogy with Marx's concept of 'primitive capitalist accumulation'.

was that the Soviet economy was now at a stage at which it had to begin to lay the foundations of modern industry and thus was in need of capital formation, of the creation of state profits which could be re-invested in industrial development and production. At this time, however, Trotsky had hardly worked out how this was to be done on a large scale and his only proposal was that the working class would have to make sacrifices, presumably in the form of lower wages and longer working hours. However, when he returned to the idea in April 1923, at the twelfth Congress of the party, he made his intentions clearer.[37] In the course of a by now, for him, recurrent call for planning, he again claimed that the Soviet economy must set out on a road leading to 'primitive socialist accumulation'. But now he linked this road directly with the elimination, albeit not immediate, of NEP. In effect he called for a socialist policy to be waged against NEP, against the private sector. Quoting Lenin that NEP had been established 'seriously and for a long time', Trotsky retorted: 'but not for ever'; it had been introduced 'in order to defeat it on its own foundation and to a large extent, by using its own methods'.[38] And he declared that the very successes achieved through NEP 'bring us closer to its liquidation'.[39] Implicit, if not explicit, in all this was the view that the time had come to see agriculture as the source of 'accumulation', as the basis for industrialization, and to act accordingly—agriculture, after all, constituted the overwhelming part of the private sector and the main beneficiary of NEP. Trotsky still presented the idea under the guise of planning, but his listeners could well understand now that he was urging not only planning but a major turn-about from NEP.[40] In short, Trotsky was telling the party that the foundations for the eventual transition to socialism could not be laid unless the problem of industrialization was directly tackled, and that to

[37] For the text of his address to the Congress, see *12 Syezd RKP: Protokoly* (Moscow, 1923), pp. 282–322.
[38] Ibid., p. 306.
[39] Ibid., p. 313.
[40] Deutscher, *The Prophet Unarmed*, pp. 99–101, argues that Trotsky was not basically opposed to NEP but was in favour of a very gradual change-over. However, in the light of Trotsky's subsequent views this seems too cautious an interpretation of Trotsky's position. Certainly, he did not come out for the immediate abolition of NEP; but the struggle against it which he contemplated already in 1923, and thereafter, implied more than a gradual evolution of the socialist, as against the private, sector.

postpone this task was to create obstacles to its future execution.[41]

The 'scissors crisis',[42] which had already begun to unfold at the time of the twelfth Congress, came to a head in late summer 1923 and, in a stark way, made conspicuous the fundamental and persisting conflict between agriculture and industry, as well as the difficulties of running a mixed economy. NEP had originally improved the situation of the peasant; now, however, the rise in industrial prices and the decline in agricultural ones—the separating blades of the 'scissors'—threatened to undermine anew agricultural production. The reasons for the crisis were primarily the inability of Russian industry, still handicapped and inefficient, to develop sufficiently to produce its own capital—thus seeking it through higher prices—and the relative success of agriculture: greater surplus production meant, of course, lower prices on the market. Politically, the danger of the crisis was that it would arouse the peasant against the regime and throw into disequilibrium the already delicate alliance between peasant and worker on which the regime depended.

The reaction of Trotsky to the crisis was to go to the root of the problem. On 8 October 1923 he addressed a letter to the Central Committee in which he attributed the deteriorating situation to the lack of an over-all economic policy and to the failure to deal with the necessary priorities of the objective situation of the Russian economy.[43] In his view, two failures of an economic nature were paramount: the failure to apply planning seriously and scrupulously and the failure to undertake a fundamental reform of industry. What was needed now was 'manipulative regulation' and, simultaneously, a long-term policy for the rationalization and modernization of industry.

---

[41] In this connection see also his 'Tezisy o promyshlennosti' of 6 Mar. 1923 in Archives, T2964 (first published in *Pravda*, no. 78, 11 Apr. 1923).

[42] The term itself was first coined by Trotsky, at the Twelfth Congress (see *12 Syezd RKP*, pp. 292–3).

[43] The full text of the letter was never published but lengthy extracts from it appeared in *Sotsialisticheskii Vestnik* (Berlin), no. 11, 28 May 1924, pp. 9–10. The letter went beyond purely economic issues and was, in fact, a general attack on the structure and leadership of the party. This was the beginning of Trotsky's criticism of party bureaucratization and reflected the political struggle which was emerging already during the last days of Lenin.

The solution to the agrarian problem lay in the solution to the industrial one. In any case, in Trotsky's view, the 'scissors crisis', having cut the link between the peasantry and industry, was 'equivalent to the liquidation of the New Economic Policy'.[44]

Towards the end of 1923 and the beginning of 1924 the struggle for power in the party, in the wake of Lenin's illness and death, had already begun in earnest. Partly this took the form of discussion over inner-party structure, to which Trotsky's main contribution was the book *Novyi Kurs* (The New Course).[45] Simultaneously, however, the main factions began to group themselves around differing economic positions so that future economic policy became the focus of the political struggle.[46] The result was the 'great debate', which extended until 1928 and which concerned all the fundamental issues of the Soviet economy and its reconstruction.

The differences, as they emerged in the debate, were deep, and indicated a substantial ideological split. The main spokesman for the Right was Bukharin, once an ardent leftist but now the most extreme defender of NEP.[47] The whole *raison d'être* of his approach may be said to have been the peasant–worker alliance.[48] He believed that without such an alliance the Soviet regime could not possibly survive, and he viewed peasant support especially as so crucial that he was willing to bend over

---

[44] *Sotsialisticheskii Vestnik*, p. 10. In a further letter of 24 Oct. 1923 (extracts in ibid., pp. 11–12), Trotsky wrote: 'I stood and stand on the opinion that one of the most important causes of our economic crisis is the lack of appropriate uniform regulation from above.' In the meantime, as a way of dealing immediately with the crisis, Trotsky urged the lowering of industrial prices rather than the raising of agricultural ones. In this latter connection, see especially his article 'O smychke', originally published in *Pravda*, no. 277, 6 Dec. 1923 and reprinted as an appendix in Trotsky, *Novyi Kurs* (Moscow, 1924), pp. 93–9.

[45] The book, and Trotsky's first criticism of bureaucratization, are discussed in chapter 10, below.

[46] The actual political struggle has been described in numerous works, but see especially the accounts by Schapiro, *The Communist Party of the Soviet Union*, chapters 15 and 16 and R. V. Daniels, *The Conscience of the Revolution: Communist Opposition in Soviet Russia* (Cambridge, Mass., 1960).

[47] In what follows no attempt is made to do justice either to the quantity or quality of the debate, something which would require much more space than can be devoted to it here. The very brief summaries of the two main positions are meant only to provide the context for Trotsky's views. The main accounts of the debate have already been cited, i.e. Erlich and Lewin (see note 31, above).

[48] The main source for Bukharin's views here is his pamphlet *Put k sotsializmu i raboche-krestyanskii soyuz* (Moscow–Leningrad, 1926).

backwards not to do anything which would undermine it. NEP seemed to him ideal from this point of view since it favoured the peasant, but also because it was a framework, he believed, within which it was possible to develop the state sector without unduly jolting the whole delicate economic structure. He did not think that the regime could possibly win in a confrontation with the peasants, although he admitted that the 'class struggle' could not be entirely avoided. He envisaged, however, a prolonged period during which the improvement in agriculture would lead to large-scale rationalization which, in turn, would require co-operation and eventually collectivization. This would naturally bring the peasant nearer the worker and make possible the integration of agriculture within an industrio-co-operative economy. In the meantime, as far as industry was concerned, the emphasis should be on efficiency and gradual development. Progress towards socialism would be slow—the phrase he used was 'at a snail's pace'—but surer than an impatient policy of full speed ahead.

There was much that was sane and realistic in Bukharin's analysis but much also that was based on pure optimism. In particular, Bukharin did not explain how industry in a backward country could be made to develop at all unless the major, if not the only, source of capital, agriculture, was exploited and dislocated. This criticism of Bukharin, and of NEP as well, formed the basis of the position of the Left, whose main theoretical spokesman was Preobrazhensky.[49] The latter took up the concept of 'primitive socialist accumulation' and concentrated directly on the fundamental dilemma of the backward society: where to find capital resources for industrial development? In Preobrazhensky's opinion the unavoidable reply to this was: among the peasants. The socialist or state sector was both too small and too undeveloped to provide more than a token flow of capital from within itself; besides, in Preobrazhensky's view, a workers' government could not expect the workers to bear

[49] Preobrazhensky's major work is *Novaya Ekonomika* (Moscow, 1926). The main arguments of the book first appeared in the form of articles published in 1924 in *Vestnik Kommunisticheskoi Akademii*. The work has been translated into English as *The New Economics* (Oxford, 1965), with an introduction by Alec Nove. On Preobrazhensky, besides the works previously cited, see also the article by Alexander Erlich, 'Preobrazhensky and the Economics of Soviet Industrialization', in *Quarterly Journal of Economics* (Feb. 1950), pp. 57–88.

the brunt of the sacrifices necessary. Only the private sector, which meant primarily the peasants, could be made to supply capital since it was, in effect, the only productive sector of the backward society. Preobrazhensky realized that the peasants could hardly co-operate on a voluntary basis and thus advocated 'exploitation' through taxation and unequal exchange. He did not, it is true, carry the argument to its logical, if extreme, conclusion—the forced and complete domination of the whole private sector—but the implications of his arguments were abundantly clear. And, in any case, it was apparent to him that NEP was essenttially a self-defeating policy; so long as the private sector remained unexploited, industrialization was impossible. NEP was an attempt, in his view, to reconcile the irreconcilable, two economic forms not only in conflict with each other but each determined to destroy the other. Obviously, in a confrontation of this nature, a workers' government could not remain neutral. This latter was the political aspect of the question; the economic aspect was that there was no way, except state intervention, which led to the development of a backward economy.

If Preobrazhensky was the economic theoretician behind the Left, Trotsky was its leading political figure and spokesman.[50] He never, it is true, interpreted the concept of 'primitive socialist accumulation' in quite the extreme and rigid fashion which characterized its use by Preobrazhensky and there were not a few other differences between the two men.[51] Nevertheless, the logic of his views was not far removed from that of Preobrazhensky. We have already seen the affinity to the latter's ideas in Trotsky's economic writings and pronouncements prior to 1924. Thereafter, Trotsky pursued a line consistent with his earlier position. His main economic work of this period was a pamphlet, written in 1925, and devoted to the query of its title: *Towards Socialism or Capitalism?*[52] It was in fact an ex-

---

[50] The views of Stalin, who at the outset sided with the Bukharin position, will be referred to in the context of the discussion on 'socialism in one country' in chapter 9, below.

[51] The main difference was over the extent of the Soviet economy's dependence on the world economy: Trotsky believed it was much greater than Preobrazhensky assumed (see Archives, T3034).

[52] *K sotsializmu ili k kapitalizmu?*, originally published as a series of articles in *Ekonomicheskaya Zhizn*, in *Izvestiya* and in *Pravda* during September 1925. A separate Russian edition

tremely optimistic work, concerned to show throughout how successfully the Soviet economy had been steered in the direction of the socialist sector. With all the dangers inherent in NEP, the Soviet regime, according to Trotsky, had nevertheless been able to exploit NEP's framework for its own long-term goals. So sanguine, in fact, was Trotsky that he could hardly imagine any other development in the future. Yet throughout the pamphlet there ran one basic set of assumptions, that agriculture would be an adjunct of industry, that the priorities of the latter would take precedence, and that the struggle against the 'bourgeois' village would be intensified and extended. In arguing that the Soviet economy had been moving away from capitalism and towards socialism, Trotsky attributed this trend to the exploitation of the natural advantages which the state sector enjoyed under a socialist government. Without denouncing the original conception of NEP he nevertheless questioned its validity for the future. It was introduced, he wrote, to 'develop the productive forces as a basis for social development in general';[53] by this he clearly meant that the private sector was allowed to flourish in order the better to exploit it later for the state sector. Thus, at the outset, the two parts of the mixed economy were allowed to struggle against each other. But such a conception, in his view, was no longer adequate, and to assure the triumph of the state sector, the latter had to be given the necessary political support and economic advantages. He repeated over and over that, in any case, the fundamental problems of agricultural production could not be solved unless Russia was industrialized; thus the latter goal was as much a matter of general economic reconstruction as of socialism, and the two, of course, were, far from incompatible, in fact complementary.[54] The danger remained, however, that the continued existence of private agriculture would lead to bourgeois stratification in the countryside, thus mitigating against the eventual socialization of agriculture. The aim should therefore be to intensify industrial development; if the 'growth of industry will

---

in pamphlet form was apparently issued but it has proven impossible to trace. For convenience, all subsequent references are to the English translation, *Towards Socialism or Capitalism?* (London, 1926). Trotsky wrote a special preface for the English edition.
[53] *Towards Socialism or Capitalism?*, p. 23.
[54] The foregoing is a summary of chapter 1, primarily, of the pamphlet (pp. 13–54).

keep ahead of the process of stratification amongst the peasantry and neutralize it', it will have created 'a technical base and economic possibilities for a gradual transition to collective farming'.[55]

This last is a fair illustration of Trotsky's approach to the issue of collectivization. Like others on the Left, he did not have an immediate plan for collectivization. In his attitude to the transition to collective farming he was closer to Bukharin than the divergence of their general views might lead one to believe. Like Bukharin he did not think that this transition could be forced, but rather that it was a function of cultural and technical development and that it depended, as well, on the prior domination of the economy by industry. Nevertheless, his views—and those of the Left in general—on collectivization were at variance with the logic of the policies he advocated. Put another way, his economic arguments at least implied that a strong hand was necessary in dealing with the peasants. How else, after all, could he expect industry to get the initiative over agriculture, and how else could 'primitive socialist accumulation' be fulfilled? In 1927, as his political career was coming to an end—in November of the year he would be expelled from the party and in January 1928 deported to Alma-Ata—he became more forthright on these issues. In September he drew up, together with twelve other members of the Joint Opposition, a long document—which came to be known as the 'Opposition Platform'—for submission to the party's Fifteenth Congress; this expounded the Opposition's views on economic and political matters.[56] Although this is a collective work, Trotsky was obviously its guiding spirit and it may be taken as a faithful representation of his own views.

The 'Platform' is, of course, an attack on Stalin's leadership but it takes the form of a detailed criticism of current economic policies. Unlike *Towards Socialism or Capitalism?* it is pessimistic

---

[55] Ibid., p. 11 (this is in the preface to the English edition).

[56] 'Proekt platformy bolshevikov-lenintsev (oppozitsii) k XV syezdu VKP (b)'. A copy of the Russian original of this work is in the Trotsky Archives, T 1007. To facilitate quotation, however, references in what follows are to the English translation by Max Eastman in Leon Trotsky, *The Real Situation in Russia* (New York, 1928), pp. 23–195 (hereafter referred to as 'Platform . . .'). Incidentally, the 'Platform' was never submitted to the Congress, since in November 1927, a month before the Congress was to meet, Trotsky and other members of the Opposition were expelled from the party.

in tone, arguing that recent developments have constituted a setback for the socialist sector and are leading towards class differentiation in agriculture. Many passages are devoted to showing the growth of the *kulak* danger, and the simultaneous forsaking of the poor and middle peasants.[57] A full chapter is devoted to the condition of the workers which is seen as having seriously deteriorated.[58] The work, however, is not simply a list of indictments, but argues a central thesis of its own: this is that the only policy both for the reconstruction of the economy and its preparation for socialism is one which gives absolute precedence to industrialization. Any other approach will not only curtail industrial development but will also fail to revitalize agriculture. In fact, the whole economic portion of the work may be said to be devoted to the principle that 'only a powerful socialized industry can help the peasants transform agriculture along collectivist lines'.[59] The argument is presented in such a way as to imply that the Soviet economy is now at a crossroads, and that the pace of industrialization must be drastically stepped up if the socialist character of the Soviet regime, and of the future society, is to be preserved. The backwardness of agriculture is attributed to the backwardness of industry: 'The inadequate tempo of development in industry leads . . . to a retardation of the growth of agriculture.'[60] But how is the tempo to be accelerated? In a sub-section devoted to this very question, the 'Platform' lists a number of measures to this end;[61] but the most far-reaching is clearly the proposal to increase substantially the taxation of the 'upper layers of the peasants and the new bourgeoisie in general' in accordance with the 'growth of accumulation' amongst these strata.[62]

Yet concurrently with the attack on the *kulak* the 'Platform' proposes a positive programme aimed at winning over to collectivism the poor peasants. Clearly what it envisages is the exploitation of the class struggle in the countryside, sharpened by the

---

[57] See especially pp. 64–7 of the 'Platform . . .'
[58] Ibid., pp. 40–59.   [59] Ibid., p. 61.
[60] Ibid., p. 77.   [61] Ibid., pp. 87–93.
[62] Ibid., p. 88. Elsewhere, the 'Platform' speaks of the necessity of making the 'kulak', 'as the renter of land . . ., wholly and absolutely . . . subject to supervision and control from the organs of the Soviet power in the country[side]' and this in order to facilitate the nationalization of land. (Ibid., p. 70.)

growth of class differentiation: 'The growth of private proprie-
torship in the country must be offset by a more rapid development of collective farming. It is necessary systematically and
from year to year to subsidize the efforts of the poor peasants
to organize in collectives.'[63] In all this, there is no direct suggestion of compulsion, and the use of force may be said to be
implied only in dealing with recalcitrant *kulaks*. However, the
element of confrontation with the peasantry is clearly evident
in the whole approach of the 'Platform', and while it expresses
the belief that collectivism in the countryside will develop of
its own in the course of time and with the rise in cultural and
technical standards, it sees the need for an economic policy
which is not dependent on such standards alone but capable,
before their attainment, of consolidating the penetration into
agriculture of socialist organization.[64]

2. Social and Cultural Reconstruction

In his essay of 1912 on the Russian intelligentsia—which we
have had occasion to discuss in another context[65]—Trotsky described as follows the heritage of Russian culture and society:

That we are poor with the accumulated poverty of a thousand years
requires no proof. History shook us out of its sleeve into a severe environment and dispersed us thinly over a vast plain. No one proposed
a different habitation for us; in the place that bound us we were compelled to put our shoulder to the wheel. The invasions from the Asiatic
East, the ruthless pressure of wealthier Europe from the West, and
the state—Leviathan consuming an excessive part of the people's
labour—all of this not only impoverished the working masses but also
dried up the sources sustaining the governing layers. Hence their slow
growth and the barely perceptible accumulation of 'cultural strata'
over the virgin soil of social barbarism ... For a thousand years
we lived in a humble log cabin, the crevices of which were stuffed
with moss—to dream of vaulting arcs and Gothic spires would not
have become us![66]

This passage is merely one of the more vivid expressions of
a central theme in Trotsky's thought in general: the backward-

---

[63] Ibid., p. 68.
[64] See especially the section on 'co-operation', ibid., pp. 72–4.
[65] 'Ob intelligentsii', in *Literatura i Revolyutsiya*, pp. 255–69; see chapter 5, above.
[66] Ibid., pp. 257–8.

ness and poverty of Russian social and cultural life. He was not the only one, of course, to recognize the limitations imposed on the Soviet regime by the cultural backwardness of the masses—the reality was too pervasive to escape the notice of anyone—but he was perhaps more sensitive to its implications than others. The problem was compounded, and not eased, by the fact that Russia did not lack an intellectual and artistic tradition, for this tradition was fundamentally rootless, severed from Russian society—or rather unattached since it was never tied to it in the first place—and thus incapable, in Trotsky's view, of providing a bridge to the masses, certainly not in the initial stages. Moreover, the Soviet regime could harbour no illusions about the pre-1917 intelligentsia: for the most part the latter was either hostile to the revolution or alien to its spirit and goals. The problem, therefore, was both to nullify the influence of an old cultural élite and to create a new one alive to socialist ideals and to the needs of Russian society. But in so far as a new intelligentsia of this kind could hardly be created overnight, the immediate tasks of social and cultural reconstruction became the responsibility of the Soviet regime itself.

In this, Trotsky realized, there lay a two-fold danger: the expectation of quick results; and, to fulfil this expectation, the misuse of political power in fundamentally non-political matters. Revolutionaries are impatient men and successful revolutions arouse expectations of unbounded possibilities; carried away by their impatience and their expectations, there were not a few amongst the Bolsheviks who believed that, in the wake of October, a new age was about to be ushered in, that a new socialist man was on the verge of being created, and that on the ruins of the old society a new one would immediately rise. Not so much to dampen this enthusiasm—for no one was a more enthusiastic revolutionary—as to channel it into immediately essential and productive tasks, Trotsky from the outset urged a realistic appraisal of the possibilities of Russian society in the sphere of cultural change and innovation. This cautious approach was in contrast to his maximalist views in the field of political and economic policies, and it grew out of his recognition, firstly, of the extent of Russian backwardness, and out of his sensitivity, secondly, to the special character of things cultural. In all his writings on cultural subjects there runs one common thread: the development of cultural norms and modes of behaviour follows processes of its own, and whether it be forms of everyday life or literature and art, changes cannot be decreed or instituted by decisions taken in government or party caucuses. If Trotsky was the most unequivocal defender of the political 'dictatorship of the proletariat', he was also the most outspoken opponent of a cultural 'dictatorship of the proletariat'.[67]

(a) *The Culture of Everyday Life*

How careful Trotsky was to set his sights on immediate not ultimate cultural possibilities may be gauged from the following passage, taken from a speech of 1923, in which he attempted to define the 'tasks of communist education':

It is frequently asserted that the task of communist enlightenment consists in the education of the new man. These words are somewhat too general, too pathetic, and we must be particularly careful not to permit any formless humanitarian interpretation of the conception 'new man' or the tasks of communist education . . . Our present task, unfortunately, cannot lie in the education of the human being of the future. The utopian and humanitarian-psychological viewpoint is that the new man must first be formed and that he will then create new conditions. We cannot believe this. We know that man is a product of social conditions. But we know too that between human beings and conditions there exists a complicated and actively working mutual relationship. Man himself is an instrument of this historical development and not the least important. And in this complicated historical interaction between conditions of environment and active human beings, we do not create the abstractly harmonious and perfect citizens of the commune, but we form concrete human beings of our epoch who have still to fight for the creation of the conditions out of which the harmonious citizen of the commune may emerge.[68]

Trotsky saw, therefore, the task of the Soviet regime to be not the creation of a socialist culture—this could not be created, it had to evolve—but of the conditions for its evolution. In his

---

[67] In what follows only those aspects of Trotsky's writings on social and cultural matters which pertain to Soviet policies and measures during the period following 1917 are discussed. His general views on cultural questions—particularly on art and literature—are discussed in chapter 11, below. The main source for the present discussion is his *Sochineniya*, XXI.

[68] 'Zadachi kommunisticheskogo vospitania', in *Sochineniya*, XXI, pp. 327–8.

writings and speeches on the training of youth and on education in general he especially stressed this element, lest the hope of fashioning a new generation of communists led the party into utopian and unattainable objectives.[69] Thus it was, in his view, essential to inculcate youth with the ideals of the socialist future but no less essential at the present to create, in general, an awareness amongst them of the importance of everyday politics and of political participation even of a mundane character.[70] At the same time he was concerned with the uprooting of such cultural traditions as were both anathema to a materialist view of the world and an obstacle to knowledge and progress, as well as to the growth of that frame of mind which would one day, in his view, constitute the rationalist mentality of the new society. At the centre of such traditions stood religion, the most stultifying if not pernicious influence, in his opinion, from the point of view of inquiry and change. The fight against religion, he declared, was a fight against 'ignorance', 'superstition', 'mysticism' and 'sentimentality': 'He who believes in another world is not capable of concentrating all his passion on the transformation of this one.'[71] The acceptance of religion was, in his view, a resignation to the world as it was, an opting out of the struggle with nature and a commitment, in the end, to a mode of thought which perpetuated class society.[72]

However, uppermost in his mind, when he spoke of the initial tasks involved in overcoming Russia's cultural poverty, was the subject of everyday customs and habits. This, in his view, was where the root of the problem of mass cultural norms had to be attacked. During 1923 Trotsky published a series of articles on this subject in *Pravda* and they were later in the same year issued in book form as *Voprosy Byta* (Problems of Life).[73] The

[69] For his pronouncements on youth and education which, however, are mainly rhetorical in nature and not distinguished by any original ideas, see *Sochineniya*, XXI, pp. 289–355 and the collection *Pokolenie Oktyabrya* (Petrograd and Moscow, 1924).

[70] See, for instance, his speech of 29 Apr. 1924, 'Molodezh, uchis politike!', in *Sochineniya*, XXI, pp. 347–53, where he stated (p. 348): 'Politics fill the air; it is not possible to live outside of politics, without politics, any more than one can live without air.'

[71] 'Zadachi kommunisticheskogo vospitania', *Sochineniya*, XXI, p. 332.

[72] 'Leninizm i rabochie kluby', in *Sochineniya*, XXI, pp. 133–63.

[73] All subsequent references are to the second edition, Moscow, 1923. (The separate articles of which it consists may also be found, in a somewhat different order, in *Sochineniya*, XXI, pp. 3–44. A nearly complete English translation of this work, by Z. Vengerova, appeared in London, 1924.)

first chapter, entitled 'Not by politics alone does man live', set
the tone for the rest of the book which ranged over such diverse
topics as religion, the family, forms of entertainment and everyday speech. In it he declared that 'we need culture in work,
culture in life, culture in the conditions of life' but that this
could not be instituted 'all at once' and therefore the 'working
class must undergo a long process of self-education, as must the
peasantry'.[74] The workers having conquered power, all further
progress depended on this process. In a long passage, worth
quoting almost in its entirety because it harks back to the
central theme of his view of Russian society, Trotsky described
the paradox of the October revolution:

One might say that the richer the history of a country and, at the
same time, of its working class, the greater within it the accumulation
of memories, traditions, habits, the larger the number of old groupings—the harder it is to achieve the revolutionary unity of the working
class. The Russian proletariat is poor in class history and class traditions. *This has undoubtedly facilitated its revolutionary education leading up
to October. It causes, on the other hand, the difficulty of constructive work after
October.* The Russian worker . . . for the most part lacks the most elementary habits and notions of culture . . . The West European worker
possesses these habits. He has acquired them by a long and slow process, under the bourgeois regime. This explains why in Western
Europe the working class—its superior elements at any rate—is so
strongly attached to the bourgeois regime with its democracy, freedom of the capitalist press and all the other blessings. The belated
bourgeois regime in Russia had no time to do any good to the working
class and the Russian proletariat broke from the bourgeoisie all the
more easily and overthrew the bourgeois regime without regret. But
for the very same reason the Russian proletariat is only just beginning
to acquire and to accumulate the simplest habits of culture ... History gives nothing free of cost. Having made a reduction on one point,
in politics, it makes us pay the more on another, in culture. *The more
easily . . . did the Russian proletariat pass through the revolutionary crisis,
the harder becomes now its socialist constructive work.*[75]

Here Trotsky summarized a central aspect of his theory of
the Russian revolution, namely, that the failure of capitalism
to take root in Russia accelerated the revolutionary process. His
point now, however, was that this advantage had turned, after
the revolution, into a disadvantage, and was threatening to

[74] *Voprosy Byta*, p. 8.   [75] Ibid., pp. 12–13 (italics added).

undermine the efforts to transform society. The extent of mass cultural backwardness was so great, in his view, that at the outset the most elementary of habits and customs had to be taught: punctuality, honesty, responsibility, and the carrying out of obligations at work and in everyday life in general. Beyond this, however, it was necessary, in a country by-passed by the 'age of enlightenment' to 'rationalize life, to transform it according to the dictates of reason'.[76] What Trotsky sought was both the secularization of life and the introduction of a far more utilitarian approach to work and social organization, an approach characterizing the cultural norms of modern European societies. This would not be the end-product of socialism but it was a pre-condition for the transition to socialism. In effect, therefore, in culture as in economics, it was the task of the Soviet republic to implement what the past had failed to implement— but since cultural modernization, like economic modernization, would be carried out under the aegis of a socialist, not a bourgeois government, it would, in Trotsky's view, assume a collectivist character from the outset.

Once again, in *Problems of Life*, he stressed the importance of the struggle against religion. And he claimed that this struggle was easier than might be expected: the Russian worker and even peasant had a 'purely external relation' to the Church. The latter was 'never successful in penetrating deeply into the consciousness of the masses, nor in blending its dogmas and canons with the inner emotions of the people'.[77] The Russian Church, unlike other Churches, provided, in his view, more for social needs than spiritual ones, it offered ceremonial and theatrical diversions from the monotony of everyday life, and religious practice was more a habit than a living attachment to deeply held beliefs. To nullify the Church and religion, therefore, it was necessary to make available other diversions, other forms of 'entertainment', other attractions and 'amusements' appealing to the senses and the imagination, to 'man's desire for the theatrical' and for the breaking of the 'ordinary monotony of life'. This the modern world had invented, and none was more effective in this respect than the cinema which combined amusement with instruction, and which, while

---

[76] Ibid., p. 39.　　　　　[77] Ibid., p. 44.

entertaining, was also capable of opening new worlds to the viewer.[78]

Trotsky's concern with the importance of everyday habits extended also to what he considered a particularly ugly Russian characteristic, abusive language and swearing. He saw in it a 'legacy of slavery, humiliation and disrespect for human dignity—one's own and that of other people'.[79] It symbolized the crudity and emptiness of cultural life, and the primitiveness of the individual's reaction to his external world. A revolution devoted to the liberation of the 'human personality' of the masses could not but refashion language as an instrument for the articulation of that personality.[80] Similarly, politeness, civility, good manners in general, were essential aspects of a society in which human respect and dignity had been restored. This applied both to the relations between private individuals and between officials and citizens. The Tsarist bureaucratic tradition had left behind a legacy of condescension and disdain for the simple citizen seeking assistance from the state or justly exercising his right to voice a grievance. Besides the usual bureaucratic difficulties he was greeted by rudeness and impatience. All this was also a reflection both of the sorry state of human relations in Russia and the absence of elementary cultural habits.[81]

The transformation of everyday cultural life, however, was also largely dependent on the manner in which Soviet society approached two mutually related subjects, the woman and the family, and Trotsky expressed his views on this as well in *Problems of Life*.[82] Once again, he struck a cautious note. While welcoming the prospect of the transformation of traditional family life he pointed to the chaos and dislocation which it engendered when carried out at a rapid pace. He gave examples of families influenced, even disrupted, by progressive, socialist ideas, but he claimed that in most cases the consequence was only a tragedy for wife and children—the former unable to fend for herself, the latter abandoned, or left to the care of the state.[83]

---

[78] Trotsky devoted a separate chapter (ibid., pp. 41–6) to the importance of the cinema as an instrument in the struggle against religion and as a vehicle for inculcating new cultural norms and habits. In another chapter (pp. 57–61) he discussed the importance of developing secular festivals and ceremonials to replace those of religion.
[79] Ibid., p. 67.   [80] Ibid., pp. 68–72.   [81] Ibid., pp. 62–6 and 73–82.
[82] See especially pp. 47–56.   [83] Ibid., pp. 51–2.

The problem was that the traditional family was collapsing faster than the conception of the new family was being formed; and that the independence of the man or husband was being asserted before the concomitant liberation of the woman had been achieved. The break-up of the family in such circumstances was tragic because it worked to the disadvantage of the woman. Thus Trotsky believed that the first task was not so much the transformation of the family as the transformation of the position of the woman, both in private life and in society generally, and that only in this way could the conception of the 'new family' take shape. The aim, of course, was complete sexual equality and this meant releasing the woman from her traditional duties—the care of the home, of the children, and so on—so that she may become an individual in her own right and, like her husband, a participant in the social and political life of her society. But this in turn depended on the extent to which the economic function which the woman had performed in the past could now be undertaken by state and society; the extent, in other words, to which the upbringing of children and the provision of various household services could be transferred to specially created public institutions. In Trotsky's view it was premature to speak of such institutions, except in the most rudimentary form, at the present stage of the development of the Soviet economy; they could come into being only within the context of a general improvement of material conditions. Until then, therefore, the complete liberation of the woman, 'genuine equality', was impossible; and thus undue haste in destroying the old family could lead only to a social vacuum. Instead of plunging ahead in accordance with doctrinal views of family life and morality, it was best, in this sphere, to remain within the bounds of the possible and the practical.[84]

As he had begun so he ended his book on the 'problems of life' with a call for moderation and patience in matters pertaining to mass culture. And he warned against the exaggerated use of the state in solving such matters. He objected also to the establishment of government organizations which would, artificially, impose norms of behaviour from above. At the most, the

---

[84] Ibid., pp. 53–6. For other, similar, of Trotsky's pronouncements on family life and the woman, see in particular *Sochineniya*, XXI, pp. 44–55, 55–8, and 64–5.

task of the state was to facilitate the evolution of new cultural customs and habits. This in itself was a major undertaking. But the ultimate goal of achieving a new mass culture depended as much on private initiative, on voluntary associations, and on a long period of social gestation.[85]

In the period after 1925, as he became more and more convinced of the need for a more rapid pace of industrialization, Trotsky turned his attention to one of the most immediate obstacles to such a policy, the low level of Russian technique and expertise. This too, he believed, was fundamentally a cultural problem, or rather a function of cultural backwardness. Yet, although this was the context within which he grasped the problem of Russian technique, his attitude to its solution differed somewhat from that to other cultural problems. In this sphere he thought that new methods, new systems of organization, the rationalization of production in general, should almost be grafted onto existing economic structures. He did not believe, it is true, that the 'technological' problem could be divorced from the cultural one, nor that, in the long run, the former could be solved without a radical change in customs and values; but he assumed that the introduction of new techniques would act as a prod to cultural change. 'The growth of technique', he wrote, 'advances culture.' And between the two he saw a 'dialectical interaction'.[86] In any case, the modernization of the economic structure was for him an objective of such magnitude and urgency that to delay it unduly might mean jeopardizing the whole Soviet experiment. Technique must be raised—even if arbitrarily—to conform to the ideals of the new Soviet social order: 'If we do not succeed in doing this, our social order will inevitably decline to the level of our technical backwardness.'[87] At the same time he rejected the view that Western techniques should be avoided because they were the product of a capitalist system; on the contrary, it was in his opinion incumbent upon Soviet society to learn from others, to assimilate the scientific and technical heritage of the advanced world, always adopting it, of course, to the Soviet, and eventually socialist, framework.

The extent of his admiration for the West may be gauged from the following passage:

The Soviet system shod with American technique will be socialism. Our social order offers a different, incomparably more expedient framework for American technique. But American technique for its part will transform our order, liberating it from the heritage of backwardness, primitiveness and barbarism. From the combination of the Soviet order with American technique there will be born a new technique and a new culture—technique and culture for all, without favourite sons or stepsons.[88]

Whatever the realistic possibilities of such a 'transference' of technique, this fairly describes the kind of technical revolution Trotsky had in mind: one making for rationalism, efficiency, exactitude and, of course, quality. In urging this technical revolution, as something which needed to be imposed largely from above, Trotsky felt he was promoting the long-term cultural revolution: 'The cultural revolution must involve the opening to [the masses] of the possibility of real access to culture and not only to its wretched fag-ends. But this is impossible without creating very considerable material preconditions.'[89] And the latter, in turn, depended on the extent to which technical backwardness was overcome. Thus it followed for Trotsky that 'the decisive instrument in the cultural revolution must be a revolution in technique'.[90]

(b) *Proletarian Culture and Socialist Culture*

Every revolution, in word if not always in deed, is a break with the past. But a revolution, at least in its initial stages, does not resolve the tension between past and present (or future), between 'continuity and change'; it rather accentuates it.[91] How much of the past need be jettisoned and how much retained? And what are the criteria for the doing of the one or the other? These are not merely academic questions; the

[88] Ibid., p. 438. It should be remembered that at the time this was written, Soviet propaganda was urging the emulation of American efficiency.
[89] Ibid., p. 442.
[90] Loc. cit. In this connection see also Trotsky's speech of 1 Mar. 1926, 'Radio, nauka, tekhnika i obshchestvo', in *Sochineniya*, XXI, pp. 410–23. Trotsky's more 'philosophical' observationᵉ on science, technique and culture are discussed in chapter 11, below.
[91] For a discussion of this 'tension', in the context of the Bolshevik Revolution, see Carr, *Socialism in One Country, 1924–1926*, I, chapter 1.

power which a new revolutionary government enjoys, and the doctrines or ideals animating it, are such as both to make poss- ible, and to encourage, action in spheres not just political or economic. The controversies which broke out after the Revolu- tion within the Bolshevik leadership over issues of art, literature, science and cultural matters in general, attest to the immediate and practical importance which was attached to policy in these spheres, and to the passion which characterized the early attempts to resolve the tension between change and conti- nuity.[92]

From what has already been said about Trotsky's approach to cultural policy, it is not difficult to guess where his own sym- pathies would be in these controversies. But the unequivocal stand which he took against the conception of 'proletarian literature' or 'proletarian culture' in general, was governed not only by his scepticism about the realm of the possible in such matters, but also by his whole conception of the nature of the arts, the sciences and the intellectual domain. Although almost all of Trotsky's writings on literary and artistic subjects are characterized by his political orientation and infused with a definite political viewpoint, his interest in such subjects was fundamentally independent of politics.[93] Above all, he recog- nized that the arts were a sphere unto themselves—though affected by the external environment and in turn affecting it— and, as such, followed their own 'laws' of development, whether in style or form or even content. As he spoke out against a 'Marxist military strategy', so he spoke out against a 'Marxist literature' or a 'Marxist science'. Beyond this, however, he also refused to accept the view that the whole of the cultural heritage of the past was to be rejected indiscriminately. The notion that all culture was only an expression of economic interests or class viewpoints he considered vulgar, ignorant and wrong. Great

[92] A succinct account of the controversy over 'Proletarian Culture' (Proletkult), includ- ing the views of its leading spokesman, Bogdanov, and those of Lenin who was opposed to it, is given by Carr in ibid., pp. 57–77 and also in his *Socialism in One Country, 1924– 1926*, II (Harmondsworth, 1970), chapter 14.
[93] Trotsky's general and theoretical views on literature and the arts, as well as his literary criticism itself, are discussed in chapter 11, below. The present discussion, in keeping with the rest of this chapter, is limited to Trotsky's writings both during a particular period—the decade or so following 1917—and on a particular subject— the policies of the Soviet government (and of the party) towards artistic questions, mainly those involving the issue of 'proletarian culture'.

art, in his view, though surrounded, like everything else, by the framework of a particular social structure was yet able to transcend it and thus give expression to human emotions, dilemmas and aspirations which were universal and timeless. Such art could be appreciated without reference to its historical context and to appreciate it was in fact to be enriched by it. Thus to reject the past *in toto*, without differentiating between good and bad, was to reject also mankind's genuine achievements, its genius and spiritual wealth:

Art is one of the ways in which man finds his bearings in the world; in this sense the heritage of art is not distinguished from the heritage of science and technique . . . The art of past centuries has made man more complex and flexible, has raised his mentality to a higher level, has enriched him in an all-round way. This enrichment is a precious achievement of culture. Mastery of the art of the past is, therefore, a necessary pre-condition not only for the creation of new art but also for the building of the new society, for communism needs people with highly developed minds. Can, however, the art of the past enrich us with an artistic knowledge of the world? It can, precisely because it is able to give nourishment to our feelings and to educate them. If we were groundlessly to repudiate the art of the past, we should at once become poorer spiritually.[94]

In one of his best-known works, *Literature and Revolution*,[95] this need to absorb the past was translated by Trotsky into concrete terms, as having a direct bearing on the future development of culture in the Soviet republic:

Though the proletariat is spiritually and thus artificially very sensitive, aesthetically it is uneducated. It is far from reasonable to think that the proletariat can simply begin at that point at which the bourgeois intelligentsia stopped on the eve of the [Revolution]. In the same way as an individual traverses biologically and psychologically the history of the human race and, to a certain extent, of the entire animal world during his development from the embryo, so, to a certain extent, the great majority of a new class, recently emerged from pre-historic

[94] 'Kultura i sotsializm' (*Sochineniya*, XXI), p. 431.
[95] *Literatura i Revolyutsiya* (Moscow, 1923). All subsequent references, as previously, are to this edition. Certain chapters of this work were originally published separately in *Pravda* during September 1923. The first English translation, by Rose Strunksy, was published in London and New York, 1925, re-issued Ann Arbor, 1960. This translation has been generally followed when quoting from the book, although references to the Russian edition only are given.

life, must traverse the entire history of artistic culture. It cannot begin the building of a new culture without first absorbing and assimilating elements of the old cultures. This does not at all mean that one must retrace, step by step, slowly and systematically, the entire past history of art. Since it is a social class and not a biological individual which is involved, the process of absorption and transformation assumes a freer and more conscious character. But a new class cannot go forward without regard for the most important landmarks of the past.[96]

The argument over the value of the past was, of course, only part of the larger controversy over the future of culture under the Soviet regime. Those who spoke for a complete rejection of the past did so in order to clear the ground for the creation of a 'proletarian culture'. If the epochs of the feudal lords and of the bourgeoisie, they argued, could create cultures appropriate to their needs and aspirations, why should the proletariat, in its epoch, not do the same? It is largely to refute this kind of thinking that Trotsky wrote *Literature and Revolution.* Although the main part of the book is devoted to an analysis of contemporary literary movements as well as of certain individual writers, the final chapters deal specifically with the issue of 'proletarian culture' and Soviet policy toward art.[97] In the preface to the work, Trotsky summarized his argument in the following words:

It is fundamentally incorrect to place in opposition to bourgeois culture and bourgeois art a proletarian culture and proletarian art. These latter will never exist, because the proletarian regime is temporary and transitional. The historical significance and the moral greatness of the proletarian revolution derive from the fact that it is laying down the foundations of a culture which is above classes and which will be the first truly human culture.[98]

Trotsky claimed that for the most part it was impossible to tell what the proponents of 'Proletkult'—as it came to be known—had in mind; sometimes they spoke as if this was to be the culture of the future communist society, sometimes as

[96] Ibid., p. 167. A page earlier he wrote: 'The worker will take from Shakespeare, Goethe, Pushkin or Dostoevsky a more complex idea of human personality, of its passions and feelings, a deeper and profounder understanding of its psychic forces and of the role of the subconscious. In the end, the worker will have been enriched.'
[97] The earlier parts of the book are discussed in chapter 11, below.
[98] *Literatura i Revolyutsiya*, p. 9.

if it were to be the culture of the transitional period.[99] In either case, however, the notion was a 'dangerous' one for it compressed the possibilities of culture into 'the narrow limits of the present day'.[100] To do this was to assume that external needs and conditions would remain unchanged, and to block, albeit indirectly, the possibilities of change. Moreover, it meant to prejudge and predetermine that which only life itself could determine, and pass judgement upon, in its own ways and at its own pace. The truth of the matter was, according to Trotsky, that the period of the 'dictatorship of the proletariat' was an abnormal one and highly inimical to artistic development. It was a period marked by war and dislocation, violence and destruction, economic want and concrete, prosaic problems of organization and reconstruction. It was a period whose 'dynamics were centred on politics', the sphere of the external world, not that of the internal spiritual one.[101] In such conditions, men's minds and talents turned naturally to immediate, practical problems. To the question 'Why are there no Belinskys today?', Trotsky replied that if Belinsky were alive now he 'would probably be a member of the Politbureau'.[102] Trotsky claimed, therefore, that the poverty of current literature and of artistic activity in general was to be expected. Moreover, in conditions of material impoverishment, man's artistic genius was the first to become starved of power. The pre-condition of artistic creation was, he believed, economic well-being, the satisfaction of basic, biological needs, and the liberation of man from material worries: 'Culture is nourished on the sap of economics, and a material surplus is essential so that culture may grow, develop and become subtle . . . Art requires comfort, even abundance.'[103]

But even assuming that the present difficulties of Soviet society were at least partially overcome and that a degree of political and economic stability were established, was this reason enough to argue that a 'proletarian culture' should, and would, evolve? Only if one further assumed, Trotsky argued, that the period of the transition to socialism would last for

---

[99] Ibid., p. 144. And usually, he added, their arguments represented 'a jumble of concepts of words out of which one could make neither head nor tail'.
[100] Ibid., p. 151.   [101] Ibid., p. 140.
[102] Ibid., p. 155.   [103] Ibid., pp. 5–6.

centuries. For if, as *he* assumed, it was a matter of 'decades' only, then there would hardly be enough time to create anything complete or lasting. In contrast to the feudal or bourgeois eras, the period of the proletariat's dictatorship was not a historical epoch unto itself, a finished social structure within which it was possible to pursue the normal occupations of life; rather it was a period of transition and therefore changing, ephemeral, and lacking a definite shape. During such a period it was difficult for the arts to find roots, and for artists to orient themselves. At best, therefore, 'proletarian culture' would be an artificially created body of official decrees, at worst a fiction existing only in the imagination of narrow literary circles.[104] And, in any case, to replace one class art by another was to replace one form of bad or mediocre art by another; the point was not to create a new class culture but a new 'human' culture, not proletarian culture but socialist culture. The latter would become possible only in so far as the 'dictatorship of the proletariat' was 'dissolved':

> As the new [proletarian] regime becomes more and more secured against political and military surprises . . . the proletariat will become more and more dissolved into a socialist community thus liberating itself from its class characteristics and ceasing to be a proletariat . . . The cultural reconstruction which will begin when the need for the iron hold of a historically unparalleled dictatorship disappears, will not have a class character. This seems to call for the conclusion that there is no proletarian culture and there never will be and, in fact, there is no reason to regret this. The proletariat comes into power in order to do away with class culture forever and to make way for human culture.[105]

What then should be done in the sphere of culture during the period of transition, and what should be the role of government and party? As to the former, the paramount aim must be the 'imparting to the backward masses of the essential elements of the culture which already exists'.[106] For the proletariat

[104] Ibid., pp. 136–45.
[105] Ibid., p. 137. Trotsky made largely the same case (ibid., pp. 145–7) against the notion of a 'proletarian science', both natural and social. He did not exclude, of course, the possibility that during the period of transition individual contributions to culture, in the arts and the sciences, might be made; but he ridiculed the idea that individual genius could be attributed to a class or be given the name of proletarian culture (ibid., pp. 147–8).
[106] Ibid., p. 143.

and the peasantry this is in fact a period of education, of a raising of standards, of their entry into the social and cultural life of the country. In this task both the intelligentsia and political institutions have a direct role to play as the transmitters of culture to the masses. But as for the actual form and character of artistic creation, its style of expression, its choice of language, images and presentation, in short, creation itself, these are matters best left to the practitioners, the artists, themselves. Thus a distinction must be made between the facilitating of access to culture, and its creation. In the case of the latter, the interference of a political institution constitutes at best an intrusion:

Art must make its own way and by its own means. The methods of Marxism are not the same as those of art. The party leads the proletariat but not the processes of history. There are domains in which the party leads, directly and commandingly. There are domains in which it only co-operates. There are domains, finally, in which it only orientates itself. The domain of art is not one in which the party is called upon to command.[107]

This means that the party must be prepared to tolerate and even encourage a variety of different schools of art, recognizing that it is only in an atmosphere of free expression that culture in general can flourish. The manner in which a socialist culture will evolve constitutes a 'complex, many-sided' process and this determines the party's policy towards art: 'It is impossible to reduce this policy to one formula, to something short, like the bill of a bird. Nor is it necessary to do this.'[108]

In spite of this general attitude, however, Trotsky's conception of the freedom of art was not absolute. The party, though not commanding, retained the powers of vetoing; for it was not neutral and it could not, in his view, follow the principles of *laissez-faire* and *laissez-passer*, 'even in the field of art'. There was a limit to its tolerance and this limit began where there was a threat to the revolution itself.[109] In fact, a school of art *opposed* to the revolution could not be tolerated. The party did not create art, but as its primary task was to defend the revolution, it was in this capacity that it delineated the framework of art. Trotsky's definition of the relationship between the

[107] Ibid., p. 161.   [108] Ibid., p. 168.   [109] Ibid., p. 163.

political sphere and the artistic therefore took the following form:

Our policy in art, during a transitional period, can and must be to assist the various groups and schools of art which have come over to the revolution to grasp correctly its historical meaning and to allow them complete freedom of self-determination in the field of art once the categorical standard of being for or against the revolution has been placed before them.[110]

But because this standard was so obviously political and was applied to a non-political sphere, its 'limits had to be clearly defined': 'To express my meaning more precisely, I would say: we should have a watchful revolutionary censorship, and a broad and flexible policy in the field of art, free from petty, partisan maliciousness.'[111]

Trotsky's views on cultural matters, both in *Literature and Revolution* and in other writings, were undoubtedly among the most informed and enlightened within the Bolshevik leadership; but even he, in the final analysis, defined the ultimate legitimacy of art in terms of a political criterion. On the other hand, however, he also defined the ultimate value, if not legitimacy, of politics, in this case Soviet revolutionary politics, in terms of a cultural criterion:

Only a movement of scientific thought on a national scale and the development of a new art would signify that the historical seed of [socialism] has not only grown into a plant but has also flowered. In this sense, the development of art is the highest test of vitality and significance of each epoch.[112]

The discussion in this chapter of Trotsky's views on the reconstruction of Russian society has shown that he was only too well aware of the extent to which economic change and progress were dependent upon the level of social and cultural develop-

[110] Ibid., p. 9. This quotation is from the preface to the book.
[111] Ibid., p. 163.
[112] Ibid., p. 5. For a further example of Trotsky's arguments against 'proletarian culture', see his speech of 9 May 1924, 'O politike partii v khudozhestvennoi literature', published in the second, enlarged edition of *Literatura i Revolyutsiya* (Moscow, 1924), pp. 195–203, and in the volume *Voprosy kultury pri diktatura proletariata* (Moscow, 1925), pp. 93–110. See also the interview with Trotsky by Maurice Parijanine in *Les Humbles*, July–Aug. 1932 and republished in the French anthology, Léon Trotsky, *Littérature et révolution* (Paris, 1964), pp. 322–31.

ment. Yet it has also shown that, despite this, there was a fundamental contradiction between the economic policies he propounded and the view he took of the objective capacities of Russian society. If before 1917 he tended to overestimate such capacities when arguing for the 'ripeness' of Russia for a socialist revolution, following 1917 he never failed to declare that Russia was culturally impoverished, primitive in her scientific and technological standards, pulled down by the weaknesses of her social classes, and largely devoid of such work habits, norms, and individual and collective responsibility as are essential to an organized and developing economy. Moreover, he had no illusions, as we have seen, about the prospects of any far-reaching, swift changes in these areas; on the contrary, he urged patience and realism, cautioned against wishful thinking and denounced attempts to force, artificially, cultural reforms, not to say panaceas. At the very least, therefore, it would have been logical for him to adopt and defend a similarly modest economic programme for Soviet Russia, one which emphasized very gradual change and development. Instead, however, he was, in the field of economic action, a proponent of the most radical of measures, supporting rapid industrialization and a policy of extreme socialization. The contradiction between this and his social views could hardly be more vivid.

The contradiction, however, was not confined to Trotsky alone. In fact, it reflected the contradiction in general between the Soviet government—no matter how much more restrained were the ambitions of some of its other leaders—and the society in which it had arisen, between the goals of the one and the capacities of the other. Trotsky, as we have had occasion to indicate, had shown that economic developments, particularly industrialization, in the latter decades of the nineteenth century had sealed the fate of Russia's traditional political institutions and had made the emergence of new ones a matter of time. He had not shown convincingly, however, and reality was now confirming this fact, that Russia was as yet prepared for new and radical *social* institutions, or for such a society as the Social Democratic movement, and now the Soviet government, were in principle committed to.[113] The situation in Soviet Russia

[113] See the concluding parts of chapters 3 and 4, above, where Trotsky's analysis of social change in Russia, and of the prospects of socialism, were criticized.

after 1917, as Trotsky himself recognized, could be described as a classic impasse between politics and society; and it is precisely over this impasse that the economic debate of the 1920s was conducted. That Trotsky, in this debate, should have sided with the extremist, the impatient position, does not mean that he was unaware of the contradictions it contained. It does indicate, however, the extent to which he was determined to see through to the end his theoretical preconceptions. It may be said of him, therefore, that having been convinced before 1917 that Russia's transformation into a modern society would follow a path different from that of the West, he was, after 1917, intent upon forging this path. He believed, in other words (to repeat what in this study has been taken as a central theme of his social theory) that in the twentieth century the economic problems of a backward society could be solved only by socialism and not through the encouragement of the free market and of capitalism in general. He thus continued to preach an alternative to the Western model of economic development.

Was this alternative possible or, rather, did it have anything actually to do with socialism? Having already noted the inherent contradictions between Russian reality and Soviet aspirations, it would be superfluous to add that on economic grounds alone Trotsky's alternative could not be implemented without doing damage to fundamental socialist ideals. In later years he would become the most acrimonious critic of precisely such damage. But were not the policies to be adopted by Stalin essentially the same as Trotsky had propounded during the 1920s? If so, had not Trotsky in principle, if not in fact, committed himself to the political measures Stalin was to employ in order to industrialize Russia? This question has often been raised, and on the face of it there is much to be said for the view that Trotsky was a sort of precursor to Stalin. Collectivization of agriculture was not, it is true, a part of Trotsky's programme at any time; but it could without difficulty be inferred from it.[114] The extent of the planning and of the state activities he envisaged called, it seems, for an administrative edifice not

[114] There are, however, very few references in his writings during this period (i.e. 1917–27) to collectivization and these are generally negative and cautious (see, for example, his speech of November 1925, published in *Izvestiya*, no. 272, 28 Nov. 1925). In the 1930s Trotsky, of course, denounced Stalin's policy of collectivization; see especially his article, 'Stalin—kak teoretik', *Byulleten Oppozitsii* (Aug. 1930), pp. 24–37.

unlike the bureaucracy which was to emerge under Stalin. And the opposition which his policies could be expected to arouse would have conceivably required some at least of the kind of oppression which also became in later years an integral part of Soviet reality. In general, therefore, Trotsky too had in effect urged the overcoming of the contradiction between economic objectives and social backwardness through the use of compulsion—in the sphere of politics as in that of economics.

As against these affinities, however, certain clear differences between Trotsky and Stalin must be noted—though not in order to cleanse Trotsky of the 'Stalinist' elements in his views but in fairness only to the logic, as he saw it, of his over-all position. In the first place, from 1925 onwards he continuously argued that Russia's economy must be reconstructed not in isolation from Europe but through far-reaching economic, commercial relations with European countries.[115] This would not, obviously, resolve the problems of creating a socialist economy, much less a socialist society, but, he believed, it would alleviate many internal difficulties of a purely economic kind which would in turn make easier social and political accommodations. This approach was completely at variance with the policy of economic isolationism which Stalin was to pursue, and which was in no small part to be responsible for aggravating economic conditions in the Soviet Union and thus, perhaps, for necessitating even harsher measures in the spheres of economics and politics alike.

Secondly, despite his determination, as we have indicated, to impose economic modernization upon a backward society, Trotsky was not insensitive to the objective limitations created by the latter. He was not, at any rate, committed to the absurd view that economics and economic growth were an autonomous sphere, functioning as if in a vacuum, capable of activation at the pull of a lever. Their nature and possibilities remained for him bound up with the social and cultural environment. Similarly, he never claimed that nationalized property and industrialization—which were his main initial goals—or even the general modernization of Russian institutions, constituted socialism. The latter would come into being only with the emergence of

[115] See in particular *Towards Socialism or Capitalism?* where Trotsky urged throughout that Russia must develop extensive trade ties with Europe.

new social relations and what he had once defined as a 'socialist psychology'. It was partly because the 'Stalinist' camp would equate mere state ownership and industrialization with socialism that Trotsky would be morally and intellectually, and of course politically, so repelled by that camp and its *terribles simplificateurs*. Moreover, in the same vein—and as we shall see more fully in a later chapter—Trotsky belonged to those revolutionaries who set great store by the role and importance of art, science and creative activity in general in the advance of socialist aims. All this, to repeat, did not prevent him from simultaneously propounding economic policies which seemed overly ambitious in the light of Russian social reality. Nevertheless, it does not appear credible that he would have treated society and culture with the same total and brutal disdain, and politics and the state with the same unequivocal devotion, as Stalin was to do in the 1930s.

Finally, the most conspicuous difference between the approach of Trotsky and that which was to characterize 'Stalinism' was Trotsky's persistently held view that, in the last resort, socialism in Russia depended on revolution in the West. Because of the demands of systematic presentation, we have dealt with his economic and social views separately from his views on the world revolution (which will be discussed in the following chapter). Historically this separation may be unjust, for concurrently with the economic policies he propagated, Trotsky spoke and wrote on Soviet Russia's external needs. The two were intertwined for him and they should be seen in conjunction with each other, logically as well as historically.[116] This does not mean that thereby Trotsky resolved the problem of socialism in a backward society—socialism in Europe did not

---

[116] In a speech he delivered on 14 Nov. 1922 to the Fourth World Congress of the Communist International, Trotsky declared 'socialist construction' to be dependent on the following factors: 'First, the level to which the productive forces have been developed and in particular the reciprocal relation between industry and agriculture. Second, the general cultural and organizational level of the working class which has conquered state power. Third, the political situation internationally and nationally.' These factors were, of course, interdependent and simultaneous. ('Novaya ekonomicheskaya politika Sovetskoi Rossii i perspektivy mirovoi revolyutsii', in Trotsky, *Pyat Let Kominterna*, Moscow, 1924, p. 464.) The Opposition 'Platform' of 1927 stated (p. 87) that a 'more revolutionary solution of the problem of real industrialization and a swifter elevation of the culture of the masses [are] the two problems upon whose solution depends the fate of the socialist dictatorship ...'

guarantee socialism in Russia and, in any case, the European socialist revolution was in itself far from being a certain prospect. Indeed, the importance he attributed to the world revolution, together with the confidence with which he awaited it, show again the extent to which even he underestimated the difficulties which would confront a socialist government in Russia and the manner, as well, in which he exaggerated the universal implications of the Russian Revolution. But this much at least can be said, in this context too, for his over-all standpoint on Soviet policies, that it remained consistently in keeping with all his theoretical preconceptions about socialism in Russia—whether or not, however, these were being confirmed by reality.

CHAPTER EIGHT

THE WORLD REVOLUTION

> Once upon a time the church had a saying: 'The light shineth from the East.' In our epoch the revolution began in the East. From Russia . . . it will, undoubtedly, march westward through Europe.[1]

THE BELIEF that socialism would one day spread throughout the world, that, sooner or later, though perhaps in different ways, the proletariat would rise against capitalism and bourgeois society everywhere, was from the beginning an integral part of the Marxist canon, its universal and chiliastic vision of the future. Marx had seen in socialism not just a solution to national problems but a movement, and eventually a way of life, that would transcend national boundaries, destroying once and for all what he considered the arbitrary, wasteful and estranging division of the world into nation-states. How and when such a revolution or transformation would sweep the world and what the world would look like in its wake always remained somewhat vague; certainly, Marx had no clearly formulated programme for bringing about this general dénouement of capitalism, and no rigid time-table for it.[2] But the Marxist movements which his ideas eventually gave rise to took it very much for granted. They saw themselves not only as the bearers of the socialist ideal and mission in a particular country, but as parts of a greater, international movement, unified in purpose even if not always in action, whose enemy was fundamentally the same everywhere.[3]

[1] Trotsky, *Pyat Let Kominterna*, p. 30.

[2] As was pointed out earlier (see chapter 4, above), Marx's views on revolution were not always consistent. Compare for instance his 1864 *Inaugural Address of the Working Men's International Association* with his 1871 *The Civil War in France* (in Marx–Engels, *Selected Works*, I, pp. 377–85 and 449–545 respectively).

[3] On the First International, see G. D. H. Cole, *A History of Socialist Thought*, II (London, 1954). On the Second International, see James Joll, *The Second International, 1889–1914* (London, 1955). On the special case of the British working class movement, always less revolutionary, if at all, than its continental counterparts, see Henry Collins and Chimen Abramsky, *Karl Marx and the British Labour Movement* (London, 1965).

In this doctrinal sense, the Russian Social Democratic movement adhered to the idea of the world revolution as a matter
of course. But its relationship to the international movement
and to the world revolution in general was problematic from
the outset. In the first place, at least until 1905 its revolutionary
prospects appeared to be minimal and, even after 1905, it was
relatively weak and isolated, it lacked a mass organizational
basis, and its social and political environment, of course, had
little in common with that of the advanced West. Beyond this,
however, there lay the question of the kind of revolution which
Russian Social Democracy was in pursuit of; even allowing for
differences between Mensheviks and Bolsheviks, both admitted
that while the West was, presumably, on the verge of a socialist
revolution, Russia had still to go through a 'bourgeois' stage.
In this sense, therefore, Russian Social Democracy remained
somewhat cut off from the main stream of events in Europe.
On the other hand, however, it was widely assumed that should
there be a revolution in Europe it would not only raise the fortunes of the revolutionary movement in Russia but accelerate
the process whereby the transition from purely bourgeois goals
to socialist ones becomes feasible.

On this view, Europe remained the centre of revolutionary
events and Russia the periphery. But by 1914 this generally
accepted view was shattered and Lenin, in particular, was moved
to revise the preconceived order of things. The spectacle of
European socialist parties voting for war credits and parading
their patriotic credentials in support of national interests had
the effect upon Lenin of destroying whatever illusions he and
his followers may have had about the revolutionary potential
of Western socialism or about the reality of international
socialist solidarity. It was then that Lenin began to contemplate
the prospect of the world revolution beginning with a Russian
revolution; and if this was to be so, then clearly the centre of
the World revolutionary movement had shifted to the East and
away from the West.[4]

This was, of course, precisely the view which Trotsky, follow-

[4] Lenin's famous work, *Imperialism, The Highest Stage of Capitalism*, written in 1916, was
of course an attempt to explain why the revolutionary spirit had gone out of the Western
proletariat and why the onus of revolution was now placed upon the masses of the
East. For a detailed study of Lenin's views on world revolution, before and after 1917,
see Stanley W. Page, *Lenin and World Revolution* (New York, 1959).

ing the initial speculations of Parvus, had been advocating since
1905–6. And the fact of October 1917, whatever the explanation for it, was, it seemed, a vindication of that view. Russia
had become the centre of the world revolutionary movement
and the focus now for the European proletariat and its leadership. The irony of this situation, however, was that the new
Soviet government continued to be no less dependent on a
European revolution. Undoubtedly, Lenin was realist enough
to accept that his regime may have to go it alone in the end;
but for this very reason he recognized that everything would
be more difficult. Initially, both Lenin and Trotsky believed
that the very survival of the Soviet government depended on
a European revolution. Thereafter, as survival seemed to be
assured, for the time being at least, by other, internal means,
it was the scope of the revolution which, in their view, became
dependent on European developments.

Once again, in so far as this was true, it was in accordance
with Trotsky's forecasts in *Results and Prospects*. Left to its own
resources, he had argued, the Russian revolution would have
to compromise with the peasantry or risk total collapse. But
such compromise would mean sacrificing socialist policies or,
at least, indefinitely pursuing contradictory and irreconcilable
aims; and this is in fact how Trotsky later explained the character of the NEP period: because there had been no revolution
elsewhere, because, consequently, the Soviet republic had
remained isolated economically and politically, she was compelled to make concessions, primarily to agriculture and the
peasants, allowing the free market to thrive and, thereby, pursuing a policy brazenly in contradiction with its socialist goals.
To continue maintaining NEP, however, would mean relegating socialism to an uncertain, perhaps unrealizable future; and
NEP, in any case, could not, in Trotsky's view, solve any of
Russia's fundamental economic problems. Thus he urged, as
we have seen, the immediate adoption of radical policies; NEP,
which was a stop-gap measure, had to be abandoned, and in
its stead there had to come stepped-up industrialization, exploitation of peasant resources, greater investment in the state sector, rigorous over-all planning, and so on. Only such policies,
Trotsky believed, would ultimately reconstruct the Russian
economy in a fundamental way, while at the same time laying

the groundwork for socialism. Of course, these policies would require resources—capital, machinery, untold commodities—which Russia had, and for a long time would have, in short supply only. They would have to be acquired from Europe and for this reason self-sufficiency or isolation was out of the question. On the one hand, therefore, Trotsky urged increasing economic trade, and economic ties in general, with European countries.[5]

On the other hand, however, far from de-emphasizing the question of the European or world revolution, Trotsky warned that its importance would grow. The economic policies he proposed in place of NEP were themselves ultimately dependent on that revolution: they could not be brought to a successful conclusion, that is, they could not go beyond a rudimentary socialist groundwork, unless socialist governments arose in Europe, thereby undermining capitalism and providing Russia with, as he had once said, 'direct state support'. Moreover, European capitalism, if it were to survive, would not remain complacent in the face of Soviet economic growth; though it would do business with the Soviet government it would also seek ways of undermining it. And although direct military intervention had failed in the past, it was not entirely ruled out in the future. At best, an isolated socialist government in Russia would continually have to adjust its internal economic policies to the capitalist world market in general, and to the capitalists' anti-Soviet machinations in particular. Besides, Trotsky continued to believe, the idea of a socialist society within the confines of a nation-state, such as the Soviet republic still was, remained inconceivable. His economic policies for the reconstruction of Russia were not meant, therefore, as a substitute for the world revolution. On the contrary, his over-all conception of Soviet policy may be said to have rested on two interconnected and equally indispensable pillars: on the one hand, a socialist-oriented economic programme at home, even if this involved 'business' relations with Europe; on the other, the pursuit of the world revolution abroad, even if this involved

[5] See *Towards Socialism or Capitalism?*, pp. 44–5, where Trotsky declared that, in any case, 'our economic system has become part of the world system ... Peasant grain is exchanged for foreign gold. Gold is exchanged for machinery, implements and other requisite articles of consumption for town and village'.

political struggle against Europe. It is to his assessment of the prospects and the importance of the latter that we now turn.

1. War and Revolution

Before proceeding to an analysis of Trotsky's views after 1917 concerning the world revolution, and in order to see the extent to which he conceived of the Russian revolution within the context of European affairs, it will be helpful to look back briefly at a work Trotsky composed immediately after the outbreak of World War I. *Voina i Internatsional* (War and the International)[6] was not a particularly original analysis of the relationship between 'imperialism' and the World War, which was, ostensibly at least, its main subject: it argued the well-known, even by then, thesis that the forces of world economic production had outgrown the confines of the nation-state; that the latter, seeking to readjust itself to these forces, had created colonies abroad and thus world imperialism; that this had not, however, solved the fundamental contradictions of the now outdated capitalist economic system; and that, therefore, war, now on a necessarily world scale, had become a way of prolonging this system and avoiding radical social change.[7] The work also contained the standard attack upon European Social Democracy, and the German in particular, for abandoning its principles and becoming an accessory to the machinations of the capitalist governments.[8]

The most interesting parts of the book, however, were those dealing with the effect the war was having on the prospects of the Russian revolution. Trotsky rejected the rationalization that by supporting the war the German Social Democrats were in effect accelerating the collapse of Tsarism, that, in other words, war between Germany and Russia would prove to be beyond the capacity of the latter and therefore increased the

[6] Included in the collection by Trotsky, *Voina i Revolyutsiya*, I, pp. 75–154; all subsequent references to *Voina i Internatsional* are to this edition. (Parts of the book originally appeared in Russian in the newspaper *Golos* during November and December 1914. In book form it was first published in German under the title *Der Krieg und die Internationale* (Zurich, 1914). The English translation, published in New York, 1918, bears the misleading, post-1917 title, *The Bolsheviki and World Peace*.)

[7] This thesis was summarized by Trotsky in his preface to the work (ibid., pp. 75–81) but it recurs throughout.

[8] See ibid., pp. 119–29.

prospects of revolution in Russia. This was, in Trotsky's view, a complete misunderstanding of Germany's role in the war. Ostensibly waging war against Russia, her main aims were to deal a blow to the Western powers with whom she had gone to war in order to assert her economic ascendancy. Even assuming that she succeeded on both Western and Eastern fronts, it did not follow that she would agree to the dismantling of the Tsarist autocracy. She would tolerate the Tsar for the same reasons that England and France had tolerated him in the past: he was convenient to do business with. In the event, however, that the more likely military stalemate developed on the Western front, this would be an even more propitious reason for coming to terms with Russia. Exhausted by the war with Belgium, France and England, the Germans would gladly conclude the war with Russia on terms not unfavourable to the latter. Thus 'history will witness an "honourable" peace between the two most reactionary powers of Europe' and 'the alliance between Hohenzollern and Romanov—after the exhaustion and degradation of the Western nations—will mean a period of the darkest reaction in Europe and the whole world'.[9]

Trotsky's point was, therefore, that capitalist or imperialist war is not waged against colonies or 'semi-colonies', such as Russia, but for hegemony over them, and that this, to the extent that it is successful, leads not to a transformation of local conditions but to their perpetuation. This being so, what then of the 'weakest-link' theory, the argument, once propounded by Trotsky himself, that Russia, as the weakest of the powers engaged in the 'capitalist war', would be the first to break from within? Trotsky was still convinced that this was extremely likely to happen, that 'war may bring a quicker outbreak of the revolution' but that it would be 'at the cost of its [the revolution's] inner weakness'.[10] For under circumstances of war, a revolution in Russia would immediately lead the German armies to turn their 'bayonets on the revolution', an objective which would be made all the more feasible by the support which the German workers' movement gave these bayonets.[11] War

[9] Ibid., pp. 103 and 104.
[10] Ibid., p. 99.
[11] Loc. cit. This was not, of course, what actually happened in 1917 when the Germans in fact welcomed a revolution in Russia for reasons which by then were only too obvious.

might, therefore, bring revolution closer but it would turn it into a 'historical miscarriage'.[12] The only way out of revolutionary catastrophes, both in Russia and in Germany, was for European Social Democracy to abandon support for the war and return to its proper task which was to fight against the bourgeoisie in its own countries and not for it abroad.

The gist of this analysis by Trotsky was that the revolutionary movements in Russia and Europe remained interconnected and interdependent. Without revolution in Russia, where 'peculiar' conditions favoured a seizure of power by the workers' movement, there could be no revolution in Europe, where imperialism had undermined and delayed the uprising of the proletariat; Russia could provide that 'spark', in other words, which would offset the temporary paralysis of European workers. But, conversely, without the subsequent revolution in Europe, the Russian revolution would either collapse or find itself unable to fulfill its promise. In all this Trotsky was voicing again, though now in the context of what he took to be the immediate opportunity offered by war, the notion of the simultaneity of modern revolutions, of the 'chain reaction' effect of national uprisings, a notion which embodied the dynamic aspects of his theory of the permanent revolution. So convinced was he that war and other developments had brought near a simultaneous outbreak of revolutions throughout Europe and in Russia, that in the same work he was already speaking of the creation of a 'republican United States of Europe, as the foundation of the United States of the World'; this was to be a federation of independent but interrelated socialist countries, within which the post-revolutionary international proletariat would immediately embark upon the 'socialist organization of the world economy'.[13]

This may have appeared premature, even fantastic, to others,[14] but Trotsky was not to be deterred, for about a year later, at the beginning of 1916, he was seriously propounding the idea again.[15] As before, he expressed confidence that the

---

[12] Ibid., p. 100.   [13] Ibid., p. 78.

[14] In *Moya Zhizn*, I, p. 273, Trotsky noted that Radek, for one, had told him that the idea was beyond the present capacity of the 'productive forces of mankind'.

[15] In a series of articles, later published as a pamphlet, under the title *Programma Mira* and re-published in Trotsky's *Sochineniya*, III, part 1, pp. 70–93 (to which all subsequent references are made). (The articles first appeared in the newspaper *Nashe Slovo*, during

international situation was ripe for the 'international proletariat to rise' against the war and against the 'imperialist'
government.[16] Its very success, however, depended on the element of simultaneity:

We have every reason to hope that during the course of the present
war a powerful revolutionary movement will be launched all over
Europe. It is clear that such a movement can only succeed as a *general
European one*. Isolated within national borders, it would be doomed
to failure . . . The salvation of the Russian revolution lies in its pro-
pagation all over Europe . . . and if in one of the European countries
the proletariat should snatch the power out of the hands of the bourgeoisie, it would be bound, be it only to retain the power, to place
it at once at the service of the revolutionary movement in other
lands.[17]

And, also as before, while advocating the principle of
national self-determination[18] he returned to the idea of the
'United States of Europe' as the post-revolutionary framework
of the European proletariat and of the European economy:

The United States of Europe is the motto of the revolutionary age
into which we have emerged . . . The democratic, republican union
of Europe . . . is possible only . . . by means of revolts in individual
countries, with the subsequent confluence of these upheavals into a
collective European revolution. The victorious European Revolution,
however, no matter how its reverberation may be fashioned in the
various countries, can, in consequence of the absence of other revolutionary classes, transfer power only to the proletariat. Thus the United
States of Europe represents the only conceivable form of the dictatorship of the European proletariat.[19]

In view of this, when Lenin later rejected the slogan 'The
United States of Europe' because it 'suggested to him that

January, February, and April 1916 and as a separate pamphlet in Petrograd, 1917.
They also appear in *Voina i Revolyutsiya*, II, pp. 459–81.)

[16] Ibid., p. 79.

[17] Ibid., p. 88.

[18] Ibid., pp. 81–4. In *Moya Zhizn*, I, p. 276, Trotsky related that when Woodrow Wilson
heard in 1917 that he (Trotsky) had advocated national self-determination in *Voina
i Internatsional*, he asked that the proofs of the English translation of the work be sent
to him.

[19] Ibid., pp. 88 and 92. Trotsky added, however, that 'the United States of Europe
will be only one of the two axes of the world re-organization of industry. The United
States of America will constitute the other' (ibid., p. 89).

Trotsky envisaged the Russian revolution only as part of a simultaneous Europe-wide insurrection',[20] this was a fairly exact interpretation of Trotsky's views and expectations during the World War. Thus when at the Zimmerwald socialist conference of September 1915 Trotsky drew up the conference's 'Manifesto' and concluded it with the famous words 'Workers of all countries, unite!', this was not perfunctory rhetoric on his part.[21] He was as convinced, then, of the interdependence of the European (and Russian) proletariat and of the actuality of the international revolutionary wave, as Marx and Engels had been on the eve of 1848 when they concluded *their* 'Manifesto' with the same words.[22]

2. Revolution in the West[23]

In the event, of course, things did not work out quite as Trotsky had hoped and expected. Although he proved to be right about the prospects of revolution in Russia, he was wrong about such prospects in Europe, particularly in Germany. Yet it took some time before he came to terms with the fact that the revolutions were not to follow one another in some inexorable fashion. For a year or two he still believed that the European conflagration was imminent, as did indeed other Bolsheviks, including Lenin.[24] But there was a fundamental difference of orientation between Trotsky and Lenin from the very outset and nothing illustrates this better than their respective attitudes towards a peace settlement with Germany.

[20] Deutscher, *The Prophet Armed*, p. 215.
[21] The Russian version of the 'Manifesto' is in Trotsky's *Voina i Revolyutsiya*, II, pp. 51–4.
[22] For other of Trotsky's writings on the political aspects of the World War, see in general the collection *Voina i Revolyutsiya*. For the views of the Bolsheviks on the World War, see O. H. Gankin and H. H. Fisher, *The Bolsheviks and the World War* (Stanford, 1940). On the socialist movement in general and the War, see Merle Fainsod, *International Socialism and the World War* (New York, 1969, originally published in 1935).
[23] The remainder of this chapter deals with Trotsky's views on the world revolution during the 1917–24 period only; the controversy over 'socialism in one country', which is a natural breaking-off point, forms the main subject of the next chapter (though some writings from the year 1924 are referred to in this chapter).
[24] For a detailed account of the ideological basis for Soviet internationalism from 1917 onwards, see Elliot R. Goodman, *The Soviet Design for a World State* (New York, 1960). An earlier but still useful work is Michael T. Florinsky, *World Revolution and the U.S.S.R.* (London, 1933).

The whole controversy over the treaty of Brest-Litovsk and the negotiations leading up to it have veen copiously documented by historians;[25] and the matter, in any case, is not of central importance to the scope of the present study. It will be sufficient, therefore, to note only the basis for the different attitudes of Trotsky and Lenin, in order to grasp the former's point of departure for the policies towards Europe he advocated then and thereafter. As we have seen above, Trotsky believed that a war launched with the support of the European Social Democrats was a disaster for the revolutionary movement in general. But war itself—or the particular conditions created by war—could be a precipitant of revolution; and, obviously, the more costly the war effort and the more distant the prospects of victory, the more likely did revolution become. This was certainly proven to be the case in Russia and Trotsky believed that it could also become the case in Germany. In negotiating the peace with the latter, therefore, he took the position that everything should be done with this consideration in mind. True, the main concern was peace for Russia; and Lenin was undoubtedly right that unless this was achieved the Soviet government would go the way of its predecessors. But Trotsky believed that to accept peace on the conditions stipulated by the Germans was to serve them politically and, thereby, to waste the opportunity of contributing towards an upheaval in Germany. Moreover, in the long run, should Germany succeed in avoiding revolution, this would have a disastrous effect on the progress of the revolution in Russia. The famous formula Trotsky coined—'neither war nor peace'—was, therefore, a way, in his view, of providing Russia with a relative respite from fighting while simultaneously denying Germany the benefits of a final settlement on the Eastern front. And it perfectly reflected

---

[25] The classic study, of course, is that by John W. Wheeler-Bennett, *Brest–Litovsk: The Forgotten Peace* (London, 1938). Deutscher, *The Prophet Armed*, pp. 346–404, gives an account which concentrates on Trotsky's position and his differences with Lenin. Trotsky's speeches at the negotiations are in *Mirnye peregovory v Brest–Litovske*, edited by A. A. Joffe with a preface by Trotsky (Moscow, 1920) and in Trotsky, *Sochineniya*, III, part 2, pp. 157–252 and XVII, part 1, pp. 3–151 (the latter also contains various articles by Trotsky on the negotiations). For Trotsky's views on Brest–Litovsk in later years, see in particular his *Moya Zhizn*, II, pp. 86–123; Trotsky here confessed that Lenin was right in pressing for peace at all costs and he, Trotsky, wrong in his opposition. This is another typical example of Trotsky's unabashed deference to Lenin in the years when their past differences were being resurrected against him.

Trotsky's determination from the outset that Soviet Russia play
a positive, active role in the spread of revolution and that, at
least, it do nothing to encourage the forces of 'imperialism'.[26]

Certainly Lenin shared this determination; he recognized no
less than Trotsky the importance of a German revolution and
was obviously not adverse to contributing to its outbreak.[27] But
his list of priorities was different; his first concern was to put
his own house in order. If the best, most sure way of safeguarding the Soviet regime was to conclude a peace, however humi-
liating, then this way had to be followed. This did not mean,
in his view, abandoning the revolutionary struggle abroad; on
the contrary, it meant preserving, collecting and reorganizing
one's strength to fight on another, more propitious day. Lenin,
the strategist of world revolution, was therefore like Lenin, the
strategist of the Russian revolution. Nevertheless, this element
of pragmatism or expediency reflected Lenin's fundamentally
Russian or internal-oriented approach as against Trotsky's international orientation. Here lay the source of the differences
over external policy which were to become particularly conspicuous in later years, though less so between Trotsky and
Lenin than between Trotsky and Lenin's eventual successor.
It bears repeating, however, that while Trotsky's commitment
to an internationalist position grew, perhaps, out of his own
personal frame of mind, on the level of rational argumentation
it took the form that the *Russian* revolution cannot survive without world revolution.[28] And this belief in the inter-dependence
of revolutions continued to guide his thinking in subsequent
years.

By the time, however, of the establishment of the Third
(Communist) International in March 1919, the situation in
Europe, from the point of view of Soviet Russia, was already
evolving in a complicated direction.[29] True, approximately at

[26] This brief summary of Trotsky's position regarding a settlement with Germany is based
on his various speeches and writings on the subject, the sources for which have been
mentioned in the previous note.
[27] On Lenin, Germany and the treaty of Brest–Litovsk, see Page, op. cit., chapters
6 and 7. But see also George Katkov, *Russia 1917: The February Revolution* (London,
1967) for an unorthodox interpretation of Lenin's involvement with the German
government and, therefore, of the motives for his subsequent policies toward Germany.
[28] See chapter 4, pp. 143–4, above.
[29] On the early (as well as the later) history of the Comintern, see in particular Franz
Borkenau, *World Communism* (Ann Arbor, 1962, originally published as *The Communist*

the same time a soviet regime was established in Hungary; but Bela Kun's Communists managed to last only a few months. And in Germany, still the crux of the whole revolutionary matter, the 'November Revolution' of 1918 was not leading to an equivalent of the 'Russian October'. The Berlin insurrection of January 1919 had ended in debacle and tragedy for the *Spartakus* League and, in May, army troops were to bring to a bloody end the attempt by Communists to assume power in Bavaria. In the meantime, of course, Soviet Russia was in the midst of the Civil War.

Nevertheless, the political situation in Germany and elsewhere in Europe remained sufficiently unsettled to allow the Bolsheviks the hope that in the end the European proletariat would find a way of fulfilling its promise and that the Russian Revolution would not remain an isolated event. During its first years, therefore, the Comintern, under the leadership and, eventually, the domination of the Bolsheviks, was above all concerned with a revolutionary strategy for Europe; and Trotsky, who often appeared at Comintern sessions as the spokesman of the Soviet government, in numerous speeches and writings during the period 1919–24 attempted to provide a conceptual basis for such a strategy.[30]

He did not, of course, have one single, uniform strategy for the whole period since the situation in Europe, particularly in Germany and France, was continuously changing. Nevertheless, all his policies were guided by certain assumptions about Europe which he never abandoned and by a general, consistent conception of the relation between the Soviet government and European developments. As to his assumptions about Europe, an article he wrote in April 1919 may serve as a representative text.[31] Not surprisingly, its main argument was that the tradi-

---

International, London, 1938) and Hugh Seton-Watson, *From Lenin to Khrushchev: The History of World Communism* (New York, 1960). See also Branko Lazitch, *Lénine et la Troisième Internationale* (Paris, 1951).

[30] The main source for Trotsky's views, as presented in what follows, is his *Pyat Let Kominterna* (Moscow, 1924). This consists of various speeches, declarations and writings during the period 1919 to the end of 1923. Volume XIII of Trotsky's *Sochineniya* is also devoted to the Comintern but its contents are reproduced almost entirely in *Pyat Let Kominterna* which, moreover, contains other writings not included in the *Sochineniya* volume. (For the English translation see Trotsky, *The First Five Years of the Communist International*, 2 vols., New York, 1945 and 1953.)

[31] 'V puti: mysli o khode proletarskoi revolyutsii', in *Pyat Let Kominterna*, pp. 30–43.

tionally accepted belief, that proletarian revolution was more likely the more advanced the capitalist countries, had not only to be revised but in fact jettisoned. This was, of course, the central theme of all Trotsky's writings about the Russian revolution for more than a decade; in evaluating now the 'progress' of revolution in Europe, not only the influence of the Russian case but its analogy for Europe was uppermost in his mind. Just as Russia, the most backward of countries in comparison with Europe, was the first to experience a workers' revolution, so in Europe itself it was the least advanced societies which would collapse first:

From Russia [the revolution] passed over into Hungary, from Hungary to Bavaria . . . Hungary is unquestionably the more backward half of the former Austro-Hungarian monarchy, which as a whole, in the sense of capitalist and even cultural-political development, stood between Russia and Germany. Bavaria . . . represents with respect to capitalist development not the advanced but, on the contrary, a backward section of Germany. Thus the proletarian revolution, after starting in the most backward country of Europe [i.e. Russia], keeps mounting upwards, rung by rung, towards countries more highly developed economically.[32]

As he had argued years ago against a 'mechanical' interpretation of Marxism in the case of Russia, so now Trotsky rejected the accepted, 'mechanical' view of Europe according to which the revolution would begin in England, the most developed capitalist nation, proceed to France and only thence to Germany. The order had in fact been reversed and to understand the reasons for this reversal it was necessary, in Trotsky's view, to look at the nature of modern capitalism. Here we are on familiar ground—the socio-cultural interpretation of capitalism which Trotsky first raised when discussing the weakness and vulnerability of Russian capitalism, and to which he now returned.[33] Firstly, he argued, the older capitalist development was, the more time it has had to become structured and institutionalized, to develop a complete way of life in which society and economics were one. Secondly, as in the case of England in particular, being first meant a long period of virtual monopoly over economic resources; thus an industrial structure had

[32] Ibid., pp. 30 and 32.   [33] See chapter 3, *passim*, above.

been created able to exploit its own full potential and that of its colonies virtually unhindered by competition; thus also it had been able to isolate its workers and to create internal mechanisms for preventing their access to instruments of power. Thirdly, the more developed the proletariat, the more it inclined to organize within the framework of the 'bourgeois' political structure which, in return for this adherence to its rules, was prepared to provide certain economic and social benefits; hence the conservatism of the trade-union movement; hence also the growth of economic differentiation within the proletariat, encouraged by capitalism, resulting in a relative absence of class solidarity or united interests.[34]

In contrast to this, Trotsky continued, those countries where capitalist development had been late and slow were unable to create internal equilibrium between their economic innovation and their entrenched, feudal social structure. Capitalism, in so far as it had been introduced, had imposed new forms of production without a parallel socio-cultural content. Thus the anomalies, the contradictions, the asymmetry, the instability, the fragility of the whole phenomenon. But this was as yet not enough to make for revolution; the point at which the collapse could begin was reached once capitalism extended itself beyond national borders, turned into imperialism, resorted to war and engulfed within its orbit, necessarily, the newer and weaker capitalist nations. Thus countries with a 'younger capitalist culture are the first to enter the path of civil war in as much as the unstable equilibrium of class forces is most easily disrupted precisely in these countries':[35]

Precisely because of the entire preceding development, the task of initiating the revolution, as we have already seen, was not placed on an old proletariat with mighty political and trade-union organizations, with massive traditions of parliamentarism and trade-unionism, but upon the young proletariat of a backward country. History took the line of least resistance. The revolutionary epoch burst in through the most weakly barricaded door.[36]

The phenomenon of Russia, therefore, would be repeated, Trotsky believed, within the context of Europe also; there too history would take the 'line of least resistance'. And the lesson

[34] 'V puti ...', pp. 32–8.   [35] Ibid., p. 40.   [36] Ibid., p. 42.

to be drawn from this for practical purposes was that all revolutionary efforts, through the Comintern and within individual countries, must be geared to *this* order of development and not to that of 'mechanical', outdated preconceptions.

If this constituted the first and most fundamental of Trotsky's assumptions about the European revolution, it was accompanied by a second one about the general vulnerability of European capitalism, the crisis it was going through and the eruptions it must necessarily suffer. Even by the middle of 1921, when the revolutionary wave of the previous years already appeared to have been repulsed, Trotsky remained confident that this was merely a temporary setback and that the capitalist system far from 'restoring' itself was in the process of continued disintegration.[37] His confidence, as usual, grew out of a combination of determinist presumptions about the nature of capitalism and what can only be called 'wishful thinking'. It was based, firstly, on the standard Marxist analysis of the inherent contradictions within capitalism: its class antagonisms, its inability to expand without increasing exploitation or risking war, its dependence on scarce markets, its failure to provide for the economic needs of the masses, and so on. This, he thought, was even truer now than it was in Marx's day. But beyond this, there had taken place, in his view, developments which had led to an aggravation of the endemic capitalist crisis. Having become a tightly-knit international system, capitalism was vulnerable at any one of a number of connecting points. The economy of one country was dependent on that of another, a crisis in one was a crisis for all. Moreover, the World War, far from culminating in the domination of one capitalist power over another, had ended with the whole of Europe in ruins, the victors no less than the vanquished. Europe came out of the War exhausted, her economy undermined, her people decimated and impoverished, her political leadership bankrupt and her resources for reconstruction depleted. The result, in Trotsky's view, had been the disruption of the European 'equi-

---

[37] See, in particular, the following: 'Doklad o mirovom khozyaistvennom krizise i novykh zadachakh Kommunisticheskogo Internatsionala', in *Pyat Let Kominterna*, pp. 138–86 (also in Trotsky, *Novyi Etap*, Moscow, 1921, pp. 138–86); 'Tezisy III Kongressa o mirovom polozhenie i zadachakh Kommunisticheskogo Internatsionala', in ibid., pp. 196–217 (the latter was co-authored by Trotsky with E. Varga).

librium'—economic, class, political, and international.[38] Europe, once the centre of the world, had become only a shadow of her former self, no longer the 'heart of the capitalist world', nor the master of 'all world politics'; instead, the 'centre of gravity has shifted from Europe to America'.[39] While the former slumps, the latter grows, exploiting the vacuum created by European decline, coming to dominate old markets in the West and new ones in the East.[40] Evidently, Trotsky envisaged a situation in which the main struggle against capitalism would shift across the oceans to America while an enfeebled Europe, together with Russia, would become the foundation of the socialist axis.

Nevertheless, the sudden rise and power of America seemed to him basically illusory and transient; her post-war 'flowering' was merely one of those typical capitalist 'booms', in this case the result of Europe's decline. It would, however, be followed by the inevitable, and no less typical, capitalist 'crisis', resulting from the likely loss of European markets and from competition with Eastern, particularly Japanese, ones.[41] In all this Trotsky revealed, on the one hand, an uncanny power for prophecy: at one point he even predicted that America would soon be engulfed in a 'depression',[42] and elswhere he hinted at a violent clash between American and Japanese interests.[43] But, on the other hand, his fundamental misunderstanding of the relations between the United States and Europe and, therefore, his inability to countenance a European recovery, were betrayed by further 'prophecies' about a war between England and America—which seemed to him imminent since England could not allow herself to become dominated by the United States.[44] But, in any case, even the prospect of a 'temporary' economic recovery in Europe appeared to him advantageous to the revolutionary movement: as in Russia following the economic improvements of 1910–12, so in Europe a partial economic

[38] 'Doklad ...', pp. 138–56. Trotsky quoted detailed production statistics to show the decline of the European economy.
[39] Ibid., p. 145.   [40] Ibid., pp. 156–9.
[41] Ibid., pp. 166–72; see also 'Tezisy III Kongressa ...', pp. 202–4.
[42] 'Doklad ...', p. 172.   [43] 'Tezisy III Kongressa ...', p. 209.
[44] 'Doklad ...', p. 179 and 'Tezisy III Kongressa ...', pp. 209–10. In the former, he even gave the year 1924 as the time of the probable clash between the United States and England.

restoration would enable the workers to re-organize and re-consolidate their forces, shaking themselves free of the demoralization which impoverishment had subjected them to.[45] Thus Trotsky saw light wherever he looked; the hopelessness of the capitalist world's 'struggle for survival' appeared to him incontrovertible, the propitiousness of the times for world revolution hardly questionable. Naturally, 'victory will not come to us automatically'; it will require planning, watchfulness, correct tactics and 'strategical manœuvring' on the part of the Comintern as a whole and its individual members. But, essentially, the 'world situation and the future perspectives remain profoundly revolutionary' and this 'creates the necessary premises for our victory'.[46]

These were Trotsky's assumptions regarding the nature of the post-war capitalist world. Underlying them was his conception of the relationship between this world and the fact of a Soviet 'workers'' government in Russia. We have already seen how at Brest-Litovsk he sought to give expression to the manner in which he conceived this relationship, to the role of 'provoker' which he wanted Soviet Russia to play in Europe. This was to remain very much the cornerstone of his strategy for the Comintern and, inevitably, the source of later criticism that he was pursuing an adventurous and irresponsible policy, that he was fundamentally uninterested in the fate of Russia and prepared to sacrifice internal stability for the mere promise of some dubious gains in foreign lands. This controversy, which had already begun in Lenin's time but reached its heights only after Lenin's death, shall concern us in the next chapter; here it will suffice to repeat that Trotsky's reply in self-defence was always that it was impossible to separate the fate of Russia from that of Europe, that the failure of revolution in the latter would inevitably culminate in the failure of the Russian Revolution itself. Moreover, it was certainly not true that he at any time advocated the 'export' of revolution on the point of a bayonet. He expected military confrontations between Russia and the outside world as a result of the latter's inability to tolerate the Soviet example; but he did not counsel military intervention in European affairs.[47] Nevertheless, if he could not be justly

---

[45] 'Doklad ...', pp. 171–2.   [46] Ibid., p. 186.
[47] In the case of the war with Poland, however, he did come near the position that

identified with a policy of revolutionary adventurism, there was a certain sense in which Russia seemed to him to be, ultimately, of secondary significance. As we have seen, he never had illusions about the prospects of socialism in Russia alone; and socialism without Europe appeared to him an impossibility. Soviet Russia had taken the initiative and had become the centre of the revolutionary world; but her role was temporary—it was as if she were 'filling in' for an ailing or delayed actor:

. . . we have erected in our country the bulwark of the world revolution . . . But we are defending this bulwark since at the present moment there is no other in the world. When another stronghold is erected in France or in Germany, then the one in Russia will lose nine-tenths of its significance; and we shall then go to . . . Europe to defend this other and more important stronghold.[48]

And in the previously referred to article of April 1919 he wrote:

The revolutionary 'primogeniture' of the Russian proletariat is only temporary . . . The dictatorship of the Russian working class will be able to finally entrench itself and to develop into a genuine, all-sided socialist construction only from the hour when the European working class frees us from the economic yoke of the European bourgeoisie and, having overthrown the latter, comes to our assistance with its organization and its technology. Concurrently, the leading revolutionary role will pass over to the working class with the greater economic and organizational power. If today the centre of the Third International lies in Moscow . . . then on the morrow this centre will shift westward: to Berlin, to Paris, to London.[49]

Thus while the road to world revolution began in the East, its ultimate fate remained centred on the West. And as a consequence it was in the end far more important what happened and was done in Europe than in Russia. Trotsky did not hesitate

---

war was an instrument of revolution. But this was a special and isolated case and, at any rate, the failure of this example hardly argued for its repetition. For Trotsky's writings on the war with Poland, see *Sochineniya*, XVII, part 2, pp. 375–485 and *Kak vooruzhalas revolyutsiya*, II, part 2, pp. 91–180. For his writings on the Red Army and the international situation in general, see *Kak vooruzhalas revolyutsiya*, III, part 2, pp. 15–177.
[48] From 'Rech po italyanskomu voprosu', in *Pyat Let Kominterna*, p. 222.
[49] 'V puti ...', pp. 42–3.

to reject a Comintern policy aimed at serving particular Russian interests and which was adventuristic from the point of view of the European socialist parties:

> . . . it is sheer absurdity to believe that we deem [the] Russian stronghold of the revolution to be the centre of the world. It is absurd even to claim that we believe it is our right to demand of you [i.e. the European Communists] to make a revolution in Germany or France or Italy, whenever this is required by our domestic policy.[50]

And elsewhere he wrote:

> . . . real assistance could not be rendered us by . . . artificially provoked uprisings, but only by the revolutionary victory of the European proletariat. The interests of Russia are therefore served by only those movements, those uprisings, which flow from the internal development of the European proletariat . . . For us the Russian Soviet Republic constitutes only the point of departure for the European and world revolution. The interests of the latter are for us decisive in every major question.[51]

This point of view did not, of course, exclude an active role for the Soviet government in European affairs; on the contrary, he believed it invited it, though in accordance with European possibilities not simply Russian needs. In this sense it both reaffirmed the primacy of Europe and avoided the charge of adventurism. But it was already out of step with what other Bolshevik leaders were thinking about the role and use of the Comintern, and it is doubtful whether Trotsky's words were representative of their views. The 'Bolshevization' of the Comintern was to turn it eventually into an instrument of Russian interests. And almost simultaneously world revolution itself was to be either abandoned or 'shelved'. Thus Trotsky, who would continue to affirm the primacy of Europe and of the world revolution, would be characterized as, on the one hand, a belittler of Russia and, on the other, an irresponsible adventurist.

It would be merely tedious and, today, hardly illuminating, to follow Trotsky's writings during the 1919–24 period on revolutionary prospects and developments in the various individual European countries. His book *Pyat Let Kominterna* (Five Years

---

[50] 'Rech po italyanskomu voprosu', p. 222.
[51] From 'Pismo t. t. Kashenu i Frossaru', in *Pyat Let Kominterna*, p. 127.

of the Comintern) is full of periodic appraisals of the situation in Germany, in France, in Italy and in England.[52] To trace in detail Trotsky's specific proposals for the various countries and at various times would require more space than can be devoted in the context of the present study; our concern has been rather to present his general conception of the 'progress', as he called it, of the European revolution. Nevertheless, it may be instructive to look briefly at one case, that of Germany, which is fairly representative of Trotsky's general approach to concrete questions of revolutionary policy and, equally, of the source of his misreading of the revolutionary potential of Europe.[53]

The German case is instructive because it shows that for all his awareness of the differences between Europe and Russia Trotsky had become carried away by the Russian example. This expressed itself not only in the general proposition that there was an analogy, albeit of different dimensions, between the backwardness of Russia and that of Germany, which allowed one to expect similarities of development; rather it extended also to practical, 'operational' conclusions which Trotsky formulated for the German Communists. Thus the tragedy of January 1919 evoked from him the reaction that the German party would have to study the Russian lesson again if it was to succeed in the future. In an article which opened with the words 'the German revolution bears clear traits of simi-larity with the Russian', Trotsky went on to explain why there was nevertheless a 'dissimilarity' in the end result.[54] The prob-lem, he argued, was the 'absence' in Germany of a 'centralized revolutionary party' akin to the Bolshevik model:

History bequeathed nothing like this to the German working class. It is compelled not only to fight for power but to create its organization and train future leaders in the very course of this struggle . . . In the absence of a centralized revolutionary party with a combat leadership whose authortiy is universally accepted by the working masses, in the absence of leading combat nuclei and leaders, tried in action and

---

[52] On France, see also the collection by Trotsky, *Kommunisticheskoe dvizhenie vo Frantsii* (Moscow, 1923) and the excellent French compilation, Léon Trotsky, *Le Mouvement communiste en France, 1919–1939* (Paris, 1967), part 2 of which, pp. 97–275, is devoted to the period under discussion in this chapter.
[53] His views on Germany in the 1930s are discussed in the following chapter.
[54] 'Polzuchaya revolyutsiya', in *Pyat Let Kominterna*, pp. 25–8.

tested in experience throughout the various centres and regions of
the proletarian movement, this movement, upon breaking out onto
the streets, became of necessity intermittent, chaotic, creeping in
character.[55]

Clearly, therefore, what was missing in Germany was Bolshevism, that 'pre-condition' for a socialist revolution which,
in 1917, he had come to recognize as indispensable. Why it was
missing he had already indicated in the past, and he now
emphasized the explanation: the very size of German Social
Democracy, its success in building a mass movement and an
enormous party and trade-union organization, converted it
into an institution which saw itself as an integral part of existing
German society so that, eventually, it became an 'auxiliary
organ of the bourgeois state, designed to discipline the proletariat'.[56] Thus the leadership was more interested in protecting
the parliamentary and trade-union power already attained
than risking a direct confrontation with the state; thus it had
turned 'revisionist' and conservative; and thus when all other
revolutionary conditions presented themselves, after the war,
it proved incapable of providing revolutionary leadership:

> Precisely because the German working class had expended most of
> its energy in the previous epoch upon self-sufficient organizational
> construction . . . in a new epoch, at the moment of its transition to
> open revolutionary struggle for power, the German working class
> proved to be extremely defenceless organizationally.[57]

Trotsky agreed that the more difficult conditions under
which the Marxist movement was forced to function in Russia
ironically made possible the growth of a superior revolutionary
leadership. Obviously, the German socialist movement could
not emulate such conditions, but the lesson it had to learn from
the Russian experience was that only by direct confrontation
and struggle, and not through compromise, could a truly revolutionary organization be created. It was, in his view, the 'one
and only road along which the class uprising of the German
proletariat can unfold'.[58] And the 'strikes, insurrections, and
battles' of the post-war period suggested that the German
workers had indeed set out on this road. In spite of the initial

[55] Ibid., p. 27.   [56] Ibid., p. 26.
[57] Loc. cit.   [58] Ibid., p. 27.

failures, which were in Trotsky's view analogous to the failures of 1905 in Russia, the experience of actual combat would bear fruit in the future, as did 1905 in Russia.[59] Thus Trotsky, in 1919, remained confident about Germany: 'The stubborn, unabated erupting and re-erupting, creeping revolution is clearly approaching the critical moment when, having mobilized and trained all its forces in advance for combat, the revolution will deal the class enemy the final mortal blow.'[60]

The repeated setbacks in Germany from 1919 to 1923 did not, at first, appreciably alter Trotsky's outlook. He continued to hold that the key to victory lay in the development of a 'combat' organization and leadership, though he simultaneously warned against a strategy which was so unremittingly 'offensive-oriented', in spite of objective conditions, as to verge on adventurism.[61] Even the defeat of 1923, which he himself admitted constituted a most serious blow to future revolutionary prospects in Germany, was attributed by him to instrumental factors: weak leadership, faulty strategy, bad timing and so on.[62] He was openly critical now of the Comintern and, in particular, of the Moscow leadership itself for having hesitated and, in the end, misguided the German Communists for reasons having to do with its own interests, and not those of the German revolution. But as the full impact of the 1923 defeat began to dawn on him, he seemed to realize that the opportunities of the past would not recur, at least not in the same propitious way. Looking back on the post-war period in Germany, he said, in a speech of July 1924: 'History never created and will hardly ever again create more favourable pre-conditions for the proletarian revolution and for the seizure of power.'[63]

Was it, however, the fear of confronting more fundamental doubts which compelled him to add again, on this same occasion, that what was lacking in Germany was the 'degree of tempering, the degree of vision, resolution and fighting

[59] Ibid., pp. 27–8.   [60] Ibid., p. 28.
[61] See, for example, his speech of July 1921, 'Shkola revolyutsionnoi strategii', in *Pyat Let Kominterna*, pp. 266–305.
[62] See his speech of June 1924, 'Cherez kakoi etap my prokhodim?', in Trotsky, *Zapad i Vostok* (Moscow, 1924), pp. 108–38 (pp. 127–35 deal with the reasons for the defeat of 1923 in Germany).
[63] 'K voprosu o perspektivakh mirovogo razvitia', in Trotsky, *Evropa i Amerika* (Moscow, 1926), pp. 5–40 (the quotation cited is on p. 11).

ability of the Communist Party necessary to assure timely action and victory'?[64] For by thus concentrating on, and blaming, instrumental, immediate factors he was in fact avoiding larger issues. There is little doubt that he was right in criticizing the Moscow leadership for its ineptitude in 1923;[65] and, certainly, the failure to create a 'Bolshevik-type' party in Germany could be argued to have constituted a stumbling-block to revolution there. But all this was more in the realm of the symptoms, rather than the causes, of the 'disease'. For the time had surely come instead to pose again the question whether Germany, and Europe in general, was as ripe for a socialist revolution as Trotsky had assumed over the years. And it should perhaps have occurred to him that Bolshevism was a phenomenon peculiar to a country like Russia and not easily given to reproduction in the West. Indeed, when explaining many years before the conditions which had made Bolshevism possible in Russia, he had more than hinted at this; but he could not, in any case, bring himself to contemplate a conclusion other than that a 'centralized revolutionary party' would arise in Germany through other developments and, ultimately, as a result of the revolutionary situation itself, which he took almost for granted. That it did not, or that even if it did, its chances of success would still be more limited than those of the original Bolsheviks in Russia, should surely have suggested that European 'capitalism' was a more resilient adversary than Marxism had anticipated and that, perhaps, it was the 'revolutionary situation' itself which should be taken less for granted. For the truth of the matter was that the Russian precedent was emerging as inapplicable to the West and, as always, far more relevant to the East.

3. Revolution in the East

The obvious analogy for the conditions which, in Trotsky's view, made possible October 1917 in Russia was the situation prevailing in Asia, or parts thereof, and not in Europe. True, Russia was not a 'colony', as so many of the Asian nations were, and she was, moreover, historically and socially at least partly

[64] Loc. cit.

[65] See the account of the 1923 defeat in Borkenau, op. cit., pp. 243–56.

within the European sphere. But the greater part of her population was closer to Asia than to Europe, both geographically and culturally, and, as Trotsky never tired of pointing out, because of her dependence on Western capital she had, in effect, a semi-colonial status. Strategically, and from the point of view of the concept of the world revolution as a whole, the significance of a socialist revolution in Russia lay in the fact that it had occurred in a country which straddled West and East, providing perhaps a link between the two.

If, nevertheless, the Soviet government was initially more interested in Europe than in Asia, this was for the obvious reason that the main danger to it came from the centre of the capitalist world and not its peripheries; and it was in Europe, as everyone believed, that the drama of a socialist triumph had still to be played out. In any case, it could be reasonably assumed that if Europe went socialist, Asia would inevitably and easily follow. This is not to say that the East was ignored in Bolshevik calculations. Lenin's grasp of the potential of peasant masses had led him to speculate optimistically about the prospects of an Asian revolution in which the 'toiling masses' of the world would rise against the 'imperialist exploiters'.[66] And when the Comintern was founded in 1919, Asian Communist movements were widely represented in it. But, of course, it was Europe which continued to occupy the minds of Soviet leaders during the early years of their regime.

The shift, when it came, was not sudden but gradual, and it was a direct result of defeats in Europe. The more the revolutionary tide there receded, the more were hopes transferred to the East. An Asian-oriented policy for world revolution was thus a product more of the force of circumstances than of choice, but in a sense it was more logical than the prior European orientation: it was easier for the East to identify with, and perhaps emulate, the Russian experience than it was for the West. In spite of great differences between Russia and Asian countries, and among Asian countries themselves, the common denominator of economic backwardness provided a not unreasonable basis for analogies.

In view of the fact that Trotsky's whole theoretical perspective

[66] See in particular his *Imperialism, The Highest Stage of Capitalism*. For a brief survey of Lenin's views on revolution in the East, see Page, op. cit., chapter 11.

on revolution had been founded on the element of backwardness, one would have expected him to be at the forefront
of those who faced East rather than West. But, as we have seen,
his ultimate orientation was basically Western. He saw the Russian Revolution as rooted in the peculiar conditions of non-
European development but its significance lay in the fact that,
originally, it had grown out of Western influences and now it
was an event having a direct impact on Europe. He did not,
in any case, divide the world into two unrelated spheres of East
and West; revolution in the twentieth century was for him
an international phenomenon, the meeting-point between
East and West, and, the Russian Revolution, the beginning of
this process. Having begun in Russia, the world revolution had
now to spread to the West, firstly in order to sustain the Russian
experiment, secondly, in order to bring down the stronghold
of capitalism. Although in Europe itself he expected the revolution to unfold from East to West—Hungary, Germany, Italy,
and only later France and England—he did not extend this
analogy to the world as a whole. Of course, world developments
did not wait to take their place in some pre-arranged line and
could unfold simultaneously; but in general he believed that
after Russia came Europe's turn, and only thereafter would the
East as a whole be swept up by the revolutionary tide.

For the most part, therefore, his writings on the world revolution during the period up to and including 1923 concentrated
on European affairs. There were many references to the East
but developments and prospects there were clearly of a peripheral, secondary concern to him.[67] He had no doubt that
these developments, in the form primarily of nationalist, anti-
colonial movements, were having a deleterious effect on the
stability of the imperialist powers, and were therefore an integral and important part of the struggle against world capitalism; but the emphasis was on this aspect of the question and
not on revolution within the East itself. It is possible to infer
from his brief remarks about, for example, India and China,
that he did not expect revolutionary developments there in the

---

[67] It is interesting to note that in the whole of *Pyat Let Kominterna*, a work consisting
of nearly sixty different items, not a single one is exclusively devoted to the East; and
the references which do occur, though numerous, are brief, and contain no sustained
analysis of developments there.

foreseeable future. He noted that the peasant masses were indeed in a rebellious mood; but he added that only the rise of a proletariat which would stand at the head of the peasants could translate this rebelliousness into revolution. True, as in Russia, this proletariat need not constitute a majority, and its role would be out of all proportion to its actual numerical strength, Nevertheless, a proletariat of the relative dimensions which existed in Russia on the eve of October 1917 was, in his view, absolutely essential, and its development would depend on the extent of industrialization in these countries. Although this process had already begun it was still in its elementary stages. For the time being, therefore, the value of the essentially peasant political movements lay, according to Trotsky, in the disorder and disruption which they were capable of inflicting upon their foreign masters.[68] Trotsky thus saw the East through the Russian experience, and he applied to it that precedent in full; he could not imagine a socialist movement growing on peasant foundations alone. In the future, this inability to contemplate a still further variant of the twentieth-century socialist revolution—or perhaps an extension of his own ideas—would seriously mislead him in his evaluation of political developments in the East.[69]

But, as we have noted, his interest in the East was at this time very limited. It was not until 1924 that he began to pay greater attention to that part of the world and for the same reasons which prompted Moscow and the Comintern in general to switch their field of interests. As we shall see in the next chapter, this in no sense signified that he had 'given up' on the European revolution; on the contrary, the great controversy which was to begin occupying him in the year following 1924 revolved as much around his insistence that revolution in the West remained actual and necessary and that its pursuit, therefore, must continue to be a central tenet of Soviet policy, as around internal economic issues. But by 1924 even he had come to realize that revolutionary forces in Europe had been repulsed, for the time being at least, and that while efforts should not be spared to organize anew, simultaneously it was

---

[68] For the references to the East on which this brief summary is based, see in particular the following pages of *Pyat Let Kominterna*: 183–4; 195–6; 207.

[69] See the discussion on China in the next chapter.

necessary to exploit the seemingly rising revolutionary wave in the East.

During 1924, Trotsky wrote and spoke extensively about the East, but the most interesting of his analyses in this connection is a speech delivered in April of that year on the occasion of the third anniversary of the Communist University of the Toilers of the East.[70] This is a remarkably optimistic evaluation of revolutionary prospects in Asia. For the first time Trotsky was prepared to contemplate the possibility that, in the event of prolonged stagnation in Europe, 'the centre of gravity of the revolutionary movement will be transposed to the East'. Moreover, just as he had once expected the Russian revolution to spark off a European revolution, so now he raised the prospect that it would be instead a general revolution in the East which would 'give an impetus to the revolution of the European proletariat'.[71] Clearly, it now must have become apparent to him that the Russian Revolution was not enough; just as clearly, however, he was giving expression to the same type of hope—albeit one now based on a wider geographical context—which in the case of Russia had only recently been shown to be unwarranted, namely, that revolution in a backward country would ignite the 'advanced' world. As always, he could not imagine separating developments in the one from the other.

His optimism was based on a further assumption, and this was that the pace of industrial development in the countries of the East would be even more rapid than it had been in Russia. He claimed now to perceive a process of 'feverish industrialization of colonial, semi-colonial and, generally speaking, of all backward countries'.[72] This, in his view, was the direct result of the fact that in the post-war world, economic activity had more and more shifted from Europe to the still relatively untapped colonies. While capital investments in Europe had declined, because of the uncertain economic situation there, they had spiralled in the colonial countries where the extraction of raw materials and the consequent growing demands for machinery promised sure and long-term profits to the bankers and financiers of Europe and the United States. The effect of

---

[70] 'Perspektivy i zadachi na vostoke', in *Zapad i Vostok*, pp. 30–41. For his writings on the East, see in general the collection *Zapad i Vostok*.
[71] Ibid., p. 38.   [72] Ibid., p. 33.

this would be to usher in a period of pronounced economic and social transformation in the East:

All this leads to the mobilization of countless proletarian masses who will immediately emerge from a pre-historic, semi-barbarian state and will be thrust into the whirlpool of industrialism. Thus, in these countries, there will be no time for the refuse of past centuries to accumulate in the minds of the workers. A guillotine, as it were, will be set to work in their minds which will sever the past from the future at one stroke, and compel them to look for new ideas, new forms and new ways of life and struggle. And this will be the time for Marxist–Leninist parties to make their first appearance in some countries and to pursue a bold course of development in others.[73]

His model for the East was therefore that of Russia. And as in Russia, so in the East revolution became a product of the particular impact which the penetration of the West had on backward societies: instead of 'slow, organic and evolutionary' growth of new forms, as in the West, development in the East 'assumes the form of terrible convulsions and drastic changes'.[74] This was the same phenomenon of sudden social disruption, economic imbalance and political instability which Trotsky had described, in the context of Russia, as constituting the conditions under which backwardness became a source of revolution.[75] He claimed that the breakdown of traditional ways of life was already apparent; the influence of old 'creeds, prejudices and customs', he believed, was waning; a good example of this was that women, the most oppressed element in the East, were beginning to liberate themselves and to assume a role in political movements;[76] and everywhere new forms of critical thought were superseding the old.[77]

Perhaps the most striking aspect, however, of Trotsky's speech is the manner in which he now interpreted the appeal of Bolshevism to the East. It is striking because it is so obviously

---

[73] Ibid., pp. 33–4.
[75] See chapter 3, above.
[74] Ibid., pp. 31–2.
[76] Ibid., pp. 39–40.
[77] 'Why is it', he wondered, 'that during the nineteenth and the opening years of the twentieth centuries, Germany produced Marx and Russia, Lenin?' His explanation was that the disrupting effect of sudden changes upon hitherto backward societies aroused, inspired and finally liberated the mind, unleashing new modes of social perception. (Ibid., pp. 31–2.) There was in this the obvious implication that the East too will now produce someone of the stature of a Marx or a Lenin. Would, in Trotsky's view, Mao qualify, one wonders?

Leninist in character and so unrepresentative of his own past attitudes towards the assimilation of Marxism among the masses. Where he had once believed that social and political ideas had to penetrate the consciousness of men, and of working-men at that, in order to become effective, it was their *emotional* impact upon undifferentiated masses which now seemed to him paramount. Thus he wrote in a passage for which there is no precedent in all his previous work:

The strength and meaning of Bolshevism consist in the fact that it appeals to the oppressed and exploited masses and not to the upper strata of the working class. That is why Bolshevism is being assimilated by the countries of the East, not because of its theories, which are far away from being fully understood, but because of its spirit of freedom and liberty . . . the name of Lenin is known not only in the villages of the Caucasus but even in the remotest parts of India. We know that the workers of China, who probably never read anything written by Lenin, are irresistibly drawn to Bolshevism. Such is the powerful influence of this great historic movement! They feel in their inner-most hearts that it is a teaching for the oppressed and exploited, for hundreds of millions to whom it is the only possible salvation.[78]

This was not, perhaps, an incorrect interpretation of the appeals of Leninism to backward societies; but it constituted at least an implicit admission that in the context of the East the old concepts of Marxism—class, consciousness, economics—were being superseded and even negated by the new concepts of Leninism—'toiling' masses, spontaneity, ideology—as the components of revolution. Coming from Trotsky, this was an amazing admission; had he reached the conclusion—in view of the success of the revolution in Russia, its failure in Europe and its apparent prospects now in Asia—that Leninism, not Marxism as such, had emerged as the standard-bearer of revolution, that subjective, instrumental, even emotional, factors were more important than the objective preconditions for a socialist revolution?

In fact this seems to have been mainly a rhetorical slip for in subsequent years Trotsky hardly ever spoke in a similar vein.[79] And the 1924 speech itself, if we neglect the above pass-

[78] Ibid., pp. 38–9.
[79] Although, as will be seen in the next chapter, he continued to believe that the failure of revolutions to materialize in Europe was due to the lack there of Bolshevik-like parties.

age, remained true to the traditional Marxist view. Thus, Trotsky argued, a nationalist, peasant movement, though 'progressive' in some ways and for certain purposes, was no substitute for a movement based on and led by the proletariat.[80] And this latter must not be isolated from the West, lest it degenerate into a 'national democratic' movement; it was to be a part, as socialist movements everywhere, of the world revolutionary movement as a whole.[81] Substantially, therefore, Trotsky remained faithful to his original Russian model. But, as we shall see, eventually this was to be at the price of neglecting or underestimating two elements which, although not entirely absent from the Russian experience, were nevertheless particularly characteristic of the East proper: the force of nationalism and the potential of the peasantry, combining to form the ideological and material spearheads of a socialist movement.

Conclusion: Theory and Practice

The Bolshevik Revolution was the first revolution in history carried out in the name of a complete and systematic social and political theory. Other revolutions, before 1917, had been made in the name of social ideologies and in accordance with preconceived political goals and aspirations. But none could claim to be motivated by a body of thought so all-encompassing, and to be so clearly identified with a definite doctrine as was the Bolshevik Revolution. There is therefore a natural fascination in following the fortunes of this Revolution—and of its leaders—as it unfolded in practice against the background of its theoretical preconceptions and guidelines. In the case of Trotsky, the fascination is all the greater because beyond the Marxist doctrine which he shared with others, he himself had before 1917 formulated a specially adapted 'scenario' for the Russian revolution. Of course, it may be said in general of the period which has been discussed in this and the previous two chapters, that it was the laboratory within which, not so much Marxism, as a particular adaptation of Marxism, was initially put to the test. For Trotsky, however, the decade or so which followed October 1917 was a period during which he attempted—albeit after 1923 with progressively declining

<hr/>

[80] Ibid., p. 35.   [81] Ibid., p. 40.

personal political powers—to translate into practice the theory
of the permanent revolution specifically. This theory claimed,
firstly, to postulate the logic of a historical development in
which a backward society comes under the aegis of a 'proletarian dictatorship'; and, secondly to sketch out, in advance,
the process which would dissolve this dictatorship in a socialist
society.

The policies he advocated after 1917 may certainly be taken
to represent, as he claimed then and thereafter, the practical
application of those parts of the theory of the permanent revolution pertaining to the period following the actual seizure of
power. These were policies which, whether in politics, in economics, in social and cultural matters, or in external affairs,
would, in his view, assure the transition from ostensibly 'bourgeois', 'liberal' beginnings to the first signs of collectivism and,
ultimately, to the framework at least of the socialist society.
They were for him the concrete expression of the elements of
'stages, process and momentum', of the central, dynamic
character of the Russian revolution, which he had already
postulated at the time of 1905 and which constituted the
'uninterruptedness' of the revolution of backwardness.

The whole theoretical conception did not, of course, work
out, either on the eve of October 1917 or afterwards, quite in
the way in which Trotsky expected it would. The source of the
conception, backwardness, proved to be its major stumbling
block as well. As he himself admitted, there was a high price
or penalty to be paid for the initial advantages of backwardness.
The years which follow 1917 show him grappling with the
dilemmas of this price and, on the whole, resigned to paying
it, though he does not quite grasp its ultimate magnitude.
Naturally, there was a choice of better or worse policies, and
the final choice was a legitimate subject for debate and controversy. But the more one follows Trotsky's own choice, the
more one is struck by how far it was fundamentally prejudged,
how far it was imposed upon him by the preconceptions of his
own theory. He was forcing this theory upon reality, and
reality, as usual, proved to be stronger. There was no way in
which the two could be made to fit together. The world revolution was the last gambit, though it too had been postulated in
advance by theory. But here as well, though in a context outside

Russia, reality was proving to be no more accommodating. For the rest of his life Trotsky was to remain convinced that this was not so, that world revolution had failed to materialize because of 'subjective' factors and errors, not 'objective' conditions. To have admitted otherwise would have meant, obviously, raising doubts about Marxism in general, and about the prospects of socialism in Russia, in particular; it would have amounted to the recognition that theory and practice remained forever irreconcilable. In that case, socialism would prove to be an illusion. It was essential, therefore, to persist with the original theory—with the idea of the world revolution and with much else besides. This, of course, was the view of Trotsky; it was not, however, a view shared by the new Soviet leadership emerging in the later 1920s.[82]

[82] An excellent recent work, Richard B. Day, *Leon Trotsky and the Politics of Economic Isolation* (Cambridge, 1973) reached the present writer too late to be referred to in this study and only a few brief remarks are possible here. Day's thesis is that the controversy between Stalin and Trotsky was not one between 'socialism in one country' and 'permanent revolution' but between economic isolationism and economic integrationism. Thus, he argues, Trotsky objected not to 'socialism in one country' but to 'socialism in a separate country'. Day's book is primarily a study of the economic debate in the Soviet Union between 1917 and 1927 and considers Trotsky's economic pronouncements without, in general, dealing with his over-all views. He is right, of course, that Trotsky after 1925 was an 'integrationist' (as was pointed out in this and the previous chapter), but there is no basis for the claim that Trotsky believed socialism could be established in Russia without revolution in Europe. On the contrary, Trotsky believed that a *socialist* society could not be created in Russia until Europe as a whole had become socialist; he supported economic integration with Europe not as a substitute for world revolution but as the only alternative possible if the Soviet experiment were not to collapse altogether. He did not confuse the 'reconstruction' of the Russian economy (i.e. economic development as such) with socialism. Beyond this, however, Day's book is a much-needed corrective to numerous misconceptions—many of them engendered by Deutscher's work—about Trotsky's position in the 1920s *vis-à-vis* Stalin.

Part III

THE PERMANENT REVOLUTION 'BETRAYED'

CHAPTER NINE

'SOCIALISM IN ONE COUNTRY': THE END OF WORLD REVOLUTION

Marxism has always taught the workers that even their struggle for higher wages and shorter hours cannot be successful unless waged as an international struggle. And now it suddenly appears that the ideal of the socialist society may be achieved with the national forces alone. This is a mortal blow to the International.[1]

THE ARGUMENT as to whether revolution in Germany in particular, but elsewhere as well in Europe, failed in the years after World War I because of miscalculation and missed opportunities, or whether the failure resulted from objective conditions, is as old as the events themselves of those years. Trotsky, as we have seen, attributed the failure to instrumental factors chiefly: even in May 1924 he declared unequivocally: 'The causes for [the German failure] lie wholly in tactics and not in objective conditions. We have here a truly classic example of a revolutionary situation allowed to slip by.'[2]

Yet in the same year, and only a month later, he was delivering a speech in which, in spite of himself, he made out a good case for the opposite view.[3] True, in a section of the speech

---

[1] Trotsky, *The Third International After Lenin* (New York, 1936), p. 71. (For bibliographical details regarding this work, see note 15, below.) The present and the next chapter deal with the period 1924–40 and take as their sources Trotsky's writings during these sixteen years. Works of a purely polemical character, of which Trotsky produced an abundance during this period, and which are of no theoretical interest today, have been more or less ignored; largely ignored too are his numerous writings devoted to 'setting the record straight', that is, to refuting Stalin's 'falsifications' about past and present. The author feels justified in ignoring such writings since this study is not concerned with personal controversies but with fundamental differences over the main issues of the period. Some mention of such writings, however, occurs in the notes, primarily in order to provide bibliographical information.

[2] From the preface to *Pyat Let Kominterna*, p. 41.

[3] This is the previously referred to speech, 'Cherez kakoi etap my prokhodim?', published in *Zapad i Vostok*, pp. 108–38.

devoted specifically to the German events of 1923, he repeated the view that success could have been achieved were it not for tactical errors. But the main body of the speech dwelt on the objective reasons why capitalism in the West was proving so resilient and managing to survive in spite of all predictions to the contrary. Taking as his example the case of England in particular, he argued that the source of the strength of capitalism in such an 'advanced' country was the long period it had had to develop in an 'organic, evolutionary' way, thus avoiding sudden jolts and disruptions in the social fabric and allowing for continuous adaptations of political to social and economic forms. New social antagonisms were always arising but the system as a whole was resourceful and flexible enough to adjust itself to the emergence of new political forces. Thus the growth of the proletariat was accompanied by its absorption into, rather than exclusion from, the cultural and political framework of society. The result, on the one hand, was change by way of piecemeal and pragmatic reform; and, on the other, an ubiquitous 'conservatism' which impregnated all segments of society, including the working class. The latter evolved traditions and organizations which though ostensibly at odds with the 'ruling classes' functioned in accordance with their principles and rules. Thus did advanced capitalism succeed in disarming all its potential adversaries by seducing, and overpowering, them with its embrace.[4]

Trotsky naturally hastened to add that all this was a temporary phenomenon, the effect of which was merely to postpone the day of reckoning. But the more he and others appended this reassurance, the more it seemed to assume the character of ritual lip service. True, as subsequent years would affirm, though others were beginning to lose hope, Trotsky never did so. But having made out a convincing case for the 'staying power' of capitalism, he avoided asking himself whether this was not a situation which could persist if not indefinitely, then for so long a period as to make the whole question of a world revolution irrelevant in any case. Clearly the Russian example was remote from European reality and therefore non-exportable, except perhaps as a somewhat artificial product having no indigenous roots in the West. The creation of an 'Eastern

[4] Ibid., pp. 108–20.

front' against the West was, of course, a reasonable alternative strategy. But what assurance was there that a backward, impoverished and isolated East, even if ruled over by socialist governments, could confront the full might of the capitalist West? Was it not possible, therefore, that the kind of revolution which had transpired in Russia, being peculiar to that kind of society, was essentially a 'local affair', albeit with serious repercussions on international relations, but with no permanent impact on the internal character of a different and older social system? If so, there was a chasm between East and West and the history of each had to follow its own prerogatives.

1. 'Socialism in One Country': Pro and Con

Numerous factors made the period from 1924 onwards a propitious one for the introduction of a doctrine such as 'socialism on one country'.[5] Without weighing the relative influence of each—it is the general climate which is important—we may note some of these: the death of Lenin which both necessitated and made possible new initiatives; the revolutionary failures in Europe capped by the fiasco of 1923 in Germany; the general mood of the country—tired of 'revolutionary sacrifices' and uncertainties, eager for concrete benefits and stability; the growing necessity of attacking the problems of the economy directly and fundamentally and not only through stop-gap measures; the impatience of the growing party and state apparatus; and the need for a new national ideological framework within which the objectives and tasks of reconstruction could be accommodated and co-ordinated. To all this one must append, of course, the constant factor of the struggle for the succession to Lenin

---

[5] Trotsky pointed out (see *The Third International After Lenin*, pp. 43–4), that the first to raise the idea of socialism in a single country had been the German right-wing Social Democrat G. Vollmar in the article 'Der Isolierte Sozialistische Staat', published in the *Jahrbuch für Sozialwissenschaft und Sozialpolitik* (Zurich, 1879). But Vollmar, according to Trotsky, made the projected 'isolated socialist state' (in this case Germany) dependent on 'lively economic relations with world capitalist economy'. In the course of time, Vollmar believed, the socialist state would triumph peacefully over capitalism as a result of its more efficient economic system, thus making actual revolutions in other countries unnecessary. Trotsky did not accept Vollmar's thesis but he considered it at least more convincing than that of Stalin's doctrine of 'socialism in one country' which, he would argue, assumed that socialism could be built in an isolated *backward*, non-industrialized country and without economic ties with Europe.

and, in particular, Stalin's already evident determination to create a monopoly of power for himself.

In the event, however, Stalin originally does not seem to have conceived of the idea of 'socialism in one country' as a doctrine aimed at exploiting all of these factors, and it was only later that its wider usefulness became apparent to him. At the outset it appeared to be yet another ideological tactic in the ongoing campaign to discredit the views and status of Trotsky, a campaign which had begun in 1923 and which by the time of Lenin's death had already proven partly effective.[6] Stalin first raised the idea in an article he wrote in December 1924, but it was then presented in a somewhat moderate form.[7] The gist of it was that since in Russia the dictatorship of the proletariat had been established through an alliance between workers and peasants, a wide enough social basis existed for organizing a socialist economy without waiting for revolutions to break out elsewhere. Trotsky, in Stalin's view, had overestimated the dependence of Russia upon outside aid by underestimating the importance of peasant support. Therefore his theory of the permanent revolution was 'a variant of Menshevism' since, like Menshevism, it was disdainful of the possibilities of socialism

---

[6] For a succinct account of the Stalin–Trotsky controversy, see H. Brahm, 'La "Révolution Permanente" de Trotski et le "Socialisme dans un Seul Pays" de Staline', *Cahiers du Monde Russe et Soviétique* (Jan.–Mar. 1965), pp. 84–99. In what follows, only the ideas and arguments of Stalin and Trotsky are juxtaposed and no attempt is made to deal with the history of the actual political struggle between the two men, nor with Stalin's road to power in general. This intricate 'chapter' in the history of the Soviet Union has been amply documented and extensively written about; see, in particular, Carr, *The Interregnum, 1923–1924*, part III and *Socialism in One Country*, II, part III, as well as Schapiro, *The Communist Party of the Soviet Union*, chapters 15–22. Deutscher's second volume of the Trotsky biography, *The Prophet Unarmed*, is largely devoted to this subject. See also the same author's, *Stalin: A Political Biography* (London, 1961), chapters 7 and 8. Nor is any attempt made to deal with the vast anti-Trotsky diatribes which now began to appear in the Soviet Union and which were written by such figures as Kamenev, Zinoviev, Bukharin and, of course, Stalin. For a compilation of such material, including contributions from the above, see *Za Leninizm: sbornik statei* (Moscow, 1925).

[7] The article was originally called 'October and Comrade Trotsky's Theory of Permanent Revolution' and published in the 20 Dec. 1924 issues of *Pravda* and *Izvestiya*. In January 1925 it was re-published, this time under the title, 'The October Revolution and the Tactics of the Russian Communists'. The English version of this article is in Stalin, *Problems of Leninism* (Moscow, 1953), pp. 113–48. As late as April 1924 Stalin, in his *Foundations of Leninism*, a series of lectures delivered at Sverdlov University, argued that socialism in a single country was impossible and that revolutions in other countries were an essential pre-condition for the establishment of socialism in Russia.

in Russia. Nevertheless, Stalin was careful to add that although 'socialism in one country' was possible in the conditions of Russia, the 'complete victory of socialism' still depended on revolutions in other countries. Thus world revolution, he agreed, remained an essential objective.

The article, and the idea it contained, did not at first arouse any particular attention. Only gradually did the subject enter into party ideological discussions. Its ascendance there was less due to its usefulness as a weapon against Trotsky than to the fact that it seemed to offer some alternative hope to the growing despair at the prospects of a European revolution. If socialism could be established in one country—even without 'complete victory'—then the Soviet Union need not feel herself impotent in the face of revolutionary failures in Europe; she could proceed with her objectives in a spirit of optimism, however guarded, and with the sense that she was implementing some, at least, of the original aims of the revolution. All was not lost after all; on the contrary, the more the Soviet Union reconstructed herself along socialist lines, the greater impetus this would give in the long-run to socialist movements in the West. 'Socialism in one country' was becoming, moreover, a popular slogan with its appeal to national sentiments and to the independent potentialities of Russia.[8]

Sensing this climate, Stalin at the beginning of 1926 decided to turn what was originally no more than a modest idea into a major doctrine. In January of that year he published the essay 'On the Problems of Leninism' and here he formulated what was to become the official version of 'socialism in one country'.[9] It may be briefly summarized as follows. World revolution is and will always remain a prime objective of Soviet policy. But the problems facing the Soviet Union at this time were more of an internal than an external nature. If world revolution was not forthcoming for the time being and if nothing was done to deal with internal problems, the Soviet Union would inevitably collapse. Fortunately, the reconstruction of the economy did not depend on the outside world; Russia had sufficient internal resources, both human and material, to be self-reliant. Moreover, these resources were large enough not only to effect

[8] See Carr, *Socialism in One Country*, II, pp. 59–61.
[9] For the English version, see Stalin, *Problems of Leninism*, pp. 149–212.

reforms but to create a 'full' socialist society. It was all a matter of 'resolving the contradictions between the proletariat and the peasantry with the aid of the internal forces of our country ... with the sympathy and support of the proletariat of other countries but without the preliminary victory of the proletarian revolution in other countries'.[10] The psychological element was uppermost in Stalin's argument:

Without such a possibility [of the victory of socialism in one country] building socialism is building without prospects, building without being sure that socialism will be completely built. It is no use engaging in building socialism without being convinced that we can build it completely, without being convinced that the technical backwardness of our country is not an *insuperable* obstacle to the complete construction of a fully socialist society. To deny such a possibility is to show a lack of faith in the cause of building socialism, to abandon Leninism.[11]

Stalin made a distinction between this, 'the victory of socialism in one country', and 'the complete, final victory of socialism in one country'. The latter he defined as the ultimate elimination of the threat of outside intervention—and this, he admitted, was dependent on revolutions in other countries. But the possibility of building a socialist society itself was not thereby affected. In the long-run, it is true, the Soviet Union would have to hope for the direct support of the European proletariat; in the meantime, however, socialism was a task which the Soviet people alone could undertake.

Stalin's essay hardly delved into the full complexities of the doctrine he was proposing; the economic and social implications of it were only perfunctorily discussed, and arguments against it were dismissed as merely symptoms of 'scepticism' and 'lack of faith'. It was as if socialism had been reduced to a matter of a proper psychological frame of mind. But there was a certain common sense in Stalin's position; after all, reality had to be faced and reality quite clearly revealed two incontrovertible facts: world revolution was at best an uncertain prospect and the Soviet Union was still in dire economic straits. To continue linking these two facts was to sink deeper into the impasse of a vicious circle. What was needed, Stalin believed,

---

[10] Ibid., p. 192.   [11] Loc. cit.

was a positive, alternative programme emphasizing the possibilities of self-reliance. The doctrine of 'socialism in one
country' seemed to offer such a programme; whether it would,
in fact, lead to socialism appeared to matter less than the immediate prospects it raised of some progress, and the sense it gave
of at least 'doing something'. Finally, Stalin's position was of
course strengthened by the fact that others seemed unable to
offer, or to agree upon, any other realistic way out of the
impasse.

Tactically, Stalin had won a victory by defining his doctrine
as the direct antithesis of Trotsky's 'permanent revolution': the
latter was thus made to appear both defeatist and adventuristic—defeatist about the potentialities of the Soviet Union,
adventuristic in its insistence on revolutions abroad. This was,
of course, a gross misrepresentation of the views Trotsky was
in fact advocating at the time; it was he, after all, who was
arguing for more fundamental economic reforms, for a more
rapid rate of industrialization, for a generally more positive
approach to internal possibilities—all measures which Stalin
himself was eventually to adopt as part of the drive for 'socialism
in one country'; and although Trotsky was certainly more prepared to encourage revolution in Europe, he did not at any
time propose reckless confrontations with the might of the capitalist world. But Stalin had grasped the initiative by contrapos-
ing his ideas to those of Trotsky and the latter found himself
more and more identified, however unfairly, with a negative,
pessimistic, and unrealistic position. At first Trotsky appeared
to want to avoid a confrontation on Stalin's terms; already in
a letter of January 1925, sensing the danger of being 'labelled',
he had written that the attack on his theory of permanent
revolution was irrelevant since the theory belonged to the past
and had nothing to do with present issues.[12] Ultimately, however, the confrontation proved unavoidable; the theory of permanent revolution did become the antithesis of 'the theory of
socialism in one country' and Trotsky himself came to accept the
complete incompatibility of the two: 'The theory of socialism

---

[12] 'Pismo Plenumu TsK RKP(b)', in *Pravda*, 20 Jan. 1925. He would make a similar
statement at the fifteenth Party Conference in 1926, again trying to avoid a confrontation on Stalin's terms (see *15 Konferentsiya VKP(b): stenograficheskii otchet*, Moscow, 1927,
p. 473).

in one country', he would write in 1929, 'is the only theory that consistently and to the very end is opposed to the theory of the permanent revolution.'[13]

For the truth of the matter was that although Stalin had intentionally exaggerated the antithesis, and had so out-manœuvred Trotsky that the latter was himself forced into exaggerating it, the differences between the two theories were real and substantial. It was, of course, patently incorrect to make the extreme claim, as Stalin had done, that while he, Stalin, proposed to reconstruct the home front, Trotsky was prepared to sacrifice that front to external objectives. But neither would it be correct to reduce the differences to the fact merely that while Stalin wanted to concentrate on internal problems, Trotsky urged the simultaneous pursuit of internal and external goals. There was some truth in this on the surface but it was only a partial expression of more profound differences of outlook and orientation. For Trotsky, the concept of 'national socialism', which is what he believed 'socialism in one country' to amount to, was a contradiction in terms. The idea that one country, and a backward one at that, could by itself create a socialist society negated everything that he had always believed in. Naturally, his whole international orientation rebelled against the idea; but so did his whole conception of socialism. It is on the basis of both the one and the other, therefore, that in innumerable writings, which occupied him to the end of his life, he set out to refute the theory of 'socialism in one country'.

Enough has been said in the course of this study about Trotsky's views on the relationship—both before and after 1917—between Russia and Europe as to make any further comment on this subject merely superfluous. We need only note here that the peculiarity which he attributed to this relationship—first in the form of the impact of the advanced West on a backward society, then in the form of the impact of a revolution in that society on the West—was the historical basis for his condemnation of a doctrine which, in his view, sought artificially to rend asunder what history had forever joined. Nor is it necessary to refer again to a concomitant view of his— the *international* character of modern revolutions—which also underlay his rejection of 'socialism in one country'; he believed,

---

[13] *Permanentnaya Revolyutsiya*, p. 168.

as we have seen, that no twentieth-century revolution could be restricted to 'local' or national proportions if only because of the nature of the world economy. Finally, we may similarly only mention in passing the universalist aspect of his thought which equally dictated his opposition to Stalin's thesis: he inherited from Marx the view that capitalism was a universalizing force which, however, unable to break through national boundaries was destined to be replaced by socialism, a system literally called forth by the universality of the modern age.

With these general tenets in mind—they were really intrinsically related and parts of a single credo—we may concentrate in what follows on Trotsky's more specific arguments against the doctrine of 'socialism in one country'. For the sake of clarity—as well as brevity—these may be summarized under three headings: (a) the dependence of the Soviet economy upon the world economy; (b) the socio-economic pre-conditions for the building of socialism; and (c) the effect of the doctrine on the pursuit of world revolution.[14]

(a) *The dependence of the Soviet economy upon the world economy:* The greatest danger of Stalin's policy of 'socialism in one country' was, according to Trotsky, the isolation of the Soviet Union which it entailed. If the Soviet Union were to be isolated, that is, not just by remaining the only country in which a revolution had triumphed but also by being cut off economically from the capitalist world, not even a start could be made on the actual reconstruction of the economy. For even the most rudimentary implementation of Stalin's proposals was dependent on foreign trade, imports, capital, know-how, and so on; and thus, ironically, 'socialism in one country' accentuated reliance on others.

The era of purely national economies, Trotsky believed, had long ended. No country could plan and run its economy without large-scale foreign trade, and without in some measure being dependent on international sources of capital. Thus the interdependence, in good times as well as bad, of individual economies. In the case of Russia, Trotsky argued that the problem

---

[14] As this chapter concentrates on the international implications of Stalin's doctrine of 'socialism in one country', those of Trotsky's arguments which dealt with the implications of the doctrine for the character of Soviet society itself have been relegated to the next chapter.

went beyond this normal state of relations: it was a matter not so much of interdependence as one-sided dependence. Being poor, undeveloped, and incapable of producing from her own resources those means and implements necessary for development, Russia had to rely on imports. Still very much as in Tsarist times, capital and goods had to be paid for by agricultural produce. Thus internal production always stood in danger of being governed by the size of exports needed, the internal market by the world market, internal policy by external demands. Nevertheless, economic ties with the West were unavoidable if the Soviet economy was to be developed. Gradually, though never completely, Russia's position *vis-à-vis* the West could be improved.

Stalin's alternative, according to Trotsky, because it was based on unrealizable internal potentialities, would not only isolate the Soviet Union but bring about the complete subordination of its economy to that of the capitalist world. There was no prospect whatever, in Trotsky's view, that the economy on its own resources could withstand the powerful pressures from the West. The solution to internal economic problems, therefore, lay in the international arena—in the first instance through economic relations with the West. This, admittedly, would only suffice to encourage initial economic growth but not to create a socialist economy. That is why, according to Trotsky, world revolution ultimately was the only final solution to the problem of socialism in a backward society.[15]

(b) *The socio-economic pre-conditions for the building of socialism:* For Trotsky, as for Marx, a socialist society was a society of plenty not of want; it was one which had solved all the main problems of economic production and distribution, not one which had merely 'equalized scarcity'. But this presupposed a number of developments: advanced technology and mechan-

---

[15] For various formulations of this argument by Trotsky, see in particular the following: *The Real Situation in Russia*, pp. 83–7; 'Problemy razvitiya SSSR', in *Byulleten Oppozitsii* (Apr. 1931), pp. 2–15; 'The Draft Programme of the Communist International: A Criticism of Fundamentals', in Trotsky, *The Third International After Lenin*, pp. 1–230, especially pp. 43–51. The Russian original of the 'Draft Programme ... A Criticism of Fundamentals', written in June 1928, is in the Trotsky Archives, T3115–7. All subsequent references are to the above English edition. *The Third International After Lenin* was published as volume I of a projected multi-volume *Selected Works of Leon Trotsky* under the editorship of Max Shachtman. However, only this and one other volume (*The Stalin School of Falsification*, New York, 1937), appeared.

ization; optimal accessibility to, and exploitation of, natural resources; a unified international economy as opposed to one consisting of hostile, competitive national units; and a cultural milieu encouraging education, science, and continuous research. It is because of the impetus which it gave to these and related developments that Marx saw capitalism as a progressive force, and as the precursor of socialism. Trotsky took all this for granted and, consequently, considered implicitly absurd the notion that a backward society, which far from solving problems of economic want was still in their grip, could 'leap' into a socialist millennium. This was to him merely utopian rhetoric, in itself a function of what he called 'national Messianism'.[16] To presume that the vast natural riches of Russia were sufficient to eliminate poverty and backwardness was to presume that the problem was a purely quantitative one. In fact it was here that economics and qualitative social and cultural development were most intertwined. To extract natural resources required know-how; their proper utilization was a matter of over-all social arrangements; and the conditions of plenty which such resources could provide were therefore dependent on work habits, education, and general customs of life. To build socialism on a low technical and cultural basis was to bring forth a situation in which everyone simply shared equally in poverty. Once again, therefore, the Soviet Union was dependent on the West, through which alone it could assimilate the socio-economic pre-conditions for socialism; and backward societies in general could make the leap to socialism only within the framework of a world socialist development.[17]

(c) *The effect of 'socialism in one country' on the pursuit of world revolution:* Since Stalin had declared that the only danger to socialism in the Soviet Union was foreign intervention, it followed, in Trotsky's view, that everything would have to be done to placate the enemies of the country. And this was in keeping

---

[16] *Permanentnaya Revolyutsiya*, p. 169.

[17] This argument is, of course, a recurrent theme in all of Trotsky's work. But for a concise statement of it in relation to 'socialism in one country', see his *The Revolution Betrayed* (New York, 1937), pp. 291–304. This work, among the most important of Trotsky's writings while in exile, was never published in Russian and will be referred to in this English translation by Max Eastman (the Russian version, under the title *Chto takoe SSSR i kuda on idet?*, is in the Archives, T3946–53). The work is discussed in detail in the next chapter.

with the general philosophy of isolation and self-centredness. 'Socialism in one country' meant not only reneging on world revolution but discouraging it everywhere in order not to provoke the West. Turning in upon itself, the Soviet Union would deny revolutionary intentions abroad and would redefine its ties with workers' movements in Europe. The effect on the Comintern would be catastrophic: it would become merely an instrument of Soviet interests, and a pacifist one at that, a 'subsidiary' and 'decorative' institution devoted primarily to a maintenance of the *status quo* in Europe:

The task of the parties in the Comintern assumes, therefore, an auxiliary character; their mission is to protect the U.S.S.R. from intervention and not to fight for the conquest of power ... [The Comintern's] main role, the role of an instrument of world revolution, is then inevitably relegated to the background. And this ... flows from the internal logic of the new theoretical position ...[18]

The conclusion Trotsky therefore drew from these considerations was that 'socialism in one country', being fundamentally incompatible with world revolution, would not only not encourage progressive forces in Europe and elsewhere, but would, albeit unwittingly, serve the interests of the forces of reaction.[19]

2. The Fate of World Revolution

From the time of his exile in 1929, and until his death in 1940, Trotsky wrote voluminously about events and developments in Europe. Almost daily he produced articles and pamphlets, not to mention an inexhaustible stream of letters, on Germany, France, Britain, Spain and Italy, as well as the United States.[20] At the same time he took a particular interest in events in China, and on this subject alone his writings could fill two or three substantial volumes. To attempt to deal with the full scope of this material is to become embroiled in the detailed history of the decade or so which it covers. We cannot even begin to do so here, not only for reasons of space but also because these

[18] 'The Draft Programme of the Communist International: A Criticism of Fundamentals', pp. 61 and 62.
[19] In this connection, see also Trotsky's article of July 1928 (written in the form of a letter): 'What Now?', in *The Third International After Lenin*, pp. 231–307.
[20] His vast correspondence of this period is preserved in his Archives at Harvard; some of it, however, is in the closed section.

writings are, on the whole, of purely historical interest today and only peripherally valuable as sources for Trotsky's social and political thought.[21] However, in the case of writings on two of the countries mentioned above—Germany and China—a brief summary of them will throw additional light on the theoretical issues dealt with in the course of this study. This is so because Trotsky was convinced that the success of the Nazi movement in Germany, and the blow to the Communist movement—in the late 1920s—in China, were in large part the result of Soviet and Comintern policy towards these movements, a policy dictated by the demands of the doctrine of 'socialism in one country';[22] therefore analysis of developments in these countries was for him a kind of empirical aspect of the theoretical controversy with Stalin and, in turn, a part of the older debate on the significance and implications of a Russian revolution. Aside from this, however, in the case of Germany, his analysis of the nature of Nazism is in itself of intrinsic value; and, in the case of China, it is instructive to see how his Russian, as well as Western, preconceptions misled him, and undermined his grasp of revolutionary realities in the East. In what follows, therefore, we shall attempt to bring out these aspects of his thought.

[21] For a brief survey of his commentaries on the international situation, see Giuliano Procacci, 'Trotsky's View of the Critical Years 1929–1936', *Science and Society* (Winter 1963), pp. 62–9. On France, Trotsky's main writings are collected in the following: *Où va la France?*, published as volume II of Trotsky, *Écrits, 1928–1940* (Paris, 1958) (for the English version of this, with, however, some variation in the contents, see Trotsky, *Whither France?* New York, 1936); Trotsky, *Le Mouvement Communiste en France* (Paris, 1967). On Britain, see in particular his *Kuda idet Angliya* (Moscow–Leningrad, 1925) and *Kuda idet Angliya? Vypusk Vtoroi* (Moscow–Leningrad, 1926) which contains extracts from English reactions to Trotsky's 1925 book and Trotsky's answer to these reactions. See also the compilation, *Leon Trotsky on Britain*, published by the Monad Press, New York, 1973. For his main writings on Spain, see the excellent compilation (issued by Pathfinder Press), Trotsky, *The Spanish Revolution, 1931–39* (New York, 1973). Some of the items on Spain can also be found, in French, in Trotsky, *De la Révolution* (Paris, 1963), pp. 373–439 and in volume III of *Écrits, 1928–1940* (Paris, 1959), pp. 401–557. His writings on Italy are much more sparse but still too numerous to list individually; see, as an example, his letter to Italian Communists, published in *Byulleten Oppozitsii* (May 1930), pp. 37–8. For his writings on the United States, see *Evropa i Amerika* (Moscow–Leningrad, 1926), and the items listed at note 175, chapter 11, below. The Russian versions of the writings on France and Spain mentioned above are to be found chiefly in the Archives and in *Byulleten Oppozitsii*.

[22] The failures of communist movements in general, and in France in particular, were also largely attributed by Trotsky to Soviet and Comintern policies, but the cases of Germany and China were, for him, especially conspicuous.

(a) Germany[23]

For Trotsky, the passage of time did not diminish the importance of Germany for the future of the world revolution. On the contrary, as the 1930s opened, he was more convinced than ever that everything hinged on the course of events in Germany:

Socialist construction in the U.S.S.R., the course of the Spanish revolution, the development of the pre-revolutionary situation in England, the future of French imperialism, the fate of the revolutionary movement in China and India—all this directly and immediately rests upon the question of who will be victorious in Germany ...: Communism or Fascism?[24]

In 1931, however, when this was written, the German Communist Party had long ceased to be an independent entity; like most other Communist parties, its leadership consisted of men obedient above all to Moscow, and subject to policies chosen and dictated from thence.[25] These policies were, as a result, determined in accordance with immediate Soviet considerations and had become, in fact, an extension of Soviet foreign policy in general. In June 1928, when the Sixth Congress of the Comintern met, it was decided that a new period—the 'third'—had now opened in Europe, one characterized by a renewed 'decay' of capitalism and a consequent intensification of the class struggle.[26] But this was interpreted as meaning above all

[23] The following are Trotsky's main writings on Germany (in chronological order): 'Povorot Kominterna i polozhenie v Germanii', in *Byulleten Oppozitsii* (Nov.–Dec. 1930), pp. 45–54; 'Klyuch k mezhdunarodnomu polozheniyu—v Germanii', in ibid. (Nov.–Dec. 1931), pp. 1–9; *Nemetskaya Revolyutsiya i Stalinskaya Byurokratiya* (Berlin, 1932); *The Only Road* (New York, 1933)—references are to the reprint of this edition in Trotsky, *The Struggle Against Fascism in Germany* (New York, 1971), pp. 272–328 (the Russian original of *The Only Road* has not been traced); 'Chto takoe natsional-sotsializm?', in Archives, T3557. References to some other of Trotsky's writings on Germany are given in the footnotes below. The writings here mentioned, as well as many others, are included in English and French compilations of Trotsky's writings on Germany; for the English, see the above-mentioned *The Struggle Against Fascism in Germany*; for the French, see Trotsky, *Écrits, 1928–1940*, III, pp. 21–399.
[24] 'Klyuch k mezhdunarodnomu polozheniyu—v Germanii', op. cit., p. 4.
[25] For an account, by one of the leaders of German Communism, of the manner in which Stalin came to dominate the KPD, see Ruth Fischer, *Stalin and German Communism* (Cambridge, Mass., 1948).
[26] The revolutionary period up to 1923 was referred to as the 'first period' and the non-revolutionary one from 1924 as the 'second period'.

a struggle against the Social Democratic parties, which were now declared to be no less dangerous than Fascism. A new term was launched—'social fascism'—and identified with Social Democracy, the defeat of which was now seen as the first priority. In subsequent years Communist parties in Europe, and especially in Germany, devoted all their efforts to this task, while concurrently putting off a confrontation with Fascism itself.

The consequences of this policy are too well known to need restating. That it split and demoralized the Left while simultaneously leaving the Right largely unchallenged is obvious. To what extent, however, can it be said that were it not for this policy, the Right, that is Fascism, could have been stopped? This is a question which raises again the relationship of 'subjective' to 'objective' factors, the importance of instrumental means—tactics, organization, and so on—as against social and historical realities—classes, economic conditions, cultural phenomena. We have already seen that since 1917 Trotsky had been convinced that all the objective factors were ripe for revolution in Europe, and that its actual manifestation depended mainly, if not only, upon the proper choice of instrumental measures. In the case of Germany during the crucial years preceding 1933, he continued to argue this same case. It would not be an exaggeration, in fact, to say that not only did he believe that Fascism could have been stopped, and a Communist revolution carried out, but that the success of Fascism was directly attributable to the errors of the Communist movement in Germany or, rather, of the Soviet regime which controlled it.

From the outset he considered Fascism the main threat to the working-class movement and—as we shall presently see—because of its social roots, a real and immediate, not a passing, danger.[27] He had, of course, little if any admiration for the Social Democrats: they were in his view a conservative, non-revolutionary force, pacifying the German workers, and interested mainly in maintaining the democratic-parliamentary structure as the framework for their socialism. But to consider them Fascists, or no better than Fascists, seemed to him

[27] See, for example, his warnings in 1930 in 'Povorot Kominterna i polozhenie v Germanii', op. cit., especially pp. 46–7.

conceptually and historically absurd, and politically disastrous.[28] There was no question but that Social Democracy was fundamentally an enemy of the Communist movement, nor that eventually the Communist party would have to undermine the hold of Social Democracy over German workers. But in view of the growing success of Fascism, the confrontation between Communism and Social Democracy had to be grasped in its proper tactical context. Strategically it was obviously true that before Communism could succeed, Social Democracy had to be defeated; but this general proposition, in Trotsky's view, did not answer all possible immediate, tactical questions. If, as was true in Germany, the main immediate threat to Communism came from elsewhere and, as was also the case, this immediate threat could not be beaten down without, temporarily at least, joining forces with some, similarly threatened, of one's enemies, then it was tactically not only legitimate but essential to forge such an alliance.[29] The point of this was that to continue concentrating on a long-term threat while being endangered by an immediate one was to fall into one abyss before even reaching subsequent ones: Fascism threatened destroying Communism before the latter could fight Social Democracy. Again, this was not a matter of one abyss being better or worse than another but of the choice of tactics and timing. Trotsky phrased the matter in the form of the following analogies:

There are seven keys in the musical scale. The question as to which of these keys is 'better'—do, re, or sol—is a nonsensical question. But the musician must know when to strike and what keys to strike. The abstract question of who is the lesser evil [Social Democracy or Fascism] is just as nonsensical . . . Let us cite another example: when one of my enemies sets before me small daily portions of poison and the second, on the other hand, is about to shoot straight at me, then I will first knock the revolver out of the hand of my second enemy, for this gives me an opportunity to get rid of my first enemy. But this does not at all mean that the poison is a 'lesser evil' in comparison with the revolver.[30]

[28] *Nemetskaya Revolyutsiya i Stalinskaya Byurokratiya*, pp. 8 and 22–32.
[29] See the article 'V chem sostoit oshibochnost segodnyashnei politiki germanskoi kompartii?', in *Byulleten Oppozitsii* (Mar. 1932), pp. 16–21.
[30] Ibid., p. 19. In *Nemetskaya Revolyutsiya* . . . (p. 157) he recounted the following 'fable' by way of illustrating the same point: 'A cattle dealer once drove some bulls to the slaughterhouse. And the butcher came nigh with his sharp knife. "Let us close ranks

Given the distribution of forces in Germany, it was impossible to defeat Social Democracy and Fascism at one and the same time. Moreover, the latter was pointing the revolver at the former as well. There was a natural, if negative, basis for an alliance here as there had been, for instance, in Russia in 1917 between Bolsheviks, Mensheviks and others against Kornilov.[31] Without harbouring illusions about the future—and without abandoning ultimate strategic goals—a tactical, 'united front' was necessary between the Communists and the Social Democrats. Neither partner would or could give in on the differences separating the one from the other; but in so far as there was a common enemy and therefore a common interest, collaboration was possible. This did not mean that as a result the Communist struggle against Social Democracy would have to be entirely suspended. On the contrary, in a sense such an alliance would serve this struggle since it would allow the Communists access to the working masses, and an opportunity therefore to offset the conservative influence of Social Democracy.[32]

Between 1930 and 1933 Trotsky was thus amongst the most vociferous opponents of the concept of 'social fascism' and, instead, a proponent of the 'united front'. He was convinced that the victory of Fascism would be not only a catastrophe for Communism in Germany but for the Soviet Union itself. It would, he predicted in 1931, 'signify an inevitable war against the U.S.S.R.'.[33] When, in the end, that victory came, he did not hesitate to attribute it to the 'stupidities' of Stalinist leadership which, in his view, were a direct consequence of the doctrine of 'socialism in one country' proclaimed in the mid-1920s. This doctrine, he claimed, had obliged the Soviet Union to pursue internecine warfare abroad rather than revolutionary objectives. In Germany, far from stopping Fascism, far from uniting

---

and jack up this executioner on our horns", suggested one of the bulls. "If you please, in what way is the butcher any worse than the dealer who drove us hither with his cudgel?" replied the bulls ... "But we shall be able to attend to the dealer as well afterwards!" "Nothing doing", replied the bulls, firm in their principles, to the counsellor. "You are trying to shield our enemies from the left, you are a social-butcher yourself." And they refused to close ranks.'

[31] *Nemetskaya Revolyutsiya* ..., pp. 61–7.
[32] On Trotsky's conception of the 'united front', see ibid., pp. 55–60 and 74–81, as well as the article 'V chem sostoit ... germanskoi kompartii'.
[33] 'Klyuch ... v Germanii', p. 6.

the working class, the doctrine had made the workers more vulnerable than they already had been. By denouncing Social Democracy as a branch of Fascism it so alienated it as to re-inforce its reformist, capitulative tendencies so that in the end its weakness in the face of Fascism itself was accentuated. And by imposing sectarian interests upon the German Communist party it turned it into a servant not of revolution, but of the private political machinations of the Stalinist regime. Thus, while supposedly staving off the 'poison', it was shot by the 'revolver'.[34]

In retrospect, it is impossible to deny that there was a great deal of truth in Trotsky's contention that Stalinist policy only served to make things easier for Fascism in Germany. But the conclusion he drew from this, that, had a different policy been followed, Nazism could have been stopped, certainly emerges as a simplification. Perhaps it should be attributed to the fact that Trotsky had come to be so repelled by the Stalin regime as to see in it the source of all evil, both in the Soviet Union and in the world at large. Whatever the case, his own subsequent analysis of the nature of Fascism—and of German Nazism in particular—shows that he was at least alive to the more profound social and historical roots of the Fascist phenomenon. The 'theory of Fascism' which he formulated was also in part a simplification, since it made too much of the standard Marxist economic explanation; but it at least had the advantage of putting the phenomenon into social and historical perspective.

Already in 1932 Trotsky had defined Fascism as a political system to which the bourgeoisie resorts during the period of the 'decline of capitalism'.[35] The notion that the bourgeoisie was tied to a parliamentary, democratic form of government was true, in his view, only of a particular stage of its development, the stage at which capitalism, having emerged from its Jacobin-ist, revolutionary struggle for dominance, settles into a period of unchallenged growth and maturity. During such a period orderly, democratic, and reformist government parallels, and

---

[34] See the articles 'Tragediya nemetskogo proletariata', in *Byulleten Oppozitsii* (May 1933), pp. 7–11 and 'Nemetskaya katastrofa: otvetstvennost rukovodstva', in ibid. (July 1933), pp. 1–6.
[35] *The Only Road* (in *The Struggle Against Fascism in Germany*), p. 280.

facilitates, peaceful competition, the latter being the source of capitalism's growth. It is otherwise once the system begins to disintegrate. The commitment to democracy then emerges to be not axiomatic and eternal, but pragmatic and ephemeral. Since it is the economic system itself which is now at stake, all political measures needed to save it, including dictatorship, become legitimate. But the particular form of dictatorship which the crisis of capitalism encourages is not simply a political artifice hastily assembled to mete out force whenever necessary. It is that too, but it is first of all a reflection of the kind of social alliance which must be forged in order to deter the objective forces making for disintegration. These forces grow out of the conditions of mutual alienation and animosity, themselves a product of the decline of capitalism, which separate the three main classes: the big bourgeoisie (now mainly finance capital), the petty bourgeoisie, and the proletariat. Looked at in the context of the relationship among these classes during a period of the threat of economic collapse, Fascism emerges as that political system which the big bourgeoisie finally must accept in order to effect an alliance with the petty bourgeoisie against the proletariat.[36]

In order to give a more detailed explication of this, Trotsky's social analysis of Fascism, we need turn to various articles which he wrote following the triumph of Nazism in 1933.[37] Here Trotsky began with the observation that although Germany was once a comparatively backward capitalist country, she had in the decades prior to 1914 managed to build an industrial edifice which catapulted her into the forefront of the capitalist world. As in all backward countries which undergo rapid change, pockets of the agrarian, feudal past remained, retaining a partial hold over social and political power, and, in general, social anomalies were aggravated. But for all intents and purposes Germany had become an integral part of the capitalist orbit, and thus subject to the 'ills' affecting this orbit as a whole:

[36] Ibid., especially pp. 272–85.
[37] What follows is based on the following articles in particular: 'Chto takoe natsional-sotsializm?', in Archives, T3557; 'How Long Can Hitler Stay?', in ibid., T3563; 'Bonapartizm i fashizm', in *Byulleten Oppozitsii* (Oct. 1934), pp. 3–6; 'Bonapartizm, fashizm i voina', in ibid. (Aug.–Sept.–Oct. 1940), pp. 29–33 (this last article was left unfinished at Trotsky's death and the editors of the *Byulleten* inserted some interpolations, in brackets, to complete sentences and provide transitions).

'over-ripeness' of the productive facilities—leading to the 'imperialist' chase after markets and colonies and, eventually, to war—and the growth in the potential power of the proletariat. In a period of economic expansion, the big bourgeoisie was able to prevent the workers' power from becoming actual by applying placating measures—parliamentary enfranchisement, freedom of organization, economic rewards and so on. However, in a period of economic decline, the big bourgeoisie was more and more forced into a direct confrontation with the workers. At first, in the years following the World War, this took the form of suppression by force: thus the growth of a Bonapartist regime, drawing its main office-holders from the army—Hindenburg, von Papen, etc.—and using the police and military as its main props. This, however, could only be a temporary measure; in an industrially advanced nation such as Germany, force could not in the end overcome the constant social pressures. What was needed was a more fundamental solution, one which took account of the reality and distribution of social classes and power.

The clue lay in the petty bourgeoisie which, during a period of economic depression, had become a huge element of discontent seeking a political vehicle for its grievances. Because of its threatened economic condition it leaned towards radical formulas, whether from the Left or the Right. Thus the struggle which developed between Communism and Fascism for the 'soul' of the petty bourgeoisie and the workers, and which—for reasons Trotsky had elucidated in his criticism of Communist tactics—was resolved in favour of Fascism. Without the support of the petty bourgeoisie, the workers—and thus the Communist movement—were unable to make a breakthrough; but the big bourgeoisie as well was unable to assert its hegemony without the petty bourgeoisie. And as for the petty bourgeoisie itself, now making up the main support of the Fascist movement, it could not become a dominant political force on its own since it lacked real economic power.

In this situation of a polarization of the two 'exploited' classes in separate and radical political movements, neither of which was strong enough to seize power yet both of which were large enough to prevent others from exercising it effectively, disorder, violence, virtual anarchy became normal everyday phenomena; 'street politics' took over from institutional politics. This was obviously inimical to the interests of the big bourgeoisie; and the latter, though separated by an abyss from the petty bourgeoisie, and reluctant to share power with it, finally saw that its only salvation lay in an alliance with it. Thus did the big bourgeoisie, finance capital, join forces with Fascism to produce the Nazi government of 1933.

There was no doubt in Trotsky's mind that the Nazi government scrupulously served the interests of big capitalism; although political power became monopolized in the hands of Hitler, the big bourgeoisie retained its economic power base. It is in this sense, therefore, that Fascism became a new variant of capitalist government, albeit one appearing during the decline or degeneration of capitalism. That it almost immediately took on such an extreme form of brutality and oppression must partly at least, in Trotsky's view, be attributed to the main goal it set itself: the virtual liquidation of the proletariat as a social force. From this flowed all the main elements of totalitarianism: the ideological negation of class divisions, and the attempt to atomize society in one ubiquitous collective; a nationalist and racist ideology to provide the semblance of unity and homogeneity; economic and cultural regimentation; and state power personified in the figure of the *Fuehrer*. Because natural class divisions in German society were stronger than this new ideology could cope with, the Nazi government retained and refined the characteristic features of a Bonapartist regime, relying on the police and special organs of suppression. But it was more than just a form of Bonapartism, and thus more stable and more dangerous, because it represented the social and political union of both the higher and the lower bourgeoisie.

Trotsky's analysis of German Fascism, for all the sweep and power of its generalizations, suffered from an exaggerated imposition of the Marxist theoretical framework. As a result it overemphasized the subsequent, if not original, role of big capital, and neglected the extent to which Hitler was ultimately able to exercise power, almost independently of particular economic interests, by creating autonomous political organs—the party, the secret police, the bureaucracy.[38] Yet Trotsky was not

[38] For an example of a work which argues the thesis that after 1936 economics in Germany became subordinated to the political power structure, see David Schoenbaum,

entirely blind to this evolution of Nazi power; although he persisted in the view that economic interests remained supreme,
it was just this Bonapartist tendency of Nazism which seemed
to him to assure its eventual downfall. For the more politics
became severed from economics and society, and the more
terror replaced institutional government, the more did this
signify that the regime was becoming isolated, and unable to
cope with social problems and divisions. The need to resort
with ever-growing regularity to force, the failure to cure
society's ills, were not accidental. They grew, according to
Trotsky, out of the fact that Fascism, although it was meant
to conceal the decline of capitalism, through its ideology and
policies exposed all the underlying elements of capitalism's
decay and degeneration:

Fascism has opened up the depths of society for politics. Today, not
only in peasant homes but also in city skyscrapers, there lives alongside
the twentieth century the tenth or the thirteenth. A hundred million
people use electricity and still believe in the magic power of signs and
exorcisms. The Pope of Rome broadcasts over the radio about the
miraculous transformation of water into wine. Movie stars go to
mediums. Aviators who pilot miraculous mechanisms created by
man's genius wear amulets on their sweaters. What inexhaustible
reserves they possess of darkness, ignorance and savagery! Despair
has raised them to their feet, Fascism has given them a banner. Everything that should have been eliminated from the national organism
in the form of cultural excrement in the course of the normal development of society has now come gushing out from the throat; capitalist
society is puking up the undigested barbarism. Such is the physiology
of National Socialism.[39]

(b) China[40]

In the midst of one of his many polemics against Stalin's policies
toward a Chinese revolution, Trotsky, dissecting the reasons for

---

Hitler's Social Revolution (London, 1966). See also a similar argument in T. W. Mason,
'The Primacy of Politics—Politics and Economics in National Socialist Germany', in
S. J. Woolf (ed.), The Nature of Fascism (New York, 1968), pp. 165–95.
[39] 'Chto takoe natsional-sotsializm?', Archives, T3557. See also Trotsky's article
'Nationalism and Economic Life', Foreign Affairs (Apr. 1934), pp. 395–402.
[40] The most important of Trotsky's writings on China are the following: 'The Draft
Programme of the Communist International: A Criticism of Fundamentals' (in The
Third International After Lenin), chapter 3 ('Summary and Perspectives of the Chinese
Revolution'), pp. 167–230; Problems of the Chinese Revolution (London, 1969) (this work

the Communist débâcle in China during the 1925–7 period, felt obliged to point out that all his warnings and prophecies had been only too tragically vindicated. 'The strength of Marxism', he noted in this context, 'lies in its ability to foretell.'[41] Yet nothing so reveals the limits of Marxist prophecy as the Chinese experience; and nothing so conspicuously bares the limits of Trotsky's own prophetic powers as the eventual evolution of the Chinese Communist movement. Though he took special pains to acquaint himself with conditions in China, Trotsky's grasp of Chinese reality proved to be almost totally misconstrued. In part this grew out of the difficulties inherent in attempting to assimilate the peculiarities of Chinese politics and society into a Marxist framework; largely, however, it was a product of Trotsky's assumption that the Russian experience of 1917 could be generalized for the East, and that this experience had established once and for all the logical link between backwardness and socialism.

This is not to say that he was less prescient about Chinese affairs than Stalin. On the contrary, with regard to the fiasco of 1927 he had every right to claim that it had proven the correctness of his criticism of Soviet and Comintern policy in China. This policy had been based on the primary objective of creating as wide a front as possible in China against the Western Powers and Japan. Thus the Comintern had urged the Chinese Communist party to enter the nationalist movement, the Kuomintang; this the party did in 1923. Thus also, in subsequent years, whenever conflicts arose between the Communists and the nationalists, the Comintern sought to preserve the

---

consists of various pieces written between 1927 and 1931; each originally appeared independently in Russian, but the compilation as a whole was issued in English; for convenience, therefore, all references are to the English compilation which first appeared in 1932 and of which the above edition is the latest); 'Revolyutsiya i voina v Kitae', in *Byulleten Oppozitsii* (Dec. 1938), pp. 2–15 (this was published in English as the preface to Harold Isaacs, *The Tragedy of the Chinese Revolution* (London, 1938), pp. xi–xxv). References to some other of Trotsky's writings on China are given in footnotes which follow. Among Trotsky's writings on the East are two articles on India: 'Revolyutsiya v Indii, ee zadachi i opasnosti', in *Byulleten Oppozitsii* (June–July 1930), pp. 5–10 and 'Indiya pered imperialistskoi voinoi', in ibid. (Aug.–Sept.–Oct. 1939), pp. 22–5. These concentrate on the issue of imperialism, but their interpretation of the prospects of an Indian revolution is very similar to that made by Trotsky of the Chinese case which will be here discussed.
[41] 'The Draft Programme . . .', p. 198.

alliance even if in a way disadvantageous to the Communists. The consequence of this policy eventually was the strengthening of the Kuomintang and the undermining of the Communists; in 1927 it culminated in clashes in Shanghai and Canton which left the Communists in virtual disarray with their urban base entirely destroyed.[42]

The Comintern's policy towards the Communists in China, though motivated primarily by immediate political considerations, was provided by Stalin from the outset with doctrinal arguments. These were, briefly, as follows: The Kuomintang was a revolutionary, progressive force because it was anti-imperialist; although it was nationalist and bourgeois in character, this suited the particular revolutionary stage at which China found herself. What was needed in China was in fact a bourgeois-democratic revolution, one which would assert the independence of China, carry out large-scale agrarian and other economic reforms and thus, eventually, prepare the ground for a subsequent socialist revolution. In the meantime, the Communist movement, too weak to pursue power on its own, had to join forces with the nationalists in order to create a powerful 'bloc of four classes'—the national bourgeoisie, the petty bourgeoisie, the peasants and the workers—against feudal landlords and foreign imperialists. In this way, the interests of the ultimate socialist revolution would be best served.[43]

It was only natural that Trotsky should brand this doctrine as a form of 'Menshevism'; the affinity was quite striking, and he made the most of it in his attacks on Stalin. He ridiculed, firstly, the notion that the Kuomintang represented a force which was fundamentally hostile either to landed interests or to foreign capital. He claimed that although purporting to be a movement for social reform, the Kuomintang had allied itself to old feudal elements which, in turn, were closely interconnected with urban capital. Foreign-inspired capitalism had already made significant inroads into the Chinese economy,

---

[42] On the history, both political and ideological, of the Chinese Communist movement during the period discussed, see in particular: Conrad Brandt, *Stalin's Failure in China* (Cambridge, Mass., 1958); Isaacs, op cit. (in the third edition of this work (Stanford, 1961) Isaacs revised considerably his earlier 'Trotskyist' viewpoint); Benjamin Schwartz, *Chinese Communism and the Rise of Mao* (Cambridge, Mass., 1951).

[43] For Stalin's political and doctrinal views on China see his *Ob oppozitsii* (Moscow, 1928).

and the Kuomintang, in an effort to protect these inroads, was basically a 'lackey' of Western imperialism. Thus the situation was substantially no different from what it had been in Russia before 1917. True, Russia had not been under foreign rule like China; but the dependence of the Tsar on foreign capital was in many ways tantamount to the same thing. The Russian bourgeoisie, like the Chinese, was not an independent force; it too was tied to landed interests and foreign capital, and so greatly feared peasant and worker discontent that it was prepared to compromise with the existing political and social structure. Under the circumstances, a bourgeois revolution in Russia had been impossible; and the period from February to October 1917 confirmed this conclusively. This, according to Trotsky, should have been enough to bury Menshevism forever; instead a new generation of 'Mensheviks', Stalin and his followers, was attempting to impose the 'mechanistic' theory of revolutionary 'stages' upon China. Here too it was bound to fail; support for the bourgeois revolution, for the Kuomintang, meant in effect support for the *status quo*. As in Russia, the only policy which could bring about real change was one which worked towards the creation of an independent workers' party, supported by the peasantry. Any other policy, based on collaboration with the bourgeoisie, would in the end betray the workers' and peasants' interests. Instead of bringing a socialist revolution closer it would push it into the distant future. And this is, in fact, what, according to Trotsky, had happened in China in 1927.[44]

In presenting this argument, Trotsky was, of course, advocating anew his theory of the permanent revolution. Admitting that there were certain important differences between China and Russia—the tradition of 'Oriental despotism', the more remote impact of the West, the experience of foreign rule, the even greater preponderance of the peasant population—he was nevertheless convinced that the theory of the permanent revolution was as valid for China as it had been for Russia. This meant, as in Russia, that the immediate goal, an agrarian revolution, could not be realized in China outside the framework

---

[44] This summary of Trotsky's critique of Stalin's policies is based on the writings mentioned in note 40, above. See also *The Real Situation in Russia*, pp. 146–55 and *Permanentnaya Revolyutsiya*, pp. 23–8.

of a socialist revolution; that revolutionary developments would not follow preconceived stages, but would be 'combined', making possible a direct 'passing over' from democratic to socialist tasks; that the only social class capable of undertaking such revolutionary tasks was the proletariat, 'leaning' on the support of the peasantry; that, however, the resulting workers' government would eventually lose the support of the peasantry and have to turn elsewhere for assistance; and that therefore this loss of support, combined with the limitations imposed by backwardness, would make it impossible for China to complete her socialist revolution on her own—like Russia, she would have to turn to the international arena and become dependent on the world revolution. Thus all the central elements of the theory of the permanent revolution, originally derived from the case of Russia, appeared to Trotsky to be applicable to the Chinese case as well.[45] That they were not applied in China, either in theory or in practice, was, in his view, due entirely to the leadership in the Soviet Union and in the Comintern, and to the doctrine of 'socialism in one country'. The events of 1927, he therefore believed, confirmed the theory of the permanent revolution in a new way, 'this time not in the form of a victory but of a catastrophe'.[46]

Stalin's policies in China had indeed proven to be disastrous for the Communist movement there. Did it follow, however, that had Trotsky's alternative been adopted the result would have been a Communist success?[47] In fairness to Trotsky, it should be noted that he nowhere claimed that a Communist revolution in China was necessarily imminent in the 1920s, but only that it was in the *process* of becoming imminent from the point of view of 'objective' conditions, and that it was therefore essential in the meantime to create a 'Bolshevik–Leninist' party equipped with the right theoretical outlook. Thus to judge the validity of the position Trotsky advocated—as against the validity of his criticism of Stalin—one need look at it not so much in the context of the 1920s as in the light of that sub-

[45] For his discussion of the Chinese case in terms of the theory of the permanent revolution, see in particular *Problems of the Chinese Revolution*, pp. 125ff. and 'Revolyutsiya i voina v Kitae', pp. 6–11. See also *Permanentnaya Revolyutsiya*, pp. 129–47 and 167–9.
[46] 'Revolyutsiya i voina v Kitae', p. 12.
[47] In this connection, see Steven Levine, 'Trotsky on China: The Exile Period', *Papers on China*, vol. 18 (Harvard, 1964).

sequent development of the Chinese Communist movement which ultimately—and nearly a decade after Trotsky's death—did lead to success. In a general way it may be said that 1949 confirmed one central aspect of the theory of the permanent revolution, namely that in a backward society a socialist revolution can break out before a bourgeois one or, at least, before a bourgeois revolution has been completed. Although China may have had what amounted to a bourgeois revolution, in a political sense, as long ago as 1911, socially and economically nothing that happened in the intervening period could be defined as a culmination of what Marxism has described as Western capitalist development. Thus 1949 in China, like 1917 in Russia, was, from an 'orthodox' Marxist point of view, premature, and appeared to confirm what Trotsky had always claimed : that only a socialist, and not a bourgeois, regime could undertake the solution to problems of backwardness in the twentieth century.

But beyond this general, though important, proposition, the post-1927 development of the Chinese Communist movement not only does not bear out other important aspects of the theory of the permanent revolution but sets certain limits to the theory's universal validity for backward countries. Two elements in particular came to distinguish the Communist movement in China : its almost exclusively peasant basis, and its force as a focus for nationalist sentiments.[48] Both these elements were either ignored or deprecated in Trotsky's prognosis for China. He did not, it is true, discount or underestimate the importance of peasant support ; in fact, as in his analysis of Russia, he was prepared to admit that without initial peasant support a Communist revolution was inconceivable. But throughout his writings on China, as indeed in all his writings where the subject of the peasantry arose, he categorically rejected the possibility of a revolution under peasant leadership or based primarily on the countryside. Again and again he stressed the limitations of the peasantry, its backwardness, narrowness of vision, lack of political experience and of ideological consciousness, and its economic weakness. Even in China, he believed, town towered over village, and the road to power lay through the urban

---

[48] On the role played by nationalism in the development of Chinese Communism, see Chalmers Johnson, *Peasant Nationalism and Communist Power* (Stanford, 1962).

centres. He was convinced that the Chinese Communist movement could triumph only as a workers' movement. The alliance with the peasantry had therefore to be an unequal one, with the proletariat clearly at the helm. Thus in the Chinese context as well, he spoke of a 'dictatorship of the proletariat', and not of the proletariat and peasantry.[49] Even towards the end of the 1930s he wrote of the prospects of greater industrialization in China which would reinforce the political supremacy of the working class.[50] It is no wonder, therefore, that he looked askance at the evolution of Chinese Communism as a rural movement, with its base of power in the countryside and not in the cities.[51] And he denounced as 'adventurism' the guerilla warfare which it practised.[52]

His attitude toward Chinese Communism as a nationalist movement was similarly uneasy and sceptical. On the one hand, he appreciated the importance to be attached to anticolonialism, the political value which accrued to those who could mobilize national support against foreign powers; but, on the other, he stressed that national liberation should be understood only as a form of social liberation, that the struggle against external rule was in essence a struggle against one and the same enemy, capitalism and the bourgeoisie, and was therefore a class struggle. He appeared to have little appreciation for the sense of nationhood which existed in China and, in any case, his anti-nationalist attitudes would not allow him to gauge objectively the significance of the Communist–nationalist hybrid which was emerging in Asia generally.[53]

It should not be difficult to guess what Trotsky's reaction to the Chinese Revolution of 1949 would have been had he lived to witness it: assuming his views remained consistent with his lifetime convictions, he would have welcomed the Revolution in so far as it put an end to Kuomintang rule, but he would

---

[49] For typical examples of his views on Chinese peasants and workers and on the 'dictatorship of the proletariat', see 'Draft Programme of the Communist International: A Criticism of Fundamentals', pp. 212–27, and *Problems of the Chinese Revolution*, pp. 99–108.

[50] 'Revolyutsiya i voina v Kitae', pp. 14–15.

[51] See 'Krestyanskaya voina v Kitae i proletariat', in *Byulleten Oppozitsii* (Dec. 1932), pp. 10–14.

[52] See, for example, *Problems of the Chinese Revolution*, pp. 187–8.

[53] See, for example, ibid., pp. 3–6 and 82–4.

almost certainly have had serious reservations about its socialist character. It quite clearly negated both the direct link which he claimed existed between a socialist revolution and the proletariat, and the subsidiary revolutionary role which he always attributed to the peasantry. He would surely have argued that under the circumstances the possibilities of socialism in China were even more limited than in Russia.

Yet the fact remains that in terms of ideology, party leadership and goals, the Chinese revolution was no less 'socialist' than the Russian. If there was a difference in its class basis and in the manner of its coming to power, this may suggest that the link between a backward society and a socialist movement was in the last resort dependent no less on peasants than on workers and, perhaps above all, on party organization. Had Trotsky, after all, underestimated the peasantry as a revolutionary force? And, in spite of his 1917 conversion to Lenin's conception of the revolutionary party, had he perhaps still not grasped, in a 'Leninist' way, the importance of this instrument of revolution? In both the Russian and Chinese cases, it would seem, the crucial factors were organization, leadership, strategy and tactics and, despite the undoubtedly more direct mass element in the Chinese case, total control by a determined élite of professional revolutionaries.[54] As we have seen, Trotsky, after 1917, had come to appreciate the dependence of twentieth-century Marxism on 'Leninism', not only in Russia but in Europe as well.[55] But he continued to insist on relating 'Leninism' to traditional Marxist assumptions about classes and revolution, more

---

[54] On the role of organization and leadership in Chinese Communism, see Franz Schurmann, *Ideology and Organization in Communist China* (Berkeley and Los Angeles, 1966).

[55] The extent to which Trotsky made the European revolution dependent on 'Leninism' may be gauged from the following (written in 1928): 'In the German revolution of 1918, in the Hungarian revolution of 1919, in the September movement of the Italian proletariat in 1920, in the English general strike of 1926, in the Vienna uprising of 1927, and in the Chinese revolution of 1925–7—everywhere, one and the same political contradiction of the entire past decade, even if at different stages and in different forms, was manifested. In an objectively ripe revolutionary situation, ripe not only with regard to its social bases but not infrequently also with regard to the mood for struggle of the masses, the subjective factor, that is, a revolutionary mass party, was lacking, or else this party lacked a farsighted and intrepid leadership.' ('Draft Programme ...' p. 85.) This was followed by a sentence which suggested that Trotsky was not unaware of the more complicated reasons for the failures of revolution in Europe: 'Of course', he wrote (ibid., p. 86), 'the weaknesses of the Communist parties and of their leadership did not fall from the sky but are rather a product of the entire past of Europe.' See

so than it was apparently essential in practice to thus relate it. This is not to say that 'Leninism'—or its Chinese off-shoot 'Maoism'—was merely a political artifice, functioning in a social vacuum. On the contrary, that it achieved successes in backward societies could be seen as a reflection, in fact, of Trotsky's own thesis about the particular vulnerability of such societies to radical, socialist movements. But it did mean that 'Leninism's' scope for manœuvre was much wider, and more autonomous, than Trotsky had assumed; that, given the fundamental revolutionary conditions existing in backward countries, revolution itself became a function of political skills and organization, not class development. To put it another way, the agent of change had come to be one particular party but not any one particular class.[56] Finally, the scope for ideological innovation also was wider than Trotsky had assumed: nationalism too could be a vehicle for the socialist revolution.

---

also Trotsky's *Uroki Oktyabrya* (Berlin, 1925), and *Istoriya Oktyabrskoi Revolyutsii* (in *Sochineniya*, III, part 2, pp. 255–329) for his *ex post facto* rationalizations of the role of the Bolsheviks in the success of the *Russian* Revolution, and the lessons to be learned from this.

[56] Trotsky always refused to acknowledge this and assumed that Lenin too would have opposed building a Communist movement based almost exclusively on the peasantry. The point, however, is not what Lenin would have thought—even if Trotsky's assumption was right, which is far from certain—but what 'Leninism' came to mean to others, like Mao, who claimed to be guided by it. Ironically, it was Stalin perhaps who in the end grasped more fully than Trotsky the realities of revolutionary power and, in spite of his many mistakes, was prepared to make greater allowance for the peculiarities of the Chinese situation. In this connection, see the introduction by Benjamin Schwartz to the third American reprint of Trotsky's *Problems of the Chinese Revolution* (New York, 1966).

CHAPTER TEN

STALINISM: THE REVOLUTION BUREAUCRATIZED

'L'État, c'est moi' is almost a liberal formula by comparison with the actualities of Stalin's totalitarian regime.
Louis XIV identified himself only with the State. The
Popes of Rome identified themselves with both the State
and the Church—but only during the epoch of temporal
power. The totalitarian state goes far beyond Caesaro–
Papism, for it has encompassed the entire economy of the
country as well. Stalin can justly say, unlike the Sun King,
'La Société, c'est moi'.[1]

MARXISM, LIKE other nineteenth-century socialist movements—only more so—promised that once society had reor-
ganized its economic life in accordance with collectivist principles it would liberate itself from the state and perhaps—
though the meaning of this was never clear—from politics altogether. In a country such as Russia, where state had always
dominated society in a particularly oppressive manner, the
appeals of Marxism, if not its immediate relevance, were
obvious. In the event, however, the triumph of a Marxist movement in Russia had the ironic, though not wholly unexpected,
consequence that the state became more powerful, more dominating than at any time in the country's history. And this relationship of state to society was not reversed in the course of time
but was extended, reaching a peak in the 1930s when the state
asserted its dominance in a manner hitherto unprecedented
anywhere, though almost simultaneously reproduced—under
different circumstances and different ideologies—elsewhere, in
Europe.

The most general explanation for this phenomenon in the
Soviet Union is one which has been frequently anticipated
theoretically in the course of this study: it grew out of the
attempt to impose upon society a social revolution for which

[1] Trotsky, *Stalin*, p. 421.

it was unprepared and which, therefore, could be carried out only through the largely autonomous activity of the state and its institutions of coercion. As we shall see in this chapter, Trotsky wholly condemned Stalin's methods of coercion. But as was previously argued, Trotsky himself while in power had become committed, if not to the manner and extent, then to the principle of the approach adopted under Stalinism: his attempt to be consistent with the assumptions of his theory of the Russian revolution created a continuity between theory and practice which was artificially evoked—it did not grow of itself but had to be forced; it was governed not so much by what reality could absorb as by what theory demanded; it constituted therefore the imposition of theoretical preconceptions and goals (or ideals) upon a recalcitrant reality which could not assimilate them in any organic way. It too meant, finally, that politics would have to dominate society.

There are those who would say that Trotsky's determination—as against that of Stalin—to impose his ideals upon Russian society contained one redeeming feature at least: it had as its genuine aim the creation of a socialist society. It is a moot point, however, whether the imposition of one ideal, however noble, can be construed to be more legitimate than the imposition of any other ideal, however ignoble: surely it is the element of imposition itself which is at issue? Trotsky did not always recognize this. Indeed in a general sense it may be said that the violent controversy which was to unfold between him and Stalin from the mid-1920s could be reduced to essentially a clash over *which* ideals should be imposed. This is admittedly to simplify matters somewhat—for at issue also was the *manner* of the imposition, in itself a question of not insubstantial importance, and a central object of Trotsky's critique of Stalinism. Nevertheless, it is the case that the element of imposition remained unresolved in Trotsky's own position and thought; and, moreover, that he saw the justice of his case against Stalin to reside not so much in differences over this, as in the fact primarily that he, Trotsky, spoke in the name of the socialist ideal while Stalin, whatever *his* goals or ideals, represented the 'betrayal' of socialism.

The notion of 'betrayal' raises, however, a further, though

not unrelated, issue: was Stalinism largely a product of Stalin himself and of other 'contingent factors' and therefore in principle avoidable, or was it the necessary consequence of that historical conjunction which joined a backward society to a socialist revolution? It is one of the weaknesses of Trotsky's analysis of Stalinism—to which this chapter will be devoted—that while it clearly invited the latter conclusion, it sought refuge in the former. Throughout the 1930s Trotsky argued as if Stalinism were inevitable and unavoidable only to conclude that it was neither, but rather the result of personality and of mistakes, miscalculations and generally perverse policies. No one did more than he to show the social and historical roots of Stalinism; and no one remained so adamant that, despite everything, Stalinism was merely an aberration, an accident almost, that it represented an unnecessary 'betrayal' of the October Revolution and of socialism.[2]

It is, of course, not difficult to understand why Trotsky could not reconcile himself to the view that Stalinism derived from the Revolution itself and the conditions in which that revolution took place; to have admitted as much would have been tantamount to conceding that the conception of the permanent revolution had finally foundered upon the reality of Russian society and, perhaps, that of European society as well. This does not mean that Trotsky's analysis of Stalinism was merely an exercise in 'wishful thinking'; on the contrary, in so far as it probed the social and political roots and character of the whole phenomenon, it was, and in many ways still is, one of the most perceptive theoretical accounts of it. But the more he dissected the realities of Stalinism, the more all the contradictions of his own socialist vision for Russia re-emerged.

1. The 'New Course'

At the end of 1923, with Lenin ill, and the struggle for the succession already underway, Trotsky published a series of articles in *Pravda*, later collected in a pamphlet under the title

---

[2] On this conflict in Trotsky's critique of Stalinism between the 'accidental' and the 'necessary' theses, see the article by John Plamenatz, 'Deviations from Marxism', *Political Quarterly* (Jan.–Mar. 1950), pp. 40–55.

Novyi Kurs (The New Course),[3] in which, for the first time, he raised some of the issues over which he would eventually become irreconcilably estranged from the post-Lenin history of the Soviet Union.[4] Although a number of years were to pass between the publication of this pamphlet and Trotsky's more complete critique, during the 1930s, of Soviet society and its institutions, this is a seminal work, prescient in its grasp of the emerging dangers to the Revolution, and anticipating many of the phenomena which later became institutionalized as permanent components of the Soviet system. A summary of its ideas, therefore, will provide an appropriate introduction to Trotsky's later analysis of Stalinism.

The role of the revolutionary party and its inner structure, the influence of organizational exigencies upon doctrinal precepts and ideals, the need, on the one hand, for a strong, select leadership and, on the other, for mass participation and democracy— all these were problems which had concerned Trotsky from his earliest days as a revolutionary, and as a member of the Russian Social Democratic movement. We have seen how suspicious he had been, from 1903 onwards, of Lenin's attitudes towards these problems, and how tenaciously he had fought against

---

[3] Moscow, 1924. Except for one appendix, written in 1920, the whole of this work was composed at the end of 1923. Although parts of it originally appeared separately in *Pravda* during December 1923, the book is here treated as one whole. (For the English translation see Trotsky, *The New Course*, Ann Arbor, 1965.)

[4] The title of the pamphlet is a reference to the so-called 'new course' initiated by the party leadership, ostensibly to bring about the democratization of party institutions, though in fact it amounted to no more than a ploy against Trotsky and the 1923 Opposition in general. In order not to appear as an opponent of greater inner-party freedom, Trotsky had no choice but to append his name to the proclamation announcing the 'new course', though he fully understood that it was a tactical manoeuvre against him. He also understood that its initiators not only did not take the 'new course' seriously, but intended to bring about the very opposite of democratization; this was, therefore, the context in which he wrote *Novyi Kurs*. (For the text of the 'new course' proclamation, see *Pravda*, 7 Dec. 1923). Trotsky's *Uroki Oktyabrya* (Lessons of October), written in September 1924 as the preface to volume III of his *Sochineniya*, is generally considered to be his main initial attack on the post-Lenin leadership. It is true that this preface had a sensational effect and was the main object of the subsequent anti-Trotsky counter-attacks; but it is largely partisan and polemical—in the narrow sense—in character, resurrecting old controversies from 1917 and constituting a paean to Lenin. In terms of ideas it is far inferior to *Novyi Kurs* which is a more fundamental analysis of social issues, as opposed to those of political leadership alone. In this sense, *Novyi Kurs* is less directly but more profoundly a condemnation and critique of Stalin, Zinoviev *et al.* than *Uroki Oktyabrya*.

Bolshevism.[5] In 1917, however, his views changed abruptly and, as long as Lenin remained alive and he himself—next to Lenin—the central figure in the Soviet leadership, these problems hardly recurred to him. On the contrary, he allowed himself to be so carried away by his enthusiasm for Lenin and for Bolshevism that he seemed to shut his eyes to the fact that the so-called 'dictatorship of the proletariat' was turning into a 'dictatorship *over* the proletariat', a danger he himself had foreseen in his anti-Bolshevik days. He had become, in fact, the most ardent defender, if not apologist, of a regime which was rapidly becoming thoroughly authoritarian.[6] It was not until virtually 1923 that he awoke once again to the dangers inherent in this, though it was not the rule of the party as such but its internal character which aroused his concern. By then, the apparatus and composition of the party, as well as the men in direct control of it, and their manner of decision-making, had become very different from what they had been before, and in the first years of, the Revolution. The changes had begun before Lenin's illness but now, with Lenin incapacitated, and organizational matters entirely in the hands of Stalin, the process was being accelerated. Leaving aside for the moment the question to what extent such changes could later be seen as the consequences of 'Leninism', and of Lenin himself—we shall speak of this later in this chapter—what was ominous at this stage was the fact that they now appeared to be largely premeditated and intentionally sought after. It had evidently become the aim of Stalin and his allies to encourage the trend towards the emergence of a new type of party member, and of the primacy of the organizational apparatus.[7]

It is in the context of these developments, as well as of the personal campaign being waged against him, that Trotsky wrote *The New Course*. Nothing could be further from the truth than to present Trotsky in the subsequent controversy as the voice of freedom and democracy striking out against the forces of darkness. The issue was not the liberalization of the regime, nor the legitimacy of the one-party system, nor even the scope

---

[5] See chapter 5, above.   [6] See chapter 6, above.

[7] For an account of the party apparatus under Lenin and the manner in which it came under the control of Stalin, see Schapiro, *The Communist Party of the Soviet Union*, chapters 13–19.

of the authority of the one party, and it is not in the name of a new
political structure that Trotsky spoke. On the contrary, he
wanted above all a return to the kind of regime created by
Lenin; and though for him that regime was far more enlightened, it could hardly be described as democratic. Moreover, he was no less interested in party unity and discipline than
his opponents, and no less intolerant than they of party factions
and groupings. Both the dictatorship of the party in general,
and the principle of 'centralism', remained for him inviolable
foundations of Soviet society and government. Not the dictatorship of the party, but dictatorship *within* the party was his
concern.

   The issue, therefore, was the internal character of the party,
and the distribution of power in it; and within the limits of this
issue Trotsky was certainly on the side of what may be legiti-
mately called democratic principles. Thus one of the central
demands which he made in *The New Course* was for a policy
which would widen the mass basis of the party, increase membership from among workers, encourage genuine mass participation, and compel party officials to be open to the influence
of the rank-and-file.[8] Moreover, it was the new generation of
Communists, the youth, with what he saw to be their new ideas
and initiative, that he wanted not only to win over to the party
but also to enable to influence it in new directions. Though he
himself obviously belonged to the Old Guard, the pamphlet
was a warning against the dangers of allowing veteran members
to retain unchallenged hold over the party.[9]

   No less striking was his plea for freedom of expression, for
the values to be attached to criticism, independence of thought,
truth, and the possibility of open debate.[10] He denounced the
whole concept of the 'yes-men', and all those other kinds of
'empty well-wishers who know what side their bread is buttered
on'.[11] Finally, he totally rejected every tendency toward personal, not to mention one-man, rule; he believed that the main
principle of Bolshevik centralism was always the rule of the 'col-
lectivity', and that this principle had to be restored now. Of
course, he nowhere defined it as meaning the elimination of
hierarchical organs, and their substitution by some kind of

[8] *Novyi Kurs*, pp. 14, 15–16.   [9] Ibid., pp. 7–14, especially.
[10] Ibid., pp. 81, 88–90, 92.   [11] Ibid., p. 92.

organizational equality; but the reaching of decisions should, in his view, represent the 'collective will' at each level, and not that of a single individual strategically placed by virtue of his party function.[12]

However passionate Trotsky's plea for the democratization of party organs may have sounded, it would seem that it was not so much democracy as such—as an end in itself—which moved him, as the purpose which he believed it would serve. The real concern running through *The New Course* is the preservation of the revolutionary spirit. At a time when the social revolution in the Soviet Union, not to mention the revolution in the West, had hardly begun, it seemed to him that already the party was turning into a conservative, institutionalized force, more concerned with protecting the little that had been achieved, than pursuing the much that remained unfulfilled. New blood, new ideas, criticism, discussion, mass enthusiasm— all these, he believed, would not only democratize the party, but preserve its *revolutionary* character, its original sources of inspiration, its very obsession with the real goals of socialism, its determination not merely to hold power, but to use it to change human society. Now it appeared to Trotsky that the spirit was being banished, and in its place a new driving force, entirely different in its implications and possibilities, was being implanted. This new force, he declared, was 'bureaucratism', the very antithesis and the scourge of revolutionism.[13]

In *The New Course* Trotsky did no more than raise the most general characteristics of bureaucratism, and we shall have to wait until his writings of the 1930s for his more original analysis and theory of this phenomenon. Yet already here his understanding of its implications for Soviet society was profound. He did not doubt that it was a driving force, in its own way capable of providing certain needs—order, stability, security and so on—which were obviously still absent from Soviet society. And he recognized its potential, when backed by unlimited power— and force—for reshaping that society, even if in a manner hardly consistent with either his or the revolution's ideals. Yet it was precisely these ideals which, in Trotsky's view, were here at stake. A bureaucratic system would, he believed, automatically

[12] Ibid., pp. 20, 81.
[13] The whole of *Novyi Kurs*, in fact, may be seen as a tract on bureaucratism.

exclude the fulfilment of those very goals which the revolution had set out to realize; thus whatever immediate advantages would accrue from it were as nothing compared with the irreparable damage it would do to the whole *raison d'être* of the regime.[14] One needed only to consider, according to Trotsky, the sources of bureaucratism, to recognize its incompatibility with socialist aims; for it was a phenomenon growing out of those very social ills which socialism was committed to eradicating, and was itself a symptom of the fact that socialism had not yet succeeded in this objective: bureaucratism was a substitute, and an artificial one at that, for the kind of social harmony which still remained unrealized:

It is unworthy of a Marxist to consider that bureaucratism is only the aggregate of the bad habits of office holders. Bureaucratism is a social phenomenon in that it is a definite system of administration of men and things. Its profound causes lie in the heterogeneity of society, the difference between the daily and the fundamental interests of various groups of the population. Bureaucratism is complicated by the fact of the lack of culture of the broad masses. With us, the essential source of bureaucratism resides in the necessity of creating and sustaining a state apparatus that unites the interests of the proletariat and those of the peasantry in a perfect economic harmony, from which we are still far removed.[15]

In *The New Course*, it was not so much the sources, however, as the nature and consequences of bureaucratism which occupied Trotsky. He saw it, firstly, as a system in which the administrative apparatus, whether of the state or of the party, becomes the dominant organ of government; rather than implementing decisions and policies, which is its proper function, it makes them. Functionaries and specialists are either appointed to political posts, or political questions are referred to the administrative structure they control. Moreover, decisions are reached in accordance with administrative considerations which now become the supreme criteria. Discussion of the issues involved is thus primarily technical, and involves only those who are supposedly competent to deal with such matters. Since, in any case, the kind of economic and social reconstruction confronting the post-revolutionary society demands an increase in governmental offices and functions, it

---

[14] Ibid., pp. 32–9.   [15] Ibid., pp. 37–8.

is precisely the man with specialist or administrative abilities who is both drawn by, and welcomed into, the state institutions, while the uneducated worker, or the educated but non-administratively minded revolutionary, find themselves excluded. Thus party and government organs become the virtual monopoly of a new kind of 'revolutionary', the bureaucrat, whose approach to all problems is business-like and down-to-earth.[16]

The problem of the exclusion of the idealistic elements in the new generation was, however, compounded, in Trotsky's view, by the fact that the old generation, once itself moved by idealistic motives, also developed, in the wake of its revolutionary success, an interest in the bureaucratization of the revolution. Partly this grew out of its determination to retain power, and prevent new men and ideas from supplanting it; and partly it was the consequence of sheer exhaustion, a desire to reap immediate results rather than persevere with long-term goals. Thus the revolutionary dictatorship of the Old Guard could be said to have been transformed into an 'opportunistic' clique:

Does bureaucratism bear within it a danger of degeneration, or doesn't it? He would be blind who denied it. In its prolonged development, bureaucratization threatens to detach the leaders from the masses, to bring them to concentrate their attention solely upon questions of administration, of appointments and transfers, of narrowing their horizon, of weakening their revolutionary spirit, that is, of provoking a more or less opportunistic degeneration of the Old Guard, or at the very least a considerable part of it.[17]

The danger, therefore, was not only that all power would become concentrated in the hands of a few men who controlled the apparatus, but that the dictatorship of the apparatus which they would institute would inevitably lead to a virtual 'petrification' of the revolution.[18] Nothing was more certain, in Trotsky's view, than that bureaucratism encouraged and, in fact, thrived on, conservatism. It enshrined the past and the present at the expense of the future. It 'killed initiative', discouraged inventiveness, and negated in principle all that appeared in the least new and untried, bold and original. Thus it preserved a static tradition, applying formally but fanatically

[16] Ibid., pp. 15–21.   [17] Ibid., p. 13.   [18] Ibid., p. 44.

methods and thinking which, though perhaps successful in the past, could prove unsuitable in new and different contexts.[19] Under bureaucratism tradition had no prospect of evolving, and the men who inherited it no prospect of being enriched by it; tradition became a body of absolute criteria instead of a dynamic source of guidance:

> If we ... take our Bolshevik party in its revolutionary past and in the period following October, it will be recognized that its most precious fundamental tactical quality is its unequalled aptitude to orient itself rapidly, to change tactics quickly, to renew its armament and to apply new methods; in a word, to carry out abrupt turns ... This is not to say, naturally, that our party is completely free of a certain conservative traditionalism: a mass party cannot have such an ideal liberty. But its strength and potency have manifested themselves in the fact that inertia, traditionalism, routinism, were reduced to a minimum by a far-sighted, profoundly revolutionary tactical initiative, at once audacious and realistic.[20]

In this same connection, defining Leninism, which he identified with true revolutionism, Trotsky wrote:

> Leninism is genuine freedom from formalistic prejudices, from moralising doctrinairism, from all forms of intellectual conservatism attempting to bind the will to revolutionary action ... Leninism is orthodox, obdurate, irreducible, but it does not contain so much as a hint of formalism, canon, or bureaucratism ... To make out of the traditions of Leninism a supra-theoretical guarantee of the infallibility of all the words and thoughts of the interpreters of these traditions, is to scoff at genuine revolutionary tradition and transform it into official bureaucratism.[21]

Trotsky did not deny that party discipline, obedience and unity are indispensable components of revolutionary action, and characteristic of a 'Leninist' party. But he rejected the identification of these with the kind of regimentation which was a function of purely dictatorial methods, based on 'orders from above', divorced from all sense of collective responsibility, and functioning in accordance with bureaucratic regulations. The pre-conditions for real unity and effective discipline were debate, criticism, the free airing of opinions, and a collective form of decision-making. Once a decision was made it was in-

---

[19] Ibid., pp. 40–9.   [20] Ibid., pp. 43–4.   [21] Ibid., pp. 47 and 48.

cumbent upon each party member to abide by it scrupulously. But he would best carry it out, in Trotsky's view, if he knew that the decision had been reached following open discussion in which his own, even if opposing view, was also allowed a hearing. Thus Trotsky praised what he called the Leninist principle of joining 'critical, bold elaboration of questions, with iron discipline in action'.[22] Bureaucratic regimentation, he believed, would only result in 'passive obedience', in the 'suppression of personality', in 'servility' and 'careerism':[23]

A Bolshevik is not merely a disciplined man; he is a man who in each case and on each question forges a firm opinion of his own and defends it courageously and independently, not only against his enemies, but inside his own party. Today, perhaps, he will be in the minority in his organization. He will submit, because it is his party. But this does not always signify that he is in the wrong. Perhaps he saw or understood before the others did a new task or the necessity of a turn. He will persistently raise the question a second, a third, a tenth time if need be. Thereby he will render his party a service helping it meet the new task fully armed, or carry out the necessary turn without organic upheavals, without factional convulsions.[24]

This statement of Trotsky's position on discipline reveals both the scope and the limits of his commitment to inner-party democracy. Although he supported complete freedom of opinion, he was opposed to any activity which aimed at providing minority views with an organizational base. Thus throughout *The New Course* he spoke out against any form of factions or groupings within the party.[25] The tendency towards factionalism was, he admitted, inevitable in a one-party system since the one party had to be broad enough so as to contain within itself a wide variety of opinions and even interests. This was particularly so in the case of the Bolshevik party since it attempted to be a bridge between workers and peasants. But the tendency had to be resisted, in Trotsky's view, because every faction created both internal dissension and was potentially the source of the coming into being of opposed class interests, or rather of the division of the party into class groupings. In a party

---

[22] Ibid., p. 49.
[23] Ibid., p. 82. For his similar views of the effects of bureaucratism and functionarism on the army, see ibid., pp. 87–92.
[24] Loc. cit.   [25] Ibid., especially pp. 22–31.

of the proletariat, the rise of factions would signify the rise of interests opposed to the proletariat. Thus it was not only the danger of rival organizations within one party which factionalism threatened to make real, but of the transformation of the party into an arena for class conflicts.

How then did Trotsky justify his own position, which, as he knew well, had itself already inspired, and become associated with, various party groupings?[26] His reply to this was that the bureaucratism which he was attacking was itself fundamentally anti-proletarian in character, and a form of factionalism. For Trotsky it was those who supported bureaucratism who were deviating from the correct revolutionary policy by introducing methods which would alienate the workers and paralyse their ability to take a part in, or even influence, revolutionary policy. 'If', he wrote, 'factionalism is dangerous—and it is—it is criminal to shut your eyes to the danger represented by *conservative bureaucratic factionalism.*'[27] Thus it was his, the anti-bureaucratic position, which represented the 'right road', the road of the proletarian, socialist revolution, while it was bureaucratism which constituted a faction, and one moreover which threatened to lead to the 'degeneration' of the workers' revolution.[28]

This last point was to become one of the central theses of Trotsky's later analysis of Stalinism. At the time of writing *The New Course*, however, he could as yet hardly imagine the extent which such 'degeneration' could reach, and he still believed that bureaucratism was a 'deviation' or a 'tendency' which could be arrested if only the party were to renew its ties with the masses and reassert the Leninist principle of 'subordinating to itself its own apparatus'.[29] 'It is necessary', he wrote, 'to regenerate and renovate the party apparatus and to make it feel that it is nothing but the executive mechanism of the collective will ... "The new course" must begin by making everyone feel that from now on nobody will dare terrorize the party.'[30]

Yet even his own conviction of being on the side of, so to

---

[26] Trotsky did not sign the platform of the 'Forty-Six' issued on 15 Oct. 1923, and generally held aloof from the group; but the ideas in the platform were almost identical with his, and among those who comprised the group were some of Trotsky's closest political associates. See Carr, *The Interregnum*, pp. 305–7 and Deutscher, *The Prophet Unarmed*, pp. 113–17.

[27] *Novyi Kurs*, p. 30.

[28] Ibid., pp. 28–31.   [29] Ibid., p. 78.   [30] Ibid., p. 81.

speak, the 'truth' and his belief that the bureaucrats were the betrayers of that truth, were insufficient to cause him to break faith with his oath to the party, or to violate the principle of obedience. Why Trotsky did not strike out with more than words against the new, post-Lenin leadership of the 'triumvirate', why he did not attempt to make a real thrust for power, remains the great enigma both of his personality and of his political judgement.[31] This is a subject which cannot be considered within the scope of the present study but it is clear that Trotsky's overriding sense of loyalty to the party in general, and to party unity in particular, was a not insubstantial factor in his reticence. In *The New Course* he had stated, as we have seen, that a Bolshevik who is in the minority in his party will nevertheless 'submit because it is his party'. And in May 1924, at the thirteenth Congress of the party, he repeated this principle of obedience in a manner which not only revealed again his sense of loyalty, but betrayed also the contradiction of his own position, and that of the 'Leninist' conception of the party on which it was based. Answering the attacks against him at the Congress—he had previously sat quietly throughout the proceedings and this was to be his only address to the delegates—he said:

Nothing is simpler, morally and politically easier, than to confess before one's party to this or that mistake. For this, I think, no great moral heroism is needed ... None of us wishes to be right or can be right against his party. Ultimately, the party is always right because it is a unique historical instrument given to the proletariat for the realization of its fundamental tasks. I have already said that nothing would be easier than to say before the party: 'All this criticism, all these declarations, warnings and protests were simply mistaken in their entirety.' I cannot, however, say so, comrades, because I do not think that it is so. I know that one cannot be right against the party. One can be right only with the party and through the party since history has not created any other paths for the realization of that which is right. The English have a saying: 'My country, right or wrong.' With far greater historical justification we can say: 'Right or wrong—wrong on certain specific, concrete questions—but it is my party.' ... It would be ridiculous perhaps, almost indecent, to express

---

[31] In this connection see the essay by Joel Carmichael, 'Trotsky's Agony', *Encounter* (May and June 1972), pp. 31–41 and 28–36, which, quite unconvincingly, attributes Trotsky's hesitations to an innate 'shyness'.

personal statements here, but I hope that should the need arise I shall not prove to be the lowest soldier on the lowest of Bolshevik barricades.[32]

Nothing expresses so well the full agony of Trotsky's position as this statement. He could not admit that he was wrong, and he reserved the right to think as his mind and conscience dictated; but neither could he bring himself to doubt what he considered to be the fundamental infallibility of the party. Faced by a conflict between his own views and those of the party, or a majority of it, he bowed to the latter. In this way he himself chose to defend and preserve the principle of ultimate obedience, a principle he took to be enshrined in Lenin's conception of Bolshevism. Admittedly, it was a principle he now embraced uneasily, as the verbal contortions in the above statement show. But accept it he did, and in so doing he identified himself with what he would in later years recognize as one of the characteristic features of Stalinism.

2. **Stalinism**

A. THE BUREAUCRATIC PHENOMENON

In November 1926, at a time when his own political demise and the ascendancy of Stalin could no longer be in doubt, Trotsky jotted down in his diary some 'theses on the inter-relation between revolution and counter-revolution'.[33] These show that Trotsky was now beginning to see developments in the party as not merely the results of an internal political struggle, but as deriving from the general post-revolutionary situation in the Soviet Union. He admitted here that the 'hopes engendered by revolution are always exaggerated' and that the inability of the revolution to fulfil rapidly the high 'expectations' of the masses led to 'disillusionment'.[34] This in turn drained the revolutionary energy of the masses and created a 'more cautious, more sceptical' mood among them.[35] The peasants now wanted only to retain their immediate post-revo-

---

[32] *13 Syezd RKP(b): stenograficheskii otchet* (Moscow, 1924), pp. 165–6.
[33] 'Theses on Revolution and Counter-Revolution', in Isaac Deutscher (ed.), *The Age of Permanent Revolution: A Trotsky Anthology* (New York, 1964), pp. 142–5. The Russian original of this diary is in the Archives.
[34] Ibid., p. 142.   [35] Ibid., p. 143.

lutionary gains—land and the expulsion of the landlords—and showed no interest in socialism; and 'considerable layers of the working class' were unable to maintain their revolutionary enthusiasm.[36] In these conditions, conservative elements in party and state came to the fore, their aim being the 'stabilization' of the regime. These elements expressed themselves through 'bureaucratism' which exploited the post-revolutionary disillusionment and which, in effect, represented a kind of 'bourgeois restoration', a 'counter-revolution'.[37]

These 'theses' of 1926 may be seen to have contained in succinct form some of the main ideas which would, in the 1930s, comprise Trotsky's analysis of the phenomenon of bureaucracy under Stalin. Trotsky was much influenced, of course, by the standard Marxist interpretation of modern bureaucracy. Thus he took over from Marx the view that the bureaucracy does not and cannot constitute an independent power, that it does not rule, but is an instrument in the hands of wider social or class interests.[38] On the whole, however, Trotsky adapted and widened such Marxist axioms so as to take account of the special character of the Soviet case. This character, he believed, derived from the fact that the Stalinist bureaucracy, unlike the Western bureaucratic model, was a consequence of economic and social backwardness. This is a recurrent, central theme in Trotsky's analysis of Stalinism and the first, therefore, which should be discussed.[39]

(a) *Bureaucracy and Backwardness*

The incompatibility of backwardness—understood both in its economic and socio-cultural senses—and socialism was, of course, always a persistent theme in Trotsky's writings, both before and after the Revolution. He took for granted the proposition that socialism was dependent on the highest development

---

[36] Ibid., p. 145.   [37] Ibid., pp. 143 and 145.
[38] For Marx's views on bureaucracy, see Avineri, *The Social and Political Thought of Karl Marx*, pp. 48–52.
[39] The discussion of Trotsky's view of the Soviet bureaucracy, as indeed the whole of this chapter, will be based primarily on his major work dealing with Stalinism, *The Revolution Betrayed* (for bibliographical details see chapter 9, note 17, above). References to other works, however, will be made throughout. Also, as will become apparent, his views did not remain static, but rather developed, and the changes will be duly noted by citing different writings.

of productive capacities, and on the consequent possibilities of solving once and for all the problems of economic
want. Before 1917 Trotsky had tended to exaggerate the extent
to which forces making for socialist change had evolved in
Russia; but even then, and certainly after 1917, he often
warned of the 'vengeance' of backwardness—the successful
workers' revolution unable to deal fundamentally with social
problems because of poverty, primitive technique, the absence
of an appropriate cultural and ideological consciousness, and
lack of support from the European proletariat.[40] It is these very
problems which he now saw to be the root of the Soviet bureaucracy of the 1930s. In *The Revolution Betrayed*, one of his best-
known works, and his most comprehensive critique of Soviet
society under Stalin (it was written in 1936), he defined the
origins of the bureaucracy in the following simple terms:

The basis of bureaucratic rule is the poverty of society in objects of
consumption, with the resulting struggle of each against all. When
there are enough goods in a store, the purchasers can come whenever
they want to. When there are few goods, the purchasers are compelled
to stand in line. When the lines are very long, it is necessary to appoint
a policeman to keep order. Such is the starting point of the power
of the Soviet bureaucracy.[41]

   The utopian aspects of Marx's view of the future, and those
of Lenin as well in his *State and Revolution*, had consisted of the
belief that once scarcity was eradicated and affluence achieved,
problems of distribution will have disappeared, and with them
the necessity for specialists, administrators or bureaucrats
whose function it had been to regulate once limited supplies.
Trotsky took over this view in its entirety; but he noted that
neither Marx—who did not think of the question in the context
of a backward society—nor Lenin had realized how really
serious the problem of poverty could become on the morrow
of a socialist revolution:

Two years before the *Communist Manifesto*, young Marx wrote: 'A development of the productive forces is the absolutely necessary practical premise [of Communism], because without it want is generalized,
and with want the struggle for necessities begins again, and that means

[40] See, for instance, the quotation in chapter 7, p. 284, above.
[41] *The Revolution Betrayed*, p. 112.

that all the old crap must revive.' This thought Marx never directly developed, and for no accidental reason: he never foresaw a proletarian revolution in a backward country. Lenin also never dwelt upon it, and this too was not accidental. He did not foresee so prolonged an isolation of the Soviet state. Nevertheless, the citation, merely an abstract construction with Marx, an inference from the opposite, provides an indispensable theoretical key to the wholly concrete difficulties and sicknesses of the Soviet regime. On the historic basis of destitution, aggravated by the destructions of the imperialist and civil wars, the 'struggle for individual existence' not only did not disappear the day after the overthrow of the bourgeoisie, and not only did not abate in the succeeding years, but, on the contrary, assumed at times an unheard-of ferocity.[42]

Trotsky hinted at Lenin's naïveté in believing (in *State and Revolution*) that bureaucratism merely reflected the 'unfamiliarity of the masses with administration', and thus failing to draw 'all the necessary conclusions as to the character of the state from the economic backwardness and isolatedness of the country'. Lenin had assumed that merely 'political measures' would be sufficient to overcome 'bureaucratic distortions' and, in so far as they were applied, 'the state would gradually and imperceptibly disappear from the scene'.[43] In fact, in Trotsky's view, the problem was not fundamentally a political, nor even an administrative, one in origin but a social and historical one. The bitter truth that backwardness and socialism *were* incompatible had to be fully confronted:

The tendencies of bureaucratism, which strangles the workers' management in capitalist countries, would everywhere show themselves even after a proletarian revolution. But it is perfectly obvious that the poorer the society which issues from a revolution, the sterner and more naked would be the expression of this 'law', the more crude would be the forms assumed by bureaucratism, and the more dangerous would it become for socialist development. The Soviet state is prevented not only from dying away, but even from freeing itself of the bureaucratic parasite, not by the 'relics' of former ruling classes, as declares the naked police doctrine of Stalin, for these relics are powerless in themselves. It is prevented by immeasurably mightier factors, such as material want, cultural backwardness, and the resulting dominance of 'bourgeois law' in what most immediately and sharply

[42] Ibid., p. 56.　　　　[43] Ibid., p. 58.

touches every human being, the business of ensuring his personal existence.[44]

It was in the context of these 'mightier factors' that Trotsky saw the triumph of Stalinism. It was true, he admitted, that the actual political struggle which followed the death of Lenin, the personalities involved, the tactics, stratagems, and arguments employed were all relevant to an analysis of Stalin's success. But they were only that layer of the iceberg which protruded above the surface. 'A political struggle', Trotsky wrote, 'is in its essence a struggle of interests and forces, not of arguments. The quality of the leadership is, of course, far from a matter of indifference for the outcome of the conflict, but it is not the only factor, and in the last analysis is not decisive.'[45] What is decisive is the social milieu, the burden of history which the Russian Revolution inherited and which, at a certain point, became so overpowering as to appear unbearable. Every revolution, Trotsky noted, was in any case an almost traumatic experience which drained the strength and emotions of its participants; it was, he said, 'a mighty devourer of human energy, both individual and collective. The nerves give way. Consciousness is shaken and characters are worn out.'[46] How much worse it was, therefore, when, as in the Russian Revolution, the real work of changing society does not precede but, on the contrary, only begins on the morrow of the political revolution. Thus the burden of backwardness, together with the inevitable post-revolutionary exhaustion, combined to create the conditions for the triumph of Stalinism or, what was for Trotsky synonymous with it, bureaucratism:

It is for the very reason, that a proletariat still backward in many respects achieved in the space of a few months the unprecedented leap from a semi-feudal monarchy to a socialist dictatorship, that the reaction in its ranks was inevitable. This reaction has developed in a series of consecutive waves. External conditions and events have vied with each other in nourishing it. Intervention followed intervention. The Revolution got no direct help from the West. Instead of the expected prosperity of the country, an ominous destitution reigned for long. Moreover, the outstanding representatives of the working

---

[44] Ibid., p. 56. For an earlier (1931) but similar definition by Trotsky of the relationship between bureaucratism and backwardness, see his 'Problemy razvitiya SSSR', op. cit.
[45] *The Revolution Betrayed*, pp. 86–7.   [46] Ibid., p. 88.

class either died in the civil war, or rose a few steps higher and broke away from the masses. And then after an unexampled tension of forces, hopes and illusions, there came a long period of weariness, decline, and sheer disappointment in the results of the Revolution. The ebb of the 'plebeian pride' made room for a flood of pusillanimity and careerism. The new commanding caste rose to its place upon this wave.[47]

Was the Stalinist bureaucracy therefore inevitable, the necessary consequence of a socialist revolution in Russia? In pointing to backwardness as the source of the bureaucracy this is surely what Trotsky appeared to imply. Yet as we already know, and as we shall see again, he in fact believed that an alternative development was possible. This contradiction between his social analysis and his political conclusion recurs again and again in his writings of the 1930s. It reflects, of course, the dilemma of the phenomenon he was trying to account for, and we shall return to the significance of the contradiction at the end of this chapter; in the meantime, it is to Trotsky's description, and attempt at definition, of the bureaucratic phenomenon that we now turn.

(b) *'What is the Soviet Union and Where is it Going?'*

'What is the Soviet Union and Where is it Going?' is the subtitle[48] Trotsky gave to *The Revolution Betrayed*, and it accurately describes Trotsky's purpose in the book: to define the nature of the Soviet regime and of Soviet society as these emerged in the 1930s. Much of the book's analysis is concerned with the question whether the Soviet Union under Stalinism constitutes a model of society fundamentally different from any other social model. As we shall see below, though Trotsky reached an equivocal, negative conclusion, his analysis itself was ambivalent.

The starting point for his inquiry was the Soviet claim that the nationalization of property constituted its transformation into 'social' property, and thus that the Soviet Union was already fundamentally a socialist society. This claim Trotsky rejected entirely. Quoting from the 1936 Soviet constitution where state property was said to be synonymous with 'the

---

[47] Ibid., p. 89.
[48] In the original Russian manuscript deposited in the Trotsky Archives (T3946–53) this appears as the main title (*Chto takoe SSSR i kuda on idet.'*).

possessions of the whole people', Trotsky called this identification 'the fundamental sophism of the official doctrine'.[49] And
he continued:

In order to become social, private property must as inevitably pass
through the state stage as the caterpillar in order to become a butterfly
must pass through the pupal stage. But the pupa is not a butterfly.
Myriads of pupae perish without ever becoming butterflies. State
property becomes the property of the 'whole people' only to the degree
that social privilege and differentiation disappear, and therewith the
necessity of the state. In other words: state property is converted into
socialist property in proportion as it ceases to be state property. And
the contrary is true: the higher the Soviet state rises above the people,
and the more fiercely it opposes itself as the guardian of property to
the people as its squanderer, the more obviously does it testify against
the socialist character of this state property.[50]

We need not pursue Trotsky's argument in detail here for
the fact that state ownership cannot be equated with that system of production and distribution which Marx envisaged for
the socialist society is fairly obvious; it is important only to note
that Trotsky had correctly pointed to the direct relationship
or, as he called it, 'the dialectic of interaction',[51] which existed
between production and distribution. To change proprietor-
ship while retaining the old principles of distribution was, for
Trotsky, to effect a mere 'juridical change' in social relations.[52]
It meant that inequality, favouritism, social and economic distinctions were to be sustained, though under a different name.
In practice, it made little difference to the worker whether his
place of work was privately owned or in the hands of the state
if in both cases the conditions of work were the same. And, in
Trotsky's view, state ownership in the Soviet Union was *not*
accompanied by a change in conditions of employment. The
principle of wage differentiation had not only not been jettisoned but in its 'Stakhanovite' guise had been raised to a sacred
level. The hierarchical relations of production, according to
which some work while others employ and manage, were similarly sanctified: the capitalists were simply replaced by the
bureaucrats, and the 'free workman' was as much a fiction

[49] *The Revolution Betrayed*, p. 236.   [50] Ibid., p. 237.
[51] Ibid., p. 239.   [52] Loc. cit.

under state ownership as under private. The principle of workers' participation in the running of their industries could find no place in a system of management which was 'super-bureaucratic'; instead workers became subject to the decrees of a new 'corps of slave drivers'.[53] The final, over-all result was not equality, nor even a system encouraging a spirit of egalitarianism, but the very opposite, the emergence of an almost oligarchical stratum of bureaucrats, appropriating to themselves material comforts and luxuries while the masses continued to struggle for simple existence. State ownership was thus a far cry from the goal of 'collective' ownership:

The Soviet press relates with satisfaction how a little boy in the Moscow zoo, receiving to his question, 'Whose is that elephant?' the answer, 'The state's', made the immediate inference: 'That means it's a little bit mine too.' However, if the elephant were actually divided, the precious tusks would fall to the chosen, a few would regale themselves with elephantine hams, and the majority would get along with hooves and guts. The boys who are done out of their share hardly identify the state property with their own. The homeless consider 'theirs' only that which they steal from the state. The little 'socialist' in the zoological garden was probably the son of some eminent official accustomed to draw inferences from the formula: 'L'état—c'est moi.'[54]

In spite of this, Trotsky rejected the temptation to define the system which had arisen under Stalin as another form of capitalism, specifically 'state capitalism'. Such a definition seemed to him to ignore the nevertheless profound differences which characterized the Soviet Union when compared with capitalist society. It was true that a privileged group, exploiting and living off the work of others, had come to dominate the economy of the country. But this group did not own the means of production, nor could it accumulate wealth in the manner of capitalists. Property had not been made 'collective' or 'social', but it had been 'socialized' in so far as *private* ownership had been abolished. It was meaningless to apply the term 'capitalism' to a system in which there was no private capital and in which production was based not on free competition but on state regulation. 'Capitalism' was a term describing a specific, historical form of economic organization; to use it now to describe the

[53] Ibid., p. 241.   [54] Ibid., pp. 239–40.

Soviet system meant abstracting the term from its social and historical context. It meant simplification through analogy, and an inexact one at that, instead of precise social analysis. The iniquities of the Soviet system and those of capitalism *were* analogous and, in practice, sometimes even identical; but this was not sufficient, in Trotsky's view, to reach the conclusion that the source of the evil was the same in each case.[55]

Not the least of the reasons, however, for Trotsky's rejection of the 'state capitalism' thesis was his conviction that however powerful and dominating the Soviet bureaucracy had become it did not, and could not, constitute a 'class'. The view that Soviet society had given birth to a 'new class' was gaining support amongst critics of the Soviet Union and, towards the end of the 1930s, this would become the subject of one of the final and major theoretical controversies in which Trotsky was to be involved.[56] But already at the beginning of the 1930s Trotsky was concerned to refute this contention. In an article of 1933 he wrote as follows:

Class has an exceptionally important and moreover a scientifically restricted meaning to a Marxist. A class is defined not by participation in the distribution of the national income alone, but by its independent role in the general structure of economy and by its independent roots in the economic foundation of society. Each class ... works out its own special forms of property. The bureaucracy lacks all these social traits. It has no independent position in the process of production and distribution. It has no independent property roots. Its functions relate basically to the political *technique* of class rule. The existence of a bureaucracy in all its variety of forms and differences in specific weight, characterizes *every* class regime. Its power is of a reflected character. The bureaucracy is indissolubly bound up with a ruling economic class, feeding itself upon the social roots of the latter, maintaining itself and falling together with it.[57]

Trotsky thus adhered to the orthodox Marxist view that a bureaucracy could not constitute a class unto itself. He

[55] Ibid., pp. 245–8. See also the article by Trotsky, written in 1933, 'Klassovaya priroda sovetskogo gosudarstva', in *Byulleten Oppozitsii* (Oct. 1933), pp. 1–12. Here, as in *The Revolution Betrayed*, he also argued that 'state capitalism' was in fact characteristic of Fascist regimes, that is, of declining capitalism, where the state intervened in order to restrict competition and thus secure the interests of monopoly capital.
[56] The controversy is discussed later in this chapter.
[57] 'Klassovaya priroda sovetskogo gosudarstva', p. 7.

admitted that the Soviet bureaucracy had achieved a 'degree of independence' previously unknown in history, and that it had become 'the sole privileged and commanding stratum in Soviet society'.[58] Nevertheless, he argued, its power derived from the function it performed, and not from social or economic foundations:

The bureaucracy has neither stocks nor bonds. It is recruited, supplemented and renewed in the manner of an administrative hierarchy, independently of any special property relations of its own. The individual bureaucrat cannot transmit to his heirs his rights in the exploitation of the state apparatus. The bureaucracy enjoys its privileges under the form of an abuse of power. It conceals its income; it pretends that as a special social group it does not even exist. Its appropriation of a vast share of the national income has the character of social parasitism.[59]

The Soviet bureaucracy, according to Trotsky, like every other bureaucracy, served, and lived off, a class. But unlike other bureaucracies, the Soviet one emerged when its class, the proletariat, was only just shaking off 'destitution and darkness' and had as yet 'no tradition of dominion or command'.[60] Thus at one and the same time it both 'served' the interests of the proletariat and dominated it, its power a function of the weakness of the class. The resulting relationship, however, did not make of the bureaucracy an independent class, nor did it amount to 'class exploitation':

... the privileges of the bureaucracy by themselves do not change the basis of Soviet society, because the bureaucracy derives its privileges not from any special property relations peculiar to it as a 'class', but from those property relations which have been created by the October Revolution and which are fundamentally adequate for the dictatorship of the proletariat. To put it plainly, in so far as the bureaucracy robs the people ... we have to deal not with *class exploitation*, in the scientific sense of the word, but with *social parasitism*, albeit on a very large scale.[61]

What then *is* the Soviet Union? If it is neither socialist nor capitalist, does it constitute some new and unique social phenomenon, or is it merely a mixture of different social forms? It

[58] *The Revolution Betrayed*, pp. 248–9.   [59] Ibid., pp. 249–50.
[60] Ibid., p. 248.   [61] 'Klassovaya priroda sovetskogo gosudarstva', p. 8.

must be admitted that throughout *The Revolution Betrayed*, as
in the rest of his writings of the 1930s, Trotsky could not quite
make up his mind as to how to define precisely the social character of the Soviet regime and the society it was creating. In principle, he was prepared to accept the conventional view that
formally at least it was a 'dictatorship of the proletariat' and,
as such, a '*preparatory* regime *transitional* from capitalism to
socialism',[62] and therefore fundamentally temporary in character. On this view, in so far as classes and social antagonisms
continued to exist, the state, and thus the bureaucracy,
remained unavoidable evils, essential for applying force and decreeing policies where voluntary consent and consensus did not
exist: 'Bureaucracy and social harmony are inversely proportional to each other.'[63] In this sense too, it was possible to
describe the Soviet regime in conventional Marxist terms, as
having a 'dual character': 'socialistic, in so far as it defends
social property in the means of production, bourgeois, in so far
as the distribution of life's goods is carried out with a capitalistic
measure of value and all the consequences ensuing there-
from.'[64]

The validity of this definition, however, depended on the
assumption that a workers' state must evolve *away* from 'bourgeois' or 'capitalist' characteristics and *towards* socialist ones.
It must be a bridge between the bourgeois and the socialist
society, but a bridge open in one direction only. But this,
according to Trotsky, was precisely where the difficulty in
applying the standard definition to the Soviet regime began.
As it appeared at present, that is in the 1930s, it was far from
certain, in Trotsky's view, that it had unequivocally set course
in the socialist direction. The growth rather than the diminution of the bureaucracy, the increase in the power of state
organs, the intensification of rule from above and, what is but
the social and economic source of these phenomena, the pur-
poseful perpetuation of 'bourgeois norms' of economic rewards
and distribution, suggested that the ultimate character of the
regime remained in doubt, and that a transition in an opposite,
non-socialist direction was at least a possibility. Nearly two
decades after a workers' revolution, the state was not 'withering
away' but growing more and more omnipotent, 'more and

---

[62] *The Revolution Betrayed*, p. 47.   [63] Ibid., p. 52.   [64] Ibid., p. 54.

more despotic'; the bureaucracy was not dying away but 'rising above the new society'.[65] The matter of the ultimate character of the Soviet Union was thus, in Trotsky's view, far from settled, and either one of two alternatives was realistically conceivable:

Two opposite tendencies are growing up out of the depth of the Soviet regime. To the extent that, in contrast to a decaying capitalism it develops the productive forces, it is preparing the economic basis of socialism. To the extent that, for the benefit of an upper stratum, it carries to more and more extreme expression bourgeois norms of distribution, it is preparing a capitalist restoration. This contrast between forms of property and norms of distribution cannot grow indefinitely. Either the bourgeois norm must in one form or another spread to the means of production, or the norms of distribution must be brought into correspondence with the socialist property system.[66]

Trotsky categorically declared that 'the question of the character of the Soviet Union [had] not yet [been] decided by history'.[67] The most that could be done at this stage by way of definition was to describe the Soviet Union as a 'contradictory society halfway between capitalism and socialism' in which opposing forces were vying with one another in a struggle whose outcome was far from predetermined.[68] It would be a 'mistake' to believe, Trotsky wrote, 'that from the present Soviet regime *only* a transition to socialism is possible; in reality, a backslide to capitalism is wholly possible'.[69] It would appear, therefore, that only two alternatives, either capitalism or socialism, were conceivable. And, indeed, this was precisely Trotsky's conclusion; although he wrote that 'to define the Soviet regime as transitional, or intermediate, means to abandon such finished social categories as *capitalism* (and therewith "state capitalism"), and also *socialism*',[70] in fact, he could not conceive of the ultimate result in any but these 'categories'. Either socialism would triumph, or a 'bourgeois restoration' would take place; either 'old Bolshevism' would oust the bureaucrats, or a 'bourgeois, counter-revolutionary' party would overthrow them. A third possibility, that the bureaucrats would perpetuate indefinitely their hold on power, and that the Soviet Union would remain forever a kind of 'intermediate' society, neither

[65] Ibid., p. 55.   [66] Ibid., p. 244.   [67] Ibid., p. 252.
[68] Ibid., p. 255.   [69] Ibid., p. 254.   [70] Loc. cit.

socialist nor capitalist, appeared to Trotsky to be highly improbable. Even if the bureaucracy were to succeed in consolidating its power and in repulsing the danger both from the 'left' and the 'right', the end result would be no different from the second of the two original alternatives, namely, the restoration of capitalism:

We cannot count upon the bureaucracy peacefully and voluntarily renouncing itself on behalf of socialist equality [should it remain in power]. If at the present time . . . it has considered it possible to introduce ranks and decorations, it must inevitably in future stages seek supports for itself in property relations. One may argue that the big bureaucrat cares little what are the prevailing forms of property, provided only they guarantee him the necessary income. This argument ignores not only the instability of the bureaucrat's own rights, but also the question of his descendants . . . Privileges have only half their worth if they cannot be transmitted to one's children. But the right of testament is inseparable from the right of property. It is not enough to be the director of a trust; it is necessary to be a stockholder. The victory of the bureaucracy in this decisive sphere would mean its conversion into a new possessing class.[71]

The conception of this new class which Trotsky had in mind had nothing in common with the new class idea which would begin to gain prominence only a few years after this had been written. On the contrary, the 'new class' was for Trotsky nothing else but the 'old class', the bourgeoisie, re-emerging, albeit via a circuitous route, but in a form fundamentally no different from that which it had assumed in the past. Should the bureaucrats hold on, they would, sooner or later, become the 'new-old' bourgeoisie, and the society a 'new-old' capitalism. A third alternative, a society fitting neither the socialist nor the capitalist category, thus remained out of the question for Trotsky. We shall see later in this chapter how this 'either-or' proposition, despite a momentary though significant reconsideration, persisted in his mind until the very end and how, and why, Trotsky resisted a conclusion which not only in retrospect, but already at the time, appeared more realistic than either of his own alternatives.

B. THE BUREAUCRATIC DICTATORSHIP

Nothing is more natural for a Marxist—though, of course, not

71 Ibid., pp. 253-4.

only for a Marxist—than to make historical comparisons, to
draw parallels with the past. It is for him the basis for understanding the present and, perhaps, the future as well. But the
search for historical parallels, even precedents, is never more
urgently felt than when the same Marxist finds himself engulfed
in a historical enterprise of his own making. At such a time,
the multiplicity and pace of events, and proximity to them, tend
to conceal from him the essential character of that which is
happening around him. It is hardly surprising, therefore, that
as the Russian Revolution became more and more immersed
in the problems and details of day-to-day life, its leaders should
turn to an event in history of at least comparable dimensions
in order to better define the emerging pattern of their work.
This event was, of course, the French Revolution of the eighteenth century which more than any other phenomenon in
modern history provided the Russian Revolution with a constant source for analogies, a model with which to identify, or
otherwise, the developments—confusing and indefinable as
they sometimes must have seemed even, perhaps especially, to
those directly involved—in the Soviet Union. From the point
of view of its declared goals and the circumstances within which
it took place, the Russian Revolution was certainly an unprecedented event in history, obviously different at least in ideological essentials from the French Revolution. But the latter
belonged, as Marxist canon never tired of stressing, to the same
genus of events in modern history, and to anyone with a sense
for the historical, the temptation to draw direct parallels must
have been immense indeed.

Moreover, the eventual fate of the French experience soon
seemed less remote from the Russian, less a matter for historical
curiosity, and more a source of anxious fascination about the
repetitive ways of revolutionary history. In the years following
the death of Lenin, as opposing tendencies began to confront
each other more and more directly so that the Revolution was
pulled now in one direction, now in another, it became impossible to avoid analogies with the fate of the original French
model. To some it now seemed that that fate was about to
be repeated in an almost exact pattern—from the phenomenon of Jacobinism, to that of Thermidor, and culminating
finally in the rise of Bonapartism. Thus, the more the Russian

Revolution held up a mirror to itself, the more the French precedent appeared to be reflected in it.

(a) *Thermidor*

We have seen in a previous chapter how, already in 1904, Trotsky had used the example of the French Revolution to identify certain developments within the Social Democratic movement in Russia.[72] At that time, denouncing the 'dictatorial' tactics of Lenin, he claimed to perceive the first, to him ugly, stirrings of Jacobinism within the Russian revolutionary movement, in the form of Bolshevik 'substitutionism'. He was then an opponent of both Jacobinism and Bolshevism. Following 1917, however, he had of course not only come to terms with the latter, but had wholeheartedly embraced the revolutionary spirit of the former. Thus, when in the late 1920s, the character of the Russian Revolution began to be debated by analogy with the French, it was Trotsky who, invoking the memory of Lenin, appeared as the defender of the Bolshevik Jacobinist tradition.[73] The danger which he claimed to perceive now, and against which he was now determined to fight, was not 'substitutionism' as such, nor even its concomitant, dictatorship, but a particular kind of 'substitutionism' which he believed would lead to an anti-revolutionary dictatorship. This was the danger of 'Thermidor', that other ghost from the French arsenal, which, just as it had once destroyed the revolutionary fervour of French Jacobinism, was now, in Trotsky's view, threatening to liquidate what still remained of Russian, or rather Bolshevik, Jacobinism.

Trotsky's definition of Thermidor, as well as his evaluation of the extent of its inroads into Soviet society and of its further prospects, were revised and reformulated by him intermittently so that it is a subject on which his views, if not wholly lacking cohesion, are at best inconsistent. He was himself aware of this, and admitted as much, and it was only in the mid-1930s that he adopted a more or less unambiguous position on this question. Until then he could not quite decide what to make of the Thermidor label or how to make it stick within the Soviet con-

[72] See chapter 5, above.
[73] The irony of this has been well noted by Deutscher in *The Prophet Unarmed*, pp. 346–7.

text. In 1927, when he first broached the subject, he recalled that the 'ultra-left', by now extinct, had some years previously been up in arms about the extent to which Thermidorian elements had by then already triumphed in government and society.[74] Although Trotsky at this time dismissed this alarm as premature, he agreed that the danger of Thermidor existed. He took the view, however, that it was a purely right-wing danger, emanating from those whose policies were clearly aimed at a virtual 'bourgeois restoration'. Thus it was men like Bukharin, Rykov, Kalinin and Tomsky—the 'right-wingers'— who worried him from this point of view rather than Stalin and the other 'zig-zagging' bureaucrats, or 'empirical' apparatus men, whom he considered as more 'centrist' in their views. It was this 'rightist' danger which he stressed in a speech of June 1927 before the Praesidium of the Central Control Commission, and in which his nearly hysterical denunciation of Thermidor was accompanied by an impassioned defence of Jacobinism, that of Robespierre as well as that of Lenin.[75] Trotsky here clearly feared the re-emergence of the 'bourgeois classes' in society using the right-wing of the party as their instrument.[76]

The defeat of the right wing in 1928–9, however, and the consequent shift to the left under Stalin, appeared to Trotsky to constitute a major blow against the Thermidorian danger. Already in October 1928, in a 'Letter to Friends' written from his exile in Alma Ata, Trotsky admitted that for the time being at least the forces of Thermidor had been effectively pushed back if not entirely eliminated.[77] And in an article of 1929 he felt obliged to defend Stalin—in spite of the fact that the latter

---

[74] The alarm about Thermidor appears to have been first raised by 'ultra-left' communists, the so-called 'democratic centralists'.

[75] The speech is reproduced in Trotsky, *Stalinskaya Shkola Falsifikatsii* (Berlin, 1932), pp. 133–53. Trotsky had been arraigned before the Commission to answer charges of 'factionalism'.

[76] Although the right-wing faction appeared to him to be the real Thermidorian enemy, Trotsky did raise the possibility later in 1927 that Stalin's 'bureaucratic Centrist faction, ... staggering between two class lines ... in sharp zig-zags' would also help to 'prepare' Thermidor. See 'The Fear of Our Platform', in *The Real Situation in Russia*, pp. 3–19. The term 'centrism', which Trotsky was to use until 1935 in relation to Stalin's 'faction', was defined by him as describing those 'trends within the proletariat and on its periphery which are distributed between reformism and Marxism, and which most often represent various stages of evolution from reformism to Marxism—and vice versa' (*The Struggle Against Fascism in Germany*, pp. 210–11).

[77] 'Pismo Druzyam', 21 Oct. 1928, Archives, T3145, 3146.

had at the beginning of that year banished him from the Soviet Union—against those who condemned Stalin's regime as Thermidor triumphant.[78] Trotsky here defined Thermidor as nothing less than a counter-revolution, in which power passed from one class to another, and which could succeed only through civil war; this, in his view, is what had happened in France with the defeat of the plebeians, the *sans-culottes*. But nothing of the sort, he claimed, had occurred in the Soviet Union; here, in spite of the bureaucratic degeneration represented by Stalin, the means of production remained in the hands of the state and had not passed into those of the bourgeoisie—and this was what counted in the end. There had been no counter-revolutionary civil war, and it was inconceivable to him that Thermidor could be carried out peacefully, through quiet bureaucratic change.[79] In this same article he also rejected the view that the bureaucracy could constitute a new exploiting class while having no property of its own, and fulfilling only managerial functions. Thus Trotsky persisted in seeing Thermidor as a right-wing, bourgeois class phenomenon which the Stalin regime did not, in his view, conform to, and which therefore remained a largely unfulfilled danger in the Soviet Union.

It was not until the 1934–5 period, a crucial one in the Soviet Union, that Trotsky began revising his conception of Thermidor in general, and within the Soviet context in particular.[80] This was the period of the assassination of Kirov, of the swing from the previous left-wing course in the Comintern to 'popular-front tactics', and of the new wave of purge trials and terror.[81] Trotsky was now convinced that the Soviet regime had

---

[78] 'Zashchita sovetskoi respubliki i oppozitsiya', in *Byulleten Oppozitsii* (Oct. 1929), pp. 1–17. The condemnation of Stalin, which Trotsky here rejected, was made by the 'Leninbund', a German ultra-left group led by Hugo Urbahns, to whose journal, *Die Fahne des Kommunismus*, Trotsky was at this time contributing.

[79] He also refused to accept the analogy, drawn by the 'Leninbund', according to which his own expulsion was like the execution of Robespierre (ibid., p. 9).

[80] By the beginning of 1933 Trotsky had become much more alarmed about the prospects of the Thermidorian threat, but he continued to insist that it could triumph only as a 'petty-bourgeois counter-revolution' generated by the peasantry primarily; see Archives, T3498.

[81] In an article written in December 1934, a few weeks after the assassination of Kirov, Trotsky was not yet prepared to discard his position on the Soviet Thermidor; but he now conceded that the bureaucracy could no longer be relied upon to preserve even the gains of October 1917; see 'Stalinskaya byurokratiya i ubiistvo Kirova', *Byulleten Oppozitsii* (Jan. 1935), pp. 1–10.

become 'Bonapartist' in character.[82] But, as he knew only too well, Bonapartism in France had followed Thermidor and, as he would argue, was in fact a higher, more entrenched form of Thermidor. If, therefore, Stalin was the 'Soviet Bonaparte', if *this* analogy was to be sustained, it was necessary to re-evaluate the 'Soviet Thermidor' analogy. This is precisely what Trotsky did in an essay first published in April 1935 and in which he now admitted that having grasped the nature of the French Thermidor incorrectly in the past, he had failed to appreciate its reincarnation in the Soviet Union under Stalin.[83] The error he had made, he now confessed, was to think that the original Thermidor had been a counter-revolution. To have been such it would have had to restore the feudal property relations which existed prior to 1789. But nothing of the sort had happened. On the contrary, Thermidor had anchored itself to the social foundations of the bourgeois revolution. What it had amounted to, therefore, was a reaction *within* the revolution, the transfer of power from the left Jacobins to the moderate and conservative ones, from the great masses of the bourgeoisie to a well-to-do minority. Looked at in this way, it now seemed clear to Trotsky that the same process, though now in the context of a proletarian revolution, had been repeated in the Soviet Union some 130 years later:

Today it is impossible to ignore the fact that in the Soviet Revolution as well, a shift to the right took place a long time ago, a shift entirely analogous to Thermidor, although much slower in tempo and more masked in form . . . Socially the proletariat is more homogeneous than the bourgeoisie; but it contains within itself an entire series of strata which become manifest with exceptional clarity following the conquest of power, during the period when the bureaucracy and a workers' aristocracy connected with it, begin to take form. The smashing of the Left Opposition implied in the most direct and immediate sense the transfer of power from the hands of the revolutionary vanguard into the hands of the more conservative elements among the bureaucracy and the upper crust of the working class. The year 1924—that was the beginning of the Soviet Thermidor.[84]

[82] Trotsky's interpretation of Soviet 'Bonapartism' is discussed in the next section of this chapter.
[83] 'Rabochee gosudarstvo, termidor i bonapartizm', *Byulleten Oppozitsii* (Apr. 1935), pp. 2–13.
[84] Ibid., p. 8.

Trotsky was now prepared to accept the view—originally propounded by the 'ultra-left' Communists and at the time rejected by him—that Thermidor had become an established fact within a year or two of its beginnings, that is by about 1926.[85] He now also claimed that the doctrine of 'socialism in one country' was in fact the doctrine of Thermidor. The contradictions raised by a workers' revolution in a backward society could have been resolved only by grasping that revolution as part of a world revolution. Since this conception was rejected, the contradictions not only persisted, but threatened to destroy all that had been accomplished. Thus the doctrine of 'socialism in one country', to protect the Revolution at least of 1917, had but one recourse, the bureaucratic domination of state and society, that is, the undermining of mass organizations and mass participation, and their substitution by a bureaucratic apparatus manned by managerial functionaries and supported only by 'the upper crust of the working class'. In this way the 'dictatorship of the proletariat' was replaced by the 'dictatorship of the bureaucracy'; the latter, however, was a dictatorship in the worst sense of the word since it was not that of a class but of a ruling caste, and it was wielded for the purpose not of resolving social contradictions but of politically manipulating them.[86]

As in France, so in the Soviet Union, this was the triumph of Thermidor. Nevertheless, Trotsky added, just as in France Thermidor solidified itself on the basis of changes created by the Revolution, so the Soviet Thermidor based itself on the changes brought about by 1917. Thus it was not a counter-revolution, though it constituted a major victory for conservative, even reactionary elements within the revolution. In this sense he claimed to have been correct at least in his rejection during the 1920s of the 'ultra-left' view that the Soviet Union had then embarked on the restoration of private property, and on the liquidation of the 1917 Revolution.[87] In fact, the usurpation of power by the bureaucracy 'was made possible and

---

[85] 'The Thermidorians', Trotsky wrote in this essay of 1935, 'can celebrate, approximately, the tenth anniversary of their victory.' Ibid., p. 12.

[86] Ibid., pp. 5–7. In *The Revolution Betrayed*, p. 105, Trotsky defined the 'Soviet Thermidor' as 'a triumph of the bureaucracy over the masses'.

[87] 'Rabochee gosudarstvo ...', pp. 2–4.

can maintain itself only because the social content of the dictatorship of the bureaucracy is determined by those productive relations which were created by the proletarian revolution'.[88] Had it sought to erase 'October 1917', had it chosen to re-establish bourgeois property relations, it would have lost the basis for its power and been swept aside by a truly counter-revolutionary regime.[89] 'In this sense', Trotsky added, 'we may say with complete justification that the dictatorship of the proletariat found its distorted but indubitable expression in the dictatorship of the bureaucracy.'[90]

Trotsky's revision of his views, as outlined above,[91] meant that he no longer saw Thermidor as a necessarily right-wing, bourgeois counter-revolution, but as the bureaucratization of revolution, or of those essential changes which the revolution had introduced. This did not imply, however, that as a result of Thermidor even these changes had been permanently safeguarded. In Trotsky's view, the dictatorship of the bureaucracy did not constitute a permanent solution to the social contradictions in Soviet society but merely an interim and artificial palliative whose dubious advantage was that it had created the *illusion* of internal stability and consolidation. In fact, the possibility of a social upheaval and of a reversal to pre-Soviet society could not be ruled out. As the social contradictions became more and more irreconcilable, the regime had found it more and more difficult to exercise control by purely bureaucratic means. The original French Thermidor, confronted by analogous problems, eventually gave way to the dictatorship of Napoleon Bonaparte; a similar development, Trotsky believed, had now taken place in the Soviet Union: the Soviet Thermidor had been succeeded by Soviet Bonapartism, a form of dictatorship which, though retaining the bureaucratic structure, added

[88] Ibid., p. 7.
[89] Clearly, therefore, however deep his contempt for Stalin's bureaucracy, Trotsky still preferred its triumph to that of the, now defunct, right-wing of the party which in the 1920s he saw as the spearhead of the bourgeois restoration.
[90] Loc. cit.
[91] Trotsky's discussion of the 'Soviet Thermidor' in *The Revolution Betrayed* adds nothing substantial to the analysis contained in his 1935 article. This is also the case with the various other writings, too numerous to list, of the post-1935 period in which he repeated the Thermidorian analogy; see, for example, his *Stalin*, pp. 404–10. For a brief account of Trotsky's views on Thermidor from the late 1920s onwards, see Siegfried Bahne, 'Trotsky on Stalin's Russia', *Survey* (Apr. 1962), pp. 27–42.

the element of personal rule. The introduction of this element, Trotsky believed, now emerged as the final, desperate attempt at preserving the changes of 1917 within the regime's political and ideological framework of 'socialism in one country'.

(b) *Bonapartism*

If Thermidor was, for Trotsky, the social consequence of the bureaucratic phenomenon in the Soviet Union, Bonapartism was its political culmination. By the mid-1930s, therefore, Trotsky had become convinced that the original French scenario would be played out in full within the Soviet context. Yet until then, having resisted, as we have seen, the Thermidorian analogy, but unable to deny what he took to be clear signs of the development of personal rule, Trotsky toyed with the idea that Bonapartism in the Soviet Union might triumph without a prior Thermidorian stage. Thus already in 1928, in the 'Letter to Friends' in which he defended Stalin against the Thermidorian charge,[92] he considered conditions nearly ripe for a Bonapartist take-over. It could assume, he wrote, one of two forms: either a military *coup d'état* or the complete monopolization of power by Stalin himself. If the former succeeded,[93] this would be because the present regime had alienated its mass base—workers as well as peasants—thus creating a power vacuum which the army could exploit. Such a *coup* would have as its main goal the maintenance of order and stability and, in pursuit of this goal, sooner or later its leaders would bring about a capitalist restoration. However, though an army *coup* seemed to Trotsky the most likely prospect, there was in his view the possibility that Stalin, fearing the loss of power, would strike first. In this case, one could expect the very rapid transformation of his rule into an all-powerful personal dictatorship. All pretence to collective or party government would disappear, and a period of outright suppression of all real, potential or imaginary opponents would be ushered in. The consequence would be the undermining of all institutions, not least the party and the bureaucracy both of which would become subjugated to the dictator. Though such a dictatorship, with

[92] Archives, T3145, 3146.
[93] Trotsky here mentioned the names of two generals, Voroshilov and Budenny, as possible leaders of an army *coup*.

Stalin as its Bonaparte, would be less overtly counter-revolutionary than the military alternative, in the long-run, because of its instability and permanent conflict with all elements of society, it too would lead to the collapse of socialism.[94]

This conception of 'Bonapartism before Thermidor' persisted in Trotsky's writings in the following years. In 1931 he wrote that while the Stalin regime could not yet be identified with Bonapartism, the 'degeneration' of the bureaucracy which had taken place was 'one of the pre-conditions' for Bonapartism.[95] In contrasting the latter with Thermidor, he defined it as a 'more open, "riper" form of the bourgeois counter-revolution'. And he added:

The crushing of the right wing of the party and the renunciation of its platform diminish the chances of the first, step-by-step, veiled— that is, Thermidorian—form of the overthrow [by the bourgeoisie]. The plebiscitary degeneration of the party apparatus undoubtedly increases the chances of the Bonapartist form.[96]

By 1932 it had become clear to him that Stalin, not a military dictatorship, would be the Soviet counterpart of the French Bonaparte. He now condemned Stalin for introducing the 'principle of a super-monarchical authority', and by virtue of this principle alone throwing into doubt the character of his regime.[97] But even now he was prepared to attach the Bonapartist label to 'Stalinism' only if it was recognized at the same time that it was a regime which continued to be grounded in 'Soviet soil'.[98] Thus in spite of his earlier pronouncement that Bonapartism was a form of the 'bourgeois counter-revolution', he persisted in attributing fundamental importance to the fact that Stalin had so far preserved the nationalized character of the Soviet economy. As a consequence Trotsky appeared undecided as to whether Bonapartism was a social phenomenon or a purely political one.

[94] Of the two evils, Trotsky clearly preferred that of Stalin. In fact, to prevent a military *coup*, he was prepared to unite with Stalin and urged the Left Opposition not to rule out such co-operation..
[95] 'Problemy razvitiya SSSR' (*Byulleten Oppozitsii*, Apr. 1931), p. 20.
[96] Ibid., p. 10.
[97] 'Otkrytoe pismo prezidiumu TsIK''a Soyuza SSR', *Byulleten Oppozitsii* (Mar. 1932), pp. 1–6.
[98] 'Klassovaya priroda sovetskogo gosudarstva', op. cit., p. 5.

When, in 1935, he reformulated his position on the Soviet
Thermidor, he was able to state more clearly the relationship
between it and Bonapartism. He had, in any case, never
claimed to take a schematic view of the distinction between
them; they were, he had written in 1931, 'only stages of development of the same type, in which the living historic process
is inexhaustible in the sphere of creating transitional and combined forms'.[99] What emerged now, according to Trotsky, was
that the two had evolved simultaneously, so that the conservative social content of the regime—its Thermidor—was buttressed by a dictatorial political form—its Bonapartism. First
bureaucratism had been enshrined, involving inevitably a shift
to the right. This immediately came into conflict with the needs
of the masses and with the idea of a workers' state. Deprived
of mass support, the bureaucracy was forced to acquire an independent power base in order to survive. It did so in two ways:
by 'strangling' the party, the Soviets, and the working class,
and by creating institutions of suppression concentrated in the
hands of the single ruler. And the more this process advanced,
the more did Stalinism, which began as 'bureaucratic
centrism', turn into Bonapartism.[100]

Trotsky took pains to point out that Soviet Bonapartism was
not to be confused with the Bonapartism of Fascist regimes, a
phenomenon he had analysed elsewhere.[101] The latter had
arisen in response to the crisis threatening bourgeois society,
and its goal was to restore and defend capitalist property. Moreover, Fascist Bonapartism appeared at a time when bourgeois
society was in disarray, declining and decaying, and it represented the last, despairing grasp of a drowning class. As against
this, Soviet Bonapartism was distinguished not only by its protection of non-capitalist, nationalized property, but by the fact
that it arose at the outset of the establishment of this form of
property and of the coming to power of a 'young' class, the
workers. Thus, it was analogous not with the dictatorship
which the 'last days' of bourgeois society threw up, but with
that of its beginnings, its ascent:

We always strictly differentiated between the Bonapartism of decay

[99] 'Problemy razvitiya SSSR', op. cit., p. 10.
[100] 'Rabochee gosudarstvo, termidor i bonapartizm', op. cit., p. 12.
[101] See chapter 9, above.

and the young advancing Bonapartism which was not only the grave-digger of the political principles of the bourgeois revolution but also the defender of its social conquests ... The present-day Kremlin Bonapartism we juxtapose, of course, with the Bonapartism of bourgeois rise and not decay: with the Consulate and the First Empire, and not with Napoleon III and, all the more so, not with Schleicher or Doumergue.[102]

Stalin, therefore, was the Napoleon I of the Russian Revolution. The parallels between him and his historical antecedent were all the more striking for showing the extent to which the same political form could be utilized to protect entirely different social forms:

In the former case [i.e. Napoleon I], the question involved was the consolidation of the bourgeois revolution through the liquidation of its principles and political institutions. In the latter case [i.e. Stalin], the question involved is the consolidation of the worker–peasant revolution through the smashing of its international programme, its leading party, its soviets. Developing the policies of Thermidor, Napoleon waged a struggle not only against the 'rabble' but also against the democratic circles of the petty and middle bourgeoisie; in this way he concentrated the fruits of the regime born out of the revolution in the hands of the new bourgeois aristocracy. Stalin guards the conquests of the October Revolution not only against the feudal-bourgeois counter-revolution but also against the claims of the toilers, their impatience and their dissatisfaction; he crushes the left-wing which expresses the ordered historical and progressive tendencies of the unprivileged working masses; he creates a new aristocracy by means of an extreme differentiation in wages, privileges, ranks, etc. Leaning for support upon the topmost layer of the new social hierarchy against the lowest—sometimes vice versa—Stalin has attained the complete concentration of power in his own hands. What else should this regime be called if not Soviet Bonapartism?[103]

Despite all the distinctions which Trotsky wished to make between Soviet Bonapartism and the Fascist variety, here too he was prepared to admit that the two were in some important ways similar. Both, in the first place, represented the rupture

---

[102] 'Rabochee gosudarstvo, termidor i bonapartizm', p. 12. 'We apply', Trotsky wrote, 'a common name to these two manifestations because they have common traits: it is always possible to discern the youth in the octogenarian despite the merciless ravages of time.'
[103] Loc. cit.

which had been wrought between politics and society. Trotsky
had described Fascist Bonapartism as the final 'statagem' of a
dying capitalist class; he had also, however, recognized that
the capitalist class, by resorting to Fascism to save itself, was
relinquishing direct rule in favour of rule by a leadership whose
origins were not capitalist but petty bourgeois, and this latter
represented, in a sense, the rootless 'dregs' of a decaying capitalist society. When this leadership came to power it pretended
to speak not in the name of a class but in that of an abstraction,
the 'nation-state' as a whole. To be sure, Fascist Bonapartism
continued to rest upon and serve not the nation but the capitalists; yet it also encouraged the impression that it was politically
independent, a regime drawing its legitimacy not from this or
that class, or even from a particular economic and social
structure, but from a popular plebiscite rising supposedly above
all individual or group distinctions. However illusory this was,
there was a sense, according to Trotsky, in which politics *were*
severed from, or stood above, society and its foundations: the
capitalists' original agreement to sacrifice the formal parliamentary institutions was followed by the Fascists' creation of
autonomous organs—bureaucracy, police, leader—over which
there was no social or constitutional control. In this way,
politics were given an independent base and came to dominate
society. The same process, Trotsky believed, could be seen to
unfold and come to fruition under Soviet Bonapartism: a regime
raised to power by the workers, it renounced its class character
by glorifying state power, resorting to the sham 'democratic
ritual' of the popular vote, the 'plebiscite', while at the same
time destroying the only legitimate popular institution, the
party, and replacing it with the bureaucracy, the police, the
single leader.[104]

There were, however, further similarities between Soviet and
Fascist Bonapartism. Both, Trotsky noted, were 'crisis regimes',
characterizing societies living through a period of pronounced
economic difficulties, and sharpened antagonisms between
social reality and social needs. Both reacted by suppressing
antagonisms through force rather than by confronting the real
social problems. Both, moreover, owed their 'birth' to 'one and

---

[104] *The Revolution Betrayed*, pp. 277–8. Trotsky here spoke of Bonapartism as the modern
form of ancient 'Caesarism'.

the same cause': 'the belatedness of the world revolution ... the dilatoriness of the world proletariat in solving the problems set for it by history'. Thus Trotsky was able to conclude: 'Stalinism and Fascism, in spite of a deep difference in social foundations, are symmetrical phenomena. In many of their features they show a deadly similarity.'[105]

Nothing, however, so clearly expressed this 'deadly similarity', in Trotsky's view, as the role which the one ruler, Stalin, had forged for himself. Like Fascism, Soviet Bonapartism appeared the moment that institutionalized forms of rule no longer sufficed to protect a social and political system lacking popular or mass support. The device of 'the leader', whether he was naturally charismatic or pretended to be so as in the case of Stalin, served a number of functions: in the first place, to personalize, and thus popularize, an impersonal bureaucracy; secondly, to create a national 'symbol', above and beyond class differences, which would provide a focus for national identification and national effort, and thus an alternative to what should have been such a focus—the socialist and revolutionary content of the regime—but which had been undermined by the policies of 'socialism in one country'; thirdly, to provide the semblance of stability, the impression of power entrenched, wielded, and dispensed, and thereby to conceal the fundamental social weaknesses of the regime.[106] Thus the more the original Thermidorian bureaucracy ran up against social antagonisms of its own making, the more it resorted to a purely political, personalized device for staving them off:

The increasingly insistent deification of Stalin is, with all its elements of caricature, a necessary element of the regime. The bureaucracy has need of an inviolable super-arbiter, a first consul if not an emperor, and it rains upon its shoulders him who best responds to its claim for lordship. That 'strength of character' of the leader which so enraptures the literary dilettantes of the West, is in reality the sum total of the collective pressure of a caste which will stop at nothing in defence of its position. Each one of them at his post is thinking: *l'état, c'est moi*. In Stalin each one easily finds himself. But Stalin also finds in each one a small part of his own spirit. Stalin is the personification of the bureaucracy. That is the substance of his political personality.[107]

[105] Ibid., p. 278.   [106] Ibid., pp. 273ff.   [107] Ibid., p. 277.

Of course, the personalization of the regime was only secondarily motivated by concern over its external image. The fundamental ambition was the monopolization of power, not only in appearance but in reality, and it was an ambition which the regime, through Stalin, set out to pursue in the most single-minded, ruthless manner yet conceived of. It is here, Trotsky believed, that the full significance of the terror—the purges, the show trials, the physical regimentation of millions—manifested itself, at two levels simultaneously. Firstly, as the psychopathology of a bureaucracy alienated from society, and of a leader driven to virtual paranoia by his ubiquitous mistrust of all men : between the bureaucracy and the leader a necessary though uneasy partnership emerged, a virtually symbiotic relationship—necessary, because neither could survive without the other or by means of any other alliance, uneasy, because it was, in effect, a partnership in crime.[108] At a second level, however, the terror appeared as the logical *political* instrument of the regime, as 'functional' from the point of view of the regime and not simply a psychological, irrational phenomenon. Having years ago committed itself to the doctrine of 'socialism in one country', having isolated the Russian masses from the outside world, and having thereby created insoluble internal problems which led to antagonism between these masses and itself, the regime found itself compelled to use the means of oppression for the purpose of self-preservation. In Trotsky's view, therefore, terror, far from being an essential feature of a socialist government was, in fact, characteristic of a regime which had renegued on socialism. True, in the early years of the Revolution, terror had been widely used against all opposition and he, Trotsky, had been amongst the first to justify it;[109] but whereas terror then had been a necessary result of civil war and of the struggle against the old regime and society and, as such, a temporary phenomenon, terror now was the consequence of a reactionary bureaucracy which had turned against those very elements that had once supported the Revolution. Stalinism therefore perpetuated, though on a scale hitherto unprecedented, that terror which was meant only for a particular, critical

[108] 'Psychopathology', 'paranoia', and 'crime' are words which abound in Trotsky's writings on Stalinism.
[109] See chapter 6, pp. 247ff., above.

period, and transformed it into a kind of permanent system of rule. And this, in Trotsky's view, was hardly surprising since Stalinism continually engendered what was in effect a condition of permanent civil war. How else, except by the use of ever-increasing terror, could it survive this civil war?[110]

The new wave of purges, the 'Yezhovshchina', which began in 1936 was, therefore, a further example for Trotsky of the extremes to which the Soviet bureaucracy was forced to go in order to preserve itself both as a privileged 'caste' and a ruling élite. By this time, Trotsky declared in a speech of 1937, its alienation from society had become complete:

It is time ... to recognize ... that a new aristocracy has been formed in the Soviet Union. The October Revolution proceeded under the banner of equality. The bureaucracy is the embodiment of monstrous inequality. The Revolution destroyed the nobility. The bureaucracy creates a new gentry. The revolution destroyed titles and decorations. The new aristocracy produces marshals and generals.[111]

All this, in Trotsky's view, merely reinforced the resentment of the masses whose fundamental problems remained unresolved. As antagonism increased, so the position of the regime became more and more unstable. Once again, therefore, it resorted to terror to protect itself. But it could hardly admit that its use of brute force was governed by its determination to defend its social status, nor that there existed any real estrangement between it and the masses. Instead, the leaders of the regime were 'forced to hide the reality, to deceive the masses, to cloak themselves, calling black white'.[112] One example of this was the pretence to 'constitutionalism' and 'legality'. In 1936 the regime had introduced a new constitution according to which every Soviet citizen was assured the most

---

[110] For an example of Trotsky's analysis of Stalinist terror in these terms, see 'Terror byurokraticheskogo samosokhraneniya', in *Byulleten Oppozitsii* (Sept. 1935), pp. 2–5.
[111] 'I Stake My Life!', printed as an appendix to the English, not American, edition of *The Revolution Betrayed* (London, 1937), pp. 292–312 (the quotation is from p. 310). This is a speech Trotsky prepared for delivery in English by direct telephone wire from Mexico City to a meeting held in New York on 9 Feb. 1937 under the auspices of the American Committee for the Defence of Leon Trotsky. A break in transmission prevented the audience from hearing Trotsky's delivery and the speech was instead read out at the place of the meeting. (The Russian version, under the title 'O protsesse', was published in *Byulleten Oppozitsii* (Mar. 1937), pp. 1–8.)
[112] Ibid., p. 310.

complete array of democratic rights, including universal suffrage and the secret ballot. In fact, of course, Trotsky immediately pointed out, these rights, like the constitution as a whole,
were entirely fictitious since the possibility of electing other than
the existing leadership was inconceivable.[113] No less meaningless, he argued, was the formal legality of the trials against the
opponents, real and imaginary, of the regime. Behind the
façade of legal proceedings every illegal method was employed
to force confessions and assure conviction. Could anyone be
taken in by the trumped-up nature of these trials? Yet the
façade, Trotsky believed, was essential from the point of view
of the authorities in order to create the illusion, at least, of
legitimacy.[114]

The trials and purges, or the 'frame-up-system' as Trotsky
called them, had, in his view, an additional function, however,
extending beyond simple deception. Unwilling to admit the
'bankruptcy' of its social and economic policies, yet unable to
conceal the ugly reality they gave rise to, the regime embarked
on a witch-hunt in search of 'enemies of the people', scapegoats
who would divert attention from itself. Thus failures could be
attributed, not to the bureaucracy or its leaders, but to 'traitors'
who had supposedly infiltrated government and society, sabo-
taging the 'advances' of the Soviet Union. Thus the obsession
with 'Trotskyism'; thus the unending 'exposés' of the trials for
all to see; thus the sensational revelations that formerly un-
blemished Bolshevik revolutionaires—among them Zinoviev,
Kamenev, Bukharin and Radek—were really 'agents' in the
employ of hostile foreign governments; thus the 'permanent
purge'.[115] This is not to say that the regime did not feel itself
genuinely threatened. On the contrary, 'fear ... imbues the
Stalinist bureaucracy throughout' so that the slightest provoca-

[113] For Trotsky's views of the 1936 constitution, see in particular his 'Novaya konstitutsiya SSSR', in *Byulleten Oppozitsii* (May 1936), pp. 1–7 and *The Revolution Betrayed*,
chapter 10. At this time Trotsky was arguing that opposition parties—though not anti-
Soviet ones—should be allowed in the U.S.S.R. (see next section, below).
[114] Trotsky devoted innumerable articles and pamphlets to the subject of the Moscow
trials; for his general view of this phenomenon, as well as specific comments on various
trials, see *The Case of Leon Trotsky: Report of Hearings on the Charges Made Against Him
in the Moscow Trials* (Before the Preliminary Commission of Inquiry, John Dewey, chairman), (New York and London, 1937).
[115] See, in particular, Trotsky's concluding statement to the Dewey Commission in
The Case of Leon Trotsky, pp. 459–585.

tion becomes a pretext for striking out; and this hysteria too 'explains the mad character of its persecutions and its poisonous slanders'.[116]

But this victimization, Trotsky stressed, was only part of a larger drama. Concurrently with the trials there was taking place the systematic and large-scale extermination, not only of lesser political figures, but of unknown peasants, workers, soldiers and even bureaucrats, who for one reason or another constituted an actual or potential threat to the regime. Method was being joined to madness in order to destroy the cohesion of social groupings, and to uproot all areas of independent human activity. At one level, according to Trotsky, this persecution was meant to prevent the evolution of competing centres of political power; at another, its aim was nothing less than the complete elimination of all distinctions between the political and the social, the public and the private. In each case, the ultimate objective was a uniform, undifferentiated society, not a classless but a faceless one. Since, however, Soviet society was infinitely heterogeneous, that is, divided into classes, and refused to adapt spontaneously, terror and compulsion had to be dispensed all the more widely and brutally. True, economic differences, privileges and rewards were not only encouraged but turned into a cornerstone of the regime's policy; yet economic *power*, outside the bureaucracy, was not allowed to develop. Inequalities, it was assumed, could persist without giving rise to conflict and antagonism; classes could continue to exist but in a castrated form. Simultaneously, however, the fiction was circulated that the dividing line between classes was being obliterated or had already disappeared; and if this was so, what need was there for politics? All that was necessary in terms of popular participation was the unanimous 'plebiscite', the expression of ultimate consensus. And this semblance of unity was to be both concretely and symbolically enshrined in the figure of Stalin, the 'leader' who now stood for ideological purity and was thus the purveyor of all legitimacy.[117]

In all this, Trotsky believed, Stalinist Bonapartism was playing out the logic of its inherent character. It had arisen as a

---

[116] *The Revolution Betrayed*, p. 283.
[117] See, in particular, *The Revolution Betrayed*, chapters 6, 7, and 10, and 'Novaya konstitutsiya SSSR', op. cit.

political artifice against the disintegration of the social Thermidor. The more the latter became untenable, the more did the artifice impose itself. However artificial the political homogeneity it sought, it was inexorably driven into realizing it. Thus social groupings, not least the workers, had to be undermined lest they exploited their potential social power; thus political institutions, not least the Bolshevik party, had to be virtually liquidated lest they exercised their political power. The bureaucracy was turned into the dominating social stratum; the secret police into the instrument of total control. Politics came to lord it over society: 'Thus was created the present totalitarian regime.'[118]

3. The Future of the Soviet Union

(a) *'The Degenerated Workers' State': For and Against*

If the Soviet Union under Stalin had become so debased as to throw into doubt its socialist aspirations, if its policy was such as to sabotage the prospects of world revolution, if its government was so tyrannical as to make complete nonsense of the idea of a workers' democracy—was there then any reason left why a socialist should still defend the Soviet Union, even in special circumstances? Had not Trotsky himself argued that Stalinism, should it survive, would issue in the triumph of capitalism in the Soviet Union? Indeed, for many of Trotsky's followers and sympathizers, the abandonment of the Soviet Union was a decision which appeared to follow naturally from their—and Trotsky's own—analyses of the nature of Stalinism. This complete and final rejection of any common cause or identity with the Soviet Union had already begun in the 1920s when first the 'ultra-left' Democratic Centralists and then Trotskyist adherents or sympathizers in Germany, France, and Belgium declared their inability as revolutionists to support the Soviet Union any longer, under any circumstances.[119] And it was to come

[118] *The Revolution Betrayed*, p. 279. In his writings on the Stalinist regime, Trotsky frequently described it as 'totalitarian'. The term had, of course, originally come into usage in connection with Mussolini's Italy and, later, Hitler's Germany; Trotsky, in employing the term, clearly intended to emphasize the similarities between the Fascist and Stalinist dictatorships.
[119] For an account of the early disputes and splits among European Trotskyists, see Deutscher, *The Prophet Outcast*, chapter 1.

to a head, albeit, as we shall see, on the basis of a new interpretation of Soviet developments, during the last year of Trotsky's life. Yet Trotsky himself, despite the virulence of his critique of Soviet developments, stopped short of propounding a complete break with the Soviet Union. His abiding loyalty to the Revolution, though not, of course, to the regime, persisted, and he continued to believe that the Soviet Union remained still worthy of preservation, that, in other words, a Stalinist Soviet Union was better than no Soviet Union at all. Thus whenever his more chagrined and embittered followers threatened to abandon the Soviet Union altogether, it was Trotsky who assumed the mantle of the devil's advocate. He did not believe, as they did, that there was a contradiction between this role and that of acting as the international leader of the anti-Stalin 'opposition'. Rather, since he saw himself waging a war on two fronts, against the 'capitalist world' on the one hand and against Stalin on the other, he believed that its successful outcome depended on a unique combination of tactics: the defence of the Soviet Union as if there were no Stalin, and opposition to Stalin as if there were no 'world capitalism'.

The reasons why the Soviet Union was still worth defending—in spite of Stalin, in spite of the bureaucracy, in spite of 'socialism in one country'—seemed to him as valid in the 1930s as they had been in the 1920s. The Soviet Union was still the only country in which a workers' revolutionary party, espousing the tenets of Marxist socialism, had seized and retained power. Despite the capitulations of Stalin, it still represented a threat to the capitalist West and, potentially, a source of encouragement to the proletariat of the world. It remained, Trotsky believed, the only real bulwark against the spread of Fascism. Virtually from the moment of Hitler's triumph in Germany, Trotsky was convinced that a world war was inevitable and one, moreover, which would have as its main purpose the conquest of the Soviet Union.[120] He was despondent, though not actually surprised, when he learned of the Hitler–Stalin

---

[120] For one of Trotsky's early predictions that the rise of Hitler meant, sooner or later, a new world war, see, for example, his 1933 article 'Chto takoe natsional-sotsializm?', Archives, T3557. 'The date of the new European catastrophe', Trotsky here wrote, 'will be determined by the time necessary for the arming of Germany. It is not a question of months, but neither is it a question of decades. It will be but a few years before

pact but the latter did not, in his view, detract from the fact
that Nazi Germany and Soviet Russia remained implacably
hostile to each other: whatever the momentary tactical
manœuvres of their leaders, a direct confrontation between the
two countries was inevitable and, in that case, there could be
no doubt, not only where the sympathies of a Marxist lay, but
also about his active support.[121] As war became more and more
imminent, he pointed to it as an overriding reason for supporting the Soviet Union. In so doing he urged his followers to distinguish between the Soviet leadership—which was, of course,
anathema and to be condemned and fought—and the Soviet
Union itself, which was still the 'home' of the Russian Revolution, its ideals, aspirations and hopes—and thus worthy of protection against the onslaughts of 'world imperialism'.[122]

But it was not only nostalgia for the Revolution, nor even
the greater contempt for Fascism, which moved him to defend
the Soviet Union. Trotsky, as we have seen, also continued to
hold that even under Stalin the essential, most fundamental
character of the Soviet Union remained intact. By this he meant
that property was kept nationalized. This did not guarantee,
he agreed, socialism in the future, but it preserved, at least, the
basic pre-condition for socialism. Moreover, it was what differentiated between Soviet and capitalist societies, it was the
one characteristic which made the Soviet Union socially unique
in a positive sense. True, it was not yet clear which way the
Soviet Union would evolve, and a 'return' to capitalism was
not entirely out of the question; but, on the other hand,
nationalized property was compatible only with socialist goals,
and so long as it remained nationalized such goals were not
completely eradicated from within Soviet society—whatever
the personal aspirations of a Stalin. In this sense, therefore, the
Soviet Union was still a workers' state for Trotsky and, as such,
deserved to be defended against its enemies.

Europe is again plunged into a war, unless Hitler is forestalled in time by the inner
forces of Germany.' For Trotsky's analysis of the impending World War, see, in particular, 'Pered novoi mirovoi voinoi', *Byulleten Oppozitsii* (Sept.–Oct. 1937), pp. 5–17.
[121] For Trotsky's reaction to the Soviet–German treaty, see, in particular, 'Dvoinaya
zvezda: Gitler–Stalin', Archives, T4653–5. He had been predicting a Soviet–German
pact since the end of 1938.
[122] This distinction is a major theme which runs through all of Trotsky's writings on
the 'defence' of the Soviet Union.

It was, nevertheless, what he called a 'degenerated workers' state',[123] and this for reasons which Trotsky had argued at length in his on-going critique of Stalinism; and while a 'degenerated workers' state' was better than no workers' state at all, the extent of degeneration, in Trotsky's view, was of such magnitude as to make opposition to Stalin, and to the Soviet leadership in general, not only urgent but, from the point of view of the 'workers' state', a matter of life and death. If the defence of the Soviet Union against its 'capitalist' enemies had to be conducted as if Stalinism did not exist, the attack against Stalinism, so ran Trotsky's argument, had to be pursued as if the enemies of the Soviet Union did not exist. In fact, of course, this 'second front', in so far as it was aimed at preserving a 'workers' state' and thus the foundations of 'world socialism', was for Trotsky simultaneously an integral part of the over-all struggle against 'world capitalism'.

This is why, as early as 1933, Trotsky's conception of the opposition to Stalin had as its focus the formation of a new Communist International. He had by then reached the conclusion that it was no longer possible to fight the 'imperialist West', much less Stalinism, within the framework of Stalin's Comintern which was, in his view, criminally responsible for the débâcles in Germany and elsewhere.[124] Although he urged the almost immediate establishment of a new International, it was not until September 1938 that the Trotskyist Fourth International came into being.[125] Trotsky conceived of it as a rival organization which would, presumably, draw followers away from the Comintern and act as the real voice and spearhead of the international proletariat, and of the 'world revolution'.

---

[123] Although Trotsky had already used the epithet 'degenerated' early in the 1930s, the actual term 'degenerated workers' state' does not occur until 1935 (see his previously referred to article 'Rabochee gosudarstvo, termidor i bonapartizm'). Thereafter the term became famous as the 'label' identifying the Trotskyist view of the Soviet Union, and was incorporated into the 1938 'Transitional Programme' of the Fourth International.

[124] His original proposal for a new International appears in the article, 'Nuzhno stroit zanovo kommunisticheskie partii i Internatsional', in *Byulleten Oppozitsii* (Oct. 1933), pp. 19–22.

[125] The 'Transitional Programme' of the Fourth International, composed by Trotsky himself, and adopted at the founding conference (which Trotsky, however, was unable to attend), appeared under the title: 'The Death Agony of Capitalism and the Tasks of the Fourth International'. For the Russian version, see *Byulleten Oppozitsii* (May–June 1938), pp. 1–18.

Above all, it would be the framework, both theoretical and political, for opposition activities against Stalin.[126] In fact, of course, it was to succeed in none of these tasks; its membership remained small, its activities ineffective, and its leaders torn by controversies. Its only real function was as a podium for Trotsky's periodic pronouncements on the world situation.[127]

Trotsky's decision, in 1933, to urge the founding of a new International, marked, however, a turning point in his attitude towards the possibilities of change within the Soviet Union. Until then—and, we may add, quite incredibly—he had believed that the Soviet bureaucracy could be removed, more or less peacefully, through internal reforms of the party.[128] Now he was convinced that this was no longer feasible. In the first place, the oppressive methods of Stalin had made it impossible to work either within the party or within the Comintern; the 'Left Opposition' was now so purged or victimized that it was effectively excluded from all influence, institutional or other. In the second place, the regime had become so dictatorial and so entrenched that even a 'peaceful' assault upon it, that is, one which used the means of argument and persuasion, would immediately elicit a violent reaction. 'No normal "constitutional" ways remain', Trotsky wrote in October 1933, 'to remove the ruling clique. The bureaucracy can be compelled to yield power ... only by *force*.'[129]

Even now, however, Trotsky did not envisage using 'measures of civil war', of 'armed insurrection', but rather 'measures of a police character' only, though he did not specify what he meant by this.[130] It was, in fact, not until 1936 that he began talking in terms of a revolution against the Stalin

[126] For Trotsky's conception of the Fourth International, see, beside the 'Transitional Programme', the following of his writings in particular: *Chetvertyi Internatsional i Voina* (Geneva, 1934); 'Discussion on the Transitional Programme' (in English originally) in *Internal Bulletin* (Socialist Workers Party), (July 1938); 'Manifest Chetvertogo Internatsionala. Imperialistskaya voina i proletarskaya revolyutsiya', in *Byulleten Oppozitsii* (Aug.–Sept.–Oct., 1940), pp. 11–28.

[127] For a brief history of the Fourth International, written by a French Trotskyist, see Pierre Frank, *La Quatrième Internationale* (Paris, 1969).

[128] Thus, for instance, as late as 1932, in his book, *Nemetskaya Revolyutsiya i Stalinskaya Byurokratiya*, op. cit., he rejected the extremist step of creating a 'new Communist party'; instead he urged the 'Opposition' to work for 'reform' from within the existing party (see, especially, pp. 154–6).

[129] 'Klassovaya priroda sovetskogo gosudarstva', op. cit., p. 9.

[130] Ibid, p. 10.

regime. Convinced now that 'state and society' had grown completely apart, with the populace alienated, yet towered over by a tyrannical dictatorship, he saw no way out except through a popular uprising, led by the workers, organized by the 'Opposition' and the emerging new International, and carrying the banner of the tradition of 'Bolshevism–Leninism'. The 'inevitability' of such a revolution was the concluding message of his book *The Revolution Betrayed*:

... the further course of development must inevitably lead to a clash between the culturally developed forces of the people and the bureaucratic oligarchy. There is no peaceful outcome for this crisis. No devil yet voluntarily cut off his own claws. The Soviet bureaucracy will not give up its positions without a fight. The development leads obviously to the road of revolution.[131]

This revolution, however, would be a *political*, not a social, one; its purpose would be to bring down a political regime not a social system:

It is not a question this time of changing the economic foundations of society, of replacing certain forms of property with other forms. History has known elsewhere not only social revolutions which substituted the bourgeois for the feudal regime, but also political revolutions which, without destroying the economic foundations of society, swept out an old ruling upper crust (1830 and 1848 in France, February 1917 in Russia, etc.). The overthrow of the Bonapartist caste will, of course, have deep social consequences, but in itself it will be confined within the limits of political revolution.[132]

Nevertheless, the changes Trotsky envisaged as emanating from this political revolution were, indeed, of a 'deep social' significance. In the penultimate paragraph of *The Revolution Betrayed* Trotsky seemed almost carried away by the vision of a new, democratic Soviet society:

It is not a question of substituting one ruling clique for another, but of changing the very methods of administering the economy and guiding the culture of the country. Bureaucratic autocracy must give place

---

[131] *The Revolution Betrayed*, p. 287. Conscious of the irony of the Russian proletariat having to make a revolution for the second time in less than twenty years, Trotsky added (ibid., p. 289): 'The proletariat of a backward country was fated to accomplish the first socialist revolution. For this historic privilege, it must, according to all evidence, pay with a second supplementary revolution—against bureaucratic absolutism.'
[132] Ibid., p. 288.

to Soviet democracy. A restoration of the right of criticism, and a genuine freedom of elections, are necessary conditions for the further development of the country. This assumes a revival of freedom of Soviet parties, beginning with the party of Bolsheviks, and a resurrection of the trade unions. The bringing of democracy into industry means a radical revision of plans in the interests of the toilers. Free discussion of economic problems will decrease the overhead expense of bureaucratic mistakes and zigzags. Expensive playthings—palaces of the Soviets, new theatres, show-off subways—will be crowded out in favour of workers' dwellings. 'Bourgois norms of distribution' will be confined within the limits of strict necessity, and, in step with the growth of social wealth, will give way to socialist equality. Ranks will be immediately abolished. The tinsel of decorations will go into the melting pot. The youth will receive the opportunity to breathe freely, criticize, make mistakes, and grow-up. Science and art will be freed of their chains. And, finally, foreign policy will return to the tradition of revolutionary internationalism.[133]

Even here, Trotsky was not prepared to contemplate the kind of reforms which would usher in an era of complete political democracy—the 'freedom of elections' and freedom of parties meant for him the 'freedom of Soviet parties' only. Nor was he sufficiently optimistic to think that 'bourgeois norms of distribution' could be entirely abolished. Nevertheless, assuming Trotsky's intentions were genuine, this was a radical programme of change and one which could leave no doubt, in the light of its contrast with the existing Soviet reality, about its revolutionary implications.

The concept of a political revolution seemed logical from the point of view of Trotsky's critique of Stalinism. He had, after all, argued that Stalinism constituted not the abolition of the October Revolution, but its subservience to a political dictatorship, to a vast personal and bureaucratic power structure which, without liquidating the foundations of a socialist society, atrophied them. It was necessary, therefore, to change not so much the basis of the social structure as the form of political rule; what was needed was a revolution which would restore the balance between politics and society and, in the process, do away with the 'autonomy of politics' rampant under Stalin.

But such distinctions between the political and the social in the Soviet Union were soon to become irrelevant nuances as

[133] Ibid., pp. 289–90.

far as a part of Trotsky's retinue of followers was concerned. Even as the Fourth International was being formed, many 'Trotskyists' were already having second thoughts about their leader's interpretation of Soviet developments. For some of them, Trotsky now appeared to be involved, at best, in theoretical sophistications and, at worst, in a hopeless exercise to salvage what was left of the original Soviet experiment. In particular, the distinction which Trotsky attempted to draw between the Soviet Union and Stalinism, as if the two were independent entities, and as if the condemnation of the latter did not mean casting aspersions on the former, seemed to some of his followers to constitute a misreading of what had actually occurred in the Soviet Union. In fact, they were now beginning to believe, Stalin, the bureaucracy and the terror had to be related integrally to the whole phenomenon of the October Revolution. Far from signifying a new advance in human history, that Revolution now emerged for them as the begetter of a typically twentieth-century monstrosity which, in their view, was at the same time yet another variation on the age-old theme of the 'master-slave' society. Thus, by 1939, among 'Trotskyists', a new view of the Soviet Union began to take hold, and compete with that of Trotsky.[134] It was most notable among the American 'Trotskyists', who constituted the largest and most important branch of the Fourth International.[135] Its effect was to isolate Trotsky even further and to render the Fourth International even more impotent than it had been to start with.

Yet Trotsky himself, in spite of the characteristically energetic campaign which he was to conduct in the last year of his life against this new 'heresy', was not entirely immune to

[134] Many of Trotsky's most loyal followers, among them Max Eastman and Victor Serge, had already begun to desert him before 1939, as a result of personal conflicts, or over such issues as Trotsky's role, now recalled, in the suppression of the Kronstadt revolt of 1921. The most complete account of Trotsky's always uneasy relationships with his followers is in Deutscher's *The Prophet Outcast* which relies, for this subject in particular, on correspondence in the closed section of the Trotsky Archives. For the views of one ex-Trotskyist, see Victor Serge, *Mémoires d'un révolutionnaire* (Paris, 1951).
[135] For an account of the American movement, by one of its leaders who remained loyal to Trotsky, see James Cannon, *The History of American Trotskyism* (New York, 1944). For the manner in which American Trotskyists, with Trotsky's blessings, infiltrated and exploited—only to be finally expelled from—the Socialist Party of America (the party founded by Eugene Debs and, at the time, led by Norman Thomas), see M. S. Venkataramani, 'Leon Trotsky's Adventure in American Radical Politics, 1935–37', *International Review of Social History*, IX, 1964, part 1, pp. 1–46.

'second thoughts' and reconsiderations. Though still convinced that the Soviet Union exhibited redeeming features, in 1939, for the first time, he seriously took into account an alternative course of Soviet development which, until then, had hardly occurred to him. While this reconsideration of the nature of the Soviet Union was concerned, for him, with the realm of the possible only, and not the inevitable or even highly probable, and though he would immediately deny its significance, it brought him as near as he ever came to entertaining doubts about the October Revolution itself.

(b) *Bureaucratic Collectivism?*

Trotsky's readiness, in the last resort, to defend the Soviet Union against wholesale condemnation had been based on the supposition that, in spite of political and social degeneration, the fundamental economic structure of a socialist-oriented society had been preserved even by Stalin. Thus if for no other reason than that the means of production had been nationalized and kept out of the reach of private hands, the Soviet Union, in Trotsky's view, remained a potentially 'progressive' society and, in essence, *different* from the capitalist world. The bureaucracy, though undermining socialism, was in spite of itself unable to forsake the socialist foundations of Soviet society; however elementary these foundations, they were sufficient to mark them off from capitalism, including 'state capitalism'. Of course, the danger persisted that Stalinism would in the end destroy even these foundations. In that case there would be a return, in Trotsky's view, to the one possible alternative, bourgeois forms of property. Thus Trotsky insisted that the twentieth century continued to offer a choice between, and to be a battleground for, two options only: either capitalism or socialism.

Yet it is precisely this line of thinking, so markedly confined to Marxist categories, which, at the end of the 1930s, began to be widely questioned. Some of Trotsky's followers, influenced in part by Trotsky's own critique of the Soviet Union, and unable to come to terms with Stalinism, could no longer accept the standard Marxist framework for analysis. Was the Soviet Union really different, they asked, or was it actually the paradigm of a new phenomenon, the bureaucratized society, which was evolving everywhere and throwing into doubt the old capi-talist–socialist division of the world? Was the bureaucracy still, as the Marxist view would have it, in the service of one class or another, or had it become the new ruling class of twentieth-century society, no less—perhaps more—so in the Soviet Union than elsewhere?

One work in particular, entitled *La Bureaucratisation du monde*,[136] and written by an Italian identifying himself only as Bruno R., was symptomatic of the changing attitude amongst Trotsky's sympathizers towards the Soviet Union, and towards the bureaucratic phenomenon in general. Bruno R., whose full name was Bruno Rizzi, had been a former Italian Communist —and, it was then believed, an ex-Trotskyist—of no particular repute, though he had met Trotsky and discussed his ideas with him.[137] His book, which appeared in 1939, was written in a stilted, Italicized French and consisted, for the most part, of ideas which had already been voiced elsewhere in different forms.[138] But it brought these ideas together in one central thesis which had the attraction and the virtue of its simplicity. Even then it may have been less noticed than it was, were it not for

---

[136] Paris, 1939. Published by Hachette, this book is now virtually a collector's item.

[137] Rizzi had previously written one other work, in Italian, *Dove va L'URSS*, published in Milan in 1937, which apparently contained the kernel of his later, 1939, book. After the publication of the latter, Rizzi seems to have been virtually forgotten. But nearly twenty years later there appeared an article about him in the French journal *Le Contrat Social* which subsequently gave rise to a correspondence—including a letter from Rizzi himself—revealing some piquant details about his views and political tendencies (he considered capitalism to be a Jewish conspiracy and he had not been unsympathetic to Italian Fascism). See Georges Henein, 'Bruno R. et la "Nouvelle Classe"', *Le Contrat Social* (Nov. 1958), pp. 365–8 and the same journal, Jan. 1959, pp. 60–1, and Mar. 1959, pp. 119–21. See also Daniel Bell, 'The Strange Tale of Bruno R.', in *The New Leader*, 28 Sept. 1959, pp. 19–20 and Dwight Macdonald's letter in the same journal, 16 Nov. 1959, p. 29. The best and, it seems, almost the only study of Rizzi's ideas, is an article by James M. Fenwick, 'The Mysterious Bruno R.', in *New International* (Sept. 1948).

[138] To trace the origins of the idea of the bureaucracy as a 'new ruling class' one can go back to, for instance, Bakunin who once predicted, and warned, that Marx's concept of the 'dictatorship of the proletariat' would lead to nothing more than the conversion of the masses into 'industrial and agricultural armies under the direct command of the State engineers who will constitute the new privileged scientific-political class'. (*The Political Philosophy of Bakunin*, edited by G. P. Maximoff, New York and London, 1964, p. 289.) Max Nomad's article 'White Collars and Horny Hands', in *Modern Quarterly* (Autumn 1932), attributes the idea to the Polish anarcho-syndicalist Waclaw Machajski, especially to his 1899 work *The Evolution of Social Democracy*. (Trotsky, in-cidentally, noted in *Moya Zhizn*, I, pp. 153–4, that during his first exile in Siberia, in 1900, he had come across some essays by Machajski, but reading them he had

the fact that Trotsky himself was so impressed—or rather felt himself so challenged—by its propositions, that he devoted one long and major article directly to it,[139] and in not a few others indirectly argued with the issues raised by Rizzi's book.

The main thesis of *La Bureaucratisation du monde* may be easily summarized, especially as shortly afterwards a work was to appear which did much to popularize a similar thesis.[140] In Rizzi's view, the Marxist prediction that capitalism would be superseded by socialism had been proven to be false, by virtue of developments both in the Soviet Union and in the West. Not socialism but a new form of bureaucratic rule was emerging everywhere and was embodied in such, ostensibly different, political forms as Stalinism, Fascism and even Roosevelt's New Dealism. What they all had in common, according to Rizzi, was a bureaucratic élite determined to rationalize the organization of society, and make economic production and distribution more efficient. In fact, Rizzi thought, this élite had largely succeeded in these objectives, and this was the reason why it was able to push the less efficient capitalism and its entrepreneurs aside, and create for itself a monopoly of political power. Against the view that the bureaucracy could not be a class since it did not own the means of production, Rizzi argued that in effect it was a possessing class since it had complete control of the state and, through it, of the economy; while it was not legally the owner of state property, it reaped its benefits by supervising the distribution of the profits accruing from production. The difference between the new élite and the possessing classes

---

acquired a 'powerful inoculation against anarchism, a theory very sweeping in its verbal negations but lifeless and cowardly in its practical conclusions'.) From a different perspective, the writings of Pareto, Mosca and Michels may be seen as having contributed to the later crystallization of the idea. In Trotskyist circles the idea was raised before Rizzi by the Frenchman Yvan Craipeau (see *Quatrième Internationale*, June 1938), and the Yugoslov Anton Ciliga (see his *Au Pays du grand mensonge*, Paris, 1937). As an editorial note in *Le Contrat Social* (Mar. 1959, p. 121) points out, to trace the full history of the idea would make for a 'good thesis subject for a future doctorate in the social sciences'!

[139] This is the article, to be discussed presently, 'The U.S.S.R. in War'. All subsequent references are to the English version which was included in the posthumous collection of letters and articles—written by Trotsky during 1939 and 1940—under the title *In Defence of Marxism* (New York, 1942). The Russian original, under the title 'SSSR v voine', appeared in *Byulleten Oppozitsii* (Aug.–Sept.–Oct. 1939), pp. 1–9.
[140] This was, of course, James Burnham's *The Managerial Revolution*.

of the past was that the former prospered not as competing individuals but as a collective unit. Thus, Rizzi declared, the new
era in world social development was that of 'bureaucratic collectivism'. This was neither a temporary development nor accidental; it would persist for an indefinite period, and it was as
socially and historically rooted as capitalism had been in its own
time. Though Rizzi believed that eventually 'bureaucratic collectivism' would give way to socialism, for the time being it had
nothing in common with the latter. On the contrary, it was
a system in which the workers were reduced to virtual slavery,
exploited and regimented by the bureaucracy in the name of
economic efficiency and complete social control. The Soviet
Union—and Hitler's Germany and Mussolini's Italy as well—
amply demonstrated, in Rizzi's view, the truth of this analysis.[141] It was neither a workers' state nor even a 'degenerated
workers' state' but a society in which the workers were under
the tutelage of the ruling bureaucracy. And the bureaucratization of the Soviet Union had marked merely the first stage in
the 'bureaucratization of the world' as a whole.[142]

What seemed to impress Trotsky about the thesis of 'bureaucratic collectivism' was that it was, in his view, an attempt at
a 'major historical generalization'[143] and, as such, a theoretical
challenge to be seriously dealt with. His reply to the thesis—
in his article 'The U.S.S.R. in War'—was, ostensibly, a taking
up of this challenge and a reaffirmation of his own stand. But
the change in Trotsky's thinking about the Soviet Union, and
his open-mindedness about Rizzi's analysis, were apparent
throughout. Though protesting that he saw no reason to alter

---

[141] Because Stalin, Hitler, and Mussolini each stood, in Rizzi's view, at the head of
a system of 'bureaucratic collectivism', a Soviet–Fascist alliance, he believed, would
be a logical development.

[142] From his analysis it clearly emerges that Rizzi welcomed 'bureaucratic collectivism'
as much for the reason that it was doing away with capitalism as that it would prepare
the way for socialism. It was, in any case, a historically necessary development in his
view. This attitude perhaps explains why some socialists and Communists—Henri de
Man in Belgium and Jacques Doriot in France are only two examples—having reached
a similar conclusion found it logical to support a victory over Europe by Hitler: such
a victory, they believed, was an essential pre-condition for the collapse of capitalism.
James Burnham, who abandoned socialism, but not his dislike for modern capitalism,
also looked forward to, and predicted, a German victory (see in particular chapter
15 of *The Managerial Revolution*, Penguin edition, 1962).

[143] 'The U.S.S.R. in War', op. cit., p. 10. This article, which is Trotsky's main reply
to Rizzi, was written on 25 Sept. 1939.

his known views, he in fact explicitly abandoned the old 'capitalist or socialist' alternative when, contemplating the future of the Soviet Union, he declared:

The historical alternative, carried to the end, is as follows: either the Stalin regime is an abhorrent relapse in the process of transforming bourgeois society into a socialist society, or the Stalin regime is the first stage of a new exploiting society. If the second prognosis proves to be correct, then, of course, the bureaucracy will become a new exploiting class. However onerous the second perspective may be, if the world proletariat should actually prove incapable of fulfilling the mission placed upon it by the course of development, nothing else would remain except openly to recognize that the socialist programme, based on the internal contradictions of capitalist society, ended as a Utopia. It is self-evident that a new 'minimum' programme would be required—for the defence of the interests of the slaves of the totalitarian bureaucratic society.[144]

And, in a later passage, he again contemplated the once 'unthinkable', giving expression to a pessimistic frame of mind such as had never before appeared in his writings:

Have we entered the epoch of social revolution and socialist society, or, on the contrary, the epoch of the declining society of totalitarian bureaucracy? ... It is absolutely self-evident that if the international proletariat, as a result of the experience of our entire epoch and the current new war, proves incapable of becoming the master of society, this would signify the foundering of all hope for a socialist revolution, for it is impossible to expect any other more favourable conditions for it ...[145]

There can be little doubt but that Trotsky's inveterate confidence in the future, which had sustained him throughout the worst periods of his life, was now intensely shaken. Stalin's complete and now virtually unchallenged mastery of the Soviet Union, the decline of the 'Left' and the rise of the 'Right' in

[144] Ibid., p. 9. Two weeks earlier he had written, in a similar vein: 'Either the Stalin state is a transitory formation, a deformation of a worker state in a backward and isolated country, or "bureaucratic collectivism" ... is a new social formation which is replacing capitalism throughout the world. Who chooses the second alternative admits, openly or silently, that all the revolutionary potentialities of the world proletariat are exhausted, that the socialist movement is bankrupt, and that the old capitalism is transforming itself into "bureaucratic collectivism" with a new exploiting class.' ('Letter to Cannon', 12 Sept. 1939, in *In Defence of Marxism*, pp. 1–2; written originally in English.)
[145] 'The U.S.S.R. in War', op. cit., p. 15.

Europe, the outbreak of war and the Soviet–German pact—
all these must have impressed themselves upon him as unmistakable signs that the future did not necessarily belong to the
'workers of the world'. And, indeed, for the first time he was
now prepared to countenance the possibility that a socialist
future was not the only alternative to capitalism; this is clearly
evident from the passages quoted above, but even more striking
is the following:

> If ... the present war will provoke not revolution but a decline of
> the proletariat, then there remains another alternative: the further
> decay of monopoly capitalism, its further fusion with the state and
> the replacement of democracy wherever it still remained by a totali-
> tarian regime ... an analogous result might occur in the event that
> the proletariat of advanced capitalist countries, having conquered
> power, should prove incapable of holding it and surrender it, as in
> the U.S.S.R., to a privileged bureaucracy. Then we would be com-
> pelled to acknowledge that the reason for the bureaucratic relapse
> is rooted not in the backwardness of the country and not in the im-
> perialist environment but in the congenital incapacity of the prole-
> tariat to become a ruling class. Then it would be necessary in retro-
> spect to establish that in its fundamental traits the present U.S.S.R.
> was the precursor of a new exploiting regime on an international
> scale.[146]

Trotsky must have been aware, in writing this, that it
amounted in effect to the admission that Marxist theory—regarding the evolution of modern society in general, and the role
of the proletariat in particular—might be proven to have been
totally in error. Moreover, the passage could be read as implying that the true nature of the Soviet Union—a 'degenerated
workers' state' or a new, bureaucratic, social order—was still
in the balance: the 'temporary' character of Stalinism now
emerged, in Trotsky's view, as certainly no longer a foregone
conclusion, as he had previously always argued. And a society
which was neither capitalist nor socialist appeared to be, after
all, a distinct possibility. In short, it was almost as if Trotsky
were suspending final theoretical judgement on these issues until events themselves decided one way or another.[147]

---

[146] Ibid., p. 9.
[147] Trotsky's equivocation on these issues in 1939 is in striking contrast with two major
articles, dealing with the same questions, written by him in November 1937: 'Once

'The U.S.S.R. in War' marked, indeed, a major departure for Trotsky from his long-held views on the Soviet Union, and some of his American followers were quick to notice this. They had, in any case, reached a similar though more extremely stated position independently, and they now pounced upon Trotsky to draw the necessary conclusions. James Burnham, for instance, the most extreme among the 'disillusioned' Trotskyists, declared that developments in the Soviet Union and elsewhere had proven Marxism to be bankrupt; by May 1940 he had not only left the Trotskyist movement but adopted an explicitly anti-Marxist stand.[148] Less volatile and more ideologically stable Trotskyists, however, could also no longer abide the 'defence of the Soviet Union'; among these was Max Shachtman, to whom Trotsky felt particularly close, and who had been a devoted follower since 1929, but who now looked upon the Soviet Union as a bureaucratic monster with imperialist policies and designs indistinguishable from those of the West.[149] The Soviet Union's invasions of Poland and Finland exacerbated, of course, the disillusionment. The upshot of all this was

---

Again: The U.S.S.R. and Its Defence', Archives T4229, 4230 published in *Fourth International*, July–Aug. 1951; and 'Nerabochee i neburzhuaznoe gosudarstvo?', *Byulleten Oppozitsii* (Feb. 1938), pp. 15–19. Here he was not prepared to entertain the slightest doubt about the correctness of his earlier prognoses.

[148] See Burnham's 'Science and Style: A Reply to Comrade Trotsky' and 'Letter of Resignation', published as appendices to Trotsky's *In Defence of Marxism*, pp. 187–206 and 207–11, as well as 'The Politics of Desperation' in *New International*, Mar. 1940. Burnham, of course, soon adopted a position on the opposite end of the political spectrum; besides *The Managerial Revolution*, see also his *The Machiavellians* (New York, 1943) and, among a spate of post-World War II, anti-Communist polemics, *The Coming Defeat of Communism* (New York, 1950).

[149] For Shachtman's views at the time of his break with Trotsky, see in particular his 'The Crisis of the American Party—An Open Letter to Trotsky' and 'The U.S.S.R. and the War', both in *New International*, Mar. 1940. See also the following works by Shachtman: *The Struggle for the New Course* (written in 1943) in Trotsky, *The New Course* (Ann Arbor, 1965); *The Bureaucratic Revolution: The Rise of the Stalinist State* (New York, 1962); '1939: Whither Russia?', in *Survey* (Apr. 1962), pp. 96–108. In the last-mentioned article, Shachtman argued that, in 'The U.S.S.R. in War', 'Trotsky turned a corner in his thinking so abruptly as to bring him into violent collision with the main pillars of the theory of Stalinism he had long and stoutly upheld'. Shachtman himself, in all his writings after 1939, propounded the 'bureaucratic collectivism' thesis about the Soviet Union. While Rizzi, however, believed that 'bureaucratic collectivism' was historically necessary, Shachtman attributed it to the misconceptions of Marxism and of its offspring, the October Revolution. Although he was eventually to abandon Trotskyism altogether, Shachtman, unlike Burnham, remained a socialist: in 1958 he joined Norman Thomas' Socialist Party.

that the Fourth International in general, and the American wing of it in particular, were left in shambles.[150]

Trotsky, however, despite the 'concessions' of his article, refused to accept the conclusions of a Shachtman, much less those of a Burnham. In a series of articles written between October 1939 and August 1940 he launched a counter-attack against those who were now abandoning the Soviet Union completely.[151] Although he admitted that his article, 'The U.S.S.R. in War', had, for the first time, taken seriously the 'theoretical possibility' of 'bureaucratic collectivism', he claimed that his position, nevertheless, remained unchanged, and that his speculations in print had been misunderstood.[152] True, Trotsky could point to the fact that his article had, in the end, apparently rejected Rizzi's theory of 'bureaucratic collectivism', and that it had not forsaken the future. Thus Trotsky had written:

Marxists do not have the slightest right ... to draw the conclusion that the proletariat has forfeited its revolutionary possibilities and must renounce all aspirations to hegemony in an era immediately ahead. Twenty-five years in the scales of history [i.e. since 1914] ... weigh less than an hour in the life of man ... In the years of darkest Russian reaction (1907 to 1917) we took as our starting point those revolutionary possibilities which were revealed by the Russian proletariat in 1905. In the years of world reaction we must proceed from those possibilities which the Russian proletariat revealed in 1917 ... Our road is not to be changed. We steer our course toward the world revolution and by virtue of this very fact toward the regeneration of the U.S.S.R. as a workers' state.[153]

---

[150] The American Trotskyists (the Socialist Workers' Party) split into a 'majority', led by James Cannon and loyal to Trotsky, and a 'minority', led by Burnham and Shachtman. In April 1940 the 'minority' set up a separate organization (the Workers' Party) which, however, itself split when Burnham, declaring that he was no longer a Marxist, declined to join it. The 'majority' view of the split is presented in James Cannon, *The Struggle for a Proletarian Party* (New York, 1943). For an account of internal controversies by an 'ex-Trotskyist', see Dwight Macdonald, *Memoirs of a Revolutionist* (New York, 1958).
[151] The articles comprise the volume *In Defence of Marxism*.
[152] *In Defence of Marxism*, p. 30.
[153] 'The U.S.S.R. in War', op. cit., p. 15. Elsewhere (pp. 8–9) in this article, Trotsky stated that he 'firmly' believed that the world war would 'provoke ... a proletarian revolution' which 'must inevitably lead to the overthrow of the bureaucracy in the U.S.S.R. and the regeneration of Soviet democracy on a far higher economic and cultural basis than in 1918'. And in the previously quoted 'Letter to Cannon' he wrote that now, in view of the war, 'the perspective of the socialist revolution becomes an imminent reality'.

Yet just as the rejection of Rizzi's thesis sounded merely per-functory[154] in the light of the over-all theme of his article, so this expression of confidence in the future had the unmistakable ring of rhetoric based on wishful thinking. He continued, it is true, to argue cogently and passionately against Burnham, Shachtman and others;[155] he fought against the split among his American followers, and sought to preserve his traditional line of thought and action;[156] and he persisted in defending the Soviet Union 'unconditionally' against the 'menace' of Western 'imperialism',[157] going so far as to justify the invasions of Poland and Finland.[158] But that faith in the inevitable flow of history which had characterized his struggles in the past had quite clearly been jolted. The future was no longer certain; though one should persevere in striving for the best, one should also be prepared for the worst. And the worst meant nothing less than the 'eclipse of civilization' and a 'relapse into barbar-ism'.[159] It would be no exaggeration to say, consequently, that Trotsky's commitment to socialism assumed in 1939 a virtually moral, personal character. If in the past he had no doubts about the tide of history, now he contemplated a future lying in ruins; but the prospect that socialism would be devastated, and that the October Revolution would consequently emerge as an illu-sory cause, would not deter him. He, at least, would remain a socialist, out of moral conviction if not out of 'scientific' cer-tainty: though it could no longer be said to be inevitable, social-ism was still an ideal worth pursuing. 'The contradiction', he wrote, 'between the concrete fact and the norm constrains us not to reject the norm but, on the contrary, to fight for it by

---

[154] Rizzi's thesis, he had written (ibid., pp. 10–11 and 13–16), was overly schematic and, moreover, assumed that 'bureaucratic collectivism' was a fact in the Soviet Union rather than a possibility.

[155] Noting that even after breaking with him, Shachtman continued calling himself a 'Trotskyist', Trotsky remarked: 'If *this* be Trotskyism then I at least am no Trotskyist. With the present ideas of Shachtman, not to mention Burnham, I have nothing in common.' (*In Defence of Marxism*, p. 168.)

[156] See his re-affirmation of Marxism and of Marxist method in *In Defence of Marxism*, pp. 48ff., 72ff., and 116ff.

[157] *In Defence of Marxism*, p. 29.

[158] See, for example, ibid., pp. 56–9 and 130–7. The gist of his justification for the invasions was that they were necessary if the Soviet Union was to fortify itself for the eventual and inevitable confrontation with Germany in particular, and the West in general.

[159] 'The U.S.S.R. in War', op. cit., pp. 9 and 11.

means of the revolutionary road.'[160] By choice, if not by necessity, he would remain true to his revolutionary past and to the cause, however, hopeless it might now appear, of the workers of the world, threatened to become the 'slaves of the totalitarian bureaucratic society'. This was the essence, therefore, of his final reaffirmation of allegiance to an ideal first declared and embraced forty years previously.[161]

Conclusion: The Bureaucratic Revolution—Backwardness, Bolshevism, Totalitarianism

In spite of the concessions, both explicit and implicit, which he made in his article 'The U.S.S.R. in War', Trotsky remained an adamant, albeit qualified, 'defender' of the Soviet Union. Was this so irrational? It has sometimes been suggested that Trotsky's refusal, even in the last year of his life, to make a break with this loyalty to the Soviet Union was rooted primarily in psychological factors: how could he, it has been argued, bring himself to renegue on the Soviet Union when that, in effect, would have meant becoming an apostate to his own past? According to this psychological interpretation, Trotsky's defence of the Soviet Union was really an unconscious effort to salvage his honour and conscience. Be that as it may—and Trotsky himself laughed off 'psychoanalytical' explanations[162]

---

[160] Ibid., p. 3.

[161] See, in this connection, George Lichtheim's perceptive essay, 'Reflections on Trotsky', in his *The Concept of Ideology* (New York, 1967), pp. 204–24. Lichtheim, noting that Trotsky could not bring himself to break completely with his past as did some of his followers, concludes nevertheless (p. 224): 'Still it remains that by 1940 Trotsky had wrung from himself the admission that a long, dark, totalitarian night seemed about to precede the dawn, and that the "slaves" would need someone to defend them. Whatever honour Communism still retains was saved by its arch-heresiarch.' Even Deutscher, who treats the proponents of the 'bureaucratic collectivism' thesis and, in general, all those who broke with Trotsky in 1939–40, with ill-concealed disdain, acknowledges that Trotsky's position had radically changed and that his commitment to Marxism was now more moral than 'scientific'; see *The Prophet Outcast*, pp. 464–9.

[162] In *In Defence of Marxism*, p. 24, he wrote: 'Certain comrades, or former comrades ... attempt to explain my personal estimate of the Soviet state psychoanalytically. "Since Trotsky participated in the Russian Revolution, it is difficult for him to lay aside the idea of the workers' state inasmuch as he would have to renounce his whole life's cause", etc. I think that the old Freud, who was very perspicacious, would have cuffed the years of psychoanalysts of this ilk a little. Naturally, I would never risk taking such action myself. Nevertheless I dare assure my critics that subjectivity and sentimentality are not on my side but on theirs.'

(though this in itself does not, of course, invalidate them)—this is not the only approach possible, nor even the most convincing, to understanding Trotsky's intransigence. The trouble with the psychological approach is not so much its speculative character as its assumption that Trotsky's position was so incongruous, irrational, and perverse as to defy a non-psychological explanation. In fact, however, Trotsky's loyalty to the Soviet Union was perfectly rational and consistent, given his own assumptions about the character and meaning of the October Revolution. And it is when one examines his evaluation of Stalinism in the light of these assumptions that one best understands the logic of his position as well as the source of his misconceptions about the nature of the Stalin phenomenon. Trotsky's position does not, thereby, emerge any less misconstrued, but it can be seen as the consequence, not of personal motives, nor even of this or that specific misjudgement, but of his over-all conception of the Russian Revolution. In a sense, therefore, this approach involves a more far-reaching critique of Trotsky.[163]

In August 1937 Trotsky wrote an essay entitled 'Stalinism and Bolshevism'[164] in which he attempted to show how utterly at odds with each other these two 'isms' were. The essay contains nothing that Trotsky had not already argued elsewhere in one form or another. But it is a concise and direct confrontation with a central issue, indicated by the title, and, inadvertently and summarily, it reveals the manner in which since 1917 Trotsky had misconceived the meaning of the Bolshevik capture of power.

At one time, as in his 1903-4 attack on Lenin and Bolshevism, Trotsky believed that a revolution was justified only when there was a correspondence between objective social conditions and the revolutionary consciousness of the masses. In the absence of such a correspondence, a revolutionary party acting in the name of the masses was no more than a conspiracy. In 1917, however, he reassessed Lenin's position and adopted the view

---

[163] This approach has the added advantage of taking his written work at face value, and not as an unconscious camouflage for some inner psychological motives; that is, it avoids engaging in psychological reductionism and remains within the realm of the rational discussion about the validity of theories and ideas.

[164] 'Stalinizm i bolshevizm', in *Byulleten Oppozitsii* (Sept.–Oct. 1937), pp. 4–20.

that although mass support was ultimately essential, a revolution was justified when there was a correspondence between objective social conditions and the revolutionary consciousness of the *party*, acting as the 'vanguard'.[165] Thereafter, he never seriously considered the possibility that the Bolsheviks in 1917 may have acted largely independently, and ran ahead, of both the masses and the objective social conditions prevailing in Russian society at the time; that, in other words, there was no correspondence between any two of the three variables, or between the necessary and sufficient justifying conditions for social revolution. Thus, in this essay of 1937, as throughout his post-1917 writings, the Bolshevik triumph twenty years earlier is taken for granted as the logical and necessary result of, so to speak, Russian history. In the essay he extolled the vanguard role of the Bolsheviks in inserting themselves into the flow of events and thereby bringing to fruition the course of history.[166] And while Bolshevism, he admitted, was only one factor, the 'conscious', subjective one, in making possible the Revolution, it was at one with the 'decisive factor', namely the objective one—deriving from the 'existing basis of productive forces'— the 'class struggle'.[167] The point of all this for Trotsky was, of course, that Russia in 1917 had been ripe for Marxism–Bolshevism.

Yet, curiously, when he turned to consider how it was that Bolshevism, in spite of its being the 'will' of Russian history, was eventually succeeded by Stalinism—which Trotsky saw as the virtual antithesis of Bolshevism—he took refuge in very different factors. Stalinism was seen as the consequence of a 'heritage of oppression, misery and ignorance', of the 'cultural level of the country, the social composition of the population, the pressure of a barbaric past, and of a no less barbaric world imperialism'.[168] This was clearly meant to imply that Bolshevism and Stalinism belonged to two different worlds, that the former represented the progressive forces of Russian society,

---

[165] See chapter 6, above. The ideal situation, of a correspondence between conditions, masses, and party, seemed to Trotsky a purely mechanical reconstruction or view of reality, and therefore never reproducible *in* reality.

[166] Thus he wrote: 'No one has either shown in practice or tried to explain articulately on paper how the proletariat can seize power without the political leadership of a party that knows what it wants.' ('Stalinizm i bolshevizm', op. cit., p. 14.)

[167] Ibid., p. 8.   [168] Ibid., p. 7.

and the latter the backward ones, and that in the 'dialectical' confrontation between the two it was Stalinism, or backwardness, which persevered.

As against this, one can, of course, raise the obvious question: if Bolshevism was really the 'will' of Russian history in 1917, why did it not maintain itself? The logical answer would seem to be that it was not the 'will' of history; or, one could argue, whether it was or was not the 'will', it in fact did maintain itself, though in an extreme form, as Stalinism. But leaving aside the matter of simple logic, it is the historical character of Bolshevism which needs to be assessed. Its triumph in Russia, and later —though under different names—in other largely non-capitalist societies, has long suggested that a relationship should be looked for not only between Marxism as such and backward societies, but between Bolshevism and backwardness.[169] It is to the credit of Trotsky that already in 1905 he was able to explain why social forces and movements other than those of Russian Social Democracy were too weak to bring down and replace the Tsarist autocracy and why, moreover, the Social Democratic movement was strategically so well placed. In 1917 he also recognized the importance which must be attributed to party organization and leadership if the movement were finally to attain power. What he was never able fully to perceive was the extent to which not only the seizure of power, but the subsequent survival as well of a Bolshevik government, were made possible by the inchoate character of the population, by the absence of strong and organized class traditions and interests, by the political vacuum created immediately with the fall of the autocracy. Politics, as is known, abhors a vacuum, and the Bolshevik genius, in 1917 and thereafter, for political organization and decisiveness was, not unnaturally, rewarded. Backwardness, understood in this sense as a condition of insufficient social differentiation and political consciousness, posed, as Trotsky feared, the permanent danger of undermining whatever prospects Bolshevism had of introducing socialist measures and institutions in Russia; but without this backwardness, Bolshev-

---

[169] Obviously the Communist movements in China and in other backward societies were not merely carbon copies of Bolshevism; but the influence of Lenin and the adoption of Bolshevik principles of organization and tactics were crucial factors in their success.

ism itself would either not have arisen or, at the very least, would not have succeeded in seizing and holding power.

In his 1937 essay Trotsky rejected entirely the contention that Stalinism was rooted in the Bolshevik tradition. Yet it is a fact that that which characterized Stalinism—rule from above and independently of the masses—was also characteristic of Lenin's regime. That it was also characteristic of the Tsarist autocracy merely accentuates the pervasiveness of the Russian political tradition deriving from the poverty of social institutions and of economic foundations—and the extent to which Bolshevism inherited this reality. Unlike Tsarism, however, Bolshevism was in principle committed to popular legitimacy; and, again unlike Tsarism, it was dedicated to revolutionary change. Yet to the extent that social and economic changes, not to speak of political ones, were already embarked upon during Lenin's lifetime, they were introduced from above and, if necessary, through coercion. Could it have been otherwise in a society which was, in fact, neither ripe for, nor even clearly aware of the meaning of, socialist change? Bolshevism responded to the lack of a political culture in Russia, to the poverty of ideological consciousness, and to the disorganization of social and economic life, by perfecting rule in accordance with the principle of the 'autonomy of politics', that is, political power as a self-sufficient instrument of social change. It is this principle which Trotsky so perceptively analysed as characteristic of Stalinism. That it was already a central feature of Lenin's rule, that the dictatorship of the party and of the institutions of coercion were established at a time when Trotsky himself shared the helms of power, appeared to Trotsky to reflect only temporary exigencies.[170] But these exigencies, as Trotsky recognized in his grasp of economic and social problems, grew merely more intense with the passing of time.

If we assume, therefore, that Russian society could be transformed radically only through the political determination and decree of its ruling élite, that, moreover, its resources, both material and human, were so impoverished, and of such quality, as to preclude the active and intelligent participation

---

[170] In 'Stalinizm i bolshevizm', p. 15, he again justified the dictatorship of the party under Lenin by pleading the danger of counter-revolution, a plea which, by the same logic, Stalin too could employ.

of any significant sector of the population in the reconstruction, much less the modernization, of the economic structure, and that, finally, such reconstruction depended on virtually complete economic control and planning, it is hardly surprising that the regime should sooner or later become extensively bureaucratized. In his autobiography and elsewhere Trotsky made much of a conversation he had with Lenin in 1922—shortly before the latter suffered his second, this time fatal, breakdown in health—in which the subject of 'bureaucratism' was raised.[171] According to Trotsky, Lenin was not only worried by the bureaucratic danger but 'appalled' by the fact that it had already begun to materialize; [172] moreover, Lenin agreed that it had infested not only state institutions but the party as well, and he offered to form a 'bloc' with Trotsky 'against bureaucracy in general, and against the Organizational Bureau [of the party] in particular'.[173] Be that as it may, it would be somewhat far-fatched to believe that bureaucratism was a phenomenon which could be eliminated without reverting to conditions of virtual chaos or, alternatively, without perpetuating indefinitely the NEP period—neither of which were prospects that could have appealed to Lenin, much less to Trotsky. The more radical the economic measures adopted and the popular resistance to them, the more concentrated in fewer and fewer hands did political power have to become; and the more systematic and planned the politics, the more did their implementation and supervision have to be entrusted to a technical and administrative élite. Bureaucratization may therefore be seen as the direct function, one the one hand, of backwardness and scarcity and, on the other, of the primary and domineering role which state institutions had to assume, particularly if private enterprise were to be eliminated.[174] Moreover, it should be noted that aside from those conditions peculiar to Russian

---

[171] *Moya Zhizn*, II, pp. 215–16; see also *The Real Situation in Russia*, pp. 304–5.

[172] Trotsky quoted Lenin as saying: 'Yes, our bureaucratism is something monstrous.' (*Moya Zhizn*, II, p. 215.)

[173] Ibid., p. 216.

[174] Whatever the relative merits of a capitalist as against a nationalized (or socialized) economy, there can be no doubt about the less omnipotent role of bureaucracy in the former; Max Weber predicted this in 1917 when he wrote: '. . . let us assume that sometime in the future [private capitalism] will be done away with. What would be the practical result? . . . The abolition of private capitalism would simply mean that also

society which necessarily encouraged bureaucratic growth, the fundamental economic objective of the Soviet regime—industrialization—itself necessarily entailed the creation of bureaucratic bodies and procedures. In the light of the Western experience, no one in Russia could be unaware of the fact that the modern industrial state could not function without large, formal, and impersonal bureaucratic institutions. If this were so in capitalist economies, where the state supposedly refrained from large-scale intervention, how much more so would it be the case in a socialist economy where the state took upon itself the control and direction of the whole economy and, in particular, of the industrial sector? Neither Lenin, who in his *State and Revolution* had vastly underestimated the complexities of economic administration, nor Trotsky, who, though he did not underestimate them, frequently evaded the implications of the problem, could resolve the contradiction between their economic objectives and their socialist ideals.[175]

The Stalinist system represented, nevertheless, only in part the rule of bureaucracy; the latter was in fact subject to, and frequently decimated by, a ruler and an institution which stood largely outside the bureaucratic, formal framework. Stalin and the secret police leaned on the bureaucracy but were not so dependent on it—as Trotsky sometimes implied—as to preclude autonomy of action. Together, Stalin and the secret police contributed those elements which transformed the Soviet system into one of 'totalitarianism', using this term in its

the top *management* of the nationalized or socialized enterprises would become bureaucratic ... State bureaucracy would rule *alone* if private capitalism were eliminated. The private and public bureaucracies, which now work next to, and potentially against, each other and hence check one another to a degree, would be merged into a single hierarchy.' (Quoted in Daniel Bell, 'The Post-Industrial Society: The Evolution of an Idea', *Survey*, Spring 1971, footnote 66, pp. 140–1.)

[175] This feature of modern bureaucracy, i.e. its necessary and indispensable relationship to industrial society, as well as its rational character, was also first emphasized by Weber; see Max Weber, *The Theory of Social and Economic Organization* (Glencoe, Ill., 1947). Since Weber, of course, the literature on bureaucracy has become enormous, as well as characterized by manifold approaches and interpretations. For a general survey of the subject, see Martin Albrow, *Bureaucracy* (London, 1970). Particularly useful in understanding the origins and nature of the Soviet bureaucracy is Barrington Moore, Jr., *Soviet Politics—The Dilemma of Power* (New York, 1965). Robert Michels' well-known *Political Parties* (New York, 1962, first published 1915), which dwells on the bureaucratization of Marxist parties in general, is especially relevant in the context of the issue here discussed, namely, the relationship of Bolshevism to the Soviet bureaucracy.

descriptive, not emotive, sense. Trotsky, by making a distinction between the bureaucratic apparatus—the source of Thermidor for him—and the political one—Bonapartism—recognized the peculiar nature of modern totalitarian dictatorships which, though based on a vast bureaucratic edifice, are nevertheless not to be identified with it alone.[176] Yet here again he was reluctant to go beyond the period and person of Stalin for the origins of Soviet totalitarianism. In 'Stalinism and Bolshevism', as throughout his writings of the 1930s, we find him not only defending Lenin's rule as far more democratic and enlightened than that of Stalin, but also arguing that had Bolshevism—as against Stalinism—prevailed, totalitarianism would not have emerged, much less taken the excessive form it eventually did.[177] Thus he points to such factors as the primacy of the party, its openness to theoretical discourse and internal democracy, and its dedication to collective rule, as Leninist features totally alien to Stalin's regime.[178] One need not deny that there was a difference between Lenin's dictatorship and that of Stalin—in spite of Trotsky's obvious tendency to idealize the former—nor that a ruler other than Stalin may have been less zealous, certainly less psychopathic, in his pursuit of absolute power, to maintain that the two regimes were of the same pedigree: though their progeny differed, the difference was one of degree not of kind. Neither need one dismiss out of hand the relevance of Trotsky's claim that the 'degeneration' of Bolshevism, as of the Soviet regime, was a consequence also of the failure of the 'world revolution' to materialize, in order to argue that the over-all developments in the Soviet Union had a

[176] Among the numerous works dealing with the unique nature of totalitarianism, see in particular the following: Hannah Arendt, *The Origins of Totalitarianism* (New York, 1958); Raymond Aron, *Democracy and Totalitarianism* (London, 1968); Carl J. Friedrich and Zbigniew Brzezinski, *Totalitarian Dictatorship and Autocracy* (2nd, revised edition, New York, 1966); Erich Fromm, *The Fear of Freedom* (London, 1942); William Kornhauser, *The Politics of Mass Society* (London, 1960); Franz Neumann, *The Democratic and the Authoritarian State* (New York, 1964); Leonard Schapiro, *Totalitarianism* (London, 1972); and J. L. Talmon, *The Origins of Totalitarian Democracy* (London, 1952). What follows draws freely, though summarily, from these works.
[177] Ridiculing Norman Thomas, who had apparently written that the Soviet Union under Trotsky would have been no better than under Stalin, Trotsky remarked that it was not a question of personalities, but of the bureaucracy as against the proletariat, and if the latter were to prevail it would 'politically and morally regenerate the Soviet regime'. ('Stalinizm i bolshevizm', op. cit., p. 18.)
[178] 'Stalinizm i bolshevizm', pp. 15ff.

momentum of their own, largely irrespective of external factors—whatever the impact of the latter on this or that specific
policy—and that this momentum, for reasons outlined above,
was irrevocably pulling in the direction of a new form of political absolutism. Despite his perceptions about Stalin's totalitarianism, Trotsky's final misunderstanding of it was not unlike
his misunderstanding of the bureaucracy—he could not, or
would not, see that it was rooted not only in the conditions of
the October Revolution but in the very aspirations of the latter.

From an institutional point of view, the issue is surely not
whether Lenin was or was not more enlightened, or even more
tolerant than Stalin; the issue is the relationship of politics to
society—and so it is of direct relevance that under Lenin too
dictatorship and the one-party system were the cornerstone of
political legitimacy and action.[179] But, in any case, totalitarianism, whether of the left or of the right, is not a system of government which is sufficiently defined or explained by having
recourse to its institutional aspects only. Its uniqueness lies in
two additional features: the politicization of all areas of social
and individual life, and total economic mobilization, regimentation, and control of the population. In the Soviet Union
—as elsewhere—these features grew simultaneously out of
the critical nature of the economic and social problems, and
out of the radical manner in which they were to be resolved
by the revolutionary movement taking power. For this latter
purpose Marxism had to be transformed into a mass ideology
having two functions: providing a system of beliefs—and thus
solutions to problems—and acting in itself as a gravitating,
mobilizing force. From this, in turn, devolved the tradition of
ideological legitimization and exclusivity—so that while the
ideology could be adjusted or adapted to specific needs in practice, it always remained the criterion for pronouncing upon the
legitimacy of private and public behaviour.[180]

---

[179] For a detailed account of how Lenin set about destroying all opposition and creating
a monolithic party during 1917–22—and thus establishing the foundations and precedent for Stalin's autocracy—see Leonard Schapiro, *The Origin of the Communist Autocracy* (London, 1955).
[180] For a psychological interpretation of Bolshevik ideology and of the Bolshevik mind
and personality, see Nathan Leites, *A Study of Bolshevism* (Glencoe, Ill., 1953). On the
element of fanaticism in revolutionary movements, see Eric Hoffer, *The True Believer*
(New York, 1951).

The fanaticism usually associated with Soviet ideology during the Stalin period—and with Stalin himself—should not lead
to the conclusion that the Stalinist system was without its economic and social rationale, or that it was always 'dysfunctional'
from the point of view of the ultimate goals of Soviet society.
In so far as Stalin was determined to carry out a social and
economic revolution—and collectivization in itself constituted
such a revolution—total regimentation was a pre-requisite,
given the economic conditions, the unreliability of spontaneous
support and, in fact, the real and anticipated popular resistance. The role of the trials, the purges and the terror was crucial
in this connection—as an affirmation of legitimacy, a dis-
couragement of opposition, and a demonstration of potential
and actual power. Trials, purges and terror prevented peripheral focuses of political power from forming—in the party, the
army, and even the bureaucracy—and thus pulling in a direction other than that decreed by the economic revolution.[181] And
terror against the population as a whole had the additional purpose of creating and maintaining an 'atomized', mass society,
if not classless then as powerless, non-differentiated, and
homogeneous as possible. Though this did not exclude the
phenomenon of 'Stakhanovism' nor, as Trotsky sometimes
overemphasized, a system of favouritism and privileges for the
bureaucrats, the general tendency was towards underplaying
social differences—and not merely for reasons of Marxist
dogma—except in the sense of 'revolutionary' as against
'counter-revolutionary elements', terms general and vague
enough to be applied politically, not sociologically. As Trotsky
pointed out, the declaration—however absurd—in 1936 that
the Soviet Union was then a socialist society, had this purpose
of creating at least the semblance of unity and homogeneity.
Stalin's excesses cannot be explained rationally alone—that is,
by pointing to either aims or results—since the reign of terror
was also in many ways counter-productive, creating instability
and uncertainty, economic mismanagement and confusion,
and large-scale decimation of army officers, administrative
experts, and of the scientific, not to speak of the humanistic,

---

[181] For an analysis of Stalinist totalitarianism, see Robert C. Tucker, *The Soviet Political
Mind* (revised edition, London, 1972).

intelligentsia.[182] But the function of totalitarianism cannot be dismissed when considering the nature of Stalin's aims or successes. This is certainly not to justify Stalinism or Soviet totalitarianism but to see both in their historical context of backwardness, Bolshevism, and the bureaucratic revolution.

The fact that Trotsky, though raising some of these issues, did not bring them to a full conclusion, or join them together in this context, may explain the source of the many unsatisfactory interpretations in his otherwise trenchant assessment of the Stalinist period: directly or indirectly such interpretations derived from his failure to grasp Stalinism as part of a historical continuum stretching back to 1903, not 1924. Consider, for instance, Trotsky's obsession with Stalinism as a reincarnation of the French Thermidor—following, supposedly, upon the 'Jacobin' phase of Lenin. It is clear that if Lenin was a 'Jacobin' it was not in the sense in which Trotsky painted him—as a revolutionary concerned above all with ideological principles, even purity—but rather in the sense of a professional, élitist revolutionary prepared to exercise political power in a practical, concrete way, albeit to bring about radical change, but without undue concern for ideological or theoretical implications; this was surely the great strength of Lenin.[183] But was Stalin, in this latter sense, any less a 'Jacobin'? Surely it was Stalin who— for better or for worse—carried out a programme of fundamental, revolutionary change in the economic structure of Soviet society? How was it possible, then, when comparing Stalin's with Lenin's rule, to claim that the former constituted a period of retrenchment, stabilization and conservatism, those features which Trotsky identified with Thermidor? That he should make this claim shows how Trotsky's determination to place Stalin outside the Bolshevik tradition could lead to a common-sense absurdity.

In fact, of course, the absurdity was also the consequence of Trotsky's *idée fixe* concerning the nature of bureaucracy and the

---

[182] See in this connection (and in general on the 'indispensability' or otherwise of Stalin), Alec Nove, *Was Stalin Really Necessary?* (London, 1964).

[183] For the relationship between Lenin the thinker and Lenin the 'doer', and for many other aspects as well of Lenin's character and talents, see the collection of papers edited by Leonard Schapiro and Peter Reddaway, *Lenin: The Man, the Theorist, the Leader* (London, 1967).

character of Stalin. He believed that every bureaucracy is prepared to pursue only such policies as best conserve order and stability; and since Stalin had built his empire on the shoulders of the bureaucracy instead of those of the—revolutionary—party, his reign had to be conservative of not reactionary, regressive if not counter-revolutionary. This obviously underestimated the extent to which a bureaucracy, in the conditions of Soviet society, could be mobilized for, and could see its interests bound up with, radical change leading to rationalized, modern, and efficient economic arrangements, whether or not these were finally achieved.[184] But Trotsky also underestimated the political, non-bureaucratic mentality of Stalin himself. Though accumulating his power through organizational work, he was not himself a prisoner of the organization.[185] Trotsky partly recognized this by identifying Stalin's rule as Bonapartist in character; yet the image of Stalin as embodying the bureaucratic and thus non-revolutionary personality persisted in his analysis. And this, in turn, led him to underestimate the extent to which Stalin remained independent of the bureaucracy, using it but ruling through less formal, more personal instruments of power. The Thermidorian analogy was out of place indeed, and Trotsky's uneasy modifications of it were a reflection of the difficulties of adapting Soviet reality to the French model.[186]

There was much that was out of place also in Trotsky's obsession with the Soviet Union as a workers' state, albeit a 'degenerated' one. This involved a concession that Stalin did not altogether mark a break with the Bolshevik Revolution; conversely, however, it revealed again Trotsky's illusion about

---

[184] See, in this connection, Moore, *Soviet Politics—The Dilemma of Power.*

[185] See Robert Tucker, 'Several Stalins', *Survey* (Autumn 1971), pp. 165–75 (also included in the 1972, revised edition of his *The Soviet Political Mind*). See also the same author's recent biography, *Stalin as Revolutionary 1879–1929* (London, 1974) as well as that by Adam Ulam, *Stalin: The Man and His Era* (London, 1974).

[186] A further example of how the Thermidorian analogy led Trotsky into misjudging Stalin's intentions is Trotsky's prediction that 'on the soil of a bourgeois regime' Stalin would maintain and defend 'bourgeois forms of property' (see his article 'Nerabochee i neburzhuaznoe gosudarstvo?', *Byulleten Oppozitsii*, Feb. 1938, p. 17). Later he was forced to revise this prediction—in view of Stalin's policies in occupied Poland—and admit that the occupation of eastern Poland would 'result in the abolition of private capitalist property so as thus to bring the regime of the occupied territories into accord with the regime of the U.S.S.R.'. ('The U.S.S.R. in War', op. cit., p. 18.)

that Revolution, namely that it had in fact created a workers' state. Those of Trotsky's followers who in the late 1930s began to propound the 'new class' or 'bureaucratic collectivism' thesis divested themselves precisely of this illusion by looking for the source of Stalinism not in Stalin, but in Bolshevism, and in the relationship between the state and the modern economy. Whatever the validity of the thesis, it had the merit of having escaped the pitfall of thinking in terms of fixed Marxist social categories.[187] It cannot be said that Trotsky avoided this pitfall; he made too much of the formal fact that the means of production in the Soviet Union were nationalized, and too little of the substantial fact that they were under the control, and at the beckoning of, the political leadership. As he himself had to admit, the practical effect of nationalization, or of state management, could be no different, from the point of view of the worker's control of his product, than that issuing from a system of private ownership. As a statement of universal application, the thesis of 'bureaucratic collectivism' was in itself an oversimplification of social and economic phenomena;[188] but it correctly perceived that the kind of society developing in the Soviet Union fitted neither the capitalist nor the socialist category—nor even an intermediary or transitional stage between the two, as Trotsky believed—but required a classification of its own in terms of that particular form of development and modernization in which the state plays the dominating—and domineering—role.[189]

---

[187] Among those who later proposed variants of the 'new class' and 'bureaucratic collectivism' idea was Rudolf Hilferding: see his article, 'State Capitalism or Totalitarian State Economy', *Modern Review* (June 1947), pp. 266–71. However, the best known of these variants is Milovan Djilas, *The New Class* (London, 1957). For a Marxist view that the Soviet Union represents a system of state capitalism, see Raya Dunayevskaya, *Marxism and Freedom* (London, 1971). For a survey of the history and evolution of the 'new class' idea, see the previously referred to article by Daniel Bell, 'The Post-Industrial Society', in the Spring 1971 issue of *Survey*.

[188] It may be taken to have been an early version of a 'convergence' view about East and West. However, whatever its applicability in the case of the Soviet Union—particularly during the post-Stalin era—it was obviously an exaggeration as far as Western industrial societies are concerned. Certainly, Rizzi's and Burnham's prophecies now appear fantastic if not ridiculous. For a brief criticism of the thesis of 'bureaucratic collectivism', see David Lane, *The End of Inequality?* (Harmondsworth, 1971), chapter 2.

[189] For a useful survey of the various theories and interpretations of the Soviet system, see Daniel Bell, *The End of Ideology* (revised edition, New York, 1962), chapter 14.

Until 1939, nevertheless, Trotsky insisted that the traditional, nineteenth-century Marxist categories were still the only
valid ones. Thus it was necessary to explain Stalinism in terms
of 'degeneration', of 'betrayal', of 'crisis' conditions, of the
failure of the 'world revolution', even in terms of Stalin himself.[190] This left—in the eyes of those who could no longer abide
what they took to be rationalizations—the impression that
Trotsky was begging the question: was he not taking Marxism,
as well as the October Revolution, too much for granted?[191]
Perhaps he himself agreed this to be the case when, re-evaluat-
ing in 1939 his conception of Stalinism, he felt compelled to
voice doubts about the truth of those Marxist assumptions
which he had so long held to be self-evident. He hastened immediately to reaffirm his allegiance to these assumptions, and to
the hopes based on them, but by then his was a solitary voice
from a very distant past.

The irony of Trotsky's failure in the 1930s to derive Stalinism
from Bolshevism and Bolshevism from Russia's peculiar social
and economic conditions is that it was precisely such derivations
that he himself had anticipated in his condemnation of Lenin
in 1903–4. But he had in the meantime, of course, travelled
a long road and found his 'way', as he once wrote, to Lenin
and Bolshevism. If he did not at the time recognize that his
1917 reconciliation with Lenin involved the tacit acceptance
of the principle of 'substitutionism', then the phenomenon of
Stalinism should have finally and vividly demonstrated the
truth of this. It should also have brought out more starkly than
ever the limitations of his own theory and practice of the permanent revolution, the contradictions of which proved in the

---

[190] These 'contingent' reasons which Trotsky gave for Stalinism were also partly the
reasons which led him to believe for so long that Stalinism must either collapse or be
overthrown. In 'The U.S.S.R. in War' (op. cit., pp. 13–14), for instance, he argued
that Soviet totalitarianism was a product of 'severe social crisis'; thus it could not be
a 'stable regime' but only a 'temporary transitional' one, doomed to fall sooner or later.
It did not occur to him, apparently, that it could be compatible eventually also with
stability and longevity.

[191] In contrast to such Marxist critics of the Soviet Union of the 1920s as the 'democratic
centralists' who, while rejecting Soviet policies and developments, remained socialists
or Marxists, many of those who became disillusioned with the Soviet Union in the
late 1930s, especially not a few of Trotsky's own followers, drew conclusions about
Marxism in general, and the October Revolution in particular, and abandoned both
the one and the other as well.

end unresolvable and which, in a sense, culminated in the 'bureaucratic revolution'. In this there is even greater irony for it was Trotsky who, in his early years, having denounced the 'orthodox' Marxists for thinking within the framework of the purely Western historical experience, both predicted a revolution unique to backward societies in the twentieth century, and anticipated the 'vengeance' of backwardness. Yet even he could not imagine how really unique this revolution would be, how extreme the vengeance, how unlike anything he, as a Marxist, could foresee or contemplate, would be the political system and the society it gave rise to. And the irony of *this* may be best epitomized by some words of encouragement which the co-founder of Marxism, Friedrich Engels, once offered to a co-founder of Russian Marxism, Vera Zasulich.[192] Writing in 1885,[193] Engels expressed much satisfaction that a party had been founded in Russia espousing the 'great economic and historical theories of Marx'.[194] There were clear signs, he continued, that Russia was approaching her '1789'; this, however, should not lead the Russian Marxists to think that their revolution was still far off for, in his view, what began as a '1789' could easily, in Russian conditions, turn into an even greater 'flood', into a '1793'. And this prompted Engels to make a general observation about the fate of revolutions and revolutionaries:

People who boast that they *made* a revolution always see the day after that they had no idea what they were doing, that the revolution *made* does not in the least resemble the one they would have liked to make. That is what Hegel calls the irony of history, an irony which few historical personalities escape.[195]

---

[192] Vera Zasulich was, of course, a 'charter' member of the Emancipation of Labour Group which Plekhanov established in 1883.

[193] See Engels' letter of 23 Apr. 1885 to V. I. Zasulich, in Marx–Engels, *Selected Correspondence* (Moscow, n.d., 1953?), pp. 458–61.

[194] Ibid., p. 459.

[195] Ibid., p. 460. Engels' words are recalled in a similar context by Bahne, op. cit., p. 42.

Part IV

THE REVOLUTIONARY AS MAN OF LETTERS

CHAPTER ELEVEN

ON ART, LITERATURE, AND PHILOSOPHY

In my eyes, authors, journalists and artists always represented a world which was more attractive than any other,
one open only to the elect.[1]

TROTSKY, IT needs hardly reminding, was a political animal
par excellence and his writings, like his life, were devoted to
politics. Yet he was amongst the least narrow-minded of the
Russian revolutionaries; his intellectual curiosity was boundless, his interests wide and varied, and his attitude to politics
never so crude as to see in it the complete essence of human
life and endeavour. He often regretted that the times he lived
in were such as to make political problems and, thereby, political activity dominant in terms of urgency, so that other pursuits
and interests had to be set aside.[2] He could not be said, of course,
to have chosen a political 'career' reluctantly and, in view of
his temperament, he would certainly not have been content to
live out a tranquil, uneventful life; but he claimed, on the whole
honestly one feels, that that which gave him greatest satisfaction
was a good book and quiet study.[3] For most of his life he did
not have time to read or study anything but political literature;
however, he made an effort, and to a surprising extent

[1] Trotsky, *Moya Zhizn*, I, p. 86.

[2] 'It is clear that the twentieth century is the most disturbed century within the memory
of humanity. Any contemporary of ours who wants peace and comfort above all, has
chosen a bad time to be born.' (From Trotsky's article, 'On the New Germany',
published in the *Manchester Guardian*, 22 Mar. 1933; also in Archives, T3519.)

[3] For instance, in the foreword to his autobiography he observed: 'A well-written book
in which one can find new ideas, and a good pen with which to communicate one's
own ideas to others, for me have always been and are today the most valuable and
intimate products of culture. The desire for study has never left me and many times
in my life I felt that the revolution was interfering with my systematic work.' (*Moya
Zhizn*, I, pp. 14–15.) And towards the end of the autobiography he wrote: 'In prison,
with a book or a pen in my hand, I experienced the same sense of deep satisfaction
that I did at the mass-meetings of the revolution. I have felt the mechanics of power as
an inescapable burden, rather than as a spiritual satisfaction.' (Ibid., II, pp. 336–7.)

managed, to keep abreast of developments outside politics, in literature in particular, but also in the sphere of art in general and, though to a much lesser degree, in philosophy and science. He held strong opinions on these subjects and he did not hesitate to express them in writing.

It is true that his writings on art, literature, and philosophy cannot be taken to constitute any major contribution to these fields, so that their importance in this respect should not be exaggerated. It is also true, as will become apparent, that his approach to 'non-political' subjects was almost always patently political; although he acknowledged that artistic creation was governed by its own criteria and principles, he could never quite bring himself to judge it in independence entirely of other factors, without regard, that is, for its social and political context or for its potential influence upon such a context. Moreover, his writings on these subjects are not of a uniform standard: some obviously betray a dilettantism and superficiality deriving from insufficient study and incomplete knowledge; and others are so clearly motivated by his political interests as to make them only incidentally works of artistic or literary criticism.

Nevertheless, many of these writings also show him to have had a natural sensibility for the artistic. His political predispositions, whether personal or such as devolved from Marxism, were never so crude as to turn art and literature, or scientific knowledge, into sub-departments of politics. His critical judgement was always conscious of the sensitivities and concerns of the artist and his appreciation of the latter's work was more often than not marked by a satisfaction derived from the purely artistic qualities of the work. This aside, from the point of view of the present study, his writings on artistic, literary, and philosophical or scientific subjects are important in that they constitute an integral part of his thought, and thus throw light on his political ideas, his intellectual personality, and his over-all conception of human creativity. What follows, therefore, should be seen in conjunction with his social and political thought in general.

1. **Art and Revolution**

In a previous chapter we discussed Trotsky's attitude towards
the relationship between art and politics;[4] we there noted his
opposition—as it was expressed during the party debate of the
early 1920s on art and literature—to the concept of 'proletarian
art' (or literature) or 'proletarian culture' in general. Here we
shall not return to this issue but turn rather to Trotsky's pronouncements on art during the 1930s when he attempted to
define once again both the principles of artistic creation and
the place of art in society.

As he had once denounced the attempt to prostitute the universality of art by transforming it into merely an instrument
of class and party politics, so in the 1930s Trotsky reflected bitterly on the extent to which this attempt had finally succeeded.
In *The Revolution Betrayed* he noted that the 'life of Soviet art is
a kind of martyrology'; one after another, artists were being
called upon to sacrifice themselves on the altar of Stalin's cultural decrees. Writers of real talent and conscience 'either
commit suicide ... or become silent'. As a consequence, the
epoch of Stalinism would 'go into the history of artistic creation
pre-eminently as an epoch of mediocrities, laureates and
toadies'.[5] Elsewhere, commenting on the absurdities of the concept of 'socialist realism'—a 'name ... evidently ... invented
by some ... functionary'—Trotsky pronounced thus upon the
state of Soviet art:

It is impossible to read Soviet verse and prose without physical disgust, mixed with horror, or to look at reproductions of paintings and
sculpture in which functionaries armed with pens, brushes and
scissors, under the supervision of functionaries armed with Mausers,
glorify the 'great' and 'brilliant' leaders, who are actually devoid of
the least spark of genius or greatness. The art of the Stalinist period
will go down as the most concrete expression of the profound decline
of the proletarian revolution.[6]

---

[4] See chapter 7, pp. 289ff., above.
[5] *The Revolution Betrayed*, pp. 184, 185.
[6] 'Iskusstvo i revolyutsiya', in *Byulleten Oppozitsii* (May–July 1939), p. 8. This article
was originally written as a letter to *Partisan Review* and was published in English in
the August 1938 issue of that journal under the title 'Art and Politics'. See also Trotsky's
1938 message to the founding conference of the Fourth International, where he
repeated this 'disgust' with Soviet art (in Archives, T4356).

In opposition to this degeneration of art in a society declaring itself to be socialist, Trotsky attempted to reaffirm those conditions which were essential for the development of art, and which he therefore considered to be both inviolable and in the true spirit of socialism. 'Spiritual creativeness', he declared, 'demands freedom.'[7] Marx had once written that an artist necessarily regards his work not as a 'means' but as an 'end in itself':[8]

It is more than ever fitting to use this statement against those who would regiment intellectual activity in the direction of ends foreign to itself, and prescribe, in the guise of so-called reasons of state, the themes of art ... In the realm of artistic creation, the imagination must escape from all constraint and must under no pretext allow itself to be placed under bonds. To those who urge us ... to consent that art should submit to a discipline which we hold to be radically incompatible with its nature, we give a flat refusal and we repeat our deliberate intention of standing by the formula *complete freedom for art*.[9]

Trotsky believed that 'art, like science, not only does not seek orders but, by its very essence, cannot tolerate them'.[10] Thus to 'command' art was to stifle and destroy it. This did not mean, however, that art was either politically neutral or politically uninvolved; it meant only that it could not be regulated by directives from above. As for its commitment to social and political causes, this was both unavoidable and desirable. Just as a political revolution sought to break down old institutions in order to create new forms of political life, so an artistic revolution sought to break out of old styles and manners of expression

---

[7] *The Revolution Betrayed*, p. 180.
[8] Karl Marx and Frederick Engels, *Literature and Art: Selections From Their Writings* (Bombay, 1956), p. 55.
[9] 'Manifesto: Towards a Free Revolutionary Art', in Archives, T4394. This 'manifesto' was first published in the autumn 1938 issue of *Partisan Review* under the signatures of the French surrealist writer André Breton and the Mexican painter Diego Rivera. Breton later revealed, however (in his *La Clé des champs*, Paris, 1953, p. 41, note 1), that it was drawn up during discussions with Trotsky in Mexico in 1938 and that it was Trotsky and Breton who in fact composed it: 'For tactical reasons, Trotsky requested that the signature of Diego Rivera be substituted for his own.'
[10] 'Iskusstvo i revolyutsiya', op. cit., p. 11. However, see also Trotsky's 1933 letter, published as 'O politike partii v oblasti iskusstva i filosofii', in *Byulleten Oppozitsii* (July 1933), pp. 21–2 where Trotsky, while emphasizing the need for artistic liberty and tolerance, stipulated two conditions for party interference in an artist's work: when the latter is directed against the 'revolutionary tasks of the proletariat' and when 'generalization in the field of art passes directly into the field of politics'.

in order to create new forms of spiritual life. The two 'revolutions', however, were not unrelated since both were dependent upon, and contributed to, a new human consciousness. Without a change in man's spiritual capacities, political freedom would remain unfulfilled; and without a free political climate, art could not flourish:

It should be clear ... that in defending freedom of thought we have no intention of justifying political indifference ... We believe that the supreme task of art in our epoch is to take part actively and consciously in the preparation of the revolution. But the artist cannot serve the struggle for freedom unless he subjectively assimilates its social content, unless he feels in his very nerves its meaning and drama and feely asks to give his own inner world incarnation in his art.[11]

This should not be read as implying that Trotsky held the crude view that artistic and political movements either necessarily coincided or paralleled each other in terms of their ideological content or even that the artist was motivated by the same goals as the political revolutionary. At the most, he believed, one could speak of a kind of *Zeitgeist* which, having its origins in particular social conditions, affected the artist as it did the man of political action. Themes directly voiced by a political movement would be echoed, though in a way characteristic of creative expression, in works of art. It was not surprising, therefore, that there should be a certain coincidence between the content of a political rebellion and that of an artistic one. But this did not mean that only one particular form of artistic expression was either legitimate or necessary from the point of view of political goals. And it certainly did not mean that artistic expression need adopt the terminology or the language in general of politics; were it to do so it would cease to be artistic and would become an adjunct of politics, at best a form of propaganda, masquerading as art but neither having any effect beyond the immediate political goal it was serving—and even here a dubious effect—nor contributing anything to the sphere of spiritual and cultural life:

... a truly revolutionary party is neither able nor willing to take upon itself the task of 'leading' and even less of commanding art, either before or after the conquest of power. Such a pretension could only

[11] 'Manifesto: . . .', op. cit.

enter the head of a bureaucracy—ignorant and impudent, intoxicated with the totalitarian power—which has become the antithesis of the proletarian revolution ... Artistic creation has its laws—even when it consciously serves a social movement ... Art can become a strong ally of revolution only in so far as it remains faithful to itself. Poets, painters, sculptors, and musicians will themselves find their own approach and methods ...[12]

If there was no direct parallel between the interests of art and those of politics, there was, nevertheless, Trotsky thought, common ground for an alliance between art and socialism. To understand why this should be so it was only necessary, in his view, to look at the condition of art under capitalism. Great art, he believed, was always timeless and classless; it transcended the limits imposed by the consciousness of its period and the tastes and interests of its ruling patrons. Art flourished in a bourgeois society so long as the latter was itself a liberating force; it did not, of course, always welcome new artistic movements but it could eventually accommodate itself to them, even offer them 'official recognition', in so far as the society was itself still vital enough to appreciate and pursue that widening of horizons which also increased the scope of economic change and activity. In this sense, it could be said that art played a social role which benefited the bourgeoisie but which was not directed by the bourgeoisie, nor even motivated by the interests of the bourgeoisie; rather it grew out of its natural tendency to break through limiting boundaries. According to Trotsky, the atrophy which set into bourgeois society, and which was itself a symptom of its inability to develop further, had a debilitating effect on art. Its economic vitality gone, its preparedness to experiment and change replaced by conservatism, its future threatened by social forces it could no longer control, bourgeois society began to fear anything which might disturb its fragile internal equilibrium. Art which did not conform to a class interest became immediately suspect; thus bourgeois society, in its period of decline, could no longer offer 'the minimum conditions' for the development of tendencies in art which corresponded to new needs and aspirations. The artist, as a result, either became a servant of the bourgeoisie—and his art classriddled, conformist, provincial and ultimately without value—

[12] 'Iskusstvo i revolyutsiya', op. cit., p. 11.

or he severed himself completely from society and took refuge
in varieties of 'bohemianism'—cubism, futurism, dadaism, sur-
realism. These new tendencies, lacking a social base and committed, as it were, to a conception of freedom which was indistinguishable from anarchy, took on a 'more and more violent
character, alternating between hope and despair'. Little
wonder then that one artistic school followed another without
any reaching a full development. This was the source of the
decadence of art which coincided in the capitals of Europe with
the First World War and its political and economic aftermath.
Thus: 'Art, which is the most complex part of culture, the most
sensitive, and at the same time the least protected, suffers most
from the decline and decay of bourgeois society.'[13]

The point of all this for Trotsky was that the 'crisis' in art
could not be resolved by art in isolation from its social environment—that way lay only further decadence—for it was a crisis
of society as a whole, of all culture, from the economic base
to the 'highest spheres of ideology'. As such it was a crisis which
could be resolved only within the framework of a society that
liberated itself from the bourgeoisie and its obsolescent institutions, and which created social relations and institutions which
were themselves liberating. If capitalism at its height was con-
ducive to artistic development, how much truer would this be
of socialism, that is, of a society which would transcend class
distinctions altogether, and which would therefore openly encourage the universal aspirations of art and, thereby, the
liberating forces of art itself? This, Trotsky believed, was the
connection between art and socialism: '[Art] will rot away inevitably—as Grecian art rotted beneath the ruins of a culture
founded on slavery—unless present-day society is able to
rebuild itself. This task is essentially revolutionary in character.
For these reasons the function of art in our epoch is determined
by its relation to the revolution.'[14]

Thus, paradox though it may be, only by returning to society
could art become independent of it: for by 'returning' it contributed to the transformation of society and to the creation
of that social framework which had no interest in interfering
in the sphere of art, thus enabling art to follow its own independent course, in accordance with its own 'laws':

[13] Ibid., p. 5.　　　　　　　　　　[14] Loc. cit.

True art, which is not content to play variations on ready-made models but rather insists on expressing the inner needs of man and of mankind in its time—true art is unable *not* to be revolutionary, *not* to aspire to a complete and radical reconstruction of society. This it must do, were it only to deliver intellectual creation from the chains which bind it, and to allow all mankind to raise itself to those heights which only isolated geniuses have achieved in the past.[15]

We may pass over in silence the question how valid was Trotsky's claim that the future of art was bound up with social-ism—or, for that matter, with any particular social system—since the weaknesses and limits of this claim are only too obvious to anyone having even a minimal familiarity with the un-predictability of artistic development. Trotsky would have been on much surer ground had he merely put forward the proposi-tion that art cannot escape the effects of its political and social environment—but that this does not make it dependent upon, or committed to, one specific social system or another. Given, however, Trotsky's view of socialism as constituting the freest of societies, it is not altogether surprising that he should have prejudged the political and social conditions for the flowering of art. This did not, in any case, lead him into the pitfalls of those who would interpret the influence of environment upon art in a crude, mechanistic fashion; he was always careful to point out that the relationship between an individual work of art—or the talent of an artist—and social factors was never direct and seldom obvious. 'The opinion', he wrote in 1940, 'that economics presumably determines directly and imme-diately the creativeness of a composer or even the verdict of a judge, represents a hoary caricature of Marxism.'[16] And he was no less careful to warn against the absurdity that political commitment obligated an artist to select only certain subjects for treatment, or confine himself to a particular form of artistic expression. About this he had already commented in 1923: 'It is not true that we regard only that art as new and revolutionary

---

[15] 'Manifesto: . . .', op. cit. The 'Manifesto' ended with the following words: 'The inde-pendence of art—for the revolution. The revolution—for the complete liberation of art.' For Trotsky's earlier, largely similar, formulation of the relationship between art and socialism as well as for his general view of the social roots of art, see his *Literatura i Revolyutsiya*, especially pp. 123–35.

[16] 'Ot tsarapiny—k opasnosti gangreny', in *Byulleten Oppozitsii* (Feb.–Apr. 1940), p. 25.

which speaks of the worker and it is nonsense to say that we demand that the poets should describe inevitably a factory chimney, or the uprising against capital!'[17]

Perhaps the real reason why he found it natural to ally 'great' art with socialism had as much to do with his conception of the nature of the former as with his political commitment to the latter. Trotsky took it for granted that all artistic expression was a form of human rebellion, whether against a concrete material reality or against a spiritual one and its tribulations. This is a theme to which he returned again and again in his writings on art: 'Generally speaking, art is an expression of man's need for a harmonious and complete life ... That is why a protest against reality, either conscious or unconscious, active or passive, optimistic or pessimistic, always forms part of a really creative piece of work. Every new tendency in art has begun with rebellion.'[18]

Not only may the external, social environment oppress the artist; art itself may be a source of disharmony. Rebellion in art thus often takes the form of rebellion against art itself, or rather against the accepted, conventional forms of artistic expression. Thus a new artistic movement is first of all a rebellion *within* art: 'Every new artistic or literary tendency ... has begun with a "scandal", breaking the old respected crockery, bruising many established authorities.'[19] Art, in fact, like all human endeavour that aimed at widening man's horizons, may be seen as a struggle against established convention:

When an artistic tendency has exhausted its creative resources, creative 'splinters' separate from it, which are able to look at the world with new eyes. The more daring the pioneers show in their ideas and actions, the more bitterly they oppose themselves to established authority which rests on a conservative 'mass base', the more conventional souls, sceptics and snobs are inclined to see in the pioneers impotent eccentrics of 'anaemic splinters'. But in the last analysis it is the conventional souls, sceptics and snobs who are wrong—and life passes them by.[20]

[17] *Literatura i Revolyutsiya*, p. 125.
[18] 'Iskusstvo i revolyutsiya', op. cit., p. 4.
[19] 'Letter to Dwight Macdonald', written on 20 Jan. 1938 and first published in *Fourth International*, Mar.–Apr. 1950, reprinted in *Leon Trotsky on Literature and Art*, edited by Paul N. Siegel (New York, 1970), pp. 101–3.
[20] 'Iskusstvo i revolyutsiya', op. cit., p. 10.

For Trotsky, this 'progress' in art was obviously analogous to the development of social thought, and social and political movements.[21] This being so, it seemed natural to him that art should become aligned with that social movement—in the twentieth century, socialism—which represented the most complete rebellion against 'conventional' reality, and which promised to enlarge the scope of human freedom.

Lest the tendentious nature of Trotsky's conception of art in the twentieth century mislead us as to his intentions, it should be stressed again that his view of 'socialist art' had nothing in common with the theory of 'socialist realism' which was decreed under Stalin. Not only Trotsky's protestations against 'socialist realism' attest to this; in the early 1920s, when in power, he fought against this tendency and, in the 1930s, the whole spirit of his writings on art was opposed to it. Whatever the limitations—deriving from his political preconceptions—of his view of art, he at least respected and defended the one principle of artistic expression, namely truth, which was incompatible with the policies of 'socialist realism': 'The struggle for revolutionary ideas in art must begin once again with the struggle for artistic *truth*, not in terms of any single school, but in terms of the *immutable faith of the artist in his own inner self*. Without this there is no art. "You shall not lie!"—that is the formula of salvation.'[22]

2. Literature and Society

Throughout his life Trotsky wrote profusely about literature. Almost the earliest of his writings deal with literary subjects: during his first banishment to Siberia, from 1900 to 1902, he contributed regularly to the Irkutsk newspaper *Vostochnoye Obozrenie* (Eastern Review) and his articles almost invariably discussed works of contemporary literature.[23] Between 1908

---

[21] In an earlier passage (loc. cit.) he remarked that Christianity was originally a 'splinter' of Judaism, and Marxism a 'splinter' of the Hegelian left; both were 'pioneers', both eventually acquired a mass base, and both—each in its own time—represented the progress of man in the process of self-liberation.

[22] 'Za svobodu iskusstva', in *Byulleten Oppozitsii* (Feb. 1939), p. 16. This is a letter Trotsky wrote at the end of 1938 to André Breton. In 'Iskusstvo i revolyutsiya', op. cit., p. 11, he declared: 'Truly spiritual creation is incompatible with lies, falsehood and the spirit of conformity.'

[23] See chapter 1, p. 13, above. These articles were later republished in volume XX of his *Sochineniya*, the source for subsequent references to them.

and 1914, during the period marked by the temporary decline of the revolutionary movement in Russia and his own isolation from revolutionary activity, Trotsky frequently wrote about literary themes.[24] After 1917 he took an active part in the party discussion concerning literature and his *Literature and Revolution*, besides defining the role of the party and government in artistic matters, was also a broad critical survey of the main literary currents of the time.[25] Finally, in the 1930s, he renewed his interest in the novel and wrote numerous essays on contemporary works of fiction.[26] 'Politics and literature', he stated in 1935, 'constitute in essence the content of my personal life.'[27] It was not altogether an exaggeration.

He did not, however, write pure literary criticism and it would be senseless to berate him for this. Those of his critics who have taken him to task for, among other things, mixing social with literary criticism, and subsuming the whole under political commentary, have surely missed the point: he could appreciate literature on its own terms but he wrote about it as a social critic and, as such, he was primarily interested in literature for the light it threw on social phenomena—as well as for the reflection of such phenomena within it.[28] He did not, on the whole, pretend to do much more than probe these dimensions of literature.

[24] His writings on literary subjects during this period are collected in his *Literatura i Revolyutsiya* (1923 edition), pp. 193–392 and *Sochineniya*, XX, pp. 249–497.

[25] Parts of this book were discussed in chapter 7, above. Its more purely literary views will be discussed presently.

[26] His *Diary in Exile* also contains many entries in which he commented on the novels, particularly French ones, which he was then—1935—reading. All references to the *Diary* are, as previously, to the London, 1959 edition.

[27] *Diary in Exile*, p. 51. Trotsky also took an interest in painting (see *Moya Zhizn*, I, pp. 172–3) and wrote some articles about art exhibitions he visited in Vienna before World War I (see *Literatura i Revolyutsiya*, pp. 372–92); but, as he himself admitted in his autobiography, his knowledge of painting 'never went beyond the stage of pure dilettantism'. As for music, about which he wrote nothing at all, he remarked elsewhere (*Diary in Exile*, p. 37) that 'for the most part' he listened to it 'superficially, while working'.

[28] Among his critics were T. S. Eliot ('A Commentary', *Criterion*, XII, 1932–3) and F. R. Leavis ('Under Which King, Bezonian?', *Scrutiny*, I, 1932). For a more generous appreciation of Trotsky's literary criticism, see Edmund Wilson, *The Triple Thinkers* (Harmondsworth, 1962), pp. 226 and 296. George Lukacs, however (in his article 'Propaganda or Partisanship?', *Partisan Review*, I, no. 2, 1934) for no reason easily comprehensible—unless it was his well-known endeavour at the time to serve Stalin—denounced Trotsky for supposedly distinguishing between 'pure art' in the socialist future and propagandist art during the transition to socialism.

The earliest of his writings on literary subjects show how ingrained was this concern with and fascination for the social content of literature. From the outset, Trotsky rejected the view that literature, or art in general, could be divorced from society or that it could pursue no end beyond itself. He readily admitted that the means of literature could be non-empirical and non-realistic; in fact, symbols and images were characteristic of literary expression. But these means were used to evoke a social reality, not only an aesthetic one, even if they were themselves not part of an empirical reality. To turn the means into an end in itself was to sever literature from human life, and leave it suspended in a vacuum. The value of a writer's work thus depended, in his view, on two separate, though interacting, elements: his art itself, that is, his talent for words, description, the evocation of images and so on, and his social conscience, that is, his concern for the condition of man.[29]

It is not surprising, therefore, that already in his early essays on literature Trotsky took a dim view of the 'modernist' trends, particularly Symbolism, which had begun to appear in Russian writing during the 1890s.[30] Trotsky's preference was quite clearly for those writers for whom, he believed, literature was virtually a confrontation with social reality and a weapon for transforming it. Thus, for example, he was deeply moved by the work and person of the Populist Gleb Uspensky; Uspensky's life, he wrote, had ended tragically—he died insane in 1902— as a direct consequence of his struggle against the 'ugliness' of the present. Yet in his work he had retained faith in the future and everything that he wrote shone with the spirit of the true revolutionary, rejecting the past and present, searching for a new identity.[31] Similarly, Trotsky admired the critic Dobrolyubov for emphasizing the relation between literature and social

---

[29] See his 1901 essays, 'O Balmonte' and 'Poslednyaya drama Gauptmana i kommentarii k nei Struve', in *Sochineniya*, XX, pp. 167–70 and 170–81.

[30] For Trotsky's first critique of Symbolism, along the lines of literary 'means' and 'ends' described above, see his essay 'O Balmonte' referred to in the previous note. For an account of the 'modernist' trends in Russian literature—first Symbolism and later Acmeism and Futurism—see: Elisabeth Stenbock-Fermor, 'Russian Literature from 1890 to 1917', in Katkov *et al.* (eds.), *Russia Enters the Twentieth Century*, pp. 263–86; and Marc Slonim, *From Chekhov to the Revolution: Russian Literature 1900–1917* (New York, 1962).

[31] See Trotsky's two obituary essays, 'Gleb Ivanovich Uspenskii' and 'O Glebe Ivanoviche Uspenskom', in *Sochineniya*, XX, pp. 33–40 and 41–67.

and political progress, for his disdain for cheap platitudes, and for his satire upon those who avoided the burning problems of the day by filling their heads with 'petty matters'.[32] Trotsky's esteem for literature that did not recoil from direct social observation and comment extended also to non-Russian works. The plays of Ibsen, for instance, in particular *An Enemy of the People*, in which Trotsky saw the dramatist exposing the subtle but crushing ways in which 'bourgeois society' destroyed its non-conformists, had an obvious appeal for him, even if he simultaneously denounced Ibsen's élitism, his fear of the 'people', and disdain for mass democracy.[33]

Trotsky's preparedness, however, to appreciate a writer's literary talent and powers of social observation, without regard for the same writer's political views or underlying ideology— a preparedness which was to mark him off from the shrill and narrow attitudes of some of his co-revolutionists of 1917—comes out particularly vividly in an essay he devoted to Gogol, in 1902, on the fiftieth anniversary of the latter's death.[34] Here too Trotsky's partiality for realistic fiction is only too apparent, as is his distaste for what he called Gogal's later 'didactic mysticism' and 'ascetic moralism', his lack of a coherent social critique going beyond the 'strictures of civic decency, far beyond such rules as those forbidding us to take bribes and rob public funds'.[35] Yet the essay is in fact a defence of Gogol against his detractors, against those who, because they cannot stomach Gogol's social conclusions, allow this to colour their appreciation of Gogol's literary talents. 'Before Gogol's appearance', Trotsky declared, 'Russian literature merely tried to exist. After him, it exists.'[36] He paid tribute to Gogol as the 'father of Russian comedy and the Russian novel', the first 'truly national writer ... free of the impulse toward imitation' of European literature and, in this sense, a forerunner of Goncharov, Tolstoy, Dostoyevsky.[37] The ultimate source of his greatness was, of course, his individual genius; but it also derived, in Trotsky's

---

[32] 'N. A. Dobrolyubov i *Svistok*', *Sochineniya*, XX, pp. 27–32. Dobrolyubov was a leader of the critical school which advocated the principle of social utilitarianism in judging the value of a literary work, i.e. the merit of the work was to depend not only on its artistic qualities but the extent, as well, to which it served the cause of progress.
[33] 'Ob Ibsene', in ibid., pp. 181–95.
[34] 'N. V. Gogol (1852–1902)', in ibid., pp. 9–20.
[35] Ibid., p. 19.   [36] Ibid., p. 10.   [37] Ibid., p. 11.

view, from the fact that Gogol was the first to see the connection between literature and life:

> Before Gogol ... our life and the convictions aroused by it went one way, our poetry another. The link between the writer and the man was feeble. The most vital men, when they took up their pens to write, concerned themselves mainly with theories of taste and not with the meaning of their work ... Letters were dissociated from life, literature created its works from itself, in obedience to the laws of poetry. But Gogol in his fiction ... put an end to this stifling autonomy.[38]

The result of this new 'linkage' between life and literature, according to Trotsky, was the birth of the Russian novel, where social reality could be portrayed as in no other literary form. Referring to Gogol's main work—*Dead Souls*, published in 1842—Trotsky summarized Gogol's accomplishment:

> By the power of his artistic intuition Gogol stormed the fortress of barbarism, daily brutality, common crime and invincible meanness, infinite Russian meanness. He took everything accumulated by history, consolidated by custom, covered by the dust of centuries and crowned by mystical sanction and proceeded to shake it, lift it, lay it bare and make it into a problem for our thought, a question for our conscience. All this he did without the aid of systematic reason: his creative genius came to grips with reality through the use, so to speak, of its bare hands.[39]

After attempting to explain why Gogol later turned into a 'didactic mystic'[40]—he gave as the main reasons, firstly, the fact that during Gogol's time there was as yet no 'coherent intellectual atmosphere', no leading 'political ideology ... accessible to literature' and, secondly, the limitations of Gogol's 'inherited moral codes', his 'traditional upbringing'[41]—Trotsky declared that Gogol's creative work nevertheless 'produced in the public conscience a coherent body of thought that went beyond the limitations of Gogol's own social outlook'.[42] By showing the contradiction between the 'rigid *forms* of Russian life and its fluid

[38] Ibid., pp. 10 and 12.   [39] Ibid., p. 17.
[40] In denouncing Gogol's 'mysticism' and 'moralism', Trotsky referred in particular to Gogol's 1847 work, *Selected Passages from Correspondence with Friends*. Although Gogol had always been a conservative in his social and political views, it was in this work that he most openly appeared as a supporter of the autocracy and the Orthodox Church, as an adherent of religious mysticism, and as a defender of serfdom.
[41] 'N. V. Gogol', op. cit., pp. 17 and 18.
[42] Ibid., p. 19.

content', Gogol's work, particularly *Dead Souls*, contrasted reality with an ideal, 'that which is' with that 'which should be'.[43] Thus his sometimes 'narrow-minded and quietistic homilies'[44] notwithstanding, Gogol's contribution to literature and social consciousness was enormous. Trotsky concluded his essay on Gogol thus:

If he tried to weaken the social meaning of his own books by the explanations he provided for them, let this not be held against him! If in his publicistic work he seduced some petty-minded creature, let him be forgiven! And for his great artistic merits, for the elevating and humane influence of his work, eternal and undying glory to him![45]

Trotsky's first essays on literary subjects were written at a time when he was only in his early twenties. But his taste in, as well as approach to, literature, though they became more refined in the course of time, did not change in any fundamental way. Political subjects and events occupied him after 1902, but he resumed writing about literature in 1908, and from then until 1914 he composed numerous essays on literary topics. The most interesting of these—and which show him to be pre-occupied by the same themes as in 1901–2—are two essays on Tolstoy, the one written in 1908 on the occasion of Tolstoy's eightieth birthday,[46] the other in 1910, on Tolstoy's death.[47]

---

[43] Loc. cit. Here, as elsewhere throughout this essay, Trotsky quoted from V. G. Belinsky—the influential Russian literary critic who was a contemporary of Gogol's—on Gogol's work. In fact, the essay is partly an appreciation of Belinsky himself, whom Trotsky venerated as the 'intellectual godfather' of the social consciousness of Russian literature which first emerged with Gogol. Belinksy, who believed that the writer must serve the cause of social and political change and describe the world realistically or naturalistically, and who was an extreme opponent of religion and of the Orthodox Church, had been an early admirer of Gogol's work. However, in 1847, when Gogol's *Selected Passages from Correspondence with Friends* appeared, Belinsky wrote his famous *Letter to Gogol* which denounced, in the most intense language, Gogol's religiosity, acceptance of Russian institutions and, in Belinsky's view, betrayal of vocation. For an account of Belinsky and, in general, for a fascinating survey of intellectual and literary life in Russia during the years 1838–48, see Isaiah Berlin, 'The Marvellous Decade', *Encounter*, June, Nov., Dec. 1955, and May 1956.
[44] 'N. V. Gogol', op. cit., p. 16.
[45] Ibid., p. 20.
[46] 'Lev Tolstoi', in *Sochineniya*, XX, pp. 249–60. (This essay was originally written and published in German, in Karl Kautsky's *Die Neue Zeit*, 15 Sept. 1908.)
[47] 'Tolstoi', in *Sochineniya*, XX, pp. 260–4. (Originally published in the Viennese *Pravda*, 20 Nov. 1910.)

The first of these contains an almost panegyrical tribute to
Tolstoy's talent for evoking character, atmosphere, panorama,
and for binding the whole together in a seemingly effortless
style—'what a miracle of reincarnation is a genius capable of'.[48]
Predictably, however, both essays concentrate on the social
aspects of Tolstoy the man and Tolstoy the writer. Trotsky was
hardly able to control his disdain for Tolstoy's moral philosophy, the flight, as he saw it, from reality, from society, from
history even, into nature, religion and the 'abstract com-
mandments of love, of temperance and of passive resistance'.[49]
Why is it, he wondered, that Tolstoy, though still living and
whose writings remained so captivating, nevertheless already
appeared to be a figure from 'a different historical world'—
and claimed to find the answer in the fact that in the 'deepest
and most secret recesses of his creativeness' and 'despite all his
... spiritual crises', Tolstoy had remained an 'aristocrat'.[50] By
this Trotsky meant nothing so crude as the fact of Tolstoy's birth
and upbringing, but rather his mentality, his psychology which
was incapable of abiding the turmoil, the dislocation, the pace,
and the depersonalization of the modern world, above all the
material and scientific changes this latter had introduced; it
was a psychology rooted in simplicity, in gentility, in changelessness, in the 'eternal cycle of birth, love and death'.[51] Tolstoy
had revolted against the nobility, against his own background,
against serfdom, against all forms of oppression of man over
man; but his distaste for change, progress, the emerging environment of city, commerce and industry resulted in a virtual
withdrawal from the world altogether. And this was reflected
in his literature where only the 'landlord and muzhik', especially the former, were given 'creative sanctuary'.[52] Without
directly identifying himself with this world of Russia's seemingly infinite past, Tolstoy was able to populate his works only
with aristocrats and peasants, so intimately interwoven in
Russia's history, and both representing for him that quality of
changelessness and continuity which was at the root of his soul's
yearning:

---

[48] 'Lev Tolstoi', op. cit., p. 252.
[49] Ibid., p. 259. On pp. 257–8 Trotsky summarized Tolstoy's well-known anarchist
philosophy.
[50] Ibid., p. 249.   [51] Ibid., p. 254.   [52] Ibid., p. 250.

[Tolstoy's] whole heart was fixed there where life is reproduced changelessly from one generation to the next, century after century. There where sacred necessity rules over everything; where every single step hinges on the sun, the rain, the wind and the green grass growing. Where nothing comes from one's own reason or from an individual's rebellious volition and, therefore, where no personal responsibility exists either. Everything is predetermined, everything justified in advance, sanctified ... And this perpetual hearing and obeying, converted into perpetual toil, is precisely what shapes the life which outwardly leads to no results whatever but which has its result in its very self.[53]

As for the new world, new social relations, new social figures—the merchant, the intellectual, the factory worker— these rarely appeared in Tolstoy's works and, when they did, they passed 'before his artist's eye like so many insignificant and largely comical silhouettes'.[54] Reality was being transformed but 'psychologically [Tolstoy] turned his back on this immense process and forever refused it artistic recognition'.[55]

The first of Trotsky's two essays on Tolstoy ended with a final homage to the genius of the artist and to the moral courage of the man who, compromising with no earthly power, insisted on going his own 'solitary' way.[56] The second essay was meant as an ironic comment on the effect of Tolstoy's ideas: rather then turning men away from politics and earthly concerns, they had contributed to that climate of dissatisfaction and revolt which turned Russia into an arena for revolutionary struggle. 'Although not a revolutionary, Tolstoy nurtured the revolutionary element with his words of genius ... And in this sense one might say that everything in Tolstoy's [social] teaching that is lasting and permanent flows into socialism, as naturally as a river flows into the ocean.'[57]

This last was so transparently facile an attempt by Trotsky to 'adopt' or 'mobilize' Tolstoy for revolutionary socialism that it is difficult to believe that he did not write it with tongue in cheek. Yet it symbolizes both the scope and the limits of his general approach to literature, particularly as this was to be

[53] Ibid., p. 251.
[54] Ibid., p. 250.
[55] Ibid., p. 251.
[56] Ibid., p. 260.
[57] 'Tolstoi', op. cit., pp. 262 and 263.

expressed in his 1923 book, *Literature and Revolution*.[58] On the one hand, it was an approach governed by a liberal attitude in principle to all literature, an openness to the artistic merits of a creative work without regard for its or the author's political views. On the other hand, however, he could not free himself of the need to ask the utilitarian question: what is the worth of the work from the point of view of one's social and political interests and goals? There was in him, therefore, a tension between the respecter of literature and the committed revolutionary. The latter, however, tempered by the former, could work as much to the 'advantage' of an ideologically suspect writer as against him—as the attempt, quoted above, to 'legitimize' Tolstoy shows.

This is amply evident in *Literature and Revolution*, written at a time when Trotsky was not only a revolutionary but a revolutionary in power.[59] Consider, for example, his views on three 'modernist' schools of the time—Symbolism, Formalism and Futurism.[60] We have already noted that Trotsky always preferred, whether as a matter of taste or ideological disposition or both, literature which was realistic and socially conscious—Belinsky was his 'mentor' in this. His attitude toward Symbolism was that it was in essence an attempt to escape human experience by using forms as far removed from any recognizable reality as possible. In *Literature and Revolution* he wrote that such an escape was in any case hopeless: the Symbolists, alienated from their environment—the ugly, stifling culture of old Russia—merely gave expression to this alienation by so obsessively avoiding contact with reality; ironically, therefore, they came to reflect a very specific situation, the particularity of their environment, belonging to a definite but limited historical

---

[58] As between 1903 and 1908, so between 1914 and 1923, Trotsky wrote almost nothing on literary topics. But as the work to be presently discussed shows, he did not stop reading literature during this period.

[59] Parts of this work, dealing with the question of a 'proletarian literature', were discussed in chapter 7, above. Here the earlier sections, devoted to a critique of contemporary or 'modernist' trends in literature, will be considered. All references, as previously, are to the Moscow, 1923 edition.

[60] The Symbolist school had, in fact, become a spent force long before 1923, giving way to the school of 'Acmeism' whose best-known members were Osip Mandelstam and Anna Akhmatova; see Stenbock-Fermor, op. cit., pp. 273–4. As for Formalism, it was, of course, primarily a school of literary *criticism*, not of imaginative literature itself.

period. Unable to transcend its environment because it was, so to speak, nurtured by it, Symbolism thus could not outlive its time or its authors.[61] Alexander Blok—who was, together with Andrey Bely, the best-known of the Symbolists—in Trotsky's view eventually recognized this and overcame it; he escaped the confines of his period and 'entered the sphere of October' when he wrote the poem 'The Twelve', his 'most important work and the only one which will live for ages'.[62] Using symbols and images as in the past, but now anchoring himself to the hopes of the present and the vision of a new future, Blok was able to create a work of art inconceivable before 1917, and transcending its immediate surroundings. 'The Twelve' was not, to be sure, 'a poem of the Revolution'; it was, Trotsky wrote, 'the swan song of the individualistic art that went over to the Revolution' but which, born in a different age, having the 'psychic needs' of its origins, could not entirely adapt itself to a new age.[63] This did not detract from its greatness, and the attempt to frown upon it because it used such images as that of Christ was merely a narrow-minded campaign to make literature a direct and immediate reflection of daily events.[64] Blok, at least, 'reached out towards us' and 'the result of his impulse is the most significant work of our epoch'.[65] As for Bely, however, he has remained, in Trotsky's view, mired in his mystical individualism, a captive entirely of the past, for whom the present hardly exists. His work, therefore, was an expression of himself alone, of his individual problems—though through himself he recalled also the problems, now merely a historical curiosity, of the pre-1917 age.[66] Thus: 'Bely is a corpse and will not be resurrected in any spirit.'[67]

This brief summary of Trotsky's comments on Blok and Bely

---

[61] *Literatura i Revolyutsiya*, p. 84.

[62] Ibid., p. 85. Blok wrote this poem at the beginning of 1918.

[63] Ibid., pp. 86 and 87.

[64] At the beginning of the book (ibid., p. 15), Trotsky wrote: 'The nightingale of poetry, like that bird of wisdom, the owl, is heard only after the sun is set. The day is a time for action, but at twilight feeling and reason come to take account of what has been accomplished . . . all through history, mind limps after reality.'

[65] Ibid., p. 90.

[66] Ibid., pp. 34–40. These pages are full of the most derogatory comments about Bely's writings. Trotsky also made fun of the fact that Bely was a follower of the German anthroposophist Rudolph Steiner.

[67] Ibid., p. 40.

serves to point up both the attraction and the exasperation which one feels with Trotsky as literary critic. On the one hand, there is a liberal-mindedness in him, a rejection of narrow and petty ideological demands, a refusal to subscribe to some mechanistic Marxist view of art, a readiness to enrich the 'Revolution' through art which is universal, and a complete acceptance of the principle that art must not be a handmaiden of politics. On the other hand, he is unable so much as to contemplate the possibility that art was a personal vocation, that it was, perhaps above all, the voice and the feelings of the artist himself, and that therefore it could function outside of collectivist goals; nor can he see any value whatever in the artist's obsession, to the exclusion of all other concerns, with words in themselves, with their music, rhythm, inner laws, their independent and, in the eyes of the artist, self-sufficient, life. It is a measure of this blindness that Trotsky failed to appreciate the work of so important a figure in Russian literature as Bely.[68]

Trotsky's impatience with the Formalist school of literary scholarship was no less pronouned, though here perhaps more justifiably so since, unlike a Symbolist like Bely whose interest in words was above all artistic and imaginative, the Formalists' approach was primarily intellectual and systematizing, as their name indicates.[69] He admitted that the 'methods of Formalism, confined within legitimate limits, may help to clarify the artistic and psychological peculiarities of literary form'.[70] But to see the essence of poetics in the study of forms, and in the descriptive and statistical analysis of syntax, vowels, consonants and syllables was to raise art merely 'to the position of chemistry'.[71] Form in literature was a question of technique and as such of

[68] For a brief account of Bely's work—which brings out the extent to which Trotsky both misunderstood and was unfair to him (Bely also wrote novels which *were* socially conscious and in later life his sympathies for the revolution led him to seek a union between Symbolism and socialism)—see Slonim, op. cit., pp. 189–96.
[69] For a detailed study of the history and doctrine of the Formalist school, see Victor Erlich, *Russian Formalism* (3rd edition, The Hague, 1969). On pp. 100–4, Erlich summarizes, with some degree of agreement, Trotsky's strictures against Formalism and says (p. 103) that Trotsky's 'awareness of the peculiar claims of artistic creativity distinguished [him] markedly from the cruder practitioners of Marxist criticism'.
[70] *Literatura i Revolyutsiya*, p. 120.
[71] Ibid., pp. 119 and 120. However, as Erlich (op. cit., p. 101, n. 11) points out, it was a misrepresentation or misconception on Trotsky's part to claim that the Formalists were mainly engaged in 'counting' words and letters.

utmost importance; it was also important to study forms objectively and not merely in accordance with arbitrary 'tastes and moods'.[72] 'But the Formalists are not content to ascribe to their methods a merely subsidiary, serviceable and technical significance—similar to that which statistics has for social science, or the microscope for the biological sciences.'[73] Their 'science', according to Trotsky, aims at nothing less than a cult—and a soulless one at that—of the word, and this inevitably leads to 'the superstition' of the word.[74] But literature was not exhausted by its forms and mechanics; its content and the circumstances—social or psychological—of its development were no less important for understanding its character. Trotsky had little difficulty in disposing of one Formalist's claim for the complete independence of literature from factors extraneous to its language.[75] He agreed with this Formalist that Marxism was not necessarily an infallible guide to aesthetic qualities. But Marxism could provide a social explanation for the forms which literature took; it 'alone can explain why and how a given tendency in art has originated in a given period of history':[76]

The architectural scheme of the Cologne cathedral can be established by measuring the base and the height of its arches, by determining the three dimensions of its naves, the dimensions and the placement of the columns, etc. But without knowing what a medieval city was like, what a guild was, or what was the Catholic Church in the Middle Ages, the Cologne cathedral will never be understood. The effort to set art free from life, to declare it a craft self-sufficient unto itself, devitalizes and kills art. The very need of such an operation is an unmistakable symptom of intellectual decline.[77]

And he concluded his attack on Formalism with the following literary 'credo':

The Formalist school represents an abortive idealism applied to the question of art. The Formalists show a fast-ripening religiousness.

[72] *Literatura i Revolyutsiya*, p. 126.
[73] Ibid., p. 120.   [74] Ibid., p. 126.
[75] One of the leading Formalists, Viktor Shklovsky, had argued in an essay that Marxism was either mistaken in its interpretation of art or simply irrelevant since, firstly, literary forms seemed to be universal and, secondly, literary themes were not necessarily definable in terms of a national or ethnic environment. Though Trotsky devoted some five pages to arguing with Shklovsky, he did admit (ibid., p. 128) that the characteristics of 'human imagination' have a partially independent effect on creativity.
[76] Ibid., p. 131.   [77] Ibid., p. 133.

They are followers of St. John. They believe that 'In the beginning was the Word'. But we believe that in the beginning was the deed. The word followed, as its phonetic shadow.[78]

Despite his extreme strictures against Formalism, Trotsky never suggested—the idea did not so much as occur to him—that it be eliminated, artificially, by political decree. He believed that in the post-1917 social climate it would naturally wither away.[79] In the field, in any case, of literary creativity itself, of imaginative literature, it was Futurism which was the rising movement in Russia, and had been since at least 1912.[80] Indeed, with its emphasis on urbanism, technology, dynamism and a variety of 'futuristic' portents, Futurism, ostensibly at least, seemed to be closest in spirit to the vision of 1917.[81] Trotsky's view of this movement, however, was, to say the least, ambivalent. He appreciated the fact that Futurism had directly aligned itself with the Revolution, which it was prepared to serve; yet he attributed this to largely accidental factors rather than to any intrinsic political character which the movement may have had. He pointed out, justly, that in Italy the Futurist movement had identified itself with Mussolini's Fascist regime[82] and he hinted that this was more natural than the self-identifi-

[78] Ibid., p. 135.

[79] In fact, however, when by 1930 it ceased to exist to all intents and purposes, it was the *political* climate which decreed its extinction; see Erlich, op. cit., pp. 118–39. In a subsequent chapter, pp. 140–53, Erlich describes how during the later Zhdanov era Formalism became one of those terms of abuse—of the like of 'Menshevism', 'Trotskyism', 'Cosmopolitanism'—which the Soviet authorities trundled out whenever they wished to be done with something or someone.

[80] This was the year in which Vladimir Mayakovsky—the most brilliant and famous of the Futurists—and others published their manifesto 'A Slap in the Face of Public Taste', rejecting most of Russia's classic writers as obsolescent.

[81] Because of this affinity it was allowed to flourish somewhat longer than other literary movements. And, in Mayakovsky, who was an ardent supporter of the Revolution and a member of the Bolshevik party—his doubts, ending in suicide, came later, at the end of the 1920s (see his play 'The Bed-Bug')—the Soviet Union produced perhaps its only original and truly great talent (as opposed to other notable writers who never wholly identified with the Soviet regime). For accounts of Russian literature since 1917, see Max Hayward and Leopold Labedz (eds.), *Literature and Revolution in Soviet Russia, 1917–1962* (London, 1963) and Gleb Struve, *Russian Literature under Lenin and Stalin, 1917–1953* (London, 1972).

[82] When, in 1914, Marinetti, the leader of the Italian Futurists, visited Russia, he shocked the Russian Futurists by talking of the 'glories' of war, authority, heroism, capitalism, and virility. The Russians hurried to dissociate themselves from these views and thereafter kept largely to themselves. Following the rise of Mussolini, Marinetti became the head of the Fascist Academy.

cation of its Russian counterpart with Communism.[83] The latter phenomenon was to be explained, in his view, by the fact that at the time of October 1917 Russian Futurism had been still in its infancy, its views not yet formed and, having been primarily a movement of non-conformism, it had been persecuted by its milieu. The Revolution swept the Futurists along— they yearned for action and change, they were eager to reject the past, and they saw in the Revolution the vehicle for all this. Beyond such generalities, however, there was no inherent common ground, according to Trotsky, between them and socialism.[84]

Still, the issue, Trotsky conceded, was not the nature of Futurism's political affiliation but the merits of its creative work. Some of its achievements, he believed, were beyond any doubt. It had rejuvenated the vocabulary and syntax of the Russian language, it had discovered and created new rhythms and orchestrations; moreover, its experimental attitude, its refusal to be cramped by old styles, its opposition to literary conventions, together with its determination to adapt language to the new age of science, machines, speed, and the modern man in general, had made it a living and creative force in literature.[85] But in its eagerness to break down the old barriers it had allowed itself to be carried away by the pretension that it could simultaneously create a new culture—as if the latter were simply a matter of the will-power of a few writers. The Futurists wished to 'anticipate history' by giving birth in the present to the art of the future.[86] Art, they said, was 'not a mirror, but a hammer: it does not reflect, it shapes'.[87] Thus

---

[83] See *Literatura i Revolyutsiya*, p. 93, where he wrote that the fact that Italian Futurism merged with Fascism is 'entirely in accord with the law of cause and effect'. At the end (ibid., pp. 116–18) of his chapter on Futurism, Trotsky appended a 1922 letter from the Italian Communist Antonio Gramsci concerning the political fate of Italian Futurism. The letter reported that most of the Futurists had turned to Fascism.

[84] Ibid., pp. 91–5 and 105–6. That a movement was critical of the bourgeoisie, Trotsky wrote, did not of itself imply that the movement was not bourgeois in character: Russian Futurism was Bohemian in origin, and Bohemianism was a form of bourgeois culture characteristic of certain periods. As for its opposition to the past, its call for jettisoning the literary tradition, of what relevance, Trotsky wondered, was this to the proletariat which had no part in the literary tradition? Even assuming that Pushkin, for example, had to be rejected—Trotsky in fact thought this ridiculous—did not the working class, Trotsky asked, first have to master and absorb him before it could overcome him?

[85] Ibid., pp. 102–6.   [86] Ibid., p. 97.   [87] Ibid., p. 99.

they had set themselves up as the begetters of the new art and language of socialism and of the workers. But this, in Trotsky's view, not only ignored the depth of the cultural poverty, and therefore the actual limited potential, of the masses; it also flew in the face of all that was known about cultural development: art could prod society on, but it could not run ahead of it, as if it were an independent entity standing outside society:

To tear out of the future that which can only develop as an inseparable part of it, and to hurriedly materialize this partial anticipation in the present day dearth and before the cold footlights, is only to make an impression of provincial dilettantism ... The effort to reason out a [new] style by the method of deduction from the nature of the prole-tariat, from its collectivism, activism, atheism, and so forth, is the purest idealism ... One must have a little historic vision ... to under-stand that between our present-day economic and cultural poverty and the time of the fusion of art with life, that is, between the time when life will reach such proportions that it will be entirely formed by art, more than one generation will have come and gone.[88]

In view of its pretensions, Trotsky continued, it was not sur-prising that the work of the Futurists was often sloppy, childish and vulgar. In a long analysis of the poetry of Mayakovsky, Trotsky attempted to demonstrate how the good and the bad in Futurism were embodied in its leading figure.[89] Dissecting Mayakovsky's images and word formations, the structure of his poems and their content, he argued that this 'enormous talent' combined genius with lapses of the worst mediocrity. Lacking an internal equilibrium and maturity, still very much the Bohemian he was at the outset of his career, he had no 'sense of proportion', no 'capacity for self-criticism', no 'sense of the measure' of art.[90] This dynamic personality failed to create dynamism in his poetry because he was always shouting at high pitch; every image, phrase, stanza was a climax, and the reader was given no sense of development, a sense without which literary dynamics were impossible. The uncontrolled enthusiam and excitement of the poet issued in imprecise and even absurdly false images. In the end one was left with a highly individualistic poetry which fell far short of doing what it had set out to do, namely, arouse social passion. It spoke of the revolt

---

[88] Ibid., pp. 97–9.   [89] Ibid., pp. 106–14.   [90] Ibid., pp. 107 and 109.

of the poet but not of society. Mayakovsky, Trotsky concluded, was still young,[91] and one could hope that in the course of time he would outgrow his immaturity and lack of discipline.[92] As for Futurism in general, it had to reject the 'pretension' that it represented the 'art of the proletariat'.[93] The maximal task it should set itself is to be a bridge and a link between the creative intelligentsia and the people, at a time when a 'wide chasm' still separated the two.[94]

Whatever one may think of its literary opinions, *Literature and Revolution* is one of Trotsky's most fascinating works. True, it is written in a characteristically opinionated, almost arrogant tone; its criticisms are sometimes based on an unfair summing up of the views of the writers and movements discussed; the language is always scathing, sometimes mocking, and not infrequently rhetorical; and the professional critic will find much in it that is both imprecise and simplified, whether it be the terminology used, or the analyses made of poetic and literary concepts. But its intelligence is undeniable, as is its knowledge of works of literature and of the artistic—not just political— issues they raise. A genuine curiosity about literature runs through it, and a sensitivity to the world of letters and imagination. It is itself written in a colourful, flowing style, full of images, aphorisms, vivid allusions. There is hardly a trace of dilettantism in it, and the author has obviously read and digested all the works of fiction, poetry and criticism which he discusses.[95] He is a Marxist and leaves no doubt about it, and the consequence is that not a few arguments are predictably tendentious and certainly derive from many ideological preconceptions; but he makes no pretension to detachment and, above

---

[91] In 1923 Mayakovsky was 30 years of age.
[92] This hope, however, did not materialize, in Trotsky's view; in an article written in 1930, following Mayakovsky's suicide, Trotsky repeated his earlier criticism of the poet—see 'Samoubiistvo V. Mayakovskogo', in *Byulleten Oppozitsii* (May 1930), pp. 39–40.
[93] *Literatura i Revolyutsiya*, p. 115.
[94] Ibid., p. 116.
[95] The summary of the book presented in the previous pages has not been exhaustive; Trotsky wrote also (ibid, pp. 41–83) about such other trends or groups in Russian literature as the Imagists, the 'Serapion Fraternity', and the 'Changing Landmarks' group. See also his observations on comedy and tragedy in the theatre (ibid., pp. 175–82) and on architecture and sculpture (182–4).

all, eschews all narrowmindedness: his Marxism does not lead him into instant, mechanical judgements and it does not prevent him from appreciating politically inimical works. Though he knows what he likes, he does not allow this to limit his range of reading. Finally, while adamantly insisting that literature is a part of social life and subject to all its ups and downs, he fully recognizes that it also unfolds in accordance with its own inner momentum, and its own ways and powers of grasping and influencing the world. 'A work of art', Trotsky writes, 'should, in the first place, be judged by its own law, that is, by the law of art.'[96] And, elsewhere: 'Artistic creation ... is also a deflection, a changing and a transformation of reality, in accordance with the peculiar laws of art.'[97]

Trotsky never again wrote so intensely or so sweepingly about literature. During the later 1920s he reiterated, on a number of occasions, his opposition to the idea of a 'proletarian literature',[98] but he made no further attempt to survey the state of Russian letters and hardly any to analyse the work of particular Russian writers.[99] In the 1930s his interest in literature revived

---

[96] *Literatura i Revolyutsiya*, p. 131.

[97] Ibid., p. 129. Compare this with a definition Mayakovsky once gave of the relation between art and reality: 'Art is not a copy of nature, but the determination to distort nature in accordance with its reflections in the individual consciousness.' (Quoted in Erlich, op. cit., p. 46.)

[98] Particularly in the speech (referred to in chapter 7, note 112) of May 1924, 'O politike partii v khudozhestvennoi literature'. The speech was delivered during a conference on party policy in the field of imaginative literature. (An account of this conference is given by Carr, *Socialism in One Country*, I, pp. 91–5.) One observation in this speech is particularly illuminating. Attacking those who saw in the works of Dante, Shakespeare, Byron, Goethe and Pushkin merely historical documents describing the state of mind of particular class societies, Trotsky counterposed the concept of art as transcending its time and milieu; in this lay the genius of these writers and, Trotsky continued, the pleasure which was derived from reading their works was beyond history or classes—it was an artistic pleasure, an 'artistic delight'. The speech was punctuated by interruptions and outcries from the proponents of a 'proletarian culture', with Trotsky replying in kind. It may be seen, without exaggeration, as a confrontation between an enlightened defender of literature and its worst philistine enemies.

[99] A notable exception to this is an article of 1926 on Esenin, written following the latter's suicide; see 'Pamyati Sergei Esenina', *Pravda*, 19 Jan. 1926 (also in Archives, T2978). This was a gentle, almost tender tribute to Esenin's lyricism, expressing pain at the loss of a 'fine poet, so genuine and of so lovely a freshness'. Here too, however, Trotsky repeated a recurrent theme in his literary writings of the 1920s: that for most writers reared in pre-1917 Russia, the opening of a new era was a traumatically disorienting experience—uprooted and alienated from the past, they were yet so influenced by it that they could not sink roots in the new present. As he had written about Blok, who after 'The Twelve' produced almost nothing, so in the case of Esenin

but this time it turned to European writing, particularly the French novel, and occasionally he would make jottings in his diary,[100] or write brief essays, about the fiction he was reading. These are tiny vignettes which add little to our knowledge of his literary views in general; but they are interesting for the light they throw on his appreciation of non-Russian literature.[101]

As was his habit when reading Russian works, so in the novels of European writers Trotsky sought a reflection of social reality—this time, of course, European reality. This is perhaps one reason why he was so fond of the French novel.[102] He was particularly impressed by Louis Ferdinand Céline's *Voyage au bout de la nuit*.[103] Aside from expressing praise for its purely literary qualities—'the artist has newly threshed the dictionary of French literature'[104]—he was full of admiration for the

Trotsky believed that a time of revolution, with its disharmony, violence and suffering, led, in one way or another, to the silencing of the poet. Trotsky concluded his essay on Esenin with the words: 'The poet is dead, long live poetry!' See also his earlier remarks on Esenin in *Literatura i Revolyutsiya*, pp. 48–50.

[100] See *Diary in Exile*, especially pp. 45–6, 48–9, 50, 68–9, 72, 95–8 and 115.

[101] About Russian literature Trotsky wrote almost nothing in the 1930s as well: apart from brief comments on Aleksey Tolstoy and one or two lesser-known contemporary Russian authors (see *Diary in Exile*, pp. 45–6, 50, and 96–8), and general observations on the decline of art and literature under Stalin (see the first section of this chapter), Trotsky's only excursion into Russian letters during this period was a brief evaluation of Maxim Gorky, written in 1936, following the latter's death (see 'Maksim Gorkii', in *Byulleten Oppozitsii*, July–Aug. 1936, pp. 8–9). Trotsky praised Gorky's humanism and the spontaneity and authenticity of his early writings but regretted his later decline into 'didacticism'. His verdict on Gorky's stature as a writer was that he was a 'great literary talent, not touched, however, by the breath of genius'. See also an early (1902) essay by Trotsky on Gorky: 'O romane voobshche, o romane "Troe" v chastnosti', *Sochineniya*, XX, pp. 210–15.

[102] His interest in French literature was of long standing; in a 1939 article (see below, note 118) he wrote that he began reading French classics while in prison after 1905 and that his taste for French novels never subsided during the next three decades or so. Even during the Civil War, he noted, he had a current French novel in the car of his military train, and after being banished, in 1929, to Turkey he accumulated a private library of contemporary French fiction, which, however, was destroyed in 1931 in a fire. He first commented on French literature in an introduction he wrote to a Russian edition of Marcel Martinet's play *La Nuit*, republished in French, under the title 'Le Drame du prolétariat français', in Trotsky, *Littérature et révolution* (Paris, 1964), pp. 258–68.

[103] See his essay 'Céline and Poincaré: Novelist and Politician', originally published in *Atlantic Monthly*, Oct. 1935, pp. 413–20 and republished in Irving Howe (ed.), *The Basic Writings of Trotsky* (London, 1964), pp. 343–55 (all subsequent references are to the latter source). The Russian original is in Archives, T3546.

[104] 'Céline and Poincaré . . .', in Howe, op. cit., p. 345.

manner in which, in his view, Céline had stripped the glossy veneer off French bourgeois society, exposing its lies, falsehoods, and ugliness.[105] Céline, who had 'walked into great literature as other men walk into their own homes', had written a novel full of pessimism, fright, and despair.[106] In this, Trotsky believed, lay the source of its greatness but, as well, of its limitations: the artist was able to tell the truth about French society by descending, psychologically, into its lower depths; he was unable to transcend it, to even emerge from it, because instead of anger and indignation he felt only weariness and desolation. Rejecting all conventions, literary and moral, he failed to find his way to 'light's glimmer', and ended in hopelessness.[107] 'Céline', Trotsky concluded, 'will not write a second book with such an aversion for the lie and such a disbelief in the truth. The dissonance must resolve itself. Either the artist will make his peace with the darkness or he will perceive the dawn.'[108]

Another French novelist whom Trotsky respected, though not without reservations, was André Malraux. After reading *La Condition humaine* he wrote to a New York publisher recommending that an American edition be brought out of this novel, 'which is free from philosophical didacticism and remains from the beginning to end a true work of art'.[109] He was, however, much less enthusiastic about Malraux's earlier novel, *Les Conquérants*, dealing with Chinese events of 1924–7.[110] Although granting that it was a 'work written with talent',[111] he could not help but be disappointed at the fact that Malraux had in effect defended Stalin's policy in China, without even realizing that this policy had actually 'strangled' the Chinese revolution. Borodin, the emissary of the Comintern, was presented in the novel as a 'professional revolutionary' whereas, Trotsky claimed, he was merely a bureaucratic 'functionary' carrying out orders from his employers.[112] The Chinese masses were

---

[105] In order to emphasize the reality which he believed Céline wanted to expose, Trotsky devoted part of the essay to painting a scathing portrait of Poincaré, 'the purest distillate of a bourgeois culture' (ibid., p. 346).

[106] Ibid., p. 343.   [107] Ibid., p. 354.

[108] Ibid., p. 355. Céline, of course, eventually became a supporter of Fascism.

[109] Quoted in Deutscher, *The Prophet Outcast*, p. 269. Deutscher's source is a 1933 letter to Simon and Schuster in the closed section of Trotsky's Archives.

[110] See his article, 'Zadushennaya revolyutsiya', in *Byulleten Oppozitsii* (May–June 1931), pp. 30–5.

[111] Ibid., p. 30.   [112] Ibid., p. 32.

treated by Malraux with a certain 'blasé superiority'.[113] These elements, according to Trotsky, gave the impression that Malraux was more fascinated by the manipulatory possibilities of revolutionary times and by power-seekers than by the social significance itself of revolution. And this, Trotsky believed, had had a deleterious effect on the literary merits of the novel since the main characters, having been distorted, did not ring true, and the real issues involved in China, having been side-stepped, were deprived of their full poignancy.[114]

Trotsky's reading was not confined entirely to French fiction: he read Ignazio Silone's *Fontamara* and wrote an exceptionally laudatory notice about it;[115] in 1937 he wrote a letter to Jack London's daughter praising highly her father's novel *The Iron Heel* which he had only then read for the first time; he was particularly impressed by its gloomy though 'prophetic' vision of a Europe devastated by a new tyranny.[116] On the whole, however, he retained throughout a preference for the French novel.[117] Perhaps the last of his literary pieces was an enthusiastic review of the novel *Les Javanais* by Jean Malaquais.[118] In it he expressed admiration not only for this particular work but for French literature in general, declaring the technique of the French novel to be the highest in the world. Whatever the truth of this, it seems clear that it was the refinement of language,

---

[113] Ibid., p. 31.

[114] Malraux, who was at the time an admirer of Trotsky, replied to the latter's criticism of his novel. Trotsky then wrote a rejoinder in which he repeated, in even harsher terms, his original strictures; see 'Ob udushennoi revolyutsii i ee udushitelyakh', in *Byulleten Oppozitsii* (Aug. 1931), pp. 20–2. In August 1933 Malraux visited Trotsky during the latter's stay in France and the two held a wide-ranging conversation, described by Malraux in his 'Leon Trotsky', originally published in English in *The Modern Monthly*, Mar. 1935 and republished in Trotsky, *Writings, 1933–34* (New York, 1972), pp. 331–8.

[115] See his brief article 'Fontamara', in *Byulleten Oppozitsii* (Oct. 1933), p. 32.

[116] The letter was published in the *New International*, Apr. 1945. London's novel first appeared in 1907 and described the disaster which would ensue if socialism were to be defeated in Europe. Trotsky noted that Fascism had confirmed London's worst fears.

[117] At one time he attempted to read a novel by Edgar Wallace; this led him to express amazement at the fact that this 'mediocre, contemptible and crude' author was so popular. As if unaware that English literature had produced works somewhat greater than those of Wallace, he added: 'By this book alone you can judge to what a degree enlightened England ... remains a country of cultivated savages.' (*Diary in Exile*, p. 115.)

[118] Written in August 1939, the review was first published, under the title 'A New Great Writer: Malaquais', in the *Fourth International*, Jan. 1941 (see also Archives T4608–10). Malaquais' novel, which received the Goncourt Prize, was translated into English as *Men From Nowhere*. It dealt with the spiritual plight of certain Europeans torn out of their native soil and tradition and thrown together by their mutual fate.

combined with a realistic or naturalistic treatment of subject matter, which attracted him to French as to other literature.

There seems no point in pretending that Trotsky's literary criticism was governed by purely artistic interests, and it is perhaps too much to expect from so political an animal that he should judge literature by purely literary criteria. He was quite clearly interested above all in the social side of literature and this affected his attitude towards individual works. As a Marxist he had quite definite views about the place and significance of art; sometimes this very nearly led him to judge a work according to whether it served social and political 'progress'. His preference for 'realism' was no doubt initially a matter of personal taste but it was certainly reinforced by Marxism. And, in any case, he could never agree that literature, or art in general, was an independent domain, a world unto itself, something which existed for its own sake only.

Nevertheless, he belongs to that small number of Marxist critics whose observations on literature are both enlightened and enlightening. Though writing from a Marxist point of view, his judgements were not vulgar: the economic 'sub-structure' was not made to emerge and peer out at every turn and the 'class struggle' was not perceived to be bursting out of every poem or novel. Though partial to 'realism', he was not narrow-minded: he recognized that literature would not be literature were it merely to photograph reality, and that creativity consisted of facility with language, and of the talent for evoking worlds and experiences which were of a different reality, one residing in the imagination and therefore transcending and enlarging the horizons of the material world. As for the uses to which literature could be put, he was certainly not averse to mobilizing it for revolutionary goals; but he was totally opposed to turning it into propaganda, whether as 'proletarian literature' or as a 'department' of government. 'The actual development of art', he wrote in 1923, 'and its struggle for new forms are not part of the party's tasks, nor are they its concern.'[119] This was not merely the paying of lip-service to the freedom of art; it was written when Trotsky was still a powerful

---

[119] *Literatura i Revolyutsiya*, p. 101. Trotsky's opposition to the interference of politics in art was also discussed in chapter 7, above.

political figure and taking an active, leading part—in party discussions—against the first attempts to circumscribe the style
and content of literature. Whatever one may predict for his
policies in other areas had he remained in power, it seems
hardly imaginable that in the field of literature he would have
decreed the dictatorship of the party (or the 'proletariat').

The fact that he saw art and literature as in themselves revolutionary by nature, seeking forever to break out of the con-
straints of past literary traditions and conventions, did not
prevent Trotsky from perceiving the ambiguous impact of
social revolution upon creative work. On the one hand, radical
social and political change could liberate the artist in a way
that he himself, depending upon his own powers only, could
never do. On the other hand, no artist was or could be entirely
free of the roots of his past, and an artist working at a time
of revolution was no less, perhaps more, a victim of the shock
of disorientation created by such a time than other men. Perhaps Trotsky's most valuable contribution in the field of literary
criticism was this understanding of the unsettled nature of art
in unsettled times. In his analyses of the work of Russian writers
in the years following 1917, he continuously emphasized what
he took to be the almost schizophrenic state of mind which
characterized their work—psychologically rooted in the past,
ideologically striving to reach out to the present and future.
For these writers, he believed, adjustment could never be complete and it was fundamentally wrong, in his view, to impose
it upon them, just as it was fundamentally wrong to assume
that the goals of a revolution were a sufficient guide to the role
and character of art. Perhaps this sensitivity to the impact of
revolution on creative pursuits was the reason why Trotsky
maintained in the end that the crisis in post-revolutionary art
must be confronted and resolved by art itself, and that the forms
art takes in the future were a matter for the future itself, and
not for the preconceptions of the present.[120]

[120] In his *Diary in Exile* (p. 46), he noted: 'Art is always carried in the baggage train
of a new epoch, and great art . . . is an especially heavy load. That there has been
no great new art [in the Soviet Union] so far is quite natural and . . . should not and
cannot alarm anyone. What can be alarming, though, are the revolting imitations of
a new art written on the order of the bureaucracy . . . The first condition for [artistic
creativity] is *sincerity*. An old engineer can perhaps build a turbine reluctantly . . . But
one cannot . . . write a poem *reluctantly*.'

3. Philosophy, Science and Marxism

In the whole of the voluminous writings of Trotsky spanning some forty years there are very few which can be defined as 'philosophical'. As a young man he took an interest in works of philosophy—and even wrote a perceptive essay on Nietzsche[121]—but this interest derived primarily from that sense of obligation towards works of the intellect which a normally curious and ambitious nature engenders in someone embarking upon the early stages of self-education; and, in any case, the interest did not last long. Very much later in life he professed to have rediscovered an interest in philosophy and expressed the ambition to write a 'big and serious' philosophical work;[122] but this never materialized and it is doubtful whether, even given the time and conditions, he would have had patience for it. The fact is that both by temperament and by natural capacity his mind was at its most content, and at its greatest ease, when dealing with political, sociological or historical subjects. Although allusions to Hegel, to Kant and to other philosophers and philosophies abound in his writings, it is difficult to see him writing a 'treatise' such as, for instance, Lenin's *Materialism and Empirio-Criticism*—whatever the actual philosophical merits of that work—not to mention the same author's jottings on Hegel, Feuerbach, Marx, and others (posthumously published as *Philosophical Notebooks*). Unlike Lenin, Trotsky made no pretensions to philosophical expertise and, on the whole, avoided dabbling even in Marxist philosophy. He had, in any case, an aversion to textual analysis and exegesis. In the case of Marxism, he generally accepted its fundamental axioms without further ado; as a system of thought he took it, above all, to be a 'method' which should be utilized for further explorations into social and political developments. Con-

---

[121] See 'Koe-chto o filosofii "sverkhcheloveka"', *Sochineniya*, XX, pp. 147–62. This was among the very first of Trotsky's published writings and first appeared in December 1900 in *Vostochnoye Obozrenie*.

[122] See his *Diary in Exile*, p. 109, where he wrote: 'My philosophical interests have been growing during the last few years, but alas, my knowledge is too insufficient, and too little time remains for a big and serious work.' He says that he has just (May 1935) written 'a little about the interrelationship between the physiological determinism of brain processes and the "autonomy" of thought, which is subject to the laws of logic'; but he does not appear to have preserved this 'essay'.

sequently—and as should be abundantly clear from all that has been written in this study—his thought dealt with theoretical problems of a socio-political nature, not with more abstract issues of a philosophical kind.

From time to time, however, excursions into such philosophical subjects as 'dialectical materialism' proved unavoidable, particularly in the late 1930s when, amongst his former followers, Marxism came under general attack. He then felt it necessary to return to fundamentals since not only some specific tenets of Marxism were being questioned but its very foundations. In the event, as we shall see, his defence of Marxism was neither original nor very convincing; in fact, it showed that he was not altogether free of the kind of obsession for attributing to Marx a grandiose and inflated philosophy of 'man and nature' which so often took a hold of Engels and, in some of their writings, Lenin, Plekhanov, Bukharin and others.[123] He too, it would emerge, insisted on attaching great importance to some of the 'sacred cows' of Marxist philosophy.[124]

Before turning, however, to these 'philosophical' writings of the late 1930s it will be useful to look back at some of Trotsky's somewhat more tempered reflections on Marxist philosophy of a decade or so earlier. His position on 'dialectical materialism'

[123] It is by now fairly clear that Marx made fewer 'philosophical' claims for his work—especially as concerns the subject of 'dialectical materialism'—than some of his followers later attributed to him (this is not to say anything about his 'early' writings, which eventually became so fashionable but which are not an issue here since neither Trotsky nor most of his contemporaries were aware of them). Despite Engels' frequent protestations that he was merely summarizing, so to speak, Marx's theoretical conclusions, there seems no doubt that he went far beyond Marx in this sphere, even allowing for their collaboration on such 'philosophical' works as *The Holy Family* and *The German Ideology* and for the fact that some of Engels' own philosophical tracts were written while Marx was still alive. Engels' main treatises on 'dialectical materialism' are *Herr Eugen Duhring's Revolution in Science* (*Anti-Dühring*) (first published 1878) and *Dialectics of Nature* (written 1873–83). Lenin's major excursion into this field is *Materialism and Empirio-Criticism* (1909). Plekhanov's best-known philosophical work is *The Development of the Monist View of History* (1895). For Bukharin's contribution, see his *Historical Materialism* (1921). For an account of these works, as well as of the subsequent history of the idea of 'dialectical materialism' in the Soviet Union, see Gustav A. Wetter, *Dialectical Materialism* (London, 1958). Shlomo Avineri's *The Social and Political Thought of Karl Marx* is an interpretation which, *inter alia*, seeks to liberate Marx from Engels. Amongst Marxists, George Lukacs attempted to do the same in his *History and Class Consciousness* (English translation, Cambridge, Mass., 1971). See also Karl Korsch, *Marxism and Philosophy* (English translation, London, 1970).

[124] For the 'unimportance' of 'dialectical materialism' to Marxist social theory, see Plamenatz, *German Marxism and Russian Communism*, pp. 8–17.

may be said to have originated when, in the mid-1920s, during a brief lull in his political activities, he developed an interest in science, or rather the philosophy of science, and, by way of this, in the relationship between science and Marxist philosophy.[125] It would be a gross exaggeration, of course, to claim that Trotsky himself formulated anything so comprehensive as a philosophy of science; his writings on science were sparse and neither particularly original nor free of the novice's dilettantism. But he had a clear grasp of the issues raised by 'dialectical materialism' for the sciences in general, and of the impact, conversely, of scientific development and discoveries upon the foundations of Marxist philosophy. He defended and sought to vindicate the principles of 'dialectical materialism'; but he did so—at this time—without the usual sententiousness and pomposity found in Marxist literature on this subject. Moreover, while he obviously considered its philosophical scaffolding to be an integral part of Marxism, he was aware of the distinction between Marxism as philosophy and Marxism as science.

All this is most evident in a long lecture he delivered in 1925, to a scientific congress, on the subject of the work and thought of the famous Russian chemist Dimitri Mendeleyev.[126] Mendeleyev, Trotsky pointed out, had frequently denounced dialectics; he believed in the immutability and stability of chemical elements, in their non-transformation into one another. In fact, however, Trotsky asserted, Mendeleyev's discovery of new elements, like his drawing up of the 'Periodic Table of Elements' in general, was a vindication of 'dialectical materialism', according to which quantitative differences eventually result in qualitative change.[127] The same could be said for Darwin's theories of evolution which, Trotsky believed, were in effect an application of Hegel's laws of the dialectic to the sphere of

---

[125] This interest in science was prompted by the fact that in 1925, after being relieved of his duties at the Commissariat of War, Trotsky had been appointed head of the Board for Electro-Technical Development and chairman of the Committee for Industry and Technology. These appointments, Trotsky observed in his autobiography (*Moya Zhizn*, II, pp. 261–2), were meant to isolate him from political activity; nevertheless, he approached them seriously, and gladly took a 'rest from politics, concentrating on questions of natural science and technology'. He recalled that he visited laboratories, watched experiments, and studied 'textbooks on chemistry and hydro-dynamics'.
[126] 'D. I. Mendeleev i marksizm', *Sochineniya*, XXI, pp. 268–88.
[127] Ibid., pp. 279–80.

organic life.[128] That neither Mendeleyev nor Darwin were aware of the 'dialectical' implications of their discoveries had to be attributed, in Trotsky's view, to their conservative frame of mind, shaped as it was by their social backgrounds and environments.[129]

Mendeleyev, Trotsky noted, had done much to free science of the need for postulating the existence of some 'superphysical' or 'superchemical vital force' to explain the relationships between various scientific phenomena.[130] He believed that chemistry could in the end be reduced to the physical and mechanical properties of its compounds thus creating a unitary foundation for all the sciences. Trotsky agreed that, in the last resort, psychology was reducible to physiological processes, physiological processes to chemical ones and these, in turn, to physical and mechanical ones.[131] The same, he added, could in principle be said about sociology, since society was a 'product of the development of primary matter'; scientific thought, therefore, cut through the complex layers and phenomena of social behaviour to the underlying components of matter, with their 'physical and mechanical properties'.[132]

Nevertheless, Trotsky hastened to point out, this was only so in principle; in practice the sciences, whether physiology and chemistry, or psychology and sociology, were not 'directly' reducible to mechanics. In principle, science had to subscribe to some unitary conception of the universe, otherwise scientists could not relate the different areas in which they worked. In fact, however, each science functioned in accordance with its own discoveries and laws. One could not understand a chemical reaction, for example, by simply resorting to the philosophical

[128] Ibid., p. 277. Trotsky was always an ardent admirer of Darwin's scientific ideas, if not of his social ones. In 1901 he wrote a short essay in which he mockingly described the backwardness of Russian social thought which, in the example he gave, expressed itself through an attempt to substitute for the 'materialist, English Darwin' an 'idealist, Russian' one; see '"Russkii Darvin"', *Sochineniya*, XX, pp. 116–18.
[129] This 'social explanation' is, of course, transparently feeble but, inadvertently, perhaps, it suggests that Trotsky was aware of the fact that commitment to 'dialectical materialism' had more to do with one's political outlook than one's scientific convictions.
[130] 'D. I. Mendeleev . . .', op. cit., pp. 274–5.
[131] Ibid., pp. 273 and 275.
[132] Ibid., p. 275. By thus momentarily conceding the reducibility, in principle, of all phenomena to mechanical properties Trotsky perhaps went further towards a mechanical, not dialectical, view of nature than he may have wished to do.

contention that chemistry was rooted in physics and mechanics: 'Chemistry has *its own keys*. One can find them only through experience and generalization, through the chemical laboratory, chemical hypothesis and chemical theory.'[133] The whole trend in the sciences was toward greater and greater specialization, for only in this way could detailed laws be established and empirical experimentation carried out. Thus each field of science was autonomous, and the laws governing one were not transposable to, or deducible from, another: 'A scientist would hardly carry over without modification the laws governing the movement of atoms into the movement of molecules, which is governed by other laws.'[134] And if this was so as regards the relationship among the natural sciences, how much more evident was it in the relationship between them and social science. The latter too was an autonomous field; from the laws of nature one could neither learn very much about social behaviour nor deduce social laws:

Of course, the life of human society, interlaced with material conditions, surrounded on all sides by chemical processes, itself represents in the final analysis a combination of chemical processes ... However, public life is neither a chemical nor a physiological process, but a social process which is shaped according to its own laws, and these in turn are subject to an objective sociological analysis whose aim should be to acquire the ability to foresee and to master the fate of society.[135]

Trotsky concluded, therefore, that it was fallacious to look to the natural sciences for a key to, or perspectives upon, society; and, conversely, that it was no less fallacious to presume that Marxism, as a social science, offered a 'universal master key' to the physical universe: such a presumption meant 'ignoring all other spheres of learning'.[136]

This was a forceful plea for recognizing the heterogeneity of the sciences. Trotsky contraposed it to the mechanistic views of Mendeleyev in order to stress the supposedly dialectical, not uniform, relationship between the sciences. By pointing out the extent of scientific specialization and diversification he also

---

[133] Ibid., pp. 275–6.   [134] Ibid., p. 278.   [135] Loc. cit.
[136] Ibid., p. 283. The irrelevance of Marxism, as argued by Trotsky in connection with military strategy, was discussed in chapter 6, pp. 256–8, above.

sought to emphasize the need for an over-all philosophy of science which would, presumably, transcend the limits of each science and thereby offer the scientist a general conception of the nature of man and the universe. This philosophy, he believed, was to be found in 'dialectical materialism'. Less than a year after his lecture on Mendeleyev, Trotsky delivered a speech in which he argued that the phenomena of radio-activity had confirmed the dialectical principle of the transmutation of quantitative differences into qualitative changes.[137]

It may be argued, however, that, in a sense, Trotsky's defence of 'dialectical materialism' did much to deflate its more ambitious pretensions. The view that each science was an autonomous principality with its own laws but incapable of decreeing laws for others, suggested that the kind of general laws of nature upon which 'dialectical materialism' depended, were not within the realms of science to establish. 'Dialectical materialism' could therefore be seen as a philosophical outlook accompanying scientific work but not necessarily integral to the latter's creativeness. Moreover, Marxism itself could be grasped as, first of all, an independent 'science' applying the methods of historical materialism, while the dialectical variety remained a matter for its philosophical afterthoughts. At the very least Trotsky agreed, as we have noted, that Marxism was not the 'universal master key' which some of its exponents had made it out to be.

If, however, the 'dialectic' appealed to Trotsky—as it obviously did—this was, it seems, because intellectually it was more fascinating to him than the dry mechanism of the purely empirical or behavioural approach to scientific investigation. It is interesting to notice in this context Trotsky's attitude toward two very different schools of psychology—that of Pavlov, which was

[137] 'Radio, nauka, tekhnika i obshchestvo', *Sochineniya*, XXI, pp. 410–23. This speech, delivered in March 1926 to the First All-Union Congress of the Society of Friends of Radio, contained the following prediction (ibid., p. 415): 'The atom contains within itself an enormous hidden energy and the greatest task of physics today consists in pumping out this energy, pulling out the cork so that this latent energy may burst forth like a fountain. Then the possibility will open up of replacing coal and petrol by atomic energy which will become the basic motive power. This is not at all a hopeless task. And what prospects it promises to open up! It alone gives us the right to declare that scientific and technical thought is approaching a great turning-point, that the revolutionary era in the development of human society parallels a revolutionary era in man's understanding of matter and his mastery over it.'

much favoured in the Soviet Union, and that of Freud, which was much frowned upon. Trotsky did his best to pay respect to Pavlov's work but he could conceal neither his fundamental distaste for a theory which reduced everything to 'reflexes' nor his fascination with the opposite theory which, he believed, endeavoured to plumb the depths of human consciousness and was, at the same time, full of suggestive, albeit speculative, ideas about human motivation. Beneath a tactful but not convincing attempt to reconcile the two schools, Trotsky clearly preferred, though not without reservations, the less rigidly empirical approach of the Freudians. In 1923 he wrote a short letter to Pavlov in which he tried to convince the latter that his school and that of Freud had much in common since both were ultimately based on given physiological phenomena, in the case of Freud that of the sexual urge.[138] Although Freud's hypotheses, Trotsky admitted, were sometimes 'arbitrary' from a scientific point of view, they had much to offer in the way of comprehending the unconscious motivations behind physiological responses. Thus the two schools were not really incompatible: 'Your theory of conditioned reflexes encompasses, it seems to me, Freud's theory as a particular case. The sublimation of sexual energy—a favourite theme of the Freudian school—is a formulation on sexual bases of the conditioned reflexes $n+1$, $n+2$, and so on.'[139]

This was a muted plea for at least keeping one's mind open to Freud's teachings. Some three years later, however, when he broached the Freud–Pavlov comparison again, he was less reserved. He raised it, in his article on 'Culture and Socialism', as part of the general theme that the socialist revolution must be receptive to all currents of enlightening scientific and cultural thought, no matter what the ideological milieu in which

---

[138] 'Pismo Akademiku I. P. Pavlovu', *Sochineniya*, XXI, p. 260. Deutscher (in *The Prophet Unarmed*, p. 178), who incidentally erroneously dates this letter as from 1922, suggests that although Trotsky included it in his *Sochineniya*, he may never have actually sent it to Pavlov. In the letter Trotsky reveals that already during his years in Vienna, prior to World War I, he had read the works of the Freudians and had even attended their gatherings.

[139] Loc. cit. Some two months after this letter to Pavlov was written, Trotsky, in a letter to a congress of scientific workers, chided Pavlov for presuming that the scientific study of physiology could solve all problems of human, social relationships; see *Sochineniya*, XXI, pp. 261–8.

they originated.[140] On the one hand, he again praised Pavlov's 'experimental' and 'painstaking' work, the fact that he erased the frontiers between physiology and psychology, and that he proceeded 'entirely along the paths of dialectical materialism', accumulating 'physiological quantity' which produced 'psychological quality'.[141] In the same breath, however, Trotsky sarcastically rebuked Pavlov for assuming that his methods could throw as much light on poetry as they had on the saliva of dogs: 'The paths that bring us to poetry have yet to be revealed.' If they could be revealed, however, Trotsky suggested that it was Freud's psychoanalysis which was more adequately equipped to do so:

The psychoanalyst does not approach problems of consciousness experimentally, going from the lowest phenomena to the highest, from the simple reflex to the complex; instead, he attempts to take all those intermediate stages in one jump, from above downwards, from the religious myth, the lyrical poem, or the dream, straight to the physiological basis of the psyche.[142]

Summarizing the differences between Pavlov and Freud, Trotsky painted the following picture of their 'methodological' approaches:

The idealists tell us that the psyche is an independent entity, that the 'soul' is a bottomless well. Both Pavlov and Freud think that the bottom of the 'soul' is physiology. But Pavlov, like a diver, descends to the bottom and laboriously investigates the well from there upwards; Freud, on the other hand, stands over the well and with penetrating gaze tries to pierce its ever-shifting and troubled waters and to make out or guess the shape of things down below.[143]

The drawbacks of a theory which could not as a rule rely on empirical experimentation to verify its claims were only too obvious. But this, Trotsky concluded, was no reason to exclude psychoanalysis from one's intellectual and cultural environment:

The attempt to declare psychoanalysis 'incompatible' with Marxism

[140] 'Kultura i sotsializm', *Sochineniya*, XXI, pp. 423–46. The main theme of this 1926 article was discussed in chapter 7, pp. 288–9, above.
[141] Ibid., p. 430. What Trotsky meant by this last statement is, to say the least, highly abstruse.
[142] Loc. cit.   [143] Loc. cit.

and simply turn one's back on Freudism is too simple, or, more accurately, too simplistic. But we are in any case not obliged to adopt
Freudism. It is a working hypothesis which can produce and undoubtedly does produce deductions and conjectures which proceed
along the lines of materialist psychology. The experimental procedure
will in due course provide the tests for these conjectures. But we have
no grounds and no right to put a ban on the other procedure which,
even though it may be less reliable, yet tries to anticipate the conclusions towards which the experimental procedure is advancing only
very slowly.[144]

That Trotsky should attempt to give a 'materialist' gloss to
psychoanalysis—whatever the basis for this—may be easily dismissed as a bit of ideologically wishful thinking aimed at 'legiti-
mizing' what was ideologically, in fact, problematical.[145] Its
supposed materialist foundation was not, in any case, the main
motivation behind Trotsky's plea on behalf of psychoanalysis.
As the passages quoted above partly show, he was drawn to
psychoanalysis primarily because it was, he thought, intellectually stimulating, because it dared to speculate upon the most
profound issues of human behaviour, whether conscious or unconscious, and because it was more imaginative and enterpris-
ing than the productive but plodding, and ultimately limited
and limiting, behaviourist school of Pavlov.[146] Perhaps in this

[144] Ibid., pp. 430–1. In a footnote Trotsky added: 'This question has, of course, nothing
in common with the cultivation of a sham Freudism as an erotic indulgence or piece
of "naughtiness". Such claptrap has nothing to do with science and merely expresses
decadent moods; the centre of gravity is shifted from the cortex to the spinal sord.'
[145] In an earlier passage (ibid., p. 430) Trotsky wrote: '[Psychoanalysis] assumes in
advance that the driving force of the most complex and delicate of psychic processes
is a physiological need. In this general sense it is materialistic, if you leave aside the
question whether it does not assign too big a place to the sexual factor at the expense
of others, for this is already a dispute within the frontiers of materialism.' Already in
1923 (in *Literatura i Revolyutsiya*, p. 162), Trotsky declared that in his view psychoanalysis could be 'reconciled' with materialism.
[146] In later years Trotsky often made observations on psychoanalysis and did not abandon his over-all admiration for it. For example, in his 1932 speech at Copenhagen
(Archives, T3469–72) he said: 'Psychoanalysis, with the inspired hand of Sigmund
Freud, has lifted the cover of the well which is poetically called the "soul". And what
has been revealed? Our conscious thought is only a small part of the work of the dark
psychic forces. Learned divers descend to the bottom of the ocean and there take photo-
graphs of mysterious fishes. Human thought, descending to the bottom of its own
psychic sources, must shed light on the most mysterious driving forces of the soul and
subject them to reason and to will.' In the preface to his autobiography (*Moya Zhizn*,
I, pp. 9–10), Trotsky candidly remarked that it is for 'psychoanalytical criticism'
to decide whether, in this work, his memory 'expels or drives into a dark corner episodes

he anticipated the later fascination of some Marxists—though not Soviet ones—with Freud.[147] At any rate, the compatibility or incompatibility of Freudian psychology with materialism and the 'dialectic' was, if not altogether an irrelevancy from a scientific point of view, largely an ideological or political issue; and Trotsky himself clearly sensed this when he urged that psychoanalysis at least be given a dispassionate hearing to prove—or disprove—itself, over time, in accordance with scientific criteria.

The example of his attitude to Freud, however, should not lead us to underestimate the significance which Trotsky ultimately attached to the materialist philosophy of Marxism. If in the 1920s one could sense a general reasonableness, a lack of pedantry, cant and sanctimoniousness in his approach to the 'dialectic', the impression is quite the opposite when one turns to some of his pronouncements on the subject in 1939 and in 1940. Perhaps it was the intensity and proximity of the then attack on Marxist philosophy—it came from such hitherto loyal followers as Max Shachtman and James Burnham—which animated Trotsky at this time to take so extreme, passionate and almost consistently wrongheaded and dogmatic a position on the essentiality of 'dialectic materialism' to Marxism; or perhaps it was the doubts about the future of socialism, voiced in his article 'The U.S.S.R. in War',[148] which prompted him to restate—lest it be suspected—his faith in Marxist doctrine. Whatever the case, he argued as if the whole future of the Marxist movement, not to mention Marxist social theory, depended

---

not convenient to the vital instinct that controls it—usually ambition'. At the outset of Trotsky's comments on Lenin's testament ('Zaveshchanie Lenina', Archives, T3487), there is a scathing disparagement of Emil Ludwig for 'hawking' in his books a vulgar and dishonest popularization of Freud's techniques; Freud, as against this, is portrayed as a heroic figure, ruthlessly breaking with all conventions in order to arrive at the truth.

[147] Of the many Marxist or neo-Marxist works which have since attempted to 'synthesize' Marx and Freud, two are particularly well-known: Erich Fromm, *The Fear of Freedom*, and Herbert Marcuse, *Eros and Civilization*. Not surprisingly, both these authors were among the first to resurrect the 'early' or 'young' Marx, i.e. the Marx who spoke about 'alienation'. Marcuse, in particular, has also emphasized the importance, in this as in other connections, of the Hegelian origins of Marx's thought. Ironically, therefore, it may be that the 'reconciliation' between Marx and Freud, to the extent that it has been effected, has been a consequence of the 'dematerialization' of the former.

[148] See chapter 10, pp. 421–7, above.

on rescuing the philosophy of the 'materialist dialectic' from its detractors; and he unhesitatingly seemed to take upon himself this mission.

His polemic—for such it basically was, despite the ostensibly rarefied atmosphere of its subject-matter—was unleashed, in the characteristically scathing style he reserved for such occasions, in a series of articles and letters written in 1939 and 1940, and later published in English in the posthumous—but appropriately entitled—*In Defence of Marxism.*[149] Its main contentions may be readily and briefly summarized for they are neither complicated nor original, and it is their general tenor and import which are of interest.

Burnham and Shachtman, as well as others, had argued that acceptance of Marxist social theory and political goals need not commit one to accept Marxist philosophy, specifically 'dialectical materialism'; one could adopt a different world outlook, or none at all, and still remain a loyal and effective Marxist. To this Trotsky retorted that to divest Marxism of its own philosophical underpinnings and claim that it could carry out its theoretical and practical tasks just as well without them, or with others, was like depriving a worker of his good tools and assuming that he could do his job just as well with no tools, or with defective ones.[150] Or, what was fundamentally the same, it was like defending the right of a Marxist to subscribe to some religious philosophy: who would deny that *this* was not detrimental to practical revolutionary activity?[151] That the opponents of 'dialectical materialism' proposed to substitute for it not religion but empiricism, or the American 'national philosophy' of pragmatism, did not, in Trotsky's view, make matters any better.[152] Marxist social theory, political strategy, and philosophy were, in the first and last analysis, inseparable, mutually dependent, virtually symbiotic; concrete problems could not be isolated from abstract ones. Nothing so much attested to this, he believed, as the fact that those who had begun by rejecting the 'dialectic' only, finished by rejecting Marxism virtually

---

[149] Most of these articles and letters originally appeared in Russian in *Byulleten Oppozitsii*. For convenience, however, all subsequent references are to the English versions in *In Defence of Marxism* (the original, 1942 American edition). Some have already been referred to, in a different context, in chapter 10, above.

[150] *In Defence of Marxism*, pp. 44–5.

[151] Ibid., p. 73.   [152] Ibid., p. 44.

altogether—witness the 'revisionism' of Bernstein and Kautsky, not to mention that of Struve and other 'Legal Marxists'.[153] These were manifestations at the time, as their counterparts were today, of 'petty-bourgeois opportunism'.[154] As against this, it was no accident that all the genuine revolutionaries— Marx, Engels, Lenin, Rosa Luxemburg, Franz Mehring and others—always insisted on the inviolability of 'dialectical materialism'.[155]

What *is* this 'dialectical materialism'? In three or four condensed pages Trotsky summarized its fundamental principles, its 'ABC', as he called it—without, however, avoiding the well-known clichés and simplifications which usually accompany Marxist explanations of the 'dialectic'.[156] Thus he reverted first to the old Aristotelian logic about 'A' never being equal to 'A'; all things exist in time, time never stops and existence itself is therefore a permanent process of transformation. From this logic it was merely a step for him to the notion of the dialectic, according to which at a certain critical point quantitative changes have qualitative consequences; this was true of chemical phenomena as well as those of physics and biology. 'Dialectical' processes, therefore, are to be found in nature: quantity and quality are there, as are the reconciliation between opposites and development through contradictions. Thus from the syllogisms of Aristotle's logic we arrive at the 'laws' of Hegelian dialectics. But the 'dialectic' is not real in the idealistic sense given it by Hegel; it is real by virtue of its material character. Its roots are 'neither in heaven nor in the depths of our "free will", but in objective reality ... consciousness grew out of the unconscious, psychology out of physiology, the organic world out of the inorganic, the solar system out of nebulae'.[157]

What, however, did all this have to do with the study of

[153] Ibid., p. 75. Among more recent examples, Trotsky offered Max Eastman and Sidney Hook (ibid., pp. 46 and 75). For Trotsky's much earlier (1933) rebukes—also aroused by their rejection of 'dialectical materialism'—of these two former sympathizers of his, see 'M. Istman i marksizm', *Byulleten Oppozitsii* (Mar. 1933), p. 31 and 'Marxism as a Science', *The Nation*, 5 July 1933 (letter to Hook apparently written in English only).

[154] Trotsky used this 'label' frequently, both as a term of abuse and as a definition of what he saw as the historical tendency within certain elements in the Marxist movement to revise the basic tenets of Marxism by way of accommodation to 'bourgeois' norms.

[155] *In Defence of Marxism*, pp. 74-5.

[156] Ibid., pp. 48-52.　　　　[157] Ibid., p. 51.

society and the formulation of Marxist revolutionary policy and strategy? Nowhere did Trotsky give a satisfactory answer to this question, beyond the truism that from the general one can learn about the particular, from 'dialectical materialism' about 'historical materialism'. Politics, he believed, was 'concentrated economics'; and economics, in the Marxist sense, was a particular manifestation of the material world.[158] In any case, the issue, as he saw it, was whether practical activity was ensconced within the shell of a defined and consistent philosophical outlook. For, removed from the shell, or deprived of it, it not only lost a 'roof' over its head but became exposed and vulnerable to every passing wind. True, Marxist philosophy was not 'eternal and immutable'; like all 'scientific thought' it would undergo development and be incorporated into a more refined 'doctrine'.[159] But to reject it now because it was imperfect was analogous to a physician refusing to utilize the present knowledge and tools of medicine on the grounds that they were incomplete.[160] Thus it should be made clear to every Marxist that if he were to 'divorce sociology from dialectical materialism and politics from sociology' he would, in the end, paralyse his capacity for political activity.[161]

This was the gist of Trotsky's defence of Marxism in general, of 'dialectical materialism' in particular. The merest glance at his arguments shows that this was Trotsky at his dogmatic, hortatory worst. In the first place, it was clever, but hardly honest, of him to transform every past and present controversy within the Marxist camp into one involving Marxist philosophy. Did Bernstein, for example, break with orthodox Marxism because of 'dialectical materialism' or because he had become convinced that Marxist social theory and practice were erroneous? For the most part Trotsky was putting the proverbial cart before the horse. Even worse, however, was Trotsky's appeal to authority: Marx, Engels, Lenin and so on, the 'founding fathers' of the creed he was defending. Since they had presumably venerated 'dialectical materialism', this philosophy had to be considered sacred and to deviate from it was therefore tantamount to committing a sin. But this was, of course, no argument at all, merely the trundling out of holy

---

[158] Ibid., pp. 123-4.   [159] Ibid., p. 76.
[160] Ibid., p. 77.   [161] Ibid., p. 93.

apparitions from the Marxist pantheon. This, and the over-all intolerant tone of Trotsky's polemic, was not entirely unlike, in fact only too reminiscent of, the manner in which his arch-fiend Stalin had decreed in ideological, not to mention other, matters—and against Trotsky himself above all. Was Trotsky here exposing a similar strain in his character? And, if so, was it not significant that this strain should emerge at a time when his own authority—in this case as the leader of his own Marxist 'opposition' movement—threatened to be undermined by desertions and deviations?

As to the substantive part of Trotsky's argument, who could take seriously the almost naïve, and certainly absurd, explanation of scientific phenomena in terms of dialectical processes? Even Engels' writings in this connection appear at least more learned by comparison. The idea, moreover, that 'dialectical materialism' was the method and tool of Marxism, like surgery and the scalpel were of medicine, was patently false historically: the method, if anything, was the economic analysis of society, and the tool, if anything, was the party, its organization and leadership.

The one possibly rational explanation for Trotsky's un-characteristically crude argumentation may, however, be contained in another of his points, namely in the claim that to become hostile, or even indifferent, to 'dialectical materialism' was to begin chipping away at the whole structure of Marxism. This in itself was no argument for the validity of the 'dialectic', of course, but it was a psychological insight into the often fragile character of a revolutionary movement. Trotsky may be seen to have sensed that its stability and confidence depended on a comprehensive, even totalist, ideology, impregnable at every point. The less all-encompassing it became, or the more it was penetrated by ideas having their source elsewhere, the greater was the danger that, firstly, internal loyalty would become disturbed and, secondly, the rest of the edifice would become susceptible to questioning, then scepticism, and would finally come under general attack. In this wide sense Trotsky was right to see in the turning upon Marxist philosophy the beginning of a possibly total renunciation of Marxism. This fear would explain why he should have chosen to appear, at this time, as the virtual spokesman for Marxist dogma. But he performed this function in a particularly intolerant, extremist fashion. His argument that a Marxist could not remain a Marxist, no matter what his social and political commitments, if he adopted, for example, the 'American pragmatist' philosophy, was perhaps analogous to the view that a Jew could not remain a Jew, no matter what his national and cultural loyalties, if he converted to, for example, the Catholic faith; this in itself was not an unreasonable contention. The difficulty began, however, when Trotsky argued that the avoidance of 'conversion' was not enough: as if to remain a Jew—or Marxist—one had to be an Orthodox Jew—or Marxist.

Nevertheless, at the time of Trotsky's 'philosophical' polemic, the fear that the other, social and political, tenets of Marxism would also come under attack, had in any case largely materialized. It is doubtful whether this had anything to do with questions of 'dialectical materialism'; the causes were more obvious, more empirical and more pragmatic. Amongst them one could list, firstly, the general failure of the 'proletarian revolution' in the West; secondly, the relative stability and powers of recovery of the capitalist economic system; and, thirdly, the very doubtful—certainly from a socialist point of view—character of the developments in the Soviet Union. All this, and more, suggested that Marx's social and historical theories had not stood the test of time and experience, and that the heyday of revolutionary activity had receded into the past. The 'crisis' in Marxism, therefore, was, as usual, both theoretical and practical.

In defending Marxism, Trotsky had thus now to carry the fight onto a second level as well—not only the validity of Marxist philosophy had to be maintained and safeguarded but the very stature of Marxism as a 'science'. It cannot be said that the latter was an easier task; nor can it be said that Trotsky was any more successful in carrying it out than he was in arguing the case for 'dialectical materialism'. Though he was at greater ease in this field, and though his tone and arguments were less shrill, less crudely dogmatic, and less bullying, they too did not amount to much more than a standard restatement of points as if taken from a Marxist textbook. Worst of all, however, was the fact that they exuded an optimism and a certainty which, given the situation at the time, were remarkable for their excesses.

Consider, for example, one of Trotsky's first forays, in the 1930s, into this field of Marxist apologetics. This is a preface he wrote in 1937 to an Afrikaans translation of the *Communist Manifesto*.[162] Half of the preface consists of a list of some twelve 'ideas' contained in the *Manifesto* which, according to Trotsky, 'retain their full force today'.[163] Amongst these are items as general as the 'materialist conception of history' and as specific as the well-known prediction by Marx and Engels about the 'impoverishment' of the working class. The first, of course, is a matter of Marxist doctrine and Trotsky may be forgiven the mere expression of faith in its validity. But the impoverishment of the workers is surely an empirical point, requiring hard evidence. That the evidence was, to say the least, uncertain does not seem to have bothered Trotsky unduly. One should not confuse, he says, the 'labour aristocracy' with the proletariat and, in any case, one should not take a 'fleeting tendency as permanent'.[164] So much for empiricism! The case he makes for the other ten 'ideas' is not much better.[165] In the second half of the preface Trotsky lists eight points in the *Manifesto* which, in his view, require 'corrections and additions' in the 'light of experience . . . the supreme criterion of human reason'.[166] However, this time the reader will be forgiven if, after perusing these eight points, he wonders what it is in Marxism that requires 'corrections and additions' that has not already been corrected and added to by Leninism: for the points are nothing else than a concise summary of the main tenets of Lenin's thought, from the theory of imperialism as monopoly capitalism to the revolutionary role of national liberation movements in the 'oppressed, colonial' countries.[167]

Less than two years later Trotsky wrote another preface, this time to a popular English abridgement of the first volume of

---

[162] 'Ninety Years of the Communist Manifesto', first published in English in *The New International*, Feb. 1938 and included in *The Age of Permanent Revolution: A Trotsky Anthology*, pp. 285–95. All subsequent references are to the latter source. (See also Archives, T4223–5.)

[163] Ibid., p. 286.   [164] Ibid., p. 287.

[165] In fact, most of these 'ideas', not surprisingly, are in the 'general' category, e.g., the class struggle, the 'withering away of the state', which perhaps gives Trotsky the feeling that he is free not to bother with direct empirical evidence.

[166] Ibid., p. 290.

[167] One point of 'correction', however (ibid., pp. 292–3), is Trotsky's own, namely, the theory of permanent revolution in the context of backward societies.

On Art, Literature, and

Capital.[168] This too must be seen as a feeble exercise in Marxist apologetics. It begins as, ostensibly, a summary of Marx's economic views; before long, however, we are into an analysis of the American economy which, Trotsky finds, perfectly confirms most, if not all, of Marx's predictions for capitalism in general. The example of the United States is seen to bear out the thesis of the 'increasing misery' of the workers and the parallel 'pauperization' of the middle classes.[169] American capitalism, Trotsky believes, has no hope of peaceful development; the New Deal, which is a policy of 'sops' to the labour and farmer aristocracy, cannot avert the 'collapse' of the economy, a collapse as inevitable as is the coming socialist revolution in America.[170] Marx's teachings, hitherto largely ignored in the United States, will soon gain in influence and Marx 'will become the mentor of the advanced American workers'.[171] Finally, colonial uprisings will aggravate and accelerate the catastrophe of capitalism; the proletariat in the imperialist countries will join hands, against its own governments, with the oppressed of the colonies.[172]

Most of this, of course, does not require the advantage of hindsight to be seen for what it is: it was already either wrong or grossly far-fetched when it was written. If nothing else, then the gradual recovery of the American economy from the depression which began a decade earlier should have given Trotsky reason to at least temper his over-confident prognostications concerning the socialist future. But Trotsky had never had much success predicting developments in the West: in the mid-1920s he made an almost wild foreboding of doom for Britain;[173] in the 1920s also, he greatly overestimated, for one reason or another, the prospects of revolution in Europe in

---

[168] 'Marxism in Our Time', in *The Living Thoughts of Karl Marx*, presented by Leon Trotsky (London, 1940), pp. 1–45 (see also Archives, T4519 and T4523–30). The title of the preface, as here given, does not appear in this, its original publication, but is the title Trotsky gave to it in subsequent, separate reprintings of it (although it has also sometimes appeared under the title 'Marxism in the United States'). In the original version a few passages were deleted, apparently by the publisher, but these are insubstantial since they concern mainly the style of some harsh remarks about certain American public figures.

[169] Ibid., pp. 15–21.

[170] Ibid., pp. 22–6 and 32–5.

[171] Ibid., p. 38.   [172] Ibid., pp. 40–3.

[173] In his *Kuda idet Angliya.'*

general.[174] Now, in the 1930s, he compounded his past errors by drawing a picture of the United States which was so one-sided as to mislead him entirely about its future.[175]

Given this confidence, the 'crisis of Marxism' hardly existed for Trotsky, or if it did he preferred to largely ignore it. Thus he could declare in 1939: 'Marx has been proved right in every, yes, every element of his analysis, as well as in his "catastrophic" prognosis. In what then consists the "crisis" of Marxism?'[176] For those who had abandoned Marxism because of disillusionment with its 'scientific' claims, Trotsky had nothing but contempt.[177] The only Marxist 'crisis' he was prepared to recognize as real and serious was of a different kind, prevailing in the Soviet Union: there, he agreed, Marxist philosophy and science, as sources of intellectual advancement, had been stultified by the intellectual bankruptcy of Stalin's regime. Not a single Marxist work, he claimed, had emerged under Stalin—in philosophy, history or the social sciences—which 'deserves attention' or which 'transcends the limit of scholastic compilations'.[178] To flourish, he maintained, Marxism, like every science, needed to be free of every 'shadow of compulsion';[179] so long as it remained under the official aegis of the state it would produce nothing but the 'same old ideas', the 'same old quotations'.[180]

[174] See chapters 8 and 9, above, on his evaluation of the then situation in Germany in particular.
[175] Of his numerous writings and statements on the United States, the following are further examples of a fundamental misunderstanding of American society: 'Perspektivy amerikanskogo marksizma', *Byulleten Oppozitsii* (Dec. 1932), pp. 22–5; 'If America Should Go Communist', originally published in *Liberty* magazine, 23 Mar. 1935 (Archives, T3665); the discussions of 1938 with his followers on the formation of an American Marxist Labour party: Archives, T4328, 4329, 4352, 4353, 4390.9; and the 1940 interview with the *St. Louis Post-Dispatch*, published in Russian as 'Mirovoe polozhenie i perspektivy', *Byulleten Oppozitsii* (Feb.–Apr. 1940), pp. 4–12.
[176] 'Eshche o "krizise marksizma"', *Byulleten Oppozitsii* (Mar.–Apr. 1939), p. 30.
[177] See, for example, his article: 'Eks-radikalnaya intelligentsiya i mirovaya reaktsiya', *Byulleten Oppozitsii* (Feb. 1939), p. 11.
[178] *The Revolution Betrayed*, p. 183. During the early 1920s Trotsky had attempted to encourage empirical studies, using Marxist methods, of social and historical development. He himself once suggested a research project which would investigate the historical correlations, over a period of about a century, between capitalist economic development and political events. The aim of the project would be to see how economic changes were reflected in the 'superstructure' of society. Although he warned against 'vulgar schematization', his own approach to this project was not entirely free of a certain schematism; see 'O krivoi kapitalisticheskogo razvitiya', *Sochineniya*, XII, pp. 357–63.
[179] *The Revolution Betrayed*, p. 180.   [180] Ibid., p. 183.

No doubt Trotsky expressed a sincere sentiment when thus calling for the emancipation of science in general and of Marxism in particular in the Soviet Union.[181] But his own approach in the late 1930s to the doctrines of Marxism raises doubts about the extent of free opinion which he himself was prepared to tolerate. In effect, his views on Marxist dogma left little room for any genuine debate over central issues. And his exercises in 'Marxology' themselves produced largely the 'same old ideas', the 'same old quotations'. Reading these exercises, one should perhaps be grateful that he wrote as little as he did in this field; it was obviously not his forte. Trotsky's mind was at its most creative when pursuing the independent analysis of social and historical problems, away from texts and issues of doctrine; he was at his best when conceptualizing concrete phenomena, at his worst when interpreting, and preaching, dogma.

---

[181] To his credit, it should be pointed out that he also pleaded for the freedom of science while he was still in the Soviet Union. In the previously referred to 1925 speech on Mendeleyev, he stressed that while science should aim at being 'useful' to society, theoretical research, even if its practical consequences were doubtful or unforeseen, was absolutely essential ('D.I. Mendeleev i marksizm', op. cit., especially pp. 286–8).

CHAPTER TWELVE

ON THE GENERAL AND THE PARTICULAR

The feeling of the supremacy of the general over the particular, of law over fact, of theory over personal experience, took root in my mind at an early age and gained increasing strength as the years advanced.[1]

THE FIGURE of Leon Trotsky, wandering after 1929 over a 'planet without a visa', only to find in the end isolation and violent death in a suburb of Mexico City, has entered the popular imagination as the classic example of the 'outcast' revolutionary, betrayed and defeated by the cruel ironies of history.[2] It is not an altogether mistaken image for it was certainly the fate of Trotsky to become the most disinherited of revolutionaries. But from the point of view of intellectual vitality it does not do complete justice to this last period of his life; though politically he was to remain almost completely ineffective, exile did not defeat him intellectually nor did it terminate his creative work. On the contrary, during the next decade or so he produced some of his best writing. In a previous chapter we discussed his analysis and critique, during this period, of the Soviet Union under Stalin.[3] Beyond this, however, he directed his energies towards a concerted, even if not systematic, reevaluation of that historical enterprise in which he had played so direct a role. The result, in particular, was *The History of the Russian Revolution*, which, with all its flaws and limitations, remains—and probably will always remain—one of the great

[1] Trotsky, *Moya Zhizn*, I, p. 110.
[2] 'The Planet Without a Visa' is the title Trotsky gave to the final chapter of his autobiography (*Moya Zhizn*, II, pp. 318ff.) in which he described his initial attempts to be granted asylum in a European country following his expulsion, in 1929, from the Soviet Union. These attempts having failed, he remained in Turkey until 1933; thereafter he spent brief periods, until expelled, first in France and then in Norway, and it was only in January 1937 that he reached Mexico, where he was allowed to stay in the Mexico City suburb of Coyoacan.
[3] See chapter 10, above.

works of the art of historical writing. Moreover, it was during this period also that he tried to deal with the obvious and persistent, but for a Marxist uncomfortable, issues concerning the role of the individual, and the importance of personal factors in historical events. Thus he wrote biographies of Lenin and Stalin, and what may be called a 'biography' of himself.[4] Finally, he attempted to justify the ethical basis of the history he had helped create, and thereby define the relationship in politics between means and ends. All this was done while he simultaneously carried on his struggle from afar against Stalin; but when he wrote in 1935 that 'the work in which I am engaged now, despite its extremely insufficient and fragmentary nature, is the most important work of my life',[5] he had in mind not only—perhaps not even mainly—his political struggle of these years, but his self-imposed mission of leaving to posterity the record of what he believed to have been a noble enterprise—the Russian Revolution of 1917.

Trotsky's historical and biographical writings, as well as his essays on political morality, may all be seen to revolve around the theme of the relationship between the general and the particular, the universal and the unique. It seems appropriate, therefore, to discuss in conjunction with these writings—and so within the framework of the same chapter—two other subjects which do not belong to the post-1929 period only, but which bring out particularly sharply Trotsky's attitude to this theme. The one concerns the 'Jewish question', to which Trotsky paid marginal attention until the 1930s but which thereafter, in the light of its renewed urgency, forced itself upon him. Here 'the general and the particular' confronted him in the form of the conflict between internationalism and nationalism. The second subject is that of Trotsky's view of the future and his conception of the 'good society'; here the above-mentioned theme was given its most forceful expression and reflected also the fundamental characteristics of Trotsky's social and political thought.

---

[4] In 1924 Trotsky published a book of biographical sketches of Lenin; this work, although not belonging to the post-1929 period, will be discussed in this chapter together with his other biographical writings (see note 52, below for bibliographical details).
[5] *Diary in Exile*, p. 53.

1. History and Biography: Masses and Leaders

(a) *History as Drama*

When *The History of the Russian Revolution* first appeared,[6] it evoked from some the expected, predictable response that it was not the work of an impartial, and therefore objective, historian.[7] No criticism could have rankled more with Trotsky. In the preface to the work as a whole, and in the introduction to its second and third volumes, he had already declared his disdain for the 'so-called historian's "impartiality"' which, in his view, was a fiction, piously resorted to by those who either had no method by which to explain historical events or merely sought to conceal, or detract from, their own partialities.[8] He, for his part, had made no attempt, he wrote then, to conceal his 'sympathies and antipathies'—had it even been possible to do so—but these had nothing to do with the question of objectivity. The latter, he believed, grew out of 'an honest study of the facts, a determination of their real connections, an exposure of the causal laws of their movement',[9] and out of the 'inner logic of the narrative itself'.[10] Now, replying to his critics, he reiterated this argument, accusing them of confusing impartiality with the issue of 'scientific method' and 'scientific objectivity': 'History is a science no less objective than physiology. It demands not a hypocritical "impartiality" but a scientific method . . . I attempted to base my *History* not on my own political sympathies, but on the material foundations of society.'[11]

There is, of course, much to be said for the view that a historian need not be impartial, detached or disinterested in order to be objective. The writing of history is judged by criteria which are independent of the historian himself and of his personal preferences, and the validity of his interpretation therefore stands or falls on the evidence and the arguments he

---

[6] The first volume of the Russian edition was published in Berlin in 1931, the second in 1933. The first English translation, in three volumes, appeared in 1932. As previously, all references are to the single-volume edition reissued by Gollancz in 1965.
[7] Aside from this, however, it was widely praised; see, for example, Kingsley Martin's review of volumes II and III in *The New Statesman and Nation*, 21 Jan. 1933, p. 77.
[8] *The History of the Russian Revolution*, especially pp. 20–1 and 508–9.
[9] Ibid., p. 21.   [10] Ibid., p. 509.
[11] 'Chto takoe istoricheskaya obyektivnost?', *Byulleten Oppozitsii* (July 1933), pp. 19–21 (the quotation is from page 19).

presents. Trotsky certainly did not attempt to conceal his 'sympathies and antipathies' in *The History of the Russian Revolution*. On the contrary: turn to almost any one of its more than 1,200 pages[12] and immediately the author's personal biases and predilections, all his likes and dislikes, are evident. But this need not, and does not, detract from judging the work on Trotsky's own grounds or on the basis of independent historical criteria. And, in any case, his choice and presentation of facts—as opposed to their interpretation—are neither wilfully misleading nor significantly inaccurate. Trotsky was too honest and too intelligent—and too confident that the facts were in any case on his side—to consciously falsify, conceal or omit. In a work of this scope there were bound to be errors and inaccuracies, particularly since it was written on the Turkish island of Prinkipo, where access to sources and libraries was so obviously limited. But one never feels that these inaccuracies are intentional and, at any rate, they have no direct bearing on the character of the issues which the *History* raises: the faults and qualities of the work have nothing to do with facts as such. One may, of course, berate Trotsky for failing to provide the historian's usual trappings of sources, footnotes and bibliography.[13] But this is surely a marginal complaint; Trotsky was not an academic or professional historian and he made no pretence to having carried out the work in accordance with the customary research procedures. The absence of such procedures is also not of any particular importance in judging the merits of the work, and its objectivity or lack of it.

Nor does the source of the 'problematics' of the *History* lie in the fact that it was written by a participant in the events it describes. One need not belabour the point that the author had a personal stake in the presentation of his story and in its culmination and consequences. It is no secret that he was one of its leading architects, or 'instruments' as he himself would

---

[12] The single-volume English edition reaches 1,266 pages; the two-volume Russian edition, printed on smaller-sized paper, takes up 1,406 pages.

[13] In the preface to the *History*, Trotsky merely mentioned (pp. 21–2) that he had used various periodicals, journals, memoirs and so on, some published by the Institute of the History of the Revolution in Moscow and Leningrad, but he did not specify which. He considered it 'superfluous', he remarked, 'to make reference in the text to particular publications, since that would only bother the reader'. In fact, however, occasionally he did give sources in the text itself.

have preferred to call it, and no reader of his account needs to be reminded that one should be sceptical about Trotsky's ability to be objective, much less impartial or detached, from this point of view alone, particularly if one keeps in mind that the *History* was written at a time when Trotsky's name was being systematically erased or debased in Soviet historical texts. True, and not surprisingly, Trotsky comes out well from his account; his views at the time of the events it deals with, his anticipation of developments, his position, policies and actions in the course of their unfolding, emerge as vindicated sooner or later. But this is not crudely done; in fact, Trotsky bent over backwards in order to keep himself as much out of the narrative as possible—so much so that one could fairly say that a really objective rendering of the events by a different hand would have been less reticent in making Trotsky a central figure.[14] There was no hypocrisy in this on Trotsky's part; during his long revolutionary career he had been accused of many things but no one had ever attributed false modesty to him (nor even genuine modesty for that matter). His reticence in this work is mainly a reflection of the fact that he was determined not to write a personal history; this was to be not a memoir nor an 'I was there' account but—*The History of the Russian Revolution*. It is not, for this reason, necessarily more objective and, as we shall presently see, Trotsky in fact hovers over this history in a quite compulsive manner: the absence of the usual kind of self-glorification should not, therefore, blind us to its emergence at another level. But the personal element is not obviously interpolated; it *is* subdued, and it is never allowed to particularize the history that is described.

The more serious criticism of the work is that its objectivity is undermined by the author's sweeping, unmitigated and unquestioning Marxist approach. Indeed Trotsky appears to have missed, or ignored, the point of much of the criticism against the *History*. Its lack of objectivity was attributed not so much to its lack of impartiality as to the method which it followed. From this point of view the critics were certainly right: *The History of the Russian Revolution* is not an objective work in so

[14] The fact that Trotsky referred to himself throughout in the third person is, however, neither here nor there; it does not make the *History* any more or less objective; it is merely a convenient literary device.

far as its assumptions are concerned. It is, of course, not illegitimate to write history in terms of a Marxist interpretation and
the fact that it is Marxist does not make it *ipso facto* wrong;
the very opposite may be the case. However, the difficulty with
Trotsky's history is that it does not seek to establish the validity
of Marxist 'laws', axioms, or concepts but merely assumes—
in advance and throughout—that they are valid. As a result
Marxist hypotheses are not so much tested by the experience
of the Russian revolution as imposed upon it; events are not
shown to confirm these hypotheses but are merely explained
by them. There is method in this approach but it hardly con-
forms to the rules and criteria of 'scientific objectivity'. '[I]
merely wished to interpret . . . the verdict of the historical process itself', Trotsky noted in his rejoinder to critics.[15] Indeed,
but the 'verdict' is clearly predetermined from the very outset
and is claimed to be incontrovertible, no matter how uncertain
the stages leading to it may appear to be. In a sense, the *History*
is a study in teleology and Trotsky himself, in his preface to
the work, admitted as much: 'A historical work only then completely fulfils its mission when events unfold upon its pages in
their full natural necessity.'[16] And later in the work he was even
more forthright: 'The present author has been true to objectivity in the degree that his book actually reveals the inevitability of the October Revolution and the causes of its victory.'[17] Objectivity is therefore identified with inevitability;
and since the goal of history is immanent in the events themselves it is the historian's task merely to reveal the 'natural laws
. . . of the historical process itself'.[18] In fact, however, Trotsky
did not so much reveal these laws as simply assert them.

But all this is fairly obvious to anyone who reads the *History*
and it would be merely tedious to harp on the issue of Marxist
bias. Moreover, however valid this criticism, it does not turn
the work into yet another exercise in Marxist or Bolshevik
hagiography. Despite all his theoretical preconceptions,
Trotsky wears his Marxism lightly. It permeates the work but

[15] 'Chto takoe istoricheskaya obyektivnost?', op. cit., p. 20.
[16] *The History of the Russian Revolution*, p. 20.
[17] Ibid., p. 509.
[18] Ibid., p. 21. See also p. 17 where Trotsky observed that the 'discovery of these laws
is the author's task'.

it does not inundate it; it governs the interpretation of events but it does not detract from the events themselves. He neither preaches nor moralizes, and only seldom does he stop to lecture the reader on the finer points of Marxist dialectics. It is difficult to believe that the author of the *History* is the same writer who some years later would so dryly and unimaginatively pontificate on the virtues of 'dialectical materialism'.[19] One is, of course, always aware that this is a history written by a Marxist but, once accepting all that this entails, one can read on without allowing this to spoil the story itself, or the flow of it.

Let us therefore admit that while Trotsky did not write a 'scientific history'—whatever that may mean—neither did he compose a crude piece of political propaganda. Let us further admit, however, that whatever our reservations about its unverified theoretical assumptions, the *History* is a work of great force and originality from which those assumptions do not detract. In fact, its lack of objectivity, as well as its Marxist view of history, must be seen in the light and in the context of its over-all character, for it is there that their full dimensions emerge. This character is not that of a Marxist history as such, but of a different historical genre: that of a work of dramatic art which, though it takes for its material historical and sociological phenomena grounded in actual facts, transforms them into theatrical forces. Trotsky would not have agreed with this formulation for he claimed that there were affinities between the *History*'s artistic qualities and its Marxist—or 'scientific' as he interchangeably called it—viewpoint. In the previously cited rejoinder to his critics, he wrote as follows:

A literary work is 'truthful' or artistic when the inter-relations of the heroes develop, not according to the author's desires, but according to the latent forces of the characters and the setting. Scientific knowledge differs greatly from the artistic. But the two also have some traits in common, defined by the dependence of the description on the thing described. A historical work is scientific when facts combine into one whole process which, as in life, lives according to its own internal laws.[20]

But whatever the relationship between art and science—and we shall argue in what follows that the two clash—there can

---

[19] See chapter 11, pp. 485ff., above.
[20] 'Chto takoe istoricheskaya obyektivnost?', op. cit., p. 20.

be no doubt about which category the *History* belongs to directly. It is almost literally a drama, unfolding upon the stage of history, which characters enter and exit, displaying their noble as well as petty qualities, playing out, inevitably, and in progressively more tense acts and scenes, some eternal plot of human folly and grandeur, the full meanings and ironies of which are only vaguely or subconsciously apparent to them, but which are intellectually and theatrically grasped and assimilated, and conveyed to the audience, by the dramatist. He too was once a character, or perhaps an actor, in the original, unrehearsed enactment of the drama, and therefore his conceptual grasp of the conscious and unconscious forces at play is reinforced by an experienced sensitivity for both the mundane and epic manner in which these forces first emerged in time and place.

To look at the *History* as a work of dramatic literature is to see the source both of its merits and faults, and to do so in a way different from what would emerge if one were to concentrate on it as simply an example of Marxist political history. Consider the question of the lack of objectivity: in a work of art this is both unavoidable and, perhaps, intrinsically desirable, since art is not documentation, and since the power of an artistic work, in part at least, depends on the individual manner in which an artist grasps reality. It is precisely this obsession with a particular point of view, or fascination with some element in human nature and behaviour, which animates much of art, not least drama. It is this also which at once so enraptures the spectator and so enrages him: enraptures because it purveys a consistent way of looking at the world which may never before have occurred to the spectator, and which reveals some truth about reality; enrages because it is so obviously only a partial representation of the world, and therefore at some point always a distortion of reality, however ubiquitous and *artistically* true it may seem to the dramatist. This is very much the effect of Trotsky's *History*. Reading it one cannot help but be fascinated by the sustained dramatic presentation of facts in the light of an over-all single theme and point of view, in this case the epic, unavoidable, almost apocalyptic confrontation between, on the one hand, corrupt, obsolescent but obstinate rulers and, on the other, the oppressed, primitive but awakening, and instinctively progressive masses, a theme buttressed, of course, by the Marxist elements of class struggle, of economic determinism, of largely imperceptible but universal, impersonal forces generating the inevitable dénouement and rebirth which meet in revolution. Who could deny that this view of the year 1917 captured some essential truth? Yet one also cannot help but be exasperated by the fact that this theme is too exclusively and too frequently imposed upon the facts, distorting the connections between them, and finally doing violence to other essential truths. In view of this approach, it is not surprising that Trotsky avoided as far as possible a documentary account of 1917—not in order to conceal facts but to rise, so to speak, above them, or rather above what he would have called an 'empiricist' investigation of the Russian Revolution.

The artistic and the dramaturgical virtues of the *History* are many and conspicuous. No reader can fail to notice, for instance, its qualities of language, its elegance of style, the smooth and accelerating flow of the narrative. Images, metaphors, striking phrases, analogies and descriptions abound in the work. There is, it seems, an almost uncanny correspondence between the story itself and the manner in which it is told: colourfully, sometimes poignantly, always vitally, without, however, spilling over into florid, exaggerated strokes, and without degenerating into either glibness or sententiousness. The movement and the momentum of events are sustained by avoiding a dry recitation of facts and by concentrating, instead, on a descriptive evocation of the events themselves. True, Trotsky is seldom content to let facts speak for themselves; but his protrayal of the atmosphere, moods and feelings seems integral to reality itself. Other of the dramatic elements are, undoubtedly, no less a product of the author's imaginative talent, and of his self-immersion in the story, than of the reality from which they are supposed to arise: thus suspense, tension, uncertainty are met at almost every stage. But they are surprisingly effective for being dramatically consistent and this in spite of the fact that, after all, the historical outcome is no secret and that it is, in the view of the author, largely inevitable anyway.[21] Frequently, Trotsky

[21] See, in particular, the description of the initial vacillations among the Bolsheviks and, later, of Lenin's 'summons to insurrection' (*The History of the Russian Revolution*, I, chapter 15, and III, chapter 5).

introduces conversations between participants or extracts from speeches at meetings and assemblies in order to further dramatize the unfolding of events or, specifically, the conflict between different views.[22] He switches to and fro, from the streets to the inner chambers of government or opposition parties, from the tumultuous masses to the behind-the-scenes goings on. In the welter of elements at play, individuals are not forgotten. In fact, one of the best things in the *History* is the portrayal of the individuals involved, the clash between personalities, the reactions— sometimes petty or narrow, sometimes heroic—of the participants to the escalating, confusing developments around them. The description, for instance, of the doomed Tsar and Tsarina is unforgettable for the combination of fascination and repulsion which it arouses—fascination for their serenity and almost complete indifference towards the outside world; repulsion for their inanities, stupidities, and total scorn and complacency towards their subjects. And the power of the debauched Rasputin over the Tsarina in particular is given extra significance by setting it not only within a personal context but in that of the whole climate of aristocratic decay and emptiness.[23] Throughout, finally, there are analyses of the concrete issues involved at each stage of the account, of the alternatives available to the figures at the centre of the drama, and of the wisdom of the decisions taken, without these analyses intruding upon the pace of the narrative, and without their becoming mere theorizing;[24] rather they are like a linking commentary between acts, provided by a narrator on stage turning periodically to the audience.

Above all, however, the dramatic character of the *History* is brought out through the presence—now in the background, now in the forefront—of the Russian masses, the peasants and workers, engulfed in and engulfing the course of historical events. Sometimes inchoate and faceless, always volatile and threatening, they move across the *History*'s pages as the demiurgic force behind the revolution. They are the real heroes of the drama and since, in the dramatist's view, their role has

[22] See, for example, ibid., I, chapter 7.
[23] Trotsky devoted a separate chapter to the description of the royal court (ibid., chapter 4).
[24] See, for example, the analysis of the 'July Days', ibid., II, chapter 3.

often remained unsung, he takes it upon himself to give them their rightful place in the centre of the stage, even when, ostensibly, it is occupied by individual, better-known figures. In the preface to the work, Trotsky makes this aim clear:

The most indubitable feature of a revolution is the direct interference of the masses in historic events. In ordinary times the state, be it monarchical or democratic, elevates itself above the nation, and history is made by specialists in that line of business—kings, ministers, bureaucrats, parliamentarians, journalists. But at those crucial moments when the old order becomes no longer endurable to the masses, they break over the barriers excluding them from the political arena, sweep aside their traditional representatives, and create by their own interference the initial groundwork for a new regime. Whether this is good or bad we leave to the judgement of moralists. We ourselves will take the facts as they are given by the objective course of development. *The history of a revolution is for us first of all a history of the forcible entrance of the masses into the realm of rulership over their own destiny.*[25]

What is presented, therefore, is the development of a kind of mass character and psychology, from the largely spontaneous, almost instinctive stirrings which erupt in the February Revolution—the *overthrow* of an old regime[26]—to the mature, conscious, confident and determined movement which culminates in the October Revolution—the *creation* of a new regime.[27] 'The masses', Trotsky adds in his preface, 'go into a revolution not with a prepared plan of social reconstruction, but with a sharp feeling that they cannot endure the old regime . . . The fundamental political process of the revolution . . . consists in the gradual comprehension by a class of the problems arising from the social crisis—the active orientation of the masses by a method of successive approximations.'[28] In *The History of the Russian Revolution* Trotsky treats the masses as a collective dramatis personæ, with feelings, moods, moments of fear, and moments of elation, not unlike a single character, groping his way in the midst of the confusion and turbulence towards a clear 'comprehension' of his 'destiny', and thereby also determining it. They are not a chorus commenting from the side,

[25] Ibid., I, p. 17 (italics added).
[26] See, in particular, ibid., chapter 8.
[27] See, in particular, ibid., III, chapter 9.
[28] Ibid., I, p. 18.

ironically and ominously, upon the follies of rulers and leaders, but an independent force acting upon both. True, they are not always—especially in the early stages—aware of the significance of what they do, nor do they always rise above the passions of the moment, and in such cases it is again the dramatist who, in arranging his material, conveys to the audience greater clarity and purpose than the facts themselves reveal. But consciousness cannot, in Trotsky's view, but be expected to lag behind events, and it is, after all, the dramatist's prerogative to telescope the two together.

As a work of dramatic art, therefore, *The History of the Russian Revolution* is truly a *tour de force*, amongst the outstanding examples of this genre of historical writing.[29] It is as such also that it succeeds in giving sense, if not resolving, some of the central enigmas of history in general, of the history of revolution in particular. Thus, for instance, Trotsky continuously confronts the problem of the personal element as against the social, the accidental as against the pre-designed and, in terms of drama, manages to convince, not by theorizing on the relative importance of each, but by relating the one to the other. The 'great, moving forces of history', he notes, 'are super-personal in character' but they 'operate through people';[30] and, indeed, throughout the work, whenever he illustrates this through dramatic description, the relationship between the personal and impersonal seems nearly self-evident; so much so, in fact, that another of his observations on this relationship has the ring of truth: rejecting speculations about the 'ifs' and 'might have beens' of personalities in history, he writes:

We do not at all pretend to deny the significance of the personal in the mechanics of the historical process, nor the significance in the personal of the accidental. We only demand that a historical personality, with all its peculiarities, should not be taken as a bare list of psychological traits, but as a living reality grown out of definite social conditions and reacting upon them. As a rose does not lose its fragrance because the natural scientist points out upon what ingredients of soil

[29] Not surprisingly, it has been compared to Carlyle's *The French Revolution*; see, for example, A. L. Rowse, *The End of an Epoch* (London, 1948), p. 282, who also sees similarities between Trotsky and Churchill, a dramatizer of history if ever there was one. Deutscher (in *The Prophet Outcast*, pp. 221 and 233) also draws comparisons between Trotsky and Carlyle, pointing out both affinities and differences.

[30] *The History of the Russian Revolution*, I, p. 73.

and atmosphere it is nourished, so an exposure of the social roots of a personality does not remove from it either its aroma or its foul smell.[31]

Similarly, when pondering the enigma of what it is that in the end unleashes an insurrection, what moment finally determines whether the army, for instance, whose role is crucial to the 'fate of every revolution',[32] will or will not join the opposition forces, Trotsky is at his best when he captures the dramatic uncertainty of that moment, not its theoretically predetermined inevitability. He gives a memorable description of such a moment, as it emerges when an army unit is confronted by a rebelling crowd:

The critical hour of contact between the pushing crowd and soldiers who bar their way has its critical minute. That is when the grey barrier has not yet given way, still holds together shoulder to shoulder, but already wavers, and the officer, gathering his last strength of will, gives the command: 'Fire!' The cry of the crowd, the yell of terror and threat, drowns the command, but not wholly. The rifles waver. The crowd pushes. Then the officer points the barrel of his revolver at the most suspicious soldier. From the decisive moment now stands out the decisive second. The death of the boldest soldier, to whom the others have involuntarily looked for guidance, a shot into the crowd by a corporal from the dead man's rifle, and the barrier closes, the guns go off of themselves, scattering the crowd into the alleys and backyards. But how many times since 1905 it has happened otherwise! At the critical moment, when the officer is ready to pull the trigger, a shot from the crowd . . . forestalls him. This decides not only the fate of the street skirmish, but perhaps the whole day, or the whole insurrection.[33]

The concrete example within the context of which the above reflection occurs is that of the final days preceding 27 February 1917, and it is an example of large-scale desertions and mutinies in the army to the side of the 'crowd'. But the dramatic force of Trotsky's reflection is that it could just as easily have been otherwise. Here Trotsky, in fact, appears somewhat as a latter-day Tolstoy, agonizing over those unpredictable, largely fortuitous, chance-governed elements which disturb and defy the

<hr/>

[31] Ibid., pp. 115–16.   [32] Ibid., p. 139.   [33] Ibid., p. 141.

best-laid plans of men, and which throw doubt on the supposedly ineluctable, rational march of history itself.[34]

Yet this comparison between Trotsky and Tolstoy can only
be a superficial and fleeting one. Unlike Tolstoy, for whom the
seeming irreconcilability of reason and chance was a fixed preoccupation, Trotsky merely takes momentary notice of this
dilemma; and again unlike Tolstoy, who sought to give a
rational explanation to history but who remained forever tormented by its accidents, Trotsky does not allow contingencies
to detract him from certainties. For beyond the dramatist, who
is himself in any case convinced of the general trend of things,
there is the professed 'historicist',[35] sure of himself, overflowing
with optimism about the course and direction history will take,
implicitly and absolutely trusting its higher 'reason' which, he
believes, is governed by predictable and irreversible laws. We
have emphasized Trotsky's dramatic approach to the writing of
history; but this, the over-all character of the *History*, must be
seen in conjunction with its other aspects. Had Trotsky chosen
to pursue this dramatic approach only, it would have been possible to judge the work at an artistic level alone—at which it
is an undoubted success—and to make allowances, accordingly,
for its over-all thematic unity. Trotsky, however, sought also—
and from the point of view of conscious intention, as opposed
to stylistic and literary temperament, above all—to write a
treatise on history itself, and on sociology. The moment, however,
that the dramatist in him turns into a 'historiologist' or sociologist, the moment that dramatic artifices and devices are made
to seem to exist in reality itself, the virtues of the *History* abruptly
change into its faults; what was dramatically legitimate and
convincing becomes historically and sociologically merely arbitrary; thematic unity becomes dogmatic uniformity.

A perhaps marginal, though telling, example of this is the
moralistic treatment of individuals. In drama, as in literature

[34] On Tolstoy's struggle to comprehend history, see Isaiah Berlin, *The Hedgehog and the Fox* (New York, 1957).
[35] This term is here used in the sense defined by Karl Popper, *The Poverty of Historicism*. See also, in this connection and in relation to what follows, Isaiah Berlin, *Historical Inevitability* (London, 1954). For the opposite case, which is in effect a defence of 'histori-cism', see E. H. Carr, *What is History?* (London, 1961). The most comprehensive study of Marx's views of history is still M. M. Bober, *Karl Marx's Interpretation of History* (2nd, revised edition, New York, 1965).

in general, the division of protagonists into heroes and villains, so long as it does not degenerate into stereotyping, is not only legitimate but perhaps artistically expedient in so far as it brings into relief conflicts between good and evil, as these are conceived by the dramatist. But what is the point of this in a work of history? What is gained by consistently presenting all those who did not share Bolshevik convictions—more narrowly even, Lenin's convictions, since, as Trotsky emphasizes, not all the Bolsheviks were at first prepared to carry out the eventual insurrection—as wicked, selfish, obstinate, and governed by narrow class interests? Thus not only the Tsar and his ministers, but the liberals and the Socialist Revolutionaries, the Mensheviks and all the 'Compromisers', are portrayed as totally blind, ignorant men unable to grasp the inevitable 'process' of history. It is in this disparaging, almost vindictive mood that Trotsky recalls his celebrated statement, made after the October seizure of power, shouted at Martov but intended for all those who still doubted the wisdom of what had been done: 'You are pitiful, isolated individuals; you are bankrupts; your role is played out. Go where you belong from now on—into the rubbish-can of history!'[36] As against this, Lenin and, later, the Bolsheviks in general, appear as the very personification of good, selflessness, and intelligence. Nothing is gained, in fact, from these moral distinctions except a schematic stereotyping of personalities. Judgement of character and record is not outside the historian's province; but surely it should be above such an artificial and predictable, not to say simplistic, Manicheism.

This example is, however, part of a larger problem in the *History*, one which again arises from the intrusion—for this is the reaction of the reader fascinated by the drama itself—of the historian-sociologist. It may be called the problem of 'objective necessity'.[37] In earlier chapters we noted how facilely Trotsky was able to discover, in the *History* and elswhere, a direct correspondence between the will of the Bolsheviks and that of 'objective conditions', not to mention that of the 'people'.[38] It would be superfluous to repeat the doubts and suspicions which this

[36] *The History of the Russian Revolution*, III, p. 1156.
[37] On this, and in general for a cogent criticism of Trotsky's *History*—which also praises its dramatic qualities—see Louis Gottschalk, 'Leon Trotsky and the Natural History of Revolutions', *The American Journal of Sociology* (Nov. 1938), pp. 339–54.
[38] See chapter 5, pp. 225ff. and chapter 6, pp. 243ff., above.

arouses; suffice it to say that the correspondence which Trotsky perceives is not obvious from the course of events themselves. If anything the events leave open the question of what political forces were playing out that which was—if it was—'historically, objectively necessary'. In spite of a brilliant chapter on 'The Art of Insurrection'[39] which argues the relationship between revolution and conspiracy, and which attempts to show that the Bolshevik seizure of power was, in effect, historically determined, the suspicion lingers that Trotsky has simply equated 'objective necessity' with success. On an individual level, this is also the case where the significance of Lenin is concerned; the surprising—for a Marxist—admission by Trotsky that without Lenin the 'revolutionary opportunity' might not have materialized is immediately juxtaposed by the claim that Lenin was not 'accidental' but a 'product of the whole past of Russian history'.[40] It emerges, therefore, that although Lenin was indispensable he was also inevitable. This being so, nothing is actually lost or given away by the admission.[41] But one is left wondering how far here too inevitability, necessity and so on are not simply *post facto* rationalizations, ideological conclusions drawn from end-results. As we have seen throughout this study, Trotsky's infatuation with Lenin and with Bolshevism, which began in 1917, was to become the source of subsequent political and theoretical dilemmas, none of which can he be said to have ultimately resolved.[42] Nothing so failed him as the Bolshevik success itself and *The History of the Russian Revolution*, when it deals with that success self-consciously, becomes an exercise in impassioned but transparent apologetics.

There is, therefore, a tension, if a not a conflict, in the *History* between, on the one hand, the freedom afforded by art and,

---

[39] *The History of the Russian Revolution*, III, chapter 6. This chapter was discussed in greater detail in chapter 6, pp. 243ff., above.

[40] Ibid., I, pp. 343–4. This question will be raised again in the next sub-section of this chapter where Trotsky's writings on Lenin are discussed.

[41] Deutscher (in *The Prophet Outcast*, pp. 241–51) castigates Trotsky at length—though in a manner of a teacher gently admonishing a wayward pupil—for his 'startling conclusion' about the indispensability of Lenin, and gives it the dimensions of a heresy. This is in keeping with Deutscher's own determinism in his biography of Trotsky—as in his biography of Stalin—which refuses to countenance the critical significance of personal factors. But, in any case, Deutscher seems to have missed the point completely since Trotsky's admission was not quite what it seemed.

[42] See chapter 10, pp. 427ff., above.

on the other, the demands made by history and sociology, and what succeeds at the one level often fails at the other.[43] That this is not invariably so is due to the fact that as a historian and sociologist Trotsky is also capable of acute observations. Thus, for instance, his reflections on changes in mass moods provide insights into the psychology of mass behaviour under prolonged stress.[44] The relationship between spontaneity and consciousness, though too often based on developments in Petrograd to the exclusion of the provinces, is, on the whole, cogently described.[45] And, when his theoretical analysis concentrates on the peculiarities of Russian society, on the anomalies, contradictions, and non-uniformities of the social and political structure, it is of the highest order of sociological observation: the brief and intensely compressed opening chapter—whose theoretical generalizations we have discussed elsewhere[46]—shows Trotsky's powers for independent analysis not to have been overwhelmed by the otherwise standard, if not commonplace, Marxist interpretation of history. Here, of course, Trotsky was in his own domain—that of the relationship between backwardness and revolution—which had been the source of his earliest social thought.

Nevertheless, *The History of the Russian Revolution* is, above all, a work of literature. Its qualities as pure history are, at best, of a minor nature and its flaws as such are far more conspicuous. Its power is an imaginative one and it would be no exaggeration to say that, in a sense, it can be best enjoyed when read as one would read a work of fiction, suspending somewhat one's belief but allowing oneself to be carried away by its evocation of scene, of atmosphere, and of drama.[47] It is in this sense too, perhaps,

[43] Gottschalk, op. cit., pp. 340–1 and 347–53, argues convincingly that there is in the *History* also a conflict between the historian—as a recorder of unique events—and the sociologist—as a generalizer, with the latter getting the upper hand; this comes out in Trotsky's continuous indication of analogies, particularly with the French Revolution, even when such analogies are at best far-fetched.
[44] See, for example, vol. II, chapter 11 of the *History*.
[45] See, for example, ibid., I, pp. 169–70. In this connection, see the observations by Fred Weinstein, 'Trotsky and the Sociological Dimension: An Analysis of Social Action', *Social Forces* (Oct. 1961), pp. 8–14.
[46] In chapter 3, above.
[47] Most critics of the *History* have readily acknowledged its literary merits; see, besides Gottschalk, op, cit., also: Robert D. Warth, 'Leon Trotsky: Writer and Historian', *Journal of Modern History* (Mar. 1948), pp. 27–41; and Bertram D. Wolfe, 'Leon Trotsky as Historian', *Slavic Review* (Oct. 1961), pp. 495–502.

that one can see the point of what Edmund Wilson has called Trotsky's 'identification of history with himself'.[48] We noted earlier that Trotsky took pains to subdue and understate his own role in the events described in the *History*; and it is a measure of his success in this respect that one has the impression that he has done himself less justice than he deserves. Yet this is a, so to speak, purely empirical impression: beyond the specific events, the spirit, if not the physical presence, of Trotsky is discernible. Partly this is expressed in the emotive language; partly in the numerous judgements—positive and negative alike—passed on the personal characteristics of the protagonists involved; and partly in the over-all efforts to justify and condemn—as if what history had begun to justify and condemn, the writing of it must complete. In the main, however, it emerges in the sense one gets of the author's total, unqualified immersion in his subject. In writing the *History* Trotsky was also writing a history of himself, or at least of that extended moment in his life upon which all that went before and after focused. If we remember the nature of Trotsky's own personality—his romantic panache, his flair for the theatrical, his aristocratic individualism, his disdain for the mundane and the everyday—then we can appreciate how much the drama of the Revolution was also a personal drama. He identified himself with the *History* and, in this dramatic sense, he identified history with himself.

At one point in the narrative Trotsky paused to remark:

If a symbol is a concentrated image, then a revolution is the master-builder of symbols, for it presents all phenomena and all relations in concentrated form. The trouble is that the symbolism of a revolution is too grandiose; it fits in badly with the creative work of individuals. For this reason artistic reproductions of the greatest mass dramas of humanity are so poor.[49]

If this is generally true, then Trotsky's own 'artistic reproduction' may be readily granted the status of an exception which proves the rule. *The History of the Russian Revolution*, for all its other faults, remains a classic of literature. It is an exception even among Trotsky's own writings. Of these, only *1905* com-

[48] Edmund Wilson, *To the Finland Station* (Fontana edition, London, 1960), pp. 432–48.
[49] *The History of the Russian Revolution*, II, p. 669.

pares with it, though it is only in part a work of history.[50] His other attempts at historical writing were far less successful as literature, and as history as well.[51] But the reader of Trotsky's vast *oeuvre* will have noticed that there is hardly a work in it, and hardly an idea, which is not partly marked by the same dramatic element which emerged so prominently in the *History*. 'Le style est l'homme même'; and the style is recognizable in the thought of the man as well.

(b) *Biography as History*

If we count his autobiography, Trotsky may be said to have written 'lives' of the three leading personalities to have emerged from the Bolshevik Revolution. This, however, needs to be qualified: of his two books on Lenin, neither is a full biography, the earlier[52] consisting of separate essays and the later[53] dealing with Lenin's youth only, since Trotsky did not manage to complete it; and the biography of Stalin also remained uncompleted, and was edited by a different hand for publication after Trotsky's death.[54] Moreover, his own autobiography stops

---

[50] *1905* differs from the *History* in that it consists of largely independent essays, though together they form a continuous account of the main events of the 1905 Revolution. Its historical sections are very similar to the *History* in their style of dramatic narrative.

[51] Of his other historical or semi-historical works, the main ones are *Istoriya Oktyabrskoi Revolyutsii* (written in 1918) and *Uroki Oktyabrya* (written in 1924). These works are, however, more in the nature of historical-political tracts than histories. Trotsky's many writings after 1929 in which he attempted to expose Stalin's historical 'falsifications' can hardly be considered works of history; however justified by the circumstances, they remain polemics.

[52] *O Lenine: materially dla biographa* (Moscow, 1924). The book contains as appendices a number of articles on Lenin originally published elsewhere: references to these will be provided below. The first English translation of this work, under the title *Lenin*, appeared in London, 1925; a more recent translation (by Tamara Deutscher) is *On Lenin: Notes Towards a Biography* (London, 1971) which includes some additional articles not included in the Russian original.

[53] *The Young Lenin*, translated by Max Eastman (London, 1972). For a long time this work was available only in a French edition: *Vie de Lénine: Jeunesse* (Paris, 1936), translated by Maurice Parijanine, reissued as *La Jeunesse de Lénine* (Paris, 1970). The Trotsky Archives contain the English translation and various clippings and notes which Trotsky had presumably prepared for subsequent volumes (see Archives, T3741–890). All subsequent references are to the 1972 English edition.

[54] *Stalin: An Appraisal of the Man and His Influence*, edited and translated by Charles Malamuth (New York and London, 1941). This edition, already referred to, actually first appeared only in 1946, the publisher having decided, following Pearl Harbor and obviously out of deference to America's war alliance with the Soviet Union, to postpone distribution. There have been some complaints about the liberties Malamuth took in

at 1929,[55] excluding, therefore, almost the whole of the exile period.

Nevertheless, even in this sometimes fragmentary form, the 'lives' constitute a formidable feat of biographical literature and tell us a great deal not only about their subjects but about Trotsky's general conception of personality and history. This latter is a topic we have touched upon previously in specific contexts;[56] here, therefore, we shall concentrate on abstracting its wider, more generalizing aspects. This aim is made easier by the fact that Trotsky's own purpose in his accounts of the lives of Lenin, Stalin, and of himself was quite obviously to paint, through his subjects, the portrait of an era.[57] This should not be taken to mean that he exploited them merely as pretexts for other interests: it is rather intended to point up the extent to which he considered the personal and the social as inseparable and mutually reflecting. In the biographies, as in his *History of the Russian Revolution*, Trotsky did not shirk the biographer's or the historian's duty to provide as much factual information about his subjects as was relevant and available; and he did so, generally, with scrupulous attention to accuracy. But, again as in the *History*, his main aim was an interpretative one, equally of the personalities involved and of the milieu in which they flourished. The result, as we shall see, was that through the lives of Lenin, Stalin, and himself he presumed to trace the history of a period and of a society. This, of course, is not uncommon, and certainly not illegitimate in biographies; in the present case, however, the biographer chose to see his three sub-

---

editing the text; in what follows, however, references to his interpolations are given only where they prove to be absolutely justified on the basis of the Russian text, deposited in the Archives, T4668–814. Trotsky was still working on this biography when he was assassinated.

[55] *Moya Zhizn*. All references are, as heretofore, to the original Berlin 1930 Russian edition, published in two volumes. The English translation (*My Life*, reissued New York, 1960) has, however, been utilized. The autobiography ends with Trotsky's arrival in Turkey.

[56] See chapters 5, 6 and 10, above.

[57] When in the early 1920s Max Eastman asked Trotsky to co-operate with him in the writing of his biography, Trotsky was at first reluctant to do so but finally agreed in the following words: 'For better or worse, it befell me to play a certain role in the October Revolution and its further development. Many people find their way to the *general* through the *personal*. In that sense biographies have their right.' (See Max Eastman, *Leon Trotsky: The Portrait of a Youth*, pp. vi–vii.)

jects as embodying the whole of this history, as if all other types and actual figures were alien to it.

Since the issue of Trotsky's own relationship to Lenin and Stalin, and his view of his own position *vis-à-vis* others, are central to the character of his biographical writings, it is necessary to begin with some brief remarks about his actual attitude to, and relations with, people around him.[58] It would be an understatement to say that these attitudes and relations were problematical. Hardly anyone who knew Trotsky, including those who at one time or another were particularly close to him, could entirely break down certain seemingly impregnable barriers to the inner man. There was always a sense about him of a 'figure'. In part this was obviously in the very character of the man, a trait imbedded in his personal psychology and subject to it; yet there is no doubt that he also cultivated this impression—a fact which, in itself, says something about his psychology. But whatever the sources, his impact on others was almost invariably that of an aloof being: he conveyed an aristocratic bearing, had utter contempt for petty and trifling matters, did not suffer fools gladly, was impatient with those who took too long to grasp what seemed self-evident to him—or to see the correctness of his views—readily showed intolerance for the weaknesses and human flaws of others, and exuded at all times supreme self-confidence. In all this he left no doubt that he was very different from the ordinary run of men and above the things and follies of this world. Besides, he was particularly argumentative—even by the standards of that community of far from placid Russian revolutionaries—and sometimes seemed to enjoy nothing more than to pour scorn of the most scathing kind, often bordering on mockery, and which came so easily to him, upon those with whom he disagreed.

These characteristics, together with the political views he held, and his independence of groups and organizations, made him both a conspicuous figure wherever he appeared and an isolated one. They certainly put a strain upon, and complicated, his relationships with others. He had very few close

---

[58] What follows draws freely from various biographical accounts and from reminiscences by some of Trotsky's contemporaries—Lunacharsky in particular (see A. V. Lunacharsky, *Revolyutsionniye Siluety*, Moscow, 1923). There is very little disagreement in this literature about the main characteristics of Trotsky's personality.

friends—in the early years only Adolf Joffe and, perhaps, Christian Rakovsky.[59] His relations with Lenin—whom he so deprecated in 1903 and for years thereafter—were, after 1917, correct, even friendly, and on the whole unstrained, despite certain serious disagreements.[60] Lenin seems to have been the only man to whom Trotsky deferred and whom he considered superior to himself. There can be no doubt of the mutual admiration between them, and of their capacity for co-operation and common understanding.[61] But Trotsky later exaggerated the intensity of the relationship; from Lenin's point of view, at least, it does not appear to have extended beyond politics to personal friendship, much less to real affection. As for Trotsky's relations with Stalin, the less said, it seems, the better: there was an immeidate and complete antipathy between the two men.

During the years of exile, Trotsky appears to have mellowed somewhat or, at any rate, to have revealed more of his inner emotions. His *Diary in Exile* is often very moving for the expressions of love and concern for, as well as dependence upon, members of his family, particularly his wife Natalya.[62] The death of his children, and of many former comrades, seems to have sometimes very nearly broken his will to live.[63] But even during this difficult period Trotsky remained overly proud and overly self-conscious in his relations with political friends and followers. The role he was now playing out was very different from that of the 'man of destiny' of revolutionary days; but he still flaunted his sense of destiny, however tragic, and sometimes pathetic, this now appeared. To the outside world, and even

[59] Joffe committed suicide in 1927 out of despair and protest over the campaign against Trotsky. Trotsky dedicated his *Literatura i Revolyutsiya* to Rakovsky with the words 'warrior, man, and friend'. See also his almost nostalgic reference to Rakovsky in *Diary in Exile*, p. 53.

[60] Particularly, of course, over Brest-Litovsk, and over the policy towards trade unions.

[61] Lenin's opinion, expressed in his 1922 testament, of Trotsky—'the most able man in the present Central Committee' but with a 'too far-reaching self-confidence and a disposition to be too much attracted by the purely administrative side of affairs'—is well-known.

[62] See particularly pp. 51, 56–7, 72 and 131–2 of the *Diary*.

[63] Following his son Leon's mysterious death in 1938 in a French clinic, Trotsky wrote an obituary article: 'Lev Sedov: syn, drug, borets', *Byulleten Oppozitsii* (Mar. 1938), pp. 2–8. Although for the most part a tribute to Leon's political work, it ends with a very moving expression of the pain felt by the father on the loss of his son.

to those who worked with him, he remained a 'figure' to the end.

Trotsky's difficulties in his relations with others, the distance he preserved between himself and those around him, and his arrogance towards lesser men, were not, however, signs of an indifference towards people in general. On the contrary, people fascinated him; amongst his earliest writings are many descriptions of, for example, rural scenes in which the simplicity, the perseverance, the suffering, even the personal nobility of ordinary men and of village life are sympathetically and compassionately evoked.[64] But even more in the case of not so ordinary men, his fascination with individuals is evident: whether as a result of his own self-regard or out of sheer curiosity for political and other figures, Trotsky always enjoyed writing 'sketches' of personalities. A whole volume of his *Works* is taken up with such essays and articles, and a whole era of revolutionaries—in particular—emerges from its pages, amongst them Jaurès, Kautsky, Bebel, Plekhanov, Martov, Rosa Luxemburg, and Karl Liebknecht.[65] In later years he often wrote obituary tributes in which his nostalgia for that era was indirectly but unmistakably expressed.[66] Almost invariably these 'sketches' sought to discover the social in the personal and thereby also the historical dimension and significance of the personality. Like Trotsky himself, his subjects also became 'figures', some more, some less human, but all representing a certain way of life or thought or a social type. The result was generally a brilliant political portrait but often too external, too one-sided, too 'rational', and in the end, one feels, not completely real. There is one other characteristic element in these portraitures: although Trotsky could be magnanimous towards those with whom he disagreed, and could show respect for their qualities and rise above petty past disputes or quarrels, he could never

[64] Originally written in 1901, these pieces on rural life were later collected in Trotsky's *Sochineniya*, IV, pp. 17–42. Other essays of a similar nature, written in later years, may be found in *Sochineniya*, VI and XX.

[65] *Sochineniya*, VIII. The volume is entitled *Politicheskie Siluety* and contains articles, written for various journals, from 1909 to 1925. See also his collection of personality sketches, *Gody velikogo pereloma: lyudi staroi i novoi epokh* (Moscow, 1919).

[66] See, for example, 'Anatolii Vasilievich Lunacharskii', *Byulleten Oppozitsii* (Feb. 1934), pp. 19–20 and 'Karl Kautskii', ibid. (Jan. 1939), pp. 15–16. See also his analysis of Kautsky's (and Engels') personality in 'Engels' Letters to Kautsky', Archives, T3709–10.

quite distinguish between personal and political differences. As in his attack on Lenin in 1903–4, his political hates overflowed into a personal antagonism.[67] This too, it seems, was a result of his 'total', undifferentiating conception of the individual personality.

All these elements reappear, with even greater force and significance, in Trotsky's biographies of Lenin and Stalin, and in his autobiography. It would be sheer speculation, of course, to look in these works for direct reflections of his own personal relationships, but the background we have sketched, particularly of Trotsky's figure-like self-regard and presence, and of his grasp of persons as representing certain phenomena beyond their immediate selves, should help us to understand the peculiar qualities of his biographical writings. Let us examine each of these works separately, beginning with the autobiography.[68]

'All the more or less unusual episodes in my life', Trotsky wrote in the foreword to *My Life*, 'are bound up with the revolutionary struggle, and derive their significance from it. This alone justifies the appearance of my autobiography. But from this same source flow many difficulties for the author. The facts of my personal life have proved to be so closely interwoven with the texture of historical events that it has been difficult to separate them.'[69] He then went on to note, however, that the autobiography was not entirely a historical work since he had had to approach events 'not according to their objective significance but according to the way in which they are connected with the facts of my personal life'.[70] Nevertheless, to read *My Life* is to read the history of a period and, despite Trotsky's caveat, a correspondence is shown to exist between the history and the life. But the overlapping between the personal and the historical proceeds not only on the level of events: 'This is a book of polemics', Trotsky wrote in the same foreword: 'It reflects the dynamics of that social life which is built entirely on contradic-

---

[67] This has been well noted by Deutscher, in *The Prophet Armed*, p. 93.
[68] It may be objected that an autobiography is not simply a biography of which the subject happens to be the author himself, but a work essentially different from biographies of others. This is certainly true, but the legitimacy of treating it here as a biographical work derives from Trotsky's own attitude to it.
[69] *Moya Zhizn*, I, pp. 11–12.   [70] Ibid., p. 12.

tions.'[71] And, a page later, he noted that 'in this book ideas, their evolution, and the struggle of men for these ideas, have the most important place'.[72] Indeed, nothing is so striking in the autobiography as the raising of 'contradictions' to the level of a clash of ideas, so that there is a thematic unity to the work, one deriving from the confrontation of certain antithetical views of the world, a confrontation working itself out concretely in the persons of definite men, not the least amongst them, of course, Trotsky himself.[73]

All this is not to say that *My Life* avoids details of a purely personal nature, or that Trotsky unfolded his life in a cold, detached manner, or that the relationship between the personal and the social and historical was presented in some mechanical, schematic sequence. On the contrary, some of its best chapters are those which deal with the author before he became involved in history, before, as he says, he passed 'through hidden channels from one world into the other', from childhood to adult life.[74] 'Mine was the greyish childhood of a lower-middle-class family, spent in a village in an obscure corner where nature is wide, and manners, views and interests are pinched and narrow.'[75] Yet from the first, uncertain memory—'at times it has seemed to me that I can remember suckling at my mother's breast'[76]—to that moment—'The Break'[77]—some seventeen years later when political, revolutionary ideas begin to enter his consciousness, there is a vivid, almost nostalgic—though unsentimental—description of the child growing up, absorbing, taking on individuality. The pace, like the childhood, is somewhat leisurely, though already we are introduced to what appear to be certain innate characteristics: rebelliousness, a competitive spirit, ambition sometimes bordering on vanity and always expressed through a desire to stand out.[78] His father,

---

[71] Ibid., p. 8.   [72] Ibid., p. 9.

[73] He had not been able, Trotsky wrote (ibid., pp. 6–7), to enter into an account of 'complicated theoretical problems', for reasons of space and format. But the 'theory of permanent revolution ... runs through this book as a remote leitmotif'.

[74] Ibid., p. 18.

[75] Ibid., p. 17. A brief description of Trotsky's youth and home was given at the outset of chapter 1, above.

[76] Ibid., p. 18.

[77] This is the title he gave to the chapter (ibid., pp. 114ff.) which described his political awakening.

[78] See ibid., pp. 111–12 for his own self-analysis in these terms.

who was illiterate and taken up with managing the family farm, does not seem to have had any lasting influence on the boy;[79] and with the mother also there were no particularly intimate ties.[80] But the portrait of his childhood is not an unhappy one; and there is no attempt to show the 'child as father to the man', no searching for some ominous signs of destiny.

It is thereafter, of course, that personal life becomes 'interwoven' with historical events. Trotsky does not crudely identify himself with history. But the chapters describing his first political and intellectual gropings run unmistakably parallel to, as he sees it, the first awakening of Russian political consciousness, culminating in the Revolution of 1905. And the subsequent ups and downs of the revolutionary movement are reflected in Trotsky's life—or perhaps the other way around, since the two *are* so interwoven in the text. The zenith, of course, is reached in 1917 though, as in *The History of the Russian Revolution*, Trotsky understates his role. From thence until 1929 there are first the days of 'glory' and then the gradual, finally abrupt fall from power. Here history and personal fate part, or so it would seem. Trotsky, however, is far from reconciled to this impression: in 1929, at least, he still exudes self-confidence and trust in history. The parting is as if temporary, and there are no doubts about the eventual reuniting of the Revolution with, if not the man himself, then what he has represented. The final paragraphs of the autobiography quote, firstly, Rosa Luxemburg on Goethe, on the latter's rising 'above material things with a calm superiority', on the 'universality of his interests' and the 'inner harmony of the man', and on his being a 'fighter in the grand style'; and, secondly, Proudhon, who speaks of the uneven but inevitable progress of revolution.[81] This, naturally, is meant to convey Trotsky's identification with Goethe's personal qualities and with the historical optimism of Proudhon:[82] these qualities

[79] He noted (ibid., pp. 36–7) that in old age his father had tried to learn the alphabet 'in order to be able to read at least the titles of my books'. Somewhat laconically he observed that his father lost all his savings in the wake of the October Revolution; and he added: 'My father died of typhus in the spring of 1922, at the very moment when I was reading my report at the Fourth Congress of the Communist International.'
[80] He recorded (ibid., p. 265) her death without the slightest intimation of emotion.
[81] Ibid., II, pp. 337–8.
[82] Though not, of course, with the political ideas of Proudhon, whom Trotsky called 'that Robinson Crusoe of socialism'. Nevertheless, he attributed personal qualities to Proudhon—'the nature of a fighter, a spiritual disinterestedness, a capacity for despis-

and this optimism are for Trotsky intertwined, as if mutually dependent, mutually fated, as they have been, thematically, throughout the pages of *My Life*.[83]

If his autobiography, for obvious reasons, avoided direct aggrandizement of its subject, no such restraint characterizes Trotsky's accounts, incomplete though they are, of Lenin's life. The first of these is a blatantly adulatory book, an unabashed exercise in flattery, the only one of Trotsky's works about which it can be said that it is almost embarrassing to read.[84] *On Lenin* was written hurriedly in March and April 1924, shortly after Lenin's death, and supplemented, in the form of appendices, by four short articles published earlier.[85] This, and the fact that the anti-Trotsky campaign was already seeking to introduce a wedge between Trotsky and Lenin, perhaps explain the fragmentary nature of the work, its popular, journalistic style, and its exaggerated, uncritical hero-worship. Even as he was writing the book, and preparing to send it to the publisher, Trotsky himself seems to have had doubts about its merits: at one point he paused to remark upon the 'inadequacy' of his account, which had turned out to be 'poorer than I had imagined when I started' writing it;[86] and in the foreword he apologized for

ing official public opinion, and, finally, the fire of a many-sided curiosity never extinguished', all of which 'enabled him to rise above his own life, with its ups and downs, as he did above all contemporaneous reality'—qualities which Trotsky wanted to think that he too possessed.

[83] It is significant that besides *My Life* Trotsky wrote many shorter pieces dealing with some event or aspect of his life and that in these too a moment of history was described through some personal experience; see, for example, one of the earliest of these pieces, *Tuda i Obratno* (Petrograd, 1919), also in *1905*, pp. 361–422 (describing his exile to and flight from Siberia in 1907) and, of the numerous later accounts of his fall from power and banishment from the Soviet Union, *Chto i kak proizoshlo?* (Paris, 1929). See also *The Case of Leon Trotsky* (The Dewey Commission hearings) in which Trotsky directly and simultaneously defended both the personal and the historical dimensions of his 'case'.

[84] *O Lenine*, unlike the other historical and biographical works dealt with in this chapter, was, as has been pointed out, written in 1924, *before* Trotsky's exile.

[85] Three of these articles were written before Lenin's death; they are, with date of writing (page numbers refer to *O Lenine*): 'O pyatidesyatiletnem' (1920), pp. 145–50 (this article was also published separately under the title 'Lenin kak natsionalnyi tip'); 'O ranenom' (1918), pp. 151–8; 'O bolnom' (1923), pp. 159–65. The fourth article was written the day after Lenin's death: 'Ob umershem', pp. 166–8 (first published as 'Lenin net!' in *Pravda*, 24 Jan. 1924).

[86] *O Lenine*, p. 38

its 'incomplete' and 'sketchy' nature and urged that it be considered as no more than a series of personal recollections.[87] This
latter is, in fact, what it largely amounts to, and as such it is
not entirely devoid of redeeming features: Lenin is shown as
a real being with everyday human qualities, not as an enshrined
demigod. Trotsky recalls his first meeting with Lenin in 1902,
the years of the *Iskra* period, the days preceding the Revolution
and the Revolution itself, the Civil War and the initial problems
of running a revolutionary government. All this is described
from the point of view of one who worked with Lenin at the
time and is able, therefore, to recount the personal side of the
man, both in action and in moments of reflection, as it emerged
through various episodes and conversations.

Nevertheless, the work is irreparably marred by Trotsky's
amost complete inability to find any blemish in Lenin's character or historical record.[88] Lenin is shown to be human, but as
perfect as human can be. The book seeks to praise its subject
not assess him, much less analyse dispassionately the effects of
his acts and ideas. Thus in almost every instance of a past controversy in which Lenin was involved, he is seen to have been
not only right, but wiser, more farsighted, more perceptive, in
fact very nearly infallible. Even in disputes involving himself,
Trotsky readily admits the errors of his, at the time, opposition
to Lenin's views.[89] Moreover, the acrimony surrounding his
break with Lenin in 1903 and his subsequent violent attack on
Bolshevism are barely hinted at.[90] As for Lenin's character,
Trotsky finds that it combined the best elements of Russian,
national traditions, and revolutionary, international ones;
that the man was selfless, dedicated in his love for humanity,
sensitive to the pain and suffering of others, driven only by a
determination to alleviate the iniquities imposed upon mankind by distorted but remediable—through revolution—social
institutions. Lenin is, in every respect, 'the leader', as a man,
as a revolutionary, as a thinker, as a visionary.[91] In short, from

---

[87] Ibid., pp. v–vi.
[88] A rare exception to this is Trotsky's admission that it was largely Lenin who was
responsible for the 'error' of the advance on Warsaw in 1920 (ibid., pp. 87–8).
[89] See, for example, on the matter of Brest-Litovsk, ibid., pp. 78–90.
[90] See the section 'Lenin and the Old Iskra', ibid., pp. 3–48, where he recalls the opposition of the Mensheviks to Lenin in 1903—but not his own.
[91] Trotsky reaches especial heights of stylistic hero-worship in the language of the four

1903 onwards he is protrayed as the 'only one to personify the future'.[92] Had anyone else but Trotsky written this panegyric, one would have probably concluded that it was the work of an incorrigible sycophant.[93]

On Lenin, therefore, is a book whose only value lies in its personal reminiscences of past episodes; as biography and as history it tells us little about Lenin and even less about Trotsky's conception of the whole problem of the individual in history, since it hardly touches upon this problem except in a glib, simplified manner.[94] At any rate, Trotsky in 1924 was both too close in time to the Lenin period, and evidently too constrained by the political circumstances which followed it, to attempt a more serious work. The intention to do so, however, was always with him, and in the mid-1930s, when exile seemed to afford the opportunity of more tranquil reflections on the past, he began to put this intention into effect. The result, eventually, was *The Young Lenin*, the first instalment of what was to be a full-scale biography but which never materialized beyond this single volume.[95] Even in this limited form, however, this is a

---

articles, mentioned above, which appear in the book as appendices. In the last of these, for instance, obviously written in an almost hysterical state following Lenin's death, the following phrases occur: 'our great leader', 'the unique who cannot be replaced', 'the party and working class are orphaned', 'in each of us there lives a small part of Lenin, and this is the best part of each of us'.

[92] *O Lenine*, p. 48.

[93] Unfortunately, some other pieces on Lenin—not included in *O Lenine*—which Trotsky wrote later in 1924 are not much better; see 'Vernoe i falshivoi o Lenine', *Pravda*, 7 Oct. 1924 and 'Malenkie o bolshom', *Pravda*, 8 Oct. 1924. In 1926 Trotsky contributed the entry on 'Lenin' to the 14th edition of the *Encyclopedia Britannica*. This, no doubt in view of the character of the publication for which it was written, is much more constrained in its language; but here too Lenin was not so much assessed as extolled. See also Trotsky's defence of Lenin and his indignant denunciation of Winston Churchill's book *The Aftermath* in which Churchill attacked Lenin: 'Mr. Churchill is Wrong', *John O'Londons Weekly*, 20 Apr. 1929.

[94] Deutscher, in *The Prophet Outcast*, pp. 248–50, vastly overestimates the book, ignores or misrepresents its tone and contents and, incredibly, exonerates Trotsky of any tendency towards Lenin 'cultism' (see also his brief comment on the book in *The Prophet Unarmed*, p. 165). Other historians, however, have also exaggerated the value of the book, though with far greater reservations than Deutscher; see the introduction by Lionel Kochan to the 1971 English translation, and the introduction by Bertram D. Wolfe to the same translation but in an American edition: *Lenin* (New York, 1971, Capricorn Books).

[95] He began collecting material for a definitive biography of Lenin in 1933; the work, however, was often interrupted and much delayed by more pressing matters. By 1935 he had completed writing the first 15 chapters which constitute *The Young Lenin* (i.e.

work on the grand scale; all those elements characteristic of the Trotsky style and of Trotsky's dramatic sweep—so conspicuously absent from the 1924 biographical sketches—are here present in their most refined manner. True, one would not say of it that it was objective any more than one would call the 1924 work objective; here too its hero is presented in too one-sided, too uncritical, too admiring a light. But the crudities of the earlier work, both in style and approach, have been entirely eliminated. Where *On Lenin* was a simplified, personal eulogy, *The Young Lenin* is a work of historical analysis and reconstruction.

As in *My Life*, the emphasis is on the 'interweaving' of the personal and the social. From the very first chapter, which describes the geographical and social character of Simbirsk—where Lenin was born—and through it of 'old Russia', the destiny of the young Lenin and that of Russia are thematically joined.[96] There is in this, of course, not a little of the dramatic artifice and much that, as a consequence, would seem to prejudge the significance of Lenin's early life. But Trotsky is writing not so much a biography as a biographical history of the climate of the last decades of the nineteenth century; the coming to maturity of the youth is set firmly within the context of a divided society and a decaying culture. The conventions of the traditional, seemingly ageless and docile Russia are counterpoised by the penetration of new ideas, the periodic outbursts of violence, the growing confrontation between an inured, stubborn autocracy and a frustrated, restless intelligentsia.[97] At the same time, however, the limitations, immaturity and hopelessness—as Trotsky sees these—of Populism, in particular of the People's Will group, are brought out, and their impact, both conscious and unconscious, on the young Lenin, struggling to assimilate the essence of his environment, is pointedly recorded. It is in this context too that we are shown the well-known influence on Lenin of his brother Alexander, of the latter's purity of character, and of the trauma of his

---

Lenin to 1893) and which first appeared in French in 1936 (see note 53, above). In later years he made attempts to resume work on this biography but with little success and nothing further was ever completed.

[96] *The Young Lenin*, pp. 1–12.

[97] See in particular chapter 3, pp. 24–37.

attempt on the life of the Tsar, and of his eventual execution.[98] Trotsky emphasizes that this influence was moral in that it 'inculcated into [Lenin] higher demands upon himself and others'; but he rejects as psychological crudity the view that the execution of Alexander immediately provoked Lenin into the pragmatic reaction: 'Well, then, we will seek a more effective road.'[99] In truth, Trotsky believes, at this time the loss of the brother had mainly a personal meaning; Lenin had as yet no idea where, politically, his brother had gone wrong, and it would be many years of 'Herculean labours' before he would find an intellectual and political answer to Alexander's failures.[100]

The readiness to acknowledge the importance of Alexander in Lenin's early life, but the refusal to explain the latter's development in these personal terms alone, reflect again the theme of Trotsky's biography: the person of Lenin must be understood against a wider canvas, not merely his immediate family environment but the over-all impact on him of the Russian social milieu and of the 'inevitable conflict'[101] between the two. Traversing the personal and the social, Trotsky thus gives us a portrait of the revolutionary as a young man which is not unlike the portrait he presents of the social and revolutionary conditions: still uncertain, uncrystallized, lacking clear goals and, on the conscious level, their 'teleology' largely unassimilated. The story of Lenin's later early life then becomes the story of that period during which developments begin to come to a head and, through Lenin, the revolutionary ideology and the revolutionary course of action, the shape of things to come, are slowly and painfully unravelled. Trotsky's description of the six years which follow the execution in 1887 of Alexander thus show Lenin observing, learning, developing methods of abstraction and analysis and, of course, encountering and beginning to embrace the doctrines of Marxism.[102] By 1893 the future revolutionary leader has emerged; Lenin now knows

---

[98] See chapter 4, pp. 38–46 for Trotsky's portrait of the brother and pp. 107–19 for his assessment of the latter's influence on Lenin.

[99] Ibid., pp. 114 and 118.

[100] Ibid., pp. 118–19.

[101] Ibid., p. 114.

[102] For Trotsky's account in the book of Lenin's Marxist self-education, see in particular pp. 124–31 and 181–95.

what needs to be done and senses his own historic role: 'The
critical movement in the minds of the intelligentsia, like the
more profound movement in the industrial areas, required a
doctrine, a programme, an instructor.'[103] By 1893 Lenin was
already set on his, and Russia's, fateful course:

> He was still to make great strides forward, not only externally but
> internally; several clearly delineated states can be seen in his later
> development. But all the fundamental features of his personality, his
> outlook on life, and his mode of action were already formed during
> the interval between the seventeenth and twenty-third years of his
> life.[104]

One can only guess, of course, how Trotsky, had he written
the subsequent instalments of Lenin's life, would have treated
the controversies of 1903 and, in particular, his own clash with
Lenin at that time and until 1917. But the guess is not a difficult
one: we know that in other writings, whenever confronted by
this issue, he more or less avoided it, at best admitting the error
of his position but without giving any hint of the profundity
of the cleavage between his views and those of Lenin. One can
be fairly sure that he would have done exactly the same upon
reaching the year 1903 in the biography of Lenin. In view of
the fact that so much of Stalin's anti-Trotsky campaign was
based on this cleavage—not to mention other, imaginary,
ones—one can well understand Trotsky's reluctance to belabour the issue, though this political rationale hardly justifies
historical dishonesty.

However, this was not the only motive for Trotsky's glossing
over past differences. After all, he had in 1917 accepted Bolshevism and there is no gainsaying his total devotion to its principles
thereafter—even if he subsequently did not, as he did in 1903,
recognize all the implications of these principles. The old differences with Lenin therefore seemed to Trotsky irrelevant. But
not even this explains entirely his unequivocal attitude towards
the history of his relations with Lenin. There can be no doubt
that beyond purely conscious political and historical elements,
an unconscious element was at play in Trotsky's recollections
of the Bolshevik leader. No one reading what Trotsky wrote
about Lenin can fail to notice the awe which characterizes these

---

[103] Ibid., p. 206.   [104] Ibid., pp. 206–7.

writings, the genuine adulation for the man and the revolutionary. Lenin was clearly Trotsky's idol and he worshipped at his shrine, identifying with all that Lenin stood for, seeking approval and acceptance in his hero's eyes. In the process he drove out of his mind the sins committed in the years of his youth. Looking back upon their famous days together, at the head of the October Revolution and the Soviet government, all else seemed to recede into insignificance, and he saw himself as the true and loyal heir of the founder of Bolshevism.[105] Thus the perpetual astonishment of Trotsky at the fact that others could dare to blemish his relations with Lenin; thus also the seeming self-conviction that the death of Lenin was a cruel, arbitrary blow, the source of his own tragedy and that of the Soviet Union, tragedies which so paralleled one another. In his 1935 *Diary in Exile* there is a revealing entry: Trotsky records a dream in which Lenin appears and expresses anxiety about Trotsky's health; in the midst of their conversation Trotsky suddenly recalls that Lenin is dead. His reaction to this, in the dream, is wish-fulfilling, as only a dream can be: 'I immediately tried to drive away this thought [of Lenin's death], so as to finish the conversation. When I had finished telling him about my therapeutic trip to Berlin in 1926, I wanted to add, "This was after your death", but I checked myself and said, "After you fell ill . . ."'[106]

This obsession with the memory of Lenin and with Lenin's death finally led Trotsky into one of his strangest speculations: perhaps the death of Lenin was not, after all, an 'arbitrary act of nature'?[107] The thought had already occurred to him in

---

[105] See, for example, his article on Lenin's testament, 'Zaveshchanie Lenina', Archives, T3487.

[106] *Diary in Exile*, p. 131. It is in this diary also (pp. 27–8) that he recalls his attempt, while still in Turkey, to write a book about Marx and Engels (though nothing came of it). 'How well they complement one another!', he exclaims and then describes in the most glowing terms the friendship between the two men and, especially, Engels' devotion to Marx. He remembers having spoken of this once to Lenin and Lenin's similar admiration for Engels: 'Lenin loved Engels very deeply . . . I remember how we examined with some excitement a portrait of Engels as a young man, discovering in it the traits which became so prominent in his later life.' Did Trotsky unconsciously feel his relationship with Lenin to have been like that of Engels with Marx? See also *Moya Zhizn*, II, p. 252.

[107] In 1924, in the article, 'Ob umershem', op. cit., p. 167, he had described thus Lenin's death, i.e. as an 'arbitrary act of nature'.

1935;[108] but it was in his biography of Stalin, on which he worked in his final years, that the thought turned into an *idée fixe*.[109] Without the slightest scrap of real evidence and on the basis of surmises and 'theoretical' circumstances alone, Trotsky now in effect declared that far from dying a natural death brought on by illness, Lenin had been poisoned by Stalin.[110] This excursion into morbid speculation is the most striking, though not the only, example of the thin line which Trotsky trod in his biography of Stalin between fact and fantasy.[111] Much of the book is based on hearsay, gossip and patently unreliable and hostile sources. It abounds in unabashed bias, distortions, personal abuse, and generally far-fetched interpretations of Stalin's motives and activities both before and after 1917.[112] Trotsky is unable to discover a single redeeming feature in Stalin's character and it is only reluctantly and with numerous qualifications that he attributes to him any political or organizational talents. 'Stalin', Trotsky declares at the outset, 'represents a phenomenon utterly exceptional. He is neither a thinker, a writer nor an orator ... Stalin took possession of power, not with the aid of personal qualities, but with the

[108] See *Diary in Exile*, pp. 43–4.

[109] *Stalin*, pp. 372–83.

[110] Trotsky's whole case was based on the fact that in February 1923 Lenin, despondent about his physical deterioration, had called in Stalin and requested the latter to provide him with poison. Trotsky relates how Stalin informed him, and Zinoviev and Kamenev, of this suicidal request. It was, of course, unthinkable to Trotsky that it should be granted but Stalin, according to Trotsky, did not express an opinion about the matter; instead there was 'a sickly smile transfixed on his face, as on a mask' (ibid., p. 376). Trotsky 'imagines' that, following a temporary improvement in Lenin's health, Stalin, thirsting for power, decided to 'expedite his master's death' (p. 372): 'I am convinced that Stalin could not have waited passively . . .' (p. 381). In retrospect, it now also appeared to Trotsky that this was the reason Stalin did not want him to be present at Lenin's funeral lest he (Trotsky) recall the poison request and demand an autopsy.

[111] He first raised publicly the 'poison' accusation against Stalin in an article he wrote at the end of 1939. The article was intended for *Life* magazine which, however, refused to publish it; it eventually appeared, under the title 'Did Stalin Poison Lenin?', in *Liberty*, 10 Aug. 1940. The idea that Stalin may have poisoned Lenin is, of course, not inconceivable and has often been suggested by others as well. However, on the basis of the 'evidence' *Trotsky* presented, there was no case for it; that he should have made the charge on such flimsy grounds suggests that by then Trotsky had become completely obsessed by the contemplation of 'what might have been', i.e. that were it not for Stalin, Lenin might have lived and his (Trotsky's) own fate might have been completely different.

[112] Of the many examples which can be cited, it may suffice to mention Trotsky's recurring hints that Stalin may once have been an *agent provocateur* in the Russian revolutionary movement (see *Stalin*, pp. 12, 53, 116, 120).

aid of an impersonal machine. And it was not he who created the machine, but the machine that created him . . . Stalin . . . took possession of [the machine]. For this exceptional and special qualities were necessary. But they were not the qualities of the historic initiator, thinker, writer or orator.'[113] The biography of Stalin is, therefore, an exercise in demonology. There is no doubt, of course, that Trotsky's subject, by any standard, had not a few demonic attributes. But what was the point of merely harping on the demonic without really analysing those aspects of this and other attributes—and they were clearly not all merely organizational in the narrow sense—which could explain Stalin's political successes?

The biography of Stalin moves at a uniformly high, almost shrill pitch from first page to last and therefore lacks almost all sense of development. From Stalin's modest and unremarkable origins in Georgia—Trotsky somewhat unfairly emphasizes the poverty of Stalin's ethnic background[114]—to the summits of Soviet political power—'Kinto in Power'[115]—there is nothing but the figure of a sly, scheming conspirator, utterly lacking leadership qualities, and merely adept at exploiting opportunities, not creating them: 'In attempting to find a historical parallel for Stalin, we have to reject not only Cromwell, Robespierre, Napoleon, and Lenin, but even Mussolini and Hitler. [We come] closer to an understanding of Stalin [when we think in terms of] Mustapha Kemal Pasha or perhaps Porfirio Diaz.'[116] The central theme of the biography is, therefore, that Stalin had only two basic capacities which, combined with the fundamental evil in him and his bottomless thirst for power, made it possible for him to become the monolithic dictator:

[113] Ibid., p. xv. On Trotsky's misguided underestimation of Stalin's political talents, see Robert H. McNeal, 'Trotsky's Interpretation of Stalin', *Canadian Slavonic Papers* (no. 5, 1961), pp. 87–97.
[114] See *Stalin*, pp. 1–3 where Trotsky warns against venturing into 'national metaphysics' but remarks, nevertheless, that 'basic character elements . . . are less happily distributed under the southern than under the northern sun'. On the other hand, he writes, Stalin's Georgian origins did not account for everything since Stalin lacked many of the *positive* qualities of Georgians. This must be a classic example of having your cake and eating it too!
[115] This is the title of the supplementary chapter (ibid., pp. 411–20) dealing with Stalin's attributes as a ruler.
[116] Ibid., p. 413. The implication of this, incidentally, is rather unfair to Ataturk, though perhaps not altogether so to Diaz.

the one was the capacity for plotting and intrigue, the other for organizational manipulations. But this theme is not made more credible for being endlessly repeated and, supposedly, illustrated by every stage of Stalin's career. It is obviously a half-truth only and, in the end, only partly explains Stalin's rise to power and the nature of his subsequent rule. As an analysis of the personal attributes required for political dictatorship, the biography of Stalin is thus a complete failure.

In addition to this, the book is rambling, cumbersome, repetitive, too long and, for the most part, tedious. One moment we are given the facts of Stalin's life, the next we are nearly bludgeoned with an explanation for them, lest we miss their meaning, though this is hardly likely since the facts are themselves so laden and interspersed with pejorative remarks. Not hesitating to offer interim assessments, Trotsky leaves almost nothing to the reader's imagination. Even the language limps, lacking Trotsky's usual sparkle, though here and there one can find a characteristic turn of phrase. Undoubtedly many of its structural and stylistic faults, perhaps even its factual ones, would have been expunged had Trotsky lived to finish the work; yet it is clear that the problem was not so much one of editing and polishing as the incapacity of Trotsky, as biographer and as *Trotsky*, to free himself of the 'demon' who, though perhaps himself possessed, had in a sense come to possess Trotsky as well.[117]

Stalin is not, however, entirely devoid of a historical dimension. Nothing in it compares even remotely with the analysis of Stalinism which Trotsky carried out in other works during the 1930s, particularly in *The Revolution Betrayed*; but even here there is at least a tacit acknowledgement of the relationship between the personal and the social. However often Trotsky would like to to believe that Stalin is his own product, that he alone is to blame for the degeneration of the Russian Revolution, he cannot quite suppress, under the welter of personal polemics, the more historical sources of Stalinism. It is, of course, somewhat surprising that he should even try to understate this element, since the view that Stalinism reflected the

---

[117] In view of this and of the extremely personalized nature of the judgements in the book, Trotsky's protestation (ibid., pp. 371–2) that 'hatred' of Stalin and personal feelings had played no role in the biography seems merely perfunctury.

backwardness of Russia was so central to, and so openly argued in, his other writings of the 1930s on the Soviet Union. Perhaps this merely points up again the extraordinary, personalized nature of this work and Trotsky's obsession with Stalin as his cruel Nemesis. But, to repeat, the wider dimensions of the Stalin phenomenon appear here too, though in a highly derogatory manner. Note, for example, the very first paragraph of the book where Trotsky records that Leonid Krassin had once called Stalin an 'Asiatic', and Bukharin had 'simplified the appellation' to 'Genghis Khan'. This is no doubt recalled and meant as a personal slur. But Trotsky adds that what is important is not 'geography, ethnography and anthropology': 'history looms larger'.[118] And, indeed, in emphasizing throughout the biography Stalin's intellectual vacuity, his lack of culture, his provincialism, his primitive behaviour, his cruelty, vindictiveness, and petty-mindedness,[119] Trotsky wishes also to bring out certain age-old aspects of Russian society which had not only not been eradicated but which, he believes, in the person and regime of Stalin had reasserted themselves. Stalin, Trotsky recalls having once observed, was a 'mediocrity' but not a 'nonentity'.[120] And, he implies, is this not like the Russian masses' cultural heritage, mediocre, but an overbearing entity barring the way to Russia's entry into the twentieth century? If Lenin, for Trotsky, represented the progressive potentialities of Russian society, Stalin was his antithesis, representing the regressive forces, the huge residue of an impoverished but ubiquitous culture. If Lenin was the hope of the future, Stalin was the retribution of the past. But the weight of this past had now become more totally stifling for it had been joined to the machinery of modern economic production and political rule, to the instruments originally created by the Revolution as means to a socialist society but, under Stalin, transformed into ends in themselves. 'Stalin's ambition', Trotsky remarks, 'acquired an 'untutored Asiatic cast intensified by European technique.'[121] Thus backwardness, combined with the technical apparatus

---

[118] *Stalin*, p. 1. He also notes that Stalin himself had once referred to himself as an 'Asiatic' but this was only for the purpose of hinting 'at the existence of common interests between the U.S.S.R. and Japan as against the imperialistic West'.
[119] See ibid., pp. 40–1, 54, 75, 113, 117, 119, 172, 177, 194, 336, 393, 414; this list of Trotsky's negative references to Stalin's character could be multiplied endlessly.
[120] Ibid., p. 393.   [121] Ibid., pp. 393–4.

of economic and political regimentation, created modern totalitarianism.

It should now be possible to assess briefly the over-all character of Trotsky's biographical writings. The Marxist, as we know, suspects the role of the individual in history; the biographer, however, is constantly confronted by it. Trotsky, as a Marxist biographer, resolved the problem by presenting his subjects as embodiments of historical trends and processes. This explains the general absence in his autobiography of psychological intro-spection, and the almost complete correspondence in all the 'lives' between the outer and the inner man, between per-sonality and character. The result, in other words, was bio-graphical history, in itself a common genre, but made suspect in the case of Trotsky by his tendency to summarize the whole of late nineteenth- and of twentieth-century Russian history through himself, Lenin, and even Stalin. Thus while he and Lenin appear as the personifications of Russia's inevitably revo-lutionary future, Stalin is the retributive threat of her past, the counter-revolutionary force hovering over the Revolution and deriving from the dilemmas of its origins.[122] Reading Trotsky's biographies one would hardly guess that other personalities and other trends existed in Russia—except as spent forces—or that the triumph of Bolshevism, both in its Leninist–Trotskyist, and later Stalinist guises, was far from certain until the very last moments. As a historian and biographer, however, not to men-tion as a Marxist, Trotsky was first and foremost concerned with the victors of history. This explains the significance he perceived in his own and Lenin's lives. But it also explains the peculiar nature of his obsession with the figure of Stalin, his attempt in this case to personalize historical events, and the final irony of having nevertheless to provide, however reluctantly, a histori-cal dimension, a social basis, for the victory of Stalin and for his own defeat.

---

[122] In this connection see also a letter Trotsky wrote in 1938, reproduced in Pierre Naville, *Trotsky vivant* (Paris, 1963), pp. 122–4. Here Trotsky argued that changes in political leadership and personal fortunes were reflections of antagonistic historical forces, and of the 'milieu' in which they took place.

2. The Jewish Question: Nationalism and Internationalism

Trotsky's views on the Jewish question may be properly considered at this point in our study both because they concern a subject which, on the face of it, is related to the biographical fact of his own Jewish birth, and because the subject itself is in the nature of a historical phenomenon, not to say dilemma. These views, though they occupy a marginal place in his thought and writings, and though they offer little that is original or unexpected, are of interest since they vividly illustrate the nature of Trotsky's internationalist convictions, and throw further light on his unwavering conception of Marxism as a universalist creed. Before giving an account of his views on the Jewish question, two related topics may be briefly raised: the one concerns the question of the role or influence of Trotsky's Jewishness[123] in his life; the other the extent to which his thought in general, and his views on Jewish questions in particular, were affected by this Jewishness, or can be seen to have reflected it.

As to the first of these topics, it seems best to make short shrift of it here, and not only because it is primarily a biographical issue—and a speculative one at that—and therefore outside the scope of the present study: the truth of the matter is that there is very little in Trotsky's life which shows that his Jewishness played any significant, conscious role in his development, that in any direct sense it could be said to have constituted a motive force in his life. This is not to deny that at certain points in his life he took the fact of his Jewishness into account, or that at others he was reminded of it; nor is it to claim that he was completely insensitive to his Jewish background. No Jew, if we bear in mind the climate which prevailed in Russia both before and after 1917, could remain altogether indifferent to his Jewishness, however much he might have wished to do so. It is, however, too much to assume that the fact alone of Jewishness is sufficient cause for a man's life, or a large part of it, to

[123] In what follows, the term 'Jewishness' is used to signify the simple fact that Trotsky was a Jew by birth and, to a certain extent, by upbringing; it is not in itself meant to imply the existence of a Jewish cultural or other identity or consciousness. The latter is precisely the issue involved in the first topic.

be governed by Jewish self-awareness, much less by what is commonly known as the 'Jewish complex', or that this fact must be reflected in all his exterior behaviour and inner tribulations. It is, of course, true that Trotsky's involvement in the Russian revolutionary movement, like the large and disproportionate involvement of other Jews, is significant from the point of view of general sociological observations about the history of the Jews in Russia at the turn of the twentieth century. The participation of so many Jews was certainly not accidental, and it is instructive to investigate its sources and its nature, as well as its impact upon the history of the revolutionary movement.[124] But it is a common fallacy to derive conclusions about a particular individual from general observations about the 'sociological' group to which he ostensibly belongs. In some cases, what is true about the group may be true about the individual; in others, there is only the most tenuous of relationships. The case of Trotsky belongs to the latter category.

Nevertheless, probably more nonsense has been written about the 'Jewish aspect' of Trotsky's life than about any other.[125] This is surprising since Trotsky never revealed any ambiguity or uneasiness about his Jewishness. He took it for what it was— a fact of birth, and of a certain particular upbringing during the early years of his childhood. He neither concealed his Jewish background nor, conversely, attempted to attribute to it any special significance, whether positive or negative. There was nothing in him which even vaguely resembled the kind of ambivalence, bordering on, or perhaps reaching, self-hatred, which may be found in some of Marx's writings on Jewish questions, nor the intense sense of Jewish nationalism which, being disappointed, finally also ends in self-rejection, as in the case of

[124] The best brief account of this kind is Leonard Schapiro, 'The Role of the Jews in the Russian Revolutionary Movement', *The Slavonic and East European Review* (Dec. 1961), pp. 148–67. The most definitive account of the history and conditions of Jews in Russia is S. M. Dubnow, *History of the Jews in Russia and Poland* (3 vols., Philadelphia, 1916–20).

[125] See, for example, Joseph Nedava, *Trotsky and the Jews* (Philadelphia, 1972). Another, equally dubious, attempt at inferring a 'Jewish compex' in Trotsky's life is the *Encounter* article—mentioned previously in other contexts—by Joel Carmichael (see *Encounter*, May 1972, especially pp. 36–7). It is, however, also possible to exaggerate in the opposite direction; Deutscher, for example, in all three volumes of his biography of Trotsky hardly mentions the latter's writings on Jewish questions, and relegates largely to footnotes Trotsky's more moderate remarks on Zionism in the 1930s as well as even Trotsky's condemnation of Stalin's anti-Semitism.

Lassalle.[126] In his autobiography Trotsky recounted openly and, it seems, fairly and accurately, the nature of his Jewish upbringing.[127] His parents were neither religious nor particularly observant of Jewish traditions; he never mastered Yiddish or Hebrew—neither of which was spoken in the home—and although he received some instruction in Jewish subjects this was on the whole very limited in scope and of short duration. Even if we assume that Trotsky in his autobiography understated early Jewish influences, there are objective reasons for believing that they would have been fewer than those prevailing in a normal Jewish environment: he grew up neither in an urban Jewish milieu nor in a Jewish-populated small town— the typical Russian *shtetl*—but in a rural community, the son of a Jewish farm-owner, largely isolated from other Jews. It does not seem unwarranted, therefore, for him to have claimed that 'in my mental make-up, nationality never occupied an independent place, as it was felt but little in everyday life'.[128]

In later life, of course, Trotsky came into close contact with many Jews, from Martov and Parvus to numerous Social Democrats in the capitals of Europe, particularly Vienna.[129]

[126] Marx's most extreme definition of the Jewish condition which, being so extreme, has engendered the view that Marx was giving vent to more than just socio-economic opinions and, moreover, that he was abnormally sensitive about his background—in spite of the fact that, as his father had converted, he had not been brought up as a Jew—is his 'On the Jewish Question' (in T. B. Bottomore, ed., Marx, *Early Writings*, pp. 3–40). But in his behaviour as well Marx displayed hostility towards all things Jewish: this has been sometimes overstated (as in M. Glickson, *The Jewish Complex of Karl Marx*, New York, 1961), but seems undeniable (see Isaiah Berlin, *Karl Marx: His Life and Environment*, 3rd edition, London, 1963, pp. 27, 99–100, and 269). On Lassalle's transformation from Jewish nationalist to Jewish deprecator, see Edmund Silberner, 'Ferdinand Lassalle: From Maccabeism to Jewish Anti-Semitism', *Hebrew Union College Annual*, XXIV, 1952–3, pp. 151–86. On the history of anti-Semitism within the Western socialist movement, see the same author's *The Anti-Semitic Tradition in Modern Socialism* (Jerusalem, 1953).

[127] *Moya Zhizn*, I, pp. 22, 55–7, 64–5, 106–10.

[128] Ibid., p. 109.

[129] In Vienna Trotsky was compelled to choose a religion for his children; he quotes his wife's explanation for this (ibid., p. 264): 'According to the Austrian law then in force, children up to the age of fourteen had to have religious instruction in the faith of their parents. As no religion was listed in our documents, we chose the Lutheran for the children because it was a religion which seemed easier on the children's shoulders as well as their souls.' Nedava (op. cit., pp. 43–4) has a field-day with this: Trotsky, he claims, 'converted' his children and, what is more, to the Lutheran faith because Karl Marx's father had chosen Lutheranism; in this way 'Trotsky might have been trying unconsciously and vicariously to identify himself with his forerunner in the socialist conception'!

But the basis for such relationships was always political. During the Revolution, the fact of his Jewishness was no obstacle, although it was exploited by White propaganda.[130] And there is only one major instance where he himself took it into account. This was immediately after the October insurrection when Lenin offered him the Commissariat of the Interior; he turned it down arguing that, in this position, his Jewish origin would 'put into our enemies' hands an additional weapon'. This, he explained in his autobiography, was a purely 'political consideration'.[131] Instead, he accepted the Commissariat for Foreign Affairs. It was only many years later, when Stalin had ascended to power, that his Jewishness was made into a thinly veiled issue: 'Anti-Semitism', he wrote, 'raised its head with that of anti-Trotskyism.'[132]

Trotsky rarely spoke or wrote on any issue as a Jew;[133] as far as was possible he tried to avoid being categorized as one— except where it was a matter merely of factual origin—and sought to disclaim any relationship between his Jewishness and his revolutionary activities. Once, when it was suggested to him that he could not ignore the element of national loyalty, that he must seee himself either as a Russian or as a Jew, Trotsky replied: 'No! You are mistaken. I am a Social Democrat and that's all.'[134] These attitudes have been taken to mean that Trotsky was ambivalent about his Jewishness, if not entirely hostile to it, and thus obsessed by it to the point of self-denial. Is it not more reasonable to assume, however, that if he did not wish to be known as a *Jewish* revolutionary it was because he rejected what he took to be, rightly or wrongly, a form of parochialism? He did not become a Marxist or a revolutionary because of the 'Jewish problem' and it was not only this problem

---

[130] Trotsky humorously recalled, however, an episode, recorded in a White Guard publication, in which a Cossack exclaims: 'Trotsky is not a Jew. Trotsky is a fighter. He's ours . . . Russian! . . . It is Lenin who is a communist, a Jew, but Trotsky is ours . . .' (*Moya Zhizn*, II, p. 86.)

[131] Ibid., pp. 62–3.

[132] Ibid., p. 86.

[133] One exception to this is his speech, to be presently referred to, against the Bund at the 1903 Congress of the Russian Social Democrats.

[134] Quoted in Wolfe, *Three Who Made a Revolution*, p. 169. On another occasion, when a Jewish delegation approached him to defend, as a Jew, the political rights of Jews following the Bolshevik triumph, Trotsky replied in anger: 'I am not a Jew, I am an internationalist.' (Ziv, *Trotsky: kharakteristika po lichnym vospominaniam*, p. 46.)

that he wished to eliminate through his Marxist revolution-ism.[135] He did not want, therefore, to be taken for a kind of Jewish representative or spokesman among the revolutionaries, a champion of Jewish causes. To be identified as a Jew, by sympathy and inclination, not by origin, meant to him to be tied to some nation-group; he rejected such ties, as he rejected all nationalism, for he considered himself an internationalist in 'flesh and blood'.[136] For this very reason neither can he be seen as an assimilationist, that is as one who sought to escape his Jewishness by identifying himself with the national environment in which he lived.[137] Moreover, he never spoke harshly or in a derogatory way about Jews or Judaism, his strictures against the Jewish religion and nationhood were like his strictures against all religions and nationhoods, and while he subscribed to the standard Marxist interpretation of the Jewish question he never subjected it to crude and simplistic formulas. Marx's severe anti-Jewish language was not echoed in Trotsky's writings.

As to the question of the influence of Trotsky's Jewishness upon his thought and ideas—though these cannot be artificially severed from his life and activities—one could, perhaps, make out a partial case for the view that no one but a Jew lacking national roots in the Russian environment could have become so extremely devoted to purely universalist principles, to, specifically, the notion of the world revolution creating one world community in which ethnic and national differences would play no role. The theme of universalism was, of course, a well-known phenomenon amongst the Jewish intelligentsia, both in the wake of Emancipation in Western Europe and secularization in Eastern Europe.[138] It is certainly one of the most ubiqui-

---

[135] '. . . national inequality probably was one of the underlying causes of my dissatisfaction with the existing order, but it was lost among all the other phases of social injustice. It never played a leading part—not even a recognized one—in the lists of my grievances.' (*Moya Zhizn*, I, pp. 109–10.)

[136] Ibid., II, p. 63.

[137] One can, of course, describe him as an assimilationist in the sense of one who wishes to erase national distinctions within an *international* community.

[138] It should be remembered, however, that it was not the only theme and, in Eastern Europe in particular, nationalism—in the form of Zionism—was no less a potent force, so that many of Trotsky's Jewish contemporaries, both in time and place, developed very different ideas. Most East European Zionists, however, were also socialists, and many were even Marxists.

tous themes in Trotsky's thought. Be that as it may, beyond this general, somewhat abstract element, Trotsky's thought lacks any specifically *Jewish* themes, and any evidently Jewish content or allusions.[139] In part this may be due to the limited Jewish education which he received, and to the poverty of his Jewish cultural heritage. However, it is also due to the fact that Jewishness was not an issue for him. He did not agonize over it; he did not feel that he had, in this connection, anything to assert or deny or conceal. In this matter he was at peace with himself; if the Jewish question was a problem it was one which, he believed, could be resolved, like so many other problems, within the framework of a socialist revolution and a socialist society. There was therefore no reason, in his view, why one should assign to it prominence over other problems, and no reason why one should suffer from a 'complex' over it.

We may consequently consider Trotsky's views on the Jewish question, as we have his thought in general, without reference to some hidden motives behind them and without the, in any case, dubious practice of 'psychologizing' them. Here too his approach is that of a Marxist revolutionary and analyst, not that of a Jew concerned with this problem specifically or in isolation from other issues. As we shall see, he both underestimated the severity of the problem and overestimated the capacity of socialism for dealing with it. The fact that he subsumed the Jewish question under the issues of nationalism and internationalism expressed, on the one hand, the absence in him of any tension between his Jewishness and his Marxism; reading his writings on Jewish questions one would hardly guess that they were written by a Jew. However, the fallacies and misconstructions of Trotsky's analysis expressed also the limits of his Marxist approach.

In comparison with most other Russian revolutionaries, who hardly touched the subject or dealt with it only in the context of the 'nationalities question' in general, Trotsky may be said to have written fairly widely on the Jewish question.[140] In abso-

---

[139] In this connection, compare Trotsky's writings (and his person) with, for example, those of Axelrod or Martov. On the former, see Abraham Ascher, *Pavel Axelrod and the Development of Menshevism* (Oxford, 1973); on the latter, see Israel Getzler, *Martov: A Political Biography of a Russian Social Democrat* (Melbourne, 1967).

[140] For Lenin's views on this subject, see *Lenin on the Jewish Question* (New York, 1934). For accounts of socialist attitudes to the Jewish question, see (in Hebrew) Edmund

lute terms, however, these writings, mostly brief articles or essays, are sparse. He certainly did not deal with the matter systematically; and under the general rubric of the Jewish question he commented, sometimes indiscriminately, on its various, though admittedly related, aspects: the condition of the Jews, the origins of their social and economic position, anti-Semitism, Jewish organizations—the Bund in particular—and the possible alternative solutions—especially the Zionist one—to the Jewish predicament. It is best, therefore, to treat these aspects collectively, as he did. And since the Jewish question must be seen in its changing social context—its nature and ramifications under Tsarism were obviously different from those under Stalin—we shall divide Trotsky's writings into two periods, before 1917 and after.

It was in 1903 that Trotsky first expressed views on matters concerning the Jewish question, and this was also to be virtually the only time in his life that he would speak openly on this, or on any other subject, in his 'capacity' as a Jew. The occasion was the fateful Second Congress of the Russian Social Democrats.[141] The first issue to arise at the Congress was the status of the Bund—the Social Democratic organization of Jewish workers founded in 1897—within the over-all Social Democratic movement.[142] The Bund demanded organizational and cultural autonomy as well as the right to be the sole representative of Jewish workers. This was vehemently opposed by Martov and other Jewish *Iskraites*;[143] as one of the latter Trotsky

Silberner, *Ha-Sotsializm ha-Maaravi u-Sheelat ha-Yehudim* (Western Socialism and the Jewish Question), (Jerusalem, 1955) and (also in Hebrew) Yitzhak Maor, *Sheelat ha-Yehudim ba-Tnua ha-Liberalit ve-ha-Mahpechanit be-Russia, 1890–1914* (The Jewish Question in the Liberal and Revolutionary Movement in Russia), (Tel-Aviv, 1964).

[141] Earlier in 1903 Trotsky had written an article in which he commented on pogroms against Jews (the Kishinev pogrom had erupted in April of that year) but this article was less concerned with the situation of the Jews than with the general political repercussions of such events; see 'Eshche o Tartyufakh', originally published in *Iskra*, 1 June 1903 and reprinted in Trotsky's *Sochineniya*, IV, pp. 146–50. See also his later denunciations of the notorious Black Hundreds in 1905, pp. 124–30 and 358–60 and, later still (1917), of the pogrom phenomenon, 'Pogromnaya agitatsiya', *Sochineniya*, III, part 2, pp. 23–4.

[142] For an account of the ties between the two until 1903, see Harold Shukman, *The Relations Between the Jewish Bund and the RSDRP, 1897–1903*, unpublished D.Phil. thesis, Oxford, 1961.

[143] The Bund issue arose before the general issue of party organization and membership which was to lead to the Menshevik–Bolshevik split, that is, before Martov, Trotsky, and Lenin found themselves in different camps.

delivered some of the most biting remarks against the Bund and against Jewish separatism in general.[144] He made it clear that he was speaking as a Jew and that, therefore, his opposition to the Bund had an added significance.[145] He lashed out, first, at the whole idea of organizational autonomy, arguing that this would only lead to a profusion of national or ethnic groupings within the party, and ultimately to a diffusion of its powers. He rejected equally the notion that only a Jewish organization could mobilize Jewish workers: this, he claimed, not only betrayed mistrust in non-Jewish socialists, but assumed that socialism could be propagated on the basis of national feelings alone, whereas its actual appeal was founded on internationalist principles. Beyond this, however, he attacked the whole concept of Jewish cultural autonomy: this, in his view, involved not only a matter of safeguarding certain cultural traits, such as language, which was legitimate; it concerned the whole issue of whether nationalities should lead a closed, separate existence. Socialism, he argued, could not reconcile itself to the idea that people should be cut off from each other, and therefore at odds with one another, because of certain cultural differences. Its goal was to break down barriers between men, and it was consequently opposed to separatism, whether on the party level or that of society at large. The demands of the Bund, therefore, appeared to him to reflect parochial tendencies and dangers which went beyond merely party organizational considerations.[146]

How far Trotsky expected the Bund to degenerate along

[144] His various remarks on this issue are in *Vtoroi Syezd RSDRP: Protokoly* (Moscow, 1959). Trotsky's words aroused much protest among the Bundists but Deutscher (in *The Prophet Armed*, pp. 73–6) exaggerates when he makes it appear that Trotsky was the focus of the whole controversy.

[145] Those 'Jewish comrades', Trotsky said, who opposed autonomy for the Bund and who preferred to work within the framework of an all-Russian party, 'regarded themselves as representatives of the Jewish proletariat as well'. (*Vtoroi Syezd RSDRP: Protokoly*, p. 57.)

[146] Ibid., pp. 71–3. See also Trotsky's *Vtoroi Syezd RSDRP: Otchet Sibirskoi Delegatsii* (discussed in detail in chapter 7, above), pp. 9–11, where Trotsky summarized the Bund controversy. Reiterating his arguments at the Congress, Trotsky here wrote of the clash between the 'universal and the particular', of the struggle against 'provincialism', 'narrow patriotism', and 'parochialism'. 'We worked hard and persistently', he remarked (p. 10), 'to be rid of the Greek political psychology—the narrow-minded patriotism of "their" cities—and to stand on the state-minded viewpoint—that of the Romans.'

these 'nationalist' lines may be seen from an article he published shortly after the Congress, in January 1904, which was devoted partly to the subject of Zionism.[147] From his strictures against the Bund it is not difficult to guess what would be Trotsky's views on Zionism; if the Bund, which after all sought to remain within the Social Democratic fold and was a revolutionary workers' organization, had become so much of an anathema to him, how much more antagonistic would be his attitude towards a movement which made national identity and political independence—in the form of a sovereign territory—the core of its ideology, notwithstanding its devotion also to socialist principles? And, indeed, in this article Trotsky defined once and for all—or nearly so, for some thirty years later he would express a slight change of mind—his hostility towards Zionism, although he reserved the brunt of his polemic for the Bund, for at this time he did not take Zionism very seriously. Having apparently followed the Sixth Zionist Congress, held in Basle in the summer of 1903, at which the head of the Zionist movement, Theodor Herzl, had proposed Uganda as a temporary territorial solution, Trotsky mocked at this 'demonstration of impotence': 'Herzl promised Palestine—but didn't deliver it.'[148] The effect of the proposal at the Congress was indeed to plunge the Zionist movement into a deep crisis. Trotsky was convinced that this was a crisis from which it could not recover; the Zionist shibboleth of a 'fatherland' had been exposed for what it was, the 'reactionary' dream of a 'shameless adventurer'[149] who, having failed once, was now desperately groping for a new stratagem with which to delude the Jewish masses: 'It is impossible to keep Zionism alive by this kind of trickery. Zionism has exhausted its miserable contents . . . Tens of intriguers and hundreds of simpletons may yet continue to support Herzl's adventures, but Zionism as a movement is already doomed to losing all rights to existence in the future. This is as clear as midday.'[150]

Trotsky nevertheless discerned a 'Zionist Left' which, he believed, would 'inevitably' join the ranks of the revolutionary movement out of disappointment with the Zionist solution to

[147] 'Razlozhenie sionizma i ego vozmozhnye preemniki', *Sochineniya*, IV, pp. 124–8. This article originally appeared in *Iskra*, 1 Jan. 1904.
[148] Ibid., p. 124. [149] Loc. cit. [150] Ibid., p. 125.

the Jewish problem. As for the rest of the remnants of 'decaying' Zionism, they would find a home for themselves in the Bund. The latter was more and more becoming a depository for all that was 'accidental' and 'particular' among Jews.[151] Competing with Zionism for adherents, it was beginning to resemble Zionism. It could well be that as Zionism disappeared, it would leave behind a successor: 'But this successor might prove to be the General Jewish Workers' Union in Lithuania, Poland and Russia [i.e. the Bund].'[152]

This was not a very perspicacious article; Zionism did not disappear and the Bund forever remained a Jewish organization fundamentally different from and opposed to the Zionist movement.[153] Trotsky betrayed a tendency to lump together indiscriminately all manifestations of cultural or national distinctions. Above all, however, he exposed an inability to appreciate the force of national identification; he was himself so far removed from any such inclination that he found it strange that people should want to retain their 'particularism'. Much better than this political analysis, however, was his analysis of the social conditions of the Jews. After 1904 and until 1917 he wrote specifically about the Jewish question on two occasions only— both in 1913—and in each case it was to unravel its inner social manifestations and its impact upon society at large.[154]

The first of these 'Jewish pieces' is an article dealing with the condition of Jews in Rumania.[155] In 1912 and 1913 Trotsky travelled through the Balkans as the correspondent of the Russian newspaper *Kievskaya Mysl*; the article was one of his many reports on social developments in the Balkan countries.[156] 'The real Rumania', he began, 'manifests itself through the Jewish question.'[157] Three hundred thousand Rumanian Jews lived

---

[151] Ibid., p. 127.   [152] Ibid., p. 128.
[153] For a general account of the Zionist movement from its beginnings to the establishment of the State of Israel, see Walter Laquer, *A History of Zionism* (London, 1971).
[154] The only other specific reference to the Jewish question occurs in his 1905 article on the State Duma: 'Kak delali gosudarstvennuyu dumu', in Trotsky, *Nasha Revolyutsiya*, pp. 110–35. A brief section of this article (pp. 129–30) is entitled 'The Jewish Question' and merely points out that the granting of political rights to Jews, as well as the alleviation of their conditions, continue to be shirked by the state authorities.
[155] 'Evreiski vopros', *Sochineniya*, VI, pp. 402–11. (Originally published in *Kievskaya Mysl* in three instalments, 17, 20, and 21 Aug. 1913)
[156] His other reports, mainly on Bulgaria and Rumania, are also collected in his *Sochineniya*, VI.
[157] 'Evreiski vopros', ibid., p. 402.

as 'foreigners', without citizenship, without fundamental political rights, but with all those obligations, including army service, which devolve upon citizens. The country, he continued, was permeated by a hatred of the Jews: small businessmen feared competition from them; clerks, professionals, state employees were anxious lest the Jews be granted citizenship and thereby take away their jobs; teachers and priests, 'agents' of the nationalistic landlords, convinced the peasantry that all its misery was due to the Jews. 'Anti-Semitism is becoming a state religion, the last psychological cementing factor of a feudal society rotten through and through . . .'[158] Why then were the Jews tolerated? Because, according to Trotsky, the Rumanian regime needed the Jew: firstly, to act as the 'middleman'—'lease-holder, money-lender, hired journalist'—between landowner and peasant, between the politician and his clients, to carry out all the 'dirty assignments'; secondly, to be the focus for the indignation of the dissatisfied Rumanian population, to be the perennial scapegoat.[159]

Trotsky then went on to give a detailed account of the historical evolution of the Jewish situation in Rumania.[160] The gist of this was that the Jews had been turned into a bartering commodity in the hands of cynical international diplomacy and high finance. At the Congress of Berlin in 1878, Western statesmen, and Bismarck in particular, had ostensibly insisted that Rumania grant equal rights to its Jews as a pre-condition to the guarantee of its independence. Very soon, however, it became clear, according to Trotsky, that Bismarck's real interest was the acquisition by Rumania at high prices of shares in the Rumanian Railways held by German bankers, some of them Jews, whose investments in the railways had culminated in huge losses. As soon as this was settled to the satisfaction of Bismarck and the bankers, the 'Jewish pre-condition' became a minor matter: Rumania granted citizenship to 900 Jews who had fought in the 1876-8 war with Turkey; as for the other '299,100', they remained in the same servile condition. 'Reading the diplomatic papers concerning this case', Trotsky remarked, 'as well as the private correspondence of the interested

[158] Ibid., p. 404.
[159] Ibid., p. 403.
[160] Ibid., pp. 404-8

parties involved, one cannot for a moment free oneself of a
feeling of deep disgust.'[161]

The final section of the article returned to the pitiful conditions of Rumanian Jewry and described the extent of the dis-
crimination against them, their lack of security, their uneven
social and economic distribution, their inability to escape certain prescribed roles arising from legal and social inequality:

The conditions of feudal stagnation, legal deprivatio:., political and
bureaucratic corruption, not only degrade the Jewish masses economically but bring about their spiritual disintegration. There might
be endless arguments on the theme that the Jews are a separate nation,
but it is an undeniable fact that the Jews do reflect the economic and
moral conditions of the country in which they live and, being artificially isolated from the majority of the population, they are nevertheless
an integral part of it.[162]

The article ended on a mixed note: Trotsky noted sadly that
Rumanian Jews had so far been unable to organize themselves
effectively for political action—they had formed a 'Union'
which based its programme on ingratiation with the ruling oligarchy, and devotion to Rumanian patriotism; on the other
hand, he hoped that their lot would yet become bound up with
that of progressive opinion and forces throughout Europe.[163]

Without question, this article constituted one of Trotsky's
best comments on the Jewish question; it was certainly the most
openly sympathetic. There was no sense here of a demonstrative
detachment; rather one feels that Trotsky was almost identifying with the endurers of injustice whom he described. Moreover, there was in the article no facile economic dismissal of
the problem; though the economic position of the Jews entered
into his analysis, the Jews were presented as the victims of a
social system—not to mention of an international diplomatic
manœuvre, if not conspiracy—rather than its happy benefi-
ciaries. There is of course no reason to believe that Trotsky's
empathy for the Jews was any greater for his being a Jew; he
could write with no less compassion about the sufferings of non-
Jews as well. His identification was with the suffering, not with
the identity of the sufferer. But how different was the tone and
content of this article, which was in effect a definition of the

[161] Ibid., p. 408.   [162] Ibid., p. 410.   [163] Ibid., pp. 410–11.

Judenfrage, from Marx's notorious fulminations on the same subject! At least it put paid to the view, which Marx was as responsible for disseminating among socialists as anyone else, that the Jews were somehow all established capitalists, and that it was capitalism which was the source of anti-Semitism.[164] Even in Western Europe this was only partially true; as Trotsky's article made clear, it was almost completely groundless as far as the Jews of Rumania were concerned and, for that matter, those of Russia and Eastern Europe in general.

No less compassionate, however, and similarly perceptive about anti-Semitism and the Jewish condition, was Trotsky's second 1913 article devoted to a specifically Jewish topic.[165] This was originally published in November of that year in *Die Neue Zeit* and was an analysis of the notorious Beilis trial, in which a Russian Jew of that name was accused of a religious ritual murder.[166] The article may be considered a classic exercise in mockery and sarcasm, a style not inappropriate to describing the superstitions, the medieval chicanery over Biblical references, and the sheer nonsense which were paraded before the court. With his sense for the dramatically fantastic, Trotsky could hardly resist exploiting the rich material for ridicule which the trial provided.[167] But the trial, of course, was not a laughing matter as far as the victimized Beilis was concerned; and it reflected the situation not of an isolated individual but of a whole class of men, the Jews of Russia. In bringing out the absurdities of the trial—as well as the absurd figures who passed through it as witnesses, lawyers, jurymen—Trotsky sought to convey the primitive reality of Russian society, at its lowest, peasant levels as at its highest, autocratic ones. This, he believed, was the crucible of Russian anti-Semitism, ignorance joining hands with viciousness to victimize innocent persons who were declared to be the source of all evil. To bring out the peculiarity of this anti-Semitism, Trotsky compared the Beilis case with the Dreyfus affair in France:

[164] Though Marx was certainly not the first socialist to voice such and other opinions about the Jews—as the examples of Fourier and Proudhon sufficiently testify. In this connection, see again Silberner, *The Anti-Semitic Tradition in Modern Socialism*.
[165] 'Pod znakom dela Beilisa', *Sochineniya*, IV, pp. 462–76.
[166] For an account of the case and trial, see Maurice Samuel, *Blood Accusation* (Philadelphia, 1966).
[167] 'Pod znakom dela Beilisa', in particular pp. 464–71.

It cannot be denied that to a certain extent an analogy between the two cases exists, but they are as strikingly different from one another as is the French drawing-room Jesuit anti-Semitism from the Russian criminal pogromist Black Hundredism, and as is the cynical and learned Poincaré—who professes not to believe in God or the Devil— from the Tsar Nicholas—who has no doubt that witches on brooms take off at night through chimneys.[168]

The trial, Trotsky wrote, aroused in him a 'feeling of physical nausea'.[169] He believed, however, that its main impact in the end would be to hasten political disgust with the autocracy; in this sense it will have contributed, in its own peculiar way, to the revolutionary temper of the times.[170]

If Trotsky's writings on the Jewish question during the period before 1917 are few and far between, they are even more sparse during the following decade or so. Generally, in his years of power he shied away from Jewish matters and, considering their marginality to his active concerns, there is nothing sinister in this. But probably the reluctance not to appear as the spokesman for Jewish causes also played a role in his silence.[171] At

[168] Ibid., p. 470.   [169] Ibid., p. 473.   [170] Ibid., p. 476.

[171] Although he sometimes demonstratively disclaimed any special interest in matters of concern to Jews, neither did he oppose Jewish causes simply because they were Jewish. However, some of his activities must have grated on Jewish susceptibilities. Thus, for example, for a year or so, in 1921–2, he headed the 'Society of the Godless', an organization created to spread anti-religious propaganda, and which was, of course, directed against Judaism no less than against Christianity (see *Moya Zhizn*, II, p. 213). Or, again, when in mid-1922 the Living Church movement came into being, Trotsky encouraged its growth, both because it was opposed to the established Church hierarchy and because it represented, in his view, a departure from medieval religiosity and the adoption of a more modern, more rational approach to religious practice. (In *Literatura i Revolyutsiya*, p. 29, he described this movement as representing the progressive going over of the Church to a NEP of its own: 'If the Soviet NEP is a mating of socialist economy with capitalism, then the church NEP is a bourgeois grafting on to the feudal stem.') However, the Living Church aroused among the Orthodox establishment the anti-Semitic charge that the movement was a Jewish conspiracy aimed at undermining Christianity (see Carr, *Socialism in One Country*, I, pp. 51–2, note 6). Trotsky, however, did not hesitate to condemn this expression of anti-Semitism: see his *Voprosy Byta* (2nd, enlarged edition, Moscow, 1923), pp. 143–5. Trotsky also never seems to have had anything to do with the 'Evsektsia', the 'Jewish bureau' of the Communist party created to 'adapt' Russian Jewry to the Revolution. All in all, it may be said of Trotsky that, rightly or wrongly, he considered his Jewishness to be an irrelevant factor. Other Russian Jews, of course, did not see matters in the same light: in 1921 Rabbi Jacob Maze, the chief rabbi of Moscow, approached Trotsky on behalf of the Russian Jews: Trotsky told him that he did not see himself as a Jew but simply as a revolutionary, to which the rabbi retorted: 'The Trotskys make the revolutions and the Bronsteins pay the bills.' (Quoted in S. M. Melamed, 'St. Paul and Leon Trotsky', *Reflex*, Nov. 1927, p. 8.)

any rate, if he took no interest in the Jewish question, neither did he have much to say on the wider national question. He was content to defer in this matter entirely to Lenin, whose views on it he accepted implicitly.[172] 'The national policy of Lenin', he wrote expansively in later years, 'will find its place among the eternal treasures of mankind.'[173] He wrote virtually nothing on this question either before or after 1917.[174] He believed that the problem of nationalities would naturally resolve itself within the framework of a workers' government— and certainly of a socialist society—in which class loyalty would be stronger than national loyalty.[175] Beyond this the matter simply did not interest him.[176] It is hardly surprising therefore that he should have made light of the whole Jewish question

[172] For Lenin's views on the national question, see V. I. Lenin, *Izbranniye stati po natsionalnomu voprosu* (Moscow–Leningrad, 1925). On the relation between these views and the Jewish question, see Harold Shukman, 'Lenin's Nationalities Policy and the Jewish Question', *Bulletin on Soviet and East European Jewish Affairs* (May 1970), pp. 43–50. For a detailed account of Soviet policy, during Lenin's time, toward the nationalities, see Richard Pipes, *The Formation of the Soviet Union: Communism and Nationalism, 1917–1923* (Cambridge, Mass., 1954). See also Mary Holdsworth, 'Lenin and the Nationalities Question', in Schapiro and Reddaway (eds.), *Lenin: The Man, the Theorist, the Leader*, pp. 265–94.

[173] *The History of the Russian Revolution*, III, p. 913. The phraseology of this sentence is quite unlike Trotsky's usual style but it reflects, again, his adulatory manner whenever reminiscing about Lenin. The sentence concludes the chapter (pp. 889–913) devoted to 'The Problem of Nationalities'. The first part of the chapter is intended to show the inability of the Provisional Government to deal with the nationalities. On pp. 904–13 there is a note which summarizes Lenin's views and which simultaneously derides Stalin's theoretical 'pretensions' in this sphere. See also Trotsky's *Stalin*, pp. 153–9 where he not only throws doubt on Stalin's originality but asserts that the latter's well-known work on the national question—'Marxism and the National Question'— was largely the work of Lenin.

[174] For his few pre-1917 writings on the national question, see *Sochineniya*, IV, pp. 370–93. Of his post-1917 writings, the chapter from *The History of the Russian Revolution* mentioned above is in effect his only sustained comment on the subject; but see also *Pokolenie Oktyabrya*, pp. 28–37, and *The Revolution Betrayed*, pp. 170–8.

[175] See his defence of the Red Army's invasion of Georgia in 1921 (in which he argued that the principle of national self-determination had to be subordinated, at least during the transition period of the Revolution, to the principle of a unified socialist economy): *Mezhdu Imperializmom i Revolyutsiei*, in *Sochineniya*, XII, pp. 183–296 (especially pp. 268–77). When in 1923 Lenin asked him to defend the case of the 'national deviationists' in Georgia against Stalin, Trotsky did so only reluctantly, without much conviction and without success, though in later years he exaggerated the differences between himself and Stalin on the Georgian issue (see *Moya Zhizn*, II, pp. 220–6).

[176] It is, however, interesting to note in this context his 1920 article on Lenin (in *O Lenine*, pp. 145–50–see note 85, above) in which he discussed the latter's 'national (Russian) characteristics'. Though asserting the fundamental internationalism of Lenin, he

during the years following the Revolution; this problem too, he thought, would disappear in the course of time.

He was genuinely shocked, therefore, when in 1926 first intimations reached him that his own Jewishness had not remained irrelevant, least of all in the party itself, and that anti-Semitism was now being exploited by supposedly dedicated Soviet Communists. This was, of course, part of Stalin's way of undermining the Opposition, by making conspicuous the fact that so many of its members were Jews. Learning of this anti-Semitic agitation within the party and outside, Trotsky wrote a letter to Bukharin in which he was hardly able to restrain his surprise, his dismay and his fury at this development.[177]

In fact this was only the beginning of what would become a standard feature of Stalinism, and not only, or even mainly, as a weapon against Trotsky. Following his exile, the truth of this slowly dawned on Trotsky and when it did he did not hesitate to confront it directly. Of his many observations during the 1930s on the phenomenon of Soviet anti-Semitism, the most interesting was to be an article he prepared in 1937 entitled 'Thermidor and Anti-Semitism'.[178] It is interesting for the manner in which Trotsky, recognizing the intractability of Russian popular anti-Semitism, attempted to link its re-emergence with the character of the Soviet regime as he defined it in the 1930s. Thus, he admitted, the October Revolution did not, in 'one blow', sweep out anti-Semitism: 'Legislation alone does not change people.' The level of culture, traditions, thoughts, and emotions, all these were stronger than laws, and it was consequently 'impossible that national and chauvinist prejudices, particularly anti-Semitism, should not have persisted strongly among the backward layers of the population'.[179] He then

---

attributed most of Lenin's revolutionary qualities, and some others as well, to his Russian origins and upbringing and to general environmental influences. There was, of course, a great deal of truth in this, but that it should come from Trotsky, who always eschewed national characterization in the case of 'truly Marxist' revolutionaries, is surprising.

[177] The letter is in the Archives, T868. Trotsky asked Bukharin to join him, despite their political differences, in verifying the facts behind this agitation. Bukharin, however, apparently chose to avoid the matter for he did not reply.

[178] 'Termidor i antisemitizm', Archives, T4105, 4106. This article was not published until after Trotsky's death. References are to the English translation in Howe (ed.), *Basic Writings of Trotsky*, pp. 206–15.

[179] Ibid., p. 207.

explained, however, that under Stalin this hostility towards the Jews was expressed in a particular form: the Jews being largely an urban population, more educated and cultured, were naturally a main source for the large number of civil servants which the Stalin regime needed; and the fact that so many bureaucrats were Jews could not have escaped the notice of the population:

The hatred of the peasants and the workers for the bureaucracy is a fundamental fact in Soviet life . . . Even by *a priori* reasoning it is impossible not to conclude that the hatred for the bureaucracy would assume an anti-Semitic colour, at least in those places where the Jewish functionaries compose a significant percentage of the population and are thrown into relief against the broad background of the peasant masses.[180]

This explanation may have served Trotsky's purpose of linking bureaucratism with anti-Semitism but it also implied that anti-Semitism worked against the interests of Stalin and the bureaucracy. Why then should Stalin have been interested in encouraging renewed expressions of hostility towards Jews? Trotsky himself seems to have recognized the limits of his explanation for in the rest of the article he showed that it was not so much the Soviet bureaucracy which bore the brunt of the anti-Semitic venom as the opponents of the bureaucracy. Thus he pointed out that the Jewish origin of many accused in the 1930s trials was made conspicuous for all to see. Why was it, he wondered rhetorically, that the Left Opposition was made to appear as made up almost exclusively of Jews?[181] Why was it that he was suddenly being identified as Bronstein, not Trotsky, and Zinoviev as Radomyslsky, Kamenev as Rozenfeld?[182] In fact, he made it clear that it was the old Bolshevik guard, against which Stalin was struggling, that was being discredited by the means of anti-Semitism; that, moreover, the bureaucracy, faced by insuperable economic difficulties, strove to 'divert the indignation of the working masses from itself to the Jews'. Finally, he noted, the 'Thermidorian reaction' was accompanied by 'the most unbridled chauvinistic

[180] Ibid., p. 208.

[181] He denied, however, that Jews were predominant among its members and pointed to the names of a number of 'fully indigenous Russians' (e.g., Smirnov, Preobrazhensky).

[182] In this connection, Trotsky recalled his 1926 letter to Bukharin and the latter's failure to intervene.

passions, anti-Semitism among them'.[183] On his own showing, therefore, the bureaucracy was more the beneficiary of popular anti-Semitism than its victim; and 'socialism in one country' which, as he had always argued, must lead to bureaucratization, could be paraded as a nationalist ideology the opponents of which would be defined as non-indigenous by origin. He was not blind, therefore, to some of the real sources of Soviet anti-Semitism; and the fact that he nevertheless attempted to see the existence itself of the bureaucracy as a cause of popular anti-Semitism may be attributed to his hope that the 'peasants and workers' were implacably hostile to bureaucratism as such.[184]

The more specific issue of Soviet policy towards Jews to which Trotsky addressed himself on a number of occasions was that of Biro-Bidzhan, the area designated in 1934 as a Jewish Autonomous Region.[185] In principle, Trotsky appeared to favour the idea of an independent cultural community within the framework of the Soviet federation. In a letter of 1934 he wrote that a 'workers' government is duty bound to create for the Jews, as for any nation, the very best circumstances for cultural development'. And he added:

This means, *inter alia:* to provide for those Jews who desire to have their own schools, their own press, their own theatre, etc., a separate territory for self-administration and development. The international proletariat will behave in the same way when it will become the master of the whole globe. In the sphere of the national question . . . there must be an all-sided material assistance for the cultural needs of all nationalities and ethnic groups. If this or that national group is doomed to go down (in the national sense) then this must proceed in the same way as a natural process, but never as a consequence of any territorial, economic, or administrative difficulties.[186]

He repeated the same view in 'Thermidor and Anti-Semitism' though here he added that the idea of Biro-Bidzhan was

[183] Ibid., pp. 209 and 213.
[184] In *Stalin* (pp. 152, 172, 399–400) Trotsky implied that Stalin was personally anti-Semitic but that he always used anti-Semitism in a 'calculated' manner.
[185] On the history of this experiment, see (in Hebrew) Jacob Lvavi, *Ha-Hityashvut ha-Yehudit be-Biro-Bidzhan* (The Jewish Settlement in Biro-Bidzhan), (Jerusalem, 1965). On the condition, in general, of the Jews in the Soviet Union, see Solomon Schwarz, *The Jews in the Soviet Union* (Syracuse, 1951).
[186] The source for this letter, a reply to a group of Jewish Oppositionists in the Soviet Union, is the pamphlet *Leon Trotsky on the Jewish Question*, published by the Pathfinder Press (New York, 1970), p. 19. The Russian original has not been traced.

in any case a temporary solution, necessary so long as nations as independent cultural entities continued to exist, and until a truly international socialist community was created. However, as far as the actual Biro-Bidzhan project was concerned, this appeared to him to reflect 'all the vices of bureaucratic despotism'.[187] And elsewhere he defined it as a 'bureaucratic farce'.[188]

Of course, a solution to the Jewish problem had become, in the 1930s, a matter of urgency not primarily because of the condition of Jews in the Soviet Union. It was the situation in Germany which had raised anew the question whether, after all, the only way of saving the Jews of Europe was the Zionist one. Did Trotsky as a consequence become more amenable to the Zionist solution? The most that can be said is that his position became less obviously hostile, though even this must be qualified. In 1934 he told an interviewer that he remained 'opposed to Zionism and all such forms of self-isolation'.[189] The Jewish question, he said, could not be 'solved within the framework of capitalism'. He did not know 'whether Jewry will be built up again as a nation'. 'However', he added, 'there can be no doubt that the material conditions for the existence of Jewry as an independent nation could be brought about only by the proletarian revolution . . . The establishment of a territorial base for Jewry in Palestine or any other country is conceivable only with the migrations of large human masses. Only a triumphant socialism can take upon itself such tasks.' Either some mutual understanding would be reached between Arabs and Jews in Palestine or 'a kind of international proletarian tribunal' would 'take up this question and solve it'.[190]

In all this there was some implication that Trotsky was prepared to at least entertain the idea of a Jewish national home, perhaps even in Palestine. In 1937 this implication became

---

[187] 'Thermidor and Anti-Semitism', op. cit., p. 214.

[188] 'Evreiskaya burzhuazia i revolyutsionnaya borba', Archives, T4490, 4491.

[189] 'On the Jewish Problem', in *Leon Trotsky on the Jewish Question*, pp. 17–18. (This interview first appeared in the journal *Class Struggle*, Feb. 1934.)

[190] Ibid., p. 18. Asked whether Arab riots in 1929 against the Jews in Palestine represented an 'uprising of oppressed masses', Trotsky replied that he did not know enough about the subject to determine to what degree 'elements such as national liberationists (anti-imperialists)' were present and to what degree 'reactionary Mohammedans and anti-Semitic pogromists' were involved.

stronger yet. In an interview with correspondents of Yiddish newspapers, the issue of Zionism and, specifically, a territorial solution, was raised again.[191] What Trotsky had to say on this occasion has been the source of different interpretations, and it is therefore worth quoting at length. He opened by regretting the fact that he did not know Yiddish, as a result of which he could not follow the Yiddish press and could not be fully informed of the many aspects of the Jewish question. He then stated the following:

During my youth I rather leaned toward the prognosis that the Jews of different countries would be assimilated and that the Jewish question would thus disappear in a quasi-automatic fashion. The historical development of the last quarter of a century has not confirmed this perspective. Decaying capitalism has everywhere swung over to an exacerbated nationalism, one part of which is anti-Semitism...

On the other hand, the Jews of different countries have created their press and developed the Yiddish language as an instrument adapted to modern culture. One must therefore reckon with the fact that the Jewish nation will maintain itself for an entire epoch to come. Now the nation cannot normally exist without a common territory. Zionism springs from this very idea. But the facts of every passing day demonstrate to us that Zionism is incapable of resolving the Jewish question. The conflict between the Jews and Arabs in Palestine acquires a more and more tragic and more and more menacing character. I do not at all believe that the Jewish question can be resolved within the framework of rotting capitalism and under the control of British imperialism.

And how, you ask me, can socialism solve this question? On this point I can but offer hypotheses. Once socialism has become master of our planet or at least of its most important sections, it will have unimaginable resources in all domains. Human history has witnessed the epoch of great migrations on the basis of barbarism. Socialism will open the possibility of great migrations on the basis of the most developed technique and culture. It goes without saying that what is here involved is not compulsory displacement, that is, the creation of new ghettos for certain nationalities, but displacements freely consented to, or rather demanded by certain nationalities or parts of nationalities. The dispersed Jews who would want to be reassembled in the same community will find a sufficiently extensive and rich spot under the sun. The same possibility will be opened for the Arabs, as for all other scattered nations. National topography will become a part of the planned economy. This is the grand historical perspective that I envisage. To work for international socialism means also to work for the solution of the Jewish question.[192]

The only certain conclusion which can be reached on the basis of this statement is that Trotsky now recognized both the catastrophic urgency of the Jewish problem and the persistent vitality of Jewish culture and peoplehood. He remained opposed to the ideology of Zionism though he may have now become convinced that a territory to which Jews could emigrate might prevent their destruction in Europe. At the end of the interview he spoke of Zionism as a 'palliative'. In this limited sense he may have thought it to be necessary at that particular moment in history. Indeed, the measure of his concern for the fate of the Jews may be gauged from a warning he gave at the end of 1938: 'Even without war the next development of world reaction signifies with certainty the *physical extermination of the Jews*.'[193] If this was the prospect, then a territorial solution was certainly preferable. But Zionism, he argued, could not solve the problem in the long run, firstly because of the conflict with the Arabs, secondly because the Jewish problem was inextricably bound up with the future of capitalist society.[194] He had been wrong, he admitted, about the strength of Jewish consciousness, and it may be that the desire for a territorial community would need to be satisfied in the long run as well; but this could be realized in a realistic and peaceful way only within

[192] Loc. cit. For a somewhat different—though not in essence—version of this interview, based on the account of another correspondent, see *Forwaerts*, 28 Jan. 1937, pp. 6 and 8.

[193] 'Evreiskaya burzhuazia . . .', Archives, T4490, 4491.

[194] His last comment on the Jewish question is a brief note written in July 1940. It reads as follows: 'The attempt to solve the Jewish question through the migration of Jews to Palestine can now be seen for what it is, a tragic mockery of the Jewish people. Interested in winning the sympathies of the Arabs who are more numerous than the Jews, the British government has sharply altered its promise to help them found their "own home" in a foreign land. The future development of military events may well transform Palestine into a bloody trap for several hundred thousand Jews. Never was it so clear as it is today that the salvation of the Jewish people is bound up inseparably with the overthrow of the capitalist system.' ('On the Jewish Problem', *Fourth International*, Dec. 1945, p. 379.)

the framework of the final collapse of capitalism everywhere and the emergence of a socialist world. 'The very same methods', he wrote, 'of solving the Jewish question which under decaying capitalism have a utopian and reactionary character (Zionism), will, under the regime of a socialist federation, take on a real and salutary meaning.'[195]

Trotsky thus continued to urge Jews, and especially of course Jewish workers, to tie their future to that of the revolutionary socialist movement.[196] He warned them against cutting themselves off from 'progressive' elements throughout the world. He remained convinced that the Jews on their own could not save themselves, either within the framework of independent organizations in countries where they lived or by way of a national state.[197] He refused therefore to reconcile himself to what, in 1903, he called the 'particularistic'; and he persisted in putting forward the internationalist view and approach.

Yet he had obviously erred in his estimate of the force of Jewish nationalism. And he had underestimated as well the potentialities of Zionism as a solution to the Jewish problem. In view of the catastrophe which befell the Jewish people during the period of the Second World War, in view also of the nearly total failure of the socialist movement to become the international force which Trotsky had hoped it would, Zionism proved to be a more realistic response to the Jewish predicament than any other conceivable and conceived solution.[198] That Trotsky could not see this, or could not reconcile himself to it, until very late, and even then only partially, may have reflected, on the one hand, his own personal independence of

[195] 'Thermidor and Anti-Semitism', op. cit., p. 215.
[196] See, for example, the concluding paragraph of 'Evreiskaya burzhuazia . . .', op. cit.
[197] In the early 1930s he called on Jewish workers' organizations in France and the United States not to remain outside the framework of the workers' movements of their countries (this was exactly like his advice to the Bund in 1903): see 'Letter to *Klorkeit* and to the Jewish Workers in France', in *Leon Trotsky on the Jewish Question*, pp. 14–15 and 'Greetings to *Unser Kampf*', in ibid., pp. 15–16.
[198] That the conflict between the state of Israel and the Arabs has not been resolved after more than a quarter of a century does not invalidate Zionism as a solution to the Jewish problem as it existed in Europe, or in the Diaspora in general, which was the problem to which Trotsky, like others, had to address himself. And the persistence of this conflict is perhaps further confirmation of the power of national sentiments, on both sides, as against international or 'class' ones, though this would be to simplify the nature of the conflict.

national ties and sentiments; however, it also pointed up the
limits of a purely Marxist analysis of social communities which
left out of account the reality of solidarity based on elements
other than those of economic class. The absence in Trotsky himself of any tension, much less conflict, between international
sentiments and national roots did not reflect the situation
among Jews in general.

Trotsky's writings on the Jewish question should not, therefore, be seen in isolation from his other writings or his views
in general. They are, quite simply, a particular example of his
over-all hostile attitudes towards nationalism, even towards
national consciousness alone, and of his consistent commitment
to the principles of internationalism.[199] If, during the 1930s in
particular, he frequently wrote and spoke about the Jewish
question, this was not because of any special, personal interest
or any basic change in his attitudes. In part it was occasioned
by the situation in the Soviet Union; in general, however, it
was a response to what had become one of the central, and ultimately tragic, problems of Europe. 'The Jewish question', he
wrote, 'has never occupied the centre of my attention. But that
does not mean that I have the right to be blind to the Jewish
problem, which exists and demands solution.'[200]

---

[199] There appears to be, however, one surprising exception to this and it concerns his
views on the Negro question in the United States. In 1933 and 1939 Trotsky and some
of his American followers held a number of discussions of this question. Trotsky supported the idea of Negro nationalism and self-determination, even an independent
Negro state: so much so, in fact, that one has the impression of reading the words
of a contemporary proponent of Black Power. These views, however, become less surprising when one looks at the motives behind them, as expressed by Trotsky in the
discussions. Disappointed by the conservative character of the American working class,
Trotsky believed that it was the Negroes who were potentially the most radical element
in America. A Negro movement demanding self-determination would, in his view,
make for a powerful jolt to American society. His position, therefore, was not unlike
that of Lenin, before 1917, on self-determination for the nationalities in the Russian
Empire, i.e. support for self-determination not in principle but as a means of accelerating the break-up of the Empire. As the discussions make clear, Trotsky's position was
also tactical: to use Negro nationalism for wider revolutionary aims. Trotsky obviously
was not always averse to political opportunism and, it may here be said, he had learnt
and imbibed well his Leninism. See: 'Minutes of Discussion on the Negro Question',
Archives, T3511; 'Self-Determination for the American Negroes', ibid., T4561; 'A
Negro Organization', ibid., T4562; and 'Plans for the Negro Organization', ibid.,
T4563 (all these discussions were held in English).
[200] 'Thermidor and Anti-Semitism', op. cit., p. 214.

3. Political Morality: Means and Ends

In February 1938 Trotsky wrote a long essay entitled 'Their Morals and Ours'.[201] It was one of his rare excursions into the field of ethical polemics.[202] It was not, however, occasioned by any sudden or renewed interest in the subject nor by any pangs of conscience arising in old age over the moral ramifications of what had been wrought in youth, though it did afford Trotsky the opportunity of reaffirming his faith in the moral justness of the Russian Revolution. He would not have written it were it not for the fact that at the time he had come under attack over his position and actions, seventeen years earlier, during the Kronstadt rebellion.[203] The moral stature of Trotsky's struggle against Stalinism in the 1930s was being questioned by throwing doubt on the integrity of his own behaviour while in power. The implication of this was that there was really no fundamental difference between him and Stalin, and between Stalinism and Leninism.[204] Beyond the personal aspect of the accusations, however, the more general issues of means and ends, history and morality, individual responsibility and social consequences, were raised in order to expose the moral and historical bankruptcy, as the critics saw it, of the Russian Revolution, and all those who had had a hand in it. This was, therefore, a direct challenge to the value of all that Trotsky held sacred. In a number of articles he replied specifically to the Kronstadt charge;[205] but in 'Their Morals and Ours'

[201] 'Ikh moral i nasha', *Byulleten Oppozitsii* (Aug.–Sept. 1938), pp. 6–19. (The essay actually first appeared in English, in *The New International*, June 1938, pp. 163–73.)
[202] His one other work, *Terrorism and Communism* (1920), which dealt primarily with issues of a similar kind—but in the context of specific Bolshevik revolutionary policies—was discussed in chapter 6, above. 'Their Morals and Ours' argues the issues in a partly more abstract manner.
[203] The charges against Trotsky's Kronstadt 'record' were raised by such former followers as Serge, Macdonald, Eastman, and Souvarine. See, for example, the contributions by Serge and Macdonald, under the title 'Once More: Kronstadt', in *New International*, July 1938, pp. 211–14. See also Anton Ciliga, *The Kronstadt Revolt* (London, 1942) and Emma Goldman, *Trotsky Protests Too Much* (Glasgow, 1938). For historical accounts of the Kronstadt rebellion itself, see Paul Avrich, *Kronstadt 1921* (Princeton, 1970) and George Katkov, 'The Kronstadt Rising', *St. Antony's Papers*, no. 6 (London, 1959), pp. 9–74.
[204] This issue was discussed from a different point of view in chapter 10, pp. 428ff., above.
[205] See the following: 'Otvety na voprosy Vendelina Tomasa', *Byulleten Oppozitsii* (June–Aug. 1937), pp. 12–14; 'Shumikha vokrug Kronshtadta', in ibid. (May–June

he addressed himself to the general issues involved, responding in a characteristically assertive, confident manner, betraying doubts neither about the past nor about the differences between Stalinist and Leninist morality and, in the process, defining the principles of his Marxist ethics.

Marxism in general, Trotsky began,[206] and Bolshevism in particular, had been denounced as 'amoral' because they supposedly appropriated the Jesuit maxim that 'the end justifies the means'. But what else, he asked, except personal or social ends could possibly justify means, what other moral criteria were there for determining the right or wrong of human behaviour? Presumably such as stood outside society or were independent of man. Where did one find such criteria? 'If not on earth, then in the heavens.'[207] The alternative, therefore, was either some conception of 'eternal moral truths' whose sources were explicitly religious, based on divine revelation; or some conception of human nature which postulated the existence of some 'special moral sense', some kind of absolute substance, also eternal, unchanging, independent. But what was the latter except implicitly religious, a 'philosophic-cowardly pseudonym for God'? 'Morality which is independent of ends, that is, of society, whether it be deduced from eternal truths or from the "nature of man", turns out in the end to be a form of "natural theology". Heaven remains the only fortified position for military operations against dialectical materialism.'[208]

Only with Hegel, Trotsky continued, did classical idealism succeed in secularizing morality; but, 'having torn itself from

---

1938), pp. 22–6; 'Eshche ob usmirenii Kronshtadta', in ibid. (Oct. 1938), p. 10. Trotsky justified both the suppression of the rebellion and his own role at the time, though he claimed that he himself was not directly involved (a claim largely at variance with the known facts); the concluding sentences of the last of the above-mentioned articles may serve to illustrate the manner of his justification: 'Idealists and pacifists always accused the revolution of "excesses". But the main point is that "excesses" flow from the very nature of revolution which in itself is but an "excess" of history. Whosoever desires may on this basis reject (in little articles) revolution in general. I do not reject it. In this sense I carry full and complete responsibility for the suppression of the Kronstadt rebellion.'

[206] After an initial outburst against all those 'representatives of the "left"' who suddenly see no difference between 'reaction and revolution, Tsarism and Bolshevism, Fascism and Communism, Stalinism and Trotskyism'.

[207] 'Ikh moral i nasha', op. cit., p. 7.

[208] Loc. cit.

heaven, moral philosophy had to find earthly roots'. This task fell to Marxism which discovered morality in society, in man himself, where in fact it had always resided. Hegel made an enormous step forward but he was only a 'stage' between religion and materialism: 'To appeal now to "eternal moral truths" means attempting to turn the wheels backward . . . from materialism to religion.'[209] Thus:

> Whoever does not want to revert to Moses, Christ or Mohammed, whoever is not satisfied with eclectic hodge-podges, must recognize that morality is a product of social development; that there is nothing immutable about it; that it serves social interests; that these interests are contradictory; that morality more than any other form of ideology has a class character.[210]

Men, therefore, developed norms by virtue of their being members of society and these norms were based on the character of social relations.[211] This being the case, only human—as opposed to supposedly supernatural—ends could be said to justify means. It was, however, absurd, Trotsky believed, to claim that an end could justify *any* means, no matter how criminal the latter was and so long as it advanced *any* chosen end. This was not, in any case, what the Jesuits had taught and to attribute such a view to them was to accept blindly the 'malicious' distortions of their—Protestant—opponents:

> Jesuit theologians, like theologians of other persuasions, occupied themselves with the question of personal responsibility, and what they actually taught is that the means in itself can be a matter of indifference but that the moral justification or condemnation of the given means flows from the end. Thus shooting in itself is a matter of indifference; shooting a mad dog that threatens a child—a virtue; shooting with the aim of violation or murder—a crime.[212]

---

[209] Loc. cit.   [210] Ibid., p. 9.

[211] In an aside, Trotsky rejected the abstract generalization of these norms in the manner of Kant's 'categorical imperative', since this 'embodies nothing concrete, it is a shell without content' (loc. cit.).

[212] Ibid., p. 7. Trotsky's defence of the Jesuits did not, of course, extend to the content of their ends, which were for him 'reactionary' in comparison with those of the Protestants. Though the Bolsheviks may have adopted the Jesuit maxim, he wrote, in terms of their historical role they were, in the twentieth century, what the Protestants were in the sixteenth. This was not the first time Trotsky had drawn such an analogy and another example will be referred to later in this chapter (see pp. 577–8, below).

Thus not every end was legitimate by virtue of being an end; it had in itself to be justified. And thus no means was moral unless the end it was meant to achieve was moral. Besides, Trotsky continued, means and ends frequently 'exchanged places': an end could become a means, as when democracy was sought by the working class in order to be utilized as an instrument for realizing socialism. All the more reason, therefore, to concentrate on the moral legitimacy of ends and to look upon means as a subsidiary problem to be resolved by reference to the moral stature and validity of the end.[213]

In the last section of his essay Trotsky pursued this argument to its conclusion and attempted to justify in accordance with it the superiority of Marxist over other ends—and, thereby, of Marxist means. This last section, entitled 'The Dialectical Interdependence of Ends and Means', constitutes, therefore, the most important part of the essay and may be taken to define Trotsky's Marxist ethics.[214] Trotsky asserted the following:

A means can be justified only by its end. But the end in turn needs to be justified. From the Marxist point of view, which expresses the historical interests of the proletariat, *the end is justified if it leads to increasing the power of man over nature and to the abolition of the power of man over man*.[215]

From this it followed that the aim here defined—that is, increasing man's power over nature and abolishing one man's power over another—was the *ultimate* end, which in itself required no justification but was posited as a fundamental axiom. In this form, this ultimate end could be considered unobjectionable from points of view other than the Marxist alone,[216] though Trotsky did not concede this and appeared to believe that it was peculiarly Marxist in character. In any case, if this was the ultimate end then socialism, and the proletarian revolution, were means to it and were to be justified only if they advanced this

---

[213] Ibid., p. 8. Utilitarianism, Trotsky noted—in a *tu quoque* retort—that 'ethics of bourgeois book-keeping', also accepted the Jesuit maxim since the principle of 'the greatest possible happiness for the greatest possible number' was nothing else than the justification of any means which fulfilled this end (ibid., pp. 8–9).

[214] Ibid., pp. 18–19.

[215] Ibid., p. 18 (italics added).

[216] As was pointed out by John Dewey in his reply to Trotsky's essay: see John Dewey, 'Means and Ends', *The New International*, Aug. 1938 (reprinted in *Partisan Review*, Summer 1964, pp. 400–4).

end. And, indeed, this is precisely what Trotsky asserted: 'That is permissible . . . which *really* leads to the liberation of mankind. Since this end can be achieved only through revolution, the liberating morality of the proletariat of necessity is endowed with a revolutionary character.'[217]

Why, however, could this end be achieved by revolution *only*? Because, in Trotsky's view, revolution, as a 'rule of conduct', was 'deduced' from the 'laws of the development of society, thus primarily from the class struggle, this law of all laws'. This did not mean that in the 'class struggle' *all* means, however base, were permissible:

Permissible and obligatory are those and only those means . . . which unite the revolutionary proletariat, fill its heart with irreconcilable hostility to oppression, teach them contempt for official morality and its democratic echoers, imbue them with consciousness of their own historic mission, raise their courage and spirit of self-sacrifice in the struggle. Precisely from this it flows that *not* all means are permissible.[218]

If this sounds too general, lacking in precision as to what specifically may or may not be done, Trotsky himself conceded the vagueness of his criteria: there was no ready answer, he wrote, as to 'what is permissible and what is not permissible in each separate case . . . Problems of revolutionary morality are fused with the problems of revolutionary strategy and tactics'. Only in the course of actual revolutionary practice could specific answers be arrived at which were at the same time within the framework of the over-all Marxist philosophy of morals. This philosophy, he continued, did not 'recognize any dualism between means and ends':

The end flows naturally from the historical movement. Organically, the means are subordinated to the end. The immediate end becomes the means for a further end. In his play, *Franz von Sickingen*, Ferdinand Lassalle puts the following words into the mouth of one of the heroes:

---

[217] 'Ikh moral i nasha', p. 18.
[218] Loc. cit. 'Socialist ends', Trotsky once told a follower, 'could never justify *any* means. One cannot be both Robespierre and Napoleon. One has to choose.' This was said by way of explaining his decision in the 1920s to oppose the then emerging Stalinism. (See Fred Zeller, 'First Impressions of the Old Man', *Le Monde*, English Weekly Selection, 10 Sept. 1969, p. 6.)

'Show us not the aim without the way.
For ends and means on earth are so entangled
That changing one, you change the other too;
Each different path brings other ends in view.'

. . . The dialectical interdependence between means and ends is
expressed entirely correctly in the above-quoted sentences. Seeds of
wheat must be sown in order to yield an ear of wheat.[219]

The final paragraphs of Trotsky's essay were devoted to the
question of terrorism.[220] Here he restated the well-known
Marxist instrumental attitude to terror: it was legitimate if,
aimed at 'individual oppressors', it was carried out not as an
act of 'individual terror' but within the framework of a mass
movement and as a means which was 'expedient' from the point
of view of the revolutionary class struggle.[221] The relevant question therefore was as always: did terror advance the ultimate
end of the liberation of mankind? Individual, isolated terror
could not be seen to do this; terror as one possible means available to the working-class movement could have this effect,
though it was a tactical means and not a substitute for the
general strategy of revolution. Terror, Trotsky concluded, was
in any case not subject to judgement in accordance with some
'moral absolute' forbidding the 'murder of man by man'; its
morality was to be determined by its capacity for serving the
goal of human liberation.[222]

The logical fallacy of Trotsky's analysis of the relationship
between Marxist ends and means was pointed out by John
Dewey in a reply—published two months later—to Trotsky's

[219] 'Ikh moral i nasha', pp. 18–19. The lines from Lassalle, incidentally, are quoted
as an epigraph in Arthur Koestler's *Darkness at Noon* (Penguin edition, 1964, p. 193).
The English translation of these lines here is as in Koestler.
[220] Trotsky's views on terrorism, both individual and that decreed by a revolutionary
government, were discussed in chapter 6, above.
[221] 'Ikh moral i nasha', p. 19. When, in 1934, his name was linked in the Soviet Union
with the assassination of Kirov, Trotsky issued a press statement in which he declared
that throughout the whole of his life he had opposed 'individual terrorism', whether
against Tsarism or against Stalinism, since this was not in the interest of the workers'
movement (see 'Statement to the Press', reprinted in *Writings of Leon Trotsky, 1934–
35*, New York, 1971, pp. 138–9).
[222] 'Ikh moral i nasha', p. 19. The argument of 'Their Morals and Ours' appears also
in a concentrated form in the previously mentioned article by Trotsky defending Kronstadt, 'Otvety na voprosy Vendelina Tomasa' (see note 205, above).

essay.[223] Writing as one who also rejected every form of absolutist ethics based on a 'moral sense' or 'eternal truths', and as one who therefore held that 'the end in the sense of consequences provides the only basis for moral ideas and action and . . . the only justification that can be found for means employed',[224] Dewey accepted Trotsky's argument about the interdependence of means and ends and even, as it was formulated, the liberation of mankind as the ultimate end. But Trotsky, Dewey argued, had been inconsistent. If means and ends were interdependent, if those means were justified which led to the ultimate end, it became necessary to examine each means separately with a view to ascertaining, as far as was humanly possible, what the consequences of the means would be:

One would expect, then, that with the ideas of the liberation of mankind as the end-in-view, there would be an examination of *all* means that are likely to attain this end without any fixed pre-conception as to what they *must* be, and that every suggested means would be weighed and judged on the express ground of the consequences it is likely to produce.[225]

This was not, however, the course which Trotsky had chosen, Dewey continued. Instead of examining independently the efficacy of all means in terms of the end, Trotsky had decided that those means were appropriate which were derived from the 'class struggle'. Thus: '. . . means are "deduced" from an independent source, an alleged law of history which is *the* law of all laws of social development . . . Instead of *inter*dependence of means and end, the end is dependent upon the means but the means are not derived from the end.'[226]

Dewey thus rejected Trotsky's deductive approach as being inconsistent with the latter's own argument about 'interdependence'. Only the inductive approach could determine which means were or were not legitimate; Trotsky's way led to a pre-judgement of means. The class struggle, Dewey added, was not

[223] See Dewey, op. cit. Trotsky, who must have read Dewey's article—especially as it was originally published in *The New International*—never replied to it. The two, of course, knew each other as a result of the 1937 Commission of Inquiry into Soviet charges against Trotsky which Dewey chaired.

[224] Dewey, op. cit., p. 401 (all references are to the *Partisan Review* reprinting of this article).

[225] Ibid., p. 402.   [226] Ibid., pp. 402–3.

necessarily ruled out as a means for attaining the end, but it had itself to be justified and there was no reason to suppose that it was the only means. In any case, the existence of a 'fixed law of social development' was irrelevant; it could not be the source for rules of conduct if the principle of the interdependence of means and ends were to be sustained. Even if the validity of such a law were to be established as conclusively as that of a law of physics, it could not be the basis for a 'moral end' since physical laws had no moral implications, and it could not be assumed that such a law necessarily led to the 'liberation of mankind' for such an assumption was merely 'arbitrary and subjective'.[227] In this connection, Dewey may have added that it was, after all, pure chance that the law of social development which Marxism claimed to discover accorded, or so Marxism also claimed, with the advance of mankind towards increasing self-liberation; suppose Marx had discovered that history showed the opposite, that the laws of social development led to greater enslavement, would it be moral to act in accordance with such laws? It would certainly be futile not to accept the reality of such laws but acceptance of reality did not determine one's moral judgement of it; it would be merely ridiculous to claim that whosoever reconciles himself to, for example, the law of gravity sees in it a *moral* end or good. Moral ends, obviously, were determined by individual choice not by laws of nature, or even by laws of human history.[228]

But it was, of course, precisely because he was a Marxist, that is, committed to certain assumptions about the workings of human society, that Trotsky could not take a purely pragmatic approach to ends, or abandon preconceptions about such sacred axioms, and the means they generated, as the class struggle. This also governed his definition of what constituted the 'liberation of mankind'. 'Their Morals and Ours' posited an ultimate end which, as has been pointed out, may not have been objected to by non-Marxists as well, if only for the reason that it was so general in character. The essay did not, however,

---

[227] Ibid., pp. 403–4.
[228] Dewey concluded (ibid., p. 404): 'Orthodox Marxism shares with orthodox religion- ism and with traditional idealism the belief that human ends are interwoven into the very texture and structure of existence—a conception inherited presumably from its Hegelian origin.'

show why socialism necessarily constituted the greater liberation of mankind; though this also, like other 'means-ends',
could not be ruled out in advance, it needed to be justified.
Here too Trotsky's only justification was that it followed from
historical laws of development. It did not occur to him that
the concept of 'liberation' was a function of certain values and
that whatever history did or did not teach it was these values—
granted even that they were rooted in social conditions—which
determined the kind of content which each individual would
choose to ascribe to the condition of 'liberation' or to that of
liberty. He did not raise, in other words, the problem of the concept itself, nor of the potential conflicts between its various attributes, nor of the distinction between the condition of liberty
and the conditions *for* liberty.[229]

In our discussion of 'Their Morals and Ours' we have left
out referring to the middle part of the essay in which Trotsky
dealt with the difference between Stalinist morality, and that
of Leninism and his own.[230] This part may now be considered
and it is best done in conjunction with another of Trotsky's
essays, written in the middle of 1939, which also treated of this
specific subject.[231] The gist of his arguments here may be briefly
stated since they were merely an extension of what he had said
about Marxist morality in general and about Stalinism and
Leninism elsewhere.[232] The general basis for distinguishing
between the latter two was, in Trotsky's view, the very simple
one that Stalinism could in no sense be considered a doctrine
which aimed at the establishment of socialism. This being the
case, Stalin could not appeal to Marxist morality since that
morality recognized as legitimate and justified only such means

[229] The issues touched upon here have been discussed in much of the contemporary literature on political theory but the most clearly defined treatment of the subject is Isaiah Berlin, *Two Concepts of Liberty* (Oxford, 1958).
[230] 'Ikh moral i nasha', op. cit., pp. 10–18.
[231] 'Moralisty i sikofanty protiv marksizma', *Byulleten Oppozitsii* (May–June–July 1939), pp. 13–18. This article was a polemic aimed mainly at Victor Serge and Boris Sou-varine; both had by then broken with Trotsky. The 1939 French translation of 'Their Morals and Ours' was issued in pamphlet form and was preceded by a prospectus which simplified and distorted Trotsky's views. Trotsky assumed it was written by Serge but the latter later denied this. Conceding the factual error of his assumption, Trotsky nevertheless remained unimpressed by Serge's protestations: see his rejoinder to Serge, 'Ocherednoe oproverzhenie Viktora Serzha', *Byulleten Oppozitsii* (Aug.-Sept.-Oct. 1939), p. 31.
[232] See chapter 10, above.

and policies as advanced socialism. Stalin's objectives were not the 'liberation of mankind' but its enslavement in a new totalitarian form. The problem, therefore, was not that Stalin used terror, violence, lies and calumny but that these instruments were utilized for non-socialist purposes and, *on this basis*, were rendered immoral.[233]

Nevertheless, Trotsky argued, the use itself of such instruments under Stalin took a form it never had and was never intended to have under Lenin. It was not only that Lenin had represented the aspirations and interests of the proletariat while Stalin renegued on them through bureaucratic rule; it was also that under Lenin terror, violence, lies and so on had been employed during the most difficult period of revolution, the Civil War, a period which decided the very fate of the Revolution. At such times particularly excessive measures were essential and unavoidable: witness, Trotsky wrote, Lincoln's actions during the American Civil War, not to mention those of the Paris Communards. If the French Revolution, more specifically its Jacobin phase, was the begetter of democracy, then 'democracy came into the world not at all through the democratic road'.[234] And it could not have been otherwise, for great transformations in history were 'bloody' breaks with it. But the Civil War period in the Soviet Union had ended long ago and the proletariat had emerged from it triumphant. The means then used were no longer essential and were certainly avoidable. Already under Lenin they had been suspended. Stalin, however, renewed them and not for extraordinary purposes of Civil War but as a normal method of government. These methods were made necessary by, and were employed to perpetuate, the policies of his Thermidorian reaction which aroused the opposition of the masses.[235] The difference, therefore, between Lenin and Stalin was not simply reducible to the kind of 'Hottentot morality' according to which the same means when used by

---

[233] See, in particular, 'Ikh moral i nasha', op. cit., pp. 16–17. In *The Young Lenin* (p. 111), Trotsky wrote admiringly of Lenin's brother Alexander's complete devotion to the truth and his inability to tell a lie. However, he pointed out, the lie can sometimes be a revolutionary weapon; Alexander's failure to recognize this made him more a 'knight than a politican'. On Trotsky's view of the 'revolutionary function' of falsehood, see also 'Kultura i sotsializm', *Sochineniya*, XXI, pp. 445–6.

[234] 'Ikh moral i nasha', p. 12.

[235] Ibid., pp. 13–15 and 'Moralisty i sikofanty . . .', pp. 14–15.

the one were 'good' and by the other were 'bad', all depending
which side you were on;[236] it went deeper, to the fundamental
distinction between the ends of the one and those of the other:
'Only that which prepares the complete and final overthrow
of imperialist bestiality is moral, and nothing else. The welfare
of the revolution—that is the supreme law!'[237]

There was, of course, some truth in Trotsky's claim that he
and Lenin could not be simply identified with Stalin without
doing violence both to historical analogy and to common sense.
Yet one cannot help but be amazed how persistently Trotsky
continued to miss the point of the comparison of Leninism with
Stalinism: whatever the differences in degree, his critics insisted,
there was no real difference in kind between the two. The historical problem was not so much whether Lenin had resorted
to the same scope of authoritarian methods as Stalin, nor even
whether Lenin's ends had been nobler; the problem was
whether Leninism had not created a precedent for Stalinism.
Once again, therefore, the argument over Bolshevik morality
was really the argument over the extent to which the ends the
Bolsheviks sought were shared by the social classes, the workers
and the peasants, whom they presumed to represent. In both
the articles by Trotsky which we have here discussed, he spoke
of the Bolsheviks as having gauged the true 'trends' among the
masses,[238] a theme which was, of course, repeated in all his writings on the Revolution. But what were these trends in fact, or
rather how far did these trends have anything to do with the
concrete socialist ends which the Bolsheviks presumably were
intent on pursuing? The element of consensus about ends was
crucial here for upon it would depend the means chosen to bring
about the ends. In reality such consensus had proved to be
largely chimerical, as had the ripeness of Russian society for
socialist institutions, and thus the Bolsheviks had chosen to impose themselves upon society. Thereafter, means were derived
not from socialist ends but from considerations of political and
economic survival. The Bolsheviks were in any case inclined and

---

[236] 'Moralisty i sikofanty . . .', p. 14.
[237] Ibid., p. 18. See also Trotsky's observations on the moral character of Lenin in *The Young Lenin*, pp. 197ff., and on the degeneration of political morality in the twentieth century in *Stalin*, pp. xii–xiv.
[238] 'Moralisty i sikofanty...', pp. 17–18 and 'Ikh moral i nasha', p. 19.

prepared—what else was Leninism about—to use autonomous
political means in order to preserve themselves in power. But
the contradiction between backwardness and socialist ends, a
contradiction Trotsky had understood as well as anyone, reinforced this tendency and eventually made a virtue of necessity.
The moral dilemma, therefore, was not primarily that of the
use of coercion, terrorism, or violence in general, as means in
the restricted tactical sense, but rather of a form of political
rule which could not maintain itself without turning such violence into a comprehensive and habitual system. Not everyone
was bothered by the reality of this moral dilemma; Trotsky was,
but he cannot be said to have come to resolve it.

4. The Good Society, or: A Vision of the Communist Millennium

To conclude the study of Trotsky's social and political thought
with a section on his views of the future communist society may
be both superfluous and misleading: superfluous, because such
views should be more or less evident from all that has been
written already about his thought, as well as from the fact that
as a Marxist he may be expected to share the usual Marxist
notions about the future; misleading, because it may give the
very wrong impression that he, any more than other Marxists,
had any definite or systematic conception of the future—as we
shall presently see, his remarks on this subject were very general
and very infrequent, and it would be a misrepresentation to
take them for anything more than occasional, almost spontaneous observations. Still, a man's vision of the future, however
vague, cannot be discounted as an element influencing his
motives, his ideas and his behaviour and in the case of Trotsky
this is particularly so: the very style and mentality of the man
exude a kind of visionary essence. Many of his writings and
ideas, including particularly the central conception of the permanent revolution, are clearly affected by it, though they do
not for this reason cease to be works of realistic social analysis.
It may be worthwhile, therefore, to gather together in concentrated form some of his thoughts on the future communist
society and thereby take account of, without however over-

estimating its theoretical value, this characteristic element in his approach to politics and society.

Georges Sorel once observed that 'to offer a theoretical analysis of the future economic order would be to attempt to erect an ideological superstructure in advance of the conditions of production on which it must be built'; thus, he concluded, 'any such attempt would be non-Marxist'.[239] Sorel need not have worried for not only Marx, as Sorel knew, but Marx's subsequent adherents as well, made few serious attempts of this kind.[240] The best known exception is, of course, Lenin's *State and Revolution*; but this work merely vindicates the wisdom of the Marxists' general reticence to dabble in 'futurology' since from it Lenin emerges with an absurdly naïve streak.[241] The reasons for such reticence, however, were not only doctrinal (in the sense defined by Sorel); they were also rooted in the fact that as a political movement Marxism had always sought to avoid being identified with the kind of 'utopianism' which characterized the ideas of the early socialists or anarchists, and which more often than not culminated in the merely imaginary construction of ideal communities.[242] The stress in Marxism was on the unity of theory and practice, on the need to change the world, on the inevitability of the class struggle, on, of course, practical revolutionary activity. It presented itself as a doctrine and a movement acting on and in accordance with reality, and it preferred to leave model-building to the historical process itself.

In spite of this, however, Marxism was the most future-oriented of doctrines, a fact so obvious as to require little ela-

---

[239] Quoted in Carr, *The Bolshevik Revolution*, II, p. 13 from Sorel's *Décomposition du Marxisme* (3rd edition, Paris, 1925), p. 37.

[240] Of course, Marx did not always resist the temptation and general observations about the communist future may be found throughout his works, in particular the *Early Writings* and the *Communist Manifesto*. For a survey of the very nebulous views of Soviet Marxists, past and present, on this subject, see Theodore Denno, *The Communist Millennium: The Soviet View* (The Hague, 1964).

[241] Always assuming, of course, that he was serious when he spoke in *State and Revolution* of the administration of the future society as being a matter of simple 'account-keeping', a function everyone would be capable of performing. This work, however, is unique in Lenin's canon and at odds with the fundamentally unspeculative character of his thought.

[242] For a defence, however, of 'Utopian Socialism' and a critical analysis of the Marxist 'scientific Utopia', see Martin Buber, *Paths in Utopia* (London, 1949).

boration. Rejecting the whole of existing reality, it enthusiastically contemplated the necessary advent of a novel society, only the bare outlines of which were as yet discernible. The differences between it and 'utopian socialism' were obvious, but utopian elements were there nevertheless, whether they were formulated in the negative form of the disappearance of classes and the division of labour, of social antagonisms, and of the state or, in the positive form, of the establishment of truly collective relationships, of universal liberation, of abundance and creative labour. The promise of a millennium was inherent in Marxism and the chiliastic dream was certainly a part of its appeal and its motive force. What has been called the 'tension between eschatology and dialectics'[243] in Marx's thought was never resolved and the impression persisted, or was made to persist—for obvious reasons—by the political movements which embraced Marx's doctrines, not only that the 'end of pre-history' was fully imminent in the here and now but that it signified the end of history itself—in the sense of an aimless, infinitely changing, and not always salutary process.

It is within the framework of this millenarian tradition of Marxism that one can best appreciate the nature of Trotsky's vision of the future. One must stress, for this very reason, that it was a vision, not a conception, much less a programme. One will not find in it a 'theoretical analysis of the future economic order', nor the kind of mundane, albeit utopian, discussion of administrative questions as occurs in Lenin's *State and Revolution*, nor even very much about the processes of the 'withering away' of the state and of classes—beyond, of course, the taking of such assumptions for granted. In matters of a time-circumscribed nature—the revolution in Russia, developments in the West, and so on—Trotsky was not, of course, reluctant to speak in programmatic, predictive terms. In so far as the more or less remote future was concerned, however, he took the language of prophecies to be more appropriate, and that of down-to-earth analysis to be almost demeaning. Asked once to predict what American society would look like 'if it should go Communist', he offered, in an ostensibly serious manner, a long list of concrete prospects and then, as if despairing at the absurdity of such exercises, concluded in mocking irony: 'In the third

[243] Avineri, *The Social and Political Thought of Karl Marx*, p. 251.

year of soviet rule in America, you will no longer chew gum!'[244] The future, therefore, had to be conjured up through inspired vision, both because such vision was itself inspiring, as no reality could be, and because the future promised by communism was to be so glorious an era in the life of mankind. One may, of course, not unjustifiably, frown cynically at such of Trotsky's presumptions, but one cannot deny the force and the confidence with which he paraded them.

It would therefore be pointless to try and organize his observations on the communist future under clearly delineated headings and categories, as if he had thought out the implications of that future for the manifold areas of human activity.[245] Rather one should take the vision in its totality, for what it is worth, and thereby preserve at least its spirit and eloquence, for these, as becomes a vision, are its most admirable qualities. They may not convince us of the validity of the vision but they will convey its impact upon Trotsky himself. 'Without a broad political view of the future', he once wrote, 'I cannot conceive either of political activity or of intellectual life in general.'[246]

The basis of the vision, that which made it, from Trotsky's point of view, credible, and not merely rhetorical and fantastic, was the assumption that mankind was at that stage of development at which it could potentially solve all its economic problems. This had been, of course, Marx's assumption as well: capitalism, having universalized, mechanized and rationalized economic production, had become an anachronism since it continued to sustain a society based on competition, supply and demand, inequality and class supremacy—all factors characteristic of conditions of limited resources, shortage and even scarcity. These conditions now persisted not out of necessity but out of the greed of the bourgeois class. The inevitable advent of socialism would both reflect the artificiality of such conditions, and the capacity of society to provide abundance and affluence for all its members.

---

[244] 'Sovety v Amerike?', Archives, T3665. This article was commissioned by and published (under the title 'If America Should Go Communist') in *Liberty* magazine, 23 Mar. 1935.

[245] Denno (op. cit., pp. 48–58) attributes to Trotsky more defined and more schematized views about the future than Trotsky's utterances can sustain or can be interpreted to convey.

[246] Cited in Wolfe, *Three Who Made a Revolution*, p. 193.

Trotsky thus believed, like Marx before him, that once economic problems became merely technical ones, once technology became so advanced that it could both solve such problems and release man from most physical labour, once, moreover, the struggle for existence became unnecessary, men could channel their energies into truly human, creative pursuits, and live self-determined lives.[247] Was it so fantastic, Trotsky asked, to envisage therefore a future in which, economic problems having ceased to engage man, he would develop all his latent talents for other activities and rise to new spiritual heights?[248]

This optimism in the capacity of knowledge, particularly scientific knowledge buttressed by technological skill, for overcoming once and for all the barriers to unlimited economic production and distribution, explains the *theoretical* reasons why Trotsky rejected all discussion of the future in terms of economic and administrative arrangements. Mankind, according to Trotsky, having become accustomed hitherto to think that economic survival was an immanent problem of existence, could not yet imagine a future in which such a problem simply did not arise. But this was precisely the point about the future— that it would reveal the *historical* nature of the problem, its relevance to a particular stage only of development, and its being, therefore, non-immanent in existence. To understand the nature of the future one must, in a sense, forget about economics; to understand what is meant by communism one must make an intellectual leap—in this case assisted by a discriminating imagination—out of all hitherto assimilated experience into the realm of a world liberated from the dilemmas of economic survival. Is this not what Marx had in mind when he spoke of the leap from the 'realm of necessity into the realm of freedom'? This being so, one could not speak of the actual economic and administrative arrangements which would prevail under communism, one could only imagine that the *conditions* for such arrangements would be entirely different and that, therefore, the arrangements would be unlike anything known until now. Consider, Trotsky suggested, the example of money: since in

---

[247] See, in particular, *The Revolution Betrayed*, pp. 56–7, 180, 258 and 291–301.
[248] See in this connection, and in relation to what follows, the concluding part of his 1932 Copenhagen speech, 'Chto takoe oktyabrskaya revolyutsiya?', Archives, T3470.

conditions of abundance, where each will really be able to receive according to his needs, money becomes redundant in principle, one can easily imagine its disappearance. What, if anything, will replace money is a problem not worth fretting about since it will have been resolved in the context of the new conditions of abundance.[249] In general, problems of the organization of production, of the distribution of goods, of the satisfaction of material wants, of both social and economic administration, will acquire a subsidiary and spontaneous character. One can imagine also that such social institutions as the family, not to mention relations between the sexes in general, will have been entirely transformed. It is useless, and in any case unnecessary, to ask in advance what they will be like.[250] What is important is to understand that liberation from economic exigencies creates conditions of greater freedom, and that such conditions make possible new and more creative social relations. Besides, economic abundance, like communism, presupposes the existence of an international community divested once and for all of the need to waste its energies on national competition, on preparation for wars, on the investment of its human and material resources in non-productive enterprises. For Trotsky, therefore, the *possibilities* of human endeavour under communism appeared to be boundless.

Given the realization of freedom from economic anxieties, given the consequent release of human labour and capacities to be occupied otherwise, where else would they flow, Trotsky asked, except into those realms of human endeavour hitherto the exclusive property of the fortunate few? We return, therefore, to the central preoccupation of Trotsky's vision of the communist future, namely, the prospect of human creativity, particularly in the arts and the sciences, becoming universal. This theme runs through all of Trotsky's evocations of the future and one may pick almost randomly for examples of it. In early 1918, for instance, addressing an audience of workers, he spoke about the ultimate aims of the Revolution: 'We must see to it that our children, our younger brothers will have the opportunity of coming to know all the conquests of the mind, of the arts and sciences, and that they will be able

---

[249] *The Revolution Betrayed*, pp. 65–6. See also 'Sovety v Amerike.
[250] Ibid., pp. 144–5, 157 and 158–9.

to live as befits human beings who call themselves "lords of creation".'[251]

But rather than multiply the sources and citations, it seems best to quote a famous passage which concludes his 1923 book *Literature and Revolution* and which, though it sometimes reaches exaggerated heights of rhapsody, gives the most complete evocation of the vision that so evidently moved him:

Having rationalized his economic system . . . man will not preserve a trace of the present stagnant and worm-eaten domestic life. The care for food and education . . . will become the subject of social initiative and of an endless collective creativeness. Woman will at last free herself from her semi-servile condition . . . Experiments in social education . . . will take place to a degree which has not been dreamed of before. Communist life will not be formed blindly, like coral islands, but will be built consciously, will be tested by thought, will be directed and corrected. Life will cease to be elemental . . . Man, who will learn how to move rivers and mountains . . . will not only be able to add to his own life richness, brilliancy and intensity, but also a dynamic quality of the highest degree.

More than that. Man at last will begin to harmonize himself in earnest. He will make it his business to achieve beauty by giving the movement of his own limbs the utmost precision, purposefulness and economy in his work, his walk and his play. He will try to master first the semi-conscious and then the unconscious process in his own organism . . . The human species, the coagulated *homo sapiens*, will once more enter into a state of radical transformation, and, in his own hands, will become an object of the most complicated methods of artificial selection and psycho-physical training. This is entirely in accord with evolution. Man first drove the dark elements out of industry and ideology by displacing barbarian routine by scientific technique, and religion by science. Afterwards he drove the unconscious out of politics by overthrowing monarchy and class with democracy and rationalist parliamentarism and then with the clear and open Soviet dictatorship. The blind elements have settled most heavily in economic relations, but man is driving them out from there also, by means of the socialist organization of economic life. This makes it possible to reconstruct fundamentally the traditional family life. Finally, the nature of man himself is hidden in the deepest and darkest corner of the unconscious, of the elemental, of the sub-soil. Is it not self-

[251] 'Slovo Russkim rabochim i krestyanam', published as a pamphlet (Moscow, 1918), p. 37. (Also in *Sochineniya*, XVII, part 1, pp. 173–98.) Later in this speech (p. 42), Trotsky spoke of creating a 'paradise on earth . . . for all eternity'.

574 On the General and

evident that the greatest efforts of investigative thought and of creative initiative will be in that direction? The human race will not have ceased to crawl on all fours before God, kings and capital in order later to submit humbly before the dark laws of heredity and blind sexual selection!...

Man will make it his purpose to master his own feelings, to raise his instincts to the heights of consciousness . . . to raise himself to a new plane, to create a higher social biological type, or, if you please, a superman.

It is difficult to predict the extent of self-government which the man of the future may reach or the heights to which he may carry his technique. Social construction and psycho-physical self-education will become two aspects of one and the same process. All the arts—literature, drama, painting, music and architecture will lend this process beautiful form. More correctly, the shell in which the cultural construction and self-education of communist man will be enclosed will develop all the vital elements of contemporary art to the highest point. Man will become immeasurably stronger, wiser and subtler . . . The forms of life will become dynamically dramatic. The average human type will rise to the heights of an Aristotle, a Goethe, or a Marx. And above this ridge new peaks will rise.[252]

Let us not pause to inquire whether such utter optimism in the powers of man did not, in fact, spill over into the realm of sheer fantasy, for we are not concerned here with the actual credibility of the vision; suffice it to say that more than fifty years after the writing of this passage its prophecies seem no less incredible. Let us instead ask the question more immediately pertinent to the nature of Trotsky's vision and, perhaps, to his thought as a whole: what was the *source* of this enormous optimism, this complete confidence in man's powers for self-mastery, this utter faith that there were no limits to human ambition?

In part, as we have noted, it lay in the Marxist conviction that only arbitrary economic arrangements barred man's way to complete freedom and, therefore, that once these were done away with unheard of human possibilities would unfold. In this sense communism itself was a source for Trotsky's optimism. Beyond, and perhaps regardless of, this doctrinal influence it

---

[252] *Literatura i Revolyutsiya*, pp. 188–90 (pp. 253–6 in the English edition of this work).

seems that Trotsky's own innate nature was also a source:
doubts, tribulations, bewilderment, despair—none of these
found a place in his character or psychology. From earliest
youth and throughout his life he exuded confidence in the
future. Amongst his earliest writings is an essay entitled 'On
Pessimism, Optimism, the Twentieth Century and Many
Other Things';[253] it was written in 1901, that is, at the turn
of the century, and in it the young author presented a kind of
dialogue between an incorrigible 'pessimist' and, as it turns out,
a no less incorrigible 'optimist'. The former enumerates a long
list of human horrors—murder, starvation, racial hatred—
which have persisted into the new century. Nothing, he claims,
has changed or will change; these horrors are the real future.
History and reality are obviously on his side. Yet the 'optimist',
unshaken, replies: 'No, *that* is only the *present.*'

Contempt for the present, a refusal to be reconciled to its
reality and an unbreachable certainty in the capacity of the
future to transform it—these constituted an intrinsic, essential
part of Trotsky's mentality, and allowed him to nearly always
transcend his immediate environment. They combined well
with the Marxist faith and doctrine; almost forty years after
the above essay, on the eve of his death, worried about his
health, he drew up his 'Testament' and declared in it:

For forty-three years of my conscious life I have remained a revolutionist; for forty-two of them I have fought under the banner of Marxism. If I had to begin all over again I would of course try to avoid
this or that mistake, but the main course of my life would remain
unchanged. I shall die a proletarian revolutionist, a Marxist, a dialectical materialist, and, consequently, an irreconcilable atheist. My
faith in the communist future of mankind is not less ardent, indeed
it is firmer today than it was in the days of my youth.[254]

Less than a week after writing this he was contemplating
suicide as a way of avoiding a long, drawn-out illness and he

[253] 'O pessimizme, optimizme, XX stoletii, i mnogom drugom', *Sochineniya*, XX, pp.
74–9.
[254] The 'Testament' was published in *Diary in Exile*, pp. 139–40 (see 'Zaveshchanie',
Archives, T4828a). This part of the 'Testament', written on 27 Feb. 1940, ends with
the words: 'Life is beautiful. Let the future generations cleanse it of all evil, oppression
and violence, and enjoy it to the full.' But advancing years and illness had depressed
him for some time now: 'Old age', he wrote in 1935, 'is the most unexpected of all
things that happen to a man.' (*Diary in Exile*, p. 99.)

added a passage to the 'Testament', in the last part of which he stated:

The 'suicide' (if such a term is appropriate in this connection) will not in any respect be an expression of an outburst of despair or hopelessness . . . But whatever may be the circumstances of my death I shall die with unshaken faith in the communist future. This faith in man and his future gives me even now such power of resistance as cannot be given by any religion.[255]

Such faith, in the face of the bitter political and personal reality of 1940, seemed to border on the irrational. In fact, however, rationalism, or the belief in human reason, was itself a source of Trotsky's optimism. It is implicit in the above quotations from his 'Testament' and it runs through all his thought. But the belief in reason, like the scope of the faith, seemed to go beyond reason itself. Partly this was because the rationalism he inherited, and which he shared with a long line of revolutionaries, contained an element of fanaticism; and partly it grew out of the conviction that history itself was fully rational, and fully comprehensible. In this sense, Trotsky, like other Marxists, though not all equally, was a child of a revolutionary tradition which recognized no boundaries to the powers of man and his intellectual faculties. In a passage remarkable for its self-awareness, Trotsky wrote in his autobiography:

The feeling of the supremacy of the general over the particular became an integral part of my literary and political work. The dull empiricism, the unashamed, cringing worship of the fact which is so often only imaginary, and falsely interpreted at that, were odious to me. Beyond the facts, I looked for laws. Naturally, this led me more than once into hasty and incorrect generalizations, especially in my younger years when my knowledge, book-acquired, and my experience in life were still inadequate. But in every sphere, barring none, I felt that I could move and act only when I held in my hand the thread of the general. The social-revolutionary radicalism which has become the permanent pivot for my whole inner life grew out of this intellectual enmity towards the striving for petty ends, towards out-and-out pragmatism, and towards all that is ideologically without form and theoretically ungeneralized.[256]

[255] Ibid., p. 141 (Archives, T4828c). Between the two parts of the 'Testament' there is an unfinished fragment in which Trotsky bequests all his possessions and literary rights to his wife (ibid., p. 140 and Archives, T4828b).
[256] *Moya Zhizn*, I, pp. 110–11.

The joining of his optimism and his rationalism to Marxism was thus at once the most personally natural and intellectually logical of steps. Socialism represented to him an 'effort to rationalize life, that is, transform it according to the dictates of reason . . . It is only socialism that has set itself the task of embracing reason and subjecting all the activities of man to it.'[257] And from thence to Lenin and to Bolshevism was perhaps more tortuous a road but, in the end, a no less logical one: 'Rationalism implied that if anything was accepted as theory, it was of course carried out in practice.'[258] This way, he believed, lay in fact the road to progress; and what was reason if not the primary tool which man took up to create, for specific, historical tasks, all those other tools the accumulation and employment of which constituted and assured human advance? For Trotsky Marxism–Bolshevism was in this sense the most historically complete and the most refined of tools, for it both comprehended the course of progress and showed the way to it. It was, for him, the tool most in keeping with the needs of the twentieth century and its tasks. Here it is appropriate to recall that Trotsky frequently drew a historical parallel between Marxism and Protestantism, especially Calvinism. On one occasion, in particular, the parallel was strikingly formulated by him:

Calvinism, with its cast-iron doctrine of predestination, was a mystical form of approach to the causal nature of the historical process. The rising bourgeoisie felt that the laws of history were on its side, and this consciousness took the form of the doctrine of predestination. The Calvinist rejection of the freedom of the will by no means paralysed the revolutionary energy of the Independents; on the contrary, it constituted their powerful support. The Independents felt themselves called to accomplish a great historical task. We may with perfect right draw an analogy between the doctrine of predestination in the Puritan revolution and the role of Marxism in the proletarian revolution. In both cases, the great efforts put forth are not based on subjective caprice, but on a cast-iron causal law, mystically distorted in the one case, scientifically founded in the other.[259]

[257] Cited in Wolfe, op. cit., p. 193. Trotsky recalled (*Moya Zhizn*, I, p. 110) that as a boy he could not understand how people were able to accept local superstitions and irrational practices: 'People refused to see the light of reason, and this drove me to despair.'

[258] Ibid., p. 114.

[259] *Kuda idet Angliya?* (Moscow–Leningrad, 1925), p. 45.

If one reads Marxism here as Marxism–Bolshevism (and Trotsky would certainly not have objected), the full intended implications of this parallel become even clearer: like Calvinism, Marxism was not 'paralysed' by its determinist doctrine but saw in it a 'calling', a duty to carry out the will of history and its laws. In both cases these laws were as if comprehended by reason, though in the one mystically and in the other scientifically. Both saw themselves as the harbingers of progress (of 'a great historical task'). Both could therefore appeal to those 'cast-iron' laws of history for the justification of their mission.[260]

But if Marxism was to the Communist (or proletarian) revolution what Calvinism was to the Puritan (or bourgeois) revolution, were the former just another historical chapter, to be superseded, like the latter, by periodic and endless doctrines and revolutionary outbursts, whatever progress or temporary relief each might contribute to mankind? There was a difference, of course, for Trotsky, and it was the difference between a 'causal law mystically distorted' and one 'scientifically founded', and this difference bore the promise of a qualitatively unprecedented, unique era in history. There would continue to be change but as a product of factors other than social conflict. For a blow had been struck at the one remaining sphere of human life still governed by irrational, elemental forces:

The historic ascent of humanity, taken as a whole, may be summarized as a succession of victories of consciousness over blind forces—in nature, in society, in man himself. Critical and creative thought can boast of its greatest victories up to now in the struggle with nature. The physico-chemical sciences have already reached a point where man is clearly about to become master of matter. But social relations are still forming in the manner of the coral islands . . . In comparison with monarchy and other heirlooms from the cannibals and cave-dwellers, democracy is of course a great conquest but it leaves the blind play of forces in the social relations of men untouched. It was against this deeper sphere of the unconscious that the October Revolution was the first to raise its hand.[261]

---

[260] The parallels between Puritanism and Bolshevism have, of course, been often suggested and analysed in historical and political literature, but see in particular Michael Walzer, *The Revolution of the Saints: A Study in the Origins of Radical Politics* (New York, 1970), pp. 300–20.
[261] *The History of the Russian Revolution*, III, p. 1191.

In effect, therefore, the social and political revolution of the twentieth century was to be the last revolution:

> . . . it would seem that we cast an aspersion on future generations when we do not think of them as having revolutionists. But we must not forget that the revolutionist is a product of definite historical conditions, a product of class society. The revolutionist is no psychological abstraction. Revolution in itself is no abstract principle, but a material, historical fact, growing out of class antagonisms, out of the violent subjugation of one class by another. Thus the revolutionist is a concrete historical type, and consequently a temporary type. We are justly proud of belonging to this type. But by means of our work we are creating the conditions for a social order in which no class antagonisms will exist, no revolutions, and thus no revolutionists.[262]

There can be no doubt, consequently, that at some point in Trotsky's personal and intellectual 'system', optimism, rationalism, the idea of progress and, not least, Marxism, so combined as to create a vision of the millennium. And he did not abandon this vision even in the increasingly darkening days of the last decade or so of his life.

[262] From 'Zadachi kommunisticheskogo vospitaniya', *Sochineniya*, XXI, p. 328.

CONCLUSION
(BY WAY OF AN EPILOGUE)

> But the misfortunes which have overwhelmed living
> people? The fire and bloodshed of the civil war? Do the
> consequences of a revolution justify in general the sacri-
> fices it involves? The question is teleological and therefore
> fruitless. It would be as well to ask in face of the difficulties
> and griefs of personal existence: Is it worth while to be
> born?[1]

IT IS not difficult to see why the notion of birth should have
suggested itself to Trotsky—above and elsewhere—as a
metaphor for revolution. After all, the view that revolution
signified the beginning of a new life was as old as the idea itself
of revolution, and a basic component of its morphology. But
neither the facile transformation of metaphor into analogy, nor
Trotsky's characteristic flourish for aphorism, will blind the
careful reader to the logical fallacy in the words which make
up the above epigraph. Whence the source of the fallacy? The
temptations of style, of the graceful phrase, the epigrammatic
idea, to which, as a critic of his once asserted, Trotsky was often
prone and sometimes succumbed, are surely a secondary factor
here, if at all.[2] Rather, the failure to distinguish between the
chance of birth and the choice of revolution, between an exis-
tential phenomenon and one which is self-imposed, between,
on the one hand, the *telos* or purpose of life in general and, on
the other, the aims or objectives of political action, must be
attributed to that virtually inherent element of determinism
which so consistently characterized Trotsky's attitude to the
Russian Revolution. As we remarked at the close of the last
chapter, this determinism went hand in hand with a belief in
reason and in progress and with a fundamentally optimistic

---

[1] Trotsky, *The History of the Russian Revolution*, III, p. 1192.
[2] See James Burnham's 'Science and Style', in Trotsky, *In Defence of Marxism*, especially
p. 188, where Burnham accused Trotsky of using style instead of logic as 'proof' for
his claims.

frame of mind. Not for Trotsky the agonies of inevitability. 'But if it's all random then what's the point?' asks a character in a modern English novel, and is left perplexed and tormented when he hears the reply: 'What's the point if it's all inevitable?'[3] As against this, Trotsky would have had little difficulty, and much satisfaction, in making—to the extent of belabouring and savouring—the point.

So complete, in fact, was Trotsky's sedulous commitment to October 1917 that not even the horrors of Stalinism—which he himself did so much, and so early, to expose—could unhinge his loyalty to the events and aftermath of that famous month, and to the ideas that went into its making. Doubts seldom arose in his mind about the ultimate value of what was introduced into history by the Russian Revolution. In this sense, he always remained true to his youth. One is reminded, by comparison, of the 'father' of Russian Marxism, Georgi Plekhanov, who, in 1918, on his death-bed, tormented by what had happened in Russia and by a sense of his own historical complicity in it, repeatedly turned to a friend from early revolutionary days with the melancholy question: 'Did we not begin the propaganda of Marxism too early in backward, semi-Asiatic Russia?'[4] No guilty conscience accompanied Trotsky to *his* grave; and if, and in so far as, such a question as Plekhanov's ever arose for *him*, it was only because others had posed it and he felt it his duty to declare it to be meaningless, to denounce it as 'fruitless'.

Yet not even Trotsky could remain insensitive to the fact that the culmination of the Russian Revolution in Stalinism required at the very least a theoretical rethinking and reformulation of the relationship between backwardness and socialism. His attempts in this direction, since they remained anchored to the contingent and unscientific concept of 'betrayal', only show up the very limited character of the revision he was prepared to contemplate. At any rate, he proved unable to account for the phenomenon whereby the domination of society by politics, or the state, and the autonomy of the latter, assumed a permanent—not 'crisis'—character. And it must be said

---

[3] The exchange occurs in Tom Stoppard's *Lord Malquist and Mr. Moon* (London, 1974), p. 140.
[4] Baron, *Plekhanov*, p. 358. The friend was Lev Deutsch, one of the founders with Plekhanov of the Emancipation of Labour Group.

again that he himself while in power saw no alternative in principle—though certainly in degree—to this 'revolution from above'—even if in his case the appeal to 'crisis' may have constituted a more genuine pretext for what he then envisaged as merely temporary measures. Moreover, the assumptions and preconceptions of his own theory of the Russian revolution unwittingly committed him to the view that the state must play a commanding role in the transformation of a backward society, though the end result might have little to do with socialism as such.

In the course of this study we have often noted this ironic relationship between ideas and events and, in particular, the manner in which the theory of the permanent revolution was finally confronted by the realities of history. This theme was anticipated in the introduction to the present work and, one hopes, established in the course of it. The reader who has followed us this far will not require a recapitulation of even the main elements of Trotsky's thought, nor of its critique, in order to appreciate this theme; to summarize is, in any case, to trivialize.[5] There is, however, a further theme which bears restating for it provides the historical perspective within which the significance of Trotsky's thought may be grasped.

It is now a commonplace to observe that the meaning and significance of Marxism have been radically transformed since the First World War: if it originally rose in the West as a critique, even a death-knell of one modern, industrial society, Marxism finally set in the East—paradox though it may be in more ways than one—as the harbinger of another modern society. This much is clear about the changing role of Marxism and need not be belaboured. It does need to be stressed, however, that while no one can any longer pretend that there is—or ever will be—a correspondence between the society created in, for example, the Soviet Union and that dreamt of in the ancient Marxist texts, the former does represent something unprecedented until the aftermath of 1917, a unique form, in fact, of collectivism which, in the meantime, has been reproduced,

[5] The present author, eschewing a summary of Trotsky's ideas here, has nevertheless succumbed to its temptations elsewhere: see Baruch Knei-Paz, 'Trotsky, Marxism and the Revolution of Backwardness', in Shlomo Avineri (ed.), *The Varieties of Marxism* (The Hague, 1977), pp. 65–81.

mutatis mutandis, in other backward societies. Trotsky's theory of the permanent revolution serves to throw light systematically, though hardly unerringly, upon this phenomenon. This is not to deny the earlier point about the limitations of the theory or the manner in which it misconstrued the possibilities of backwardness; it is, however, to claim that Trotsky's analysis of the condition of backwardness, of the character of the modern revolution, of the concept of 'combined development' and of the relation of all this to a socialist movement, if not to the socialist society, established, at the very least, a heuristic model, and provided a theoretical paradigm, of what we have in this study called 'the revolution of backwardness' and what has emerged in this century as the characteristic revolution of our times.[6]

This revolution was partly the consequence of the impact of the West, during a particular historical juncture, upon backward societies. But the form it took put an end to expectations of a historical convergence between East and West; Marx's assumptions that the 'country that is more developed... shows, to the less developed, the image of its own future',[7] was proved to be erroneous, and perhaps a typical example of European egocentrism. Trotsky may be said to have been the first Marxist to have perceived this error—though it was Lenin and Bolshevism, the latter itself a reflection of the different revolutionary possibilities of East and West, which confirmed his prognosis in reality. It may well be, therefore, that Trotsky's main importance as a thinker lies precisely in his having postulated the impossibility of a universal history in the twentieth century.

This too, however, is an irony, perhaps the greatest irony of all: for while Trotsky's intellectual insights all pointed in this direction, in the direction, that is, of a parting of the ways between East and West, he himself remained ill-at-ease with, and unreconciled to, this prospect—as his insistence on 'world revolution', even when this came to verge on fantasy, bears wit-

---

[6] Trotsky's 'Law of Combined Development' has been acknowledged by some anthropologists, of the evolutionary persuasion, as the first scientific attempt to postulate the potentialities of evolution of backward societies; see Marshall D. Sahlins and Elman R. Service (eds.), *Evolution and Culture* (Ann Arbor, 1960), pp. 99–100.

[7] Marx–Engels, *Selected Works*, I, p. 450.

ness. To put the matter somewhat differently: the Trotsky who ultimately refuted the existence of one historical crucible, who was a theorist of the 'revolution of backwardness', a revolution belonging to a genus having no precise counterpart in, or affiliation with, the Western tradition, was also consumed by a faith originating in that very tradition, to wit, a faith in the last universal revolution and in the socialist millennium.[8]

That revolution, like the millennium of which it was to be the harbinger, proved to be an illusion, of course. Not to belabour the point, nor to savour it, but merely to make it, let us leave the last word to a character in the at once phantasmagoric and realistic anti-utopian novel *We* by Yevgeny Zamyatin, himself once a Bolshevik and later a refugee from Stalin's Russia.[9] The narrator in the novel is in the midst of a conversation with a companion when the latter suggests acting against 'The One State':

I sprang up. 'This is unthinkable! This is preposterous! Is it possible you can't see clearly that what you're stirring up is a revolution?'

'Yes, revolution! But why is that preposterous?'

'It's preposterous because there can't be any revolution. Because our revolution ... was the last. And there can't be any other revolutions. Everybody knows that—'

'Dear man, you're a mathematician ... Even more—you're a philosopher, because of your mathematics. Well, then: name the ultimate number for me ... the ultimate, the supreme, the greatest number of all.'

'Come ... that's preposterous. Since the number of numbers is infinite, what number would you want to be the ultimate one?'

'Well, and what revolution would you want to be the ultimate one? There is no ultimate revolution—revolutions are infinite in number ...'[10]

---

[8] It is this latter aspect of Trotsky which has dominated the popular view of him and which has been stressed and encouraged by, amongst others, Deutscher. It explains perhaps the cult status which Trotsky has often enjoyed in Western radical circles.

[9] Zamyatin had been a Bolshevik in his youth but had left the party before 1917. Following the Revolution he had a great influence upon the literary group known as the 'Serapion Fraternity' (a group, incidentally, which Trotsky had discussed in his *Litera-tura i Revolyutsiya*, pp. 50–5). *We* was written in 1920 but its publication in Soviet Russia was banned. In 1931, unable to publish anything, Zamyatin requested and received permission from Stalin to leave the country.

[10] Zamyatin, *We*, translated by Bernard Guerney (London, 1970), pp. 214–15.

MARX ON BACKWARDNESS AND ON RUSSIA

ON THE face of it, nothing seems more incongruous than the supposed relevance of Marx's writings to the Russia of the late nineteenth century. It has become a commonplace by now to note that that corpus of thought and social investigation which constituted the work of Marx was directly linked to a particular period in Western history and is therefore best understood and most relevant within that context. Marx wrote primarily about the West and, more specifically, about that part of it which he called 'capitalist'. By this he meant a form of society which had abandoned an agricultural economy for an industrial one, in which labour was wage-labour and the means of production in private hands, and in which two classes, the bourgeoisie and the proletariat, were predominant. He saw socialism in general—and his own version of it in particular—as a child conceived in the very womb of this form of society, as a historically rooted reaction to it, and as an emerging model of the post-capitalist future. Quite clearly, therefore, a society such as Russia was in Marx's own lifetime, or even thereafter, hardly provided a welcome context for his ideas nor an arena within which they could be tested.

Nevertheless, Marx's thought also constituted a social theory which presumed to provide at least the methodological means for analysing all societies. Marx's own interests were centred on European capitalist society but inevitably they led him to examine non-capitalist societies as well. It is necessary to distinguish between two subjects which, in this context, occupied Marx's attention at various stages of his work. The one, which will not concern us here, is what may be called *pre-capitalist* society and has to do with the purely historical question of the economic development of Western Europe. This was the 'laboratory' of Marx's materialist view of history for it provided the framework within which he could trace the stages of economic change, particularly as it took place in feudal society. The other is the more remote, but in our context the more directly relevant, subject of *non-capitalist, non-Western* society, or one characterized by the 'Asiatic mode of production', as Marx himself defined it, a subject which intermittently fascinated him but to which he devoted no systematic attention.[1] The importance of this subject grew out of Marx's recognition that the Western historical experience was hardly universal and that the existence of static or unchanging and virtually stagnant 'Asiatic' economies posed serious problems for his own dynamic, 'dialectical' view of history.[2]

A brief summary of Marx's views concerning the 'Asiatic mode of production' is here essential in order to grasp Marx's later ambivalent attitudes towards Russian society. In the famous 'Preface to *A Contribution to the Critique of Political Economy*' (1859), Marx almost offhandedly treated the Asiatic mode as if it were a part of universal economic development, and related it to the various historical stages experienced in Europe. Thus he declared: 'In broad outlines Asiatic, ancient, feudal, and modern bourgeois modes of production can be designated as progressive epochs in the economic formation of society.'[3]

The inclusion of the 'Asiatic' raises numerous questions.[4] In what sense could the Asiatic mode be seen as having given rise to the later modes? What was the dialectical relationship—a relationship which constituted the basis of Marx's view of historical change—between the first and the others? Moreover, in what sense could the Asiatic be described as a 'progressive epoch'?

Before the above-cited 'Preface', however, Marx had intermittently turned his attention to the problem of backward, Asiatic societies, particularly in his articles during the 1850s for the *New York Daily Tribune*. It is evident that the problem was a source of some disquiet to him primarily because his unifying mind was confronted by a dichotomous world: on the one hand, a developing, dynamic Europe, on the other, a stagnant, static Asia. It was obvious to him, in fact, that there was not the remotest relationship between the two, that consequently

[1] Marx's writings on this subject consist primarily of the articles he dispatched from the 1850s onward to the *New York Daily Tribune* as its London correspondent. These, together with private correspondence and relevant excerpts from Marx's general theoretical works, are collected in Shlomo Avineri (ed.), *Karl Marx on Colonialism and Modernization* (Garden City, N.Y., 1968). Such of Marx's (and Engels') writings as deal specifically with Russia have been collected in Paul Blackstock and Bert Hoselitz (eds.), *Marx and Engels: The Russian Menace to Europe* (London, 1953). Writings on China are in Dona Torr (ed.), *Marx on China* (London, 1951).
[2] This aspect of Marx's work has only recently, and infrequently, received attention; see, in particular, the introduction by Avineri (ed.), op. cit., pp. 1–28; Karl A. Wittfogel, *Oriental Despotism* (New Haven and London, 1957), chapter 9; and George Lichtheim, 'Oriental Despotism' in his *The Concept of Ideology* (New York, 1967), pp. 62–93. But see also an earlier account of Marx's views: Solomon F. Bloom, *The World of Nations* (New York, 1941), pp. 48–56 and 151–69.
[3] Marx–Engels, *Selected Works*, I, p. 363.
[4] A full analysis of the problem is given by Avineri (ed.), op. cit., pp. 4ff.

human history was not as universal as his general theoretical writings had assumed, and that it was necessary to make allowance for a serious exception—one, moreover, which encompassed an extremely large territorial and demographic area containing such nations as China and India.

The differences between the Asiatic mode and the others were noted by Marx himself. Firstly, while the latter were all characterized, in one form or another, by the fundamental institution of private property, the former was based primarily on common ownership of land. Secondly, the Asiatic world, or at least a substantial part of it, had a unique form of social organization, the village community. The peculiar features of this community were common ownership of land, the union of agriculture and manufacturing, almost complete social and economic autonomy, and minimal contact with the outside world.[5] The village system was in turn mainly responsible for the third unique feature of the Asiatic world, a feature having no counterpart in the West, namely what Marx called 'Oriental despotism'. This was a highly concentrated, bureaucratic and conservative form of government made possible by the autarchic nature of the society and the non-involvement of the various village communities in the provision of the common needs of society as a whole. Finally, and above all, what distinguished the Asiatic mode of production from the ancient, the feudal, and the bourgeois, was that it was completely unchanging. In fact for Marx, as for Hegel before him, the Orient was 'unhistorical', or simply lacking in history, since its experience was a uniform, monotonous repetition of the same thing. Contrary to all that Marx had noted about the European world, the Asiatic contained no forces within itself working for change and progress.

This clearly negated Marx's very philosophy of history, as he himself must have recognized in spite of that facile juxtaposition in the 'Preface' of 1859. Nevertheless, he made no attempt either to acount for it theoretically or to adjust his, European-centred, theoretical premises. But, in any case, in the nineteenth century, the problem of the eternal nature of Asiatic society was becoming an almost purely academic one. For by this time Asian society *was* changing, though not through its own internal mechanisms; and what really concerned Marx in his writings on the Orient was the practical, social and political, question of the impact of the West, through its economic, 'imperialist' penetration, on the societies of China, India and the Middle East. Like others, Marx clearly perceived the traumatic element in this impact: the disintegration of traditional hierarchies, the disloca-

[5] For his description of the village system, see in particular Marx's article of 25 June 1853, 'The British Rule in India', in Marx–Engels, *Selected Works*, I, pp. 345–51.

tion of populations, the transformation of work habits, and the crumbling of ancient cultures. All this, to be sure, was still in its early stages but it was, in Marx's view, an irreversible process, though made more difficult to bear for those affected by the fact that it arose not out of the 'dialectical' needs of the societies themselves, but out of conquest or penetration by foreign, alien powers. For Marx, however, the negative, destructive impact was outweighed by other considerations. In the first place, since the Asiatic mode of production *was* stagnant and unchanging, conquest by European imperialism was the only way of bringing Asia into the mainstream of progressive, universal life. Secondly, the transformation of Asia was a pre-condition both for the undermining of capitalism and the eventual triumph of socialism. This second point arose naturally from Marx's understanding that capitalism could not collapse so long as it had backward colonies to lean on,[6] and from the universal view of socialism which he had consistently advocated, a view which predicated the socialist millennium upon a general revolutionary conflagration in Europe and elsewhere, and the creation of one universal human community. What was happening in Asia was therefore cruel but unavoidable and necessary, just as capitalism had been in its own time in Europe. Whatever the paradox, Marx can therefore be seen as a 'supporter' of European imperialism, though obviously so that it may the better be destroyed eventually. This clearly emerges in many of his statements, of which the following is a striking but representative example:

> England, it is true, in causing a social revolution in Hindostan, was actuated only by the vilest interests, and was stupid in her manner of enforcing them. But that is not the question. The question is, can mankind fulfil its destiny without a fundamental revolution in the social state of Asia? If not, whatever may have been the crimes of England she was the unconscious tool of history in bringing about that revolution.[7]

That capitalism in its imperialist guise is a progressive force in the world thus follows unequivocally from Marx's analysis. But must

---

[6] This thesis was, of course, the basis later for various Marxist theories of imperialism.

[7] 'The British Rule in India', *Selected Works*, I, p. 351. The article concludes with the following stanza from Goethe's *Westostlicher Diwan*, 'An Suleika':

> 'Should this torture then torment us
> Since it brings us greater pleasure?
> Were not through the rule of Timur
> Souls devoured without measure?'

See also the article 'The Future Results of British Rule in India' (*New York Daily Tribune*, 8 Aug. 1853), *Selected Works*, I, especially p. 358. Both this and the previously quoted article were written by Marx in English.

capitalism itself be erected in Asia, must the backward but now evolving societies of this continent go through the same economic development as was once the destiny of Europe? We know, of course, that in the case of Europe Marx saw the various stages of economic transformation as necessary, inevitable, and historically logical. Before there could be capitalism there had to be feudalism, and socialism, in turn, was inconceivable without capitalism. Was this also the case as far as the non-European world was concerned? Apparently yes, for all that Marx wrote on the subject (without however answering the question directly) suggested that the Asiatic mode of production was destined to be replaced by bourgeois economic forms, though without going through the intermediary 'ancient' and 'feudal' stages, since capitalism could only 'export' itself, not its historical past. Thus, in the *Communist Manifesto*, he and Engels wrote:

The bourgeoisie, by the rapid improvement of all instruments of production, by the immensely facilitated means of communication, draws all, even the most barbarian, nations into civilization. The cheap prices of its commodities are the heavy artillery with which it batters down all Chinese walls, with which it forces the barbarians' intensely obstinate hatred of foreigners to capitulate. It compels all nations, on pain of extinction, to adopt the bourgeois mode of production; it compels them to introduce what it calls civilization into their midst, i.e. to become bourgeois themselves. In one word, it creates a world after its own image.[8]

This seems as unambiguous as it can be. But when we come to look at Marx's observations on Russia a much more complicated picture emerges, of the problem in general, and of Russia in particular, which suggests that Marx had not quite made up his mind and preferred perhaps to leave the question open.

That Marx took a special interest in Russia is obvious from a remark in a letter written in 1877: 'In order that I might be specially qualified to estimate the economic development in Russia, I learnt Russian and then for many years studied the official publications and others bearing on this subject.'[9] Some of his earliest followers were Russians and, as is well known, the first translation, in 1872, of *Das Kapital* was into the Russian language. But the real reason for his interest was undoubtedly the very peculiar, perhaps unique, nature of Russian society and the revolutionary implications of this. The problem was how to locate and define Russia on the social map: was she a European nation, Asiatic, or a combination of the two? That she did not belong

---

[8] *Selected Works*, I, p. 38.
[9] Marx–Engels, *Selected Correspondence*, p. 377. This is the well-known letter addressed to the Editorial Board of the *Otechestvenniye Zapiski*; its contents will be discussed presently.

to the mainstream of European development was clearly evident to all; but neither could she be classified as a typical Asiatic society. Marx does not seem to have used the term 'semi-Asiatic' as a practical solution, though it does appear in an article of 1853 signed by him but apparently written by Engels.[10]

During the 1850s, when he made observations about Russia in the context of commentaries on the 'Eastern Question' and the conflict with Turkey, Marx treated Russia as a patently backward, non-European and reactionary power.[11] It was Russia's role in international affairs which interested him at this time but his views were governed by the assumption that Russian government and society were hopelessly archaic. He therefore portrayed Russia as a 'menace', as a dangerous upstart dabbling in European matters. In the Crimean War, his sympathies were wholly on the side of the Turks, which meant, of course, the British and the French. This was perfectly consistent with his view of capitalism, in its imperialist dress, as a progressive, revolutionizing force. He wanted the Ottoman Empire to be overrun by 'universal' capitalism and not by the reactionary, particularistic Tsarist autocracy. A victory for Russia would thus constitute a set-back for the universalizing potentialities of European capitalism:

. . . let Russia get possession of Turkey and her strength is increased by nearly half, and she becomes superior to all the rest of Europe put together. Such an event would be an unspeakable calamity to the revolutionary cause. The maintenance of Turkish independence, or, in case of a possible dissolution of the Ottoman Empire, the arrest of the Russian scheme of annexation, is a matter of the highest moment. In this instance the interests of the revolutionary Democracy and of England go hand in hand.[12]

Between the middle of the 1850s and the 1870s there is a gap in Marx's writings on Russia. However, when in the middle of the latter decade he returned to the subject, his former attitudes towards Russian society as fundamentally reactionary appear to have undergone a considerable modification. It has been suggested that by this time Marx had come to discover certain positive factors in Asiatic society, particularly in the traditional village community.[13] However, the more probable reason for his renewed and more hopeful interest in

[10] *New York Daily Tribune*, 19 Apr. 1853, reprinted in Blackstock and Hoselitz (eds.), op. cit., pp. 133–8. Russia is here (p. 134) said to be semi-Asiatic in her 'condition, manners, traditions, and institutions . . .'.
[11] See, in particular, the *New York Daily Tribune* articles of 12 Apr. and 14 July 1853, reprinted in Avineri (ed.), op. cit., pp. 54–8 and 102–7.
[12] From the 'Real Issue in Turkey' (*New York Daily Tribune*, 12 Apr. 1853), in Avineri (ed.), op. cit., p. 58.
[13] Lichtheim, op. cit., pp. 75–6. But see the challenge to this interpretation by Avineri (ed.), op. cit., p. 19.

Russia was the growing influence of his ideas amongst Russian intellectuals, albeit particularly those connected with the Populist movement.[14] Moreover, since the Emancipation of 1861, the Russian village commune had become a central issue in Russian revolutionary debates and, for the Populists, the basis for a Russian form of socialism. Marx could hardly avoid contemplating the new developments in Russia, especially since his Russian 'students' now turned directly to him for an evaluation of socialist prospects in their country.

Marx says[15] that he began in 1870 to study Russian and to refamiliarize himself with Russian internal developments but it was not until 1877 that he apparently felt confident enough to make a more than passing statement concerning Russian social questions. The occasion which gave rise to it was an article by the Russian Populist N. K. Mikhailovsky which had appeared in the October 1877 issue of the Russian journal *Otechestvenniye Zapiski* (Fatherland Notes).[16] In interpreting Marx's 'historico-philosophical views', Mikhailovsky reached the conclusion that according to Marx a Russian socialist must first work for the destruction of the village commune (*obshchina*) in order to create the basis for the development of capitalism without which socialism was impossible. This was, of course, a strictly mechanistic reading of Marx which assumed the latter to have discovered and postulated a universal, inevitable law of economic development through which all societies were fated to travel. But it was certainly not an unreasonable interpretation, if one bears in mind Marx's concept of capitalism as a universalizing phenomenon. Nevertheless, Marx reacted immediately and in the strongest possible terms. In November he drafted a letter to the editorial board of the *Otechestvenniye Zapiski*;[17] although he failed to send it off, it was later passed on by Engels to Vera Zasulich in Geneva where it appeared in the May 1884 issue of *Vestnik Narodnoy Voli* and, later still, in 1888, it was published in Russia itself in the Moscow magazine *Yuridichesky Vestnik*.[18] The letter thus had a wide circulation and must have come to the attention of many Russian revolutionaries, both Populists and Marxists.

After dismissing Mikhailovsky's claim that he had once derided the

---

[14] For the intricate questions involved in the relations between Marx, Marxism and Populism, see Andrzej Walicki, *The Controversy Over Capitalism* (Oxford, 1969), pp. 132ff.

[15] In his letter to S. Meyer of 21 Jan. 1871, in *Selected Correspondence*, pp. 310–11.

[16] For the circumstances surrounding the writing of this article, and quotations from it, see Richard Kindersley, *The First Russian Revisionists* (Oxford, 1962), pp. 11–13; see also the bibliographical note in Blackstock and Hoselitz (eds.), op. cit., p. 274.

[17] The English version of the letter is printed in *Selected Correspondence*, pp. 376–9. But for a different translation, see Blackstock and Hoselitz (eds.), op. cit., pp. 216–18.

[18] See the bibliographical note in Blackstock and Hoselitz (eds.), op. cit., p. 274.

Russian village commune,[19] Marx comes straight to the point: 'I have arrived at this conclusion: If Russia continues to pursue the path she has followed since 1861, she will lose the finest chance ever offered by history to a people and undergo all the fatal vicissitudes of the capitalist regime.'[20] This, in his view, means that if Russia chooses to follow the capitalist path, 'she will experience its pitiless laws like other profane peoples'. He points out that in *Capital* he had been concerned to trace only that path through which in 'Western Europe' capitalism had emerged; he had not claimed that everywhere capitalism must emerge. In spite of this, Mikhailovsky had attributed to him a grandiose, universal theory:

He feels he absolutely must metamorphose my historical sketch of the genesis of capitalism in Western Europe into an historico-philosophic theory of the general path every people is fated to tread, whatever the historical circumstances in which it finds itself, in order that it may ultimately arrive at the form of economy which ensures, together with the greatest expression of the productive powers of social labour, the most complete development of man.[21]

After citing the experience of the plebeians of ancient Rome as an example of how 'different historical surroundings' can lead to totally different consequences—in the case of the plebeians, whose initial conditions were somewhat analogous to those of the modern proletariat, the result was not wage-labour or capitalism but a mode of production based on slavery—Marx concludes:

By studying each of these forms of evolution separately and then comparing them one can easily find the clue to this phenomenon [i.e. of different results] but one will never arrive there by using as one's master key a general historico-philosophical theory, the supreme virtue of which consists in being super-historical.[22]

This obviously constituted a major and unequivocal statement of Marx's theoretical position and must have been a source of encouragement to those Russians who envisaged a different path for Russian socialism. But did that path lead through the village commune, as Populists believed? About this we get no clear commitment from Marx. Following the already mentioned denial of having once derided the commune, Marx makes only one further reference to this

---

[19] In the appendix to the first German edition of *Das Kapital*, Marx had attacked Herzen for believing that the Russian village commune could serve as a basis for the regeneration of Europe. In his 1877 letter Marx says that his dismissal of this belief implied nothing about the significance of the commune in *Russian* society (*Selected Correspondence*, p. 377).
[20] *Selected Correspondence*, pp. 377–8.
[21] Ibid., p. 379.   [22] Loc. cit.

subject. In the second paragraph of the letter he notes that the 'great Russian scholar and critic', N. G. Chernyshevsky, had concluded that Russia need not destroy the village commune and pass to capitalism but can avoid the 'tortures' of the latter by 'developing the historical conditions specifically her own'. On this Marx comments:

My honorable critic [i.e. Mikhailovsky] would have had at least as much reason for inferring from my consideration for this 'great Russian scholar and critic' that I shared his views on the question, as for concluding from my polemic against the 'literary man' and Pan-Slavist [i.e. Herzen] that I rejected them.[23]

This is certainly a convoluted way of taking a stand. Besides, it is not followed, as it should be, by any analysis of the commune or by argumentation in its favour. On the contrary, in another sentence, Marx claims to have polemicized against Herzen because the latter had 'discovered the Russian commune not in Russia but in [a] book . . .'[24] Marx may therefore be taken to have implied that the commune was more a relic of the past than a living reality.

Marx returned to the question of the Russian village commune on two other occasions: the one in 1881 in a letter to Vera Zasulich, the other in the well-known preface of 1882 to the second Russian edition of the *Communist Manifesto*. The letter to Zasulich was a reply to a direct appeal for guidance: 'You understand, Comrade', Zasulich had written to Marx, 'how profoundly your opinion on this question interests us, and what a great service you would render us, if you expounded your ideas on the possible destiny of our village community, and on the theory of the historical necessity for all countries of the world to pass through all phases of capitalist production.'[25] In concluding, she requested permission to publish Marx's reply in Russia. Marx apparently now decided to go into the matter seriously and systematically for in preparing a reply he drew up four fairly lengthy drafts. These dealt in an extensive way both with the general nature of village communities and the specific Russian example.[26] In

[23] Ibid., p. 377.
[24] Loc. cit. The reference is to the book *Russian Studies* by Baron von Haxthausen, a Prussian Counsellor of State, who in 1847, after travelling in Russia, had published this work in which he extolled the village commune.
[25] The full English translation—from which this quotation is taken—of Zasulich's letter to Marx appears in Blackstock and Hoselitz (eds.), op. cit., pp. 276–7.
[26] The drafts were discovered only in 1911 and not published until 1926 by D. Ryazanov in *Marx–Engels Archiv* (see the bibliographical note in Blackstock and Hoselitz, eds., op. cit., p. 277). The latter also contains (pp. 218–26) a composite version in English of the four drafts. Only the letter which Marx actually sent off is discussed here since the drafts, remaining unknown, could play no role in influencing Russian revolutionaries.

the event, however, he chose to dispatch only a short letter, most of which was concerned with the interpretation of certain passages in *Capital* and which contained only a brief paragraph on the village commune as such.[27]

The passages from *Capital* are cited by Marx to show, as in the letter of 1877, that his analysis of capitalist development was meant to be valid for Western Europe alone, with the obvious implication that that development need not be repeated elsewhere.[28] While in the West, Marx writes, capitalism involved the transformation of one form of private property into another, in Russia, if capitalism were to emerge, it would involve the transformation of common property into private property. In stating this Marx is only denying that capitalism must everywhere be created in the same way; he is not saying explicitly that capitalism as such can be *avoided*. The letter ends with the paragraph on the village commune:

Thus the analysis given in *Capital* assigns no reasons for or against the vitality of the rural community, but the special research into this subject which I conducted, the materials for which I obtained from the original sources, has convinced me that this community is the mainspring of Russia's social regeneration, but in order that it might function as such one would first have to eliminate the deleterious influences which assail it from every quarter and then to ensure the conditions normal for spontaneous development.[29]

This is a very cautious statement. Marx is 'flirting' with the commune but stopping short of an outright commitment. He would like to believe, it seems, that there is a basis in Russia for a non-capitalist development; on the other hand, he is far from certain that this basis is strong enough or that it has not already been undermined by Western economic influences.

Less than a year later, in the Russian preface to the *Communist Manifesto*, Marx formulated the issue in the form of a question:

Can the Russian *obshchina*, though greatly undermined, yet a form of the primeval common ownership of land, pass directly to the higher form of communist common ownership? Or, on the contrary, must it first pass through the same process of dissolution as constitutes the historical evolution of the West?[30]

---

[27] The English version of the letter is in *Selected Correspondence*, pp. 411–12. It was published for the first time only in 1924 but its contents were known to most of the original Russian Marxists (i.e. the 'Emancipation of Labour' group).
[28] 'Hence the "historical inevitability" of this movement [the breakdown of agricultural production] is *expressly* limited to the *countries of Western Europe*.' (*Selected Correspondence*, p. 412.)
[29] Loc. cit.
[30] *Selected Works*, I, pp. 23–4. The 'Preface' is also signed by Engels.

Once again, he offered no definite answer. But this time he introduced a new variable: 'If the Russian revolution becomes the signal for a proletarian revolution in the West, so that both complement each other, the present Russian common ownership of land may serve as the starting-point for a communist development.'[31]

This somewhat clarifies the source of Marx's fascination, however muted, with the commune, perhaps even the source of his interest in Russia generally. Already in 1877 he had become optimistic about the possibilities of an upheaval in Russian society.[32] He then noted that 'all sections of Russian society are in full decomposition economically, morally, and intellectually'.[33] It must have occurred to him, therefore, that a backward society, subject to the sudden and thus more disorienting impact of capitalist penetration, might collapse before the more developed societies. In such a case, if there was no concomitant revolutionary explosion in the West, the backward country would in all likelihood undergo a full-fledged, bourgeois revolution; this, at least, was the most that could be hoped for against the background of a capitalist Europe. If, however, there occurred, more or less simultaneously, a proletarian, that is, socialist, revolution in Europe, this could lead to a general conflagration in which the backward nation would be swept along by the socialist flames. Thus Russia might avoid capitalism and thus the *obshchina* might yet become the basis for *Russia's* socialism.[34] Conversely, however, there was in all this the clear inference that if in the meantime the commune

[31] Ibid., p. 24. In the original manuscript, following the word 'West', a clause is stricken out. It reads: 'the decomposition of the communal ownership of land in Russia can be evaded' (see Blackstock and Hoselitz, eds., op. cit., p. 228).

[32] See his letter of 27 Sept. 1877 to F. A. Sorge, *Selected Correspondence*, pp. 374–5, in which he wrote: 'This time the revolution begins in the East, hitherto the unbroken bulwark and reserve army of counter-revolution.' This was written following the initial Russian setbacks in the war with Turkey of that year. Shortly afterwards, however, the war ended with a Russian victory. A similar idea of revolution beginning in the East seems to have struck him as early as 1853; see his article 'Revolution in China and in Europe', in Avineri (ed.), op. cit., pp. 59–70, especially the remark on p. 64 about the effect on England of a revolution in China.

[33] *Selected Correspondence*, p. 374.

[34] Walicki, op. cit., p. 189, claims that in Marx's view the avoidance of capitalism in Russia 'was not . . . dependent upon the previous victory of the socialist revolution in the West'. Walicki argues this claim partly by citing the previously quoted final paragraph from Marx's letter to Vera Zasulich. But, as we have seen, there was nothing in this paragraph to imply that the task of 'eliminating the deleterious influences' on the village commune, a task essential if the commune was to be preserved, was simply a matter of the revolutionary struggle in Russia. On the contrary, there was the clear implication that this task was dependent on successfully withstanding the invasion of European capitalism. And how could European capitalism be withstood in Russia unless it was being undermined at home? Marx clearly hoped for a war on two fronts: he continued to be optimistic about an eventual revolution in Europe and

failed to maintain itself against 'deleterious' capitalist encroachments, against the 'process of dissolution', that basis for a short cut to socialism would have disappeared and Russia, like the West, would have to pass through a capitalist stage of development. But whatever the case, the prospect of Russian developments becoming a 'signal' for the European socialist revolution explains, it seems, Marx's fascination with Russian society.

It is true that Marx's position on Russia was not so clear-cut as to make only one interpretation of it possible. And as was to happen so often with his work after his death, followers and opponents alike, Marxists, Populists, and others in Russia, found in his words whatever each wished or looked for. In spite of himself, he could be all things to all men and certainly a man for all seasons. But if Marx sometimes raised questions without categorically answering them, his life-long colleague, Engels, had the compensatory ability of quickly putting perplexed minds at rest. Thus if Marx's pronouncements on Russian social questions were sometimes the source of many contradictory interpretations, those of Engels could have left no one in doubt as to what the 'Marxist' position should be. This does not mean, however, that this was a position the essence of which, as opposed to the formulation, Marx would have rejected.

Although Engels, like Marx, had intermittently commented on Russian affairs from the 1850s onward, his most complete treatment of the subject is to be found in two main articles, the one written in 1875, the other, after Marx's death, in 1894.[35] Both are so identical in the views which they convey that they can be dealt with as one, in spite of the nearly twenty-year time lapse between them. The gist of the articles is that on the whole not much in the way of autonomous development can be expected from the phenomenon of communal agriculture in Russia. Engels argued that similar peasant communities have existed, even until recent times, in Germany, in Ireland, in Poland, not to mention India, and everywhere they were characteristic of those societies which were in a low state of productive development. Nowhere were they able to provide a basis for more sophisti-

---

he came to think Russia might provide the spark for it. He made the success of socialism in the latter dependent upon its success in the former. He flirted with the *obshchina* idea and with Russian Populism but he did not subscribe to the Populist view of the Russian future as independent of Europe.

[35] 'On Social Relations in Russia' (1875) and 'Russia and the Social Revolution Reconsidered' (1894). The English versions of both these articles (the first under the title 'Russia and the Social Revolution' and with the date, incidentally, given wrongly as 1873) appear in Blackstock and Hoselitz (eds.), op. cit., pp. 203–15 and 229–41. The 1875 article is written in the form of a polemic against the Russian Populist-socialist, Peter Tkachëv.

cated production, so that in the course of time progress came to depend, in fact, on their abolishment. It was the same in Russia where more advanced forms of production not only did not arise from the village communities but had to struggle against them to succeed. Moreover, the Russian autocracy was in great part a product of the communal system:

[The] complete isolation of the various villages from each other, which produces in the whole country identical, but the very opposite of truly common interests, is the natural basis of Oriental despotism, and from India to Russia this type of social structure has always produced despotism wherever it was paramount, and has always found its completion in this form of government. Not only the Russian state in general, but its specific form, the despotism of the Tsar, instead of being suspended in mid-air, is a necessary and logical product of Russian social conditions.[36]

Engels was not sure whether the Russian *obshchina* was any longer a viable community even in its existing form. He saw it as being in the process of disintegration, a process brought about by, on the one hand, its inability to cope with its productive, economic needs, and, on the other, by the expansion of industry, commerce, and urban life in Russia. It was a process which was, in Engels' view, nearly inevitable and certainly could not be arrested by the commune's internal forces. Salvation, if it was to be sought at all, had to be sought elsewhere:

We see that communal property long ago passed its highpoint in Russia, and to all appearances is nearing its doom. Yet there exists, doubtless, the possibility of transforming this social organization into a higher form . . . But this can happen only if in Western Europe a victorious proletarian revolution is achieved before the complete disintegration of communal property. This would provide the Russian peasant with the pre-conditions to such a transformation . . .[37]

Should this revolution occur, a society such as Russia, Engels was willing to grant, would be much better prepared for the socialist transformation since it could rely on already imbedded collectivist traditions. Thus only under such circumstances could capitalism be avoided:

It is not only possible but certain that, after the victory of the proletariat and the transfer of the means of production to common ownership among Western European peoples, the [backward] countries . . . will derive from the remnants of common ownership and the corresponding folkways a powerful means of appreciably shortening their process of development to a socialist

[36] 'On Social Relations in Russia', op. cit., pp. 211–12.
[37] Ibid., p. 213.

society and of escaping most of the sufferings and struggles through which we in Western Europe have had to labour.[38]

Like Marx at the end of the 1870s, so Engels writing in 1894 was prepared to contemplate the possibility of revolution breaking out first in Russia. Nevertheless, even in such an eventuality, its prospects as a *socialist* revolution would be determined by what followed elsewhere. Thus he concluded:

The revolution [in Russia] will give a new impetus to the working class movements of the West, and provide them with better conditions for the struggle. Thus it will hasten the victory of the modern industrial proletariat, without which contemporary Russia cannot achieve a socialist transformation arising either out of the village community or out of capitalism.[39]

On the basis of these two articles by Engels, both of which were openly published and widely read, we may justifiably conclude that whatever the controversy over Marx's own writings on these matters, there could be little doubt in anyone's mind as to the 'Marxist' position as formulated by no less an authority than Engels. In this sense, therefore, it is possible to speak of a definite Marx–Engels legacy— on the question of Russia—to Russian Marxism. But whether the legacy had any serious or lasting impact on the Russian Marxist movement is, of course, another matter.

---

[38] 'Russia and the Social Revolution Reconsidered', op. cit., p. 234.
[39] Ibid., p. 241.

BIBLIOGRAPHY

The arrangement of the bibliography is as follows:

I. WRITINGS BY LEON TROTSKY

A complete bibliography of Trotsky's writings is now available: Louis Sinclair, *Leon Trotsky: A Bibliography*, Hoover Institution Press, Stanford University, Stanford, California, 1972 (Hoover Bibliographical Series No. 50). The length of this work—nearly 1,100 pages—in itself bears witness to the task involved and anyone doing research on Trotsky owes a deep debt to Sinclair. An earlier, somewhat shorter version of this work is deposited in mimeograph form in the British Library under the title *Records of Leon Trotsky: A Chronological Bibliography of Trotsky's Works*, 2 vols., Glasgow, 1961–2.

Sinclair's bibliography (the 1972 edition) is divided into two main parts. Part I is a chronological listing of all Trotsky's writings, giving details of original publication, reprintings, and of translations into various languages. Part II consists primarily of a concordance to Trotsky's main works, and to the newspapers and periodicals in which Trotsky's writings appeared. (It includes also a concordance to the Trotsky Archives at Harvard but this is very incomplete.) The bibliography is a model of thoroughness and comprehensiveness, even if here and there a few items have escaped Sinclair's attention.

The existence of this bibliography makes it unnecessary to provide a similar listing here—although this would in any case have been impossible as it would have required a volume unto itself. Even to list only those writings which have been referred to in this study would demand an inordinate amount of space. In what follows, therefore, only *books* (and some pamphlets)—whether single works or collections—are listed. Individual articles, essays, letters, speeches, etc., have been excluded. References to a great number of the latter, however, were given in the footnotes: an attempt was there made to give as much bibliographical information as possible and to identify each item—so that a reference, for example, to Trotsky's *Sochineniya* included the title of the specific work (article, speech, etc.) involved. It is hoped, therefore, that this bibliography, together with the footnotes, will provide a guide to Trotsky's most important writings. Beyond this, however, as well as for additional details, the reader is referred to Sinclair's bibliography.

A. CHIEF SOURCES

This sub-section lists and describes the three main sources for Trotsky's writings, published and unpublished, as opposed to individual works and collections which are given in the next sub-section.

1. *Sochineniya*. According to a prospectus which was printed at the end of volume XII of the *Sochineniya*, the State Publishing House (Gosizdat) intended to issue Trotsky's complete works in a total of 23 volumes. When publication was suspended in 1927, only 12 volumes had appeared; of these three were in two parts, so that a total of 15 books were published. The *Sochineniya* therefore consist of the following (place of publication in each case is either Moscow or Moscow–Leningrad):

Vol. II: *Nasha Pervaya Revolyutsiya.*
  Part 1, 1925. (Writings 1904–6, dealing mainly with the 1905 Revolution. Many of the items here originally appeared in Trotsky's 1906 collection *Nasha Revolyutsiya.*)
  Part 2, 1927. (Writings mainly from the period 1906 to 1909. For the most part this consists of his book *1905.*)

Vol. III: *1917.*
  Part 1, *Ot Fevralya do Oktyabrya.* 1924. (Writings February to September 1917, dealing with the events of that period.)
  Part 2, *Ot Oktyabrya do Bresta.* 1925. (Writings from and about the period of the title.)
  (The dates of publication are not given in the above but are known from other sources.)

Vol. IV: *Politicheskaya Khronika.* 1926. (Writings mainly from 1901 to 1910 and some from 1911 to 1914, on Russian politics and events. Consists of articles which originally appeared in such journals as *Vostochnoye Obozrenie, Iskra* (old), *Pravda* (Viennese), etc.)

Vol. VI: *Balkany i Balkanskaya Voina.* 1926. (Writings 1908–13 on the subject of the title. Many of the articles here originally appeared in the newspapers *Pravda* (Viennese), and *Kievskaya Mysl.*)

Vol. VIII: *Politicheskie Siluety.* 1926. (Writings 1908–25, mainly sketches of political personalities. Includes articles from *Nachalo, Nashe Slovo,* and *Kievskaya Mysl,* among others.)

Vol. IX: *Evropa v Voine.* 1927. (Writings 1914–17 on Europe and the World War. Many articles from *Nashe Slovo.* A large part of this volume also appears in Trotsky's 1923 collection *Voina i Revolyutsiya.*)

Vol. XII: *Osnovnye Voprosy Proletarskoi Revolyutsii.* n.d. [1925?]. (Consists primarily of three works: *Terrorizm i Kommunizm* (1920), *Mezhdu Imperializmom i Revolyutsiei* (1922), and *Novaya Ekonomicheskaya Politika Sovetskoi Rossii i Perspektivy Mirovoi Revolyutsii* (1922).)

Vol. XIII: *Kommunisticheskii Internatsional.* 1926. (Writings 1919–21, all dealing with questions of the Communist International. Most of the items here may also be found in Trotsky's *Pyat Let Kominterna.*)

Vol. XV: *Khozyaistvennoe Stroitelstvo Sovetskoi Respubliki.* 1927. (Almost all the writings here are from the year 1920 and deal with economic questions, including the 'militarization' of labour and economic planning. Speeches, directives, etc., which first appeared in *Pravda* and official government publications, are here reproduced.)

Vol. XVII: *Sovetskaya Respublika i Kapitalisticheskii Mir.*
Part 1, *Pervonachalnyi Period Organizatsii Sil.* 1926. (Writings and speeches, mainly from the year 1918, on subjects ranging from Brest-Litovsk to economic problems and to the organization of the Red Army.)
Part 2, *Grazhdanskaya Voina.* 1926. (Writings and speeches 1918–21, mainly on the Civil War. Most of the items here may also be found in Trotsky's *Kak Vooruzhalas Revolyutsiya.*)

Vol. XX: *Kultura Starogo Mira.* 1926. (Writings 1901–2 and 1908–14 on literary and cultural subjects. The writings from 1908 to 1914 were also published in Trotsky's *Literatura i Revolyutsiya.*)

Vol. XXI: *Kultura Perekhodnogo Perioda*. 1927. (Writings mainly from 1923 to 1925 on cultural problems of Soviet Russia, including problems of science and education.)

2. *The Trotsky Archives* (Houghton Library, Harvard University). The Archives consist of thousands of items, including original manuscripts of articles and books, correspondence and miscellaneous notes, pamphlets, newspapers and clippings, and cover the period from the end of 1917 to 1940. A bibliographical guide to the whole is available: *Guide to the Papers of Leon Trotsky and Related Collections in the Harvard College Library*, Harvard, Second Version, 1959. The arrangement of the Archives is in four sections: 1. Soviet Correspondence (T1–T2950); 2. Works (T2951–T4928); 3. Ephemera (T4929–T5323); 4. Closed Section (this consists of 45 boxes of materials from the period 1919–40 and closed to readers, in accordance with Trotsky's stipulation, until 1980; Deutscher, however, was given access to this section). In addition, there are three related collections: the Van Heijenoort Papers (V1–V201)—papers entrusted to Harvard in 1958 by Trotsky's former secretary; the Harper Manuscripts (H1–H28)—materials dealing with Trotsky's *Stalin* and its translation by Charles Malamuth; and the Dewey Commission Exhibits (D1–D438)—papers and publications submitted to the Commission during its sessions.

From the point of view of the present study, the most valuable section is the second (i.e. Works, T2951–T4928) which consists in large part of the manuscripts of many of Trotsky's writings during 1929–40. A series of 796 documents from the period 1917–22 (duplicates of which are also deposited in the International Institute of Social History, Amsterdam) have been published as *The Trotsky Papers* (see next sub-section).

3. *Byulleten Oppozitsii*. This journal was Trotsky's chief political and ideological organ from 1929 to 1940. Most of his important theoretical writings during this period appeared here originally and many of the issues were written almost entirely by him. A total of 87 numbers of the *Byulleten* were published but, since some were double numbers, the actual number of separate issues was 65. The paper was managed by Trotsky's son, Leon Sedov, until his death in 1938, and edited by Trotsky himself. The last four issues appeared after Trotsky's assassination. The dates and places of publication are as follows:

Nos. 1–19 (July 1929–Mar. 1931): Paris
Nos. 20–32 (April 1931–Dec. 1932): Berlin
Nos. 33–9 (Mar. 1933–Feb. 1934): Paris
Nos. 40–3 (Oct. 1934–April 1935): Zurich

Nos. 44–78 (July 1935–July 1939): Paris
Nos. 79–87 (Aug. 1939–Aug. 1941): New York.

A complete set of the journal was republished in 1973, by the Monad Press of New York. It constitutes a reproduction, in four volumes, of all the original Russian issues and so makes the *Byulleten* readily available for the first time. It has the further advantage of identifying all those of Trotsky's articles which originally appeared under pseudonyms.

B. INDIVIDUAL WORKS

As stated previously, only books or pamphlets are here listed, not the multitude of shorter pieces which Trotsky wrote. In every case the edition given is the one which has been used; reference to another edition of the same work is made only if it too has been utilized. Similarly, translations are listed only where these have been used or consulted. The order of the items is according to date of publication:

Vtoroi Syezd RSDRP: Otchet Sibirskoi Delegatsii. Geneva, 1903.
Nashi Politicheskye Zadachi. Geneva, 1904.
Do 9-go Yanvarya. Geneva, 1905.
Nasha Revolyutsiya. St. Petersburg, 1906.
Istoriya Soveta Rabochikh Deputatov v Gorode Sanktpeterburga (ed.). St. Petersburg, 1906.
V Zashchitu Partii. St. Petersburg, 1907.
Voina i Internatsional. Parts of this work were originally published serially in 1914 in the Paris Russian newspaper *Golos.* The full work was republished in Trotsky's *Voina i Revolyutsiya,* I, pp. 75–154.
    German: *Der Krieg und die Internatsionale.* Zurich, 1914.
    English: *The Bolsheviki and World Peace.* New York, 1918.
Programma Mira. Petrograd, 1917. (Also in *Voina i Revolyutsiya,* II, pp. 459–82.)
Istoriya Oktyabrskoi Revolyutsii. Petrograd, 1918. (Also in *Sochineniya,* III, part 2, pp. 255–329.)
Itogi i Perspektivy. Moscow, 1919. (Also in *Nasha Revolyutsiya,* pp. 224–86.)
    English: *Results and Prospects,* in *The Permanent Revolution* and *Results and Prospects,* London, 1962.
Godi Velikogo Pereloma: Lyudi Staroi i Novoi Epokh. Moscow, 1919.
Tuda i Obratno. Petrograd, 1919.
Terrorizm i Kommunizm. Petrograd, 1920. (Also in *Sochineniya,* XII, pp. 7–180.)
    English: *Terrorism and Communism.* Ann Arbor, 1961.
Novyi Etap. Moscow, 1921.

Mezhdu Imperializmom i Revolyutsiei. Moscow, 1922. (Also in *Sochineniya*, XII, pp. 183–296.)
Voprosy Byta. 2nd edition, Moscow, 1923.
　　English: *Problems of Life.* London, 1924.
Kommunisticheskoe Dvizhenie vo Frantsii. Moscow, 1923.
Literatura i Revolyutsiya. Moscow, 1923.
　　English: *Literature and Revolution.* Ann Arbor, 1960.
Voina i Revolyutsiya. 2 vols., 2nd edition, Moscow–Petrograd, 1923–1924.
Kak Vooruzhalas Revolyutsiya. 3 vols. in 5 parts, Moscow, 1923–5.
Pokolenie Oktyabrya. Petrograd and Moscow, 1924.
Zapad i Vostok. Moscow, 1924.
Pyat Let Kominterna. Moscow, 1924.
　　English: *The First Five Years of the Communist International.* 2 vols., New York, 1945 and 1953.
Novyi Kurs. Moscow, 1924.
　　English: *The New Course.* Ann Arbor, 1965.
O Lenine: Materialy dla Biografa. Moscow, 1924.
　　English: *Lenin.* London, 1925.
　　　　On Lenin: Notes Towards a Biography. London, 1971.
Uroki Oktyabrya. Berlin, 1925. (Also in *Sochineniya*, III, part 1, pp. ix–lxvii.)
1905. 4th Russian edition, Moscow, [1925].
　　English: *1905.* New York, 1972.
Kuda Idet Angliya? Moscow–Leningrad, 1925.
　　English: *Where is Britain Going?* London, 1926.
Kuda Idet Angliya? Vypusk Vtoroi. Moscow–Leningrad, 1926.
Evropa i Amerika. Moscow–Leningrad, 1926.
Towards Socialism or Capitalism? London, 1926.
The Real Situation in Russia. New York, 1928.
Chto i Kak Proizoshlo? Paris, 1929.
Moya Zhizn. 2 vols., Berlin, 1930.
　　English: *My Life.* New York, 1960.
Permanentnaya Revolyutsiya. Berlin, 1930.
　　English: *The Permanent Revolution,* in *The Permanent Revolution* and *Results and Prospects,* London, 1962.
Istoriya Russkoi Revolyutsii. 2 vols., Berlin, 1931 and 1933.
　　English: *The History of the Russian Revolution,* translated by Max Eastman, single volume edition, reissued London, 1965.
Nemetskaya Revolyutsiya i Stalinskaya Byurokratiya. Berlin, 1932.
Problems of the Chinese Revolution. London, 1969 (first published 1932).
Stalinskaya Shkola Falsifikatsii. Berlin, 1932.
　　English: *The Stalin School of Falsification.* New York, 1937.

The Only Road. New York, 1933 (reprinted in *The Struggle Against Fascism in Germany*, New York, 1971, pp. 272–328).
Chetvertyi Internatsional i Voina. Geneva, 1934.
The Third International After Lenin. New York, 1936.
The Revolution Betrayed. Translated by Max Eastman, New York, 1937.
The Case of Leon Trotsky. New York and London, 1937.
The Living Thoughts of Karl Marx. London, 1940.
Stalin: An Appraisal of the Man and His Influence. Edited and translated by Charles Malamuth, New York and London, 1941 (issued in 1946).
In Defence of Marxism. New York, 1942.
Diary in Exile, 1935. Translated by Elena Zarudnaya, London, 1959.
The Trotsky Papers, 1917–1922. Vol. I, 1917–19, Vol. II, 1920–2; edited and annotated by Jan M. Meijer, The Hague, 1964 and 1971 (original Russian with English translation).
The Young Lenin. Translated by Max Eastman, London, 1972.
    French: *Vie de Lénine: Jeunesse*. Paris, 1936.
        La Jeunesse de Lénine. Paris, 1970.

C. OFFICIAL PUBLICATIONS

The following official party protocols in particular have been referred to, or consulted, for statements and speeches by Trotsky at party Congresses and Conferences:

Vtoroi Syezd RSDRP: Protokoly. Moscow, 1932 (the Moscow, 1959 edition has also been referred to).
Pyatyi (Londonskii) Syezd RSDRP: Protokoly. Moscow, 1963.
Odinadtsatyi Syezd RKP (b): Stenografcheskii Otchet. Moscow, 1922.
Dvenadtsatyi Syezd RKP (b): Stenografcheskii Otchet. Moscow, 1923.
Trinadtsatyi Syezd RKP (b): Stenografcheskii Otchet. Moscow, 1924.
Pyatnadtsataya Konferentsiya VKP (b): Stenografcheskii Otchet. Moscow, 1927.

The following publications, which contain speeches by Trotsky, have also been referred to:

Mirnye Peregovory v Brest-Litovske. Edited by A. A. Joffe, Moscow, 1920.
Voprosy Kultury Pri Diktatura Proletariata. Moscow, 1925.

D. NEWSPAPERS AND PERIODICALS

Trotsky's articles appeared in literally hundreds of Russian and other newspapers and periodicals. The following is a list only of the main ones consulted (excluded are publications to which Trotsky contributed rarely or irregularly, and those which it has proved impossible to locate, e.g. *Vostochnoye Obozrenie, Kievskaya Mysl*):

Russian: *Byulleten Oppozitsii* (see sub-section A, above); *Ekonomicheskaya Zhizn*; *Golos*; *Iskra*; *Izvestiya*; *Nachalo*; *Nashe Slovo*; *Novaya Zhizn*; *Novyi Mir*; *Pravda*; *Pravda* (Viennese); *Vpered*.

Other Languages: *Die Fahne des Kommunismus*; *Fourth International* (New York); *International Press Correspondence*; *Living Age*; *Manchester Guardian*; *Militant*; *New International*; *New Militant*; *Partisan Review*; *Permanente Revolution*; *Quatrième Internationale*; *Socialist Appeal*; *La Vérité*.

E. ANTHOLOGIES IN ENGLISH AND FRENCH

The following is a list of the main English and French anthologies or collections of Trotsky's writings. Some include complete works; others give only brief extracts. The whole, however, should provide a guide to the translations available in the above languages:

Our Revolution. Edited by M. J. Olgin, New York, 1918.
Whither France? New York, 1936. (For the French of this, see vol. II of the next listing.)
Écrits, 1928–1940. 3 vols., Paris, 1955, 1958, 1959.
De la Révolution. Paris, 1963.
The Essential Trotsky. London, 1963.
The Age of Permanent Revolution: A Trotsky Anthology. Edited by Isaac Deutscher, New York, 1964.
The Basic Writings of Trotsky. Edited by Irving Howe, London, 1964.
Littérature et révolution. Paris, 1964.
Le Mouvement communiste en France, 1919–1939. Edited by Pierre Broué, Paris, 1967.
Politique de Trotsky. Edited by Jean Baechler, Paris, 1968.
Leon Trotsky on the Trade Unions. New York, 1969.
Military Writings. New York, 1969.
Leon Trotsky on the Jewish Question. New York, 1970.
Leon Trotsky on Literature and Art. Edited by Paul N. Siegel, New York, 1970.
The Struggle Against Fascism in Germany. New York, 1971.
Leon Trotsky Speaks. New York, 1972.
Leon Trotsky on Britain. New York, 1973.
The Spanish Revolution, 1931–39. New York, 1973.
Problems of Everyday Life and Other Writings on Culture and Science. New York, 1973.

The Pathfinder Press of New York has announced the publication, in twelve volumes, of the English translations of Trotsky's writings (excluding books) of the period 1929–40. Most of these volumes, under the title *Writings of Leon Trotsky*, have already appeared. They are excellently edited and translated. One hopes that a similar collection, for the—admittedly longer—period before 1929, will also be undertaken.

II. WORKS ON LEON TROTSKY

Only such works as deal specifically with Trotsky, or have separate sections devoted to him, are listed here.

A. BIOGRAPHICAL AND HISTORICAL

Carmichael, Joel, 'Trotsky's Agony', *Encounter* (May and June 1972), pp. 31–41 and 28–36.

——, *Trotsky: An Appreciation of his Life*. London, 1975.

Daniels, Robert V., *The Conscience of the Revolution: Communist Opposition in Soviet Russia*. Cambridge, Mass., 1960.

Deutscher, Isaac, *The Prophet Armed: Trotsky 1879–1921*. London, 1954.

——, *The Prophet Unarmed: Trotsky 1921–1929*. London, 1959.

——, *The Prophet Outcast: Trotsky 1929–1940*. London, 1963.

Eastman, Max, *Leon Trotsky: The Portrait of a Youth*. New York, 1925.

Hansen, Joseph *et al.*, *Leon Trotsky: The Man and His Work*. New York, 1969.

Lunacharsky, A. V., *Revolyutsionniye Siluety*. Moscow, 1923 (English translation London, 1967).

Malraux, André, 'Leon Trotsky', in Trotsky, *Writings, 1933–34*, New York, 1972, pp. 331–8.

Melamed, S. M., 'St. Paul and Leon Trotsky', *Reflex* (Nov. 1927).

Serge, Victor, *Vie et Mort de Trotsky*. Paris, 1951.

Smith, Irving H. (ed.), *Trotsky*. Englewood Cliffs, N.J., 1973.

Venkataramani, M. S., 'Leon Trotsky's Adventure in American Radical Politics, 1935–37', *International Review of Social History*, IX, 1964, part 1, pp. 1–46.

Wilson, Edmund, *To the Finland Station*. London, 1960.

Wolfe, Bertram D., *Three Who Made a Revolution*. Boston, 1955.

Wolfenstein, E. Victor, *The Revolutionary Personality: Lenin, Trotsky, Gandhi*. Princeton, 1967.

Ziv, G. A., *Trotsky: Kharakteristika po Lichnym Vospominaniam*. New York, 1921.

Zeller, Fred, 'First Impressions of the Old Man', *Le Monde* (English Weekly Selection), 10 Sept. 1969, p. 6.

(The above is not an exhaustive list; numerous other works have been devoted to some aspect of Trotsky's life but these have not been referred to in the present study as they do not touch upon its subject matter.)

B. ON HIS THOUGHT AND WRITINGS

Angell, Norman, *Must Britain Travel the Moscow Road?* London, 1926. (On Trotsky's *Where is Britain Going?*)

Avenas, Denise, *Économie et politique dans la pensée de Trotsky.* Paris, 1970.

Bahne, Siegfried, 'Trotsky on Stalin's Russia', *Survey* (Apr. 1962), pp. 27–42.

Brahm, H., 'La "Révolution Permanente" de Trotski et le "Socialisme dans un seul pays" de Staline', *Cahiers du Monde Russe et Soviétique* (Jan.–Mar. 1965), pp. 84–99.

Brossat, Alain, *Aux Origines de la révolution permanente: la pensée politique du jeune Trotsky.* Paris, 1974.

Day, Richard B., *Leon Trotsky and the Politics of Economic Isolation.* Cambridge, 1973.

Dewey, John, 'Means and Ends', *Partisan Review* (Summer 1964), pp. 400–4.

Geras, Norman, 'Political Participation in the Revolutionary Thought of Leon Trotsky', in Geraint Parry (ed.), *Participation in Politics*, Manchester, 1972, pp. 151–68.

Gottschalk, Louis, 'Leon Trotsky and the Natural History of Revolutions', *The American Journal of Sociology* (Nov. 1938), pp. 339–54.

Knei-Paz, Baruch, 'Trotsky, Marxism and the Revolution of Backwardness', in Shlomo Avineri (ed.), *The Varieties of Marxism*, The Hague, 1977, pp. 65–81.

Krassó, Nicolas (ed.), *Trotsky: The Great Debate Renewed.* St. Louis, 1972. (Collection of articles which originally appeared in the *New Left Review*.)

Lee Chen-Chung, 'Trotsky's Theory of the "Permanent Revolution" and Mao Tse-tung's Theory of the "Continuous Revolution"', *Issues and Studies* (Apr. 1972), pp. 29–39.

Levine, Steven, 'Trotsky on China: The Exile Period', *Papers on China*, vol. 18, Harvard, 1964.

Lichtheim, George, 'Reflections on Trotsky', in his *The Concept of Ideology*, New York, 1967, pp. 204–24.

MacIntyre, Alasdair, 'Trotsky in Exile', *Encounter* (Dec. 1963), pp. 73–8.

Martin, Kingsley, 'The Art of Revolution', *The New Statesman and Nation* (21 Jan. 1933), p. 77.

Mavrakis, Kostas, *Du Trotskysme*. Paris, 1973.

McNeal, Robert H., 'Trotsky's Interpretation of Stalin', *Canadian Slavonic Papers* (no. 5, 1961), pp. 87–97.

Nedava, Joseph, *Trotsky and the Jews*. Philadelphia, 1972.

Plamenatz, John, 'Deviations from Marxism', *Political Quarterly* (Jan.–Mar. 1950), pp. 40–55.

——, 'Trotskyism', chapter 12 of his *German Marxism and Russian Communism*, London, 1954.

Procacci, Giuliano, 'Trotsky's View of the Critical Years 1929–1936', *Science and Society* (Winter 1963), pp. 62–9.

Rowse, A. L., *The End of an Epoch*. London, 1948, pp. 274–90.

Scharlau, W. B., 'Parvus und Trockij: 1904–1914. Ein Betrag zur Theorie der permanenten Revolution', *Jahrbücher für Geschichte Osteuropas* (Oct. 1962), pp. 349–80.

Schurer, Heinz, 'The Permanent Revolution: Lev Trotsky', in Leopold Labedz (ed.), *Revisionism*, London, 1962, pp. 67–76.

Vestuti, Guido, *La Rivoluzione permanente: uno studio sulla politica di Trotsky*. Milan, 1960.

Warth, Robert D., 'Leon Trotsky: Writer and Historian', *Journal of Modern History* (Mar. 1948), pp. 27–41.

Weinstein, Fred, 'Trotsky and the Sociological Dimension: An Analysis of Social Action', *Social Forces* (Oct. 1961), pp. 8–14.

Wolfe, Bertram D., 'Leon Trotsky as Historian', *Slavic Review* (Oct. 1961), pp. 495–502.

III. GENERAL BIBLIOGRAPHY

Listed here are all other works which have been referred to in the course of this study.

Adams, Arthur E. (ed.), *The Russian Revolution and Bolshevik Victory: Causes and Processes*. Lexington, Mass., 1972.

Albrow, Martin, *Bureaucracy*. London, 1970.

Alexander, Robert J., *Trotskyism in Latin America*. Stanford, 1973.

Arendt, Hannah, *The Origins of Totalitarianism*. New York, 1958.

Aron, Raymond, *Democracy and Totalitarianism*. London, 1968.

Ascher, Abraham, *Pavel Axelrod and the Development of Menshevism*. Oxford, 1973.

Avineri, Shlomo, *The Social and Political Thought of Karl Marx*. Cambridge, 1968.
—— (ed.), *Karl Marx on Colonialism and Modernization*. Garden City, N.Y., 1968.
Avrich, Paul, *Kronstadt 1921*. Princeton, 1970.
Balandier, Georges, *Political Anthropology*. Harmondsworth, 1972.
Baran, Paul A., *The Political Economy of Growth*. 2nd edition, New York and London, 1962.
Baron, Samuel H., *Plekhanov: The Father of Russian Marxism*. Stanford, 1963.
Beling, W. A. and Totten, G. O. (eds.), *Developing Nations: Quest for a Model*. New York, 1970.
Bell, Daniel, 'The Strange Tale of Bruno R.', *The New Leader* (28 Sept. 1959), pp. 19–20.
——, 'The Post-Industrial Society: The Evolution of an Idea', *Survey* (Spring 1971), pp. 102–68.
——, *The End of Ideology*. Revised edition, New York, 1962.
Berlin, Isaiah, *Karl Marx: His Life and Environment*. 3rd edition, London, 1963.
——, *Two Concepts of Liberty*. Oxford, 1958.
——, *The Hedgehog and the Fox*. New York, 1957.
——, *Historical Inevitability*. London, 1954.
——, 'The Marvellous Decade', *Encounter*, June, Nov., Dec. 1955, and May 1956.
Black, C. E., *The Dynamics of Modernization: A Study in Comparative History*. New York, 1967.
—— (ed.), *The Transformation of Russian Society*. Cambridge, Mass., 1960.
Bloom, Solomon F., *The World of Nations: A Study of the National Implications in the Work of Karl Marx*. New York, 1941.
Blum, Jerome, *Lord and Peasant in Russia from the Ninth to the Nineteenth Century*. Princeton, 1961.
Bober, M. M., *Karl Marx's Interpretation of History*. 2nd, revised edition, New York, 1965.
Borkenau, Franz, *World Communism*. Ann Arbor, 1962.
Brandt, Conrad, *Stalin's Failure in China*. Cambridge, Mass., 1958.
Breton, André, *La Clé des champs*. Paris, 1953.
Brutzkus, Boris, 'The Historical Peculiarities of the Social and Economic Development of Russia', in Reinhard Bendix and S. M. Lipset (eds.), *Class, Status and Power*, Chicago, 1953, pp. 121–35.
Buber, Martin, *Paths in Utopia*. London, 1949.
Bukharin, Nikolai, *Put k Sotsializmu i Raboche-Krestyanskii Soyuz*. Moscow–Leningrad, 1926.

Bibliography

611

Burnham, James, *The Managerial Revolution*. Harmondsworth, 1962.
——, 'Science and Style: A Reply to Comrade Trotsky' and 'Letter of Resignation', in Trotsky, *In Defence of Marxism*, New York, 1942, pp. 187–206, 207–11.
——, 'The Politics of Desperation', *New International*, Mar. 1940.
——, *The Machiavellians*. New York, 1943.
——, *The Coming Defeat of Communism*. New York, 1950.
Cannon, James, *The History of American Trotskyism*. New York, 1944.
——, *The Struggle for a Proletarian Party*. New York, 1943.
Carr, E. H., *The Bolshevik Revolution, 1917–1923*. 3 vols., Harmondsworth, 1966.
——, *The Interregnum, 1923–1924*. Harmondsworth, 1969.
——, *Socialism in One Country, 1924–1926*. 3 vols., Harmondsworth, 1970, 1972.
——, *What is History?* London, 1961.
Cherevanin, F. A., *Proletariat v Revolyutsii*. Moscow, 1907.
Ciliga, Anton, *The Kronstadt Revolt*. London, 1942.
——, *Au Pays du grand mensonge*. Paris, 1937.
Cohen, Stephen F., *Bukharin and the Bolshevik Revolution: A Political Biography 1888–1938*. London, 1974.
Cole, G. D. H., *A History of Socialist Thought*. Vol. II, *Marxism and Anarchism, 1850–1890*. London, 1954.
Collins, Henry and Abramsky, Chimen, *Karl Marx and the British Labour Movement*. London, 1965.
Dan, Theodore, *The Origins of Bolshevism*. London, 1964.
Daniels, Robert V., *Red October*. New York, 1967.
Denno, Theodore, *The Communist Millennium: The Soviet View*. The Hague, 1964.
Deutscher, Isaac, *Stalin: A Political Biography*. London, 1961.
Djilas, Milovan, *The New Class*. London, 1957.
Dobb, Maurice, *Soviet Economic Development Since 1917*. 6th edition, London, 1966.
Dubnow, S. M., *History of the Jews in Russia and Poland*. 3 vols., Philadelphia, 1916–20.
Dunayevskaya, Raya, *Marxism and Freedom*. London, 1971.
Eisenstadt, S. N., *Modernization: Protest and Change*. Englewood Cliffs, N.J., 1966.
Erlich, Alexander, *The Soviet Industrialization Debate, 1924–1928*. Cambridge, Mass., 1960.
——, 'Preobrazhensky and the Economics of Soviet Industrialization', *Quarterly Journal of Economics* (Feb. 1950), pp. 57–88.
Erlich, Victor, *Russian Formalism*. 3rd edition, The Hague, 1969.

Fainsod, Merle, *International Socialism and the World War*. New York, 1969.

Feinstein, Otto (ed.), *Two Worlds of Change: Readings in Economic Development*. New York, 1964.

Fenwick, James M., 'The Mysterious Bruno R.', *New International* (Sept. 1948).

Fischer, George, *Russian Liberalism: From Gentry to Intelligentsia*. Cambridge, Mass., 1958.

Fischer, Ruth, *Stalin and German Communism*. Cambridge, Mass., 1948.

Florinsky, Michael T., *World Revolution and the U.S.S.R.* London, 1933.

Frank, Pierre, *La Quatrième Internationale*. Paris, 1969.

Frankel, Jonathan, 'Lenin's Doctrinal Revolution of April 1917', *Journal of Contemporary History* (Apr. 1969), pp. 117–42.

Friedrich, Carl J. and Brzezinski, Zbigniew, *Totalitarian Dictatorship and Autocracy*. 2nd, revised edition, New York, 1966.

Fromm, Erich, *The Fear of Freedom*. London, 1942.

Galai, Shmuel, *The Liberation Movement in Russia, 1900–1905*. Cambridge, 1972.

Gankin, O. H. and Fisher, H. H., *The Bolsheviks and the World War*. Stanford, 1940.

Gerschenkron, Alexander, *Economic Backwardness in Historical Perspective*. Cambridge, Mass., 1966.

——, 'Patterns of Economic Development', in C. E. Black (ed.), *The Transformation of Russian Society*, Cambridge, Mass., 1960, pp. 52–61.

Getzler, Israel, *Martov: A Political Biography of a Russian Social Democrat*. Melbourne, 1967.

Glickson, M., *The Jewish Complex of Karl Marx*. New York, 1961.

Goldman, Emma, *Trotsky Protests Too Much*. Glasgow, 1938.

Goodman, Elliot R., *The Soviet Design for a World State*. New York, 1960.

Haimson, Leopold, *The Russian Marxists and the Origins of Bolshevism*. Cambridge, Mass., 1955.

Harcave, Sidney, *The Russian Revolution of 1905*. London, 1970.

Hayward, Max and Labedz, Leopold (eds.), *Literature and Revolution in Soviet Russia, 1917–1962*. London, 1963.

Heitman, Sidney, 'Between Lenin and Stalin: Nikolai Bukharin', in Leopold Labedz (ed.), *Revisionism*, London, 1962, pp. 77–90.

Henein, Georges, 'Bruno R. et la "Nouvelle Classe"', *Le Contrat Social* (Nov. 1958), pp. 365–8.

Hilferding, Rudolf, 'State Capitalism or Totalitarian State Economy', *Modern Review* (June 1947), pp. 266–71.

Hoffer, Eric, *The True Believer*. New York, 1951.

Holdsworth, Mary, 'Lenin and the Nationalities Question', in Schapiro and Reddaway (eds.), *Lenin: The Man, the Theorist, the Leader*, London, 1967, pp. 265–94.

Horowitz, David, *Imperialism and Revolution*. Harmondsworth, 1971.

Hoselitz, B. F. (ed.), *The Progress of Underdeveloped Areas*. Chicago, 1952.

Isaacs, Harold, *The Tragedy of the Chinese Revolution*. London, 1938.

Jacobson, Julius, 'Isaac Deutscher: The Anatomy of an Apologist', in Jacobson (ed.), *Soviet Communism and the Socialist Vision*, New Brunswick, N.J., 1972, pp. 86–162.

Johnson, Chalmers, *Peasant Nationalism and Communist Power*. Stanford, 1962.

Joll, James, *The Second International, 1889–1914*. London, 1955.

Katkov, George, *Russia 1917: The February Revolution*. London, 1967.

——, 'The Kronstadt Rising', *St. Antony's Papers*, no. 6, London, 1959, pp. 9–74.

——, *et al.* (eds.), *Russia Enters the Twentieth Century, 1894–1917*. London, 1971.

Kautsky, John H., *Political Change in Underdeveloped Countries*. New York, 1962.

——, *Communism and the Politics of Development*. New York, 1968.

Kautsky, Karl, *The Dictatorship of the Proletariat*. Ann Arbor, 1964.

——, *Terrorism and Communism*. London, 1920.

——, *Dvizhushchiya Sily i Perspektivy Russkoi Revolyutsii*. St. Petersburg, 1906.

——, 'Slavyane i revolyutsiya', *Iskra*, no. 18, 10 Mar. 1902.

Keep, J. L. H., *The Rise of Social Democracy in Russia*. Oxford, 1963.

Kindersley, Richard, *The First Russian Revisionists*. Oxford, 1962.

Kochan, Lionel, *Russia in Revolution*. London 1970.

Kornhauser, William, *The Politics of Mass Society*. London, 1960.

Korsch, Karl, *Marxism and Philosophy*. London, 1970.

Labedz, Leopold (ed.), *Revisionism*. London, 1962.

——, 'Deutscher as Historian and Prophet', *Survey* (Apr. 1962), pp. 120–44.

Lane, David, *The End of Inequality? Stratification Under State Socialism*. Harmondsworth, 1971.

Laquer, Walter, *A History of Zionism*. London, 1971.

Lazitch, Branko, *Lénine et la Troisième Internationale*. Paris, 1951.

Leites, Nathan, *A Study of Bolshevism*. Glencoe, Ill., 1953.

Lenin, V. I., *Polnoe Sobranie Sochinenii*. 5th edition, Moscow, 1958–65.

——, *Selected Works*. 3 vols., Moscow, n.d. [1963?].

——, *Izbraniye Stati po Natsionalnomu Voprosu*. Moscow–Leningrad, 1925.

Lenin, V. I., *Lenin on the Jewish Question*. New York, 1934.

Lerner, Warren, *Karl Radek: The Last Internationalist*. Stanford, 1970.

Lerski, George Jan, *Origins of Trotskyism in Ceylon, 1935–1942*. Stanford, 1968.

Lewin, M., *Russian Peasants and Soviet Power*. London, 1968.

Lichtheim, George, *Marxism: An Historical and Critical Study*. 2nd edition, London, 1964.

——, 'Oriental Despotism', in his *The Concept of Ideology*, New York, 1967, pp. 62–93.

Liebenstein, Harvey, *Economic Backwardness and Economic Growth*. New York and London, 1957.

Lukacs, George, *History and Class Consciousness*. Cambridge, Mass., 1971.

Luxemburg, Rosa, *The Mass Strike: The Political Party and the Trade Unions*. New York, 1971.

——, *The Russian Revolution*. Ann Arbor, 1961.

——, 'Nach dem ersten Akt', *Die Neue Zeit*, 4 Feb. 1905, pp. 610–14.

Lvavi, Jacob, *Ha-Hityashvut ha-Yehudit be-Biro-Bidzhan*. Jerusalem, 1965.

Macdonald, Dwight, *Memoirs of a Revolutionist*. New York, 1958.

——, 'Once More: Kronstadt', *New International* (July 1938), pp. 212–214.

Maor, Yitzhak, *Sheelat ha-Yehudim ba-Tnua ha-Liberalit ve-ha-Mahpechanit be-Russia, 1890–1914*. Tel-Aviv, 1964.

Marx, Karl, *Pre-Capitalist Economic Formations*. Edited by E. J. Hobsbawm, London, 1964.

——, *Marx's Grundrisse*. Edited by David McLellan, London, 1971.

——, *Early Writings*. Edited by T. B. Bottomore, London, 1963.

——, and Engels, Friedrich, *Selected Works*, 2 vols., Moscow, 1955.

——, ——, *Selected Correspondence*, Moscow n.d. [1953?].

——, ——, *The Russian Menace to Europe*. Edited by Paul Blackstock and Bert Hoselitz, London, 1953.

——, ——, *Literature and Art: Selections From Their Writings*. Bombay, 1956.

——, ——, *The Holy Family*. Moscow, 1956.

Mason, T. W., 'The Primacy of Politics—Politics and Economics in National Socialist Germany', in S. J. Woolf (ed.), *The Nature of Fascism*, New York, 1968, pp. 165–95.

Maximoff, G. P. (ed.), *The Political Philosophy of Bakunin*. New York and London, 1964.

Mendel, A. P., *Dilemmas of Progress in Tsarist Russia: Legal Marxism and Legal Populism*. Cambridge, Mass., 1961.

Meyer, Alfred G., *Leninism*. New York, 1962.

Michels, Robert, *Political Parties*. New York, 1962.

Milyukov, Paul, *Ocherkii po Istorii Russkoi Kultury*. St. Petersburg, 1896.

Moore, Jr., Barrington, *Soviet Politics—The Dilemma of Power: The Role of Ideas in Social Change*. New York, 1965.

——, *Social Origins of Dictatorship and Democracy*. Harmondsworth, 1969.

Naville, Pierre, *Trotsky vivant*. Paris, 1963.

Nettl, J. P., *Rosa Luxemburg*. 2 vols., London, 1966.

Neumann, Franz, *The Democratic and the Authoritarian State*. New York, 1964.

Nomad, Max, 'White Collars and Horny Hands', *Modern Quarterly* (Autumn 1932).

Nove, Alec, *An Economic History of the U.S.S.R.* Harmondsworth, 1969.

——, *Was Stalin Really Necessary?* London, 1964.

Owen, L. A., *The Russian Peasant Movement, 1906–1917*. London, 1937.

Page, Stanley W., *Lenin and World Revolution*. New York, 1959.

Parvus (Alexander Helphand), *Rossiya i Revolyutsiya*. St. Petersburg, 1906.

——, 'Preface' to Trotsky's *Do 9-go Yanvarya*. Geneva, 1905.

Pipes, Richard, *Social Democracy and the St. Petersburg Labor Movement, 1885–1897*. Cambridge, Mass., 1963.

——, *The Formation of the Soviet Union*. Cambridge, Mass., 1954.

Plamenatz, John, *German Marxism and Russian Communism*. London, 1954.

Polanyi, Karl, *The Great Transformation*. Boston, 1957.

Popper, Karl, *The Poverty of Historicism*. London, 1960.

Preobrazhensky, Evgeny, *Novaya Ekonomika*. Moscow, 1926. (English translation by Brian Pearce, *The New Economics*, Oxford, 1965.)

Proudhon, P.-J., *Idées révolutionnaires*. Paris, 1849.

R(izzi), Bruno, *La Bureaucratisation du monde*. Paris, 1939.

Robinson, G. T., *Rural Russia Under the Old Regime*. New York, 1932.

Rostow, W. W., *The Stages of Economic Growth*. 2nd edition, Cambridge, 1971.

Sahlins, Marshall D. and Service, Elman R. (eds.), *Evolution and Culture*. Ann Arbor, 1960.

Samuel, Maurice, *Blood Accusation*. Philadelphia, 1966.

Schapiro, Leonard, *Totalitarianism*. London, 1972.

——, *The Origin of the Communist Autocracy: Political Opposition in the Soviet State, First Phase 1917–1922*. London, 1955.

——, *The Communist Party of the Soviet Union*. London, 1963.

——, 'The Role of the Jews in the Russian Revolutionary Movement', *Slavonic and East European Review* (Dec. 1961), pp. 148–67.

Schapiro, Leonard and Reddaway, Peter (eds.), *Lenin: The Man, the Theorist, the Leader*. London, 1967.

Schoenbaum, David, *Hitler's Social Revolution*. London, 1966.

Schram, Stuart R., *The Political Thought of Mao Tse-tung*. Harmondsworth, 1969.

Schurer, Heinz, 'Alexander Helphand-Parvus: Russian Revolutionary and German Patriot', *The Russian Review* (Oct. 1959), pp. 313–31.

Schurmann, Franz, *Ideology and Organization in Communist China*. Berkeley and Los Angeles, 1966.

Schwartz, Benjamin, *Chinese Communism and the Rise of Mao*. Cambridge, Mass., 1951.

Schwarz, Solomon M., *The Russian Revolution of 1905*. Chicago and London, 1967.

——, *The Jews in the Soviet Union*. Syracuse, 1951.

Seliger, Martin, *Ideology and Politics*. London, 1976.

Serge, Victor, *Memoires d'un révolutionnaire*. Paris, 1951.

——, 'Once More: Kronstadt', *New International* (July 1938), pp. 211–212.

Seton-Watson, Hugh, *The Decline of Imperial Russia, 1855–1914*. New York, 1952.

——, *The Russian Empire, 1801–1917*. Oxford, 1967.

——, *From Lenin to Khrushchev: The History of World Communism*. New York, 1960.

Shachtman, Max, 'The Crisis of the American Party—An Open Letter to Trotsky' and 'The U.S.S.R. and the War', *New International* (Mar. 1960).

——, *The Struggle for the New Course*, in Trotsky, *The New Course*, Ann Arbor, 1965.

——, *The Bureaucratic Revolution: The Rise of the Stalinist State*. New York, 1962.

——, '1939: Whither Russia?', *Survey* (Apr. 1962), pp. 96–108.

Shukman, Harold, *The Relations Between the Jewish Bund and the RSDRP, 1897–1903*. Unpublished D.Phil. thesis, Oxford, 1961.

——, 'Lenin's Nationalities Policy and the Jewish Question', *Bulletin on Soviet and East European Jewish Affairs* (May 1970), pp. 43–50.

——, *Lenin and the Russian Revolution*. New York, 1968.

Silberner, Edmund, *The Anti-Semitic Tradition in Modern Socialism*. Jerusalem, 1953.

——, 'Ferdinand Lassalle: From Maccabeism to Jewish Anti-Semitism', *Hebrew Union College Annual*, XXIV, 1952–3, pp. 151–186.

——, *Ha-Sotsializm ha-Maaravi u-Sheelat ha-Yehudim*. Jerusalem, 1955.

Slonim, Marc, *From Chekhov to the Revolution: Russian Literature 1900–1917*. New York, 1962.

Stalin, J. V. *Sochineniya*. Moscow, 1946–53.

——, *Problems of Leninism*. Moscow, 1953.

——, *Ob Oppozitsii*. Moscow, 1928.

Stenbock-Fermor, Elisabeth, 'Russian Literature from 1890 to 1917', in Katkov *et al.* (eds.), *Russia Enters the Twentieth Century*, London, 1917, pp. 263–86.

Struve, Gleb, *Russian Literature Under Lenin and Stalin, 1917–1953*. London, 1972.

Talmon, J. L., *Political Messianism: The Romantic Phase*. London, 1960.

——, *The Origins of Totalitarian Democracy*. London, 1952.

Torr, Dona (ed.), *Marx on China*. London, 1951.

Treadgold, Donald W., *Lenin and His Rivals: The Struggle for Russia's Future, 1898–1906*. New York, 1955.

Tucker, Robert C., *The Soviet Political Mind*. Revised edition, London, 1972.

——, *The Marxian Revolutionary Idea*. London, 1970.

——, *Stalin as Revolutionary 1879–1929: A Study in History and Personality*. London, 1974.

Tugan-Baranovsky, M. I., *Russkaya Fabrika v Proshlom i Nastoyashchem*. 3rd edition, Moscow, 1934.

Ulam, Adam B., *The Bolsheviks*. New York, 1968.

——, *The Unfinished Revolution*. New York, 1960.

——, *Stalin: The Man and His Era*. London, 1974.

Veblen, Thorstein, *Imperial Germany and the Industrial Revolution*. London, 1939.

Venturi, Franco, *Roots of Revolution*. London, 1960.

Von Laue, T. H., *Sergei Witte and the Industrialization of Russia*. New York and London, 1963.

——, *Why Lenin? Why Stalin?* Philadelphia and New York, 1964.

Walicki, Andrzej, *The Controversy Over Capitalism*. Oxford, 1969.

Walzer, Michael, *The Revolution of the Saints: A Study in the Origins of Radical Politics*. New York, 1970.

Weber, Max, *The Theory of Social and Economic Organization*. Glencoe, Ill., 1947.

Westwood, J. N., *Endurance and Endeavour: Russian History, 1812–1917*. Oxford, 1973.

Wetter, Gustav A., *Dialectical Materialism*. London, 1958.

Wheeler-Bennett, John W., *Brest-Litovsk: The Forgotten Peace*. London, 1938.

Wildman, Allan K., *The Making of a Workers' Revolution: Russian Social Democracy, 1891–1903*. Chicago and London, 1967.

Willetts, Harry T., 'The Agrarian Problem', in George Katkov *et al.* (eds.), *Russia Enters the Twentieth Century*, London, 1971, pp. 111–137.

Wittfogel, Karl A., *Oriental Despotism*. New Haven and London, 1957.

Za Leninizm: Sbornik Statei. Moscow, 1925.

Zeman, Z. A. B. and Scharlau, W. B., *The Merchant of Revolution: The Life of Alexander Israel Helphand (Parvus), 1867–1924*. London, 1965.

INDEX